# Game Character Development with Maya

**Antony Ward**

New
Riders

NRG

New Riders Games
New Riders
1249 Eighth Street • Berkeley, CA 94710

Game Character Development with Maya
Antony Ward
Copyright © 2005 by Antony Ward

Published by New Riders. For information on New Riders Games books, contact:

**New Riders**
1249 Eighth Street
Berkeley, CA 94710
(510) 524-2178
Fax: (510) 524-2221
http://www.peachpit.com
To report errors, please send a note to errata@peachpit.com
New Riders is an imprint of Peachpit, a division of Pearson Education

**Editors:** Kate McKinley, Linda Harrison
**Production Editor:** Lisa Brazieal
**Technical Editors:** Phelan Sykes, Charles Shami, Jared Fry
**Copy Editor:** Carol Henry
**Interior design:** Frances Baca
**Compositor:** Owen Wolfson
**Indexer:** Karin Arrigoni
**Cover design and illustration:** Aren Howell

ISBN 0-7357-1438-X
9 8 7 6 5 4 3 2
Printed and bound in the United States of America

*I would like to dedicate this book firstly to my wife, Jade. Her continued support and understanding has been amazing, not just throughout the creation of this book but in the eight years we have been together.*

*The second dedication is to our children: Jacob, currently 18 months old, and our new baby who is growing as we speak and scheduled to make an appearance around January 2, 2005.*

*I love you all!*

# Acknowledgements

The actual idea of writing a book hadn't even entered my mind until a friend of mine, Mat Buckland (author of *Programming Game AI By Example*), suggested I give it a go. So if it weren't for a chance conversation with him, this book might never have been written.

Being a new author, I was a bit wary when I began this venture, but New Riders took me by the hand and guided me through the whole process, making it easy for me to concentrate on getting the information across to you readers.

Over the course of the book's creation, I have worked with so many wonderful people—people who have shared my vision in creating a book for those who want to make great characters for games. So to all the people I haven't mentioned here, you have not been forgotten, and thanks for your time and help.

My first contact with New Riders was with Elise Walter, whom I bugged constantly while my proposal was being scrutinized.

Next came my editors, Linda Harrison and then Kate McKinley. Both have been my guardian angels, going above and beyond to make this book the best it could be.

Technical editors Phelan Sykes, Charles Shami, and Jared Fry provided invaluable comments and advice. I have learned a lot from you all.

Toward the end of the process came copyeditor Carol Henry, who took each chapter and smoothed it out for me, ironing out all the creases and making it an easier read. Then Owen Wolfson went to heroic lengths to pull it all together and make it *look* like a book.

Finally, thank you, the reader, for buying this book. I hope you get as much out of reading it as I did writing it.

# Contents At a Glance

# Table of Contents

# Introduction

Every few years, another new game console or computer system is released that is more powerful than its predecessors. With this increase in power comes better graphics capabilities. This lifts the game artists' restrictions, giving them freedom to add more detail to their geometry. But it also adds pressure to create yet more detailed and visually stunning characters, not only on paper but also in the game engine.

As the emphasis on graphics grows, so does the size of the development team needed to create a single game. Back in the early 1980s, a team comprised a single programmer who would no doubt create his or her own graphics—all that was needed were simple shapes formed from a few pixels on screen. Today's gamers demand much more from their games and, as a result, team sizes can run into the hundreds.

With teams becoming so large, good organization is very important, and smaller subteams usually are formed to cover specific areas. On the art side, you will often have three primary teams: characters, environment, and animation. Possibly another, smaller team would cover the front end—the main startup menu, the onscreen display, and so on.

If you desire to join a character team, this book is just for you. As you work your way through each chapter, you will learn the processes of generating an in-game character, from concept to modeling, optimization, texturing, rigging, and finally animating. Along the way you'll be introduced to the Maya interface and its many tools.

## Why Maya?

"But why Maya?" I hear you ask. "Surely 3D Studio Max is the more dominant 3D application in the games industry." There was a time when this was true, but Maya is fast becoming the industry standard.

In 2002 Maya was used to create six of the top ten best-selling PlayStation 2 titles. Characters in the Tomb Raider series, Jak and Daxter, Legend of Zelda, and Halo 2 have all been lovingly crafted using Maya's extensive toolset. A recent Alias Systems press release states that in an independent survey performed by Acacia Research, 46 percent of North American games development studios said they used Maya. Within the top eight studios in Japan, 50 percent of their 3D software licenses are now Maya licenses.

All over the world, games development studios are turning to Maya. In North America, Infinity Ward, Ion Storm, Sony Computer Entertainment, Polyphony, Nintendo, Namco, and Square-Enix, to name but a few, have made the transition. In Europe, Digital Illusions, Blitz Games, Bizarre Creations, Lionhead Studios, and Electronic Arts all utilize Maya as the main tool for creating artwork for their games.

As you can see, more and more companies are switching to Maya, and this is mainly due to its continued focus on the games development market. This focus shows results—with each new release of Maya comes more features geared toward games development.

## Why I Wrote This Book

Back when I started out in the games industry, there was nothing to refer to. You had only your own enthusiasm and desire to create interactive entertainment. In the run up to achieving my first position, I spent weeks working away on my Amiga 1200, drawing 2D graphics and creating animations for games I had designed myself. These graphics won me a position at a company called Freestyle Software, a place that gave me a chance and set my foot on the ladder of this industry.

There were no books or Web sites then about how to create games, so you had to be disciplined enough to teach yourself the latest 2D package or, as time went by, the current 3D package. Now there is a wealth of knowledge available, so getting into the industry is a little more difficult due to the intense competition. Today you have to prove you have a good understanding of the tasks involved in creating game-related artwork. Here in this book I'll share some insider knowledge and techniques that will enable you to get a leg up into the games industry.

As the games market has grown over the years, the developer's job has become more recognized as a true career path and not just a hobby. Universities now offer courses dedicated to games programming, artwork, and animation. But there is still a shortage of books on the subject. Plenty of books have been written about creating high-resolution characters for films, but only a scarce few cover the restrictions involved in working with game models, and there are none that cover creating console resolution models from concept through to animation.

Not everyone gets the opportunity to further his or her education formally; this is why I want to share what I've learned over the past eleven years. I am not saying that my methods are perfect, and there's no requirement that you *have* to work this way. I'm simply showing you how I work. With that information, you can branch out and form your own, improved techniques.

## About This Book

To the seasoned game artist, some of the structure of this book may be unexpected. Once you know the basic fundamentals of game character development, all the different stages tend to blur into just a few. When you know what to look out for early on—where polygons should be placed so the character deforms correctly, and so forth—you can preempt what would normally be done further down the line. I have tried to separate each step of the character development process into its own chapter, to help you, the reader, learn and understand each individual stage. Once you've worked through the book and gained some experience, you'll find the boundaries of each section merging into a continuous process.

You may also wonder about the scope of the book; it covers a great deal. Those actually employed in the games industry tend to work in one specialized area, such as modeling, texturing, rigging, or animation. To date I have worked for five companies, and at each I have been called upon to perform a number of tasks. It's sometimes just not economical to employ five people to cover five separate areas, when one or two can cover them all just as easily. From my experience, you are less likely to be offered a position if you are not flexible in your skills. Yes, specialize in one area if you like, such as character or game world development, but learn what you can about every stage. You will no doubt be called upon at some time to perform a task that's not in your job description, so it's helpful to have at least some of the relevant knowledge.

All that said, if you already have a development studio in your sights, it's best to check out how they work so that you can focus your skills accordingly.

# On the Included CD

Supplied with this book is a CD-ROM that will work with both Windows and Mac systems. Throughout the book, keystrokes that are different on each platform are expressed in Windows/Mac format (for instance, Shift+Ctrl/Cmd).

The CD contains many tools and files associated with the book's contents. There are four primary directories: Maya, Morgue, Project Files, and Software. The following sections describe these directories and give instructions for loading and setting them up.

> **NOTE** The scripts available in the Maya/Scripts directory are free, shareware tools and are not necessary for working through this book. The shelf, however (found in Maya/Shelves), is an important part of the book's projects and should be installed following the instructions below.

### Maya/Scripts/CreatureTools_v5

Creature Tools is an automated character rigging and animation system for Maya. With Creature Tools installed, you will be able to generate a full skeleton and rig for your character in seconds.

Inside this directory you will find two subdirectories labeled Manual and Scripts. Place all the files found in the Scripts directory into your My Documents/maya/6.0/scripts folder (for Mac: {home}/Library/Preferences/Alias/maya/scripts). Replace the 6.0 in this path with the version number of Maya you are currently running; if you're using the PLE included on the CD (described in "Software" just below), it's 6.0PLE.

When you start Maya, you'll see a new menu called Creature Tools; if it doesn't appear, open the script editor and type `crToolsMenu` to load Creature Tools manually.

For information on how to use Creature Tools, refer to the manual found in the Manual directory.

### *Maya/Scripts/Misc*

In this directory you will find a selection of scripts that I use regularly. To install these, simply place them into your My Documents/maya/6.0/scripts folder (for Mac: {home}/Library/Preferences/Alias/maya/scripts). Here again, you need to change the 6.0 in the path to match your Maya version.

To run the scripts, type the filename (without the .mel extension) into the script editor and press Enter.

- ▶ instanceSplit.mel converts instanced objects into unique ones.

- ▶ notePad.mel places a note into the current scene. When the scene is reloaded, notes are displayed to remind you or a colleague of anything you have put into the scene.

- ▶ showMaterial.mel is a handy little program that opens the Attribute Editor, displaying the material assigned to the selected face. This saves you the effort of searching through the Hypershade—a useful shortcut if your scene has hundreds of textures.

- ▶ resBatch.mel simply alters the way your textures are displayed in Maya's views. It scales the size of all the textures, not physically but temporarily, speeding up the real-time display as you work.

### *Maya/Shelves*

Please make sure you install this shelf (shelf_GCDM.mel) before you begin working with the projects in this book. It contains tools that are useful—and sometimes essential—for completing the example tasks.

Copy the shelf_GCDM.mel file into your My Documents/maya/6.0/prefs/shelves directory (for Mac: {home}/Library/Preferences/Alias/maya/6.0/prefs/shelves). A new Shelf called GCDM will be available the next time you launch Maya.

### *Morgue*

In The Morgue you will find a selection of files taken straight from my own library. Feel free to use these to help develop your own skills and characters, but they are not available for commercial use.

### Project Files

All of the Maya and texture files you will need for the book's projects can be found in the Project Files directory. Each subdirectory name corresponds to the associated chapter number.

### Software

You don't actually need your own version of Maya to work through this book, because on the CD we have included the Personal Learning Edition (PLE), a free version of Maya. Although it is essentially the same application as the full version of Maya, the PLE does have some restrictions. For example, you can load the .mb files supplied on the CD, but you are only able to save them as .mp, meaning they will only work with the PLE.

Refer to Maya's help directory found in Help > Maya Help (F1) for further details on the differences between the full and PLE versions of Maya.

If you would like to keep completely up to date with the PLE, you can download the absolutely latest version from the Alias Web site; you'll find a link on the CD.

In addition, the CD contains a link to the Adobe Web site's download page. Here you will find a demo version of Photoshop. Of course, if you already have a graphics program you're comfortable with, feel free to use that.

Now that you know the where's and why's about this book and you have your environment set up, let's move on and dive into the world of *Game Character Development with Maya.*

**CD Files**

FaceScan.tif
MainScan.tif
GraeColorRender.tif
KilaColorRender.tif

# CHAPTER 1
# Designing Your Character

**PLAYING A COMPUTER GAME** is in some ways very similar to reading a book or watching a film: It is pure escapism. For the duration of the game, the player becomes the hero. During these few hours they step into another world, leaving worries and troubles behind. The overall design of the hero plays a key part in the player's distraction; a good design, combined with a good story, can encapsulate the player, immersing them fully in the game. A bad design will only serve to shatter the illusion, which could single-handedly cause your game to fail in the marketplace.

So where do you start when designing a character? This depends on the project. If you are working on a licensed project, a cartoon for example, or a comic book or movie license, you will be supplied with all the relevant materials to help you create your characters. These materials might include various models and color sheets, or even photographic references.

In theory, not having to worry about character design for your game could save time and work, but in reality you will find that the licensor will want the 3D version of their creation to stay true to its original style and design. Accomplishing this will involve a great many submissions of your artwork to get feedback from several people. First, you must be happy with the piece, and then your immediate manager—the lead artist on the project—must approve it. The work will then be passed to your art director before it is finally presented to the client. And it's not done yet: The client may have to pass it around among a few colleagues before you receive any feedback. All this can turn out to be a lengthy process and will ultimately mean your having to make plenty of minor alterations before the characters are "signed off" as complete.

If, on the other hand, you are developing a product independently, all the character designs will be developed in house. Passing through fewer people means approval times will be shorter. This also means you will have more creative freedom, as long as your project managers are happy with the result.

In this first chapter I will share my own thoughts about the character design process, and in particular my ideas about designing the two main characters that we will develop as we work through this book.

## What Makes a Successful Character?

Designing a character can be difficult; not only have you got to be fresh and original, but you must also be able to communicate your ideas to others through your artwork. You don't have to be an excellent traditional artist; all you need at this point is the ability to roughly sketch your ideas and put them onto paper for others to see. Once the sketches are approved, you can spend more time creating better renderings of the concepts to flesh out your basic ideas.

So what are key points to keep in mind when designing a successful character?

▶ **Target Audience**—One of the first things to consider is for whom you are designing this character. Who is the game aimed at? The design and style for the character should fit the target audience's age group. If you are designing for a younger, pre-teen player, the character could be more of a caricature or could have a cartoon style with exaggerated proportions and bright colors. An adult audience will connect better with a more realistic hero.

▶ **Player Identification**—As with the characters in a film, the more players can identify with the game hero, the more deeply they will be drawn into the game. Players must *want* to be the character, to step into those shoes for the duration of the game.

▶ **Character Depth**—Your characters' personalities will contribute tremendously not only to their visual design but also to the way they act. Their "background" is what shapes their personality, so it's essential that you have good knowledge of the characters' past and present.

▶ **Branding**—If you are designing the main character for the game, it could be that all advertisements will be based upon that character. With this in mind, the character must be original and memorable as well as marketable.

▶ **Technical Considerations**—We talk more about technical matters later in the chapter. Knowing the technical limitations that affect your character will have an impact on your design of that character.

▶ **The Game World**—Finally, look at what the level/world builders in your game are doing. Work together with them, so that your characters and their world fit together. If the styles compete, the character may look out of place, and you lose the player's connection with the game hero.

We now have a good idea of what qualities make up a good character, but what else can help us conceptualize that character? Inspiration certainly can, and it's all around us.

Comics are a good source of inspiration; they give us many of today's cool characters. Superman, for example, is one of the most popular heroes of our time. His "S" shield is recognized worldwide. The striking red, blue, and yellow colors of his costume, his swirling cape, and the underwear worn on the outside of his outfit are all part of his trademark. Yet his uniform is relatively simple in design. Batman is another good example derived from comics; his design demonstrates good use of color and a strong silhouette—both important factors in a character's design.

It's safe to say that comics have long been a source of inspiration for game characters. Visit any game development studio and you will be hard pressed to find an artist's desk that doesn't display some comic memorabilia.

We can also learn substantially from studying other successful game character designs. The hugely popular Final Fantasy series gives us colorful characters that hold a lot of personality and visual style. With each new Final Fantasy game come new styles and fresh new characters, each unique in its appearance. Lavish swords and weaponry, highly imaginative outfits, and well-conceived characters add to the gaming experience.

Metal Gear Solid is another example of strong character design, in this case taking a more hyper-realistic style. The chosen colors fit the character perfectly—he is a moody tactical character who uses stealth effectively, and his outfit has to represent this by being practical as well as stylish.

Finally, we have games such as the Jak and Daxter or Ratchet and Clank series, which are complete departures from the previously mentioned titles. These PlayStation games offer well-designed characters using a more abstract and cartoony style, because this sort of game needs to appeal to a wider audience, particularly the younger gamer.

## The Three Stages of Concepting

So where do we start with our concept? Do we sit down and begin to sketch? Just pour out our ideas onto paper? Nope. Not yet. If you go to this step too early, you might end up with a good design, but it will not be what your manager wants.

*Concepting* usually happens in the pre-production phase of a game, and sometimes earlier. During this time the designer, along with the concept artists, will work on the game's design and overall style. You will be approached by either your lead artist or the art director and asked to provide some concept artwork for the design. They will provide some basic information to start you off (for example, the general style and overall look of each character). You can then begin plans to flesh out this information; this is covered in more depth in the "Preparation" section.

The aim is to have a clear idea of what direction you're taking, having a vision in your mind of what the character will look like and why. Concepting a character has three stages:

▶  Research

▶  Preparation

▶  Design

As you gain more experience in concepting, you may find that you need to do less during the first two stages and can more or less move straight into the design (sketching) phase. For the novice, however, it is important to begin at the beginning: researching the character.

## Research

Our primary job when doing character research is to gain as much information as possible about the character. You can get the basic details from the lead designer, as well as information on game mechanics. All of this will tell you what the character needs to do in the game, which will have an impact on the design. Consult your lead artist and art director about the general style and look of the game. Ideally, you should have the basics—age, height, sex, and hair/eye/skin color—but if possible you should get a more in-depth description. Just being told that the main character is a "guy with a gun" will not do.

Having a brief history or biography of the character can be invaluable. Folding this insight into the character's personality will help you decide not only what they would wear but why they would wear it. Will the character have a distinguishing feature or some sort of visual scarring? What about the hair style and color? Your design should fit the brief; for example, a conservative character would not sport a bright-pink mohawk—well, not unless the game guidelines ask for it.

### A Sample Character History

To help demonstrate the importance of character history or biography, I have come up with a basic game idea and two main characters, Kila and Grae. The following introduction gives you a rough idea of the overall game and introduces you to these key characters.

*It was a crisp autumn morning; the sun shone through the trees, gently melting the frost that had formed during the night. Kila lay quietly on the park bench. She had been awake for only a few minutes, but it felt like an eternity. Shivering slightly, she dared not move or open her eyes, for the moment she did, the hangover she had so far avoided would no doubt kick in with a vengeance. She could hear movement all around her—people on their way to work, cars stopping and starting and idling in the rush-hour traffic. Life was happening all around her, and she wished it would be quiet. Carefully she lifted her head from the wooden slats of the bench. To her surprise and relief, her dizziness, nausea, and headache disappeared.*

*Confused, Kila tried to recall the events that led up to her night on the bench, but her memory was patchier than usual. She could remember finishing work at the club and having a few drinks with her friends, but that was about all; the rest was a blur. She smiled, thinking that the lack of memory probably meant it must have been a great night. No doubt the details would trickle back to her as the day went on. Feeling surprisingly well, she rose from the bench and headed home.*

*"Morning, Kila. Good night?" shouted her neighbor, Suzie.*

*Kila, fumbling for the keys to her apartment, turned to face her friend. "Yeah, what I can remember of it," she joked as she opened her door.*

*"Must have been good," teased Suzie. "You can fill me in on the details later!" As she passed on her way out of the building, Suzie added "Hey, cool contacts. Catch you later!"*

*"Yeah, see you Suzie." The door closed behind her; Kila was home at last. She walked down her hallway toward the bathroom, where she turned on the shower and removed her jacket. Wait a minute…cool contacts? She suddenly remembered what Suzie had said. "But I don't wear contact lenses." Confused, she moved in front of the mirror, wiped off the condensation from the steaming shower, and stood still in amazement. Her once brown eyes were now bright*

*green; they even seemed to glow. She moved closer to the mirror, inspecting her eyes. Maybe she'd got some contacts from her friends? After all, they were all the rage on the clubbing scene. She gently pulled her eyelids apart, and to her horror saw that the glowing green eyes were really hers. What was going on? How had this happened? She backed away from the mirror and walked into her bedroom, moving toward the full-length mirror in the corner.*

*As she approached the mirror, she caught a glimpse of something dark on her left arm. Halting in amazement, her eyes crept slowly along the long, gothic tattoo that crawled all the way from her shoulder down to her wrist. Twisting to look at the back of her arm, she was faced with another shock—the tattoo spread to her back. Frightened, she pulled off her shirt and looked in alarm at her back. The beautiful tattoo covered nearly all of her back. How had she ended up with something like this? "This has to be a joke, I don't remember having anything like this done last night." Now panicking, she licked her fingers and desperately tried to wipe the tattoo off, hoping it was temporary, maybe a practical joke. It did not budge.*

*Kila sat at the foot of the bed, her head in her hands. Steam from the shower still running in the bathroom floated into the hallway. Only one thought hammered in her mind: "What happened to me last night?" She wracked her brains, trying to remember the slightest clue to how her eyes could possibly change color, and how she could have obtained the extraordinary tattoo. A tattoo of this size would take weeks to heal, but this one looked months old—yet yesterday it hadn't existed. She would quiz her friends, the other dancers she worked with at the club. Someone had to know.*

*Later that evening, hoping to find some answers, Kila headed to the club where she worked. As she walked through quiet streets, she couldn't help but notice a car following her at a distance. Nervous, she picked up her pace and ducked down an alley that was guarded by two posts preventing vehicles from entering. Her heart was pounding in her chest and she could feel panic rising. Chancing a quick glance behind, she was reassured to see no one—she was no longer being followed. Breathing a sigh of relief, she turned and continued on her way.*

*"Hey, babe!" came a voice from the shadows. "What's a pretty thing like you doing in a place like this?" Kila spun around, squinting to see where the voice was coming from. Eventually she glimpsed six figures emerging from the*

*shadows. "Look, I don't want any trouble," she pleaded, trembling, as the men surrounded her.*

*"Well that's too bad, because we do," one of them replied. As they moved in, she could feel her heart racing, pumping adrenaline through her veins. She spun around to get her bearings, and then she felt it. Her skin began to warm; the heat grew uncomfortable, bordering on painful. She could feel something deep inside her body growing, taking over. Suddenly, as if a switch had been flicked, she stood perfectly still, no longer quivering, steady as a rock. Slowly she raised her head and stared directly at the one who had threatened her. Her green eyes were glowing wildly, her breathing heavier and deeper now. The thug hesitated but was only briefly impressed. "Nice trick, babe, but it doesn't scare me." He reached around to the back of his jeans and produced a long knife. "You see, I can be scary, too," he threatened, pointing the weapon at her. "Now hand over your cash like a good little girl. Then I think we'll have a bit of fun. What do you say, guys?" A murmur of excitement spread around the circle.*

*Kila's glowing eyes were fixed on the leader. A moment passed and then she spoke: "You want it, come and get it." He looked her up and down, then moved toward her, still brandishing the knife. Kila was very still, eyes pinned on her adversary, waiting for the right moment.*

*He was a few feet away when she made her move. In a split second, her left arm flung out in front of her, and what seemed like ribbons of flesh flew out of the tattoo, impaling the thug in his chest and throat. There was a gasp from the rest of his gang as they watched their leader seem to hang in midair, struggling to breathe, body twitching wildly. Kila smiled coldly; she seemed to enjoy seeing him suffer. She pulled back, retracting the deadly weapon, and his limp body dropped lifeless to the ground. The silence was deafening; no one moved or spoke. Through his fear, one of the others found his voice. "She…she killed Greg!" And from behind her, she heard "Get her!" There was a mad rush and they were upon her.*

*Suddenly a brilliant flash momentarily stunned Kila's attackers. Her arms seemed to be forced apart by invisible hands, and she felt herself rising slowly from the ground. As she floated, tendrils spun out of her back and began to wrap around her body, layer upon layer, enclosing her like a spider wrapping up its prey. Meanwhile, something began to take shape, a form gradually being created by the tendrils: a torso, and then arms, legs, and finally a head. What was once Kila was now a 30-foot beast, a demonic monster. The thugs were horrified. With a mighty roar, the beast took a huge swipe at the circle, knocking two of them flying, into the surrounding walls. The rest of the men fumbled for their concealed weapons and let rip with a hail of bullets.*

*The bullets entered the beast from several directions, but its body seemed to absorb them. They had no effect other than provoking it, making it angrier. It lunged for another thug who managed to dodge the attack, using the opportunity to escape. "I'm getting out of here! We weren't paid to handle this. What the hell is this thing?" He fled, closely followed by his comrades. The beast, once Kila, was alone in the alley. It looked around for another victim, its deep, rough breaths gradually slowing. As it calmed, it began to glow gently, and the wrapped tendrils began to retract back into Kila. Slowly, eventually, she was back to herself again. She glanced down and saw the lifeless body of the thug she had killed, dropped to her knees and began to cry. "What's going on? What was that?" she sobbed. Kila didn't want to kill anyone. Indeed, Kila hadn't killed anyone—it was that thing inside her who had done it.*

*As Kila wept, a dark figure of a man in the shadows at the far end of the alleyway took a long drag on a cigarette, then dropped it to the pavement and extinguished it with his foot. The stranger was pleased with what he had seen; this could work out better than expected. Satisfied there was nothing more to observe, he turned and got back into his car and drove away.*

This story sets the scene for the game. A young woman's life is turned upside-down when she finds herself part of a symbiotic relationship with Grae, the organism living inside her. Grae can manipulate Kila's DNA in numerous ways, the main one being to show his true form. Throughout the game, Kila struggles to find answers as to why this has happened, while struggling with the overpowering evil that has invaded her body.

From a design point of view, Kila should be quite average looking, nothing too fancy or flashy. There are two reasons for this:

▶ Keeping her appearance average will allow the player to relate to the character.

▶ A plain and not-too-fancy Kila will provide more of a contrast between her and the monstrous Grae.

> **NOTE** ▶ This first, unremarkable design for Kila will work well as an introductory character for this book, allowing me to discuss the basic principles associated with creating a real-time character.

Grae's design should be completely different from Kila's. To start, he will be larger and his parts will have more outrageous proportions. He should include some of the more advanced elements associated with modeling creatures for games, such as wings and double-jointed legs (dog legs).

> **NOTE** ▶ The Grae character will comprise advanced areas of character design for the reader's instruction.

At this point, you probably have a few ideas of your own about how Kila and Grae should look, but before we move on we need to gather some more information on the two characters. The following tables are a kind of "bio," presenting basic details and some set pieces of information about the characters.

| | |
|---|---|
| **Name** | Kila. |
| **Age** | 22. |
| **Height** | 5 feet, 6 inches (1.7 meters). |
| **Occupation** | Exotic dancer in a nightclub. |
| **Main Outfit** | Ripped jeans and short top. Overall outfit has a slightly stylized look. |
| **Hair Color** | Dark brown with a red tint. |
| **Eye Color** | Green (originally brown, before the evolution to Grae began). Her eyes appear to glow. |
| **Brief Background** | Taken away from abusive parents when she was 8 years old and raised by a foster family. At 16, she left home without their consent. Alone in the big city, she finds herself the target of pimps and crooks and resorts to crime to get money to live. Eventually, at 19, she got a break as a dancer in a local nightclub, where she has been earning an honest living ever since. |
| **Personality** | On the outside, Kila is quite a strong character, very confident and sometimes cocky. This is just a front, however; on the inside she is vulnerable and sensitive. |
| **Other Details** | She has a large, visible gothic tattoo that starts on her back and left arm and spreads down to the back of her left hand. |

| | |
|---|---|
| **Name** | Grae, or GX-792. |
| **Age** | Unknown. |
| **Height** | 30 feet (9 meters). |
| **Occupation** | Unknown. |
| **Outfit** | His body is made up like a mummy, with strips of flesh wrapped and layered to build his body. |
| **Hair Color** | Grae is hairless. |
| **Eye Color** | His eyes should glow green to tie in with Kila's. |
| **Brief Background** | Part of a secret experiment, Grae is almost 100% manufactured; the key component of his structure is of extraterrestrial origin. Kila is an accidental test subject, the intended subject being the scientist who created him. On the night before he is due to inject himself, the scientist goes out for one final night as a normal man. He meets Kila and they go back to his apartment. She is accidentally injected with GX-792 when thieves invade the apartment; the scientist is killed, but Kila escapes. |
| **Personality** | Grae is evil; he delights in the pain of others. The only person he looks out for is Kila. His main mission is to protect his host, although this protection is purely selfish (if his host dies, then he dies, too). |
| **Other Details** | Grae's wings will consist of tendrils. If possible, these will have constant motion when they're out, but they will be stored away in his back most of the time. Although Grae does have a mouth, he does not have the ability to talk. |

## Technical Limitations

With all this information at hand, we have a pretty good starting point. From the introductory story, we know a little of how the game begins and we have insight into the main character's personality. Next we have the set details listed in the foregoing tables. These are explicit guidelines about the character that we must follow when we begin to design.

Normally this is all you need for character design, but for the project outlined in this book we are creating a real-time character; that means there are other considerations that could affect your design. As with any game artwork, you are expected to work within certain technical limitations. Examples are polygon count, texture page size, animation data, and even joint limits (all of which are covered in later chapters). The lead artist, having worked closely with the lead programmer to come up with the numbers, will impose these restrictions.

So how does this affect your character design? Let's look at two examples.

▶ **Example A: John Doe**—In this case you are creating a generic character who will be onscreen with a hundred others, plus vehicles and the game world. The polygon count limit is between 500 and 1000, but you are urged to go as low as possible, as is always the case when creating real-time artwork. The less overall memory your character takes up the better, as the entire game will have to fit inside a tight budget. In addition, let's say you are informed that John Doe will have to use a basic skeleton, which will probably mean a limit of about 15 joints. You are not going to see him up close, so there is no need for significant detail.

With such small polygon and joint limits, you won't be able to build long flowing hair, or that complex rocket pack you had in mind. Instead, you will be better off sticking with a basic model: arms, legs, head, and probably hands that are fixed in a certain pose because you will not have enough polygons or joints for separate fingers. In addition, you won't have sufficient polygons to have nice, rounded muscle tone, so you will have to rely on the textures to show any needed detail. Since the character will always be positioned away from the camera, however, any detail in the texture will be lost.

> **TIP** ▶ When compiling your research, try to get a good idea of how big the character will be onscreen, this will allow you to get a good idea of just how much detail you will need.

▶ **Example B: Hercules**—This is the game's main character; he will be seen both close up and from a distance, but the game is predominantly viewed in the third-person perspective (from behind the character). As the game's cut scenes are rendered real-time, Hercules will also need fully posable fingers, as well as facial animation. Your polygon limit is 3000, and the character needs to look good at all resolutions.

This should give you scope to create a decent design for Hercules. You have sufficient polygons to get the detail you need. Plus, his being the main character means you can go to town on making him look great. Sufficient levels of detail can be adopted to make sure he looks good at any distance while ensuring he only uses the needed polygons. (We talk more about levels of detail in Chapter 10.)

**TIP** ▶ Here's one thing to remember when creating a character who is viewed from the third-person perspective: Chances are that 99% of the time the character will be viewed from behind, so you will want to make the character's back interesting for the player.

**TIP** ▶ An RTS (real-time strategy) game—a top-down, isometric, Diablo- or Warcraft-type game—often requires some extreme proportional distortions for its characters to read well onscreen: Head and shoulder areas often need exaggeration, and limbs might require thickening to make sure they don't "wink out" at distances (become too negligible in width to merit a pixel onscreen).

### Animation Considerations

You can see how a game's technical restrictions can affect the look of your designs. Another important question you should ask is, "Will it animate okay?"

Implementing a cape, ribbons, or hair into your character concept may look cool—but when it comes down to it, do you have the resources to animate the feature successfully? Take the cape, for instance. Essentially, if it's hand animated, you can consider it an additional character. So do you or the other animators on the project have time in the schedule to animate it? Your programmers may have a nice dynamics engine which will drive the cape cloth for you while obeying real-world physics, such as wind, drag, and gravity. This will save time, but will it give a good enough simulation? Will it move convincingly? There are dangers in employing a dynamics simulation to animate cloth or hair, and if done wrong it can destroy the player's connection with the main character and the game. If the simulation moves unpredictably or pops through the character or surrounding area, it will distract the player from the game and ultimately become annoying.

Some other animation issues to consider: When designing clothing at or near joints, think about how these areas will behave when the joint bends. Loincloths, skirts, shoulder pads, long sleeves, cuffs, and overlapping armor can cause some of the most frustrating problems when skinning your character (covered in

Chapter 11), and often require additional control bones not allowed in your joint budget.

> **TIP** ▶ Consult your technical director or lead animator about any design element that looks troublesome or that might need substantial secondary animation or many control bones. And do it before embarking on the modeling stage; you may be saving yourself a lot of rework later on.

### Summing Up the Limitations

So let's summarize the basic technical limits for our two characters.

| Technical Element | Kila | Grae |
| --- | --- | --- |
| Polygon Limit | 4500 or less | 5500 or less |
| Joint Limit | No more than 60, if possible | No more than 60, if possible |
| Texture Pages | Two; 512x512 | Three; 512x512 |

This is quite a short list, and on a real project there will be other areas to consider. How will facial animation be handled in the game—will it be joint driven or will you use blend shapes (we will discuss this in Chapter 13)? What about extra texture effects like alpha, specular, bump, or normal mapping? Will Grae's wings be joint or dynamics driven? These questions may look scary to the uninitiated, so for now we will concentrate on the basics. Other technical considerations and concerns will be covered as we work through the book, building, texturing, and rigging our characters.

Luckily, Kila and Grae are the main characters, so we have been given generous polygon, joint, and texture limits. Grae is quite large and also has wings, so he will need more joints, polygons, and (possibly) texture space than Kila.

## Preparation

Having done the research, we now have all the information we could possibly handle, right? Now do we start to draw? Nope, we move on to the next stage: preparation. We need to gather reference material and compile a *style sheet.*

At this point, we know what the character will look like and we have a pretty good idea of where to start. What I like to do next is compile a style sheet to hold all the relevant images I find while collecting my reference material. The Internet, with its unlimited image resources, is an excellent source for the gathering of material. Other great sources are magazines and even DVDs—you can get references from anywhere, really.

Looking at the information on our characters so far, we can see that Kila is a casual, average-looking girl in ripped jeans and a T-shirt. So to start, we can go to one of the many Internet search engines that have the option to search for images, and do a search for "ripped jeans" or simply "jeans." After quickly scanning the results for anything relevant and grabbing it, we move on to the next item of clothing we want to design, and so on and so forth. Maybe we even add a belt of some sort. After we have enough references for her clothing, we can move on to her hairstyle, makeup, and other elements. The earlier bio table specifies a large, gothic tattoo, so we look for references on tattoos. The main idea of a style sheet is to gather every image you will need into one location, and you then only need to refer to this when you begin to sketch. The style sheet is also useful for showing to others, to give them a feel for the style of the character.

**TIP** Good Web sites for clothing images are online catalogs and shopping sites. These contain images of people in various poses wearing entire outfits; these pictures can also be useful references for your concept drawings.

Once you have all the images you need, you can simply load them all into Photoshop and compile them into one large image, usually an 8.5" by 11" sheet at a resolution of 300 dpi. Then print it, and it's ready for you to use. Don't be afraid to compile a number of style sheets if you feel you need them. Or, if you are lucky and have access to a larger-format printer, produce one to that size.

**Figure 1.1** shows an example of a style sheet layout. (Unfortunately, due to copyright restrictions, I cannot show the actual images I compiled for Kila and Grae but this should give you a general idea.)

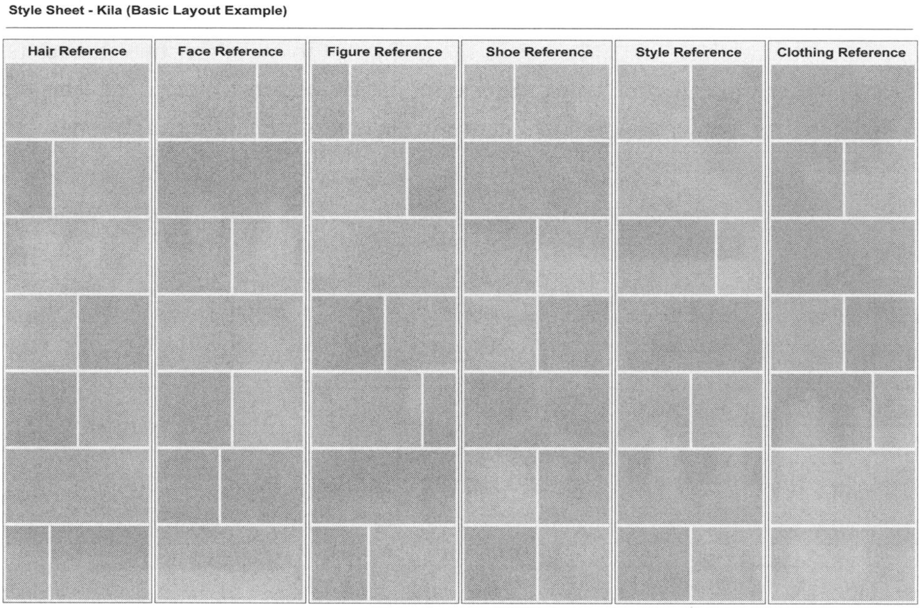

Style Sheet - Kila (Basic Layout Example)

FIGURE 1.1 Sample layout for a style sheet

# Design

We are now at the final stage, design—you are now ready to begin drawing. Although the first two stages of research and preparation may seem like a lot of work, believe me—it is worth it. Without the proper preparation, you could end up stumbling ahead blindly, but having help at hand early on will keep you from falling later. It's trite, but true: "If you fail to prepare, you prepare to fail!"

Let's have a look at some of the key points to consider when fleshing out the design of your character.

▶ **A Good, Fresh Style**—A strong visual style is important and must remain consistent throughout the whole design. Coming up with an original style can be difficult; don't be surprised if, whatever your character looks like, someone in the approval list will comment on how "it looks like such-and-such." Try not to directly copy an existing style, and instead use a mixture of different influences to come up with something original.

▶ **Contrast Among Characters**—When designing a series of characters, it is important to have contrast among them. Try not to make any two characters too much alike. A good way to check the success of your concept in terms of contrast is to line up your characters and switch off the lights so the characters are only visible in silhouette. Can you tell who is who?

▶ **Asymmetry**—To make your design more interesting, make sure the character is not completely symmetrical. Variation is the key, just as it is in the real people all around you. No one's features are completely symmetrical.

▶ **Appeal**—Your character has to be appealing to its target audience. If the game is aimed at young children, reflect this in your design by including bright colors and outrageous proportions. Make the characters fun to look at as well as play with.

▶ **Color**—The colors of your character can say a lot about them. Darker colors tend to represent evil or a rebellious nature; brighter colors are usually associated with a good, pure person.

▶ **Proportions**—The size and scale of your character can add greatly to the desired style. As a rule of thumb, a realistic humanoid character tends to be around eight heads high. Looking at the comparison in **Figure 1.2**, you can see the proportions of a more heroic, stylized male character. He would have a slightly smaller head but much larger shoulders than the average figure. The legs would be longer, but in contrast his torso would be shortened and his waist smaller.

**Figure 1.3** illustrates the difference between a realistic and stylized female. The more stylized version has longer legs, a smaller waist, and—yep, you guessed it, a larger chest. In the face she has more pronounced cheekbones, larger eyes and eyelashes, plus more voluptuous lips than the realistic version.

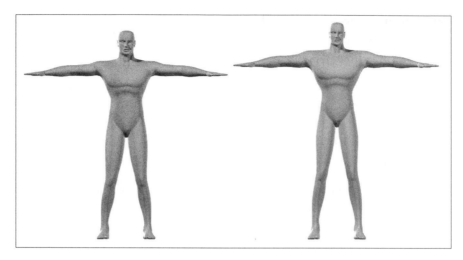

**FIGURE 1.2** Male character style comparison

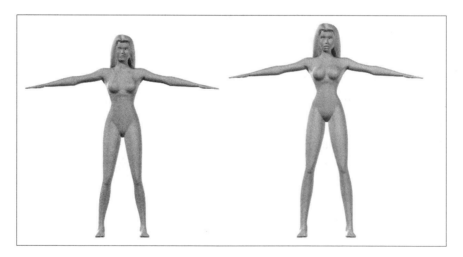

**FIGURE 1.3** Female character style comparison

With cartoon characters, you can play around with the numbers, changing them drastically to achieve exaggerated proportions. But a good starting point is to have the overall size of your character around three heads high. This will give them a larger head in proportion to the body, so add to this contrast by increasing the size of the hands and feet (**Figure 1.4**). If they are meant to be cute, you can give them large eyes, too.

**FIGURE 1.4** Example of cartoon character proportions

▶ **Anatomy**—A good knowledge of anatomy is essential when creating characters. Understanding the basics of muscle and bone structure will help you shape your figures, making them more realistic and correctly proportioned. Having a good selection of anatomy books to refer to is always a good idea.

### Your Early Sketches

Using your style sheets, you can now begin to roughly sketch out some ideas. Take your time if you have it, and spend a few days playing around with ideas. **Figure 1.5** shows a few early sketches I produced for Kila; you can probably see the progression of her design and the deep contrast between the first idea and her eventual look.

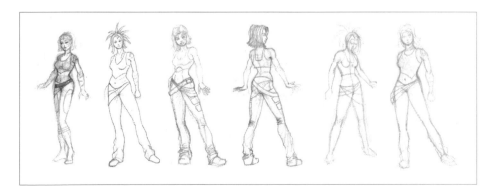

**FIGURE 1.5** Brainstorm sheet for Kila

While designing Kila, I tried to make her look normal but with subtle differences. Early on, I gave her wild hair and extravagant clothing, but this all looked over the top. I also tried to tone down the amount of symmetry she originally had. Notice that her hair is now longer on one side, and across her waist the belt and sash cross from opposite directions.

**Figure 1.6** shows the sketches I produced while creating the concept for Grae. My initial idea was to have Kila visible inside his chest, with all the tendrils wrapped around her. I eventually dropped this idea, first because of polygon restrictions, and secondly because it could have caused problems when animating.

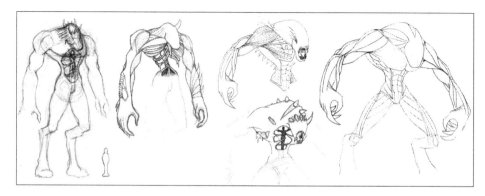

FIGURE 1.6 Brainstorm sheet for Grae

Once you feel confident and comfortable with an idea, you can create a cleaner piece, which you then show to your lead artist and game designer. Again, this should be a quick image to give an idea of the design. It's likely your collaborators will want it revised; you can pretty much be sure your first idea will not be the one they like.

If you have the time and are given the freedom to do so, why not render some nice color pieces like the ones in **Figures 1.7** and **1.8**. Some companies encourage this step. They also like you to present the characters in a well-arranged sheet showing the final render along with a few sketches. These summary sheets look professional and impressive, and at the end of the day you will end up with a nice piece of artwork to go in your portfolio.

FIGURE 1.7 Kila renders

FIGURE 1.8 A complete render for Grae

### Creating the Model Sheets

Great! They love your idea and give you the go ahead! But before you or someone else starts to model, you need to create a few model sheets to work from. These sheets show the character in many different ways; they are the blueprints for building the character.

Imagine someone else is going to be building Kila, and plan out everything for that person.

First of all, you should produce a turnaround view (**Figure 1.9**). The basic images included in this are a front view, side view, and rear view. You can also include a three-quarter view if you have time. If there are any design areas about which you can already be specific, or if you feel something needs more explanation, include these specifics in this turnaround sheet.

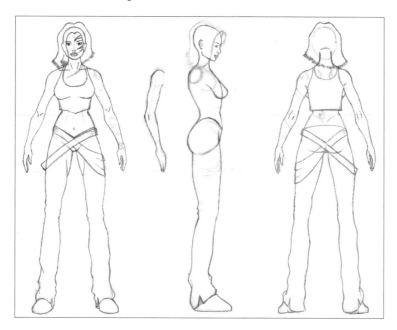

**FIGURE 1.9** Kila model sheet, turnaround view

Notice that the silhouettes for the front and back views are the same. You may be able to make out faint lines across the image; these are important because you need the proportions to be the same for each angle.

To help the person who is going to model your character, you can produce a head sheet like the one in **Figure 1.10**. This is like the turnaround view sheet but focuses on the head's front and side views along with any additional information needed.

**FIGURE 1.10**
Kila head sheet

Whew! With concepting complete, you should have a well thought out and great looking character to work with. So put your crayons away and boot up your computer—it's time to build your creation in glorious 3D.

## Summary

In this chapter, we covered the main phases of creating your own concepts for real-time characters. In addition, we examined the artwork that should be prepared before you move on to modeling a character.

What you should have at this point are some nice character concepts that have been approved by your manager. From these, you will have created the model sheets needed to move to the next stage. In the next chapter, we will start to build your characters, at the same time introducing you to Maya's environment and basic modeling tools.

CD Files

Kila_Basic.mb
Kila_Combined.mb
Kila_Primitive.mb
Kila_Start.mb

*In Scans directory:*
KilaFront.jpg
KilaSide.jpg
MainScan.tif
KilaFront.tga
KilaSide.tga

# CHAPTER 2
# Modeling Kila

**THE CONCEPTING IS COMPLETE** for our characters Kila and Grae, so it's time to move onto the computer and into Maya.

We begin this chapter by showing you how to prepare and store your artwork, as well as the procedure for configuring Maya's environment. Then we'll explore the basic modeling tools as we begin to build our characters.

# Preparation

You are now ready to create your characters. You have all the needed resources, which you have gathered yourself or have received from another concept artist. For a given character, you should have at hand the following:

▶ **Model Sheet**—The model sheet displays the full character from various angles, preferably the front, side, and rear views. Specific details may also be included on this sheet.

▶ **Head Sheet**—The head sheet gives a close-up of the character's head and facial features. Like the model sheet, the head sheet has front, side, and rear views.

▶ **Color Sheet**—The color sheet displays the fully rendered character. You will use this for color reference when it comes time to apply a texture.

▶ **Limitations**—Before you begin to model a character, it's important that you know all the applicable technical restrictions. These will include polygon counts and texture page limits.

With all the necessary information ready, let's look at how to properly store it.

## Artwork Storage

An important piece of information you should obtain at this stage concerns the storage of your artwork. Is there a specific directory structure in place? Does an area exist on the network where all the artwork for a particular project will be stored? Does this location get backed up frequently and regularly?

Many game development studios have custom-written software in place to take care of artwork storage, but deserving of mention is one of the best and most widely available: Alienbrain. A clever application, Alienbrain holds all the game assets on a server to which the development team has access. When a piece of artwork is begun, it is stored not only locally but also on the server. These server files are then locked. An individual wanting to work with a file must "check it out" and then check it back in at the end of the work session.

This is just the tip of the Alienbrain iceberg: The program is capable of much more. It has plug-ins available for Maya, Photoshop, and many other applications to speed up workflow and make things more user friendly, while all along keeping regular backups of your work in case the worst should happen.

You can find more information on Alienbrain by visiting their Web site www. nxn-software.com.

As good as Alienbrain is, it does not set up a directory structure for you. The leads on your team should establish this so that everyone knows where everything is at any given time. The directory framework can be as simple as the structure seen in **Figure 2.1**.

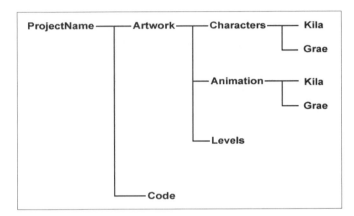

**FIGURE 2.1** A basic directory structure

## Preparing the Work Environment

Now that you know where to store your artwork, you can begin to prepare your working environment.

### Scanning in the Model

First, you need to scan in your model sheet. By having these images available on your computer, you can import them into Maya and use them as a guide when you begin to build the model. Many developers find this arrangement to be a much better way to work because you can ultimately create a more precise model. Attempting to model from memory or by referring to hard copy references will ultimately lead to errors, and the proportions of the final models will likely be off.

**TIP** You don't need the scanned image to be huge, but it should retain most of the details that exist in the artwork. Scan in the model sheet at 100% or a resolution of 300 dpi; this is quite big, but it's easier to shrink the image later on than to enlarge it. In addition, scanning it higher and then reducing it will give you a better-quality image than if you initially scan at a lower dpi.

### Preparing the Scanned Image

When you take the image into Photoshop (or your preferred digital imaging package), you first need to rotate it, in this case 90 degrees counterclockwise. Save the rotated image now for use as reference.

Once all that is done, you can shrink the image. All you need to do is adjust the ppi (pixels per inch); this will scale the overall image (**Figure 2.2**).

**NOTE** Make sure Resample Image is enabled, If you leave this option unchecked in the Image Size dialog box, changing the dpi (dots per inch) does not alter the pixel resolution of the image (or its storage size on disk). It only affects the size of the image when it is printed.

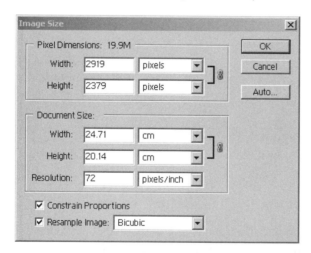

FIGURE 2.2 Scaling an image in Photoshop's Image Size window

Adjusting an image to 72 ppi usually gives an acceptable result. When you need to work with a better, more detailed image, play around with the ppi until you have something acceptable. I recommend using a lower resolution in order to consume less memory on your machine, but you do not want to end up with an image so small that you can't make out any details. See **Figure 2.3** for an example of a good and a bad reduction.

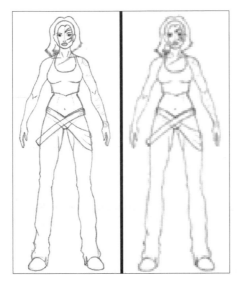

FIGURE 2.3 In the image
reduction on the right, the
ppi resolution is set too low.

### Storing the Image

Now that you have your image stored with a resolution you can work with, you
can chop it up and store the pieces (**Figure 2.4**). An ideal place to keep them would
be in a Scans directory inside the main scene folder. These pieces will then be
imported into Maya later as image planes, guidelines for modeling our characters.

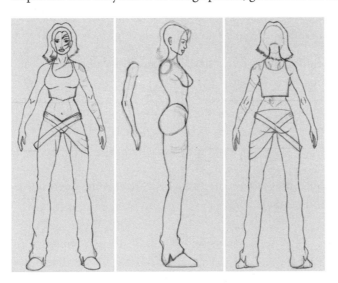

FIGURE 2.4 The
chopped images

To store the pieces of an image, normally you would follow the directory structure dictated by your project manager, but for this book's project we will use
the file system found on the book's CD. For this chapter, our characters will be
stored in the directory Project Files/02. To keep things tidy, I have added a folder
called Scans. Place the image pieces in here, along with the initial image scan
(MainScan.tif). Let's call the cropped images KilaFront.jpg and KilaSide.jpg—
there's no need to crop the rear image as we won't be importing it into Maya.

> **TIP** ▶ Making sure the images are the same height, as well as keeping the
> head and other body parts in line, will help when working with them in Maya.

## Saving Image Planes

For developers experienced with Photoshops tools, here is another way
of creating the image planes: When imported into Maya as image planes,
these images will show up as line art. There will be no white rectangle
around them to get in your way.

1   Working from a 72 ppi scan, use the Rectangular Select tool and select
the front drawing.

2   Copy the front drawing and create a new canvas with a black background.

3   Make sure the image mode is RGB by going to Image > Mode > RGB.

4   Open the Channel Editor and create a new channel; this will be an
alpha channel by default.

5   Paste the image into the new alpha channel and then select Image >
Adjustment > Invert.

6   Save the image as a 32-bit Targa file.

The KilaFront and KilaSide images saved as Targa files are also included on
the CD (KilaFront.tga and KilaSide.tga).

With the images cropped, stored, and ready, we have done all our external preparation. Next, we will move into the Maya program, so let's take a look at the basic tools it has to offer.

## Getting Started in Maya

We are now ready to load Maya and prepare it so we can begin modeling. But first let's have a look at Maya itself. In case you don't have Maya, you'll find Maya's Personal Learning Edition on the CD.

### Maya's Learning Movies and Tutorials

When you start Maya for the first time, you will be presented with the Learning Movies window seen in **Figure 2.5**. These one-minute movies cover some of the very basic elements in Maya, from moving and manipulating objects, to simple keyframe animation.

I recommend that you watch these movies before you proceed in this chapter. If you have already skipped past the Learning Movies window, you can reopen it by going to Help > Learning Movies.

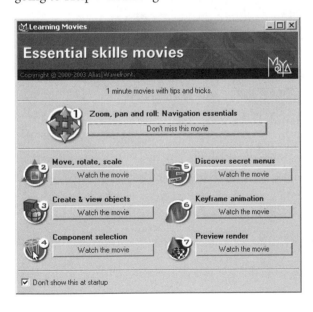

**FIGURE 2.5** Maya's helpful Learning Movies take only a minute each.

If you have time, I also recommend looking at Maya's built-in tutorials (Help > Tutorials). These cover every aspect of Maya and go beyond the fundamentals in the Learning Movies to show more advanced areas such as expressions and MEL (Maya Embedded Language).

### Navigating with Menu Sets, Marking Menus, and The Hotbox

There are various ways to navigate the menus in Maya. Each person has their own preference, but you will no doubt use every method at some point in your work with Maya.

Across the top of Maya's user interface is the *main menu bar.* This menu can be changed, depending on what area of Maya you are working in, by using the *menu sets.* The menu sets are located at the left of the status bar (**Figure 2.6**). You can change among the Animation (F2), Modeling (F3), Dynamics (F4), and Rendering (F5) menu sets. Each group opens up new tools specific to that job.

**FIGURE 2.6**
Menu sets

Right-clicking an object will open up a *marking menu,* Maya's term for a contextual menu (**Figure 2.7**). These menus give quicker access to some of the tools you will commonly use with that object—for example, component selection.

The third method is the *hotbox,* which contains every menu and menu item available in Maya and is fully customizable to suit your needs. When you want quick access to any menu without having to change menu sets, or if the menu you require is hidden, simply hold down the spacebar to open up the hotbox (**Figure 2.8**). To the right of the hotbox are the Hotbox Controls, where you can customize the appearance and contents of the hotbox.

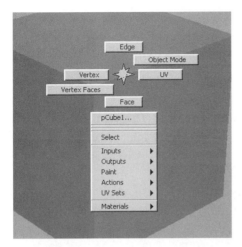

**FIGURE 2.7** Right-click an object to see its marking menu.

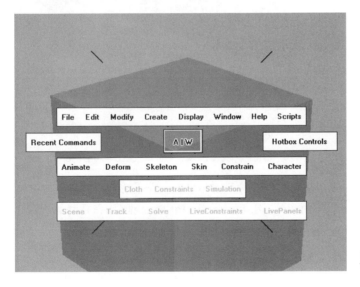

**FIGURE 2.8**
The hotbox

Now that you have some basic knowledge of Maya and its user interface, we will see how to make sure Maya is configured correctly, before we begin to model.

### Setting up Maya Preferences

Although the majority of Maya's default preferences are fine for most of what we're doing we will alter a few now to help us later. It's important to follow these steps so we're all working the same way.

**1**   Go to Window > Settings/Preferences > Preferences to open the Preferences window (**Figure 2.9**). This screen contains all the global preference settings in Maya.

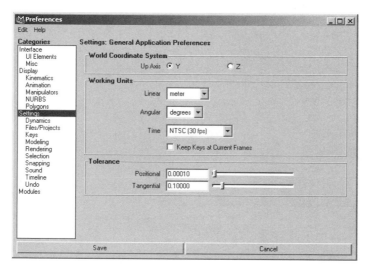

**FIGURE 2.9**
Setting Maya preferences

The first important setting to establish is the choice of units you are using (the scale you will be modeling to). It's important to make sure that everyone on the project is using the same units; differing scales can cause major problems down the line, especially when rigging and animation are involved.

**2**   In the Categories panel on the left, select Settings and see what the working units are currently set to. In **Figure 2.9**, you can see that we will be working in meters and animating at 30 frames per second. Of course, these settings may vary depending on the project you are working on.

**NOTE**   For this book we will be using meters, but feel free to work in whatever units you are comfortable with. Just remember to make the appropriate corresponding adjustments to any of the measurements or values you use from the book.

**3** While in the Preferences window, select the Interface category. Make sure Open Attribute Editor on the right is set to In Separate Window. This setting will ensure that we are working in the same environment for the discussions in this book; otherwise, some sections may be confusing.

**4** Once you have finished setting up all your global Maya configurations, click Save.

**5** Then go to Display > Grid in the main menu and click the options box to open the Grid Options (**Figure 2.10**). In the Size section, setting the Grid Lines Every and Subdivisions to 1 will set each square on the grid to represent 1 meter (or whichever unit you are working in). Length and Width dictate how far your grid expands across your virtual world.

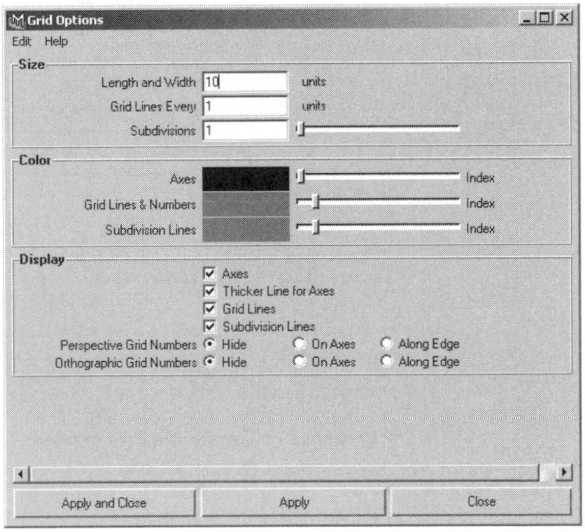

**FIGURE 2.10**
Grid Options setup

The Maya environment is now configured for our project. Remember that your settings should be the same as everyone else's on the project.

Next, you must tell Maya where you wish to work. You can do this by using Maya's *projects*. In Maya, you can work in a variety of file types and formats. By creating a project, you create subdirectories under a parent directory in which to store everything. This is Maya's way of combining in one place all the files relevant to the current scene.

6   You can, if you like, ask Maya to create a directory structure and a new project for you by going to File > Project > New (**Figure 2.11**).

Here you can specify a name and a location for the project. Clicking Use Defaults at the bottom will automatically fill in the rest of the New Project window with names for the corresponding directories. If you do not want all the directories created, you can simply leave them blank and Maya will ignore them. Once you are happy with the project structure, click Accept. Maya will build the specified directories for you and set the new project to be the current one.

If your directory structure is already in place, as it should be, another way to set the current project is by going to File > Project > Set (**Figure 2.12**). Here you simply point to the directory you wish to work in, and it's set.

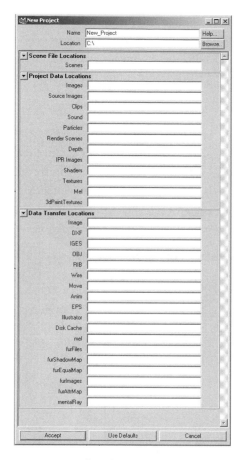

**FIGURE 2.11** Creating a new project.

7   The final work environment option to set is found in the Polygons > Tool Options menu. In that menu, make sure Keep Faces Together is activated.

As we progress through the book, we will perform operations that would otherwise involve our having to set this manually afterward. Setting it here means it is now set globally, saving us work later.

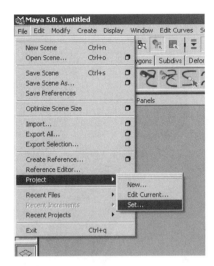

### Importing to Maya

The final part of our preparation for modeling is to import the images we
scanned and cropped earlier, bringing them into Maya's panels so we can use
them as guides.

1    To import an image into the front view, at the top of the panel, select View >
Image Plane, and click Import Image to open up the browser. You have already
set your project, so the browser will automatically open in the correct base
directory, enabling you to select the images we created earlier. For this view
we will use the file KilaFront.jpg (or you can use KilaFront.tga), which is in
the Scans directory.

> **NOTE**   To switch views simply go to the Panels menu item in the current
> view panel and select the appropriate camera.

As you can see from **Figure 2.13** the image plane is quite large. We know
that each grid square is equal to one meter, so at this setting Kila would be
30 meters tall. We know from the character details we gathered earlier that
she is 1.7 meters tall, so let's change her size.

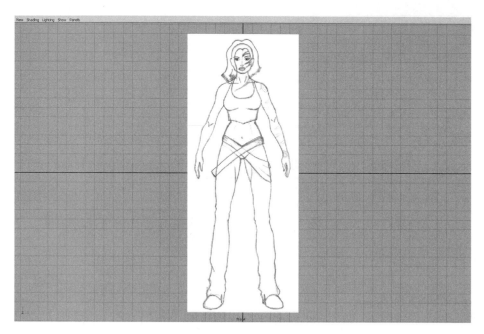

**FIGURE 2.13** The image imported into our front view, 30 meters tall

**2** If you have not selected anything else at this stage, the image's attributes will be available in the Channel Box under a heading of imagePlane1. Otherwise, if you need to make the attributes available, select View > Image Plane again. Notice that a new option is available, Image Plane Attributes. Move your mouse over this to reveal the current panel's image planes. At the moment, you should have only one, called imagePlane1; select this. A new window opens, holding the options available for this image plane; you should also see it available in your Channel Box.

**3** Set the Width and Height attributes to 1.7, and she will scale down to the size we need.

**4** Now do the same for the side view. Import the image called KilaSide.jpg (or use KilaSide.tga) and resize it to 1.7. When you're done, switch to the perspective view (**Figure 2.14**) to see how things look so far.

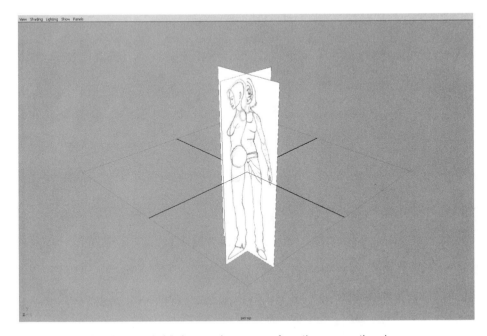

**FIGURE 2.14** The front and side image planes, seen from the perspective view.

**5**   Looking through the perspective view now, things might seem a little confusing, but this can be fixed. We simply need to move the two images so that they do not intersect.

Select the side image by dragging the mouse over a corner of the image plane. Look in the Channel Box, which now shows the attributes available for the side view (**Figure 2.15**). At the bottom, under the heading Inputs, you can see the image plane, named imagePlane2.

**6**   Click imagePlane2 to reveal the image plane's options. Select Center X and set it to -0.35, which will move the image slightly to the left. Type -0.2 into the Center Z input box, which will move the image forward.

Play around with these settings for both images until you are happy with their positions. You should end up with something resembling **Figure 2.16**, with the images no longer intersecting.

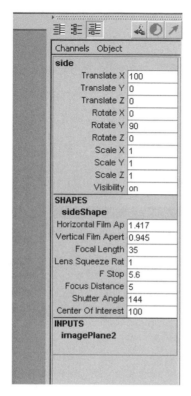

FIGURE 2.15 Side view attributes

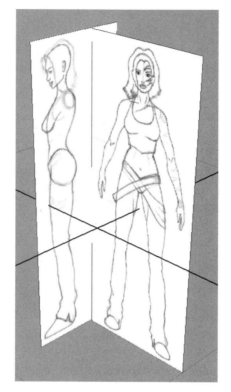

FIGURE 2.16 Adjust the image plane positions so the images don't intersect.

## Working with the Layer Editor

Before we finish this section, we will place the image planes into a layer. This will keep the scene tidy, as well as prevent the image planes from accidentally being selected and moved. You'll find the Layer Editor in the bottom-right corner of the Maya interface, under the Channel Box (**Figure 2.17**).

**1**   First create a new layer by going to Layers > Create Layer, or click the Create Layer button on the Layer Editor's toolbar (to the right and just under the menu).

**2**   A new layer is created, called layer1. Double-click this to bring up the Edit Layer options.

**3**  In the Edit Layer window, rename the layer to ImagePlanes. Set Display Type to Reference. This means whatever is in this layer will be visible but not selectable. Also, pick a color to represent the layer.

You can quickly hide everything in the layer by clicking on the V to the left of the layer name in the Layer Editor. This controls the visibility. The next indicator to the right, the R, represents the display type; you can click on this to cycle between Reference, Template, and Normal.

**4**  Select both the image planes, then highlight the ImagePlanes layer. With the layer highlighted, go to Layers > Add Selected Objects to Current Layer. The image planes will now be in the layer.

**FIGURE 2.17** The Layer Editor

**5**  Save the file, calling it Kila_Start.mb.

Our preparation is now complete; we are ready to start building the Kila character.

## Building a Placeholder Character

Using primitives (simple shapes such as cubes or cylinders) to create a basic "placeholder" version of the model gives the animators something to work with while the model is being completed. Depending on the project you are working on, getting a character approved can take time and could leave the animators waiting around for you, which in the long run will put them behind schedule. Generating this quick model will mean the animators can get to work early, transferring the animation to the final model at a later stage. Not only does this facilitate the workflow, it can also pinpoint any potential problem areas with the character's proportions.

### Basic Limb Creation

Using the file Kila_Start.mb that we have established, we can create some basic shapes and scale them to fit our character.

1   Load the file named Kila_Start.mb. Start by switching to the front view panel, and create a cube. To do this, go to Create > Polygon Primitives > Cube and open up the Polygon Cube Options dialog box (**Figure 2.18**). Make sure Width, Height, and Depth are all set to 1; then click the Create button.

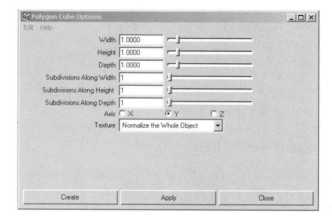

2   Select the newly created cube; this highlights it in green, and a new manipulator should appear. (If this doesn't happen, press W to get into move mode, or click the Move tool in the toolbox to the left.)

Take a look at **Figure 2.19**, which shows the four main manipulators; from the left, they are Move, Rotate, Scale, and the pivot point manipulator.

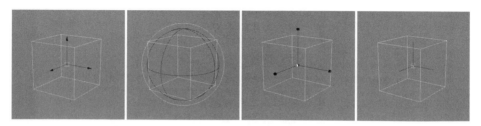

FIGURE 2.19 Move, Rotate, Scale, and pivot point manipulators

Each manipulator has four directions of movement or rotation, displayed in a particular color:

▶ Red moves or rotates around the X axis (left and right).

▶ Green moves or rotates around the Y axis (up and down).

▶ Blue moves or rotates around the Z axis (forward and backward).

▶ The yellow box/cube/circle moves or rotates the object relative to the camera's view.

The use of each manipulator is pretty self-explanatory except for the pivot manipulator. This will allow you to move the pivot point on the selected object. You can access this by pressing the Insert key.

> **TIP** You can alter the size of a manipulator by using the + and − keys.

> **TIP** Using keyboard shortcuts is a good way to work more quickly. For the manipulators, use W to switch to move mode, E to rotate, and R to scale.

**3** Using the appropriate manipulator, move, rotate, and scale the cube until it roughly fits Kila's left thigh (**Figure 2.20**).

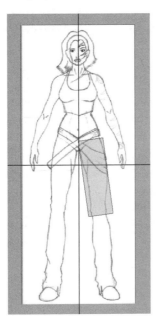

FIGURE 2.20 Thigh creation, front view

Note that it is important that you not freeze the object's transformations at this stage; this would reset the object's axis, making it more difficult to scale. **Figure 2.21** (left) shows the axis as it should now be at this point in the procedure. We can quite happily scale this object; it will scale around the correct axis. On the other hand, **Figure 2.21** (right) demonstrates the axis if it were reset. Scaling this object now would deform it incorrectly, making it difficult to achieve the desired shape.

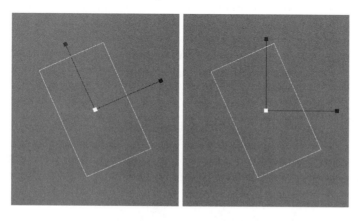

**FIGURE 2.21**
Do not reset the axis; it should be as shown on the left.

## Viewing the Geometry

Open up a view panel's Shading menu will reveal all the ways you can view your geometry as you work (**Figure 2.22**).

▶ Wireframe (key 4)—Displays the edges of all the geometry in the view panel.

▶ Smooth Shade All (key 5)—Displays all the surfaces as smooth-shaded.

▶ Smooth Shade Selected Items—Displays the selected objects' surface as smooth-shaded (not shown in **Figure 2.22**).

▶ Flat Shade All—Displays all surfaces and meshes as flat-shaded, faceted objects.

▶ Flat Shade Selected Items—Displays the selected objects' surfaces as flat-shaded/faceted (not shown in **Figure 2.22**).

**Viewing the Geometry, continued**

▶ Bounding Box—Shows the objects in the scene as boxes. This is mainly used to speed up Maya when you're navigating complex scenes.

▶ Points—Displays only the points (vertices) of objects in the scene (not shown in **Figure 2.22**).

These last two are in the Shade Options submenu:

▶ Wireframe on Shaded— Combines the smooth-shaded and wireframe views.

▶ X-Ray—Shows all objects as semitransparent.

There are other options to be found in the other menus that allow you to alter the lighting and so on, but we will discuss those as and when we come to use them later in the book.

**TIP** ▶ At this stage, you may find it easier to work in X-ray mode because it allows you to see through the geometry in the scene.

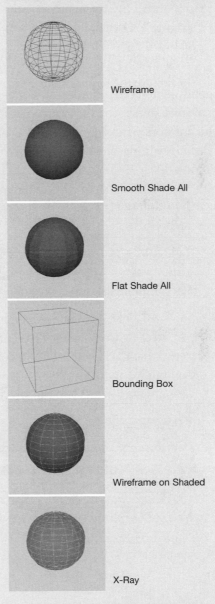

Wireframe

Smooth Shade All

Flat Shade All

Bounding Box

Wireframe on Shaded

X-Ray

**FIGURE 2.22** Various ways to view your geometry in Maya

**4** When you're happy with the front view, switch to the side view and again manipulate the cube until it fits inside the thigh on the image plane (**Figure 2.23**).

At this point, you may wish to taper the lower part of the cube so it fits Kila's thigh better, coming in slightly at her knee. The easiest way to achieve this is to work directly on the vertices. At the moment, you are working in Object mode, meaning you are selecting, editing, and manipulating complete objects. Vertices, like polygons, edges, and UVs, are all components of objects, so to edit components we need to switch to Component mode. There are a number of ways to do this:

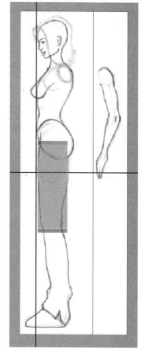

**FIGURE 2.23** Thigh creation, side view

▶ Right-click the cube itself. This will display a marking menu with options for opening up various components of the object for selection.

▶ Look at **Figure 2.24** (top). I have highlighted the Select By Component Type button in the status line. Clicking this button will switch to Component mode, and the buttons to the right will change to represent the various components you can select.

**FIGURE 2.24** Switch to component mode (top) and the selection type buttons change (bottom).

▶ Pressing F8 will toggle between Object mode and Component mode. You can then select the component you wish to edit via the marking menu or the buttons in the status line.

**5**   Switch to Component mode and open up the vertices for editing. You will notice that the box's outline turns blue and the vertices are now colored purple. You can select the vertices at the bottom of the thigh and scale them inward, so that they fit nicely around her knee. Do this in both the front and side views.

To go back into Object mode, press F8, or you can right-click to bring up the marking menu and select Object Mode.

| Shortcut Keys for Editing | |
| --- | --- |
| F8—Toggle Component/Object mode | F11—Faces |
| F9—Vertices | F12—UVs |
| F10—Edges | |

Continue using this method, creating basic cubes and manipulating them until you have Kila's left side completed; just concentrate on her limbs for now. You should end up with something like **Figure 2.25**.

### Create the Right Side

Kila's right side will require much less effort than her left. With this model, we can simply *mirror* her left limbs to create her right side.

To do this we will *group* the current geometry. Grouping objects serves two purposes. First, it keeps the scene nice and tidy, making it easier to work with and navigate among the objects. Second, it allows us to manipulate a series of objects at the same time and with the same pivot.

When grouped, all the selected objects will be placed under a *group node*. This is the parent,

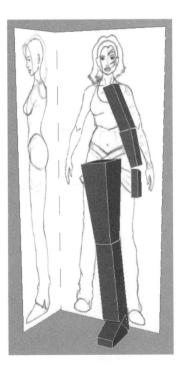

**FIGURE 2.25** Basic left arm and leg created with cubes

and the objects are children. Whatever you do to the parent will be reflected in the children.

> **TIP** ▶ When objects are arranged in a group hierarchy, you can move up and down the chain using the arrow keys. The up and down arrows will "pick walk" up and down the chain. The left and right arrows will cycle through the objects on a particular hierarchical level.

1 Select the geometry you have created for Kila's left arm and leg, and go to Edit > Group (or press Ctrl+G/Cmd+G). This groups the objects, placing the pivot for the group in the world's center.

> **TIP** ▶ When selecting objects in your scene, remember these key-click combinations: Holding down Ctrl will remove items from the current selection. Holding the Shift key will toggle the items between selected and unselected. Holding down both Ctrl+Shift will add items to your selection.

2 Create a duplicate. With the new group still selected, go to Edit > Duplicate and open up the options. Set the first input box next to Scale to –1 (this will mirror the duplicated geometry across the X axis). Also, make sure Geometry Type is set to Copy and Group Under is set to World. When you're done, click the Duplicate button.

You now have two arms and two legs in the scene (**Figure 2.26**).

### Finishing the Head, Neck, and Torso

To finish Kila, we need to create a head, neck, and torso. As before, we will use simple cubes for these. Create four cubes and manipulate them until they represent the neck, head, upper torso, and lower torso (**Figure 2.27**).

Divide the torso under the rib cage to give it a little more flexibility when it is animated.

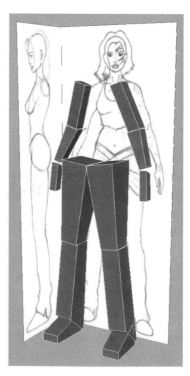

**FIGURE 2.26** The character with both sets of limbs

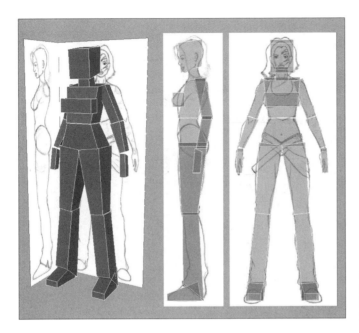

FIGURE 2.27 Cube placement for upper body—front and side views

## Cleaning Up

She's not much to look at, really, but this *Dr. Who* reject will be quite important in getting your characters animations started. All that is left at this stage is to clean up your scene and the History list.

1    Select all the geometry that makes up your character and, as before, press Ctrl+G/Cmd+G to group everything into a nice tidy group. This should be named group3.

2    Open up the Outliner (Windows > Outliner), which displays the contents of the current scene. As shown in **Figure 2.28**, you should now have three groups named group1, group2, and group3.

You can also use Maya's Hypergraph (Windows > Hypergraph)  to organize the scene's contents.

3    Delete group1 and group2, as these are no longer of use.

> **TIP** ▶ It's important to stay on top of object naming. Remember that other people may use your work, so try and make it as easy for them as possible.

**4** Next you will need to combine the objects into a single mesh. To do this, simply select all the cubes and go to Polygons > Combine. (For the first time, you will need to switch from the default Animation menu set to the Modeling menu set, or you won't see the Polygons menu.)

As you have built this character, each action you have taken has created an extra node in the construction history. Look in the Channel Box when you have an object selected, and in the Inputs section you can see this history in the form of a long list. This is helpful for going back and editing things, but it also increases the file size and eats up your system's memory. Having a long history could also throw Maya into terminal lock-up if operations such as Polygons > Combine, Edit Polygons > Extract, or Polygons > Smooth are executed on a complex model.

What we can do now to clean up the history is to bake it onto the model by first selecting the character and going to Edit > Delete By Type > History.

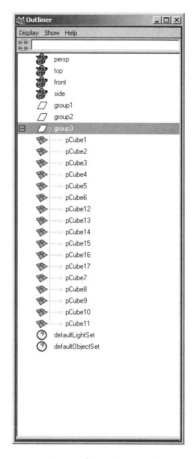

**FIGURE 2.28** Scene contents in the Outliner

Alternatively if you wish to delete the history on every object in the scene simply go to Edit > Delete All by Type > History. This does not require anything to be selected beforehand.

With this version of the Kila model, the amount of detail is really up to you. You could use cylinders, as I will in the upcoming Basic Shape tutorial, to get in a bit more of the character's shape. Or you could just stick to basic boxes. Whatever you choose, make sure you don't spend too long on this version; it is only a placeholder character, after all.

You will find my version of Primitive Kila on the CD in Project Files/02, named Kila_Primitive.mb.

## The Basic Shape for Kila

Now we'll begin building our final model. As with Primitive Kila, we first have to
block out the basic shape to get a good idea of the whole character's shape and
proportions. Don't be too concerned with details at this stage; we will cover that
stage of the modeling in Chapter 3.

### Limbs and Torso

This time we will begin with cylinders rather than cubes. If you look at the
human body from a geometric standpoint, it is made up of cylindrical shapes
(except the head, which is spherical).

We know our polygon limit: 4500. With this in mind, we can estimate the configuration of the cylinders that will make up the left arm, left leg, and torso.
Because the overall shape of the character is roughly symmetrical, we only need
to model her left side. Then we can duplicate it and mirror it across at a later
stage, saving half the work.

For a character that comes out at between 2000 and 3000 polygons, you'll get a
manageable number of polygons to begin with by starting with cylinders that
have eight subdivisions around the axis and eight height subdivisions. This also
leaves you with a smooth cylinder that won't look blocky or faceted when viewed
in the game. I have the luxury of more polygons for this character, so I am going
to begin with a 10-subdivision setup.

The beauty of this method of creating characters is that it is fully scalable; you
can begin with just a few subdivisions to create a lower-resolution character, or
more subdivisions for a smoother character with greater detail, to use for rendering or FMV (Full Motion Video).

## Mirrored Instances

Modeling just half of the model can produce challenges when you're working out proportions and getting a general feel for the overall shape. To help with this, you can create a *mirrored instance*. Although you use the Duplicate command to create the mirrored instance, Maya does not create any extra geometry. Rather, you are asking it to redisplay the same geometry in a different place, or in this case a mirrored version. So in effect, anything you do to the original will also be applied to the clone and vice versa.

To create a mirrored instance, simply select the mesh and go to Edit > Duplicate, opening up the options. Set the first input box next to Scale to -1, and for Geometry Type select the Instance option (**Figure 2.29**). Click the Duplicate button, and you have a full character.

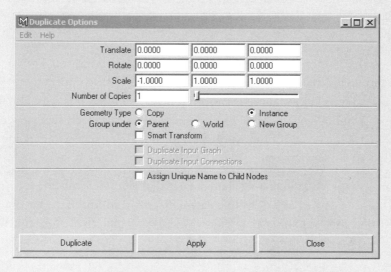

FIGURE 2.29 The Duplicate options for creating a mirrored instance

## Subdivision Surfaces

Many developers use a technique of creating low-resolution meshes with a view to creating a higher-resolution version using *subdivision surfaces.*

You first create a lower-resolution proxy model, and then go to Modify > Convert > Polygons To Subdiv to convert it to a subdivision surface. The result is a nice, smooth, high-resolution mesh with the added bonus that you control it via the lower proxy model. The vertices act as control points for the higher-resolution version.

**Figure 2.30** shows a lower proxy model on the left and its higher subdivision surface on the right.

For more information on subdivision surfaces, look at Maya's online help by going to Help > Contents and Search and selecting Modeling Subdivision Surfaces from the displayed help page.

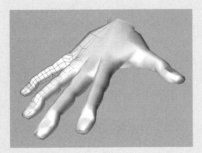 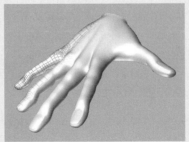

**FIGURE 2.30** An example of using subdivision surfaces

### Left Arm Creation

Lets begin building the left arm.

**1**  Load your initial file, Kila_Start.mb.

**2**  Create a cylinder (the first of three; you'll need two others for the left leg and the torso). Go to Create > Polygon Primitives > Cylinder and open up the options.

**3** Set the Radius to 0.1 and the Height to 1. Set both Subdivisions Around Axis and Subdivisions Along Height to 10 (**Figure 2.31**). Click the Create button.

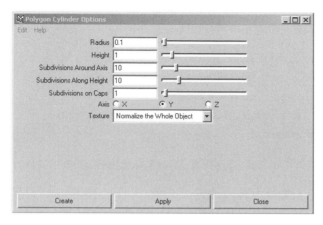

FIGURE 2.31 Polygon Cylinder creation options

**4** In the Channel Box, rename the cylinder to LeftArm. Then switch to the front view and move the cylinder up so that it lies over the character's left arm. Keep the center of the cylinder (the center row of edges) near the elbow area of the arm. Rotate the cylinder so that it matches the orientation, and then scale the cylinder until it is about the same scale as the arm in the image plane (**Figure 2.32**).

**5** Now that the geometry is in place, you can edit it further to achieve the shape you need to work with. Right-click the cylinder itself, bringing up the marking menu. Select Vertex to switch to vertex editing mode.

**6** The cylinder is now blue, with all its vertices available to manipulate. Select each horizontal row in turn and scale it inward, using the red X axis manipulator, so that the outer vertices follow the lines of Kila's arm. Make sure you only scale along one axis at a time. As you scale the vertices, feel free to move them to the correct position—but manipulate a single strip at a time; try not to edit each vertex individually. See **Figure 2.33** for a comparison of the original arm with the scaled one.

**TIP** You may find it useful to use the Lasso tool to select the vertices. This allows you to draw a line around the area you wish to select.

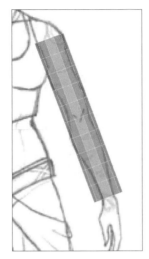 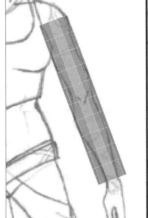 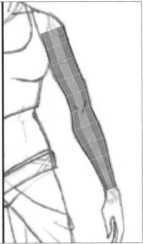

**FIGURE 2.32** Cylinder— front view　　**FIGURE 2.33** Left arm sculpting—front view

**7** Next, switch to the side view and follow the same procedure. Manipulate the cylinder until it's in the same position and orientation as the arm in the image. Right-click the cylinder and select Vertex from the marking menu to edit the vertices.

### Arm Orientation

In addition to moving and scaling the vertices to match the image, you will want to rotate them to match the orientation of the limb. As the arm bends, it's a good idea for the vertices to follow the contours of the limb. Don't try and do the entire arm in one go—take your time and do each horizontal row, moving to the next one only when you are happy with your work (**Figure 2.34**).

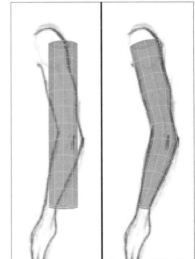

**FIGURE 2.34** Left arm sculpting— side view

### Left Leg Creation

The left arm is done for now. Next, we will create the left leg.

**1**   Create a new cylinder using the same configuration as for the left arm. Name this second cylinder LeftLeg; then manipulate and scale it until it roughly matches Kila's leg in the image plane (**Figure 2.35**).

Again, remember to try and keep the central pivot of the cylinder around the pivot of the leg (the knee).

**2**   Right-click the cylinder and select Vertex from the marking menu. As before, scale each horizontal strip of vertices until the outer ones match the outline of Kila's leg, making sure you only scale along one axis at a time (**Figure 2.36**).

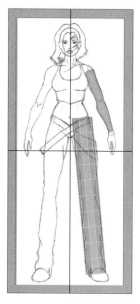 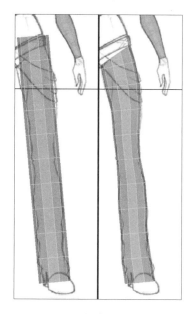

FIGURE 2.35 Positioning the left leg

FIGURE 2.36 Left leg sculpting— front view

**3**   Once you are happy with the general shape of the front, go to the side view. Again, rotate and scale the strips of vertices so they follow the contours of the leg (**Figure 2.37**).

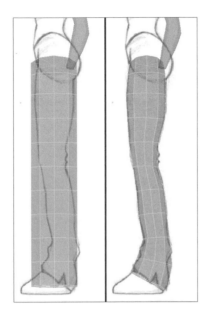

FIGURE 2.37 Left leg sculpting—side view

### Creating and Positioning the Torso

The basic limbs are complete; now let's tackle the torso. We will concentrate on the main body for now, and leave constructing the breasts for later.

1   We will follow the same procedure as before, so create a third cylinder, but this time set both the Subdivision Axis and Subdivision Height to 8. You need this configuration so that you will have a line down the center of her torso. Create this one and call it `Torso`.

2   Move the cylinder up along the Y axis and roughly scale it to fit the torso. At this point, try not to move it in any other direction.

3   Just as you did with the arm and the leg, select each horizontal strip of vertices and scale it to match the torso in the image. Move the vertices up or down to match key areas in the sketch, such as around the hips (**Figure 2.38**).

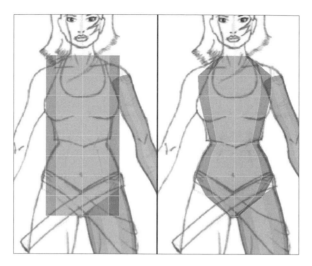

**FIGURE 2.38** Torso sculpting—front view

**4**   Switch to the side view and position the cylinder so that it lies over the image. Just move it along its Z axis, because moving it up or down will mean it won't be aligned with the front image.

**5**   Manipulate the vertices so that the cylinder fits inside Kila's torso (**Figure 2.39**).

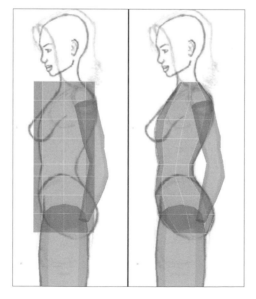

**FIGURE 2.39** Torso sculpting—side view

### Deleting Half of the Torso

We are not yet finished with the torso. Because we are only working on the left side of Kila, we need to delete half of her torso. (This is why it was important to have an edge down her center.)

Right-click on the mesh again, but this time select Face from the marking menu. You will now be in face editing mode; you can tell because the mesh has turned blue and selection handles have appeared in the center of each face. Select Kila's right side (your left), and press Delete. The faces disappear, leaving only the left side of her torso (**Figure 2.40**).

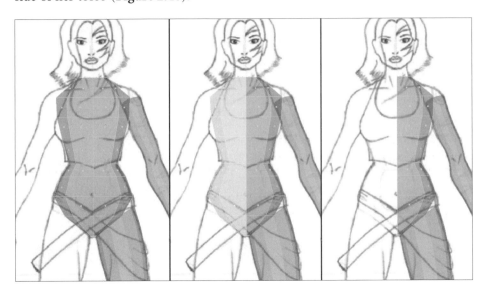

**FIGURE 2.40** Deleting half of Kila's torso

By now you can see the character starting to take shape. You should have a clean, grid-style mesh that fits the left side of your character (**Figure 2.41**). Ideally, however, what you want is for this to be one mesh, a single piece of geometry. We must combine these initial pieces and weld them together.

### Moving the Pivot

Eventually, you need Kila to be in a specific pose before you can attach a skeleton to her (more detail on this in Chapter 10). For now, we want to raise up her arms so they're easier to work on. The problem is that the pivot for the arm is currently in the center of the cylinder. To raise the arm convincingly, we must move the pivot to where the shoulder is and rotate it from there.

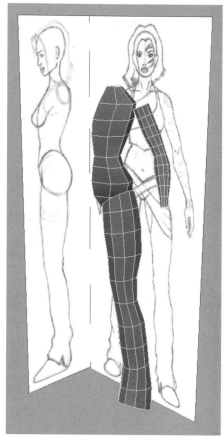

FIGURE 2.41 The model so far

1   Select the left arm. Make sure you are in rotate mode by pressing E. The Rotate manipulator will appear in the center of the arm, where the current pivot is.

2   To move the pivot, first press Insert; this changes the manipulator to represent the pivot position.

3   Move this pivot manipulator up to where the shoulder would be, and press Insert again to go back to the Rotate manipulator. See **Figure 2.42** for an illustration of this manipulation.

> **TIP** To simplify the movement of the pivot manipulator, you can use the snap tools to position it exactly on a vertex. While moving the pivot point, press and hold the V key, which will snap the pivot to the nearest vertices.

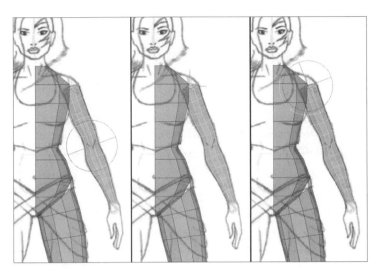

**FIGURE 2.42** Pivot point manipulation

**4**   Rotate the arm until it is raised slightly (**Figure 2.43**).

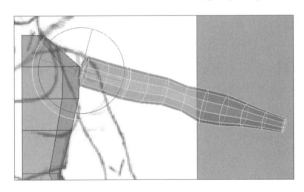

**FIGURE 2.43** The
rotated arm, raised
slightly

**5**   Before we can begin welding and stitching these elements together, we must
combine them into one object. While you still have the arm selected, hold
down Shift and select the torso and leg.

**6**   Go to Polygons > Combine, which will combine the selected objects.

**7**   We need to clean the model up a little, so remove the history by going to
Edit > Delete By Type > History. Keep in mind that it's a good idea to continue deleting the history and saving your model after you have reached a
stage where you are happy with it.

> **NOTE** Don't develop the bad habit of saving over the same file each time you work on the character. Name saved files incrementally, for example Kila_01.mb, Kila_02.mb, and so on. This makes it easy to go back to a previous version should the worst happen.

> **TIP** Maya does have a built-in incremental file saver. Go to File > Save Scene and open the options, and you'll be able to activate the incremental save. A directory called incrementalSave will be created, and all subsequent saves will be stored there.

### Stitching Together

Now comes the fun part. We have to stitch these parts together by adding, splitting, and removing polygons as well as welding vertices.

Let's start with the leg. First we have to remove the caps from the leg; the ends must be opened up so we can attach them. Plus we don't want to end up with stray polygons existing inside Kila.

Select the faces at either end of the leg. Do this just as you have done earlier, by right-clicking the actual mesh, then selecting Face from the marking menu so you can select the faces shown in **Figure 2.44**. Then press Delete to remove them.

You can also do this on the arm now, so that you don't have to do it later. Remember to do both ends, the shoulder and the wrist (**Figure 2.45**).

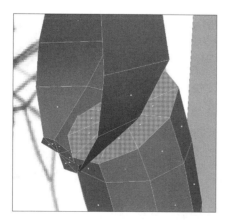

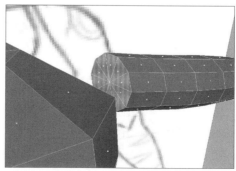

**FIGURE 2.44** Delete the caps on the leg.     **FIGURE 2.45** Delete the caps on the arm.

Returning to the thigh area, look for areas where vertices could line up and potentially be welded together. We know the leg has more polygons than the lower torso, but we can split polygons in order to connect them up. First, though, we must connect any that already line up. The first two lie down on the side of the hip. They both exist in roughly the same plane, so we can join them.

1   Select both vertices (**Figure 2.46**). Then go to Edit Polygons > Merge Vertices and open the options.

2   Set Distance to 0.1 and click Apply.

If nothing happens, it may be that the distance is too small, meaning the vertices are too far apart. Try again with a larger Distance setting. Close the options box after you've found a successful number, since we can use this distance for the rest of the welds.

Alternatively you can edit the node's Distance directly in the Channel Box. Select the polyMergeVert1 name, and the node's attributes will open below it, showing one named Distance. You can edit this, making it larger until the vertices snap together. They are now welded into a single vertex, as demonstrated in **Figure 2.47**.

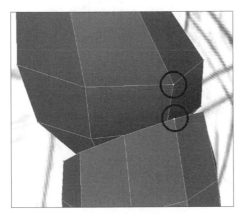
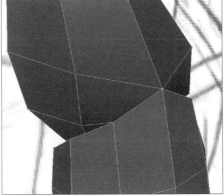

FIGURE 2.46 Vertex alignment          FIGURE 2.47 The vertices welded on the hip.

Moving around to the left, you can skip the next vertex on the leg because there doesn't appear to be a nearby vertex to weld it to. Notice that the one after that is in quite a good position to be welded to a close vertex on the torso (**Figure 2.48**).

Moving around to the back now, in a similar position to the front, you'll see another two vertices that can be welded as shown in **Figure 2.49**.

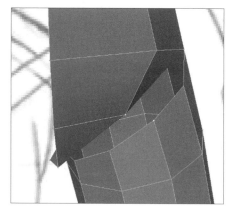

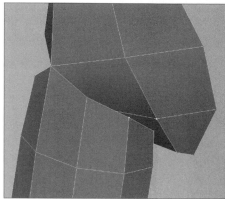

FIGURE 2.48 Vertex welding at the front of her pelvis.

FIGURE 2.49 Vertex welding on the back.

**TIP** ▶ If the image planes start to get in your way, you can quickly hide them by going to the view's Show menu and unchecking Cameras. Alternatively, you can turn off the visibility on your ImagePlane layer.

Looking between the vertices you have welded, you should see two that appear to have nowhere to go. You could weld them to the vertices just above the hips, but they are too far away.

What you need to do now is create some new vertices in the geometry so that you can weld to these. Looking from the side, select the two faces on the lower torso and delete them (**Figure 2.50**), which will open up the hip area.

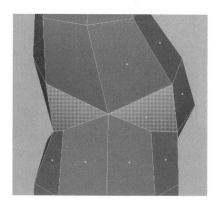

FIGURE 2.50
Removing faces

Now create some new faces to replace the ones you deleted, the difference being that these new ones will connect to the upper leg.

1   Go to Polygons > Append To Polygon Tool. This opens a tool that will allow you to create new polygons by stitching them onto the edges of existing ones. You should notice the edges of the mesh get slightly thicker when you activate this tool, to highlight the ones eligible to be appended.

2   Select one of the edges around a hole you just created. Purple arrows appear, highlighting other edges that you can now select to create a new polygon (**Figure 2.51**). The first time you clicked, you dictated the polygon's starting position, and now you are telling Maya where you next want it to go.

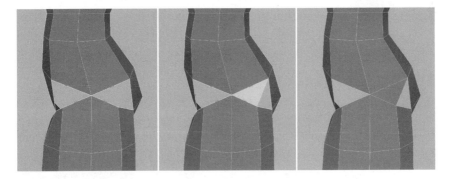

FIGURE 2.51 Adding faces to fill in the gaps on the hip

3   Select another edge around the same hole. A pink triangle appears, showing the polygon you are about to create. Now press Enter on the keyboard to complete the polygon's creation (**Figure 2.52**).

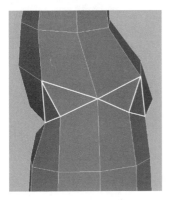

FIGURE 2.52 The hip with the new faces added

Follow this same procedure to create another three faces, connecting the leg to the hip and filling in the holes.

> **TIP** ▶ A quick way to repeat the last command is to press G or Y. This saves having to go back through the menus.

As you rotate around the mesh, you will notice that we have not removed the caps from the torso, so before you continue, select these top and bottom faces and delete them. This will also help you as you continue to weld the leg to the hip area.

Following the same pattern described for the outer thigh, move around the inner thigh, skipping a vertex then selecting one. Match this vertex to the closest one belonging to the torso, and weld them as shown in **Figure 2.53**.

Move around to the back, and select and weld two vertices from there. Every other vertex gets welded, first the ones at the front and then those in the same area but at the rear (**Figure 2.54**).

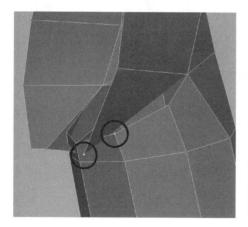

**FIGURE 2.53** Weld the vertices nearer the inner thigh.

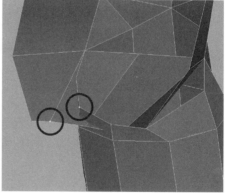

**FIGURE 2.54** Weld the vertices at the back of her leg.

You should end up with one vertex in the middle of the leg and two remaining on the torso. Don't waste time welding these, because the vertices left on the torso belong to faces we need to remove. Select the faces as shown in **Figure 2.55**, and delete them.

**FIGURE 2.55** Delete the inner faces.

Move around to the front of the figure and using the Append To Polygon Tool create two new faces, filling the gap at the front.

Now move around to the back, looking at her backside, where one polygon still remains. Instead of deleting this one, split it, making a new vertex that you can weld to. Go to Edit Polygons > Split Polygons Tool. Your mouse pointer will change to a sharp point, indicating that the tool is active.

When using the Split Polygon Tool, you must always start and end the cut on an edge. Select the edge at the upper-right of the face. A small square appears; holding the mouse button, move the square up to where the vertex is and release the button.

We now want to put a point on the edge that is closest to the final vertex of the leg, but shares the polygon of the edge we started on. Again, select the edge and hold down the mouse button until you are in the correct position, and then let go. The split is apparent as shown in **Figure 2.56**. Press Enter to complete the operation.

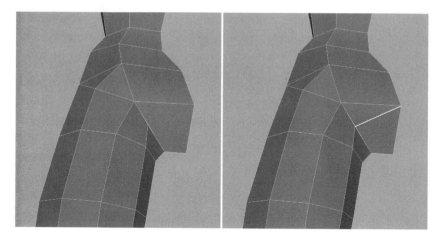

**FIGURE 2.56** Splitting faces to create an extra vertex.

**NOTE** The Split Polygon Tool will not snap to the position of the second vertex (nor should it), because it lies on an unconnected edge.

You now have a new vertex that you can weld to, so select both vertices and weld them.

Our leg is now connected to the torso, but not very smoothly. We can fix this by moving around the mesh and manipulating the vertices until we get a better shape. Take care to keep checking your image plane guides as you go; it's important you maintain the shape of the character. Keep moving around the mesh, checking the edges for stray polygons and anything that's not smooth. Take your time, making sure the shape is perfect before you proceed. Don't be afraid to split an area to smooth it out, as we did above the hip in **Figure 2.57**. At this early stage, you don't need any details, but you do want to end up with a smooth mesh.

A wise move at this stage is to slowly rotate around the model and watch how the form turns. This can reveal undesired concavity in an inappropriately turned edge. As you rotate, notice the two edges just on her hip that are highlighted in **Figure 2.58** (left). The current arrangement of these edges causes the polygons on either side to appear concave. We want them to be rotated, or flipped.

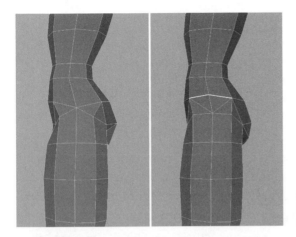

**FIGURE 2.57**
Smoothing out the
area above the hip

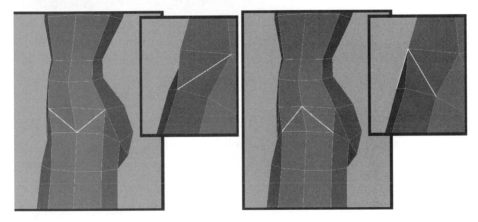

**FIGURE 2.58** Concave edges on her hip

Normally we could use the Edit Polygons > Flip Triangle Edge Tool. We would select the edges we need to flip or rotate and then choose Flip Triangle Edge from the menu.

Unfortunately, if you try and do this, Maya comes up with an error: `Warning: polyFlipEdge: Cannot flip texture border edge 218`. The error occurs because two different types of texture-mapping coordinates exist on either side of the edges we are trying to flip. So what do we do? A quick solution is to manually delete the edges.

**1**   Go into edge editing mode (F10), select the two edges, and press Delete.

**2**   Now go in with the Split Polygon Tool and split the polygons correctly. You can see the results in **Figure 2.58** (right).

Kila's thigh is at a satisfactory stage now, so let's move on and attach her arm. Before you do, take a moment to clean the history, since this can slow things down if it's not kept under control.

Looking from the front, we should probably start by scaling her arm up slightly around her shoulder. When a person's arms are raised, the shoulders become more pronounced, so let's do the scaling here, before we continue. Simply select the vertices around the top of the arm and scale them up globally, ever so slightly (**Figure 2.59** middle).

Select the edges at the same end of the arm. To do this quickly, convert the selection by going to Edit Polygons > Selection > Convert Selection to Edges. Now you have edges selected for you, but you only need the very end ones, so you need to deselect the others. You are still in vertex editing mode, so right-click on the mesh and select Edge from the marking menu. Holding down Ctrl, drag over the unneeded edges.

Kila's arm is a little too far away, so you need to extend it so it meets the body. With the edges still selected, go to Edit Polygons > Extrude Edge. Drag the green arrow (Y axis) until the polygons have cut into the shoulder (**Figure 2.59** right).

FIGURE 2.59 Arm extension

**NOTE** Because we set Keep Faces Together earlier, the faces that have been extruded will automatically be welded together. Without this option set, the polygons would be divided and fanned out.

We can now start the work of stitching this area together. Clean it up a little first, by moving some of the vertices to a more suitable place, bringing them out of the torso mesh and into daylight as shown in **Figure 2.60**.

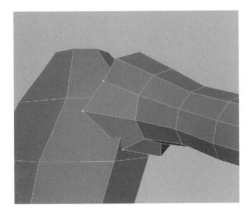

**FIGURE 2.60** Move the vertices for the shoulder out of the geometry.

We could now start matching these vertices up with vertices on the torso, but a better idea is to move the ones on the torso to match the shoulder. First do the vertices in the armpit area. Weld these together as shown in **Figure 2.61**.

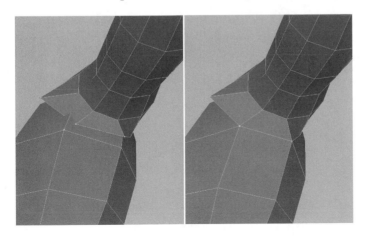

**FIGURE 2.61** Armpit welding

Moving to the front of the arm, select the three vertices right at the front, as seen in **Figure 2.62**, and weld these.

**FIGURE 2.62**
Weld the three
vertices at the
front of the
shoulder.

You will notice that we have a minor problem with a polygon cutting through another, but this can be rectified easily. To fix this you need to remove some faces now before proceeding. Select the three at the upper-rear of the torso, along with the center one from the row below it (**Figure 2.63**), and delete them all.

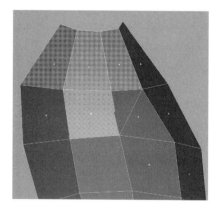

**FIGURE 2.63** Removing
some extra polygons

As shown in **Figure 2.64**, you should be left with two vertices sticking out; select them both. Holding down V, snap the selected vertices to the ones below them, and then weld them.

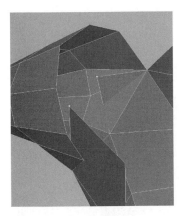

FIGURE 2.64
Polygon cropping

The area is cleaned up nicely now, and you can see things a bit more clearly. You need to go around the top now, and fill in the rest of the shoulder.

Select the top two and the rear two edges on the shoulder. Go to Edit Polygons > Extrude Edge, and drag the green arrow (Y axis) until the edges are nearly in line with what's left of the torso, as shown in **Figure 2.65**.

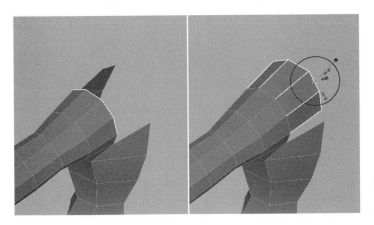

**FIGURE 2.65**
Extending the
shoulder.

All that's left to do now is fill in the holes at the front and back and do a bit of tidying. Before you do this, activate the Append to Polygon tool used earlier and fill in the holes; then spend some time cleaning up the area by moving vertices until the shape is correct. It's a good idea to refer to a good anatomy book when you're doing this, to make sure the shape matches actual human anatomy.

1   Right-click the mesh and select Edge from the marking menu to switch to edge editing mode.

2   Select all the edges on the mesh and go to Edit Polygons > Normals > Soften/Harden and open up the options.

3   Click All Soft, then Apply, and close the window.

> **NOTE**  A *normal* is a line representing the direction perpendicular to a polygon's surface. When you render polygons, the normals determine how light reflects off the surface.

Deselect the mesh and notice that it has been smoothed out—no more harsh lines (**Figure 2.66**). This gives us a clearer view of what the actual in-game mesh will look like.

Delete the history, and save your work as Kila_Combined.mb.

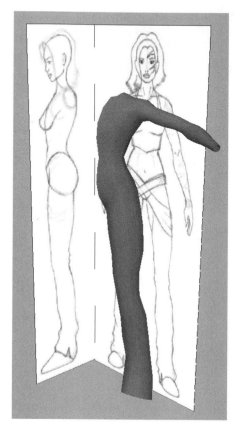

**FIGURE 2.66** Cleaned-up, stitched-together model

## Head and Neck

At this early stage of development, we only need placeholder geometry—something we can build upon later—for the head and neck. The neck can be created using a simple cylinder; as with the torso, we only need half, but it's easier to create the whole thing and delete half later.

Create another cylinder, with Subdivision Axis set to 8 and Subdivision Height set to only 2. Position the cylinder so that it lies where the neck should be. You shouldn't need to edit any of the strips of vertices for this section because it is such a small area and is pretty much cylindrical in shape to start with (**Figure 2.67**).

FIGURE 2.67 The basic neck in position

You need to remove half of the neck cylinder, along with the end caps. Right-click the neck's geometry and select Face from the marking menu. Drag over the half you don't want. Hold down Shift, select the top and bottom caps, and press Delete to remove them (**Figure 2.68**).

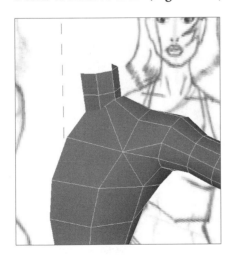

FIGURE 2.68
The cropped neck

For the head, begin with a cube, but not a simple one like what we created for the primitive version of Kila. This time, set Subdivisions Width to 4, Subdivision Height to 4, and Subdivision Depth to 4.

Move, scale, and rotate the cube so it approximately fits the size and orientation of the head in the image plane (**Figure 2.69**).

FIGURE 2.69 Head position

This time, delete half of the head first. Because you're going to be editing the vertices, it's easier to work on only one side.

In the side view, scale the vertices in so that the cube begins to resemble the image in the image plane (**Figure 2.70**).

FIGURE 2.70
Remove half of the head and manipulate it in the side view.

In the front view, select all the vertices on the right side of the cube. Switch to the side view, where you now need to scale the vertices in—because the head is rounder than it is square. First you need to smooth it out a little; when that's done, move to the next row, scaling these vertices in slightly (**Figure 2.71**).

**FIGURE 2.71**
Manipulate the front
of the head.

Now work on the vertices individually, manipulating them until the half-cube
roughly resembles the shape of half a human head. Start in the side view, and
then move around to the front, before finally working in perspective view.
Remember to use your guides, and refer to some good anatomical reference
material.

You may find it useful to smooth the head out a little by softening the normals,
as we did before. Right-click the mesh, and select Edge from the marking menu
to get into edge editing mode. Select all the edges on the mesh, and go to Edit
Polygons > Normals > Soften/Harden and open up the options. Click All Soft,
then Apply, and close the window; **Figure 2.72** shows what you should have now.

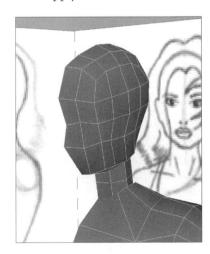

**FIGURE 2.72**
Sculpt the head to
achieve a better shape.

The final stage in creating the basic neck and head is to attach them to the body.

1   First let's attach the neck; start by hiding the head. Select it and press Ctrl+H/Cmd+H.

2   To combine the neck and body, use Polygons > Combine and proceed to weld the closest vertices. You may need to weld three together at once, as seen in **Figure 2.73**.

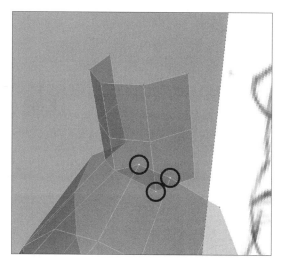

**FIGURE 2.73** Welding three vertices

Once fully welded your geometry should resemble that in **Figure 2.74**.

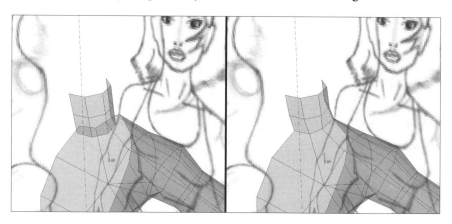

**FIGURE 2.74** Welding the neck, before and after

**3**  Press Ctrl+Shift+H/Cmd+Shift+H to bring back the head; then combine this to the rest of the body. Again, try to weld the vertices that are the closest or that make the most sense to weld (**Figure 2.75**).

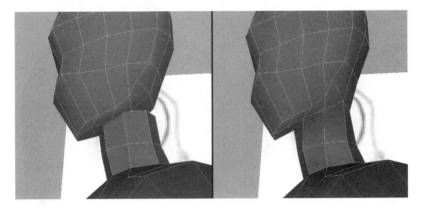

FIGURE 2.75 Welding the head

**4**  You will no doubt be left with some internal faces. It's best to remove these before you proceed, and patch up any holes that are left under the chin (**Figure 2.76**).

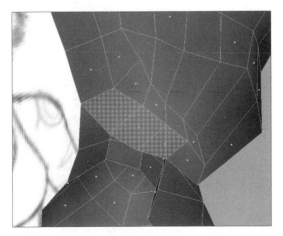

FIGURE 2.76
Remove internal faces.

**5**  Finally, clean up the area, first by selecting the edges and smoothing the normals. Then spend time working the vertices until you are happy with the final shape; your goal is shown in **Figure 2.77**.

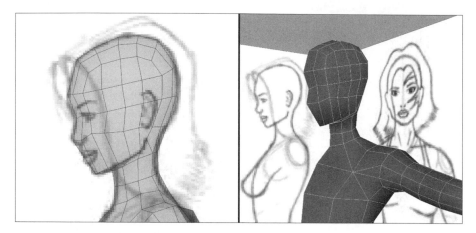

**FIGURE 2.77** Basic head and neck attached to the body

Finish off by deleting the history on the mesh and saving your work.

If you haven't already done so, now would be a good time to implement one of the mirrored instances I mentioned earlier in the chapter.

**1**   Select the mesh and go to Edit > Duplicate, opening up the options.

**2**   Set the first input box next to Scale to -1, and check Instance.

**3**   Click Duplicate to finish (**Figure 2.78**).

Now rotate around Kila and see if you can fix a few areas, filling her out and rounding her off (but don't worry too much about it at this stage because we still have a few things to add).

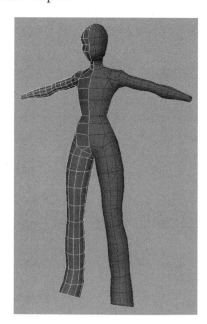

**FIGURE 2.78** Character with mirrored instance

### Feet and Hands

It's not necessary to bother with placeholder hands and feet. However, if geometry already exists for the hands and feet, you can add them just to get a sense of what the final character will look like (**Figure 2.79**).

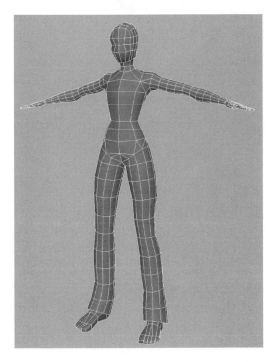

**FIGURE 2.79** The character with temporary feet and hands

Alternatively, you can include some primitive objects in order to achieve the correct proportions, giving a feel for the final character.

### Other Body Parts

Kila's basic shape is complete; now you can add any additional geometry. Skip her hair and clothing for now; you need to concentrate on getting the fundamental mesh completed and to a stage where you are happy with it. The one fundamental part remaining is the chest, so let's add this now.

To simplify things, remove the mirrored instance you created earlier; just select it and delete it.

**1**   Create a sphere, opening up the options for Create > Polygon Primitives > Sphere (**Figure 2.80**). Set Subdivisions Around Axis to 8 and Subdivisions Along Height to 6.

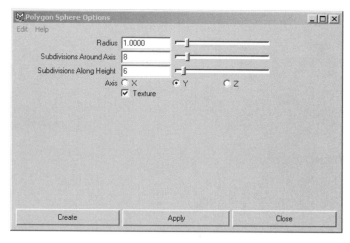

FIGURE 2.80 Polygon sphere options

**2**   In the front view, position and scale the sphere until it covers her left breast. Do the same in the side view. In addition, rotate the sphere around its X axis by 90 degrees, and 20 degrees around its Y axis; you want the tip of the sphere pointing forward and slightly to the right (**Figure 2.81**). We do this so the sphere is pointing as a real breast would, with the nipple pointing outward slightly and not straight ahead.

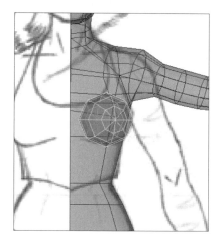

FIGURE 2.81 Breast sphere position and rotation

**3**   Combine the main mesh and the sphere. Then adjust the vertices on the top of the sphere to match the guide images (**Figure 2.82**).

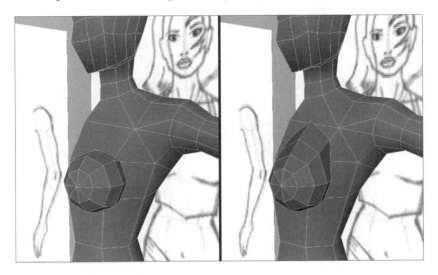

FIGURE 2.82 Sphere editing

**4**   Remove the back of the sphere (the faces that now exist inside the torso mesh), as seen in **Figure 2.83**.

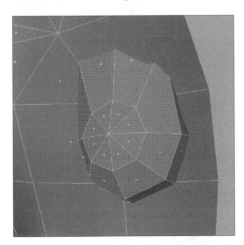

FIGURE 2.83 Remove the back of the sphere.

**5**   Your next step is to weld the sphere to the front of the torso. First, split the polygon across where her collarbone would be, and weld it to the top point of the sphere (**Figure 2.84**).

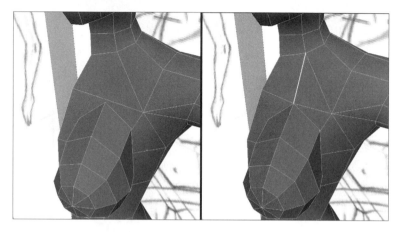

**FIGURE 2.84** Split the collarbone so you can weld to the top of the sphere.

**6**   Remove the polygons from the front of her torso by selecting them and deleting them, leaving a large hole in their place.

**7**   Using the Polygons > Append To Polygon Tool, work your way around the sphere, filling in the holes and stitching the sphere to the front of her torso. As you work your way around you can weld the vertices at the very bottom of the sphere, this will allow you to create another polygon here. The result can be seen **Figure 2.85**.

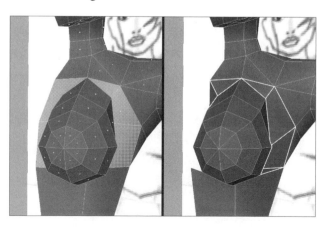

**FIGURE 2.85** Remove the torso polygons so we can stitch the sphere to her front.

Our character is wearing a short top, so you will not be able to see the breasts as separate entities. This being the case, we can edit the inside of the sphere to bring the vertices out, creating the middle of the top—the part that bridges the front of her chest (**Figure 2.86**).

Create a mirrored instance at this point to help visualize how things are looking. You can see that we have a problem (well, not a problem to some)—her chest is huge! You need to reduce it to keep it in proportion to the overall design.

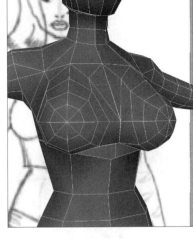

FIGURE 2.86 Bridging the breasts

**1**   First, select all the vertices at the front of the sphere.

**2**   Double-click the Move tool to open up its options. Under Move Settings, select Move Normal (**Figure 2.87**).

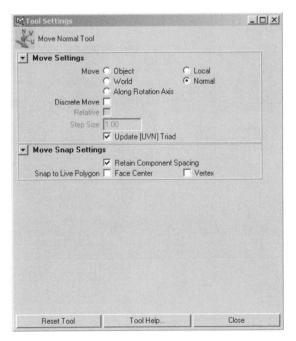

FIGURE 2.87 Move Normal tool options

**3** Move the handle via the manipulator labeled N. Notice that the vertices scale in and out while each one stays a relative distance from the other. Move them until you are happy with the size of her chest (**Figure 2.88**).

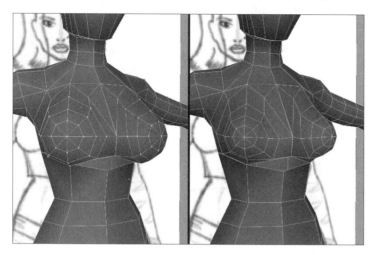

FIGURE 2.88 Breast reduction

**4** When you're finished, open the Move tool's options again and select Move Object in the Move Settings to reset the tool.

Although this is a good way to quickly reduce the size of Kila's chest, you will need to spend some time afterward tweaking it back into an acceptable shape. Take as much time as you need to rework any other areas you are not happy with. Use the Split Polygon Tool if you need to add extra polygons to smooth her out (**Figure 2.89**).

Once you're completely happy with the entire shape, delete the history and save the file as Kila_Basic.mb.

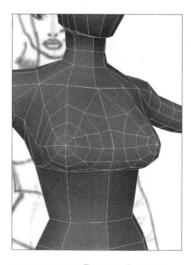

FIGURE 2.89 Breast refinement

You now have an excellent basic model with correct proportions (**Figure 2.90**). You could use this mesh, along with placeholder hands and feet, as your primitive model, passing it on to be rigged and animated. It has a lot more detail than the box version and is closer to the final model.

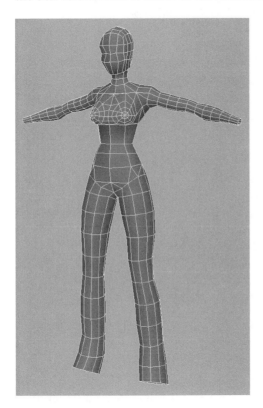

**FIGURE 2.90** The completed basic model

## The Morgue

Building up a collection of body parts is an efficient way of speeding up the modeling process as you create more and more characters. After you have completed a character, make sure the geometry is clean, optimized (more on this in Chapter 5), and ready to pass into a game engine. Once it reaches this stage, you can divide it up into specific body parts—hands, arms, feet, legs, torso, and head. Then store the parts in a special folder on your hard drive—what I like to call The Morgue—ready to be used on other characters.

This storage method isn't just for the high-end versions of your characters; it is just as helpful for holding other levels of detail. In the end, you will have, for example, a complete set of hands at various resolutions. You can then import these into your scenes, adjust them as needed, and attach them to your characters, potentially saving days, if not weeks of work.

**Figure 2.91** displays many different resolutions I have generated for the same hand. This file lies in my Morgue, ready for me to use on a new character. The models range from a fully deformable hand with working fingers, to a standard mitten-type hand typically used for lower-resolution models. Hands can take a lot of time to create—not only in their construction but in the way they deform. So once you have a good hand model, keep it safe. Even if you don't use it as-is on another character, you can refer back to its topology.

**FIGURE 2.91**
An example of various hand resolutions

On the CD you'll find a directory called Morgue. In it I've placed a number of files from my own library. Feel free to use them either as you progress through the book or on your own personal projects.

## Summary

We have successfully prepared our artwork and imported it into Maya, while examining a few of the environment settings. As we've begun the creation of the Kila model, we have experienced some of Maya's basic modeling tools, most of which we will be using again in Chapter 3 as we add further details to the geometry.

# CHAPTER 3
# Finishing and Refining

**YOU HAVE SPENT** valuable time developing your basic model and getting the size, shape, and proportions correct. Although it may look good and clean at this point, many areas still need work in order for this to be a successful game model. This chapter will help you take the base mesh you have created and build upon it by adding details to the geometry. In addition, you will make it deform convincingly by implementing real-life muscle structures into the topology.

Studying anatomy will help you be more aware of character form and movement. You'll become better at drafting and animation, and you'll build more efficient models.

Before you embark on this chapter, it's important to gather a few good anatomical references, be they books or Web sites. There are hundreds of online resources you can use. Each of these sites offers literally hundreds of images available to download. See Appendix B, "Reference and Further Reading," for a list of suggested books and Web sites.

Of course, the best and most convenient reference is *you*. Get yourself a mirror and study your own body.

## Muscle Line Mapping

Let's start working. Load the last file you saved in Chapter 2, called Kila_Basic.mb.

Look at your character model (**Figure 3.1**). So far, it's quite well defined and the proportions are correct. It is a good base model. In fact, with a bit of optimization, you could use her as a low-resolution character just as she is. She would not, however, be good as our main model. We still have a few problems to address:

▶   Taken statically, she looks fine, but once you start to animate her, the flaws will show. There will be breaks or bulges in the areas that bend, either because they don't have enough polygons or because the topology needs some work.

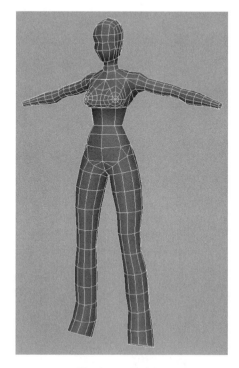

**FIGURE 3.1** Our base model

▶ The mesh as it stands has too many polygons that simply are not needed.

▶ She lacks physical detail in both her body and face.

▶ This model still has no hands or feet.

Our first step is to physically map the muscle groups onto the mesh. Doing this gives us a good understanding of how the mesh will move. In turn, when we animate the model, the polygons will deform, giving the illusion of muscles deforming under the skin. While we are adding these lines to the mesh, we can also add detail, giving additional shape to the geometry while we check its deformability.

> **TIP** ▶ A lot of detail can be gained through the texture map (more on this in Chapter 9, "Texture Painting"). Try not to get too caught up in building small details into the geometry—you'll just use up processor power, meaning fewer polygons can be used elsewhere in the game.

Use **Figure 3.2** to guide you in placing the muscle lines on the mesh. This illustration shows a simplified version of the muscles. All we need is a basic idea to work with; at this point, we're just implementing the main muscles.

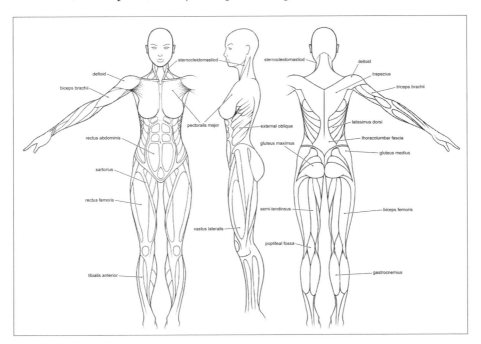

**FIGURE 3.2** Basic muscle lines of the human body

We will start at the top and work our way down, but we will skip the head for now and concentrate on that area later in the chapter. So select the left side of the mesh, and let's get started.

### The Neck

Refer to the neck in **Figure 3.2**. You can see two large muscles coming from the ears and ending where the collarbones meet in the center of the chest. These are the sternocleidomastoid muscles. Let's add these to our model.

1   We are going to split the polygons around the neck, carving these muscles into the mesh. Start by going to Edit Polygons > Split Polygon Tool.

2   As you did in the preceding chapter, click and hold on the starting edge around where the ear should be. A small icon appears, representing the starting point of the cut. Move the point up until you are at the corner where two edges meet, and release the button.

3   Select the point on the next edge where you wish to cut, and press Enter to finish that cut.

4   You need to work your way around until you get to the collarbone, as shown in **Figure 3.3**. You will have to do it a polygon at a time, selecting each edge that you encounter on the way.

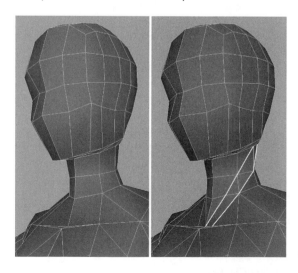

**FIGURE 3.3** Adding the sternocleidomastoid muscles

**NOTE** You don't have to always end up in the corner of two edges; you can cut anywhere along an edge. However, it's wise to begin where a vertex already exists and try to end on one, too.

**TIP** As you are cutting, you will find that occasionally you can't go any farther with the current cut. This could be caused by an unshared edge, or faces that are flipped the wrong way. It isn't a problem—just press G to finalize the current cut; this will also restart the Split Polygon tool. Then start a new cut from where the previous one ended.

If you are using a mirrored instance, you will notice that the cuts you make on one side will be mirrored across to the other. Also, when you create a cut, it automatically turns the new edge into a crease, making the normals hard. It's probably a good idea to smooth them as you go along. To do this, select the edges you wish to smooth. Then go to Edit Polygons > Normals > Soften/Harden and set the options to All Soft. Click the Apply button and close the options.

I think that's about all for the neck. As mentioned earlier, we only need a basic layout of the muscles. Adding too much detail now would be pointless because most of it will be removed later, when we optimize the geometry.

### Collarbones

Moving down, we come to the upper body, so let's implement the collarbones next (**Figure 3.4**, left).

Use the Split Polygon tool to carve out the details, as shown in **Figure 3.4** on the right. Don't be afraid to move some of the vertices to further sculpt the area until it resembles its anatomical reference.

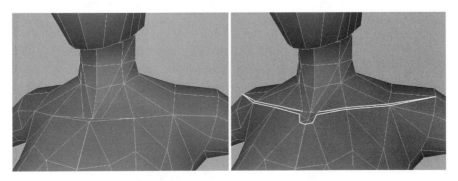

FIGURE 3.4 Adding the collarbones to the mesh

If at any point you end up with tiny triangles starting to appear, as in **Figure 3.5** (left), feel free to remove them. You can do this in one of two ways:

▶ Right-click the mesh and select Vertex from the marking menu, moving you into vertex editing mode. Select the two vertices on either side of the edge you want to remove, and weld them.

▶ Right-click the mesh and select Edge from the marking menu, moving you into edge editing mode. Select the edge you want to remove (the middle view in **Figure 3.5**), and then go to Edit Polygons > Collapse. This removes the edge, bringing in the vertices on either side and welding them (**Figure 3.5**, right).

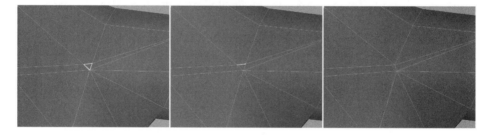

**FIGURE 3.5** Remove any tiny triangles by using the Collapse tool.

## The Chest and Shoulders

Moving on, we can start working on the chest and shoulder area. Refer to the muscle reference in **Figure 3.6**, which focuses on the shoulder area. You can see that the huge muscle on the chest, the pectoralis major, stretches across and under the shoulder muscle, the deltoid. It would probably make sense to try and sculpt these at the same time, and then work on the armpit area before progressing to the rear of the upper body section.

Using the Split Polygon tool, create a new line following the outline of the two muscles lying across the chest and over the arm (**Figure 3.7**, middle).

> **TIP** When you're done with an area, feel free to work on it further, adding more edges and manipulating the vertices until you are happy with the shape.

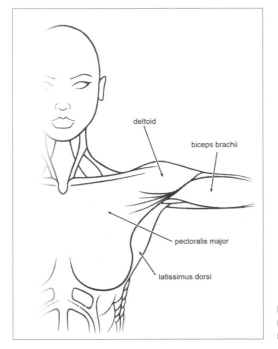

**FIGURE 3.6** Upper body muscle lines, with the arm raised

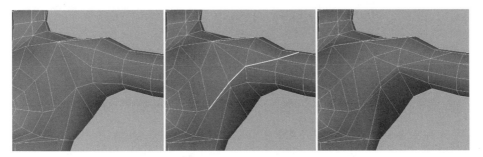

**FIGURE 3.7** Add detail to the chest, shoulder, and armpit areas.

Looking at **Figure 3.8** (left), the shoulder seems a little angular; this is because there are too few polygons here at the moment. When this area bends in animation, we will get quite a rough-looking deformation. You can prevent this by adding extra strips across the top as you continue adding the muscle lines.

Split the polygons as I have in **Figure 3.8** (middle), following them around to the back of the shoulder (**Figure 3.8**, right) while continuing the line for the deltoid muscle.

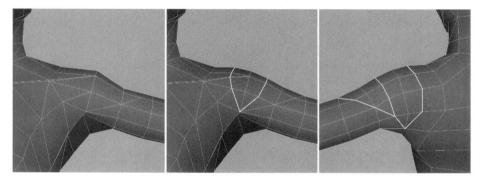

FIGURE 3.8 Insert more polygons into the shoulder.

Move the newly created shoulder vertices out slightly to round off the area.

### The Back

This brings us nicely around to the rear of the upper body. We don't need immense detail here, either, but it's important to get the basic muscles in.

Starting at the top of the back and moving downward, work in the trapezius, lattimus dorsi, and thoracolumbar fascia muscles (refer again to the anatomical reference as you go). See the left and middle views of **Figure 3.9**.

Halfway down the back, just above the hips, there is quite a large space. It will make life easier if we subdivide this area, allowing us to continue adding the back muscles (**Figure 3.9**, right). Follow the cut all the way around to the front of the mesh.

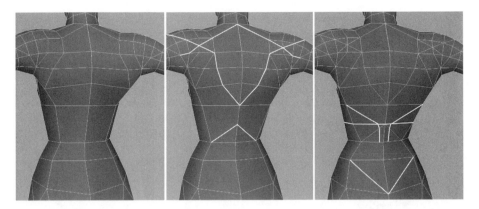

**FIGURE 3.9** Add muscle lines to Kila's back.

Still on her back, we could implement the spine at this point. This will be a simple recess down the center of her back. First, though, as you can see in **Figure 3.10** (left), there is another large area in between her shoulder blades. Take a moment to split this area, taking the cut across the center as in **Figure 3.10** (right).

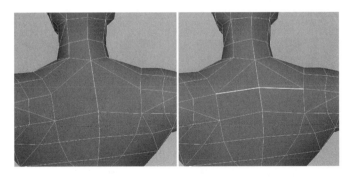

**FIGURE 3.10**
Subdivide the large polygon at the top of the back.

Now, to create the recess for the spine (**Figure 3.11**), split the polygons just on either side of the center, remembering to remove any small triangles that are created. Finally, move the vertices that run down the center slightly inward.

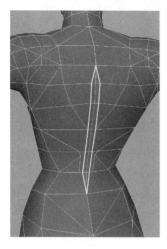

FIGURE 3.11 Insert the recess for the spine.

Now is probably a good time to delete that history that has steadily been building up.

### The Stomach

Moving around to Kila's front in **Figure 3.12** (left), we can begin to work in her stomach muscles. Split polygons and move vertices to get the general shape seen in **Figure 3.12** (right).

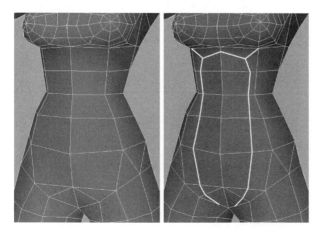

FIGURE 3.12 Add muscle detail to the stomach.

**NOTE** It's important to remember that when you split polygons, Maya places the cut on top of the current polygons. This means that although you have divided the polygon, it will still appear flat when viewed from an angle. In most cases, as occurred with the stomach muscles, you will need to pull these new vertices out slightly to round the area off.

### The Pelvis

Moving farther down the front of the model's body brings us to the next part to work on: the pelvic area. Because Kila is wearing jeans, there is not much point in mapping the muscles here, but we do need to make sure the area has clarity and deforms correctly.

Switch to the front view and make sure your image plane is visible. What you need to do first is mark out the top of her jeans. Judging by **Figure 3.13** (left), we are in a good position. The edges at either side already lie in the correct position for the hip-hugging jeans; even the edges at the rear follow where her jeans should go, so you only need to fix the front. Go ahead and split the polygons at the front of the mesh, following the top of her jeans (**Figure 3.13**, right).

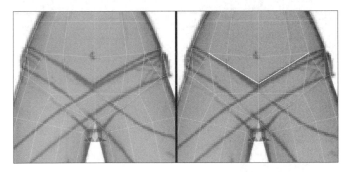

**FIGURE 3.13** Create the area at the top of the jeans.

Now you need to address the groin area. The polyons seem to have moved down slightly so they no longer line up with the reference image. Also, the creases where the upper legs meet the hips need to be realigned. We want to end up with the mesh closely resembling the image plane, as in **Figure 3.14**. Don't worry if both sides don't match exactly; as long as one side matches the guide images, we are fine.

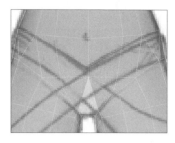

FIGURE 3.14 Fix the crotch area; position the vertices to match the guide image.

First move the vertices apart, creating a gap (**Figure 3.15**, left), and then use the Edit Polygon > Extrude Edge and Polygon > Append To Polygon tools to fill the hole. Afterward, work the vertices to round off the area, which should give you a nice, clean result like that shown on the right in **Figure 3.15**.

FIGURE 3.15 Fill in the gap, creating the crotch area.

What you can start to do at this stage is include creases in your geometry. Look at **Figure 3.16** (left); this is how the mesh looks now, with all the normals smooth, giving us a nice smooth surface.

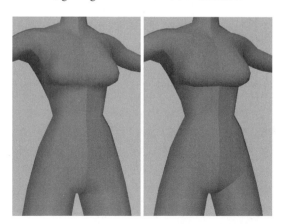

FIGURE 3.16 Add creases to your geometry by creating hard edges.

**Figure 3.16** (right) is the same mesh—but here there are creases added around the crotch, the upper part of the jeans, and under her chest. These creases are simple to do; it's just a matter of making the edges hard. Here are the steps:

**1**  Right-click the mesh and select Edge from the marking menu.

**2**  Select the edges you wish to crease, in this case under her chest and around the folds in her jeans.

**3**  Go to Edit Polygons > Normals > Soften/Harden and open up the options.

**4**  Earlier, we clicked All Soft to smooth out the geometry. This time, select All Hard. Then click Apply and close the options.

This isn't a vital part of the procedure; it just makes the geometry look better as you are working on it. To add balance to the model, as you would with a painting, you should have both hard and soft lines (edges).

### The Buttocks

Time to work on Kila's rear. At the moment it's not much to look at (**Figure 3.17**, left), but we will soon fix that. As you did for the front, move the vertices to lie roughly where the creases should be, as shown in **Figure 3.17** (middle).

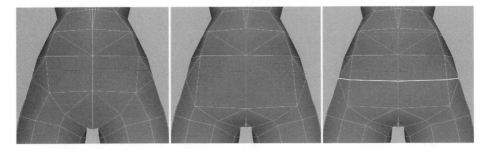

FIGURE 3.17 Move the vertices to tidy up her bum.

You are now left with a huge flat area; subdivide that by splitting the polygons, as shown in **Figure 3.17** (right). This still leaves the area flat, so switch to the side view and use your guide to round it off (**Figure 3.18**).

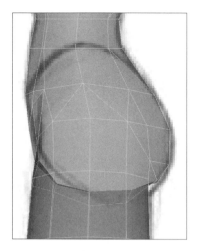

**FIGURE 3.18** Round off the flat surfaces.

Rotate the model, tweaking the vertices until you are happy with the shape of the buttocks. Switch to the perspective view and look down on it from above to make sure she is nicely rounded—remember to always refer back to your anatomical reference material.

You will probably notice that from certain angles she still seems quite flat. You can fix this by subdividing the long faces at the rear by creating vertical cuts (**Figure 3.19**, right). Before you do this, however, delete the edges designated in the left pane of **Figure 3.19**. Then add a cut at either side of the crease under the buttocks (**Figure 3.19**, middle).

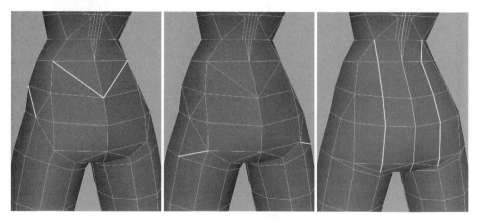

**FIGURE 3.19** Subdivide the long faces to smooth out the buttocks.

Continue tweaking, making sure you use your guide images. **Figure 3.20** illustrates another area that could benefit from a little subdivision, smoothing it out and rounding it off. Here again, you'll split the polygons horizontally to subdivide the area; in fact, you can split these all the way around, ending at the crotch (**Figure 3.20**, middle). When you're done, tweak the vertices until the shape is just right (**Figure 3.20**, right).

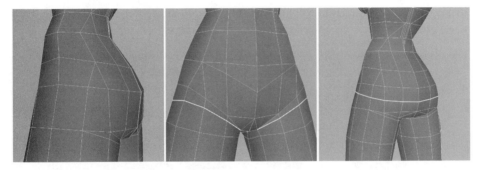

**FIGURE 3.20** Further subdivision is needed.

**Figure 3.21** shows the entire torso with all its refinements. We have added geometry not only to help the shape, but also to aid deformation.

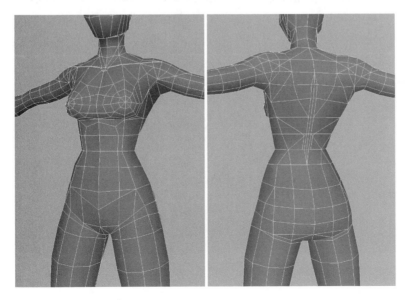

**FIGURE 3.21** The refined torso

### The Arms

The torso is more or less complete now. It has more detail, and the shape is coming along nicely. The next stage is to refine the limbs, starting with the arms.

To begin, we will build in a simple elbow. I have highlighted an edge in **Figure 3.22** (left); this is where our elbow will be. All we need to do is pull that edge out slightly, but first we need to create four cuts (**Figure 3.22**, middle). As shown in **Figure 3.22** (right), this will allow us to pull out the center edge, creating the basic elbow.

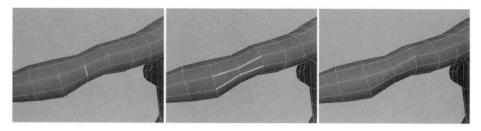

**FIGURE 3.22** Build in the basic elbow.

Having the elbow in place helps us to complete the rest of the arm. Let's work on the upper arm first, sculpting in the biceps and triceps. Most of the arm detail can be achieved by simply moving the vertices. And remember—we still need to refer to our muscle reference to get it right.

Begin to mark in the biceps by cutting the polygons to create the outline; **Figure 3.23** (middle) shows these cuts.

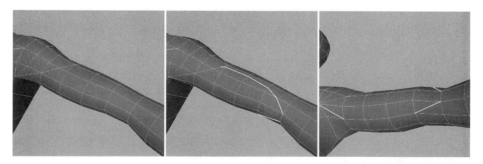

**FIGURE 3.23** Carve the biceps into the mesh.

Now work on molding the biceps into its correct shape. If you are at all unsure about how it should look, use a good arm reference to get it looking right. **Figure 3.24** shows the finished biceps on our model.

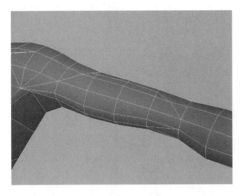

**FIGURE 3.24** Manipulate the vertices to get the biceps correctly shaped.

Moving around to the back of the arm (**Figure 3.25**, left), we can work in the triceps. First cut in the outline shown in **Figure 3.25** (right), and then move the vertices to achieve the desired shape.

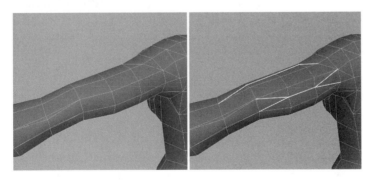

**FIGURE 3.25** Create the triceps.

You may not need to cut any polygons for the forearm; just make sure the shape is correct. The muscles run down toward the wrist, as our edges do anyway, so it would be a waste of time to work in every muscle; further detail in this area can be gained by her texture.

We now have enough definition in the upper body. You can, if you like, spend a bit more time mapping in the rest of the muscles, as I have in **Figure 3.26**. Round off this section by doing what makes up 90 percent of most modeling: rotating and tweaking. Move around the model and make sure it is smooth, anatomically correct, and clean.

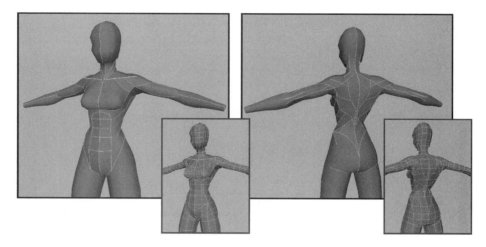

FIGURE 3.26 Upper body muscle maps

When you're done, delete the history and save your work as Kila_Muscles.mb.

## Legs

Depending on the character you are creating, you may need to add muscle lines to the legs. **Figure 3.27** shows a different character I created a while ago; she has muscles mapped on her entire body. This was done by following an appropriate muscle reference and splitting the polygons to outline the muscles.

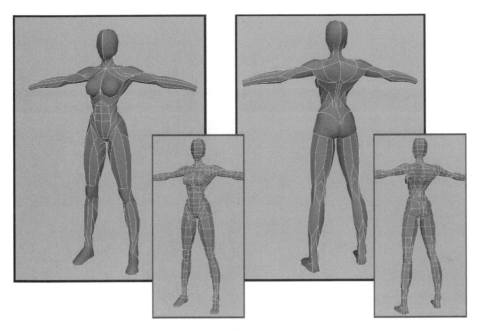

FIGURE 3.27 The muscles mapped to the entire body of another model

## Face and Upper Body Detail

Kila's torso and limbs are sculpted now to a point where we can move on to another area. We will begin by adding more details to the geometry, starting as before from the top and working our way down.

### The Face

It's about time we gave Kila a face. We will begin working on her from the side, so switch to the side panel now and focus in on her face.

The image in **Figure 3.28** (left) will do for the head, but it is of very low quality. This is where our head model sheet from Chapter 1 comes in handy. Scan in the sheet and divide it up into two sections, as you we did with the body model sheet.

Import the side image into the side panel (or load in the file 02/Scans/ KilaFaceSide.tga from the CD), and position and resize it until it is the same scale as the current head (as seen in **Figure 3.28**, middle).

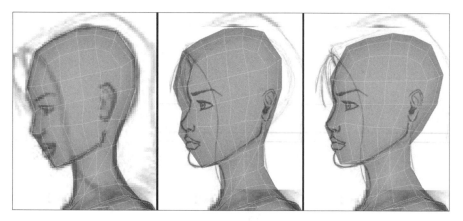

FIGURE 3.28 Import the head model sheet

You now have a better image to work with. Take a look: The first thing that stands out is that the head is tilted slightly. So we must select the vertices of the head and rotate it, so that it fits the head in the image plane (**Figure 3.28**, right).

In order to add more detail to the head, we must add some more vertices and polygons to the face. We could split the polygons where we need them, but since we need to divide a large area, we can do something quicker.

1    Referring to **Figure 3.29** (left), select the faces at the front of the head.

2    Go to Edit Polygons > Subdivide and open the options.

3    Set Subdivision Levels to 1 and Mode to quads.

4    Click the Apply button to finish, and close the options.

As illustrated in **Figure 3.29** (right), Kila's face is now divided up into smaller sections, allowing us to begin refining the area.

Switch to the side view (**Figure 3.30**, left), and begin to manipulate the vertices to better fit the image in the image plane (**Figure 3.30**, right). When you're happy with the side view, switch to perspective view and begin to work on the rest of the vertices. At this stage, you're not aiming for any details such as eyes, nose, or mouth. For now, work on achieving a smooth area and getting the overall shape of the head. See the progression in **Figure 3.31**.

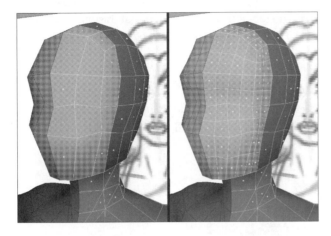

**FIGURE 3.29** Subdivide the face so we can add detail.

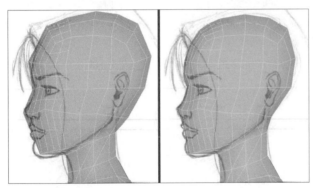

**FIGURE 3.30** Move the vertices to fit the side outline.

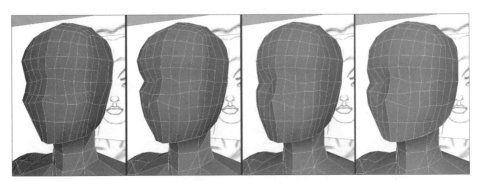

**FIGURE 3.31** Progression of the face shape

> **TIP** Depending on the accuracy of the head images, you may find it difficult to get the mesh looking exactly like the front and side images at once. Don't worry; try to find a happy medium. What's important is that it looks like the character when it's finished. The topology is your concern at this stage, especially if the character will have any lip-sync capabilities, as most characters do.

### Nose

The basic head shape is in place. Its time to work in some features; let's begin with the nose. As shown in **Figure 3.32**, switch to the front view and split the polygons as demonstrated. These should follow the line of the nose, then the eyebrow.

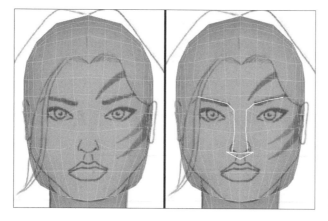

**FIGURE 3.32** Split the polygons around the nose.

Switch to the side view and move the vertices to match the nose (**Figure 3.33**). Switch to the perspective panel to see how things are looking, making any needed adjustments to retain the shape.

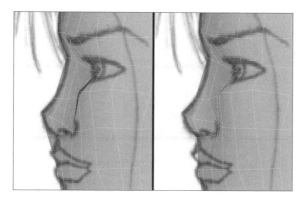

**FIGURE 3.33** Add detail to the nose.

Still in the perspective view, cut the polygons as shown in **Figure 3.34** (middle), making an X. Move the new vertex that's in the center of the X, pulling it down slightly to give her nostril more definition (**Figure 3.34**, right).

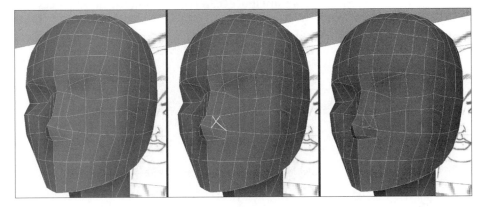

**FIGURE 3.34** Define the nostril.

### Lips and Mouth

Let's continue and create a rough version of her lips. Move to the front view and split the polygons around the outline of the mouth (**Figure 3.35**). You will see that the nose needs to be thinned out slightly to match the image, so we may as well implement this while we are here.

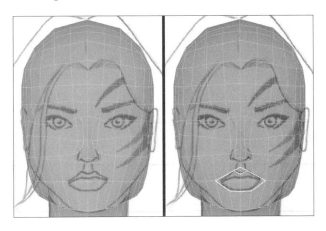

**FIGURE 3.35** Create the basic mouth.

Switch to the side view and move the vertices to match the lips in the image (**Figure 3.36**, middle). We could leave the lips as they are, but they look a little flat and we need to give them some volume. To do this, simply divide them down the center. Then, as shown in **Figure 3.36** (right), pull the new vertices outward to round off the lips.

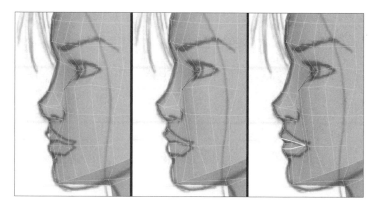

FIGURE 3.36 Round off the lips in the side view.

At this stage, we can begin to implement the muscles lines of the face (as seen in **Figure 3.37**). We are currently working on the mouth area, so let's split more polygons around the mouth to map out the muscles. This will also help us add more definition to the chin and the rest of this facial area.

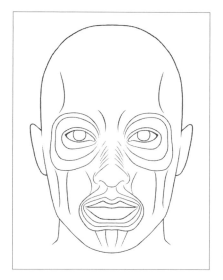

FIGURE 3.37
Facial muscle map

Following the reference in **Figure 3.37**, create a ring around the mouth (**Figure 3.38**). As in **Figure 3.39**, switch to the side panel and fill out the chin.

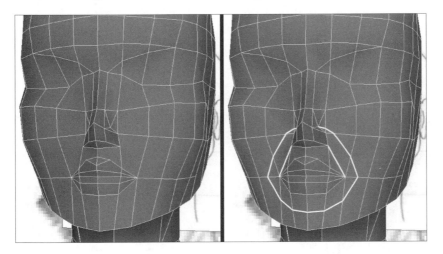

FIGURE 3.38 Create a ring around the mouth.

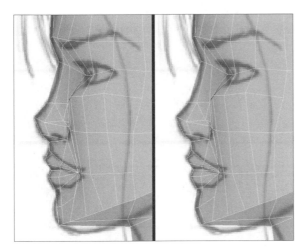

FIGURE 3.39 Fill out the chin from the side view.

Now open up the perspective view and work on the area until the shape looks correct. **Figure 3.40** shows the mouth area completed with the first set of muscle maps.

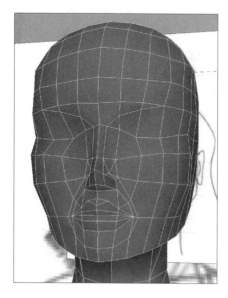

FIGURE 3.40 Kila's head with the mouth muscles completed

### Eye Area

Let's now work on the eyes. Go to the front view and, as illustrated in **Figure 3.41** (right), split the polygons, creating the outline for her eye. The polygons in the center of the eye won't be needed, so select the faces inside the eye's outline and delete them.

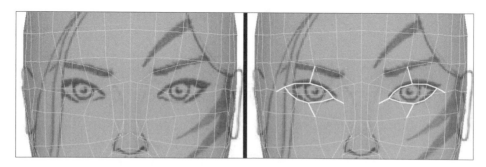

FIGURE 3.41 Build in the outline for the eye.

With the outline for the eye in place, move the vertices of this outline to fit the shape of the eyeball. You'll need an eyeball first in order to do this, so create a basic sphere and position it where the eyeball would be (**Figure 3.42**).

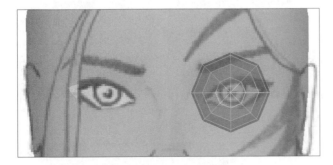

**FIGURE 3.42** Create a sphere for a placeholder eyeball.

Using this placeholder eyeball as a guide, move the vertices of the eye so that they follow the curve of the eyeball (**Figure 3.43**). Make sure to leave a small gap between each vertex and the eyeball.

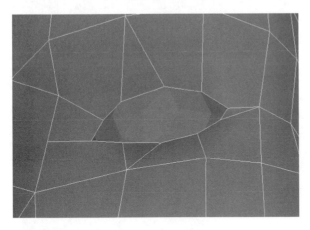

**FIGURE 3.43** Adjust the outline of the eye to make it curve around the eyeball.

With our basic facial features in place, we can start to refine them by adding more detail. Staying with the eye, carve in a ring around it (**Figure 3.44**, left). This subdivides the polygons, allowing you to smooth out the area; it also act as a muscle line. Shape these new vertices to fill out the area around the eye. Then you can build in the eyelids (**Figure 3.44**, middle). These will be quite important to the face's animation; the eyes must be able to open and close.

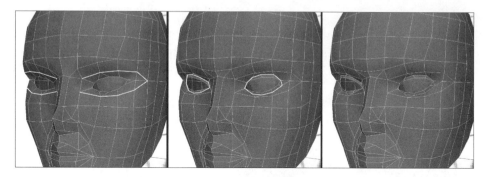

FIGURE 3.44 Refine the basic eye area, adding the eyelids.

To fill in the gap between the eyelids and the eyeball, simply select the edges shown in **Figure 3.45a** and extrude them inward (**Figure 3.45b**).

Kila has very long eyelashes. To achieve this look, all you need to do is repeat the extrusion task you just did for the eyelids. Select the edges on the rim of the eye, but this time extrude them outward, as seen in **Figure 3.45c**. Manipulate the vertices to match the shape in the front guide image, splitting the outer edges highlighted in **Figure 3.45d**, to separate the upper and lower lashes. **Figure 3.45e** shows that Kila's eyes are essentially complete.

With the basic features in place, let's continue to refine the face. Before you continue, delete the history on the geometry and save the file.

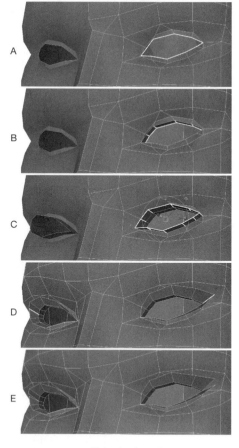

FIGURE 3.45 Extrude the edges to create the inner eye and the eyelashes.

### Face Refinement

We will begin by working on the nose. Looking in from the side, as in **Figure 3.46** (left), you can see that the nose is quite sharp and angular. Split some of the polygons, and move the vertices to smooth out the nose (**Figure 3.46**, right).

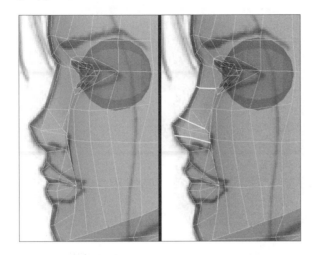

**FIGURE 3.46** Start in the side view to smooth out the nose.

Moving to the front view, edit the vertices to smooth out the nose even more, adding cuts to the underside of the nose (**Figure 3.47**, right).

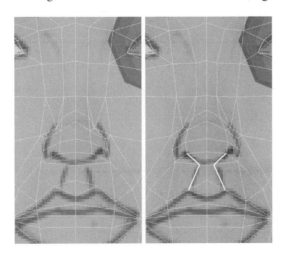

**FIGURE 3.47** Continue to smooth out the nose using the front view.

Now switch to perspective view to see how you're doing. It's coming along well—but if you look upward from the bottom, her nose is still quite sharp and pointed. In **Figure 3.48**, I have split the polygons vertically across the nostril, allowing the nose to be rounded off.

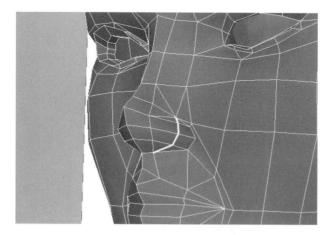

**FIGURE 3.48** Subdivide the nostril to round off the nose.

To complete the nose, insert a hole underneath to create the nostril. Split the polygons underneath, creating an X (**Figure 3.49**, middle). Move the new vertex up into the nose to create the nostril cavity.

As you've done with everything else up to now, have a final look around the nose, manipulating the vertices to fill out the shape. You should end up with the nostril as illustrated in **Figure 3.49** (right).

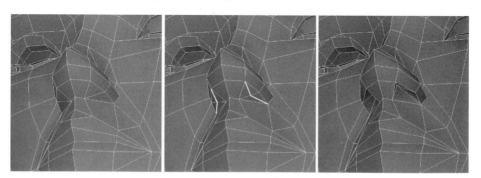

**FIGURE 3.49** Create the nasal cavity to finish the nose.

Nose and eyes are done; moving on brings us to the mouth. Switch to the side view and start working the vertices to refine the shape of the lips. Split the polygons to round off the lower lip. Look at the model in the perspective view now, and divide the lips as illustrated in **Figure 3.50** (middle). Next, it is merely a case of sculpting the area until the lips better fit your reference imagery (**Figure 3.50**, right).

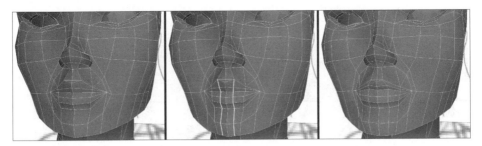

**FIGURE 3.50** Refine the lips.

Before we can leave the head and move on, we must fill out the chin. In **Figure 3.51** (left), the area under the chin is very flat and the chin itself is quite angular. To rectify this, start by splitting more polygons, following the ones on the side of the head down to the bottom (**Figure 3.51**, middle). Then adjust the vertices to fit the outline in the image plane (**Figure 3.51**, right).

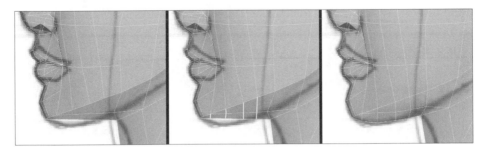

**FIGURE 3.51** Fill out the chin.

The final stage for the head is to spend time making sure the shape is perfect. We have all the features in, and now we must make sure they resemble the character we are building.

Getting the face right is crucial, so load in the original color image that was created in Chapter 1 (**Figure 3.52**). This is how the character should look and will be our reference for this part of the model.

Put as much time as possible into refining the face and head. Get it just right (**Figure 3.53**) before you go forward. Then delete the history and save your work as Kila_Face.mb.

FIGURE 3.52 The main head reference

FIGURE 3.53 Finished face and head geometry

## The Neck

Progressing down from the face, we come to the neck. There's not much you can really do here except perhaps to make the muscle you defined earlier, the sterno-cleidomastoid, a little more pronounced (**Figure 3.54**).

You can achieve this simply by creating a split all the way down the center of the muscle (**Figure 3.54**, middle). Then manipulate the vertices until you have the required shape (**Figure 3.54**, right), giving the muscle slightly more definition.

Continuing on, the shoulder area seems fine for now. We may need to add some more subdivisions to get a nice round shoulder when she lowers her arm, but we can test this out when we come to the deformation tests (Chapter 6, "Deformation Testing").

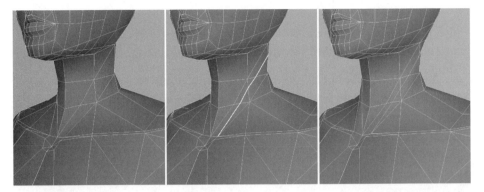

**FIGURE 3.54** Defining the neck

### The Armpit

Next comes the armpit. It is important for this part of the anatomy to be correct in order to achieve good deformation. It's wise to refer to a real armpit, so look around for a good photo to use as a guide (or use a mirror). Visit one of the links suggested in Appendix B; they will have many reference images.

To start, split up some of the larger areas as seen in **Figure 3.55** (middle), giving you more pieces to work with. Using your reference as an example, move the vertices around until you have a better shape (**Figure 3.55**, right).

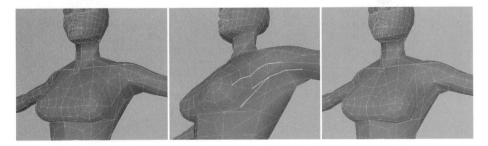

**FIGURE 3.55** Work to refine the armpit area.

I like to keep my models clean and tidy, so I prefer to work in *quads*. (A quad is simply two triangular polygons combined to make a square.) This method has a second advantage: If you are creating a subdivision surface model, using mostly quads will result in a smoother model when it's converted (see "Subdivision Surfaces" in Chapter 2).

To create a quad, select two adjoining triangular faces (**Figure 3.56**) and go to Polygons > Quadrangulate to convert them to a single quad. This technique is particularly useful if applied to a number of faces at once. Another way to create a single quad is to select the dividing edge and delete it.

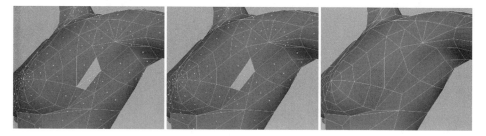

FIGURE 3.56 Convert unneeded triangles to quads.

Continue checking the model for areas to improve. Notice the polygon just under her chest (**Figure 3.57**, left), which is at a sharp angle to the polygon below, making this area look angular when you rotate around the model. It is best that we remove this polygon, rebuilding the area to smooth it out.

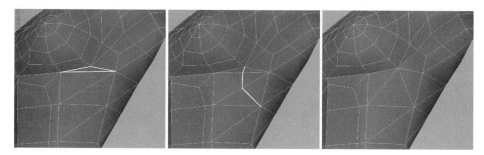

FIGURE 3.57 Rebuild any areas that don't look smooth or natural.

The quickest way to accomplish this is to split the faces as shown in **Figure 3.57**, middle. Select the new vertices and snap each one to the topmost vertex of the cut. Finally, weld them together, resulting in the simplified but smoother area seen in **Figure 3.57**, right.

### The Navel

We've accomplished a lot—except for the hands and feet, there really aren't many more details we can add to Kila's main body. (In Chapter 4, "Modeling Details," we'll get to add clothing and other areas like ears and hair.) So let's just finish this section by giving her a navel.

For a general game model, the navel could be achieved with the texture, causing no major problems. But for demonstration purposes, I will go ahead and create it using the cutting and shaping method used throughout this chapter.

1   Switch to the front view, making sure the image planes are visible. Zoom in, as in **Figure 3.58** (left), to where the navel would be.

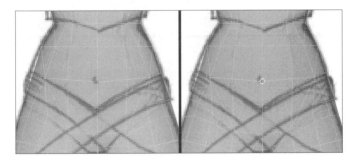

**FIGURE 3.58**
Finish the basic details by building a navel.

2   Make two small cuts, resulting in a diamond shape (**Figure 3.58**, right). The cuts need not follow the image perfectly; they just need to be in the correct place.

3   Select the faces just created (**Figure 3.59**, left). Then select Edit Polygons > Extrude Face, and move them inward slightly.

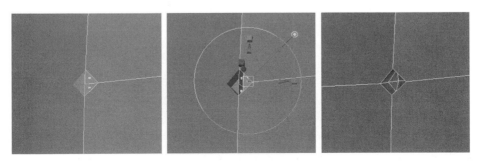

FIGURE 3.59 Extrude the faces inward, making the depression of the navel.

4    As you can see in **Figure 3.59** (middle), some faces have been created down the center of the navel. Delete these before moving on to manipulate the inside of the navel, shaping it correctly (**Figure 3.59**, right).

Kila's navel is fairly basic for now; this is because we are not sure how it will look in the game, or even if it will ever be seen up close. After the model is complete, we can come back to the navel and add details or remove it if necessary.

At this point, Kila's essentials have been modeled. She now has a face, and the primary areas of her body have been shaped and adjusted to give her an explicit form. If we require it, more-precise muscle definition can be achieved with the texture, as can many of the smaller details. For now, her shape looks good and will deform well.

Delete the history on your geometry and save your work as Kila_Details.mb.

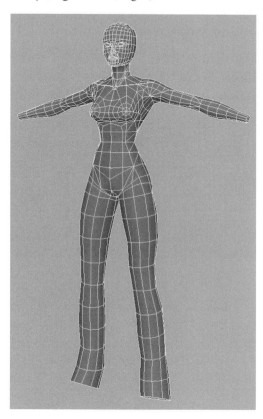

FIGURE 3.60 Kila so far

## Hands

Hands in a game environment can come in many shapes and sizes. During our research in Chapter 1, we discovered that Kila is to have a fully working hand, meaning all the fingers can be animated separately. If you are at all unsure about the number of fingers your character should have, talk it through with your lead artist.

Although we already have determined the hands we need for Kila, I will illustrate in this section how to develop various resolutions for a hand, covering any eventuality. The best starting point for this task is to build the higher-resolution version and then work down.

If you already have a selection of hands at your disposal, as I do in my Morgue, you can simply import one that's appropriate, attach it, and keep working. But let's say you're starting from scratch. You'll need some sample hand images that you can import into Maya and use as a guide. The image in **Figure 3.61** is the one we will use as a base in this discussion.

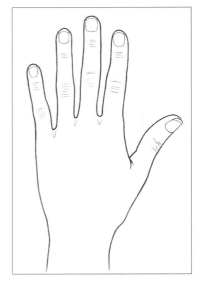

FIGURE 3.61 Hand reference image

### Building a Finger

Before we continue, let's look briefly at how the finger is going to bend, and the best way to build this. Load the file called BendingTest.ma (located on the CD in the 03 directory). It comprises five primitive fingers, as seen in **Figure 3.62** (top). If you move along the timeline, the fingers will bend (**Figure 3.62**, bottom).

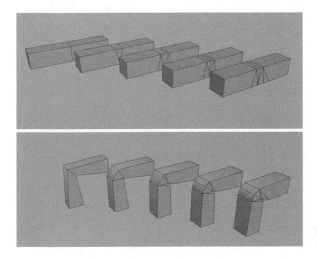

FIGURE 3.62
Finger bending test

Notice that the finger on the far left is pinching badly as it bends, while the one on the far right keeps its shape. This is an example of how adding a few polygons in the correct place can help. It may very well be, however, that in your game the character's fingers are never seen up close, so the far-left finger will do just fine. So let's begin with building a simple finger. Once we have one finger complete, we can duplicate it and use it for the rest of the hand:

1   Start with a new scene and go to Create > Polygon Primitives > Cube. Create a cube with a Width of 6, Subdivisions Along Width of 3, Subdivisions Along Height of 2, and Subdivisions Along Depth of 2 (**Figure 3.63**).

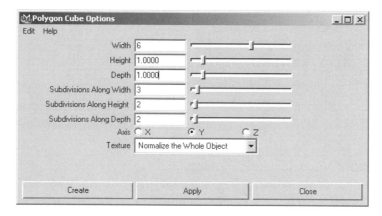

FIGURE 3.63 Cube configuration to start the finger

2   Use the Split Polygon tool to follow the cuts shown in **Figure 3.64** in the middle. This defines the knuckle areas.

3   With the knuckles in place, start to shape the rest of the finger. Move the knuckles down the finger until they are correctly positioned. Then, as in **Figure 3.64** at the bottom, taper the whole finger down toward the tip.

4   Looking from the side view (**Figure 3.65**), our finger is a little flat. We need to give it more shape. Subdivide the finger further, but this time don't use the Split Polygon tool. Instead, go to Edit Polygons > Cut Faces Tool.

Like the Split Polygon tool, Cut Faces cuts the faces for you, but in this case you define a single straight line that determines the axis of the slice. Maya then slices through the entire mesh, following this line. A word of warning: Be careful when applying this tool; it will cut through both sides of the mesh.

Try it here: Select an area between the top of the finger and the next knuckle, holding down the mouse button. A line appears, spanning the entire view panel. Move the mouse, and the orientation of the line alters, to determine the line that will be sliced across the finger.

Make sure the line is completely vertical, and then let go of the mouse button. A line has been cut all the way through the mesh, saving you the effort of having to create each cut individually.

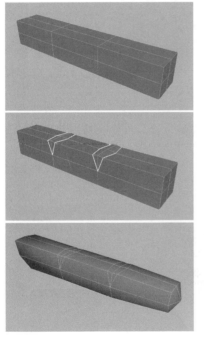
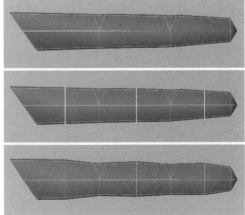

FIGURE 3.64 Add the knuckle definition, and then begin to mold the shape.

FIGURE 3.65 Divide the finger so that we can add more shape.

5    Continue to work, making a total of three slices, until the finger looks like that in **Figure 3.65** (middle).

6    Now that you have these extra divisions, you can add definition to the finger. Look at your own finger from the side and try to match it (**Figure 3.65**, bottom).

**7** Switch to the top view and continue shaping, as illustrated in **Figure 3.66**.

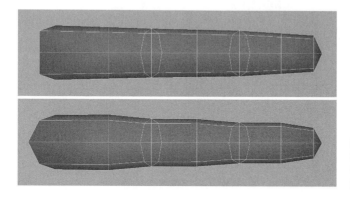

**FIGURE 3.66**
Shape the finger additionally from the top view.

**8** Moving on, create the fingernail. Using the Split Polygon tool, create a cut at the end of the finger to outline the actual fingernail (**Figure 3.67**, middle). Manipulate the vertices until you achieve the required shape (**Figure 3.67**, right).

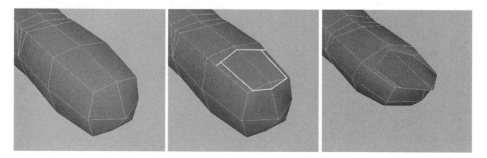

**FIGURE 3.67** Create the fingernail.

**9** While you're at the fingernail end, you can remove a couple of unneeded vertices. You should wind up with two vertices on either side of the nail, as shown in **Figure 3.68** (left). Select these and weld them to the vertices above them (**Figure 3.68**, right).

**10** Finally, using reference or your own finger, continue working on the overall shape until you are happy with the results (**Figure 3.69**).

FIGURE 3.68 Tidy up the fingernail by removing these vertices.

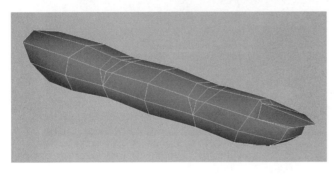

FIGURE 3.69 Using your reference, keep shaping the vertices.

**11** Referring back to our bending test in **Figure 3.62**, we can see that the finger we've just designed will more than likely pinch underneath as it's deforming. Let's try to fix that. As illustrated in **Figure 3.70**, split the polygons until you get two upside-down V shapes, almost mirroring the knuckles above.

**12** For the last time (on this finger, anyway), work on the general shape until you are satisfied.

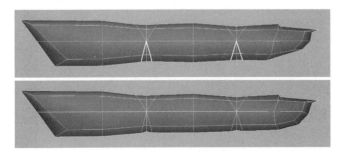

FIGURE 3.70 Create extra polygons underneath the knuckle to help the finger deform better.

What we have now is a decent finger model—although it may have a bit too much detail or too many polygons for the actual character you are building. **Figure 3.71** shows how the finger we have just built can be reduced to a lower iteration in a matter of minutes. All I did to achieve this was to snap the vertices I didn't want to the ones I wanted to keep, and then weld the whole finger using a low distance of 0.1 or 0.01.

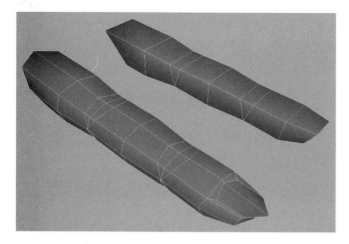

**FIGURE 3.71** The high- and low-resolution versions of the finger

Before continuing, delete the history on your finger and save as Kila_Finger.mb.

## Creating All the Fingers

As we progress with building the hand, I will demonstrate the lower-resolution version next, for comparison. The technique is the same, no matter which finger you use.

1   Now it is time to use our guide image, the one in **Figure 3.61**. Switch to the top view and import the image as an image plane. Go to View > Image Plane > Import Image and select the image called Hand_Top.jpg (on the CD in the directory 03/Scans).

2   Size at the moment is not really an issue, as long as the proportions are correct. So instead of altering the image plane, simply rotate and scale the finger until it matches the middle finger in the image, lining it up with the knuckle as in **Figure 3.73**. Keep the rotations to 90 degrees for now.

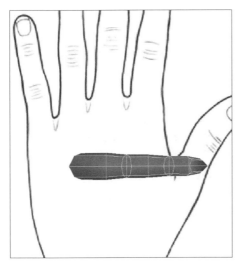

FIGURE 3.72 Import the guide image as an image plane.

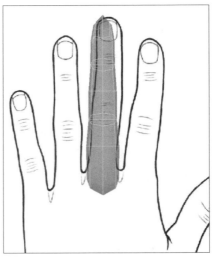

FIGURE 3.73 Position the finger so it matches the image plane.

3   Before creating the other fingers, check that the proportions are correct. As in **Figure 3.74** (left), move the finger to the right of the image's middle finger and compare the proportions. The size looks fine, so go ahead and compare the knuckles' positions. Make any necessary adjustments (**Figure 3.74**, right) before proceeding.

**NOTE** It's important to get the finger right, because any changes you make later will involve altering five fingers instead of one.

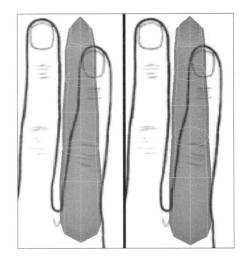

FIGURE 3.74 Double-check the proportions.

4   Once you are happy with the finger's proportions, duplicate it four times. Then position and scale each copy to fit its corresponding finger in the image (**Figure 3.75**). Don't do the thumb yet, however (you will need to edit the thumb a bit more before positioning it).

5   Now we'll look at the thumb. It's shaped differently from the fingers, and it's set on an angle. So before positioning it, we want to reshape it. Waiting to do this later would make the task more difficult. You can achieve the desired shape by simply selecting areas of vertices and scaling them up until the digit looks thicker, resembling a thumb (**Figures 3.76** and **3.77**).

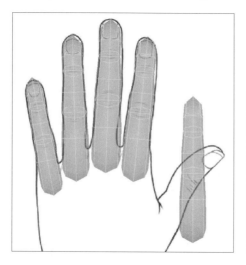

FIGURE 3.75 Create the other fingers for the hand.

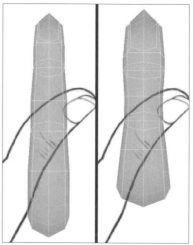

FIGURE 3.76 Adjust the fifth digit until it resembles a thumb.

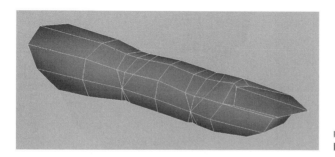

FIGURE 3.77 The finger now looks more like a thumb.

**6** To finish the thumb, reposition it so it lies over the thumb in the guide image (**Figure 3.78**, left). Then rotate it around its X axis by 45 degrees (**Figure 3.78**, right).

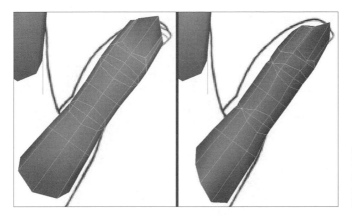

**FIGURE 3.78** Position the thumb so it matches the image.

**7** The fingers are ready; you may want to move the fingers up slightly as I have done in **Figure 3.79**, so they lie above the thumb.

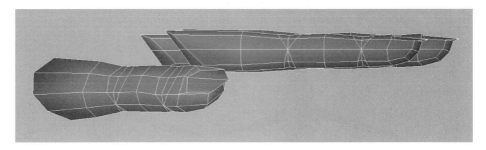

**FIGURE 3.79** Move the fingers up slightly so they lie above the thumb.

**8**  Moving on, combine all the digits so they are a single mesh. As you can see in **Figure 3.80** (top), we still have the ends of the fingers capped. Before we start work on the palm, remove these caps (**Figure 3.80**, bottom).

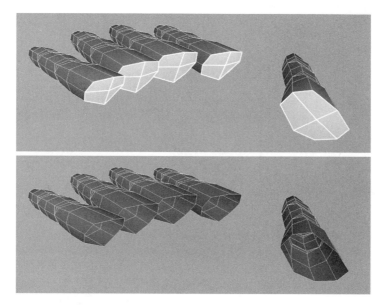

FIGURE 3.80 Combine the digits and remove the inner faces.

### The Hand

Now we can start on the main part of the hand. Use the Append To Polygon tool to bridge the gaps between the fingers and between the forefinger and thumb (**Figure 3.81**), filling in the outer areas.

Next, bring the fingers up to meet the thumb by selecting the edges (**Figure 3.82**, left) all around the outer ring of the fingers. Select them all the way underneath, too. Use the Extrude Edge tool to pull the edges out to meet the thumb (**Figure 3.82**, right). Finish by flattening the new edges. You can use the Scale manipulator, or the small square on the Extrude Edge manipulator to do this.

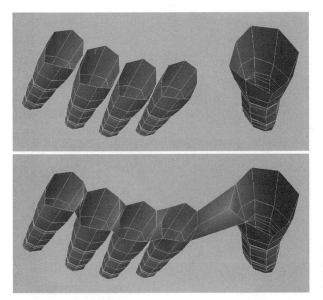

FIGURE 3.81 Use the
Append To Polygon tool to
bridge the gaps between the
fingers and thumb.

FIGURE 3.82 Extrude the edges at the end of the fingers to create the hand.

**TIP** If you are experiencing problems aligning the edges of the fingers you can align the edges manually by using the standard Move manipulator and snapping the edges to the grid. First, open up the Move tool options and deselect Retain Component Spacing. With this setting turned off, when we use the grid snap tool to align the edges they will all keep their original spacing relative to one another. Select the edges and, holding X, move them along the Z axis. All the edges will align themselves along a straight line perpendicular to that axis. Release X, and position the edges correctly.

Now it's time to work those vertices. Shape the existing palm and upper hand areas using the guide image and any reference material you have (**Figure 3.83**).

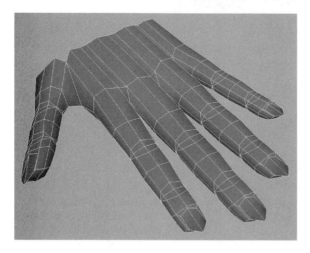

FIGURE 3.83 Work on the vertices to shape the new polygons for the palm and upper hand.

You now need to do another extrude. You should have a complete loop at the inner side of the hand (**Figure 3.84**, left). Select the edges around this loop and extrude them (**Figure 3.84**, middle). For this extrusion, pull it right down to the wrist and scale it inward, across the X axis (**Figure 3.84**, right). Look in the Channel Box; you will have all the attributes for the extrusion available. Set Divisions to 2.

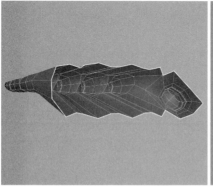

FIGURE 3.84 Extrude the edges around the upper hand again.

More work on the vertices is needed now, shaping the palm, upper hand, and upper wrist areas until the entire hand is correct. Start by rounding off the wrist area and working your way up. We appear to have quite a few polygons in the palm area, and it would be easier to edit if we removed some of the unnecessary ones. Select the edges shown in **Figure 3.85** (left); they should lie between the tendons on the back of the hand. Select the same edges on the underside, too, and then go to Edit Polygons > Collapse to remove them (**Figure 3.85**, right).

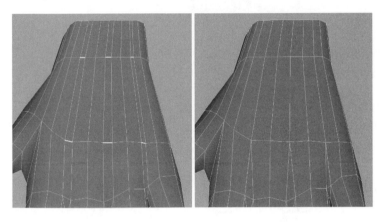

**FIGURE 3.85** Collapse some of the edges making up the hand, cleaning up the area and making it easier to edit.

Kila's arms were made up of 10 subdivisions around the axis, so the wrist area of the hand should match this. As shown in **Figure 3.86** on the left, select every other edge and collapse them. This leaves 12 remaining (**Figure 3.86**, right), but we can remove two more later after we have worked some more on the area.

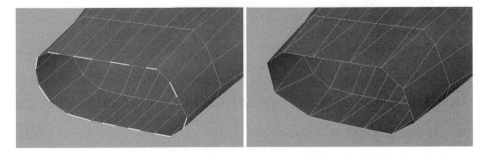

**FIGURE 3.86** Reduce the polygons in the wrist so it will match up more closely with the arm.

Now we have a simpler mesh to work with more easily. Continue shaping the palm and upper hand; use the tendons on the back of the hand as a guide, lining up the edges to follow them.

Looking at the hand on the left in **Figure 3.87**, we could use some more vertices across the middle to fill it out. As you did earlier, use the Cut Faces tool to cut a line all the way through the hand (**Figure 3.87**, right). Then shape the upper part of the hand until you are happy with it (**Figure 3.88**).

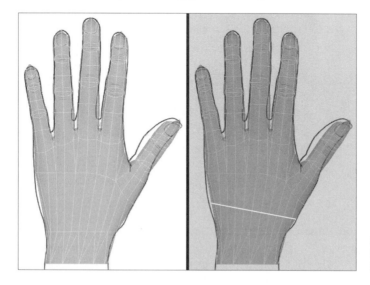

FIGURE 3.87 Split the hand using the Cut Faces tool.

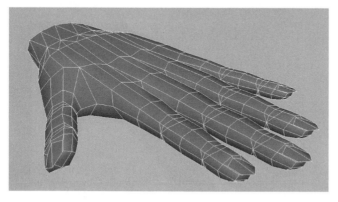

FIGURE 3.88 Shape the upper part of the hand.

Next, rotate the hand so you are looking at the palm (**Figure 3.89**, left). Our next job is to create the muscle that lies at the base of the thumb. Following **Figure 3.89** (right), split the polygons outlining the muscle, adding a second line across the center that will let you define the muscle.

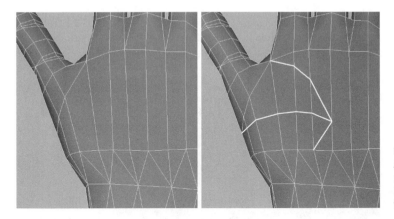

**FIGURE 3.89**
Add the large
muscle at the
base of the
thumb.

The final addition to our hand will be the knuckles. To add these, you'll add an X above each finger (**Figure 3.90**, right). Do this as you've done before, by splitting the polygons. Then pull upward the vertices that are now in the center. This will make the knuckles more pronounced.

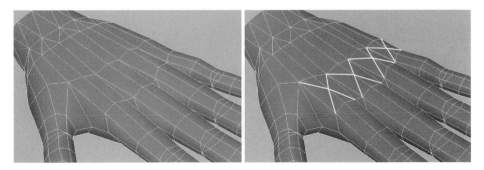

**FIGURE 3.90** Split the polygons above each finger to make knuckles.

And there you have it—a hand for Kila. Admittedly, it probably has more polygons than it needs, but we can remove these when we come to the optimization process in Chapter 5, "Model Optimization."

## Hand Resolutions

As mentioned earlier, I followed the same procedure for the other hand, but using the lower-resolution finger. **Figure 3.91** shows both hands.

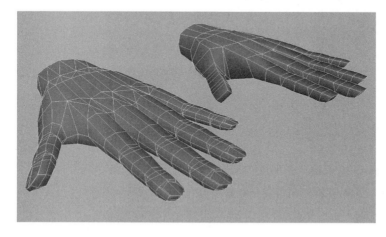

**FIGURE 3.91** Our high- and low-resolution hands, both produced using the same procedure.

The hands may look quite different up close, especially with the wireframe visible. But look at them in **Figure 3.92**, at a distance similar to how they will be viewed in a game. From afar, you can hardly tell the difference. This is the key to creating anything for games: If you can't see it in the game, don't waste time creating it.

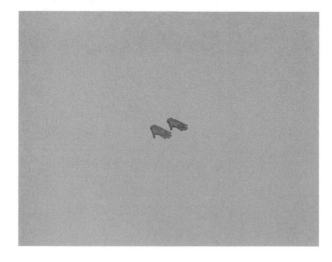

**FIGURE 3.92** Although there is a difference of 604 polygons between these two hands, you can't tell when they're viewed in the game.

One hand has 1010 polygons, but the other has only 406. Using the second, lower-resolution version could save you 604 polygons, freeing up precious processor power. And this isn't the lowest we can go; we can reduce the number of polygons even further.

Look at **Figure 3.93**; these are some of the hands in my Morgue. You can see how they differ. You could remove some of the fingers if they will not be needed, merging them so they are no longer individual; or you could merge them all, leaving a mitten-type hand.

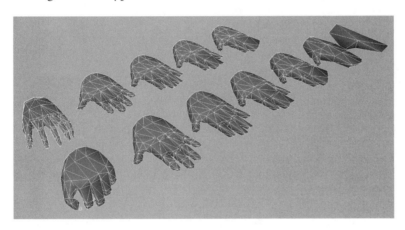

**FIGURE 3.93** A collection of hands at various resolutions

Many games use finger merging not only to cut down on the polygon count, but also the joint count. You see the mitten hand on all the main characters of the ever-popular Grand Theft Auto series on PS2. In that type of game, you need all the processing power you can squeeze out of the system in order to run everything that is happening in the background. Using the mitten-type hand can also mean you use 4 joints to animate it, rather than the 15 needed to move a fully rigged hand, again saving processing power.

Other games move the detail up a notch and just combine the pinkie, ring, and middle fingers, leaving the index finger and thumb free. This type of hand is useful for characters that need to hold weapons, or that may briefly be seen up close. The separate index finger gives the illusion of a fully working hand.

If you're on a tight budget and the hand does not need to be animated, you can always create a hand in a dynamic pose. This means you only need the wrist joint to animate it and, depending on the game engine you're using, you can swap the hand models when you need a different pose.

> **TIP** ▶ It is important to try and use the lowest version possible for a hand. This is an area that can eat up lots of power, so if you don't need a fully work-ing hand, don't use one. You can easily create a low-resolution version from the high version that we built in this chapter. Simply select vertices you want to remove and, holding down the V key, snap them to the vertex that you want to keep. Just remember you will need to weld them, or the polygons will still exist.

### Attaching the Hand to the Model

All that is left to do now for Kila's hands is to attach them to the model. We will use the higher version for this discussion. If we have enough polygons in our budget, it will be nice to keep some of the detail, since she is the main character and we may wind up seeing her hands up close.

1   Delete the history, and save your current file as Kila_Hand.mb. Then load the last active file containing the body, which was Kila_Details.mb.

2   Import the hand into Kila_Details.mb, by going to File > Import and open-ing Kila_Hand.mb.

3   No doubt the hand in your file is absolutely massive, so scale it down. As a guide, the hand should be about the same size as the span from chin to fore-head on the face (**Figure 3.94**).

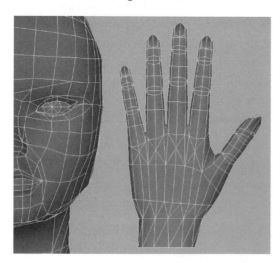

**FIGURE 3.94** Scale the hand to match Kila's face.

**4**  Position the hand at the end of the wrist, overlapping the first strip of polygons with the palm down, as shown in **Figure 3.95**.

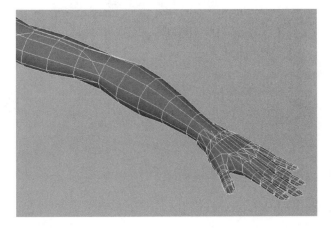

**FIGURE 3.95**
Position the imported hand at the end of the wrist.

**5**  Delete the first strip of polygons from the hand (**Figure 3.96**, left), and then combine both meshes so that you can stitch them together. If you had a mirrored instance for the arm geometry, it will have been removed and you will need to re-create it.

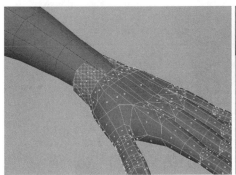 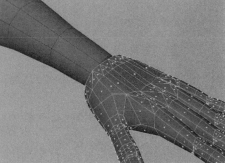

**FIGURE 3.96** Trim back the hand before combining both meshes.

**6**  Match up vertices that lie closest to one another and weld them (**Figure 3.97**), as you did when you stitched the limbs to the torso. Because you have 10 subdivisions on the arm and 12 on the hand, there will be an area where you have to weld three vertices together. Start at the top and then move to the bottom, working on the sides last.

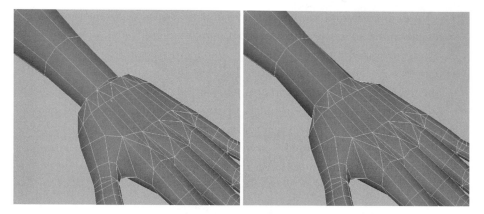

FIGURE 3.97 Stitch the hand to the arm by welding vertices that are close.

**7** Because you began with differing numbers of vertices, you will end up with an area that looks "wrong"—maybe it's just not as smooth as it should be. Since you welded the side vertices last, this is where the problem area lies. There are quite a few polygons on the hand, so you can afford to lose a few from here. Select the edges highlighted in **Figure 3.98**, and collapse them.

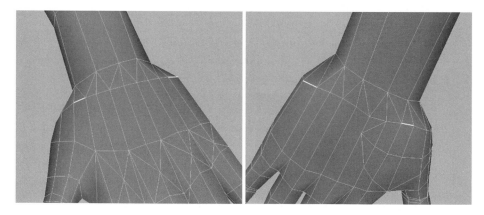

FIGURE 3.98 Collapse these edges to smooth out the wrist area.

Work some more on the problem area until you are satisfied with the shape (**Figure 3.99**).

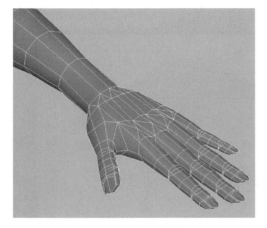

**FIGURE 3.99** The attached, finished hand

When you're done, delete the history and save your work as Kila_WithHands.mb.

## Feet

Kila is wearing shoes, and most of the time her shoes will be simple shapes. For the purposes of this discussion, however, we will explore the possibilities of bare feet.

I have in my Morgue various versions of feet, just as I do hands. **Figure 3.100** shows some of these choices, which are quite basic. As you look from the left to the right, you can see how I have duplicated and reduced the higher-resolution foot to create the next in the line. So they start at 140 polygons and end with just 25.

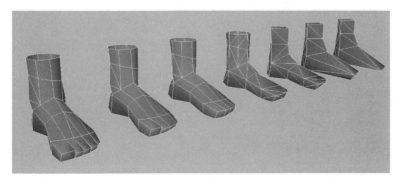

**FIGURE 3.100** Bare feet, at various resolutions

In this section, we will see how to create the higher-resolution foot. Then, if we need to, we can reduce it. Once we have our bare foot created, a few simple steps will transform it into Kila's athletic shoe. Let's start with a new scene.

1    There are 10 subdivisions around the axis of our leg, so let's keep that amount for the foot. Create a new cylinder with Subdivisions Around Axis set to 10 and Subdivisions Along Height at 3.

2    Switch to the side view. As demonstrated in **Figure 3.101**, select the faces at the front and extrude them, setting the number of Divisions to 4.

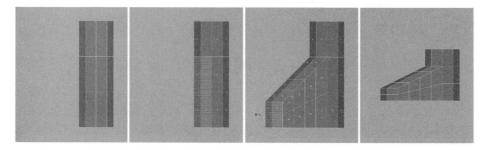

**FIGURE 3.101** Extrude the faces out of the front of the cylinder.

3    Scale the extrusion down the Y axis and move it down to line up with the base of the cylinder. The basic foot shape may be a little high, as it is on the far right in **Figure 3.101**, so scale the entire mesh down slightly.

4    Still in the side view, start to adjust the vertices as shown in **Figure 3.102**, to get a better-defined foot shape.

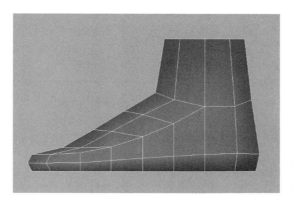

**FIGURE 3.102** Adjust the shape of the foot in the side view.

**5** Switch to the perspective view and make the same adjustments. Try to sculpt the mesh, transforming the shape until it resembles a foot (**Figure 3.103**).

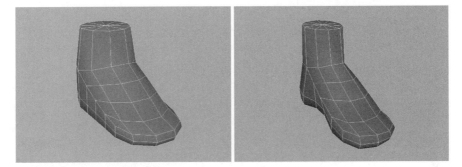

FIGURE 3.103 Work on the foot in the perspective view.

The general shape of the mesh now represents a foot, time for a quick tidy-up:

**1** First remove the faces from the top of the foot, the top cap of the original cylinder.

**2** Next, look at the bottom of the foot (**Figure 3.104**). It's a bit of a mess, so spend some time cleaning it up a little. Snap the vertices on the inner sole to the outer ring and weld them, until the sole resembles the one on the right in **Figure 3.104**.

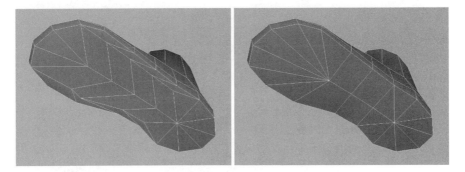

FIGURE 3.104 Tidy up the bottom of the foot.

3    A key part of the foot is the ankle, and we will add this next. Following **Figure 3.105**, split the faces, carving in a general outline for the ankle. Do this on both sides of the foot.

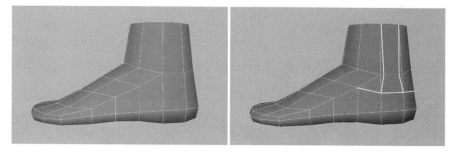

**FIGURE 3.105** Cut the outline for the ankle into the mesh.

4    Finally, pull the ankles out slightly so they are more pronounced (**Figure 3.106**). Remember that the outer ankle joint is lower than the inner one.

Hopefully, the material in this section will have given you a base to build upon. For our purposes, we just need to alter this version of the foot slightly until it looks more like Kila's shoe; you can see the result in **Figure 3.107**.

Delete the history on the foot and save it as Kila_Foot.mb.

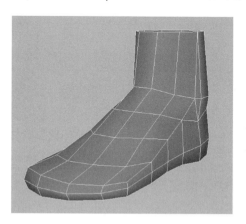

**FIGURE 3.106** The improved foot model

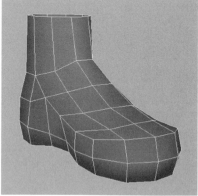

**FIGURE 3.107** Alter the shape of the foot to suggest an athletic shoe, so we can use it on Kila.

**NOTE** You can go on from here, as you wish, to add more details to the foot—individual toes, for instance. Simply divide the front of the foot into five segments, separating them to create the toes.

### Attaching the Foot to the Model

Load the file created earlier, Kila_WithHands.mb. We will now import the foot into this scene. As you did with the hand, scale and manipulate the foot until it is in the correct position (**Figure 3.108**, left).

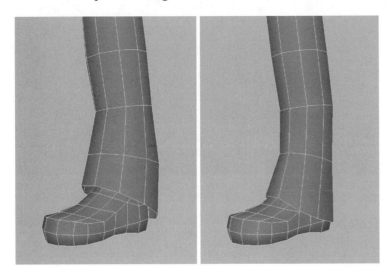

**FIGURE 3.108**
Position the foot and adjust her trousers to fit it.

Before saving this file and ending this chapter, alter the bottom of Kila's trousers to fit the new foot (**Figure 3.108**, right). Then, as always, delete the history, and save the scene—this time as Kila_WithFeet.mb.

Now when you mirror the geometry Kila will have both feet.

## Summary

Kila now has the main details she needs (**Figure 3.109**). This chapter showed you how to add detail to her face, arms, main body, and legs. We also generated a full hand and experimented with making a foot.

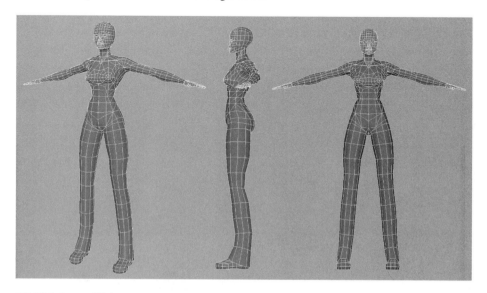

FIGURE 3.109 Kila's progress

Next, we will add details to her in the form of hair, clothing, and more.

**CD Files**

Kila_Feet.mb
Kila_Hair.mb
Kila_Ear_01.mb
Kila_Ear_02.mb
Kila_InnerMouth.mb
Kila_Head.mb
Kila_Complete.mb
KilaFront.jpg
KilaSide.jpg
KilaFaceFront.jpg
KilaFaceSide.jpg

# CHAPTER 4
# Modeling Details

**WE ARE REALLY** moving along with Kila—the end is in sight. In this chapter we will give our character's head some important details: hair, eyes, ears, and the inner mouth. Then we will work on her clothing, adding her crop-top T-shirt, and complementing the jeans with a sash and belt.

## Creating Hair

You are probably looking at your character and thinking, "She doesn't look much like what she's supposed to…." Her lack of hair is the main reason for Kila's unexciting appearance right now; you will be surprised at how much interest a hairdo adds to a character's overall look.

Let's start work on giving Kila some hair, by first loading the file you last worked on, Kila_Feet.mb. Look at the original concept artwork, or the image planes, and you'll see that her hair is not fully symmetrical, so we will, to an extent, need to model the whole coiffure. Her hair is parted down the center, so what we can do is model one-half of the hairdo, then duplicate and mirror it, and edit the copy to have the slightly different look of the other half.

To begin, let's remove some of the polygons from around the back of the head, the ones that will not be seen. Using **Figure 4.1** as a guide, mark in the hairline using the Split Polygon tool, and then delete the unwanted polygons.

> **NOTE** You will only need to work on one side of the model as the other is merely a mirrored instance.

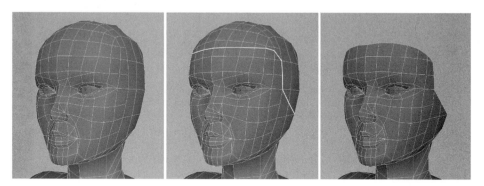

**FIGURE 4.1** Mark the hairline and then remove the polygons from the back of the head.

We are finished editing the main model now. Carving in the hairline gives us a starting point for creating the hair. We'll begin with the inner layer—the hair lying closest to her face and head.

### Inner Layer

We want the hair to look layered, giving it some depth. To create this effect, we will use strips of polygons starting at the hairline and building our way out.

1   Create a new polygonal plane like the one seen in **Figure 4.2**, by going to Create > Polygon Primitives > Plane and opening up the options window. Set the configuration to Width 0.02, Height 0.15, Subdivisions Along Width 1, and Subdivisions Along Height 5.

FIGURE 4.2 Create a new polygonal plane.

2   Move the new plane, matching it up to the polygons on the side of the head as shown in **Figure 4.3**. Duplicate the plane and position the new copy next to the original while trying to stay between the two vertices on the head, so the width of the strip matches the width of the polygon underneath it.

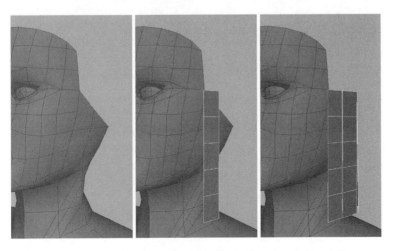

FIGURE 4.3 Position the planes to create the bottom layer of her hair.

**3**  Continue duplicating and positioning strips until you have five of them placed around the head. Remember, we are only working on half of the head for now, so don't place the strips all the way around.

We now have our innermost strips for the hair; next we will create the outer layer that starts at the top of her head and drapes over the inner layer of hair. With these two areas in place, we can create other strips to place in between, amplifying the layered effect we are after.

### Outer Layer

Start work on the outermost layer of hair.

**1**  Duplicate one of the current strips, position it at the top of the head, and rotate it by 90 degrees (**Figure 4.4**). Make sure the top of the strip lies at the same position as the center of the model; this point will act as the part in her hair.

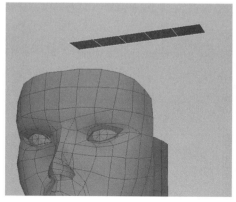 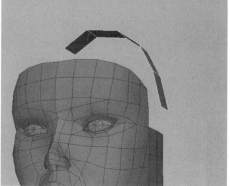

FIGURE 4.4 Add a new plane above the head and curve it to follow the shape of the head.

**2**  Edit this strip, bending it to follow the shape of her head. You will notice in **Figure 4.4** that the strip is too short. It does need to be longer, so select the edge nearest the bottom and use the Extrude Edge tool to add three more divisions.

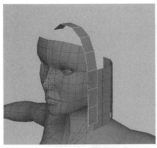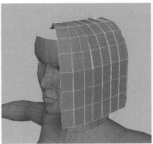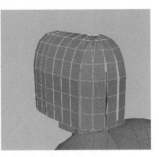

FIGURE 4.5 Duplicate the top strip to create the top of her hair.

**3**   As demonstrated in **Figure 4.5**, duplicate the new strip several times, until you have filled out the top, side, and back of the left side of her head.

**4**   Looking from the side, the hair seems very flat. Manipulate each strip individually, altering the position and scale to make the hair higher at the crown than in the front (**Figure 4.6**).

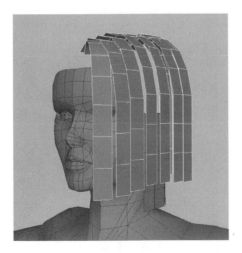

FIGURE 4.6 Move and scale the strips to lift her hair at the crown.

Time to do a bit of tidying up. In the perspective view, look down onto your hair geometry; it should look like mine in the left panel of **Figure 4.7**—a bit of a mess. Before moving on, combine the upper parts of the strips and weld some of the vertices around the top, trying for the result shown on the right in **Figure 4.7**. Don't work all the way down the strips; just concentrate on the top five rows of vertices for now.

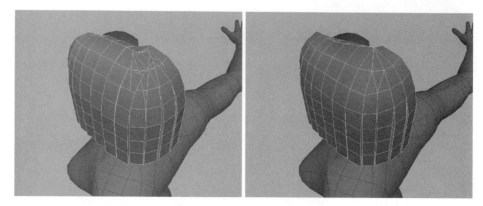

FIGURE 4.7 Tidy up at the crown of her head by welding some of the vertices.

We now have the base geometry in place for the top of her hair. Create a mirrored instance to use as reference, and you'll see something like **Figure 4.8** (left). Take some time now to work on the shape a little more. It may help to snap the vertices together between the strips, but do not weld them yet. Aim for something like **Figure 4.8** (right).

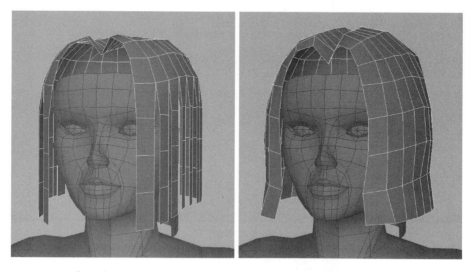

FIGURE 4.8 Spend some time shaping the upper portion of her hair.

### The Front Hairline

Let's now create the front hairline, filling in the gap between her forehead and hair. Remove the mirrored instance of the hair for now so we can concentrate on just one side.

1   First, hide the top layer of hair by selecting it and pressing Ctrl+H/Cmd+H. Leave the underneath visible because you will need it for this part of the modeling.

2   Duplicate one of the side strips and position it above her forehead, following the example in the middle panel of **Figure 4.9**.

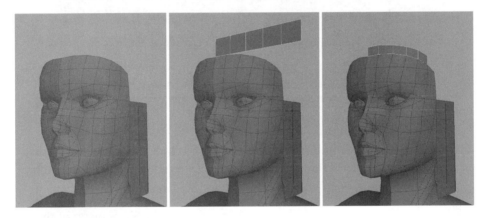

FIGURE 4.9 Add a new strip above the forehead.

3   Adjust the vertices until you have the arrangement shown in the right panel of **Figure 4.9**, snapping the lower vertices to the ones on the top of her forehead.

4   Bring back the geometry that makes up the top of her hair by pressing Ctrl+Shift+H/Cmd+Shift+H. Now snap the upper vertices of this newly added forehead strip to the front section of her hair (**Figure 4.10**).

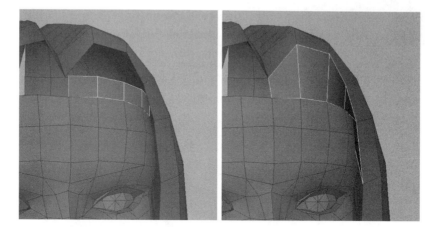

**FIGURE 4.10** Snap the upper vertices of the forehead strip to the front part of the outer hair layer.

**5**   Now combine both pieces of geometry—the hairline strip and the front parts of her hair—and weld the vertices at the front, making a single, solid object.

**6**   To complete the front hairline area, you need to hide the rest of the model, making just the hair visible. This time, instead of selecting all the geometry and pressing Ctrl+H/Cmd+H to hide it, we can simply isolate the hair.

To do this, select the upper piece of hair and go to the Show menu of the active view. Move down to Isolate Selected, and choose View Selected. You should now be presented with just the top layer of hair, as shown in the left panel of **Figure 4.11**.

**TIP**   The Isolate Select command is very useful. For example, you can isolate components such as a selection of faces rather than whole objects.

**7**   Continuing on, you need to extrude the lower edge at the temple (**Figure 4.11**, middle). This edge must be brought down to meet the bottom of her hair (**Figure 4.11**, right).

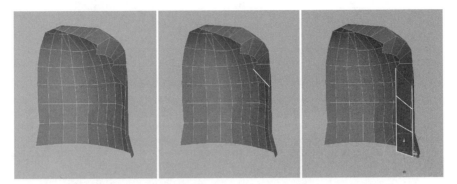

**FIGURE 4.11** Isolate the top layer of hair and extend the front.

8   Weld the side vertices of the extrusion to the first row of vertices closest
to them on the existing hair, and then adjust the vertices to create a better
shape (**Figure 4.12**).

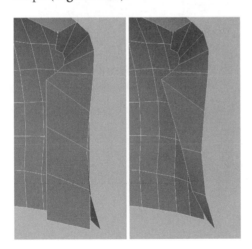

**FIGURE 4.12** Weld the bottom vertices and then adjust
the shape.

### Adding Volume to the Hair

Un-isolate the geometry so you can see the face and head again. You do this exactly
the same way as you did earlier to isolate it: Choose Show > Isolate Select >
View Selected, so that it is unchecked.

Now we will give the outer layer of hair some more shape, getting rid of the
dome it currently resembles. After that, we'll work on the rest of the hair, filling
it out and thickening it to give it more volume.

1    As shown in **Figure 4.13** on the left, select the bottom row of edges and collapse them.

Because you did not weld the vertices on the lower areas of the strips, when you collapse the edges they will form spikes as illustrated on the right in **Figure 4.13**.

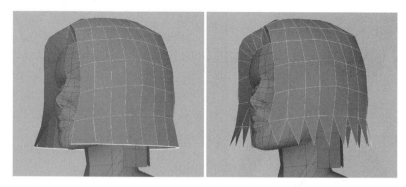

FIGURE 4.13 Collapse the bottom row of edges.

2    Move up to the next row of edges and, editing each one in turn, scale them in slightly. Do this for the next row, too, until you have long spikes running around her hair, as shown in **Figure 4.14**.

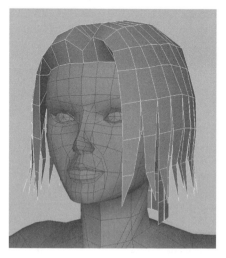

FIGURE 4.14 Scale the edges in, to create long spikes.

Apart from some final tweaking, our outer layer is complete. It needs additional work, moving the vertices to randomize the shape, but we won't do that until all the basic geometry is in place. Now we must fill out the hair, making it appear thicker, giving it more volume.

3  Using the strips on the inside layer, do as you did with the outer ones. Select the bottom edges and collapse them, then adjust the upper edges until you have long, sharp polygons.

4  Duplicate these edited inner strips, creating a total of 17, and position them between the outer layer and the head.

When you're finished working on this side of the head, you can create a mirrored version to see how the hair is looking overall. Begin by selecting all the pieces of geometry that make up the hair on Kila's left side. Press Ctrl+G/Cmd+G to group them. Open up the Duplicate options, make sure that Instance is not selected, and click Duplicate or Apply to create a mirrored duplicate of the group (setting the Scale value for the X-axis to -1).

Kila's coiffure should now resemble **Figure 4.15**. For now, the hair shape is acceptable. It still needs more work, but let's leave it for now and go on to create the left side of the hairdo (Kila's right). It will be different from the right side.

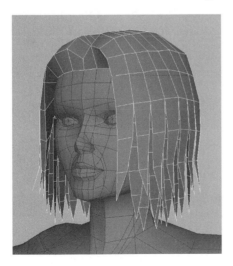

**FIGURE 4.15** Fill out the hair with additional pointy strips.

### Developing the Left Side

The hair on Kila's right side hangs down, but on the other side the hair is tucked behind the left ear. To start developing this side of the hairdo, first hide the inner strips so you can concentrate on the outer layer of hair (**Figure 4.16**).

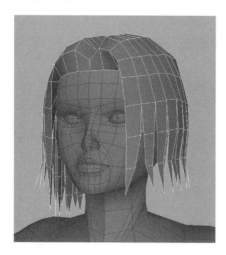

FIGURE 4.16 Prepare the hair for more work by hiding the inner layer on Kila's left.

1    Select the vertices shown in **Figure 4.17b**, and weld them all together until you are left with a single vertex (**Figure 4.17c**).

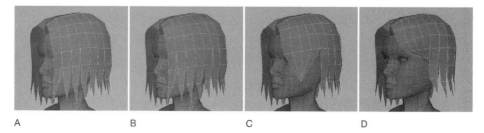

A            B            C            D

FIGURE 4.17 The steps for tucking the hair behind the ear

2    Move this remaining vertex up to roughly the spot where the top of the ear should be. Then proceed to work on refining this area of the hairdo until the tucked-in look is correct (**Figure 4.17d**).

3    Combine both the left and right sides that make up the top, outer layer of her hairdo.

4    Bring back the inner-layer strips you hid earlier, adjusting them to fit the new tucked-in arrangement. You will have to delete some of the strips that no longer fit the shape.

At this point, you have basic geometry in place to use for Kila's hair. Keep working on it until you are happy with the overall shape.

### Organizing the Strips

To keep things in order, we will now organize the strips used to fill in the hair, combining them into individual horseshoe-shaped layers. In this arrangement, not only will they be easier to work on, but applying a texture to them will be less difficult.

1    Hide everything except the strips of hair (**Figure 4.18**).

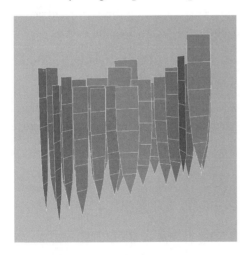

**FIGURE 4.18** Hide everything except the strips of hair.

2    Switch to the top view so you are looking down on the strips (**Figure 4.19**, left). It looks like I got a bit carried away, rotating the strips to fit. First, using the Rotate manipulator, alter the rotations so the strips appear as flat lines in the top view. You will find that the same axis needs altering for each strip.

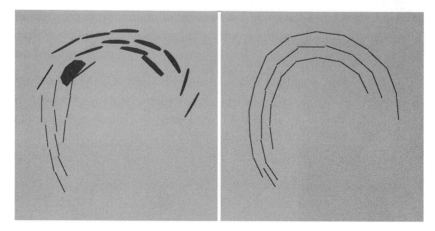

FIGURE 4.19 We want to move the strips so they follow a more organized structure.

**3**    Position all the strips so they follow a curve, making three concentric curves in total. Add more strips if you need them to complete the curves.

**4**    Combine the strips that make up each curve so that you end up with three separate horseshoe-shaped objects (**Figure 4.19**, right).

**5**    Switch to the perspective view and isolate the outermost section of hair. All you should be able to see is that particular piece of the geometry (**Figure 4.20**, left).

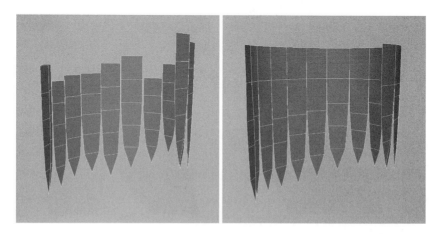

FIGURE 4.20 Level off the top and adjust the vertices to tidy up the geometry.

**6**   Scale the top row of vertices down the Y axis so that they all lie on the same level. Just using the basic Scale manipulator is sufficient here because you do not need to have an exact scale. Then weld them all together, making a complete strip running around the top. Do this again for the next row down. As needed, adjust the remaining strips to tidy up the rest of the geometry. **Figure 4.20** (right) shows what you're aiming for.

**7**   Repeat these welding steps for the other two, inner layers until you have something close to what's shown in **Figure 4.21**.

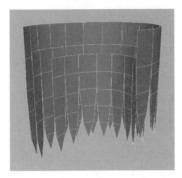

**FIGURE 4.21** Weld all the layers' strips.

Now unhide the rest of Kila to see how things are looking. As you can see in **Figure 4.22**, I've started to shape the outer hair somewhat, by curling the ends up very slightly and refining the overall shape. Notice that I have added another strip for a loose strand at the right temple.

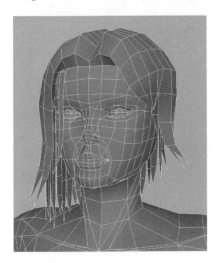

**FIGURE 4.22** Current view of Kila with hair

### Refining the Hair

To complete Kila's hair we will now spend some time working on the inner-layer strips, bending the bottoms out to follow the strands in the outer layer. We'll also add some more volume by twisting the strips at the bottom.

Because we have been working in layers, the first step is easy. On the first inner layer, select the lower row of vertices and globally scale them outward. Move up to the next row and do the same. Continue this process on the other inner rows, curling the hair slightly outward at the bottom.

To fill the hair out a little and thicken it up, we now need to twist each strip slightly, like turning the slats of a venetian blind.

1   Select every other edge on each strip (**Figure 4.23**, left and middle). Then scale them across the X and Y axes, bringing them in toward the middle as shown in **Figure 4.23** (right). Select only the bottom two edges of each strip; do not scale the top.

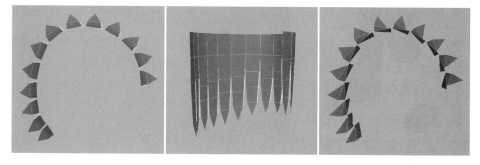

FIGURE 4.23 Twist each strip to fill out the hair.

2   Repeat this process on the next layer, this time selecting the opposite edges so that the effect will be reversed.

3   Finally, scale the third layer in the same way as the first.

All the refinement work left to do now is to work on the overall shape, trying to fill in any large gaps between the strands of her hair. Take a look at **Figure 4.24** to see an example of the end result.

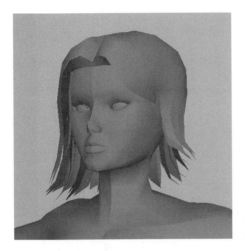

**FIGURE 4.24** Work on the overall shape of Kila's hair.

For now, do not combine all the elements that make up the hair. Just clean up the scene and save your work as Kila_Hair.mb.

### Quick Cleanup with the Outliner

If you open up your Outliner, you may notice that a lot of groups and empty nodes are starting to appear; you can also see these in **Figure 4.25a**. Most of these elements are unnecessary and only bump up the file size. Let's clean them up.

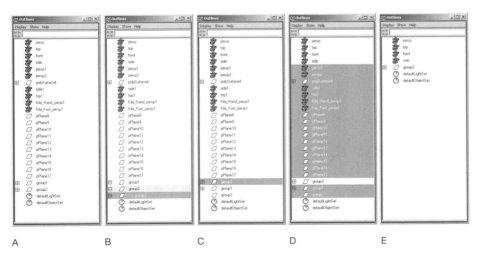

A            B            C            D            E

**FIGURE 4.25** Use the Outliner to clean up your scene.

1 Start by selecting in the Perspective view all the pieces of geometry you want to keep, and press Ctrl+G/Cmd+G to put them into a group. **Figure 4.25b** shows the new group named group3.

> **TIP** The easiest way to select what you want to keep is to drag a selection lasso over all of the geometry in the view.

2 In the Outliner, click and hold the middle mouse button on the new group, and move it up until it exists in the world root (that is, outside of any other groups), as seen in **Figure 4.25c**. As you move the group over another object, two lines will appear above and below the object; these indicate that if you let go of the mouse now, the group will be placed within this object. If a single line appears, it indicates that letting go of the mouse button here will leave the group in the world root.

3 You know that you've included everything you need in group3, so you can now select the other bits and pieces as shown in **Figure 4.25d** and delete them.

Obviously, it's very unlikely that the items in your Outliner will exactly match the ones in **Figure 4.25**, but this does not matter. In deciding what can be deleted, just look for items similar to the ones highlighted that are outside the group3 group.

4 You may also notice that a few new cameras have popped up (persp1 and persp2, for example)—the result of our having imported items earlier. Select and delete these. Do not delete the four main cameras (persp, top, front, and side), but feel free to remove any others.

5 Finally, rename group3 to Kila and save.

## Modeling the Ear

So now we've finished off the hair. Our next step is to create an ear to place on the left side of Kila's head.

> **TIP** Before you start to model the ear, find a decent picture of an ear on the Internet or in an anatomy book. This will help you create an accurate model (or texture, depending on how the ear will be represented).

1   Start with a new scene, and create the cube in **Figure 4.26** using the following configuration: Width 0.5, Height 1.5, Depth 1, Subdivisions Along Width 1, Subdivisions Along Height 5, and Subdivisions Along Depth 2.

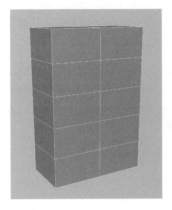 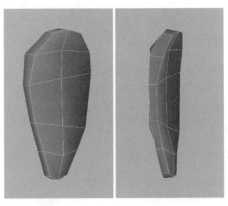

FIGURE 4.26 Create a basic cube, five divisions high.

FIGURE 4.27 Manipulate the cube until it resembles an ear.

2   Using your reference, shape the cube to achieve the basic shape of an ear. Work on it from the side and then the front, and finally in the perspective view until you are happy with it (**Figure 4.27**).

3   Before saving this version, remove some of the polygons from behind the ear, as seen in **Figure 4.28**.

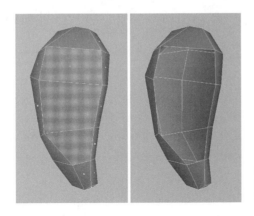

FIGURE 4.28 Remove the polygons from the back of the ear.

4   Delete the history and save this as Kila_Ear_01.mb, so you can use this version later if you choose.

We could quite happily use the ear in its present state, allowing the texture to show the detail—especially if we need to keep within our polygon budget. For the purposes of this tutorial, however, we will work on it a little more to show how to develop a more detailed ear in case we need one. Enhancing the ear is a simple case of cutting the details into the mesh using the Split Polygon tool, and then working on the geometry to achieve a satisfactory shape.

**5**   Divide the front of the ear, following the lines in **Figure 4.29**, left. Work on the entire front area until the ear is satisfactory (**Figure 4.29**, right). There is no need to put in every detail, since most of this can be achieved in the texture.

**6**   Delete the history and save this ear as Kila_Ear_02.mb.

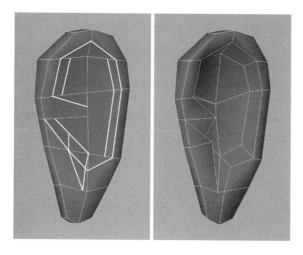

**FIGURE 4.29** Add detail to the ear by first splitting the polygons.

### Attaching the Ear

Now we have two ear models (one slightly more detailed than the other). For now, we are going to attach the higher-resolution version. When we come to optimize the mesh, we can reduce it if we need the polygons. Make sure you have both ears saved, and then load Kila_Hair.mb again.

**1**   Before you begin to attach the ear, you need to make the head whole. At the moment you only have one-half; the second, right side is simply an instance. Delete the instanced mesh and focus in on the head. It's probably best to isolate the mesh, too, so you're only working on the main body.

**2**  Select the faces shown in **Figure 4.30** (the ones that make up the head and upper neck).

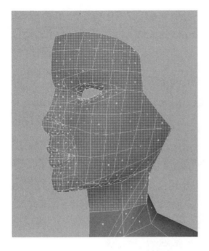

FIGURE 4.30 Select the head and upper neck, and detach the faces using the Extract tool.

**3**  To separate these pieces from the main mesh, go to Edit Polygons > Extract and open up the options. Make sure Separate Extracted Faces is on, then click Extract. The head will now be separated from the rest of the body.

What we need to do now is duplicate this half, mirror it, and merge all the vertices down the center. There is a simple way to do this—use the Polygons > Mirror Geometry tool.

**4**  Open up the options for the Polygons > Mirror Geometry tool and, as seen in **Figure 4.31**, make sure –X is selected, as well as Merge With The Original and Merge Vertices. Click Mirror to apply the tool.

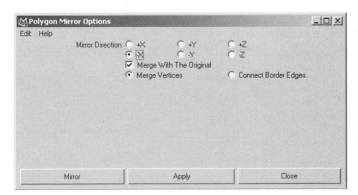

FIGURE 4.31 The Mirror Geometry tool options

You should now have a full head with all the vertices welded nicely down the center; the last thing to do is smooth out the crease that runs down the middle of her head.

5    Import the ear we were working on earlier (Kila_Ear_02.mb) and position it as shown in **Figure 4.32**.

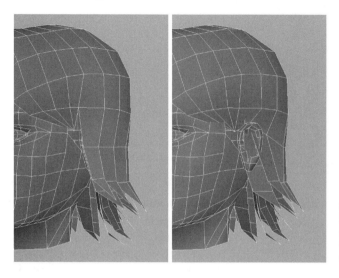

**FIGURE 4.32**
Position the ear without the hair visible; then adjust the hair to fit the ear.

Looking at **Figure 4.32**, we seem to have miscalculated where the hair should be. We can adjust this now so that the hair lies over and behind the ear (**Figure 4.32**, right). Now that we know how the hair and ear should look, we can more capably work on this area. Hide the head at this stage so we can concentrate on the hair and ear.

6    As you can see in **Figure 4.33** (left), one of the inner strips of hair is popping through the ear. Since this is quite close to the face, we can simply delete the entire strip by selecting its polygons and deleting them (**Figure 4.33**, right).

7    As illustrated in **Figure 4.34** (left), rotate around so you are looking at the back of the ear from inside the head.

**TIP**    Press F to focus the camera on the selected object or components.

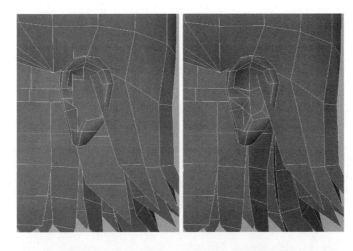

FIGURE 4.33 Remove the strip that is popping through the ear.

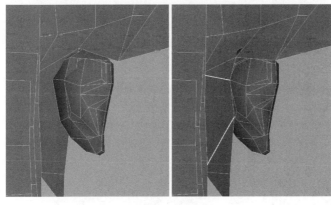

FIGURE 4.34 Fill in the gaps around the ear by snapping the vertices together.

8   Snap the two vertices belonging to the hair to the two nearest ones on the top of the ear. Then work your way around, splitting the hair as shown in **Figure 4.34** (right) and leaving no gaps around the top and side of the ear.

9   Bring back the geometry for the head, and hide the hair. Before using the same vertex-snapping technique to fill in the gaps between the head and ear, you must first combine them. As demonstrated in **Figure 4.35** (left), look from inside the head at the ear. Use the Append To Polygons tool to fill in the gap, making a seamless join between the head and the ear (**Figure 4.35**, right).

FIGURE 4.35 Attach the ear to the head by creating polygons to fill in the gap.

10 Work on the ear until the shape is satisfactory on all sides. For a start, you can collapse the edges at the front of the ear. These are highlighted in **Figure 4.36** (left). Keep working until you achieve the model illustrated in **Figure 4.36** (right).

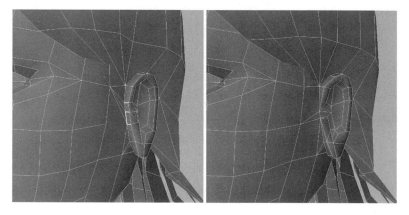

FIGURE 4.36 Work on the ear until you are happy with the entire shape.

As you can see in **Figure 4.37**, the outer head is now complete. All we need to do to finish it is test to see how it deforms, and optimize it—both of which we will cover in later chapters.

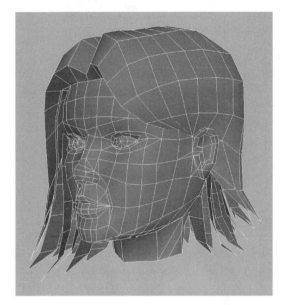

**FIGURE 4.37** The outer head is complete.

## Modeling the Eyes

If your game uses many real-time cut-scenes, chances are your character will need facial animation. The eyes play a huge part in acting; we are all drawn to the eyes when we interact with people.

Eyes are relatively easy to construct; all you need to do is create a sphere and optimize it slightly. You may have noticed that our model already has some spheres where the eyes should be. These were used earlier to create the eyelids, and we did not delete them. To demonstrate how to create the eyes, we will remove these spheres and start from scratch.

1    Create a new polygonal sphere with its Subdivisions Around Axis and Subdivisions Along Height both set to 8 (**Figure 4.38a**).

2    As demonstrated in **Figure 4.38b**, remove the back half of the sphere.

**3** Select the edges that lie down the center of the sphere, shown in **Figure 4.38c**, and then collapse them to get the eye shape (**Figure 4.38d**).

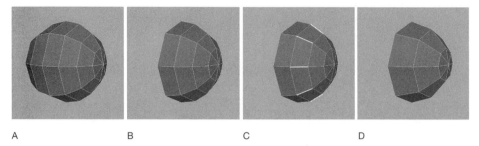

A B C D

FIGURE 4.38 Optimize a sphere to achieve an eye shape.

**4** Position this sphere so it lies where the left eye should be.

**5** To create the right eye, duplicate the left eye mesh and alter the Translate X attribute in the Channel Box to be a negative value. For example, if it reads 0.38, make it –0.38.

There we have it; the eyes are done (**Figure 4.39**). Feel free to save at this point.

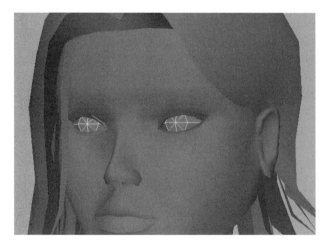

FIGURE 4.39
Kila now has eyes.

## Developing the Inner Mouth

Cut-scenes can also involve conversation, so the inside of the mouth will need to be developed to include the teeth and a tongue. Let's begin with her teeth.

### The Teeth

Most games just adopt a simple set of teeth consisting of a flat curve of polygons with a teeth texture on them. This is what we will use for Kila—it's unlikely that she would benefit from a set of fully modeled teeth because we will never get close enough to see them in detail. Besides, a full set of teeth would increase the polygon count dramatically.

**1**   In a new scene, create a new cylinder with the following configuration: Radius 1, Height 0.4, Subdivisions Around Axis 14, Subdivisions Along Height 1, and Subdivisions On Caps 1. Your cylinder should look like the one in the top panel of **Figure 4.40**.

**2**   Remove the top and bottom from the cylinder, as well as five quads from the back, giving you the shape in **Figure 4.40** (bottom).

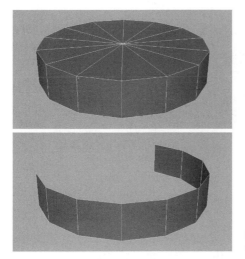

**FIGURE 4.40** Create and edit a basic cylinder.

**3**    Teeth are never perfectly round, but at the moment our mesh is (**Figure 4.41**, left). Switch to the top view and scale the geometry to match the shape illustrated on the right in **Figure 4.41**.

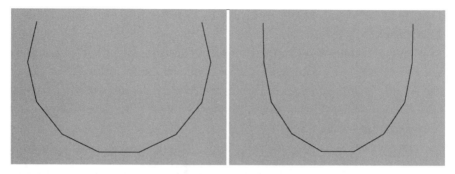

FIGURE 4.41 Scale the teeth geometry to achieve this shape.

**4**    We have our top teeth complete now. To create the bottom set, duplicate the upper set and position it below. Make sure you scale it in slightly along the X and Z axes, because a human's bottom teeth are positioned back a little from the top teeth (**Figure 4.42**).

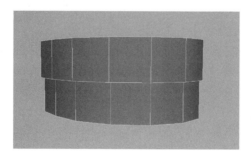

FIGURE 4.42 Duplicate the top-teeth mesh and position it underneath and slightly back from the original set.

### The Tongue

Now that the teeth are done, let's create the tongue.

**1**    First hide the teeth; we don't need them yet.

**2**    Create a cube with the following configuration: Width 0.5, Height 0.2, Depth 1, Subdivisions Along Width 2, Subdivisions Along Height 2, and Subdivisions Along Depth 3.

**3**   Following the progression in **Figure 4.43**, adjust the shape so it takes on the look of a tongue. Scale the upper and lower vertices in slightly in preparation for the next step, in which you will move the front-center ones out a little.

**4**   Select the vertices that lie down the center of the object and move them down a fraction, creating the crease in the tongue.

FIGURE 4.43 Edit the vertices to sculpt the shape of a tongue.

**5**   Rotate the front and the back to curve the tongue.

**6**   Make the teeth visible again and position the tongue inside them (**Figure 4.44**). You may need to scale the tongue further to make it fit properly. In addition, make sure you delete the faces at the rear of the tongue, as shown in **Figure 4.44** on the right.

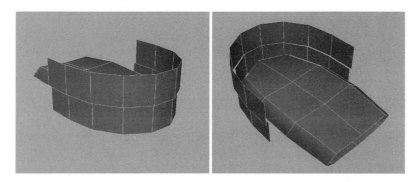

FIGURE 4.44 Position the tongue between the teeth.

The teeth and tongue elements are complete, so delete the history and save as Kila_InnerMouth.mb.

### Adding the Inner Mouth Elements

We will next merge the inner mouth elements we created (teeth and tongue) into our character.

1 Load in the last file you were working on (Kila_Hair.mb), and import the inner mouth elements into the scene.

2 Scale the geometry down and position it inside her head as shown in **Figure 4.45**. The upper teeth should just dip down below the bottom lip.

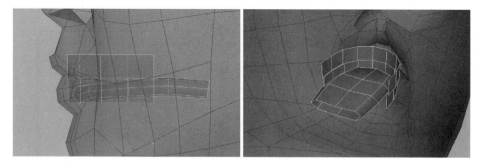

**FIGURE 4.45** Import the teeth and tongue into your latest scene and position them behind the lips.

3 Double-check the shape of the mouth. If you can see teeth popping through, then the mouth is not the correct shape. Kila's lips should lie on top of her teeth.

### The Inner Cheeks

Before we finish the mouth area, we need to do one last thing. If Kila were to open her mouth in its current state, we would see not only her teeth and tongue but also the back of her head. On some platforms, we would not even see that— we would see straight through the back of her head. What's needed now is to create the inside of the mouth, consisting of the top of the throat (upper palette) and inner cheeks.

1 At present, Kila's lips are sealed shut, so to start you need to cut them open. As shown in **Figure 4.46** (top), focus in on her lips and select the vertices that run along the opening between the lips.

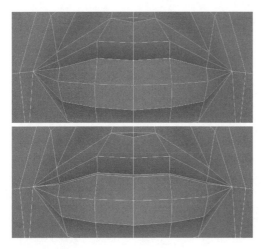

FIGURE 4.46 Split the vertices to create an opening between the lips.

**TIP** When you're zooming into your geometry, it may happen that the camera cuts into the mesh before you get close enough. To fix this, open up the attributes for the camera by going to View > Camera Attribute Editor, and reduce the value for Near Clip Plane.

2    With the vertices selected, go to Edit Polygons > Split Vertex. This will split up the vertices, "un-welding" them, so to speak. Now the vertices are all separate. Select each one in turn and move it up or down, creating a slight opening in the mouth as shown in **Figure 4.46** (bottom). Just remember to weld them again when you are done.

3    Hide the teeth and tongue for now. As illustrated in **Figure 4.47**, select the edges around the opening of the mouth.

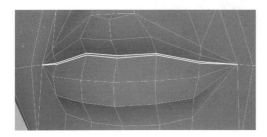

FIGURE 4.47 Select the edges around the opening of the mouth.

**4**  Extrude the edges inward, adding two divisions to the extrusion (**Figure 4.48a**). Do this by setting Divisions to 3 for polyExtrudeEdge1 in the Channel Box.

**5**  Weld together all the vertices at the very end to create a point (**Figure 4.48b**).

**6**  Select the edges on both the top and the bottom of the extrusion, as highlighted in **Figure 4.48c**.

**7**  Collapse these edges (**Figure 4.48d**).

**8**  Bring the center points on the top upward, and the ones below downward, to create a hollow in the middle.

**9**  Optimize the shape by welding the extra vertices to the top and bottom points (**Figure 4.48e**).

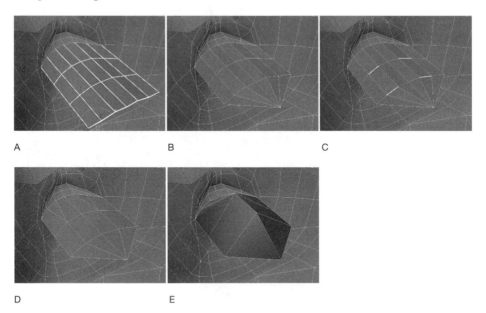

**FIGURE 4.48** Create the cavity of the mouth.

**10** Adjust the vertices to make the cavity larger. Aim for the results shown in **Figure 4.49**.

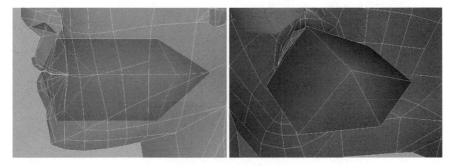

FIGURE 4.49 Enlarge the cavity to envelop the teeth and tongue.

**11** Unhide the teeth and check to see that they fit inside the cavity.

We are now finished with the head area and can move on and add some clothing. But first, clean up your scene and save your work as Kila_Head.mb.


## Dressing Kila

All game characters wear some sort of outfit—more often than not these will be weird and wonderful and will require extra polygons. In Kila's case, we have some relatively simple additions to make. These include adding details to her crop top and jeans, as well as giving her a belt and a sash that drape her waist.

### Crop Top Details

We'll enhance Kila's crop top and chest area by adding some cleavage, as well as a suggestion of a loose overhang at the waistline.

Start with the cleavage area. In the concept drawing, the low-neck top shows a bit of cleavage. What we need to do is define the neck of her crop top to implement this cleavage.

**1** Using the Split Polygon tool, carve in the cuts shown in **Figure 4.50** (right). These will allow us to edit the central area at the top of the cloth that bridges her breasts.

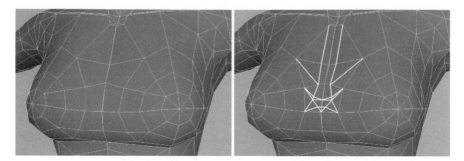

FIGURE 4.50 Cut the polygons.

2    Smooth out the extra edges you have created—all except the ones that will mark the top of the fabric. These are highlighted in **Figure 4.51** on the left.

3    Start working on the area, sculpting it to achieve the correct shape. You're aiming for the result illustrated in **Figure 4.51** on the right.

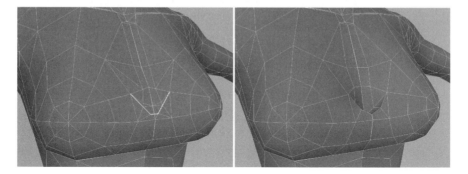

FIGURE 4.51 The cleavage, before and after

4    Move the vertices down the center first, pulling them inward, using the side view to line them up with the curve of her torso (**Figure 4.52**).

5    Continue working your way out, smoothing the area, moving downward the vertex just above the line of the fabric; this creates the crevice. Remember to convert joining triangles back to quads.

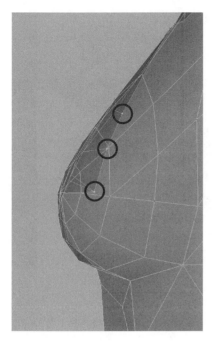

**FIGURE 4.52** Move the central vertices inward so they are in line with the torso.

Notice in the concept drawing that the crop top is not skin tight, but rather is slightly loose at the bottom. We want to create this pointed "overhang." As shown in **Figure 4.53**, we'll focus in on the middle of her body.

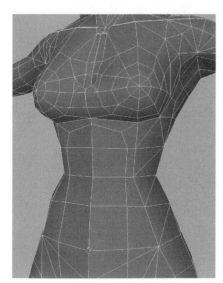

**FIGURE 4.53** To create a loose overhang, work on the area at the middle of the body.

1  Following the lines highlighted in **Figure 4.54**, cut around the center of the body. Mark out the base of Kila's crop top, making sure that there are two parallel cuts encircling the entire body mesh.

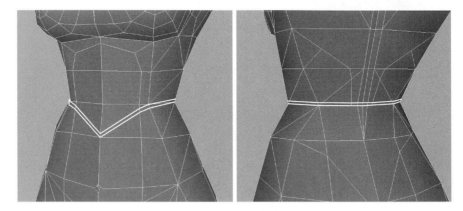

**FIGURE 4.54** Create two lines across her stomach, outlining the bottom of her crop top.

2  Scale the top line out and move it down, creating the overhang seen in **Figure 4.55**.

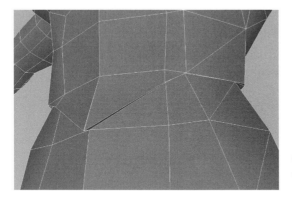

**FIGURE 4.55** Create the overhang by moving the top line out and down.

3  When you created the initial cuts, some small edges will have been created; these in turn make up small polygons, like the ones in **Figure 4.56** (top). It is best to get rid of these now, cleaning up the area.

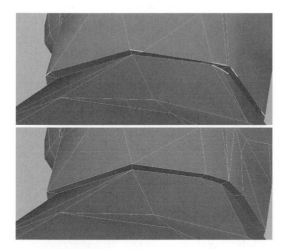

FIGURE 4.56 Remove these small edges that were created by the cut.

4  Finally, spend some time smoothing out the general shape of the crop top (**Figure 4.57**).

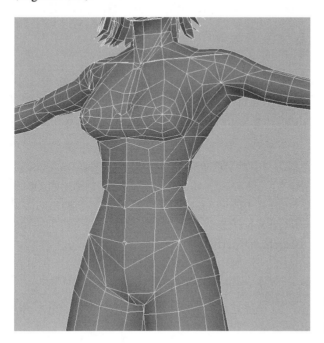

FIGURE 4.57 Smooth out the rest of the crop top.

With Kila's crop top completed, let's continue on down to the jeans, and the sash and belt that drape her waist.

### Separating the Jeans from the Body

Our next clothing task is to model the character's jeans. We could model the left side and mirror it to create the right, as we did with her upper body. Although this would save time, it would present a few problems. First, the sash around her waist cannot be mirrored; it should be built into the waist because it fits snugly at every point from the waist to the opposite hip. Also, we will be building creases into the legs of her jeans, so it would be very obvious if we simply mirrored one side to create the other.

Before we begin, we have to separate the jeans from the rest of Kila's body, then create a duplicate to become the right side, and combine the sides as we did for her head.

1  Delete the mirrored instance if you have one, and select the polygons that will make up the jeans (**Figure 4.58**). This should be easy because you marked out the top of them earlier.

2  Go to Edit Polygons > Extract; this will separate the leg from the body. You should not have to open up the options and reconfigure them because they were saved the last time you used this tool.

3  Next, you need a mirrored duplicate, so go to Polygons > Mirror Geometry. Again, you set the options last time you used this tool, so they should be at the same settings now. You don't have to open the options.

4  Since you only need to work on her legs at this point, it makes things easier if you hide the rest of the geometry. So select everything but the legs and press Ctrl+H/Cmd+H.

5  Double-check that the vertices down the center of the legs have merged correctly. If some have not, weld them now; smooth out the crease, too.

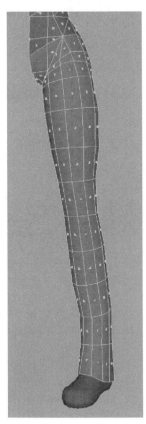

**FIGURE 4.58** Select the polygons that will make up her jeans.

Now we have a complete pair of legs and we can begin working in the clothing details.

### Creating the Sash

Because the sash fits snugly all the way around, we can simply mark in the outline so we'll know where it will be on her form. It is made of thin material, so we don't need to create an overhang as we did with the T-shirt. Our task with the sash is to work on the general area, smoothing it out and tidying it up.

Use the Split Polygon tool to mark in the outline for the sash. Follow the lines in **Figure 4.59**. I am sure your modeling skills are coming along wonderfully now, so I will leave this part up to you. Remember to remove any tiny polygons that have cropped up, and make the area as clean as possible. Your resulting mesh should resemble **Figure 4.60**.

**FIGURE 4.59** Mark in the outlines for the sash.

**FIGURE 4.60** Tidy up the sash, removing unwanted polygons and creating smooth lines.

To finish the sash, we will create a couple of folds in the fabric on the outside of the leg. We can rely on the texture to create most of the folds, but these at the thigh are quite distinct, so we will build them into the geometry.

1  Following **Figure 4.61** as a guide, cut the polygons around the outside of her left thigh. You'll need two cuts for each fold. Follow these cuts around the leg, spanning two polygons, matching the cuts on the front.

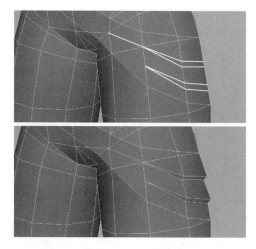

**FIGURE 4.61** Create more cuts in the outer thigh and build in two folds.

2  Select the vertices on the top of each cut and move them out, creating the upper part of the fold.

3  Finally move the lower vertices up slightly to close the gap (**Figure 4.61**, bottom).

### Creating the Jeans

Continuing on to the jeans now, we first need to get some idea of the creases in the jeans at the back of her knees, and also on the lower legs. You should have some references for this already on your style sheet. Better still, use the original color concept image (**Figure 4.62**). You can find this on the CD: Project Files/01/ KilaColorRender.tif.

**FIGURE 4.62** Use the color concept image as reference for the creases in the jeans.

Kila's upper thigh area is relatively flat, so we don't need to add any detail here. Like the folds on the sash, the creases in the jeans can be added when we apply texture. We can, however, build in some folds around the back of her knees. Move down to where her knees are; use the guide images to get the correct location.

**1**    As you did for the folds on the sash, cut the polygons here at the knees to create two segments (**Figure 4.63**, left).

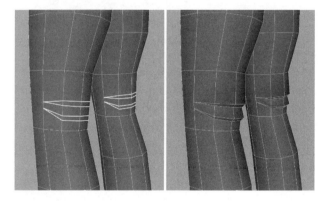

**FIGURE 4.63**
Creating folds in the denim around the back of the knees

**2**    Move the top of each segment out and the lower portion up, producing the two folds you can see in **Figure 4.63**, bottom. Because we combined the legs earlier, you will need to do this on each knee.

Moving around to the front of her legs, we will now build in some basic knees. These will function more toward deformation than for the overall look of the mesh.

**3**    Cut the polygons as shown in **Figure 4.64**. Then pull out the upper section in the middle of the knee, creating a ridge.

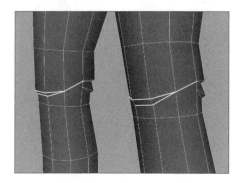

**FIGURE 4.64** Create a ridge at the front to act as her knee.

4   Adjust the overall knee areas, scaling them in slightly to get the correct shape (**Figure 4.65**).

Now we get to the lower legs. This area needs quite a bit of enhancement to achieve realistic creases and folds.

5   Following the progression in **Figure 4.66**, begin by creating a cut that will be the first fold in the jeans leg. Adjust the vertices around this first cut to fold the polygons at the front over the ones at the back. Move downward, adding in one fold at a time until you reach the bottom.

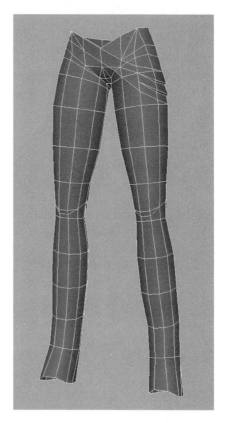

**FIGURE 4.65** The knee area is complete.

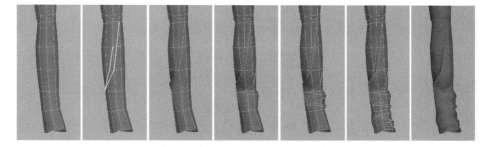

**FIGURE 4.66** The steps for adding the folds into the bottom of the jeans leg

**6**    Rotating around to the back of the leg (**Figure 4.67**, left), you can see that not much needs to be added here—just a few creases at the bottom will do (**Figure 4.67**, right).

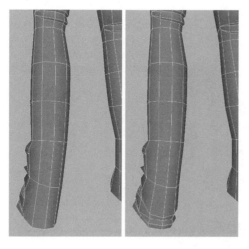

FIGURE 4.67 Add creases at the back of the leg.

**7**    Follow these same procedures for the right jeans leg, adding the extra detail to the lower leg. You can see this progression in **Figure 4.68**.

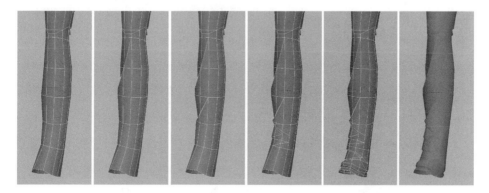

FIGURE 4.68 Add creases to the right leg of the jeans.

When they're finished, the legs of the jeans should look like **Figure 4.69**.

**FIGURE 4.69**
The finished jeans

After all this work, unhide everything and see how she looks. Check out **Figure 4.70**, left. Her feet seem wrong. They are shaped oddly; plus they are pointing forward. We want them to be pointing out slightly, as real feet do naturally.

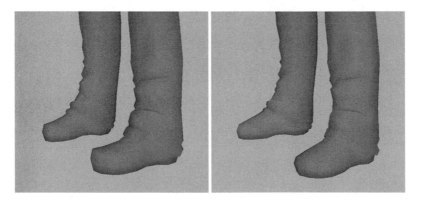

**FIGURE 4.70** Make a small adjustment to the shoes and the position of the feet.

Work a little on the shoes until they look more realistic (**Figure 4.70**, right) and then rotate each foot so the toes are pointing out slightly. You will also need to rotate the bottom of the jeans to match the feet.

## The Belt

The belt is relatively simple. It's essentially just a cylinder that wraps diagonally around Kila's hips.

1   Still in the same scene, create a cylinder with the following configuration: Radius 0.2, Height 0.05, Subdivisions Around Axis 14, Subdivisions Along Height 1, and Subdivisions On Caps 2.

2   As shown in **Figure 4.71**, delete the central polygons; then scale the remaining vertices out to create a small rim.

3   Position the cylinder as shown in **Figure 4.72**. Scale and rotate it until it just fits around her hip, draping diagonally.

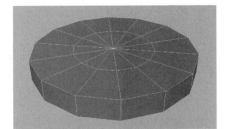
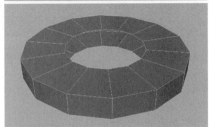
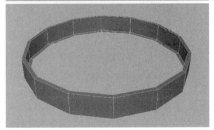

**FIGURE 4.71** Remove the center, and scale the remaining vertices out.

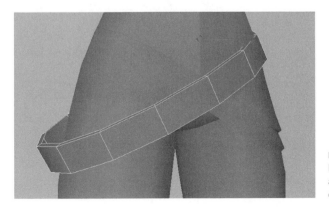

**FIGURE 4.72**
Position the cylinder at Kila's hip, draping diagonally.

**4**    Working on the vertices, adjust the belt so it lies better (**Figure 4.73**).

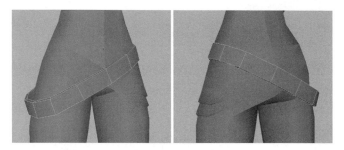

FIGURE 4.73 Adjust the belt to fit tighter around her hips.

At the point where the belt slings downward, we can actually see the inside. The problem here is that once this goes into a game engine, you may be able to see right through the belt. Because the polygons on the belt are being displayed as double-sided, we are fooled into thinking it is solid. Let's make it single-sided and see if we get an improvement.

**5**    Select the belt and press Ctrl+A to open up the object's attributes (**Figure 4.74**).

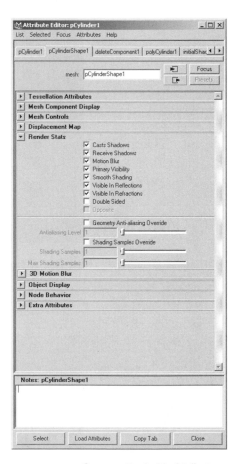

FIGURE 4.74 Open up the belt's Attribute Editor.

6   In the Render Stats pane, uncheck the Double Sided option; this will show you how the belt will look when it is displayed single-sided, as will happen in some platforms (**Figure 4.75**, left).

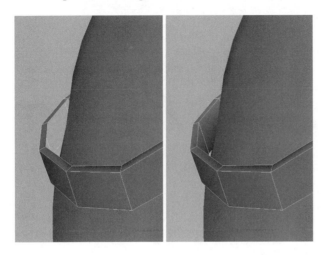

7   Using the Append to Polygon tool, fill in the gaps on the inside of the belt (**Figure 4.74**, right)—but only do this at the base. The rest of the belt should lie quite close to the character's body, so we don't need to do the rest.

And there we have it; our model of Kila is complete! You can see the finished model in **Figure 4.76**.

You can clean her up as we did before, by deleting the history. In addition, at this point you can also freeze the transforms. This will reset all translate and rotate values to 0 and all scale values to 1, without losing any of the position, rotation, scale, or pivot alterations done to the mesh so far.

Save the file as Kila_Complete.mb.

Although we're done working on this latest version of Kila, we have two more stages to go through before she can be signed off. In Chapter 5, we will examine optimization tasks, and in Chapter 6, we will look at deformation.

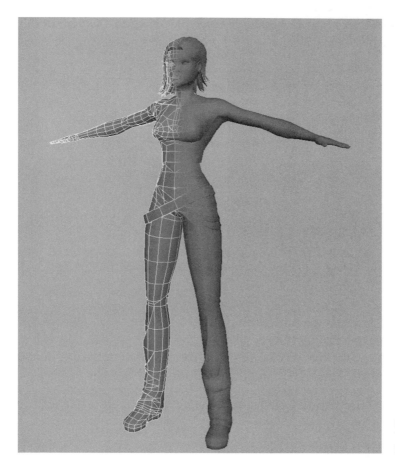

**FIGURE 4.76**
The Kila model
is complete.

## Summary

We now have a complete model of Kila, our main character. She has all the detail we need at the moment—but this also means we may have gone over our poly-gon budget. In the next chapter, we will examine areas where we can optimize, removing any geometry that is not needed.

**CD Files**

Kila_Complete.mb
Kila_Optimized.mb

# CHAPTER 5
# Model Optimization

**UNTIL NOW,** we have spent our time developing a good, clean model without worrying too much about the polygon count. That's about to change—in this chapter, we will be removing a lot of the details you have sculpted into Kila so far. Try not to think of this step as destroying all your hard work, however. What you've accomplished so far is to create a character that is complete and has all the embellishment it needs to have. With all these details in place, we can now make informed decisions about the places from which we can remove those details. That's what optimization is all about.

You will find as you gain more experience in modeling game characters that the optimization stage will gradually become less important, because you will learn to analyze the topology automatically, from the moment you begin building. For the novice artist, this chapter tells you exactly what you need to be looking for as you optimize your character.

With every model, you will find areas where polygons have been placed but are not needed. Essentially, we want the model to have as few polygons as possible. Our polygon limit for this project, established in Chapter 1, is 4500, and we don't want to use more than that number. Indeed, after optimization we may very well end up well under our budget, which is good. If not, we will start to look at areas that we can sacrifice in order to bring the polygon count down.

## Deciding What to Remove

It's important to decide carefully about where to remove polygons from the geometry. Remove the wrong ones, and the shape of our character will change dramatically. It could also result in bad deformation in the game.

The first two sorts of polygons you should consider for removal are unnecessary polygons and polygons that form shallow angles.

Your model is currently made up of hundreds of polygons, and almost all of them are needed. You may think that a polygon's actual presence means it is necessary to a model, but this is not the case.

So how do you determine which polygons will be unused? An *unnecessary polygon* is one that does not add to the shape of the mesh, nor does it aid in its deformation.

Look at the two cubes in **Figure 5.1**. They look exactly the same; the only way they differ is in construction.

Now look at their wireframes in **Figure 5.2**. You can see that the one on the right contains more polygons than the one on the left. Since the edges are straight, the cube does not need the extra polygons to create that straight edge. If we removed these polygons, the cube would look exactly the same.

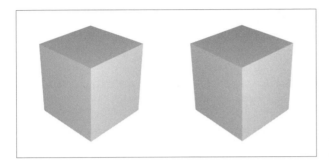

**FIGURE 5.1** Although these cubes look the same, they are constructed differently.

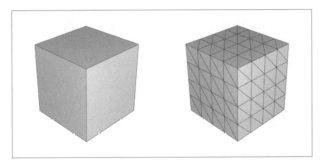

**FIGURE 5.2** In the wireframe, you can see that the cube on the right unnecessarily uses far more polygons than the one on the left.

Removing areas that contain shallow angles is also a good way to reduce the polygon count, although this will slightly affect the way the geometry looks.

Take a look at the cylinders in **Figure 5.3**. Do you see a difference? The one on the right has a very slight bump in it. This is a *shallow angle*, and it adds so insignificantly to the shape of the geometry that no one would miss it if it were gone.

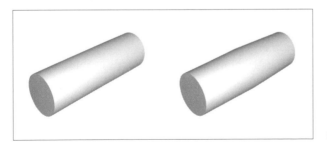

**FIGURE 5.3** Two cylinders

We now know what to look for—unnecessary polygons and shallow angles—so let's move on and begin optimizing our character model.

## Finding the Polygon Count

Before we begin optimizing, let's first look at how many polygons our model currently has.

Load in the last file you saved, Kila_Complete.mb. You first need to convert the geometry to triangles in order to get an accurate reading.

1   Select everything by dragging over the entire character in the view panel; then go to Polygons > Triangulate. The model will now be built from triangular polygons only.

2   To show the polygon count, go to Display > Heads Up Display > Poly Count. The polygon statistics (**Figure 5.4**) will be displayed in the upper-left corner of your view, although depending on your resolution setting these could even take up more space.

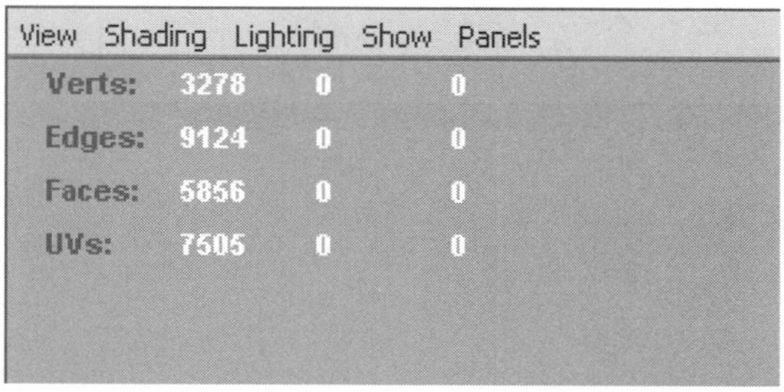

| View  Shading  Lighting  Show  Panels | | |
|---|---|---|
| Verts:  3278 | 0 | 0 |
| Edges:  9124 | 0 | 0 |
| Faces:  5856 | 0 | 0 |
| UVs:  7505 | 0 | 0 |

FIGURE 5.4 The polygon count display

In the Faces line, the far-left number is the current scene's polygon count. This includes only the polygons of objects onscreen, so make sure your entire mesh is visible. Our current polygon count is 5856. This is 1356 over our budget, which is what we expected.

Remember that we added the higher-resolution hands and ear in Chapter 4, to see if we could use them. Each hand alone is around 1010 polygons. If we replaced those with the lower version, which was 406 polygons each, we would save 1208. But we don't want to do that just yet as we first need to remove the unnecessary polygons. We will begin by looking at Kila's upper body, concentrating first on her arms before moving on to her torso, considering various places where we can cut back. Next we will look at the lower body, including waist, legs, and feet, before working on her hair, neck, and face.

After we've made some changes, we can recheck the polygon count and decide whether we need to make any additional sacrifices, such as swapping the hands for lower versions.

---

**Optimization Methods**

In this chapter I don't explain in detail how I am removing polygons. Feel free to use one of the following methods, which you have already seen used in the book so far:

▶ Simply select the edge and go to Edit Polygons > Collapse. This will collapse the edge, bringing together the two vertices it shared in.

▶ You can weld vertices by going to Edit Polygons > Merge Vertices. This method gives results similar to collapsing the edges, bringing together the selected vertices. In some cases you will want to retain one of the vertices' positions; to do this, snap the others to it by holding down V while moving the vertex, remembering to weld them afterwards.

▶ In some instances you can simply select the edges and press Delete; this will remove the edges but the vertices will remain in the geometry. You will then have to select and delete those, too.

---

## Arm Optimization

Let's begin by looking at Kila's arms. (We'll leave the hands for now, just concentrating on the arm itself.)

Before you start, make sure to press Z/Cmd+Z to undo the triangulation you used to get a polygon count. Or you can reload the file called Kila_Complete.mb.

With the model now back in quads, the polygon count will be lower, around 3342. Don't let this fool you—Maya's quads can be made from a number of triangles, not just two, so this number is not an accurate reflection of the number of triangles in the scene. We want this amount to be around 2600. When in doubt, it's always best to do a quick triangulation to check the actual count.

1   Looking from the front, you can see three sections of polygons that can be removed because they affect the shape of the arm only slightly. These areas are highlighted in **Figure 5.5**. The best way to remove these polygons is to collapse the edges, so go ahead and do that now.

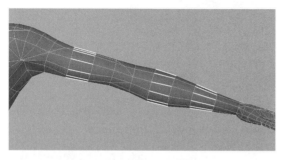

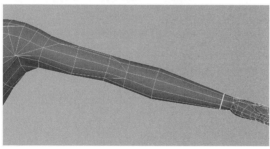

**FIGURE 5.5** Remove the shallow angles from the arm.

2   Move the row that is closest to the wrist down the arm (**Figure 5.5**, bottom). This will help when the wrist deforms.

3   On the top of the arm, you can remove some of the small polygons that exist here. Collapse the edges highlighted in **Figure 5.6**, left.

4   You will have to do a bit of repair work to the areas from which you have removed the polygons and edges. The shape of the biceps and the shoulder area will need some extra work (**Figure 5.7**).

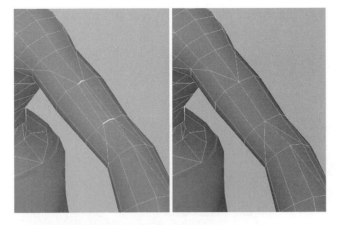

**FIGURE 5.6**
Collapse the edges that form small polygons on the top of the arm.

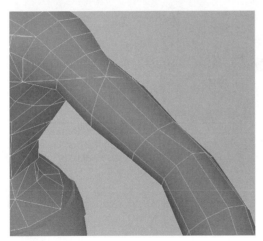

**FIGURE 5.7** Tidy up the arm area after optimizing.

**TIP** ▶ If you end up with two adjoining triangles, try converting them into quads. Select them and go to Polygons > Quadrangulate. This helps to keep the mesh clean and tidy.

**NOTE** ▶ When converting to quads, Maya will guess at the way the triangles should lie. This could result in concave areas like we saw on her hips in Chapter 2. In such instances, it will be necessary to keep the area triangulated.

5   Optimize the back of the arm by welding the vertex in the center of the X (**Figure 5.8**, top) to a vertex above it.

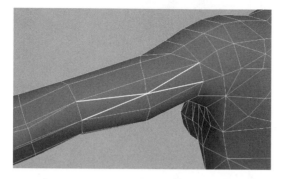

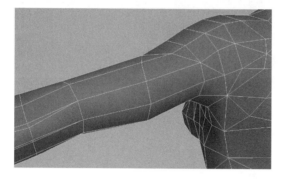

**FIGURE 5.8** Remove the vertex in the center of this X by welding it to a vertex above it.

That's about all we should do on the arm for now; if we need to, we can reduce it further later.

## Torso Optimization

Next, let's look at the torso area. At the very front, there are some edges we created when doing our muscle mapping, as you can see on the left of **Figure 5.9**. Since this area is cloth and not skin, we can remove these edges, giving us a nice, flat front (**Figure 5.9**, right).

Flipping around to her back, you can see the same situation as in the front: a few unnecessary edges because the area is cloth. In addition, there are a few unused polygons.

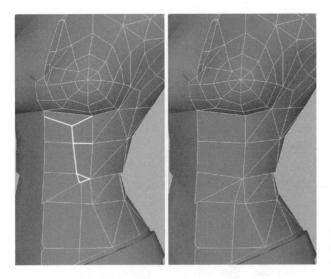

FIGURE 5.9 Take out the edges at the front of her crop top.

First remove the edges highlighted in **Figure 5.10**, left. Then remove any stray vertices that remain, giving us a cleaner back (**Figure 5.10**, right).

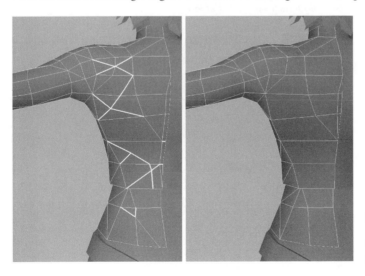

FIGURE 5.10 Remove these highlighted polygons on the back.

Finally, on Kila's side there are a few unused polygons just under her arm, as well as two edges we can collapse at the front of her shoulder. These are all illustrated in **Figure 5.11**.

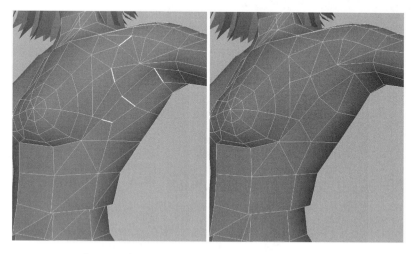

FIGURE 5.11 Remove these polygons from under her armpit.

Looking farther down the model, you will notice a few areas that are currently triangulated. Convert these to quads to clean up the area.

The topology in the breasts is sound; reducing this area would mean we'd lose the curve, making them more angular. So, with the torso optimized, let's move on.

## Waist and Leg Optimization

We next come to Kila's waist area. We will not optimize the belt at this time; it is currently quite low in resolution anyway, so reducing it more would make the overall shape suffer.

1 Hide her belt so we can concentrate on her waist.

Although we modeled all of the sash in Chapter 4, we only need certain parts of it built into the geometry. The rest will be visible via the texture. Take a look at **Figure 5.12**; there are a few areas here we can optimize. For example, highlighted on the left, along the hip, is a shallow angle comprising numerous divisions; this was created when we split the polygons for the sash.

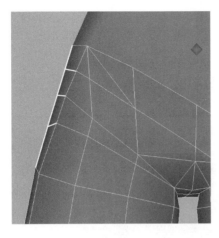

**FIGURE 5.12** The front of the waist.

**2**   Follow the line highlighted in **Figure 5.13** (left) around the mesh, removing most of the sash's polygons (**Figure 5.13**, middle).

**3**   When you're done, combine some of the triangular faces into quads to clean up the area (**Figure 5.13**, right).

**FIGURE 5.13** Remove most of the sash from the front.

**4**   Rotating around to her backside, continue removing the extra polygons of the sash. There are a couple at the top of her jeans that can go, too. These are all highlighted in **Figure 5.14**, left.

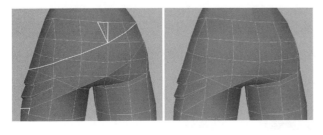

**FIGURE 5.14** Continue removing the sash from the back.

We are finished with her waist for now, so let's concentrate on her thighs before moving down the legs. There are a few shallow angles here but we will not remove all of them.

1    Select just the edges across the center of the thigh (**Figure 5.15**, left) and collapse them, giving us the results seen in **Figure 5.15**, right.

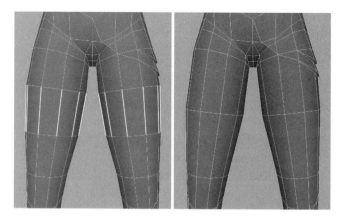

FIGURE 5.15
Collapse the central row of edges across the thighs.

2    At the very front of both knee areas, under the ridges of her knees, there is a small quad (**Figure 5.16**, top). It does not help either the shape or the deformation, so we can remove it, leaving the knees as shown in **Figure 5.16**, bottom.

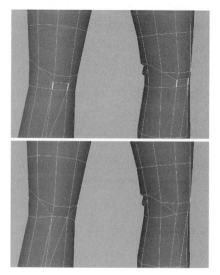

FIGURE 5.16 Collapse the edges just under the ridge of her knees.

**3** Working on the back of the knees, there are more edges we can collapse, shown in **Figure 5.17**, left. Again, they create both shallow edges and smaller polygons, so these edges won't be missed.

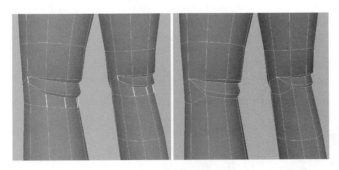

FIGURE 5.17
Collapse the central row of edges across her knees.

**4** Moving on to the calves, start by collapsing the central section of edges, shown in **Figure 5.18**, left. This extra division of polygons is not essential. Notice on your model and in **Figure 5.18** (middle) that collapsing these edges leaves some of the creases in front a bit messy. Take five minutes to fix them (**Figure 5.18**, right).

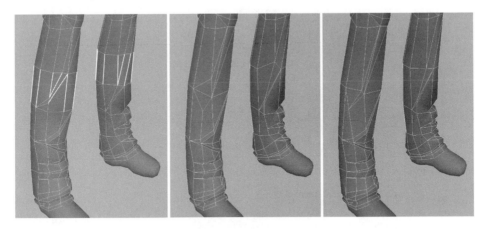

FIGURE 5.18 Remove the central division of faces from the calf area, and then clean up the creases.

5   Concentrating on just the left leg now, optimize the folds in the cloth at the bottom of her jeans. Try to maintain their shape—following the example in **Figure 5.19**, collapse the middle of each fold, leaving the peaks intact. Move over to the right leg and do the same (**Figure 5.20**).

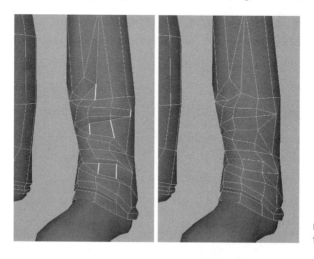

FIGURE 5.19 Optimize the folds on the left leg.

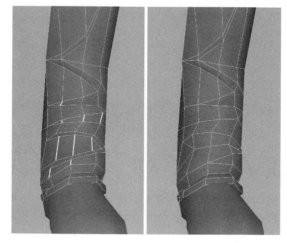

FIGURE 5.20 Optimize the folds on the right leg.

6   At the back of her lower legs, we can remove a section of polygons completely and not harm the overall shape. Select the edges shown in **Figure 5.21** (left) and collapse them. Next, optimize the area a little more by removing any small polygons or edges that are left.

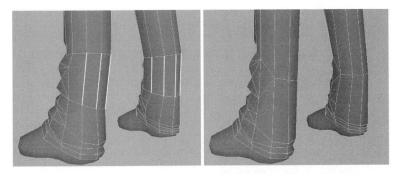

**FIGURE 5.21** Remove the unnecessary section at the back of her leg.

For now, Kila's jeans are optimized, so let's see what we can do with her feet.

## Foot Optimization

The optimization you can do on Kila's feet is fairly straightforward.

1    To start, delete any polygons that are hidden by her jeans (**Figure 5.22**), these will never be seen in the game so they don't need to exist.

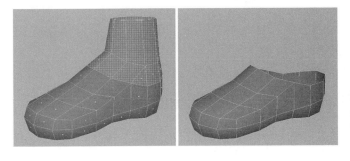

**FIGURE 5.22** Delete any faces from the shoes that are hidden by her jeans.

2    Because the tops of her shoes are relatively flat, we can remove the middle section of polygons. As illustrated in **Figure 5.23**, select the edges that span the middle and collapse them. Make sure you collapse them all the way around the foot.

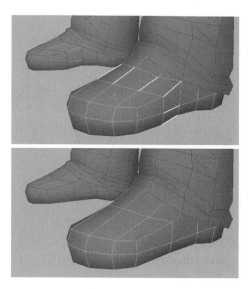

FIGURE 5.23 The tops of her shoes are flat, so remove the central section of polygons.

3    Before we finish with the feet, notice that three quads at her heel, also hidden by the jeans, could be removed; see the top of **Figure 5.24**. After removing these three quads, weld down the point on the remaining quad to create a triangle, and smooth the area.

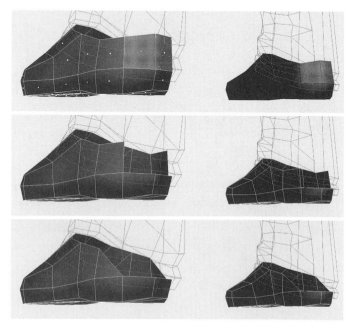

FIGURE 5.24 Get rid of the three quads at the back of her feet.

**TIP** If you want to be able to see through the jeans but keep the shoes solid, as I have in Figure 5.24, right-click the geometry you want to see through and select Actions > Template. To return it to normal, right-click again and select Actions > Untemplate.

Before we continue to her hair and face, take one final look around Kila's main body. You should now have a good idea of what to look for, so chances are you can find a few more polygons to remove. A few areas I found were in her collarbone and the backs of her shoulders. You can see these areas highlighted in **Figures 5.25** and **5.26**.

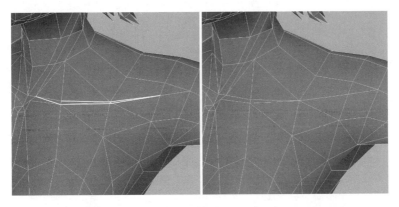

FIGURE 5.25 Check her collarbone area for opportunities for reduction.

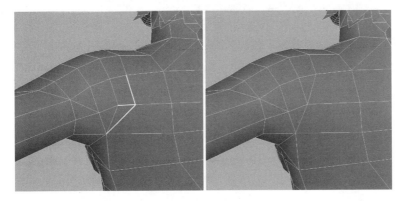

FIGURE 5.26 Behind the shoulder, you can remove a polygon or two.

**NOTE** It is very important to have the right amount and placement of geometry around the shoulder for good deformation. We will examine this in Chapter 6.

We are not at the stage where we need to sacrifice any major details yet. Our current polygon count is 2992 (remember, this is in quads)—we are only 392 away from reaching the target of about 2600.

We can leave the main body behind now, and get busy with the head area.

## Hair, Face, and Neck Optimization

The geometry that makes up Kila's head and hair is a goldmine of opportunities where we can remove lots of polygons. Let's begin with the hair.

### The Hair

Hide everything apart from her hair and face. Template the face (using the method explained earlier for working with the jeans), so we can work on just the top part of her hair.

To start, there are quite a few areas where we can collapse edges because there are so many shallow angles.

1    Select the edges shown in **Figure 5.27**, selecting them all around her hair, and collapse them.

 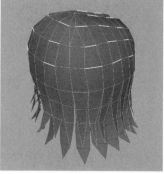

**FIGURE 5.27**
Select and collapse every other edge, to reduce the hair.

Leave the very bottom of the hair intact, however. This area is divided into separate strips, so collapsing the edges constructing the strips will remove them. Kila's hair should now look like that in **Figure 5.28**.

**FIGURE 5.28**
The hair after the edges are collapsed.

Take another look; there are still a couple of shallow angles that can be removed without affecting the overall shape of her hair.

2　As shown in **Figure 5.29**, select the middle row of edges and collapse them, leaving the hair as seen in **Figure 5.30**.

**FIGURE 5.29**
Reduce the hair further by removing this row of edges.

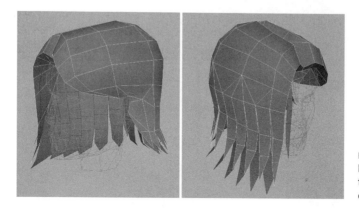

FIGURE 5.30 The hair after removing the middle row of edges.

3    Moving around now to the front of her hair, we can have a look and see if we can get away with removing a polygon or two from here. Try selecting and collapsing the edges shown in **Figure 5.31** (left); does it still look okay?

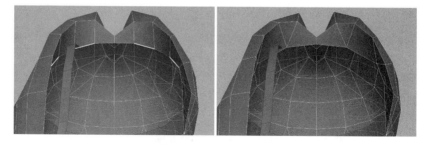

FIGURE 5.31 Try removing a few edges from the front.

Although it does looks fine (**Figure 5.31**, right), altering the hairline like this will reduce the number of vertices along that edge, thereby changing how the face mesh lines up with the hair. This will become obvious when the face is untemplated in subsequent steps.

4    Continue looking around the geometry for polygons to be removed. Another one lies right on the top; you can see it in **Figure 5.32** (left). It's a small polygon and so should not cause any major problems when it's removed.

**FIGURE 5.32**
Remove this tiny polygon from the top of her hair.

We are finished now with the top portion of the hair; let's optimize the inner layers next.

1   Isolate the first layer so we can work on it alone (**Figure 5.33**, top).

2   As shown in the middle image of **Figure 5.33**, select every other edge around the very top and collapse them. We can do this because the top layer of hair will hide most of these polygons. We still need them to exist, though, so that you don't see through her head.

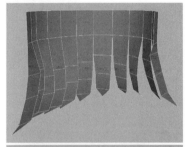

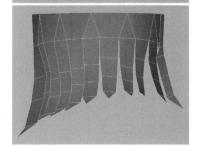

**FIGURE 5.33** Collapse the top strip of edges on the first layer of hair.

**3**  Since this is an inner layer, the curves in the geometry need not be perfectly smooth. That means we can reduce this layer some more by removing an entire row of polygons. This is shown in **Figure 5.34**.

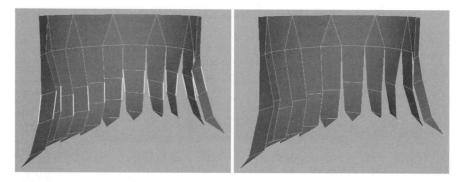

FIGURE 5.34 Further reduce the inner layer by removing a row of polygons from the strips.

Now follow the same procedure for the other inner layers of hair. When you're done, the geometry will look like that in **Figure 5.35**.

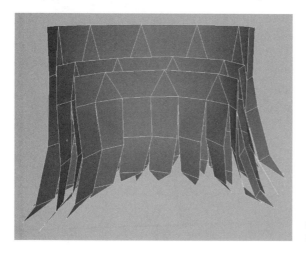

FIGURE 5.35 More reductions on the other inner layers

### The Face and Neck

The hair's done; now let's work on her face. One quick look will show many areas where you can reduce the mesh.

Start with the forehead. I chose to begin here because we've already reduced her hairline, and the vertices in her hair no longer line up with her head.

1    Follow the edges down the brow, starting with the same edges we removed from her hair, until you get to the eye area. If you're not sure which edges to choose, they're shown in **Figure 5.36** (left). Judging by the results in **Figure 5.36** (right), removing these edges doesn't cause a problem.

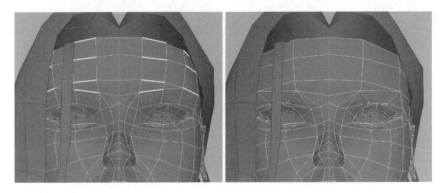

FIGURE 5.36 Optimizing the forehead

Time to make our first sacrifice; we need to reduce her ear. This is not a major loss, however, because the texture will hold all the detail we need.

2    Flatten the outer face of the ear, but try to retain the ear's general shape (**Figure 5.37**).

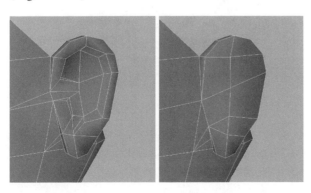

FIGURE 5.37 Flatten out the face of the ear, keeping the overall shape.

**3**   It looks like we can reduce the ear a little more by collapsing the edges high-lighted in **Figure 5.38** (left). This will ultimately affect the ear's overall shape, but not too much.

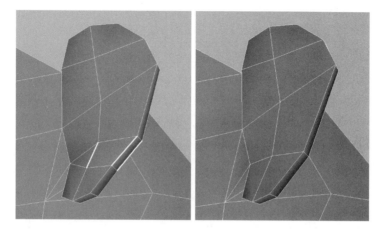

FIGURE 5.38 Collapse these three edges.

**4**   Looking around, you'll spot a small polygon nearly out of sight on the inside (**Figure 5.39**, left); remove this. Then go ahead and work a little more on the ear's general shape, and see if you can remove any more polygons.

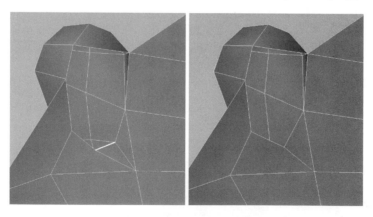

FIGURE 5.39 Collapse this small polygon hiding on the inside of the ear.

After the ear is done, the next major area to examine is under her chin. You can see in **Figure 5.40** (left) that there are lots of unused polygons here.

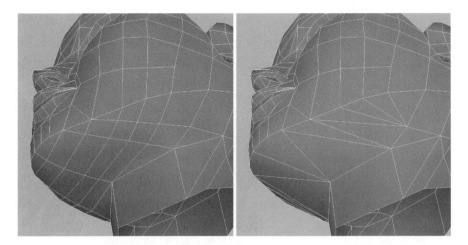

FIGURE 5.40 Flatten the area under her chin.

1   We can probably get away with flattening the area as demonstrated in **Figure 5.40** (right), although I admit I'm not entirely comfortable with removing this many polygons in one go because it does affect the shape. After we're finished, if we're under our budget, we can always add a bit back into this area to fill out the shape.

2   Removing so much from the chin will make other potential trim areas stand out. The edges in **Figure 5.41** (left), for example, lead up from a now-unused edge around her jaw.

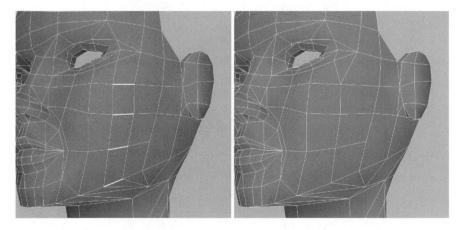

FIGURE 5.41 Working up from the jaw line, remove polygons from her cheek.

**3** Again, optimizing the underside of her chin has made other reduction possibilities leap right out at us. Look at the chin itself: We definitely don't need all six of those subdivisions. Removing the bottom edge alone, however, may cause some odd-looking results. So work your way up as I have done in **Figure 5.42** (left), optimizing the lips, too.

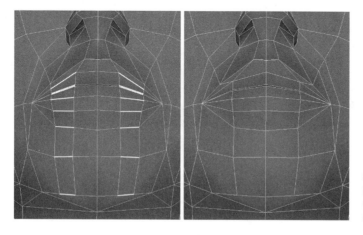

**FIGURE 5.42**
Reduce the subdivisions in her chin and lips.

**4** Removing the edges from the lips has left us with two stray vertices, shown in **Figure 5.43** at the top. Weld these vertices to the ones closest to them, smoothing out the upper lip (**Figure 5.43**, bottom).

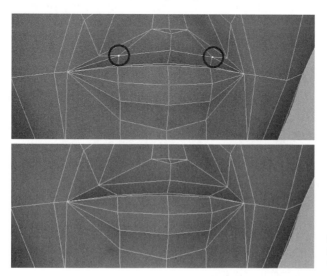

**FIGURE 5.43**
Smoothing out the upper lip

Next, we will examine Kila's eyes before moving on to the rest of her head. They are quite round, but we don't actually need this amount of detail.

**1**  We can get away with collapsing the edges highlighted in **Figure 5.44** (left), before moving the remaining vertices to reshape the eye as shown in **Figure 5.44** (right). By doing this, we'll regain 18 quads, or 36 polygons.

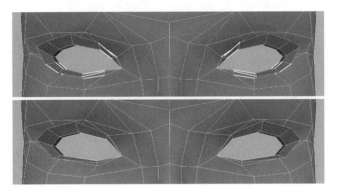

FIGURE 5.44 Reducing and reshaping the eyes

Now look at the bridge of the nose from the side. You'll spot an area that is quite flat. There are three vertical subdivisions making up this area, but we can live with just two.

**2**  Select the edges that make up the central division of the nose. Optimizing the bridge of the nose means we can also reduce her cheeks, so work your way around them and see what you can do (**Figure 5.45**).

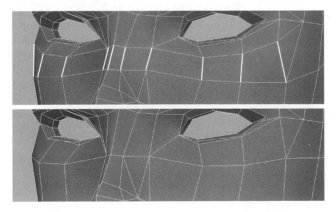

FIGURE 5.45 Optimizing the bridge of her nose and the cheeks

**3** Here's something less obvious: Notice the small polygon next to the corner of her eye, shown in **Figure 5.46**. Select and collapse this, as it is not needed.

> **NOTE** It's important to keep your eyes peeled, looking for potential areas of optimization that are less easily seen, like this one.

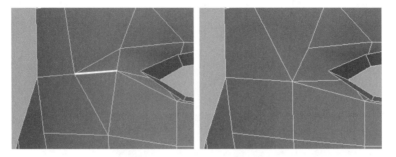

FIGURE 5.46 Here's an edge you can collapse without taking away from the shape of the eye.

> **TIP** When you are unsure about removing a particular polygon, go ahead and try it—if the geometry looks wrong, you can always press Z/Cmd+Z to undo the operation. And Shift+Z/Shift+Cmd+Z will redo the last undo.

**4** The back of Kila's head would be another good place to look for optimization opportunities, because her hair will cover it. In **Figure 5.47** (left), you can see an edge that might potentially be collapsed.

FIGURE 5.47 This area at the back of the head can be reduced.

**5** Now move around the head, scanning the surface for anything you might remove. Above the nostril we built in the crease, but this is such a small polygon we just can't justify keeping it, so collapse this edge (**Figure 5.48**).

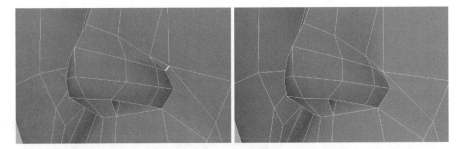

FIGURE 5.48 The small polygon above her nostril can be removed.

Returning to the back of her neck, it looks like we can do some additional reduction. Shown in the top image of **Figure 5.49**, there are two quads on the sides of the neck that do not offer much in the way of shape or deformation. These edges can be removed, but make sure to fine-tune the new geometry so that the form correctly resembles the back of a neck.

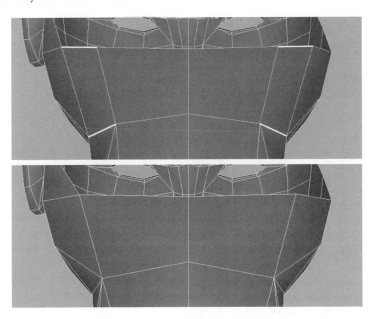

FIGURE 5.49 You can reduce these edges, but you'll need to reshape the area afterward.

Taking one last look around the head, we notice an edge under the jaw that we can remove (**Figure 5.50**). This cleans up the area nicely.

Another spot we can remove in this area is the muscle definition in the side of the neck, also shown in **Figure 5.50**. Ultimately this does not add to the character; besides, the muscle tone here can be drawn into the texture if we need it.

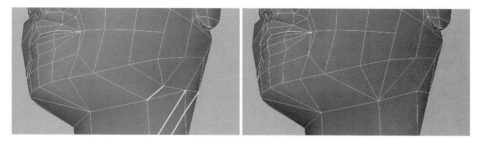

**FIGURE 5.50** On final inspection: an extra edge under the jaw and a muscle in the neck.

The face is now complete and can be seen in **Figure 5.51**. As mentioned earlier, we may have removed too much from a few areas, but we will wait and see how things shape up. If we come in well below our limit, we can go back in and rework some areas.

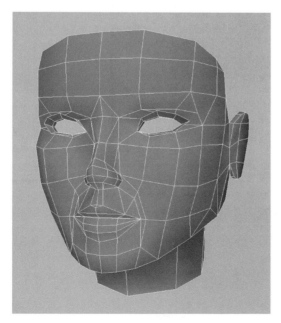

**FIGURE 5.51** The fully optimized face

Now bring back the rest of the geometry so it is visible. Because we removed the detail from the upper part of the neck, we must now remove it from the lower portion as well, so they match up (**Figure 5.52**).

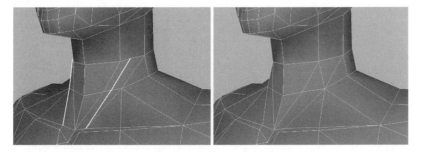

**FIGURE 5.52** Optimize the lower neck so that it matches the upper portion that we trimmed.

## Current Count

The main optimization is now complete. Before we find out how we are doing as far as the polygon count is concerned, let's look at the appearance of our character. **Figure 5.53** shows our model of Kila before and after optimization—can you tell which is which?

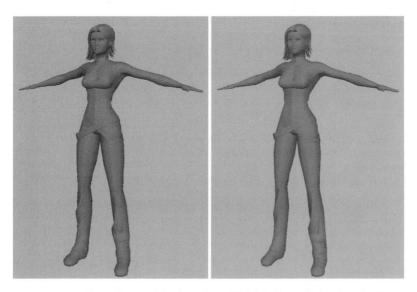

**FIGURE 5.53** Character model comparison. Which is the optimized version?

If you look closely, there are subtle differences now. The main difference, however, is that one version has 1054 more polygons. You can see from this example that removing polygons does not mean you have to sacrifice the detail or even the shape of a character. What it does mean is that you have a well-constructed and efficient model that doesn't eat up lots of processing power because it has 1000 polygons in an ear that the player never sees. It pays to be ruthless!

So where are we now with Kila? Remembering that our limit is 4500, let's see how many polygons she currently holds. Select all the geometry, and go to Polygons > Triangulate and read the onscreen display. Our current polygon count is 4802. Hmmm, not bad—but we're still 302 over our limit. There's one remaining area where we can reduce to pare down these faces a little more: the hands.

**NOTE**  Remember to undo (Z/Cmd+Z) the triangulation before you proceed.

## Hand Optimization

Kila's hands at this point do house a lot of detail, so reducing them by 151 polygons each should not significantly reduce their quality. We should be able to have all five fingers articulated, without having to resort to a mitten hand or one with frozen fingers.

So what's available for optimization? We can start by removing the fingernails. Here we have to remember that when working on the fingers, if we alter one we must do the same on the other four. They all have to match or they will look odd.

1  On all the fingernails and the thumbnail, snap the inner vertices of the nails to the outer ones and weld them, as demonstrated in the before-and-after shots in **Figure 5.54**.

   Currently we have fewer divisions of faces on the wrist than we have across the back and palm of the hand. So we should next optimize the back of the hand. **Figure 5.55** (left) shows the back of the hand currently.

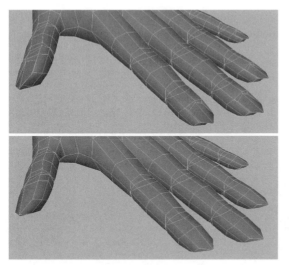

FIGURE 5.54 Start by removing the fingernails.

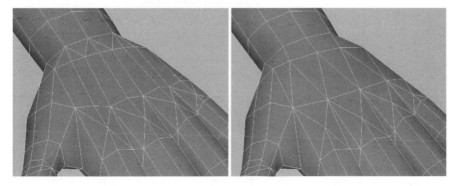

FIGURE 5.55 Optimize the back of the hand so it matches the divisions on the wrist.

2   Following the center of the X created for the knuckles, trace back to the two vertices behind it and weld them to the ones on their left (**Figure 5.55**, right).

**3**  Next, flip the hand over and do the same for the palm, reducing it to match the divisions on the wrist. **Figure 5.56** shows the palm before and after the optimization.

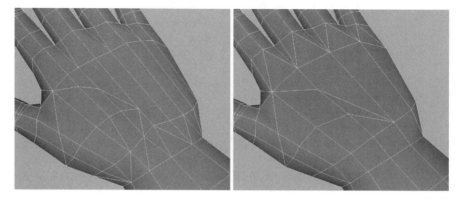

FIGURE 5.56 Reduce the palm as you did the back of the hand.

**4**  You might be left with the two edges I have highlighted in **Figure 5.57** (left). If so, you can simply collapse these because they don't add anything to the model.

FIGURE 5.57 Collapse these two edges if they exist on your model.

The main hand area is now done, but we can reduce it even further by optimizing the fingers.

1   Flatten the top of each finger as shown in **Figure 5.58**. Do this by snapping each of the vertices that run down the center to the ones directly to their right. Remember to weld them afterward, or the polygons will still exist.

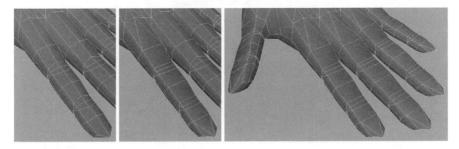

FIGURE 5.58 Flatten the top of each finger.

2   Right at the tip of each finger there is a single vertex that we no longer need. It doesn't add much to the shape, so snap it to the vertex at the tip of the nail, and weld (**Figure 5.59**).

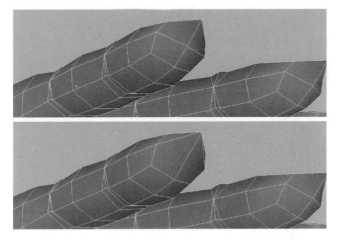

FIGURE 5.59
Remove the vertex
in the center of
each fingertip.

3    Still looking at the fingertip, there are two edges at either side of the nail; you can see these in **Figure 5.60**, left. Collapsing these on each finger will recoup another 20 polygons.

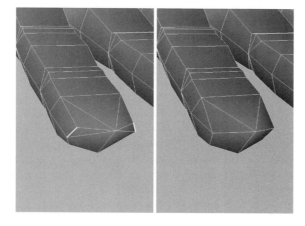

**FIGURE 5.60**
Collapse the two edges on each side of the fingernail.

That completes the first stage of reducing the hand; you can see the results in **Figure 5.61**. We could leave it as-is, but there's more we can do. I don't think we will see a major difference in quality if we move forward one more step, which will reduce the polygon count by another 160.

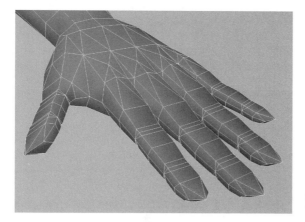

**FIGURE 5.61**
The hand model so far

4    As we did on the top of the hand, we can optimize the sides of the fingers and thumb. Select the vertices that run down both sides of each digit, and snap and then weld them to the vertices below. **Figure 5.62** shows you how this looks on just the index finger.

**NOTE** This operation not only removes the side-finger divisions but also reduces the number of mesh divisions on the underside of each knuckle from 3 to 1.

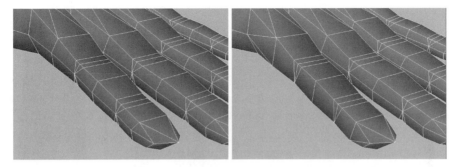

FIGURE 5.62 Flatten the sides of each finger and thumb.

We will leave the bottom curve of the fingers intact. This will provide a little more shape than they would have if we reduced them to cubes.

Once all the digits have been done, the hand is finished (**Figure 5.63**).

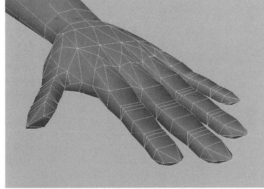

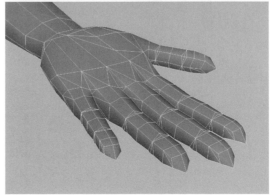

FIGURE 5.63 Final optimized hand model

## Final Check

So the model optimization is done! We have been through each section of Kila's body and optimized them all in an attempt to get the polygon count under 4500. Before we look at the final total, spend some time looking at the model to try and reduce it further. See if you can spot any areas we missed.

**Figure 5.64** shows the final model, top to bottom, after all the optimizations described in this chapter. So what's the polygon count? Triangulating the model gives it to us: 3998. We are well under our budget—which is great. But we can't afford to put any detail back in just yet, as we may need the polygons during the next chapter, "Deformation Testing." Once the model is finalized we can then go back through it, if we feel we need to, and add detail back in.

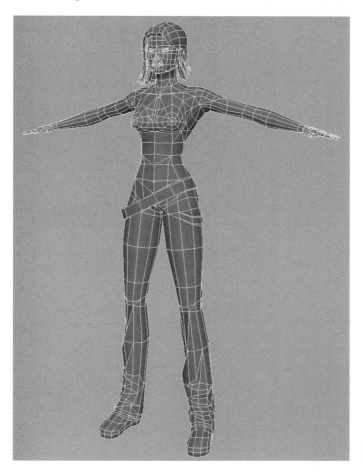

**FIGURE 5.64**
Kila, fully optimized

Before we go to the deformation stage, I recommend saving the model and leaving it alone for a day. Clean up the model and the scene then save your file as Kila_Optimized.mb. If you can, do something else before you come back to it for a final look. Taking a break from it will enable you to see it from a fresh perspective when you return. You may be able to spot some additional extra polygons that can be removed, or an area that needs reshaping. Indeed, optimizing the geometry will mean that some areas do in fact need reshaping. Usually, they will be thinner than before and so will need filling out.

Take some time to look around the entire model. Double-check the proportions and make sure the shape is perfect. Check it against your concept images; you must be positive it is correct before you proceed to the next stage.

> **TIP** Here's a good way to determine how smooth your model is: Go to the Lighting menu in your current panel and select Use No Lights. Just the silhouette of the character will remain. Now you can rotate around the model and assess her.

Following are some of the alterations I made to Kila during my final, postoptimization examination:

▶ Adjusted the bottom of her crop top so the point was smoother

▶ Generally reworked the shape of her hips, widening them slightly

▶ Moved up her navel

▶ Brought the upper body down, shortening her slightly (the distance between her chest and the bottom of her t-shirt was too great)

▶ Added more of a curve to the small of her back, making her chest and backside a bit more pronounced

▶ Shortened the legs and widened the bottom of her jeans

▶ Reduced the length of her neck

▶ Added an extra division across her waist to smooth it out

You can see the final model in **Figure 5.65**.

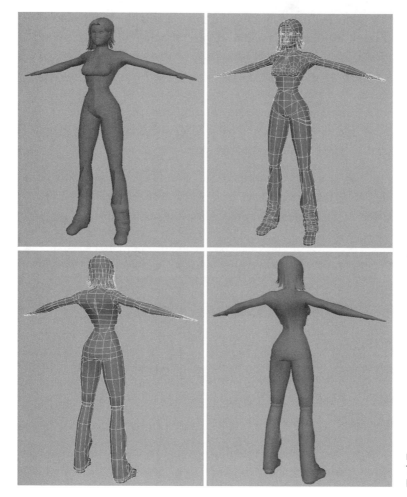

**FIGURE 5.65**
The tweaked
Kila model

When you're sure Kila is ready, clean up the model and the scene, and save your file again as Kila_Optimized.mb.

## Summary

We now have a model that is not only clean and good looking, but efficient as well. The various techniques explored in this chapter will serve you well when you need to optimize your geometry. You'll know what to look out for on future projects.

With Kila now the best she can be, we can proceed to see how she deforms.

**CD Files**

Kila_DeformTest.mb
Kila_Optimized.mb

# CHAPTER 6
# Deformation Testing

**WE ARE NOW CLOSE** to finishing sculpting the Kila model; only this chapter remains before the base model is compete. If you are like me, you could easily spend another week refining and fine-tuning the mesh to perfection, but time is *not* a luxury you can afford in the games industry, so we will push on.

In this chapter we will briefly introduce the use of joints and binding while we test that our model will deform correctly. For a game character to perform convincingly, it must deform convincingly. Using the correct topology around areas that bend, such as elbows and knees, will result in a believable character that the player can relate to. Testing Kila's deformation at this stage—with the mesh completely sculpted—will save headaches later on. Suppose the character hasn't been tested, and we go on to texture and rig her. If we then realize that she needs extra polygons in a certain place or has an area that needs altering, that will mean retexturing and possibly rerigging her. It's important to test the deformation now.

In Kila's current condition, her torso will initially deform quite well because it is essentially cylindrical in shape and does not need to bend dramatically. The arms and legs, however, will bend quite considerably at the elbows and knees and so must be checked.

## The Arms and Legs

Two of the main areas on a model that need to be tested are the arms and legs, in particular the elbows, shoulders, and knees. These areas are important because they bend the most as the character moves around the game world and interacts with the environment and with other characters.

### Setting Up the Arm Skeleton

Let's start by loading the file called Kila_Optimized.mb and focusing in on her left elbow. You can see the elbow in **Figure 6.1**, and up to now there are no major problems with it. Let's put a basic skeleton in and see how it bends.

**FIGURE 6.1** For our first skeleton area, focus in on Kila's left elbow.

**1**    Switch to the top view so that you are looking down on the arm. Switch to wireframe mode (press 4) so that you can see the joints as we place them.

> **Switching Views**
>
> Use the number keys to cycle through the viewing modes in Maya.
>
> ▶    4 switches to wireframe mode
>
> ▶    5 switches to shaded mode
>
> ▶    6 switches to textured mode
>
> ▶    7 switches to lighted mode

**2**    To begin placing the joints, switch to the Animation menu set (F2). Go to the Skeleton menu and select the Joint tool. Leave the options alone for now; we are going to use the default settings. We will explore joints in more detail in Chapter 11, "Skeleton Setup."

**3**    Following **Figure 6.2**, place the first joint just before the shoulder, then one at the shoulder itself, then at the elbow, and finally at the wrist—making four joints in all. Press Enter to confirm the placement. Don't worry about renaming the joints; they are only temporary.

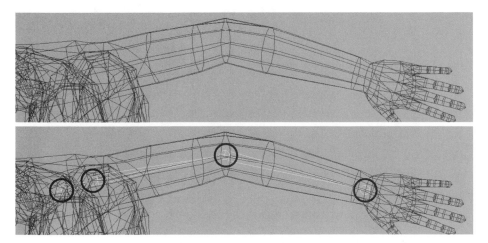

**FIGURE 6.2** Place four joints: before the shoulder, at the shoulder, at the elbow, and at the wrist.

The joints are now correctly placed in the X and Z axes, so next let's check the Y axis.

**TIP** You can adjust the size at which joints are displayed by going to Display > Joint Size.

4   Switch to the front view (**Figure 6.3**, left), and you'll see that the joints at this stage all lie in the wrong place in the Y axis. You need to move them up so they are positioned down the center of her arm. If you select and move the first joint you placed, it will also move the rest, because the other joints are parented to this one and thus inherit its movement. This will put the arm into the basic position for us.

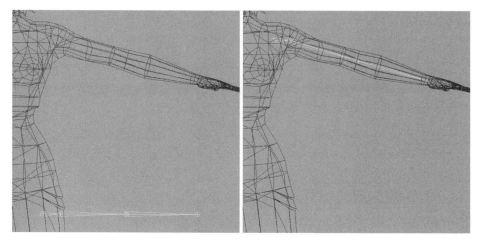

**FIGURE 6.3** Move the joints up so they lie down the center of the arm.

5   To fine-tune the positioning of the remaining joints by moving each in turn until they are all correctly positioned down the center of the arm (**Figure 6.3**, right).

Once you have the main shoulder joint in place, you can use the Rotate tool to position the rest if you prefer, although it's not essential.

**TIP** If a series of objects are placed in a hierarchy, you can select the children or parent by using the arrow keys. Pressing the up arrow will move up the chain; pressing the down arrow will move down the chain. This process is called "pick walking."

This is all we need to do at this stage to build a basic skeleton, so let's continue with our arm setup.

### Skeleton Binding

Now we need to attach the mesh to the joints. The skeleton essentially drives the model and deforms it for us.

**1**  Select the first joint of your skeleton. Then hold Shift and select the geometry so that you have both the skeleton and the mesh selected.

**2**  Open up the options for a smooth bind (Skin > Bind Skin > Smooth Bind).

**3**  Make sure your Smooth Bind options are configured in **Figure 6.4**. The important sections are Max Influences and Dropoff Rate.

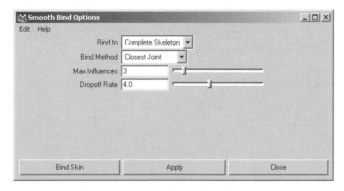

FIGURE 6.4 Setting Smooth Bind options

### Smooth Bind Settings

**Max Influences** specifies the number of joints that can influence each vertex. For example, setting this to 1 would mean that the forearm joint only influenced the vertices near it, which could make the character deform badly and look quite rigid. This number may depend on the game engine you are using, so discuss the setting with your lead artist first. Usually, 2 or 3 is a good number for Max Influences.

**Dropoff Rate** dictates how rapidly a joint's influence decreases as it moves away from the joint. The default is 4, which works well for most characters.

**4**  When you're ready, click Bind Skin to continue. The wireframe on your mesh should turn pink, indicating that the joints are connected to the mesh.

**5**  Switch to the top view and turn on Smooth Shade All in the Shading menu.

In **Figure 6.5** you can't see the joints, but it doesn't matter—Maya has a priority list that dictates which things get selected before others. Joints are higher on this list than polygons, so if you drag a selection over the forearm you will select the elbow joint.

FIGURE 6.5 Select the elbow joint and rotate it to bend the arm.

**6**  Do this now—drag a selection around the forearm and rotate the elbow around the Z axis. This is shown in **Figure 6.5**, right.

> **NOTE**  Because this is a default bind, the elbow joint may influence the torso. Don't worry about this now; we will address this issue in the next section.

Although the geometry does bend, it's not a very natural looking elbow. What we can do now is tweak the way the joints influence the elbow by painting the weights around it.

### Painting Weights

Different 3D applications use various techniques for adjusting the way joints drive geometry; Maya's is one of the best and friendliest I have used. When you *paint weights,* you paint a joint's influence onto the mesh, telling Maya what areas are influenced and by how much.

Let's get ready to adjust the weights on Kila's elbow.

**1** Select the mesh and go to Skin > Edit Smooth Skin > Paint Skin Weights Tool, and open up the options window. **Figure 6.6** shows the options now available to you.

Also notice that in the perspective view, your geometry now has grayscale shading all over it; you can see this in **Figure 6.7**. This is an interactive display of the area that the current joint is influencing. White is maximum and will inherit 100% of the joint's movement; black represents no influence.

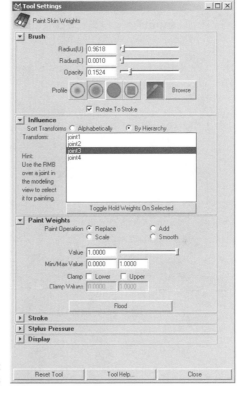

FIGURE 6.6 The Paint Skin Weights options

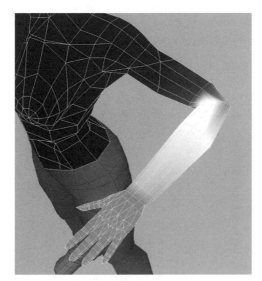

FIGURE 6.7 The influence is displayed for the currently selected joint.

**2** Leave the Paint Skin Weights window open, as you'll need to refer back to it as you paint. Move your mouse curser over the geometry and you'll notice that the pointer changes to a paintbrush icon with a red circle around it (**Figure 6.8**). This shows you where you are painting as well as how large your brush is.

**FIGURE 6.8** The mouse pointer changes to indicate where you are painting and the size of your current brush.

## Options for Painting Skin Weights

There are lots of options to play with in this tool, as you can see in the Paint Skin Weights options window. Typically, I only use the few I have high-lighted in **Figure 6.9**, but feel free to experiment with the other brushes and options until you find a way of working that you're comfortable with.

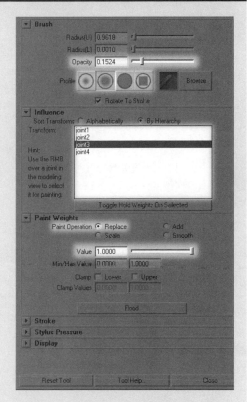

**Opacity** (in the Brush panel) and **Value** (in the Paint Weights panel) work together:

▶  Value sets the amount by which the joint influences the skin. A setting of 1.0000 will fully influence the vertices. This value is the maximum a vertex will be influenced. If you set it to 0.5, a vertex will only be influenced by 0.5, no matter

**FIGURE 6.9** The weight-painting options I frequently use are highlighted here.

how much you paint on (unless your paint operation is set to Add).

▶  The Opacity setting dictates how much of the Value will be painted by each stroke. So if your Value is 1 but your Opacity is 0.25, you will only paint one-quarter of the full value each time.

CONTINUED ▶

**Options for Painting Skin Weights, continued...**

The **Paint Operations** (in Paint Weights) you can perform are as follows:

▶ Replace is the paint operation I tend to use most often. This operation simply replaces the current influence with whatever you are painting. I find it quick and easy to get good results by only using Replace.

▶ Add will add on top of the current influence.

▶ Smooth averages the influence values of adjacent vertices, much like a blur operation would soften the edge between a black area and a white area in an image. Smooth is quite handy when, for example, you have a large area that needs a gradual, smooth deformation.

▶ Scale reduces the influence on joints that are farther away.

The various brush types are represented next to Profile in the Brush panel. These influence the way you paint; choose among a fine brush stroke, a solid brush with smooth edges, a solid brush, and a square brush.

### Elbow Weight Painting and Testing

Now that you've seen the weight-painting options, let's paint the elbow and see if we can get a good shape when it is bent.

1  Set Value and Opacity to 1 (their highest settings). Select the solid brush, which is third from the left, and choose joint3, which is the elbow joint.

2  To begin, make sure the vertices away from the elbow are fully influenced by their respective joints. While we have the settings on maximum, paint around the section of vertices highlighted in **Figure 6.10**, making them pure white. (Most of these are already fully influenced by the elbow, but it doesn't hurt to check.)

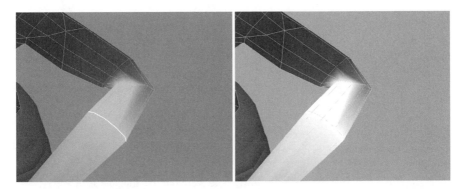

FIGURE 6.10 Set the vertices just out from the elbow, to be fully influenced by the elbow.

**3**   Reset Value to 0 and paint over the upper arm (**Figure 6.11**), removing any influence the elbow has over this area.

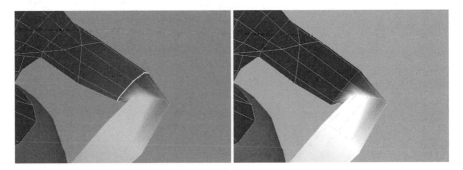

FIGURE 6.11 Remove the influence from the upper arm.

**4**   Set Value to 0.5 and paint over the middle section of the arm, highlighted in **Figure 6.12**, so that the elbow and upper arm both influence this area. You will probably have to select joint2 and paint the area again, since both joints will be influencing this bend.

FIGURE 6.12 Paint the middle of the arm so that both the shoulder joint and the elbow joint influence it.

**5**    We now have each row of vertices weighted neatly. Put Value back to 1, select the softer brush (second from the left) and move Opacity down to about 0.2.

Go ahead and work some more on the elbow area and see if you can achieve an acceptable result. You will end up with the elbow looking much like that in **Figure 6.13** (left). Not looking very good, is it? We could spend more time painting the area, but we won't get a satisfactory result. No matter how much we try, we will still end up with the sharp angle on the outer edge and the pinching on the inside.

Fixing this will involves adding more polygons to the area, as illustrated in **Figure 6.13** (right). We'll discuss that next.

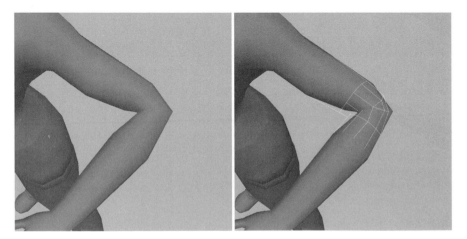

FIGURE 6.13 The elbow so far

### Adding Polygons to the Elbow

We need to add some polygons to keep the elbow from pinching as it bends. These will lie close to the actual elbow. They will only be added at the front and the rear because the elbow only rotates around one axis; we don't need to worry about the top and bottom.

1   To quickly get the joints back to their original position, right-click the first joint and select Assume Preferred Angle from the marking menu.

2   Select the mesh and open up the options for Skin > Detach Skin. Make sure the Delete History option is selected, then click Detach.

> **NOTE** In the Detach Skin options, Delete History resets the mesh back to its original shape, removing all the weighting information attached. Bake History "bakes" the bend onto the geometry, keeping the mesh in the same pose. Keep History detaches the skeleton but keeps the weighting information. This last option is handy to retain the weights from the original in case you want to add an extra joint to the skeleton after you rebind.

3   We are back to square one, but with a better idea of how the elbow should be. Let's add some polygons now. Using the Split Polygon tool, cut the front as shown in **Figure 6.14**. You're cutting from the pivot point of the elbow on the top, to the one at the bottom.

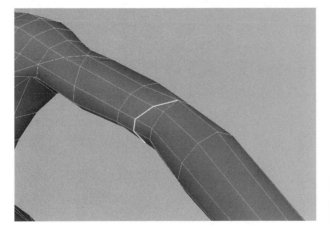

**FIGURE 6.14** Add a small section of polygons at the front of the elbow.

**4**    Farther down the arm, add a new subdivision as shown in **Figure 6.15**.

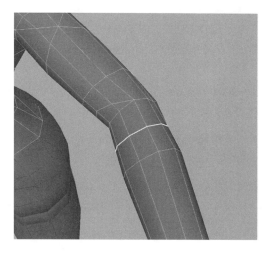

FIGURE 6.15 Insert a new section across the lower arm.

**5**    The final addition will be a section around the back of the elbow similar to the one we added to the front (**Figure 6.16**).

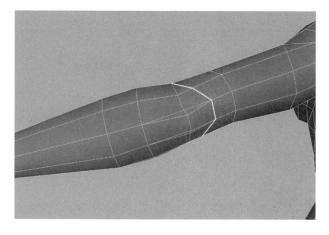

FIGURE 6.16 Add a section at the back of the elbow like the one in the front.

**6**    Now that we have these extra polygons, we may as well use them to add a little shape to the elbow area (**Figure 6.17**). You can also add a slight depression on the inside of the elbow, too, if you haven't already. Delete the history when you're done.

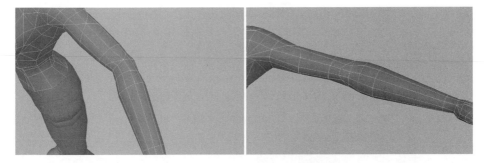

**FIGURE 6.17** With new polygons added, reshape the arm.

**7**   To rebind the mesh to the skeleton select the first joint of the skeleton and then the mesh. Go to Skin > Bind Skin > Smooth Bind, making sure its options are still set at Max Influence 3 and Dropoff Rate 4.

**8**   Bend the elbow and begin to paint the weights. Start by making sure the vertices on either side of the elbow are only influenced by the shoulder (joint2) or the elbow (joint3).

**9**   Set the middle row of vertices to be half influenced by the shoulder and half by the elbow.

**10**   Finally, as shown in **Figure 6.18**, fine-tune the area with the softer brush and smaller opacity setting to get the shape just right.

This is a game model, so we're not going to get the elbow perfect, but we have a decent elbow deformation as it now stands. So while we have the skeleton in the arm, let's continue on and check the shoulder.

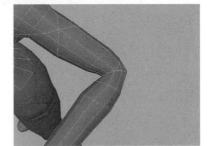
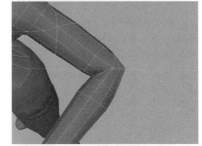
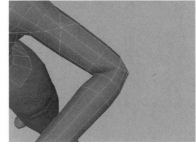

**FIGURE 6.18** Paint the elbow to achieve a satisfactory bend.

## Shoulder Weight Painting and Testing

The shoulder area can be quite tricky because it has three axes of rotation rather than one. Let's see how it looks when it is rotated.

1   To begin, make sure Kila's complete torso is fully weighted to the first joint, joint1. It should be completely white, as seen in **Figure 6.19**.

FIGURE 6.19 Fully weight the torso to the first joint in the skeleton.

2   Select the shoulder joint and rotate it down, so her arm is by her side, to see how it deforms. As you can see in **Figure 6.20**, it's not very good at the moment, but a little painting will sort this out.

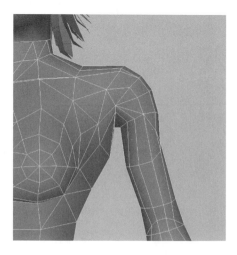

FIGURE 6.20 The shoulder before painting.

**3**  Begin by removing some of the shoulder's influence from the top of the shoulder and the area under her arm. Do this by selecting the first joint of the arm and using Add in the Paint Weights options to make these areas influenced more by this joint. This will reduce the amount they are affected by the shoulder joint.

**4**  When you're done, tweak the shoulder until it is smooth, with a gradual gradient (**Figure 6.21**).

We are almost there, but the armpit area seems too high up, making the shoulder look too thin.

**FIGURE 6.21** Adjust the weighting around the shoulder.

**5**  While still bound to the skeleton, we can adjust the vertices around the shoulder, bringing the armpit down slightly, as you can see in **Figure 6.22**. Mesh tweaks after binding are generally not a good idea, but in this case it doesn't cause a problem since we'll be detaching the skeleton toward the end of the chapter.

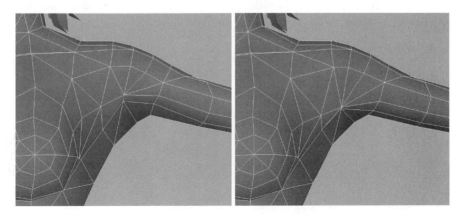

**FIGURE 6.22** Adjust the vertices to bring the armpit area down slightly.

As you can see in **Figure 6.23**, the shoulder now looks okay when deformed.

> **NOTE** ▸ Since we are still using a mirrored instance, the left side will deform just as the right does.

We're not yet finished with the shoulder. It bends in more than one direction, and we need to see how it looks when rotated around the other two axes. We've already worked on the Y axis, so let's reset the arm back to its default position and see how it looks when rotated around the X axis.

You will probably notice, as shown in **Figure 6.24**, that some minor pinching occurs. As with the elbow,

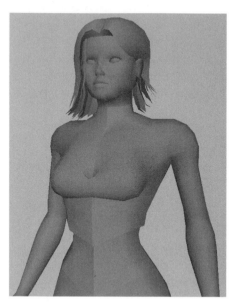

**FIGURE 6.23** The shoulder area now looks better when deformed.

we won't get the shoulder to look perfect at all angles, but the good news is that with a bit of creative weighting these problems can be minimized. There is little point in spending time to make these changes now, however. We are happy with the general topology of the shoulder at this point, so we will spend time adjusting the weights when we come to build the final rig.

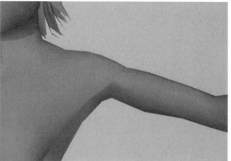

**FIGURE 6.24** Some areas still pinch, but we can fix these in the final rig.

## The Lower Body

Next we will look at how Kila's lower body reacts when we move her legs into extreme positions. The main area we will be looking at is where her legs join to her torso.

### Setting Up the Lower Body Skeleton

For our work on the lower body, we start by creating the skeleton that will drive the legs.

You only need to look at one of her legs, since they are more or less identical in construction. Just remember that if you make any changes to the left leg, you will have to copy these changes across to the right.

1    In the side view, switch your display to wireframe.

2    Create six joints at key points in the leg and foot. As illustrated in **Figure 6.25**, the first joint should be just below the waistline, at the top of the hip. This will be followed by joints placed at the hip, knee, ankle, the ball of the foot, and finally at the tip of the toes.

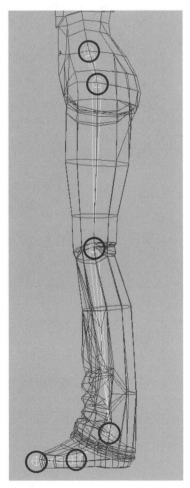

**FIGURE 6.25** Create the joints for the leg.

**3** Switch to the front view, and adjust the skeleton so it lies down the center of the left leg and foot (**Figure 6.26**).

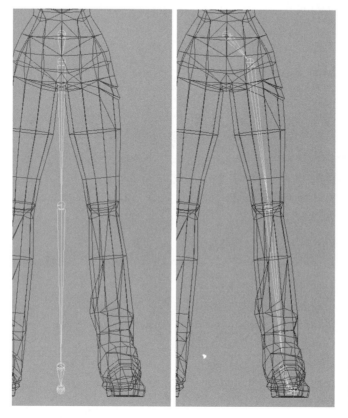

**FIGURE 6.26**
Position the joints down the center of her leg.

With the skeleton in place, we can now bind it to her trousers using the same procedure as before.

### Lower Torso Weight Painting and Testing

Let's see how the hip area of the torso looks when it is influenced by the skeleton.

**1** Before you begin properly testing the left leg, make sure the entire right leg and the top of the trousers are fully influenced by the first joint (**Figure 6.27**). This should be called joint5. You do this to pin down the leg you are not working on. If you don't, it will move when you rotate the joints and could become distracting.

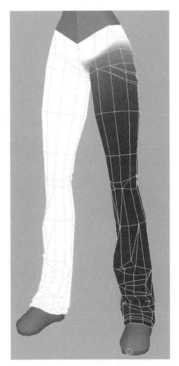

FIGURE 6.27 Fully weight the leg you are *not* working on to the first joint.

2    So let's see how things look when we bend the leg. First rotate the leg forward at the hip joint (**Figure 6.28**), and take a look at how it deforms.

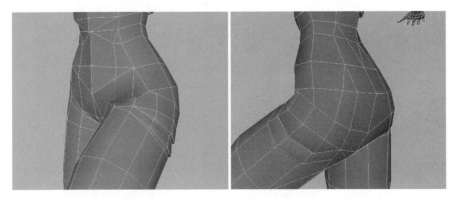

FIGURE 6.28 The initial deformation looks fair, but it needs some work.

3    Initially it's not looking too bad; now let's paint some of the weights to try
and smooth out the area. Begin by fully weighting the bulk of her thigh to
the hip joint.

Then go in with the smoother brush and, using Replace, smooth out her
backside and the crease at the front. **Figure 6.29** shows that we have a good
deformation, so there doesn't seem to be any need to add any polygons here.

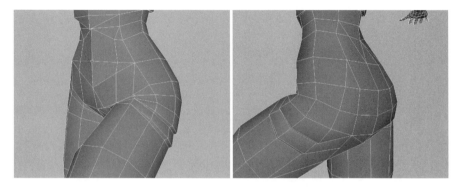

FIGURE 6.29 Tweak the weighting around her hip to smooth out the area.

4    Take a look at how the hip deforms if the leg is rotated back (**Figure 6.30**);
it reveals a few minor problems but nothing the weighting can't fix. The
same is true when the leg is rotated out to the side (**Figure 6.31**); it will look
better with some tweaking of the weights.

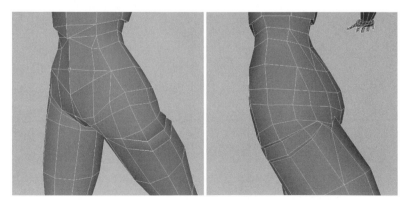

FIGURE 6.30 Rotating the leg back

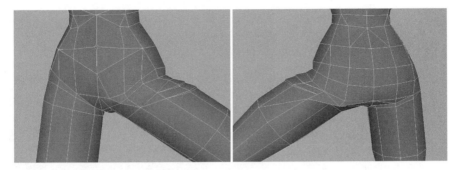

**FIGURE 6.31** Moving the leg out to the side

There are a few areas in the lower torso area that pinch and deform incorrectly, but these can be fixed by spending some time on the weighting, something we will cover in Chapter 14, "Final Character Deformation."

The thigh doesn't need any additional geometry, so let's move on.

### Knee Weight Painting and Testing

Our next painting and testing site is the knee. As you have done with the other joints, rotate it to see how it looks initially (**Figure 6.32**, top).

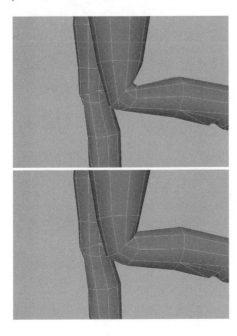

**FIGURE 6.32** Bend the knee and paint the area to fill out the shape.

By now, we know that we will need to adjust the weighting to get a proper shape. Make sure the lower leg is fully weighted to the knee, and then fine-tune the weights around the knee to retain the shape of the leg. The resulting shape should resemble **Figure 6.32** (bottom).

The knee area looks fine; like the hip area, there's no additional geometry needed.

Up to now we haven't had to make any alterations to the main leg—which is good because it means we don't have to do anything to her right leg. As you can see in **Figure 6.33** you can now deform almost all of the limbs.

### Foot Weight Painting and Testing

The final area to test in the leg is her ankle. Judging by the topology, this, too, will be fine; but you have to be certain before moving on to the next chapter. So let's take a look.

**FIGURE 6.33** Almost all of the limbs can now form correctly.

1   First, reset the joints in her leg by right-clicking the joints and selecting Assume Preferred Angle from the marking menu.

2   Go into wireframe mode, and this time select both the ankle joint and ball joint. We don't need the upper leg joints to influence her foot, so there's no need to select them or the tip of her toe.

3   Hold Shift and select the mesh that makes up her foot, then bind them (**Figure 6.34**). In the Smooth Bind options, make sure Bind To is set to Selected Joints, or the foot will be bound to the entire skeleton.

Select the ankle and ball joints before selecting the foot for binding.

4   As shown in **Figure 6.35** (left), rotate the ankle down and the ball of the foot up, so that Kila is standing on her toes. Then go ahead and edit the weighting information on the foot. We need the back of the foot weighted to the ankle joint, and the front of the foot to the ball joint (**Figure 6.35**, middle).

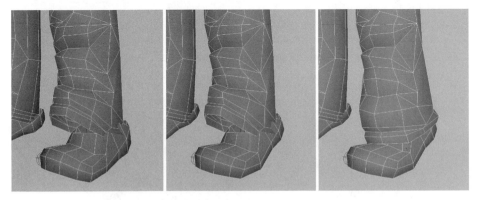

Work on weighting the foot.

5   Next, work on the base of her jeans leg, making the very bottom fully weighted to the ankle joint before gradually smoothing it out up to her shin area (**Figure 6.35**, right).

The only area that is a concern now is the underneath part of her shoe, mainly the front sole. The polygons are laid out now so that the base appears concave when the foot bends. Adjusting the topology as shown in **Figure 6.36** will easily solve this, but we will need to do it when we detach the geometry from the skeleton. In addition, notice that we can reduce the sole, removing the vertices that run down the middle.

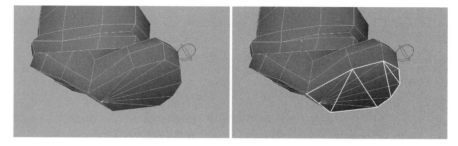

FIGURE 6.36 Adjust the topology of the sole as shown, to remove the concave look.

6   We are now happy with the way the lower body deforms, so let's detach the geometry from the skeleton. First reset the joints in the arm and leg so that they are back in their original positions. Then select the geometry and go to Skin > Detach Skin.

7   Now we can quickly fix the sole of the foot. First hide the joints by going to the view panel's Show menu and deselecting Joints. Then work on the foot until you have the sole looking similar to **Figure 6.37** (right).

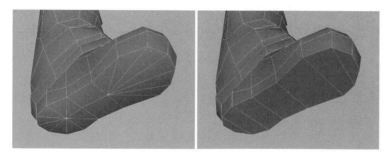

FIGURE 6.37 Optimize the base of the foot.

After finishing your work on the lower body, make sure you delete the history from each piece of geometry.

## Face Deformation

Animating facial expressions, particularly using blend shapes, can be difficult and time consuming. Early testing at this stage is imperative, to guarantee that you won't have to redo work at a later stage.

The best approach for testing the face is to try and create some of the more extreme facial expressions your lead artist has indicated will be needed for the character, and see how it holds up. These could include a shouting face with the mouth wide open, and maybe a face with the lips puckered up and eyes closed.

1    Begin by hiding everything that is not related to the face. **Figure 6.38** shows what you should be left with: just the head and eyes.

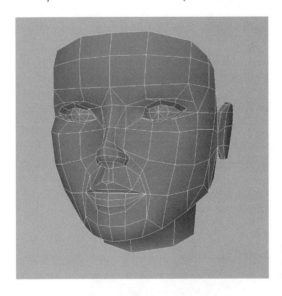

**FIGURE 6.38** Create a duplicate of the current head and eyes to work on.

2    Create a copy of these elements to work on, and hide the originals.

> **NOTE** We work on copies so that we don't inadvertently edit the main head. We'd have problems if we couldn't undo an operation or get back to the base geometry.

3    Place the duplicate head and eyes into a group, calling it Angry, and begin working on this piece to create an angry, shouting look like the one in **Figure 6.39**. You can achieve this by simply moving vertices, but make sure you edit both sides of the face.

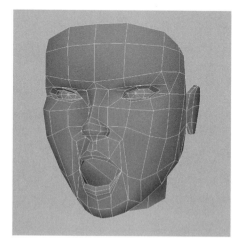

**FIGURE 6.39** Create an angry, shouting face.

4    While editing the face, look out for any areas that don't deform correctly. In particular, look for polygons that appear concave when adjusted.

The main face looks okay, but the lips may cause a problem when animated. At the moment the upper and lower lips meet in the corners; the resulting pinch is unnatural and may cause some rendering artifacts (**Figure 6.40**, left). To prevent this, we want the lips to form a complete loop, as shown in **Figure 6.40** on the right.

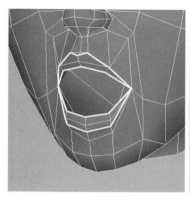 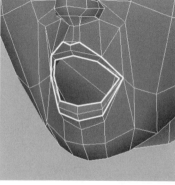

**FIGURE 6.40** As is, the lips will not animate well.

1   Focus in on the lips of the original head model (**Figure 6.41a**).

2   As shown in **Figure 6.41b**, create a cut around the outside of the corners of the lips.

3   Weld all the new vertices together, creating the new outside edge of the lips (**Figure 6.41c**).

4   Select the edges leading into the old corner of the lips and use the Flip Triangle Edge tool (Edit Polygons > Flip Triangle Edge) to rotate them (**Figures 6.41d** and **6.41e**).

5   Convert the polygons highlighted in **Figure 6.41f** into quads.

6   Adjust the lips, fixing the overall shape.

In this state, the lips don't look much different, but when we open her mouth again (**Figure 6.42**) you will see the difference.

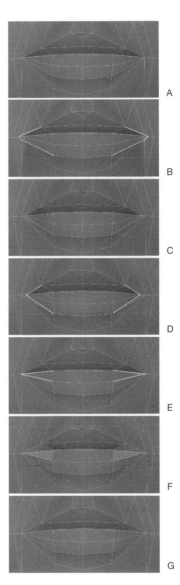

A

B

C

D

E

F

G

FIGURE 6.41 Alter the lips, removing the pinch that occurs in the corners when they animate.

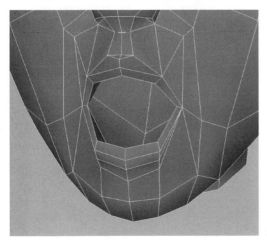

FIGURE 6.42 The new mouth

Let's test another facial expression.

**1** Hide the Angry face group, and create another duplicate of the original. Call it Pucker and group it.

**2** Test the eyes and lips by closing the eyes and puckering up the lips (**Figure 6.43**).

**3** When I generated this face, I noticed a few minor areas that could use improvement:

▶ The eyeballs were too far forward, so I had to move them back. This meant I had to edit the shape of the eyes slightly.

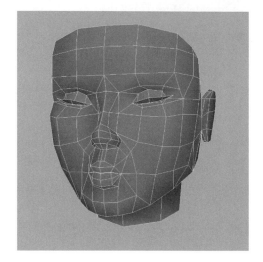

**FIGURE 6.43** Sculpt the face to close the eyes and pucker the lips.

▶ Looking from the side, the eyelids were almost flat. A real eyelid follows the curve of the eyeball, so I adjusted the vertices to correct the overall shape.

**4** Now we implement all the alterations we did for our duplicates in our main model and we are done.

The face will now hold up to the mouth being opened wide and also tightly closed. The eyes will successfully open and close, too. Deformation testing is now complete.

Save your work as Kila_DeformTest.mb.

## Summary

In this chapter, we have seen how to use Maya's binding tools. After several chapters of hard work, a great deal has been accomplished. The Kila model is now ready to be textured. We have modeled her, optimized her, and checked her to make sure she will deform correctly. It's time to set Kila aside now, and put what we've learned to use in creating our second character model—Grae.

# CHAPTER 7
# Modeling Grae

**WE HAVE ONE** of our character models complete now, but before we go on to apply mapping and texture to Kila, let's see what you have learned so far. Modeling Grae is our next task, and instead of covering each step in detail, I will briefly skim through each section of Grae's creation, highlighting any key areas that differ from Kila's creation. You'll be able to test your knowledge, and you can refer back to the previous chapters for help if you need it.

## The Torso and Limbs

We have the model sheet and, in **Figure 7.1**, the color render of the character Grae, which you should scan into the computer. To start off, we must bring these into Maya as image planes before moving on to create the base shapes that will form his torso and limbs.

**FIGURE 7.1**
Grae's render

1   Split the model sheet up and get the images imported into Maya as image planes, then positioned and scaled correctly as in **Figure 7.2**. Save the file as Grae_Start.mb.

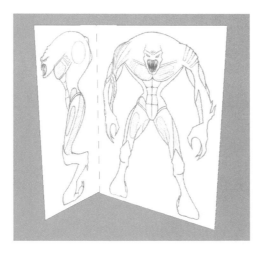

**FIGURE 7.2** Bring the front and side views into Maya.

**2**   Create the three base cylinders that will be his left arm, leg, and his torso.

> ▶   Set the first two cylinders to have a Radius of 0.4, Height of 4, and enter 10 for both Subdivisions Around Axis and Subdivisions Along Height. Leave all the other settings for now.

> ▶   Set the third cylinder to have the same dimensions, except Subdivisions Around Axis, which you'll set at 8. This will be his torso.

Position the three cylinders so they are in the correct place and orientation, using the image planes as reference.

**3**   Starting with the arm, adjust the vertices to more closely match the curves of the arm in the image plane. First work in the front view (**Figure 7.3**), before moving on to the side view (**Figure 7.4**). Remember to rotate each row of vertices to match the orientation of the arm.

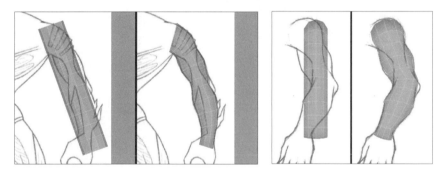

**FIGURE 7.3** Adjust the vertices on the arm in the front and side views.

**4**   Next work on the torso, first adjusting the vertices in the front view. When you're happy with it, delete the left side of the mesh, leaving you with one-half as seen in **Figure 7.4c**.

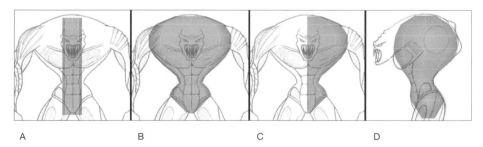

A          B          C          D

**FIGURE 7.4** Work on the shape of the torso.

**5**    Continue working on the torso from the side view (**Figure 7.4d**).

**6**    We now come to the leg. Because Grae's leg is such a unique shape, you'll find it easier to begin working on it in the side view as seen in **Figure 7.5**. Try your best to match the way the leg bends, but don't worry if you get angular areas or long polygons; we can fix these later on. As you can see in **Figure 7.5** (middle), we just want the general shape mapped out. When you are satisfied with the side, switch to the front view and continue shaping (**Figure 7.5**, right).

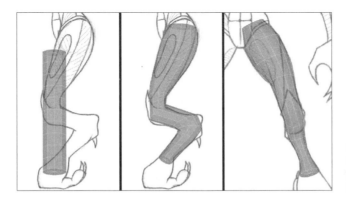

FIGURE 7.5 Map out the shape for the leg from the side and front views.

The main body is now blocked out; your geometry should now match that in **Figure 7.6**.

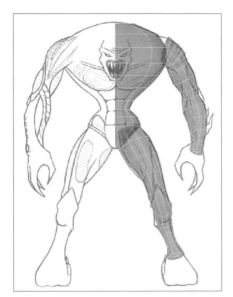

FIGURE 7.6 The main body blocked out prior to stitching

Before you continue to the next section, where we combine all three pieces (arm, leg, and torso), remove the caps from each cylinder. This opens them up so we can stitch them together.

### Stitching Together

Time now to use the modeling tools you were introduced to in the first few chapters. We will combine the separate pieces of the model, making it a whole element.

#### Arm and Torso

Begin by stitching the arm to the torso.

1  In order to stitch the shoulder to the torso, you first need to combine them, making them a single object.

2  Extrude the edges at the upper arm until they intersect with the torso. You can see this in **Figure** 7.7 (middle).

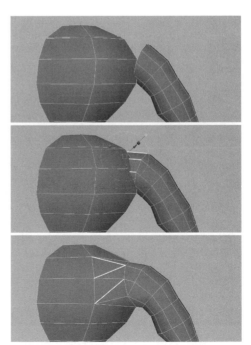

3  Snap and weld the vertices that lie closest to each other. Don't worry if you have a few spare vertices; you can split the existing polygons on the torso to create new vertices for welding, as seen in **Figure** 7.7 (bottom).

4  Adjust the vertices to smooth out the area, remembering to remove any internal faces.

Now let's attach the leg to the lower torso.

**FIGURE 7.7** Extrude the upper arm so that you can stitch it to the torso.

### Lower Torso and Leg

Before attaching the leg, it would be helpful to subdivide the large polygons at the bottom of the torso. This split is shown in **Figure 7.8**.

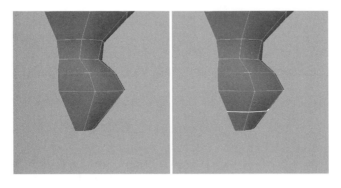

FIGURE 7.8 Subdivide the large polygons at the bottom of the torso.

**1**  Combine the leg to the rest of the body, and then snap and weld the vertices that lie closest together (or that make the most sense to weld).

**2**  You will undoubtedly have a few vertices remaining, so split the polygons on the torso to accommodate these (**Figure 7.9**).

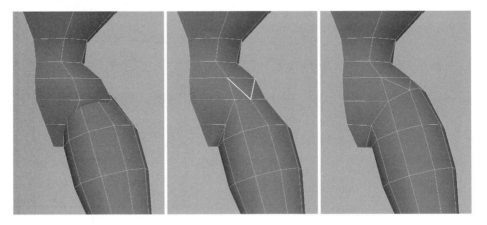

FIGURE 7.9 Join the leg using the same method used to attach the arm.

**3**  Work on the area of the join, smoothing it out and removing any internal polygons.

The basic shape of half the character is now in place, but before proceeding we will alter Grae's pose.

## Arm Position Adjustment

When we began modeling Kila, we raised her arm prior to attaching it, making it easier to work on later. We didn't do this for Grae; instead, we'll raise his arm now. Recall that a single object has a pivot, which we can manipulate. With Kila's arm, we moved it to the shoulder so that we could rotate the arm correctly. We can't do that here because Grae's arm is already attached to the torso; if we were to rotate his arm, the rest of the body would follow.

Luckily, not only objects have pivots; a selection of components has one, too.

**1**    Select the vertices that make up the arm, making sure the Rotate manipulator is active.

**FIGURE 7.10** Edit the selection's pivot so you can rotate the arm.

**2**    Press Insert to enable the selection's pivot, and move it up to the shoulder (**Figure 7.10**, middle).

**3**    Press Insert again to return to the previous manipulator, and rotate the arm upward along the Z axis (**Figure 7.10**, right).

You now have a single mesh that makes up the left side of Grae; all he needs is a head. Now would be a good time to save; call this file Grae_Combined.mb.

## Creating Grae's Head

Looking at his design, we can see that Grae doesn't really have a neck, so we will move straight on to his head.

1   As with Kila, you will begin with a cube. Create one and set Subdivisions Along Width, Subdivisions Along Height, and Subdivisions Along Depth all to 4.

2   Move, scale, and rotate the cube so it fits the size and orientation of Grae's head in the image plane (**Figure 7.11**).

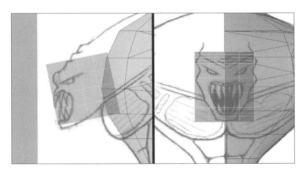

**FIGURE 7.11**
Manipulate the cube so it lies over the head in the image plane.

3   Delete half the cube, and adjust the vertices to achieve the general shape of the head (**Figure 7.12**). Use a mirrored instance to help you get a feel for the whole head.

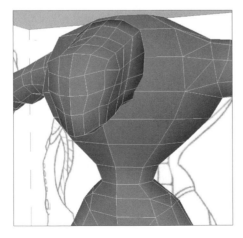

**FIGURE 7.12** Adjust the cube to get the basic head shape.

With Grae's head in place, let's now combine it with the rest of the geometry.

**Attaching the Head**

To complete the head and finish this section, attach the head shape to the rest of the body.

**1**  First we need to remove some polygons. Select the area of Grae's chest directly behind the head shape and delete them. Also, remove any polygons that exist on the back of the head geometry.

**2**  Combine the head and body geometry; then use the Append To Polygon tool to fill in the gaps, bridging the head and the torso.

**3**  Play around with the vertices, using a mirrored instance to help you work on the whole figure. Do this until you are happy with the way Grae looks (**Figure 7.13**).

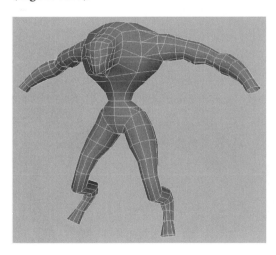

**FIGURE 7.13** The head is now attached to the rest of the body.

Delete the history on your model and save it as Grae_Basic.mb.

## Muscle Line Mapping

We now have a shape that resembles Grae, although it still needs a lot of work. He is quite a muscular character, so it's important that we map the muscle lines at this stage, sculpting in some of the more prominent muscles on his torso and upper arm.

Mapping the muscle lines will improve the model not just visually, but technically as well. Creating polygons that follow the correct muscle structure will help when it deforms later—the polygons will deform correctly and give the impression of real muscles moving under the skin.

### The Chest, Shoulder, and Arm

Let's begin work on the upper body by mapping his chest; then we'll move across to work on his armpit, shoulder, and arm.

1 Following **Figure 7.14**, add more detail to the chest, making it more pronounced. Carve in the collarbone, just above it.

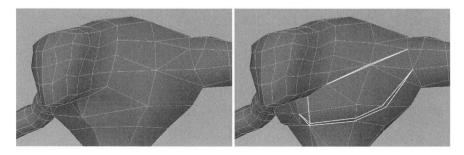

FIGURE 7.14 Add a bit more detail to Grae's chest.

**2** Add further definition to the front of Grae's shoulder before working on the armpit. The shoulder needs to be nicely rounded when it deforms, so add an extra division to help smooth out the area (**Figure 7.15**).

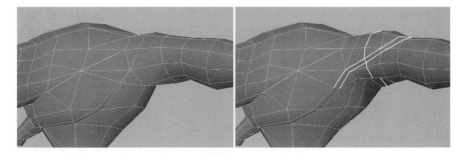

FIGURE 7.15 Defining the shoulder and armpit

**3** Now start on the front of his arm. Use the Split Polygon tool to carve in the muscles, as seen in **Figure 7.16**.

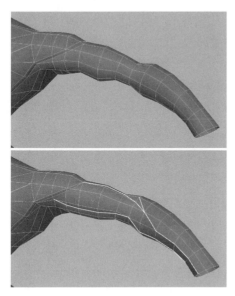

FIGURE 7.16 Carve in the muscle lines at the front of his arm.

**4** Following **Figure 7.17**, move around to the back of the arm, working on the shoulder. Don't be afraid to alter the shape of the arm slightly if the character needs it.

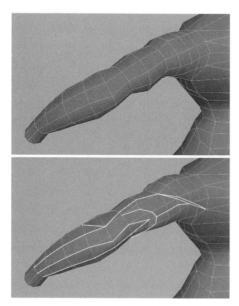

FIGURE 7.17 The back of the arm and shoulder

When you're satisfied with the chest, shoulder, and arm, we will proceed to map the muscles of his torso.

### The Torso

Let's work on his back first.

**1** Delete the edges highlighted in **Figure 7.18** (middle). This will clean the back up to get it ready for carving in the muscle detail. This is illustrated in **Figure 7.18** (right).

**2** Rotate around to Grae's front, and incorporate the stomach muscles. As happened with the back, you'll need to do some cleanup. Follow **Figure 7.19** and divide the polygon that makes up his chest so you can add more shape to it, making it less flat and angular.

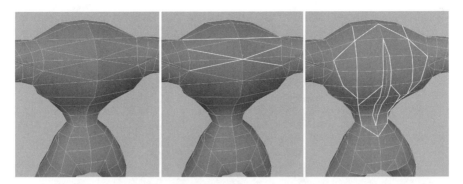

FIGURE 7.18 Map the muscles to the back.

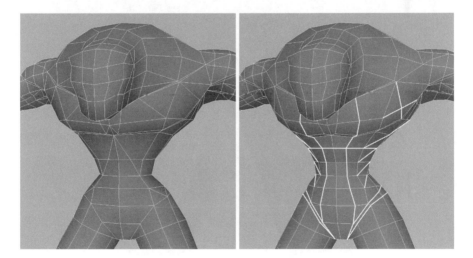

FIGURE 7.19 Split polygons to add the stomach muscles.

We are finished with the upper body, so let's move on to his legs.

## The Legs

At this point, we will add the muscles to the upper legs only, as shown in **Figures 7.20** and **7.21** (top). We won't do the lower part of the legs because they need quite a bit of work done to them, coming up in the section, "Adding Details." If we added muscle lines now, we'd just lose them.

While we are here working on the legs, we can also improve Grae's backside (**Figure 7.21**, bottom). Notice the three large polygons just below the base of his spine. Divide these and work on the overall area to smooth it out.

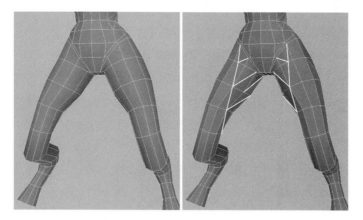

FIGURE 7.20 Cut the muscles into the front of the upper legs.

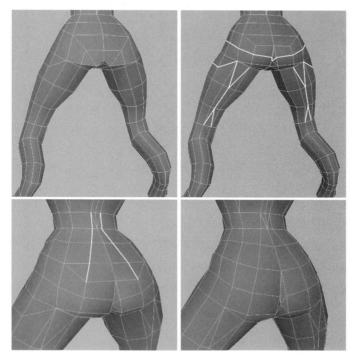

FIGURE 7.21 Move around to the back, adding muscles and detail to the legs and backside.

The basic muscles are mapped onto Grae now, and we have added definition to some areas, smoothing them out to make them look more complete (**Figure 7.22**).

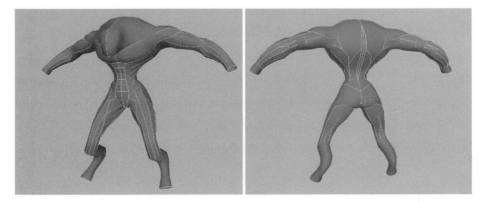

FIGURE 7.22 Grae with muscles mapped

Save Grae in his current state as Grae_Muscles.mb. He's coming along nicely, so let's start adding some details.

## Adding Details

With Grae's muscles now in place, we can begin to flesh the model out. We'll start at the top and work our way down, adding details as we go, leaving the head, hands, and feet until last.

In the color render, Grae has some impressive definition, but we don't need to model it all. Most of the detail will be drawn on with the texture, we can then use some texture effects to bring the detail out of the model (more on these in Chapter 9, "Texture Painting"). After modeling Kila, you should have a good idea of what to look for when adding particular features to Grae. Here are some reminders:

▶   Check for large polygons that make areas look flat and angular. These can be subdivided to smooth the area out while also allowing it to deform better.

▶   Keep an eye open for small polygons that add nothing to the overall look of the mesh. As the model will be viewed from a distance for the majority of the time, these can be deleted.

▶ Finish with a clean, grid-style mesh, quadrangulating the mesh wherever possible to make it easier to read.

▶ Focus on the model as a whole; rotate around it checking its silhouette to make sure the edges flow smoothly.

With these guidelines in mind, let's start with a look at the main part of Grae's body.

### Body Detail

The first area we can enhance is at the very top of the model, at the back of the shoulders; you can see in **Figure 7.23** that it is presently quite angular for such a large area.

1    Using the Split Polygon tool, divide up the larger polygons and smooth the area out (**Figure 7.23**, right).

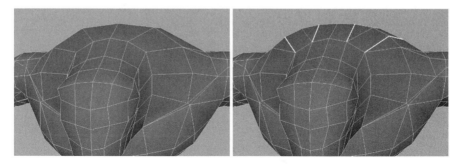

**FIGURE 7.23** Smooth out the very top of Grae, making the back of his shoulders less angular.

2    Next add some detail to his stomach muscles by extruding the faces (**Figure 7.24**). Select all the faces that make up the stomach area and go to Edit Polygons > Extrude Face. As you move the blue arrow outward, each face will be extruded along its normal, the direction it is facing.

Earlier in the book we set Keep Faces Together to always be on (Polygons > Tool Options > Keep Faces Together). With this active, all the extruded faces will be welded, making the stomach area one single mass. In this case, though, we need each face to extrude separately.

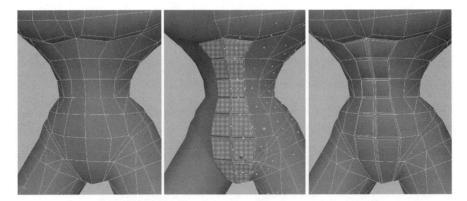

FIGURE 7.24 Extrude the faces of the stomach for more definition.

**3**   Look in the Channel Box for the attribute Keep Faces Together and set it to off. Then use the green and red cubes at the end of each arrow to scale each face inward (**Figure 7.24**, middle). Finally, smooth the hard edges and you are done (**Figure 7.24**, right).

> **NOTE** ▶ If your budget won't allow the extra geometry, you could rely on the texture to add this detail to the stomach instead. Adding a bump map (see Chapter 9), or even a normal map (see Appendix A, "Normal Mapping in Maya"), will give the illusion of detailed geometry, even where there is none. This being said, these two techniques do have their restrictions and cannot always be used effectively.

Before continuing, keep looking around the main body for areas you can improve by smoothing and adding detail. Once you are completely happy with the shape, proceed to the next area—his lower legs and feet.

## Leg Detail

We skipped the lower legs earlier because there was no point in working on them until now. At the moment, they are pretty basic and are in dire need of some detail, so let's add some.

### Lower Legs

As demonstrated in **Figure 7.25**, we will begin by dividing up this portion of the leg at the first knee-bend. There are sections of large polygons here making the area look flat and angular, so add two divisions above the knee and three more below it. Using the guide images in your image planes, tweak these new divisions to get the correct shape.

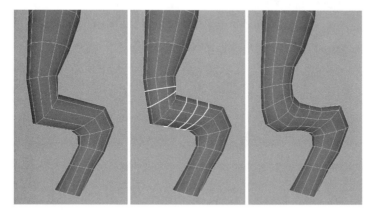

**FIGURE 7.25** Divide the flat areas around the knee.

Staying with the knee, let's add some definition. The following steps are illustrated in **Figure 7.26**.

A                                    B

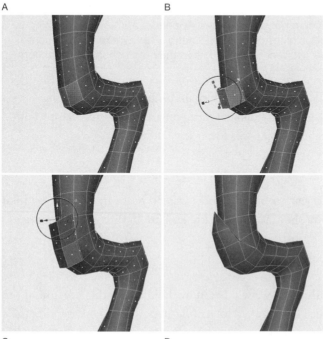

C                                    D

**FIGURE 7.26** Add detail to the front of the knee.

1   Select the three faces at the front of the knee (**Figure 7.26a**).

2   Use the Extrude Face tool (leaving Divisions set at 1) to pull these faces out (**Figure 7.26b**).

3   Select the top of the extrusion and use the Extrude Face tool again, this time setting Divisions to 2. Pull the extrusion upward in front of the leg (**Figure 7.26c**).

4   Work on the new faces, collapsing the top edges to create the point (**Figure 7.26d**). Don't delete the inner, back faces created by the extrusion as these could be seen as the character moves around.

Let's move on to the next joint in his leg, the one at the back. Again, this looks quite angular, so add some new divisions and adjust them to smooth out the joint. As you can see in **Figure 7.27**, these divisions don't need to go all the way around the leg.

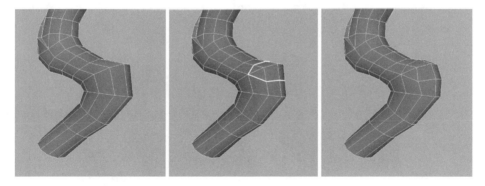

FIGURE 7.27 Add new divisions to the next joint.

With the overall shape of the leg in place, we can next work in some more detail, adding the knuckle to the back of the leg.

### *Back Leg Knuckle*

Let's begin by adding the top part of the knuckle. Do this by extruding the three faces shown in **Figure 7.28** and then adjusting the vertices to get the right shape.

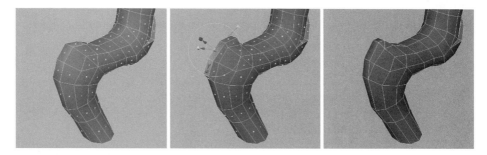

FIGURE 7.28 Extrude the faces at the back of the leg to create the knuckle.

The final leg area we will build, before moving on to the foot, is just below the knuckle at the back of the leg. This is where the first claw will exist. You can add this easily using a procedure (**Figure 7.29**) similar to that just used to create the knee.

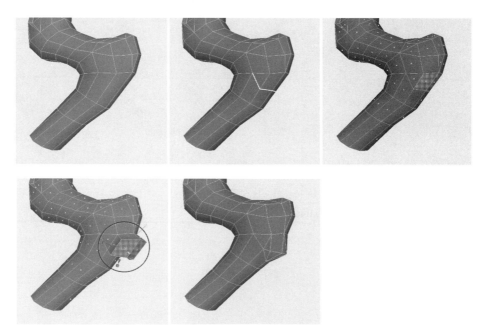

FIGURE 7.29 Add extra geometry so you can create the root for the leg claw.

## The Foot, with Three Toes and Claws

Now we've arrived at Grae's foot. Currently no geometry exists for this, so, following **Figure 7.30**, extrude the edges at the bottom of the lower leg and scale them to fit the general shape of the foot. Then switch to the front view and scale the vertices again, so that the bottom-front of the leg matches what you see in the image plane.

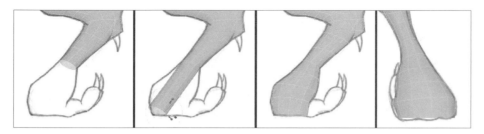

**FIGURE 7.30** Add new divisions to the next joint.

Next, we are going to create the three toes, so save your current model and start a new scene. All three toes are the same, so we can save time by creating one toe and then duplicating it for the other two.

**1**   In the new scene, create a cube with a Width and Height of 1 and a Depth of 3. Set Subdivisions Along Width to 2, Subdivisions Along Height to 3, and Subdivisions Along Depth to 5 (**Figure 7.31a**).

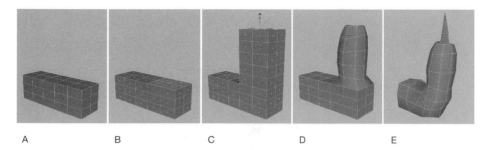

A          B          C          D          E

**FIGURE 7.31** Sculpt the toe from a basic cube and add a claw.

**2**   Following **Figure 7.31b**, select four faces on the top nearest the front.

**3**   Extrude these faces up, making sure that the extrusion has four divisions (**Figure 7.31c**).

**4**   Sculpt the block, making the shape of the toe.

To complete the toe, we will create a claw that sits on the tip. The claw is constructed out of a simple cylinder, which is then tapered to create the point. You can see the finished toe in **Figure 7.31e**.

**5**   Create a cylinder with Subdivisions Around Axis set to 4 and Subdivisions Along Height set to 3.

**6**   Remove the bottom faces that create the cap.

**7**   Weld all the top vertices together to create the point.

**8**   Adjust the other vertices to create the claw shape then position it where the claw should be.

**9**   Finally combine the toe and the claw.

Clean up the scene and save as Grae_Toe.mb.

Now let's bring the toe into the same scene as the main model and combine them.

**1**   Load your current Grae model and import the toe into the scene.

**2**   Position the central toe first. Then duplicate it twice for the other two (**Figure 7.32**), making sure you rotate the outer ones out slightly so all three toes aren't parallel.

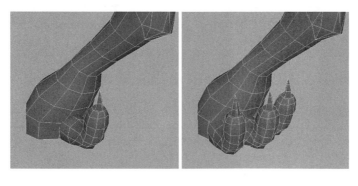

**FIGURE 7.32**
Import the toe and duplicate it, creating three.

**3**   Combine all the toes with the main model so we can stitch them together, creating a single piece of geometry.

**4**  Remove all the rear faces from the main foot, as seen in **Figure 7.33** (left).

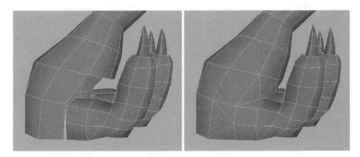

FIGURE 7.33 Stitch the toes to the foot.

**5**  Use the Append to Polygon tool to fill in the gaps between the foot and the toes (**Figure 7.33**, right).

**6**  To finish Grae's leg, spend some time adding detail to the main foot. Fill in and round the bottom, adding hooflike creases to the front, as shown in **Figure 7.34**.

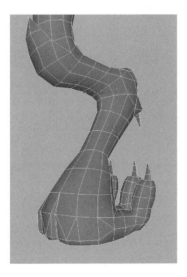

FIGURE 7.34
Add definition
to the foot.

Now create a mirrored instance of the foot and have a look at the model as a whole. Ask yourself if the model looks correct—how are the proportions? Then make any necessary adjustments.

When done, delete the history and save as Grae_WithFeet.mb.

### Creating Grae's Hands

Each of Grae's upper arms is quite different from the other, so we will tackle the hands next because these are the last parts of the model that are similar. This will bring the arms to a stage where we can edit them separately.

We are not going to waste time creating the hands from scratch, since we already have a hand model we can use: Kila's. We'll chop the hand off Kila's latest model, adjust it, and use it for Grae.

1   Load the last version of Kila you worked on, Kila_DeformTest.mb.

2   As illustrated in **Figure 7.35**, select the faces that make up her left hand.

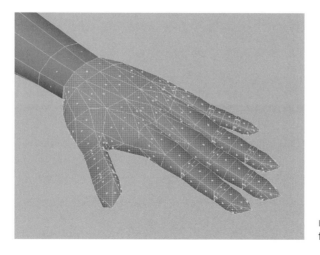

FIGURE 7.35 Select the faces you want to extract.

3   Go to Edit Polygons > Extract and open up the options for this tool. Make sure that Separate Extracted Faces is checked, and then click Extract.

4   The hand is now detached. Select it and go to File > Export Selection, and save the file as KilaOpHand.mb.

5   It's best to edit this hand while it's in its own scene, so load the hand file you just exported.

To make the hand easier to edit, it should first be leveled out. The best way to do this is to select all of its vertices and correct the rotation, first in the top view and then the front. Note that this correction has already been done to the file of the same name on the CD (07 Kila_OpHand.mb).

With Kila's hand leveled out and ready to edit, we can proceed to adjust it to become Grae's. In the artwork, it looks like he only has two joints in each finger, whereas Kila's fingers (like ours) have three.

> **TIP** ▶ If you are unsure about any specifications check with your manager. Even something as simple as one fewer joint could create problems if you make an incorrect assumption.

**6**  Remove the extra polygons used for the third joints of each of Kila's fingers (**Figure 7.36**, middle).

**7**  With these polygons removed, go ahead and alter the hand until it looks more like Grae's (**Figure 7.36**, right).

**FIGURE 7.36** Edit Kila's hand to get Grae's.

When you're finished, save the new hand as Grae_Hand.mb.

As you can see, you can easily achieve other, different hand styles by altering one base hand. There is no need to remodel a new hand completely from scratch. Next we will attach this new hand model to Grae's arm in the main model.

**1**  Load the file called Grae_WithFeet.mb.

**2**  Import the new hand into the scene, manipulating it until it's the correct size and has the proper orientation and position.

3    Combine the hand with the rest of the geometry and weld the wrist area, making it solid and removing any gaps (**Figure 7.37**).

FIGURE 7.37 Import and attach Grae's new hand.

Save the file as Grae_WithHands.mb before you continue.

**Arm Detail**

With Grae's hands in place, we can now work on the rest of his arms. This time, since the arms are very different, we will first need to create two separate arms.

1    Remove the mirrored instance, if you have one, and then select the faces that make up the left arm (**Figure 7.38**). As it's mainly the lower arms that are different, we only need to select the polygons from the middle of the upper arm.

2    As you did with the hand, go to Edit Polygons > Extract to separate the arm from the torso.

3    The pivot for the arm will automatically be in the center of the world, so you can safely duplicate and mirror it without any adjustments. Select the arm and go to Edit > Duplicate, making sure you have set the Scale value in the options to -1.

4    To finish, delete the history on all three meshes and freeze the transformations, which will reset the −1 Scale value back to 1.

5    To help balance things out, create a mirrored instance of the main body.

As you can see in **Figure 7.39**, you now have a full character again—but you can now work on each arm independently. So let's add the arm detail.

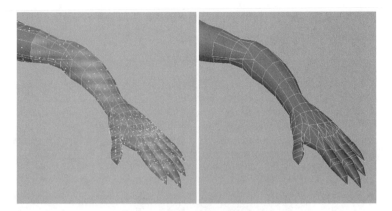

FIGURE 7.38 Detach the main part of the left arm.

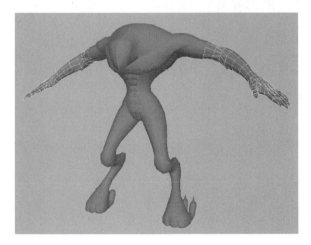

FIGURE 7.39 The full character with separate arms

**Figure 7.40** shows the progression of the left arm. Carve in the detail around the upper arm before using extrusions to create the two spikes.

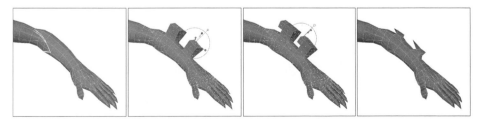

FIGURE 7.40 Add detail to the left arm.

Following **Figure 7.41**, work on the right arm. Thin down the upper section before using a cylinder to create the area underneath.

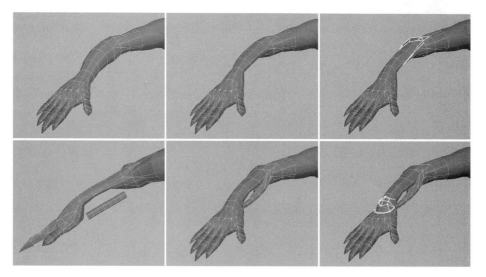

FIGURE 7.41 Add detail to the right arm.

Look around the whole mesh now for any other spots where you can add definition or improve the shape (**Figure 7.42**). When you are completely happy, save your work and move on.

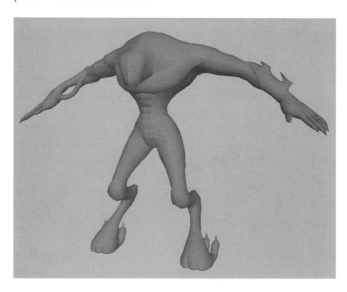

FIGURE 7.42
The Grae character
so far

### Giving Grae a Face

We have arrived at the final part of the main model for Grae, the face. To create Grae's face, including the open mouth with all those menacing teeth, we will follow the same procedure we used for Kila's more agreeable countenance in Chapter 3.

### *Outer Face*

**Figure 7.43** illustrates the following instructions for creating the majority of Grae's face.

1   Begin by selecting the polygons that make up the face, and subdivide them by going to Edit Polygons > Subdivide (**Figure 7.43b**).

2   Work on the head vertices until you get the general shape (**Figure 7.43c**).

3   When you're happy with the overall shape, move on to the mouth. Build in the lips, and remove polygons to create the cavity of his open mouth (**Figure 7.43d**).

4   Carve in the eyes by cutting the outline into the mesh and deleting the inner faces (**Figure 7.43e**). Create a sphere to act as a dummy eye so you can achieve the correct shape for the eyelids.

5   Finally, work on the whole head, making adjustments until it is correct.

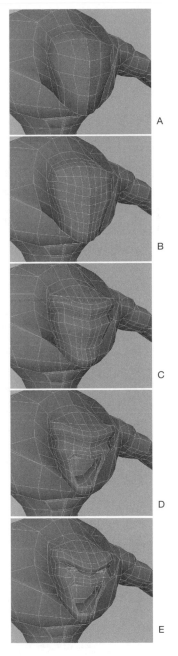

**FIGURE 7.43** Building Grae's face

### Teeth and Inner Mouth

With the outer face complete, we can build Grae's mouth, gums, and teeth. To begin, we will create a tooth the same way we created the claws for his feet. Then we can proceed to create the rest of his mouth, including his gums and inner mouth.

1   Create a basic cylinder with Subdivisions Around Axis set to 4 and Subdivisions Along Height set to 3.

2   Remove the top faces that create the cap of the cylinder.

3   Weld all the base vertices together to create the point.

4   Adjust the other vertices to create the tooth shape.

5   Position the first tooth as shown in **Figure 7.44** on the left. Then duplicate it for the rest of the teeth on the left side of Grae's mouth, scaling the new teeth to match the concept sketch.

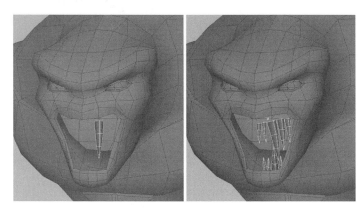

**FIGURE 7.44**
Create the teeth on the left first.

Grae's upper gums are visible in the concept artwork, so we'll follow **Figure 7.45** to build the gums into the teeth area.

1   Hide all the surrounding geometry, leaving just his teeth visible.

2   Combine all the teeth, making them a single object (**Figure 7.45a**).

3   Select the top-front row of edges and extrude them upward with three divisions (**Figure 7.45b**).

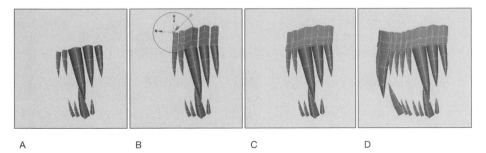

A                    B                    C                    D

**FIGURE 7.45** Combine the teeth and build in the gums.

**4**    Weld the vertices between the upper edges of the gums and the top of the teeth.

**5**    Adjust the new faces, creating the appearance of gums (**Figure 7.45c**).

**6**    Finally, duplicate and mirror the teeth, giving you the right side. Combine the two sides and weld the vertices down the center (**Figure 7.45d**).

**7**    To create the inner mouth, unhide the head geometry and extrude the edges around the lips inward to form the inside of the cheeks and throat. Remember to weld the back vertices so you can't see through the model.

Follow the procedure in the section "The Tongue" in Chapter 4 to build Grae a tongue. Alternatively, you could import Kila's and scale it up.

To finish off the head we need to give him some eyes. We can use the same method for creating them as we did with Kila in the section "Modeling the Eye" in Chapter 4. (Or we could just use the eye we've already made for her and import it into Grae.)

Grae's head is now complete (**Figure 7.46**).

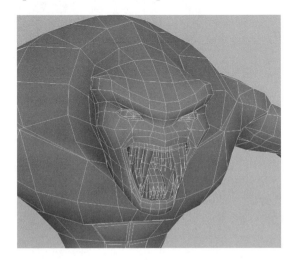

**FIGURE 7.46** The completed face of Grae

## Modeling the Wings

Grae has wings, and they're somewhat unconventional. His are constructed from separate strands rather than being two solid entities.

To build the wings, we have two options available to us:

▶   We can build the entire wing, modelling each strand separately.

▶   We can construct the wings out of several large, flat polygons; then the individual strands can be added in the form of a semi-transparent texture.

The first option would produce a better-looking result but would require plenty of polygons. In addition, we would need lots of joints in order to animate the wings; each strand would need at least 10 joints to animate successfully. Another plus is that we would need very little texture space.

What about the second option? Both wings could be created with under 60 polygons, and animation would require only a few joints. The downside: We would need more texture space for these wings. Let's go with this safer second option and see how the wings turn out.

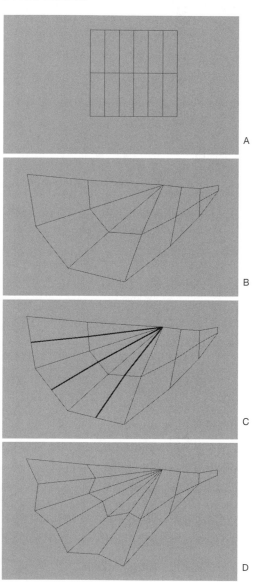

**FIGURE 7.47** Create and adjust a basic plane to get the wing shape.

Although the wings are not conventional, we still want them to animate like normal wings. That is, we want them to fan in and out as well as flap up and down. With this in mind, we will try and create the basic geometry of the wing by placing edges where the joints occur in a bat wing.

**1**  Start in a new scene. Create a polygonal plane by going to Create > Polygon Primitives > Plane. Configure the plane so it has six Subdivisions Along Width and two Subdivisions Along Height (**Figure 7.47a**).

**2**  Manipulate the plane's vertices until you have a credible wing shape, as illustrated in **Figure 7.47b**.

**3**  So that we can add a bit more shape to the wing, divide the larger spans (**Figure 7.47c**).

**4**  Edit the whole wing in the perspective view, making it less flat and more three-dimensional, as shown in **Figure 7.48**.

**FIGURE 7.48** Adjust the wing in the perspective view until it looks less flat.

**5**  Save the file as Grae_Wing.mb; then load the full Grae model file.

**6**  Import the wing and position it, duplicating it to make the wing on the other side.

Now, as you did with Kila, rotate around the entire model of Grae, making sure he is perfect before you proceed to optimization.

As shown in **Figure 7.49** the Grae model is now complete. Clean up the geometry and the scene, and save your work as Grae_Details.mb.

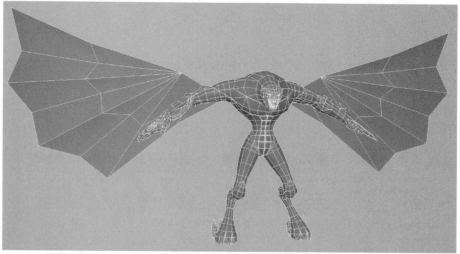

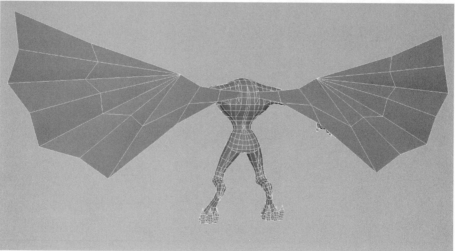

FIGURE 7.49 The Grae model, complete

## Optimization

Your next task is to optimize Grae, lowering the polygon count in the process. The limit for Grae was set at 5500; let's see how close we are to that.

**1**    Select all the geometry and go to Polygons > Triangulate.

**2**    Go to Display > Heads Up Display and make sure Poly Count is checked.

The current Grae model is 5394 polygons—not bad; we are already under our budget. As mentioned in Chapter 5, the purpose of optimization is not only to lower the polygon count; it's also a way to remove unwanted and unneeded polygons. Removing 100 polygons from Grae could mean more detail can be added elsewhere in the game—every polygon counts.

Lets recap what we're looking for as we optimize:

▶    Unnecessary Polygons—An unused polygon is one that neither adds to the shape of the mesh, nor aids in deformation.

▶    Shallow Angles—Polygons that make a shallow angle do add to the shape of the geometry, but in such a small way that no one would miss them if they were gone.

Most important during optimization is to keep zooming out of your mesh to see how it will look from the game perspective. Chances are, you will never see Grae's body up close, so don't leave too much fine detail in the model that would never be seen.

With these objectives in mind, let's begin optimization. Following is a brief overview of areas that could be optimized, starting from the top and working downward. First, the wings—they are really as low as they can go. We could reduce them further, but this could make them deform badly, so leave them alone. Hide them for now so you can concentrate on the rest of the body.

## Head and Inner Mouth

As shown in **Figure 7.50**, there isn't much we can remove from the head. What we can do is collapse a few edges, knocking a few polygons off the count. These edges are around the sides of the head, so removing them will not alter the overall shape.

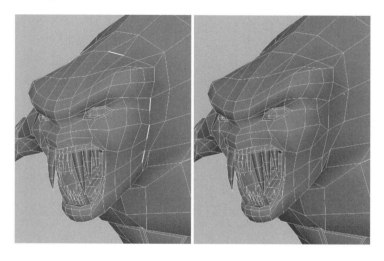

**FIGURE 7.50**
Optimizing the head

Moving on to the internal part of the head, hide everything except for the main, left side of Grae's body. Focus in on the inner mouth. There are a few edges inside here we can collapse, as highlighted in **Figure 7.51**. The inner mouth will have a basic texture and so does not need lots of detail. Removing these polygons won't cause any problems.

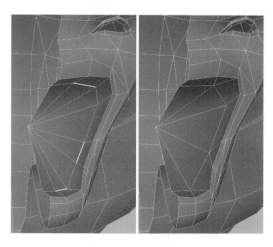

**FIGURE 7.51** Optimizing the inner mouth

Next, look at his teeth. To help your examination, isolate the teeth using the view's Show > Isolate Selected > View Selected command. The very top of the gums will be hidden inside the geometry making up the inner mouth. Therefore, we can afford to collapse some of the edges. This process is demonstrated in **Figure 7.52**.

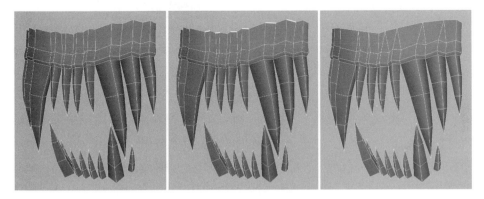

**FIGURE 7.52** Reduce the top of the gums.

We are done with the head, now let's look at the rest of the body.

## Main Body and Legs

First, there are a couple of extra polygons on his shoulder (**Figure 7.53**). These were created to show the muscles making up this area. Since these particular muscles could be defined with the texture, we can remove the detail here.

**FIGURE 7.53** Remove the extra detail from the shoulders.

Looking at the overall lower leg, we initially see two areas containing shallow curves, one on the thigh and the other on the lower leg (**Figure 7.54**). We can safely select the edges highlighted in the figure and collapse them.

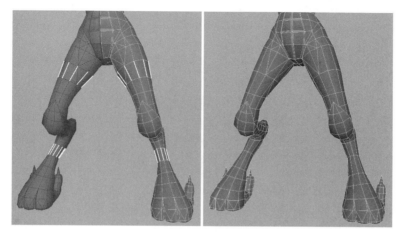

FIGURE 7.54 Remove the shallow angles from the legs.

Finally, we can do the same on the midsection of the leg, collapsing the edges shown in **Figure 7.55**.

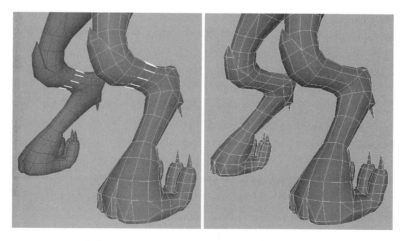

FIGURE 7.55 Collapse the edges on the midsection of the leg.

There isn't much more we can remove at this stage, but take a last look around your model and see if you can find anything. When you're ready, clean up the mesh and save the file as Grae_Optimized.mb.

# Deformation Testing

With the model complete and optimized, we've arrived at the final stage for Grae: testing how he deforms.

### Joint Creation

Initially, we need to insert joints for the arms and legs. Do this using Skeleton > Joint Tool as demonstrated in **Figures 7.56** and **7.57**.

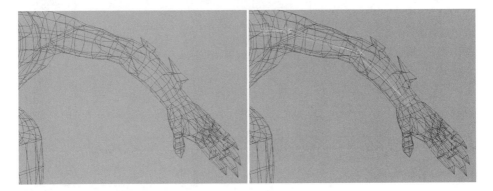

**FIGURE 7.56** Insert joints into the arm.

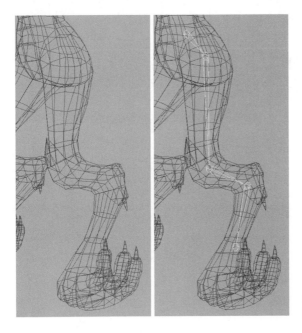

**FIGURE 7.57** Create the skeleton for the leg.

Since Grae's arms are not identical, it's best to test them separately. Instead of creating a new set of joints for the right arm, we can mirror the existing ones. The process in the following steps is illustrated in **Figure 7.58**.

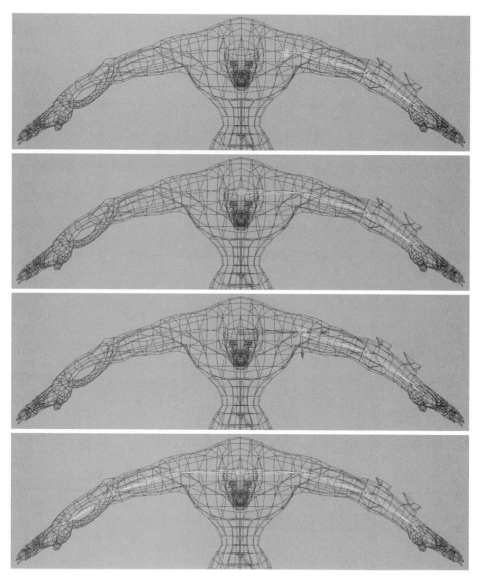

FIGURE 7.58 Mirror the joints to create the right arm.

**1**   Select the first joint of the arm, the one before the shoulder.

**2**   This joint needs to be moved across the X axis to the center of the model, so press Insert and reposition the joint as close to the center as possible.

**3**   When you're there, press Insert again to return to the normal translation mode.

> **TIP** You can make sure the joint is in the center by setting Translate X to 0 in the Channel Box.

**4**   Select the shoulder joint and go to Skeleton > Mirror Joint; make sure the options are set as shown in **Figure 7.59**. The principal setting to be sure of is Mirror Across, which dictates which way the mirror will take place. Set this to YZ.

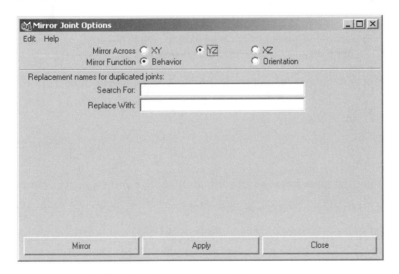

FIGURE 7.59 Options for mirroring the arm joints

Follow **Figure 7.60** to build up the joints for the wing. Initially you will have to create four separate sections, before parenting the smaller three to the main knuckle of the wing.

> **TIP** To accurately place the joints for the wing, you can point-snap each joint to the appropriate vertex by holding down V as you move them.

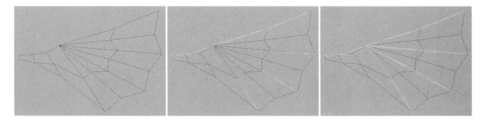

**FIGURE 7.60** Build the joints to deform the wing.

> **TIP** To parent one object to another, simply select the child, and then hold Shift and select the parent. Press P to complete the operation.

The basic joints are now in place and we are ready to begin binding them to the geometry. To make the binding process easier, we should first tidy the scene by renaming the objects that exist in it.

### Joint Renaming

Our scene is getting quite large, so let's tidy it up a little and make it easier to work with.

1   Open up your Outliner. Looking at **Figure 7.61** (left), you can see we have three main joints: joint1, joint5, and joint13. Next to these are plus icons (+), which tells us that other objects exist below these in the hierachy. Shift-click each of the plus icons to open up the joint objects (**Figure 7.61**, center).

> **NOTE** Holding Shift when you click opens the full hierarchy. Clicking without Shift will merely open the immediate child of the object.

2   Our collection of joints in the scene currently have names that aren't associated with what they will be deforming. It's a good idea at this point to rename the joints more appropriately (**Figure 7.61**, right).

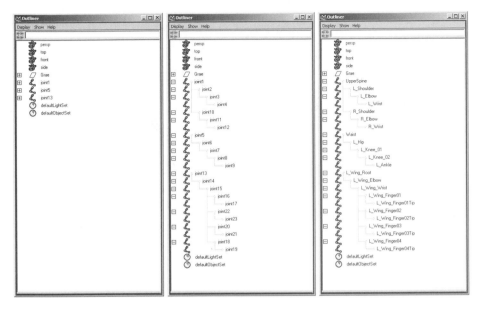

**FIGURE 7.61** Rename the joints that will move our character.

After spending time tidying the scene it would now be a good time to save.

### Binding and Testing
We will now test the deformation of the wing, so hide everything in the scene except the wing geometry and the skeleton.

**1**    Select the joints that make up the wing, so we can bind them to the wing itself. You can quickly do this by selecting the root joint and going to Edit > Select Hierarchy.

**2**    Hold Shift and select the wing; then go to Skin > Bind Skin > Smooth Bind in the Animation menu set.

**3**    The mesh will automatically be deselected, but the joints should remain selected. Rotate them around the Z axis to test the deformation (**Figure 7.62**).

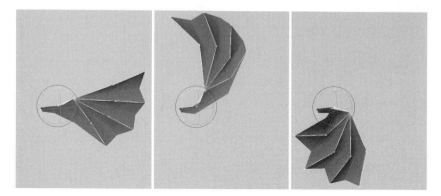

FIGURE 7.62 Rotate the wing to see how it deforms.

The wing seems to hold up fine; deforming it doesn't highlight any potential problems, so reset the joints by right-clicking and selecting Assume Preferred Angle from the marking menu. Then detach the skin and we'll move on to test the leg.

Hide everything except for Grae's left side and the joints making up the skeleton for the leg. Select the joints, then the mesh, and bind them as you did the wing. Before you work on the leg, weight the upper body to the Waist joint (Skin > Edit Smooth Skin > Paint Skin Weights Tool), making sure it won't be influenced by any other joint (**Figure 7.63**).

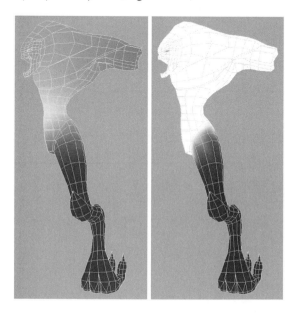

FIGURE 7.63 Weight the upper body to the Waist joint.

**NOTE** For a refresher on the weighting tools and options, refer back to Chapter 6, "Deformation Testing."

To begin testing the leg, rotate it forward and see how it looks. The topology appears to be okay; a bit of weight painting is all this area needs. Test this by adjusting the weighting information around the hip. **Figures 7.64** and **7.65** show the front and back of the upper leg before and after the weights have been adjusted.

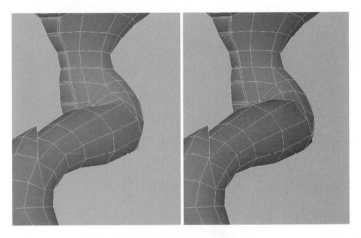

**FIGURE 7.64** The weighting before and after editing

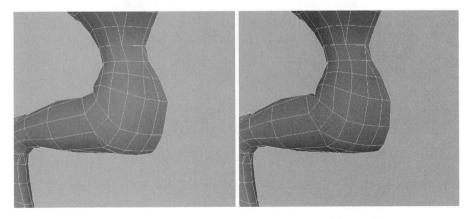

**FIGURE 7.65** With the leg rotated forward, smooth out the rear of the model.

When finished, follow **Figures 7.66** and **7.67** and rotate the leg backward to see how it deforms in this position. Again, adjust the weighting to see if you can get away without adding any more geometry to this area.

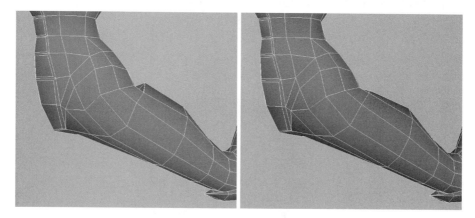

**FIGURE 7.66** Adjust the weighting with the leg back

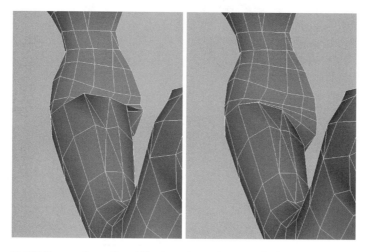

**FIGURE 7.67** Smooth out the large jagged area at the back of the leg.

To finish testing the leg, rotate the two knee joints upward and see how they hold up (**Figure 7.68**).

The knee joints seem fine—nothing that can't be fixed by adjusting the weighting information. Reset the leg skeleton and detach the skin from the main body, choosing Delete History in the options.

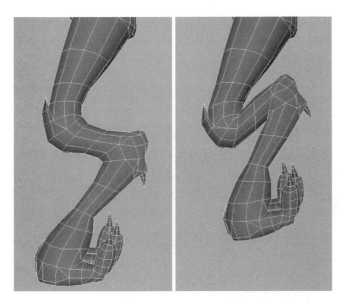

FIGURE 7.68 Rotate the knees to see how they look.

With the leg complete and not needing any deformation adjustments, we can proceed to the final part of Grae's main body, his arms. We need to test both arms, but first we must reattach them to the main model.

**1**   Remove the mirrored instance if you have one in your scene. You need to have two separate halves of Grae's body to work with; a mirrored instance will not work at this point.

**2**   Hide everything in your scene except the two arms, the main body mesh, and the joints for the arms.

**3**   Duplicate the original mesh, making sure Copy and not Instance is selected as the Duplicate geometry type. Setting Scale X to -1 will in effect mirror the duplicate to create the second half.

**4**   Combine the left arm with the left side of the body, welding the vertices where the arm was divided.

**5**   Do the same for the right side, combining it to the right arm and welding the vertices.

You should now have two meshes: the left and right sides of Grae (**Figure 7.69**). Delete the history on both before you proceed.

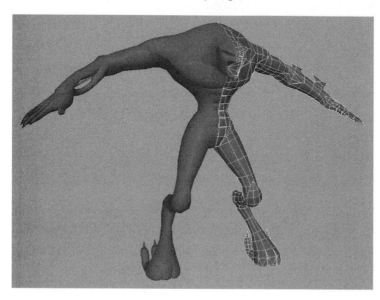

**FIGURE 7.69**
Two separate
sides for Grae

We will work on Grae's left side first, so select these joints: UpperSpine, L_Shoulder, L_Elbow, and L_Wrist. Then add the left side of the model to the selection. Apply a Smooth Bind.

As you did previously for the Waist joint, make sure the whole of his main body is weighted to the UpperSpine joint (**Figure 7.70**).

Focus in on the shoulder and bend it down to see how it initially deforms (**Figure 7.71**). As expected, some minor weights will need to be painted, especially to fill out the armpit area. But once this is done, the shape should be good enough for us to move on to the elbow.

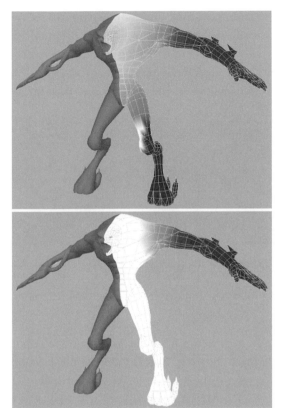

**FIGURE 7.70** Fully weight the body to the UpperSpine joint.

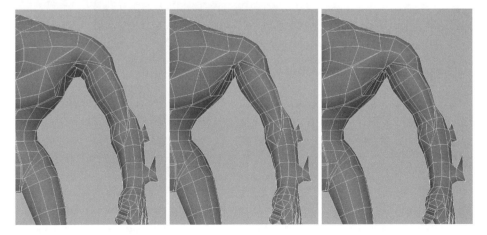

**FIGURE 7.71** Adjust the weighting on the shoulder.

Before we bend the elbow, we have to address a small problem. As you can see in **Figure 7.72** on the left, the rotation manipulator does not follow the orientation of the arm. This is because the *rotational pivot* is incorrect. The rotational pivot dictates how the joint will rotate and should match the orientation of the arm. We need to realign the pivot so that the elbow will bend correctly around the Z axis.

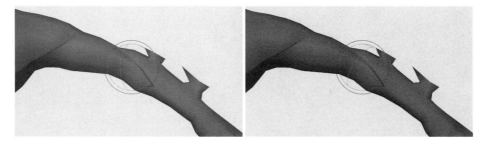

FIGURE 7.72 Fix the rotational pivot so we can rotate the arm correctly.

We will discuss rotational pivots and joint orientation in more depth in Chapter 11, "Skeleton Setup."

For now, to quickly fix the problem, go to Skeleton > Orient Joint and open up the options window. Configure this tool as shown in **Figure 7.73**: Set Orientation to XYZ and make sure the option to "Reorient the local scale axes" is *not* enabled. Then click Apply.

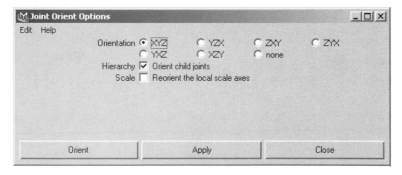

FIGURE 7.73 Setting the Joint Orient options to fix the rotational pivot

With the rotational pivot corrected, we can now bend the arm before adjusting the weights, to see how it will look (**Figure 7.74**). It appears to be fine, so let's reset the joints, detach the skin, and then repeat the process on the right arm.

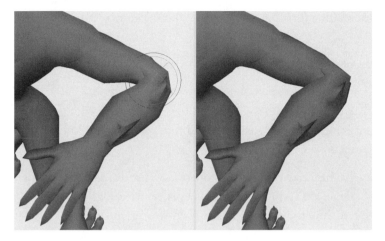

**FIGURE 7.74**
Work on the
left arm elbow
weights.

1    First bind the skeleton to the right-side mesh.

2    Weight the body to the UpperSpine joint.

3    We know the shoulder is okay because it's identical to the one on the left, so
     we will skip this area.

4    Check the joint orientation on the elbow, and fix it if it's incorrect.

5    Rotate the elbow before tweaking the weights, to see how the area will look
     (**Figure 7.75**).

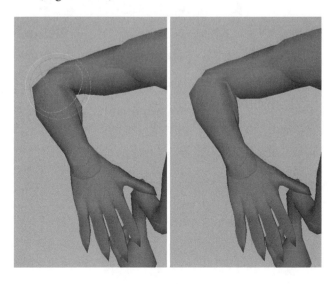

**FIGURE 7.75**
Work on the right
elbow weights.

**6** When everything is fine for all the joints, reset the skeleton and detach the skin.

Combine both sides of the mesh now, welding the vertices down the middle so we have a seamless join.

Now for the face: There isn't much we really need to test here. Grae doesn't talk, so all he really needs is a mouth that can open and that's already in place. What we *do* need to test are his eyes.

With Kila, we created a duplicate of her head to work on for testing, but we don't need to do this with Grae. We are only testing his eyes, so we can rely on the Undo command to return to the original mesh when we are finished.

Focus in on his left eye and, as seen in **Figure 7.76**, adjust the eyelid until the eye is closed. It looks good; nothing needs to be tweaked or altered. Use Undo (Z/Cmd+Z) to return to the mesh with the eyes open.

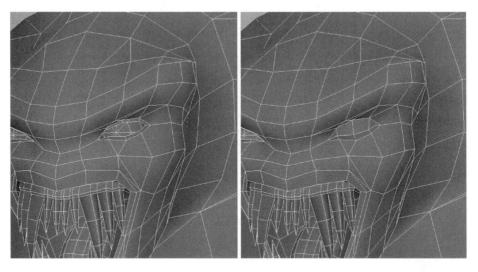

**FIGURE 7.76** Test the eyelids to make sure they cover the eye correctly.

The Grae model is now complete (**Figure 7.77**). Spend as much time as you can now, moving around the model to double-check the overall shape. As always, keep an eye out for ways to further improve or optimize the geometry.

When you're ready, delete the history on all the geometry, tidy up the scene, and save your work as Grae_DeformTest.mb.

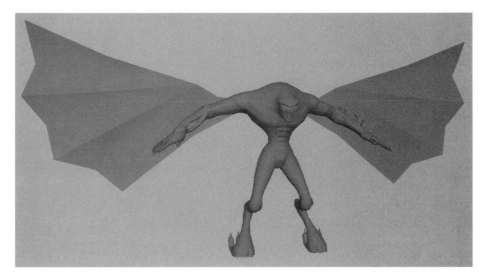

**FIGURE 7.77** The final Grae model

## Summary

In this chapter you have once again worked through the process of modeling a character, this time to build the imposing, more stylized creature, Grae. By now you should have a good grasp of modeling techniques, as well as the essential tasks associated with polygon modeling, joint creation, and binding. In addition, you should have a good idea of what to look for when optimizing your geometry.

Now that we have Kila and Grae modeled, we can proceed in a new direction and learn to apply mapping data and a texture.

**CD Files**

CheckerMap.jpg
Kila_DeformTest.mb
Kila_Divided.mb
Kila_Mapped.mb
Grae_DeformTest.mb
Grae_Divided.mb
Grae_Mapped.mb
KilaBodyUV.tga
KilaHairUV.tga
KilaHeadUV.tga
GraeBodyUV.tga
GraeMiscUV.tga
GraeWingUV.tga

# CHAPTER 8
# Texture Preparation

**THE KILA AND GRAE** models are complete, but they need color to

bring them to life. Before we can apply color to our geometry we must

prepare the surface by applying UV data.

Within each vertex that exists in your polygon model lies a UV point

("UV" for short), which stores 2D coordinates that correspond to specific

pixels on your texture. When you create any primitive objects in Maya,

UVs are assigned by default, but these UVs are often altered when further

modeling occurs—meaning that they need to be rearranged to look

correct.

We will begin this chapter by looking at ways to clean up the UV data, making it usable so that we can then apply a texture to our characters.

## Mapping Methods

There are four main ways to apply UV mapping data to a polygon object: planar mapping, cylindrical mapping, spherical mapping, and automatic mapping. All of these involve projecting the data directly onto the objects surface.

*Planar mapping* (Edit Polygons > Texture > Planar Mapping) projects UVs through a plane along one direction only onto a mesh. This method is ideal for mapping flat objects.

As you can see in **Figure 8.1**, the front of the cube is mapped fine, but because we are using a planar map the texture is stretched along the sides. To fix this you would need to apply additional mapping to the other five sides.

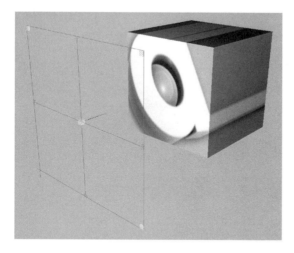

FIGURE 8.1 Planar mapping

*Cylindrical mapping* (Edit Polygons > Texture > Cylindrical Mapping), as the name implies, projects the UVs inward through a cylinder onto the selected object (**Figure 8.2**). This will work best on the outer polygons but, as with the planar mapping, you will need to add further mapping to correct the top and bottom caps.

Similarly, *spherical mapping* (Edit Polygons > Texture > Spherical Mapping) projects inward through a sphere (**Figure 8.3**).

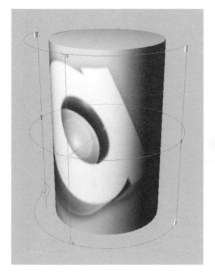 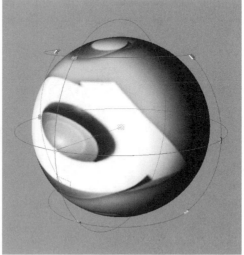

**FIGURE 8.2** Cylindrical mapping          **FIGURE 8.3** Spherical mapping

The three techniques mentioned so far have very similar options for altering the final projection. Let's have a look at some of the more common options, shown in **Figure 8.4**; these are for a planar projection but are also used on the other projections.

▶ Keep Image Ratio will lock the aspect of the projection to that of the image you are applying it to.

▶ Smart Fit will automatically fit the projection to the geometry. If turned off, the projection manipulator will be created at the world root.

▶ Mapping Direction is a setting unique to a planar projection and the one you will use most often. This allows you to dictate which axis the projection should come from.

▶ Image Center, Image Rotation, and Image Scale each adjust the position, orientation, and size of the projection.

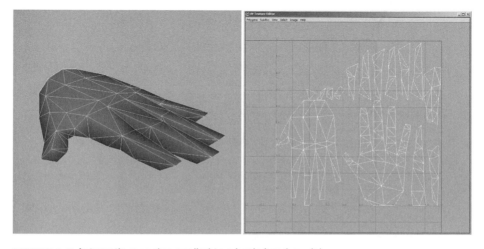

**FIGURE 8.4** The options for Polygon Planar Projection

The fourth and final mapping method is *automatic mapping* (Edit Polygons > Texture > Automatic Mapping). This will attempt to find the best UV layout for your mesh by projecting inward from a specified number of angles.

Look at **Figure 8.5**, left, where we have a basic, low-polygon hand model. If we apply automatic mapping with the default options, our UVs will be laid out for us. You can see this in **Figure 8.5**, right.

> **NOTE** To see an object's current UV layout, simply select the mesh and go to Window > UV Texture Editor. In addition to seeing the UVs, you can also edit them; we will talk more about the UV Texture Editor later in the chapter.

**FIGURE 8.5** Automatic mapping applied to a basic hand model

We will see how to use some of these mapping methods as we apply UV mapping to our characters, but first we need to prepare the geometry to make the mapping process easier.

## Dividing a Character

The most efficient way to texture a character is to divide it up into areas whose shapes lend themselves to a particular type of projection. For example, an arm could either be treated as a cylinder, or if divided lengthwise, could use two planar projections. The idea is to approach the mapping procedure with a strategy.

Here is what to look for when choosing how to break up the character:

▶   Look for areas that resemble the projection shape most closely. If you map a cylinder with, say, a planar projection, you will wind up with stretching on two sides and overlap on the back; overlap is *bad* in almost all cases.

▶   Look for areas that can share the same texture and projection information. The left and right side hand areas, and maybe even the pants legs or the face (if symmetrical) are likely candidates.

▶   When choosing where to cut, try to hide seams wherever possible. Look first for natural seams like waistbands and collars. If there is no natural seam, choose the next least conspicuous spot, such as under the armpit, between legs, under hair, and so forth.

Splitting the geometry up will make it easier to apply the initial UV projections to the character. With these in place, we can then go in and tweak the UVs individually to reduce any undesirable stretching and overlap.

We will now begin working on Kila to show how best to divide her. No mapping will be applied at this stage.

### Kila

Load the file called Kila_DeformTest.mb.

> **NOTE**   It's been a while since we looked at the Kila model because we have been working on Grae. Take this opportunity to have a fresh look at the model, making sure you are happy with it. When you're ready, we will begin by examining the torso and arms.

### Torso and Arm Preparation

Kila currently only has one-half of her upper body; the entire right side is a mirrored instance. We're going to delete the instance and create a mirrored *copy* of the left torso for her right side—but first we will extract her arm. We do this because although we want to map then entire torso, the mapping for her left and right arms can initially be the same, so we only need one arm to exist at this time.

**1** Select the faces that make up Kila's left arm and extract them, separating the arm from the torso (**Figure 8.6**).

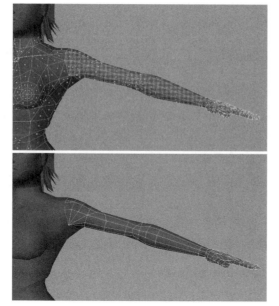

**FIGURE 8.6**
Extract the left arm.

**2** Now we can go in and finish preparing the torso. First delete the mirrored instance, so only the left half of her torso remains.

**3** Use the Polygons > Polygon Mirror tool, making sure Weld Vertices is enabled. This will create the right side.

**4** If the vertices running down the center of her torso did not all lie on the same plane when you did the mirroring step, you may need to go in now and make sure that they are welded correctly. When that's done, smooth the edges.

We now have a complete torso that is almost ready for mapping. There are two ways to approach this area:

▶ It's basically cylindrical in shape, so we could map it cylindrically. This would produce a good result, but it can be difficult to control the positions of the seams. (The seams are the areas where the cylinder edges meet. If you imagine rolling a piece of paper around your arm, this is the cylindrical projection. The position of the seams will be the places where the edges of the paper meet.)

▶ We could detach the front and back, planar-mapping both. This would give a better UV layout. We'd only have to adjust the sides and the breast area because they will initially overlap and be stretched.

Another advantage to splitting the torso would be the placement of the UV seams. They would run down Kila's sides, so we could disguise them as the seams on her T-shirt. In addition, they would also be hidden when her arms are down, which would be for the majority of the time.

Planar mapping seem to be the best option, so let's now split the torso in two.

1 Select the faces that make up Kila's front, selecting the ones that face forward more than backward. Use Extract to separate them (**Figure 8.7**).

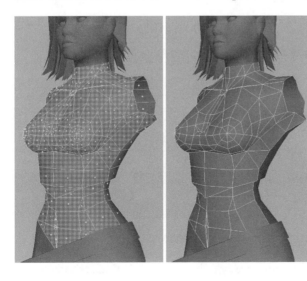

**FIGURE 8.7** Split the torso into the front piece and the back piece.

The front and back are now separated and prepped, ready to be mapped.

We will apply cylindrical mapping on the arm, because the shape is almost cylindrical and it will give us an opportunity to see this form of projection demonstrated. Alternatively, you could apply the same technique that we used for the torso, as we will with the legs later. The hand, however, will need planar mapping to both the top and bottom, so that we can apply a different texture to each side.

2   Start by detaching her hand from the arm. Select the faces that make up the hand and Extract them (**Figure 8.8**).

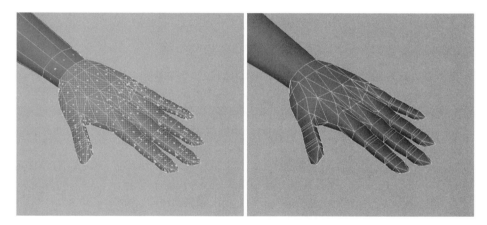

FIGURE 8.8 Extract the hand.

3   Finally, separate the top of the hand from the bottom (**Figure 8.9**).

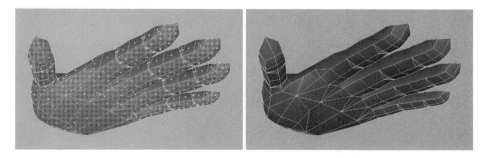

FIGURE 8.9 Separate the top of the hand from the bottom.

The torso, arm, and hand are now ready to be mapped. Let's continue down her body now and work on the legs.

### Leg Division

For Kila's legs, we can adopt the same technique we used on the torso. Her jeans will have a seam that runs down the outside and the inner leg; this can be used to disguise the UV seam.

As you did with the torso, select the front faces (**Figure 8.10**) and Extract them.

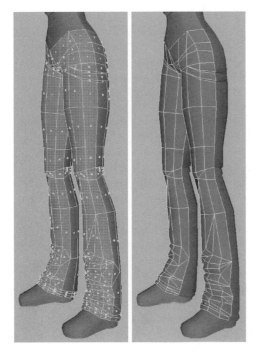

**FIGURE 8.10** Separate the front and the back of the legs.

### Shoe and Belt Division

Continuing on, we get to the shoes. Both shoes will be mapped the same, so we can delete the one on the right for now, and duplicate the left shoe once mapping has been applied.

There are a number of ways you can approach the shoes, depending on the amount of detail you wish them to have.

▶ A simple planar projection from the side is usually a good way of quickly mapping the shoe. This does mean, though, that the inner and outer sides of the shoe have to be the same.

▶ You could use automatic mapping, as demonstrated earlier with the hand model, but this might give unpredictable results—you could wind up spending most of your time rearranging the UVs.

▶ To get the most detail into the shoe, the best approach is to manually split up the model. This will also give you more control over the UVs' placement. This is the method demonstrated in this discussion.

Separate the sides, top, front, back, and bottom (**Figure 8.11**). We will apply planar mapping to each area later.

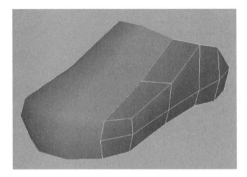

**FIGURE 8.11** Divide the foot into specific areas.

Leave the belt intact, since it was created from a basic cylinder that has not been altered enough to destroy its initial mapping coordinates.

With separation of the main body completed now, let's see what needs to be done to her head.

### Head Division

The main head will be fine as it is; a simple cylindrical or planar map will work well here. So let's concentrate on the inner mouth, along with her eyes, teeth, and tongue.

1 Detach the inner mouth (**Figure 8.12**) and the ear (**Figure 8.13**). We do this because both these areas can initially be planar-mapped.

The inner mouth will need only a simple texture, perhaps a gradient running through it. The ear will benefit from a simple planar projection.

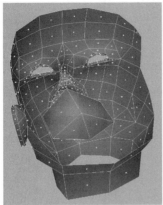 

**FIGURE 8.12**
Detach the inner mouth from the head.

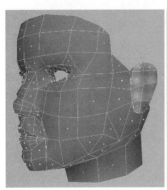 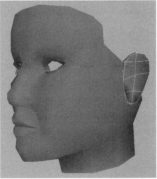

**FIGURE 8.13**
Separate the ear.

**2**  Both the eyes will be handled the same, so delete the one on the right side.

**3**  We don't need to do anything to the teeth. Like the belt, the teeth were created from cylinders and so should still retain some good mapping. You can also leave the tongue as is, because it's a basic shape (**Figure 8.14**).

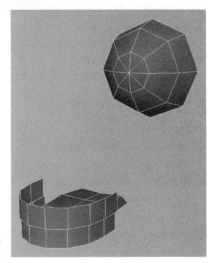

**FIGURE 8.14** The inner mouth and eye are fine as they are.

### Hair Division

The inside layers of Kila's hair were initially made from individual strips of polygons. Therefore, this part of the hair should retain its basic mapping—if we texture one strip with particular mapping coordinates, they will exist in the other strips.

Using this method will save texture space and, since the inner layers are not fully visible, we should be able to get away with repeating the texture. If, on the other hand, the texture looks obviously copied, we can apply a cylindrical map to the layers.

The outer layer of hair is a different story. No usable mapping exists on it because we have drastically edited the topology. But we only need to do a couple of things to prepare the hair.

**1** The best approach for the outer hair is to first split the hair down the middle, as shown in **Figure 8.15**.

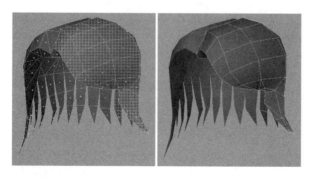

**FIGURE 8.15** Split the hair into two halves.

**2** Separate the inner polygons from both sides (**Figure 8.16**).

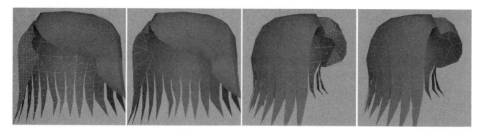

**FIGURE 8.16** Detach the inner polygons.

Kila is now prepped and ready to be mapped. Clean up the geometry by deleting the history, and save the file as Kila_Divided.mb.

### Grae

Grae is a more unique character than Kila, but a lot of the same principles will apply. We will now take the same steps with the Grae model, getting him ready to apply UV mapping.

Start by loading the file named Grae_DeformTest.mb. As you did with Kila, take some time to check the model for any last-minute changes.

#### Wings

We will initially hide the wings and concentrate on the main body of Grae.

You may be thinking that we could delete a wing, mirroring the other one across. We could do this with ordinary wings because the mirroring would not be obvious. However, Grae's wings are made up of tendrils and should not look identical. What we can do is leave the wings until last, applying them to a separate texture page. Then we can judge whether we have the space to map both separately.

So for now, go ahead and divide up the body.

#### Leg Division

With the wings hidden, the first area of Grae's body that stands out are his legs. Looking back to our concept drawing, we can see that the upper thigh sections differ in surface design and thus will each need separate mapping. The lower legs, however, are the same, which allows us to use identical mapping techniques.

1   As shown in **Figure 8.17**, detach the lower legs and delete the one on Grae's right.

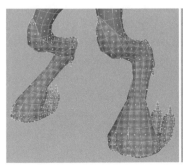 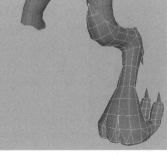

**FIGURE 8.17**
Detach the lower legs.

**2**    Because all three toes were initially created out of the same piece of geometry, we can delete the outer two and concentrate on the central one. Detach all three toes from the main foot (**Figure 8.18**), separate the toes, and delete the outer two.

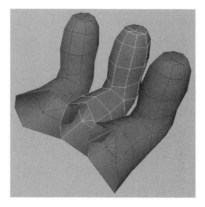

**FIGURE 8.18** Separate the toes, deleting the outer two.

**3**    As is, the lower leg section is too complex to achieve clean mapping; breaking it up will simplify the process. Detach the lower section of the leg, as shown in **Figure 8.19**.

**FIGURE 8.19** Separate the lower section of the leg.

The lower legs can be cylindrically mapped, leaving the upper thighs to be mapped with the torso, so let's look at that area next.

### Torso Division

Let's begin our work on the torso.

1    Select and detach the arms (**Figure 8.20**). This will leave us with the main area we want to work on.

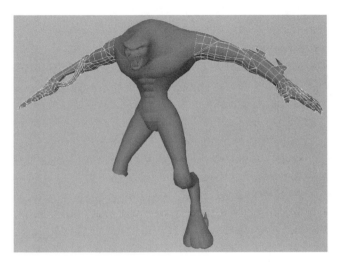

FIGURE 8.20
Detach the arms.

2    We can map Grae's upper body and thighs much the same way as Kila's torso. Separate the front and the back (**Figure 8.21**) so you can later apply planar mapping to them.

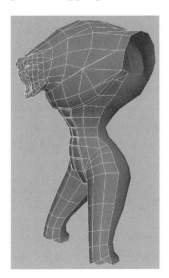

FIGURE 8.21 Split the upper body into the front and the back.

**3**  Detach the head (**Figure 8.22**) and then the inner mouth (**Figure 8.23**). You could split the head down the center, mapping one half and mirroring it. In this case, though, leave the head intact, because the texture may need to be different on each side.

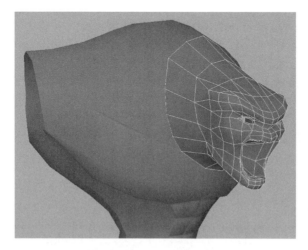

**FIGURE 8.22**
Detach the head, but don't split it.

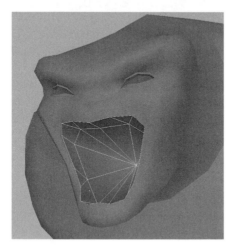

**FIGURE 8.23**
Separate the inner mouth from the head.

**4**  Separate the upper and the lower teeth so that you can map them independently (**Figure 8.24**).

> **NOTE** Because the upper and lower teeth aren't physically connected, you can simply go to Edit Polygons > Separate to detach them.

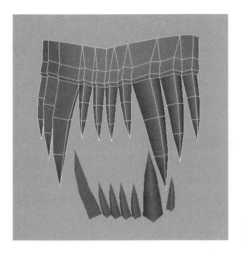

**FIGURE 8.24** Separate the upper and lower teeth.

This is all we need to do to the upper body area for now, so now let's edit the arms.

### Arm Division

Start with the left arm.

1  Following **Figure 8.25**, first detach the hand and then the upper arm. (The arm itself is bent much more than Kila's was. Detaching it will make it easier to map.)

2  Separate the spikes from the upper arm (**Figure 8.25**, right), since these can be mapped separately.

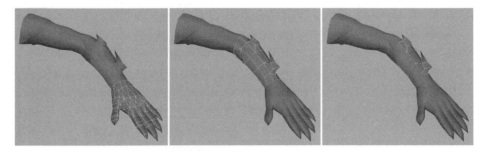

**FIGURE 8.25** Divide the left arm into sections.

3  Moving on to the right arm, divide it up into the same workable sections.

4  To finish up, divide both hands into top and bottom sections.

Grae is now divided and ready to be mapped. Save the file as Grae_Divided.mb.

With both models prepared, we can move on to apply mapping to Kila and Grae. We will use tools already mentioned in this section, as well as get our first introduction to the UV Texture Editor.

## Mapping UVs: The Checker Map Technique

Using a checkered texture as a guide while you manipulate the UV coordinates on your mesh will make it very obvious when an area gets stretched or looks distorted. Once you've corrected all these problems, you can create your texture safe in the knowledge that what you draw is what you will see on your geometry. The checkered technique is also a good way to visually verify that all areas of the model are receiving proportionally comparable texture space relative to each other.

### Create the Checkered Texture

Load in the file Kila_Divided.mb.

Before we edit the UVs, we need to see how they currently lie on the geometry. To do this, we'll first create the checkered material that will be applied to the model.

1    Go to Window > Render Editors > Hypershade. This opens the window in **Figure 8.26**. Hypershade contains all the information on your current materials and textures, as well as on various other objects such as lights and cameras in Maya.

> **NOTE** By default the Hypershade will open with split view, the top shows the current shaders in the scene and the bottom is a work area. This is useful if your scene has lots of materials, as you can drag individual shaders into the work area for closer attention. To change the Hypershade view, use the three boxes to the far right of the Hypershade toolbar, Show Top Tabs Only, Show Bottom Tabs Only, and Show Top and Bottom Tabs.

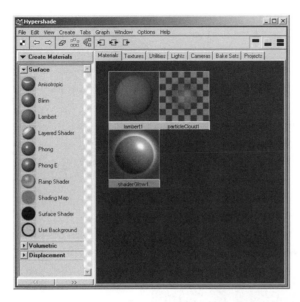

**FIGURE 8.26** Hypershade showing top tabs only.

## Hypershade Options

There are a number of materials available to you in Hypershade, so let's briefly look at some of the more common ones.

▶ An **Anisotropic** material is used to represent surfaces that have small grooves, like brushed metal or a vinyl record.

▶ A **Blinn** material is useful for shiny, metallic-looking surfaces.

▶ A **Lambert** is a material that represents flat, matte surfaces.

▶ A **Layered Shader** is used when you want to combine two materials or textures into a single material.

▶ **Phong** and **Phong E** materials are useful for shiny, plastic-looking surfaces.

**2** We don't need a shiny finish to this texture, so we will use a Lambert. There are a couple of ways to create this:

▶ Select Create > Materials > Lambert either from the Hypershade menu bar or by right-clicking in the main window and using the contextual menus.

▶ Select the Lambert icon under the Create Materials bar on the left. (If this bar is set to something else, like Create Textures, click the name and select Create Materials from the drop-down menu.)

Whichever method you choose, the result is a new material called lambert2 (**Figure 8.27**).

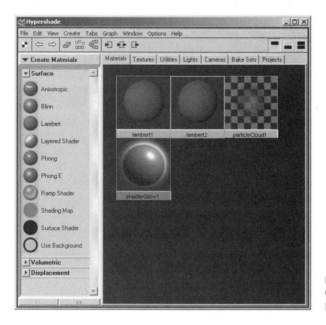

**FIGURE 8.27**
Create a new
Lambert material.

**3** Double-click the new material to open its attributes, as shown in **Figure 8.28**.

**4** Highlighted at the top of the window in **Figure 8.28**, in the lambert text field, is its current name. Change lambert2 to Check.

**5** Under the Common Material Attributes section you will see various options, from Color to Translucence Focus. We are only interested in the Color option for now.

Next to this is a colored rectangle and then a slider, and a small box with a checkered pattern in it. Click this box to open up a Create Render Node window (**Figure 8.29**).

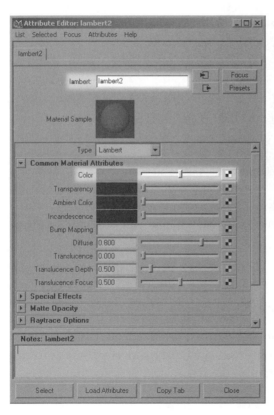

FIGURE 8.28 The new Lambert material's attributes

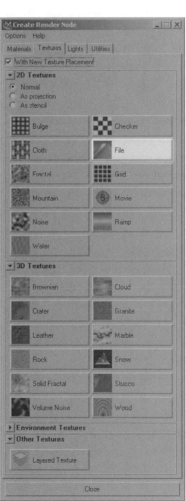

FIGURE 8.29 Defining the material in the Create Render Node window

6 Under the heading 2D Textures, select File. The Attribute Editor now changes to show the file's attributes (**Figure 8.30**).

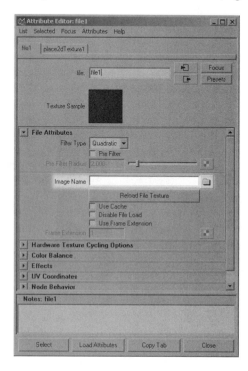

**FIGURE 8.30**
The file attributes

7 Next to Image Name, you'll see a space followed by a folder icon. Click this folder and browse to the file called CheckerMap.jpg (you can find this file on the CD in Project Files/08).

8 Click Close to complete the material's creation. Go back to the Hypershade; as you can see from **Figure 8.31**, the material is now named Check and the ball shows the checkered texture that is applied.

9 Before we apply this material to Kila, we need to make materials visible in the view panels. Go to the Shading menu and make sure Hardware Texturing is on, or press 6 on your keyboard.

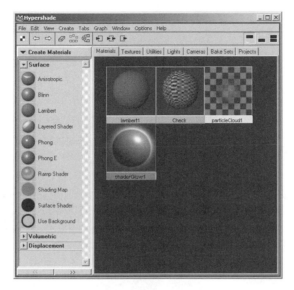

**FIGURE 8.31** The new Check texture has been created.

**10** The quickest way to apply the Check material to our character is to select all the geometry, then right-click the material in the Hypershade and select Assign Material To Selection. Make sure to right-click *only* the material—there is no need for it to be selected (highlighted) in the Hypershade. Left-clicking to select it first will only serve to de-select the geometry.

Another method is to middle-mousebutton-click your material and drag it to the geometry to which you want to apply it.

Your model now looks like the one in **Figure 8.32**. You can tell that the UVs need work at this stage, because the grid is not cleanly laid out over her body. With the material applied, we can now go in and tweak the UVs, making sure the squares on the texture are lined up correctly.

**FIGURE 8.32** Kila with the material applied

## Arm UVs

Let's begin our UV work with Kila's arm. Since the shape is cylindrical, we can simply apply a cylindrical map to this area. The problem is that since her arm is bent, a single cylinder will not suffice. So we will map her upper and lower arm separately, as shown in **Figure 8.33**.

1  Select the faces of the upper arm (**Figure 8.33b**).

2  Go to Edit Polygons > Texture > Cylindrical Mapping, to apply the mapping to the selected faces.

You are now presented with the projection manipulator; you can see it in **Figure 8.33c**. This represents how the mapping is being applied to the geometry and, like any other manipulator in Maya, you can adjust it to better suit your needs:

▶  The small light-blue squares in the corners manipulate the projection's height and horizontal sweep.

The *horizontal sweep* is the amount by which the projection wraps around an object. The default amount is 1.8, which is 180 degrees and only covers half the object. This doesn't mean, however, that only half of the object is mapped; it merely alters the aspect ratio of the UV placement. You can edit the horizontal sweep directly by moving the red squares on either side of the manipulator.

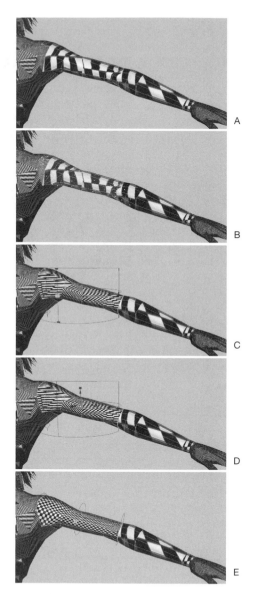

**FIGURE 8.33** Apply cylindrical mapping to her upper arm.

▶ The green squares adjust the height of the mapping, and the light-blue flat square in the center adjusts its overall scale.

▶ The last, larger cyan cube, which exists on the edge of the projection, adjusts its rotation around the object.

These handles are all good for adjusting the projection locally—but what if you need to move it globally? You should see a red T icon in the bottom-left corner of the projection manipulator. Selecting this will toggle between the projection's default manipulator and Maya's standard Translate/Rotate/Scale manipulator (**Figure 8.33d**).

We now need to adjust the cylinder's manipulator so that it fits this portion of her arm.

**3** Start by using the red cubes to adjust the horizontal sweep, making the projection spread around to the back of the arm.

**4** Click the T icon to switch to Maya's default manipulator and use this to adjust the cylinder's rotation so it matches the orientation of the upper arm (**Figure 8.33e**).

**5** Now you can either use the current Scale manipulator, or click the T icon again to return to the projection manipulator and adjust the scale to envelop the arm.

**6** With everything still selected, go to Window > UV Texture Editor.

The UV Texture Editor (**Figure 8.34**) shows how the UVs of the currently selected object are laid out. What you see is the upper arm flattened out, as if you have peeled the skin off and laid it out flat—in other words, "unwrapped." Here is where we will manipulate the UVs, adjusting them to eliminate undesired overlap, reduce stretching, and make the UVs easier to paint.

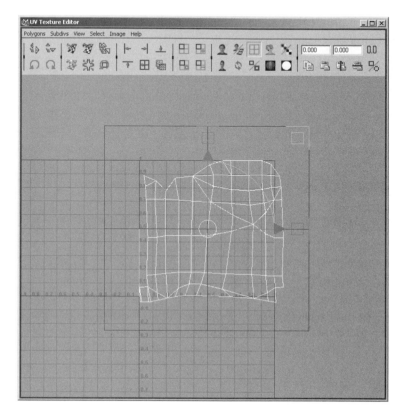

**FIGURE 8.34** The UV Texture Editor

You may still have the actual Check texture in the background. This texture is usually good to use as a guide, but for now we need to remove it. Turn off the image by going to Image > Display Image.

The upper arm is looking okay now. The UVs are nicely laid out following a uniform pattern. We can also identify key areas of the arm, such as the shoulder, which will be useful when we paint our textures.

Let's continue on now to work on the UVs of lower arm. Select the faces for the lower arm and repeat the foregoing procedure (**Figure 8.35**).

> **NOTE** It is important that the projection manipulator's orientation around the mesh matches that of the upper arm. This will ensure that both sets of UVs will follow the same lines when we come to edit them; for example, we want the elbow's UVs to line up.

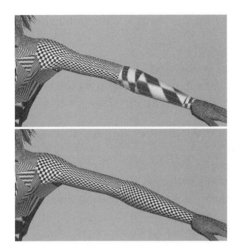

**FIGURE 8.35**
Map the lower arm.

The basic UV mapping is now in place for the arm, but we need to work on it some more before we are finished.

### UV Manipulation on the Arm

With the basic mapping in place, we can now edit the UVs in the UV Texture Editor.

1   Select the arm and look in the UV Texture Editor. You can see in **Figure 8.36** (left) that both sets of mapping overlay each other. We need them to be separate.

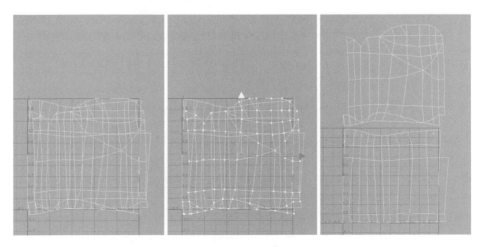

**FIGURE 8.36** Adjust the position of the mapping for the arm.

**2**  In the perspective view, select the faces of the upper arm. They will be high-lighted in the UV Texture Editor.

**3**  Move back to the UV Texture Editor and go to Select > Convert Selection To UVs. Both sections of the arm will be visible once more, but only the UVs for the upper arm will be selected (**Figure 8.36**, middle).

**4**  Press W to switch to translate mode, and move the selection up, separating the two sets of UVs (**Figure 8.36**, right).

Now the UVs are separated so we can see them clearly. We next need to combine both sections of the arm, making one complete piece and eliminating the seam between the upper and lower arm sections.

### UV Sewing

Since the upper and lower arms are already combined in the 3D view, connecting them in the UV Texture Editor is simple.

**1**  Right-click in the UV Texture Editor and select Edge from the marking menu, putting you into edge-selection mode.

**2**  Select one of the edges at the base of the upper arm. You will notice that the edge it is connected to in the 3D view is also highlighted in the UV Texture Editor, and its associated edge along the border of the other set of UVs is highlighted.

> **NOTE**  If the two edges do not lie above and below each other, right-click and select UVs; then move the upper arm UVs along until the edges match.

**3**  Holding the Shift key, continue across until you have the bottom row selected, as shown in **Figure 8.37** (left).

**4**  To weld these edges together, go to Polygons > Sew UVs.

We now have one complete map of UVs unwrapped for the arm (**Figure 8.37**, left).

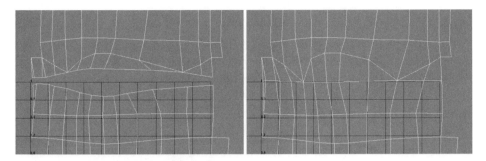

**FIGURE 8.37** Combine the upper and lower sets of UVs.

### *UV Cutting and Moving*

Look at the UVs of the arm; you will notice an area that sticks out to the left. This needs to be cut off and positioned in the gap on the right, making the UV map clean and easier to read.

> **NOTE**  Depending on how your mapping went, this projection may be severe, but don't worry—the next steps will help you fix this.

Let's first check and see where the seams lie. Select a UV on the border in the UV Texture Editor; this will also show up in the 3D view, letting you see where the seam is. We want the seam to be on the bottom of the arm, so that when the arm is lowered, the seam is not as noticeable. Currently the seam is around the back of the arm, across the elbow.

We have two problems to solve here. We will first cut the UVs where we want the seam to be, moving the remainder over to the right before sewing them again. The following steps are illustrated in **Figure 8.38**.

1   In the UV Texture Editor, select a line of edges from the top to the bottom. These will mark the underneath of the arm (**Figure 8.38a**). To find this line, go to your 3D view and switch to UV editing mode. Then select a UV under the arm; this will also show up in the UV Texture Editor, so you can tell what edges to select.

2   Now you know where to cut, so go to Polygons > Cut UVs.

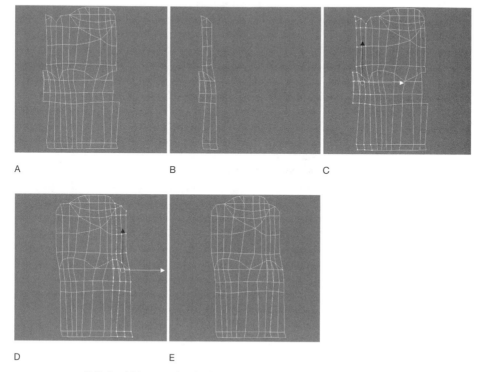

FIGURE 8.38 Edit the UVs to make the layout cleaner.

3   Still in the UV Texture Editor, switch to face-editing mode and select the faces to the left of the cut (**Figure 8.38b**).

4   Go to Select > Convert Selection To UVs so that we can edit this piece (**Figure 8.38c**).

5   Move the selection over to the right. This should fit more or less exactly (**Figure 8.38d**).

6   Finally, select the edges where the new join is and go to Polygons > Sew UVs to join them (**Figure 8.38e**).

Now comes the fun part. We have our basic UV map showing us an unwrapped version of the arm. The problem is that some areas are still stretched and do not fit correctly. We're going to edit the UVs individually in the UV Texture Editor, trying to get the grid on the arm as perfect as possible.

The checkered texture works well as a guide. Try to keep the squares square and proportionate (**Figure 8.39**). This can be a tedious job, but when the UVs are correctly laid out, your texture will not stretch or look incorrect. Once you have spent time painting the texture in Photoshop, the last thing you want is for it to appear warped on the actual geometry.

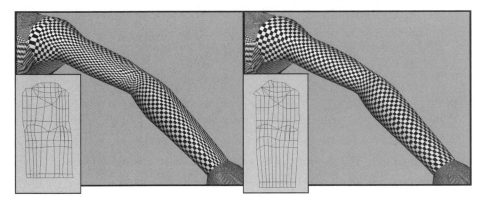

FIGURE 8.39 Work on the UVs individually, keeping the squares in the texture square.

> **NOTE** ▷ Keep in mind that you will not be able to remove all of the stretching from the texture. I suggest that you concentrate on the larger areas that will hold detail. The main forearm, elbow, and shoulder will be most visible, whereas the underneath part of her arm won't be seen most of the time.

The arm is done; let's get to the torso UVs.

## Torso UVs

We will approach the torso from a slightly different angle, this time we will begin by planar-mapping the front and back before tweaking the UVs in the UV Texture Editor.

1   Select the front and go to Edit Polygons > Texture > Planar Mapping. Make sure Keep Image Ratio is checked in the options box; this will initially keep the squares in your texture at the correct size. Your torso will now be mapped (**Figure 8.40**, right).

FIGURE 8.40 Planar mapping applied to the front of the torso

2    Flip around to the back of the torso and apply the same mapping with the same configuration (**Figure 8.41**).

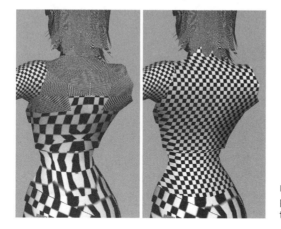

FIGURE 8.41 Planar mapping applied to the back of the torso

3    Although these areas look fine when you're looking at them straight on, the sides are stretched. Work on the front first, editing the UVs in the UV Texture Editor (**Figure 8.42**). Make sure no UVs overlap, particularly around her chest and armpit areas.

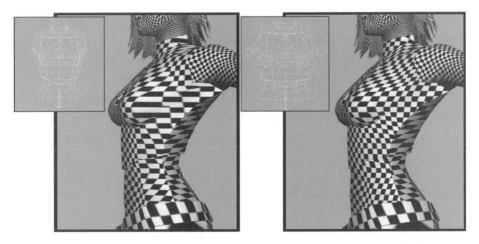

FIGURE 8.42 Edit the UVs for her front, fixing the stretched areas.

**4**  When we applied the mapping to Kila's back, it was projected from the front, so in effect the UVs are mirrored. Before you begin editing here, we need to flip all the UVs. Select them all in the UV Texture Editor and go to Polygons > Flip UVs, making sure you select Horizontal in the options.

**5**  Now work on the back, removing most of the stretched areas of the texture until it resembles that in **Figure 8.43**. Try to remove as much as you can here, because Kila will eventually have a tattoo; if the UVs are incorrect, the tattoo will stretch.

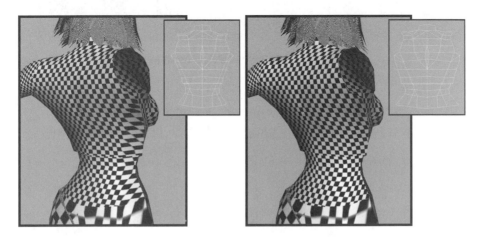

FIGURE 8.43 After flipping the UVs on her back, remove the stretched areas.

The UVs are now nicely laid out for her torso. Next up is the lower body, including waist area, legs, and feet.

### Lower Body UVs

To make it easier to generate the texture for Kila's sash and the jeans, we will keep the waist and leg UVs together.

#### *Waist and Legs*

The UVs for the waist items and the legs will be edited exactly the same as you did her torso. Let's start with the legs.

1   As seen in **Figure 8.44**, first apply planar mapping to the front and the back of the entire lower body.

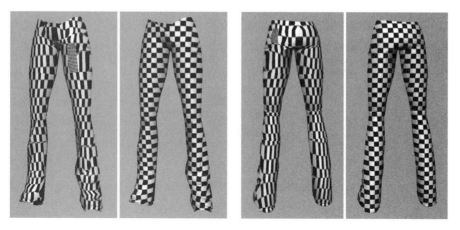

FIGURE 8.44 Apply planar mapping to the front and back of her legs.

2   Using **Figures 8.45** and **8.46** as a guide, edit the UVs in the UV Texture Editor. Your goal is to reduce the amount of stretching that can be seen. Remember to flip the UV's for the back of her legs before you edit them.

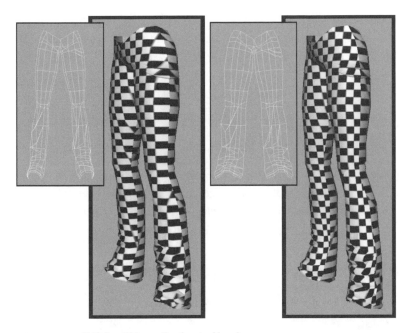

FIGURE 8.45 Edit the UVs on the front of her legs.

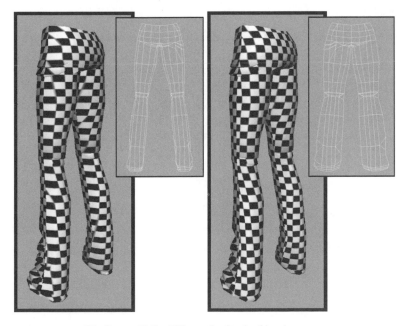

FIGURE 8.46 Flip then edit the UVs on the back of her legs.

### Feet

The feet are already split into six segments, ready for mapping. You should have front, back, left, right, top, and bottom segments.

> **NOTE** As mentioned previously, simple planar-mapping of the foot from the side will provide a good enough UV layout for you to texture, because most shoes are identical on both sides. You will then just separate the base of the foot and map this separately in order to apply the tread on the sole. Creating the UVs for the shoe, as demonstrated in this section, should be reserved for feet that hold a lot of texture detail.

1   Select each portion of the foot and apply Planar Mapping to them all individually (**Figure 8.47**). Remember to set the Mapping Direction in the options; this will save you time when you are adjusting the projection.

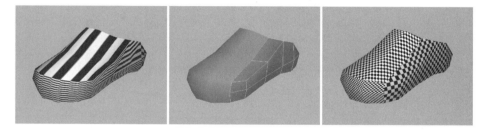

FIGURE 8.47 With the foot divided into segments, planar-map each section.

2   Select all the pieces of the foot and look at their mapping in the UV Texture Editor (**Figure 8.48a**).

3   The UVs for each piece are overlapping, so, working on each piece individually, select the UVs and move them out of the center, as in **Figure 8.48b**.

4   When they are all moved, you can combine the geometry that makes up the foot. Remember to weld the vertices as you do.

5   With the foot once again a whole object, edit the UVs some more, sewing the sides and front to the top (**Figure 8.48c**). Make sure all the pieces are the correct size—remember that you will end up with more detail on areas that are larger.

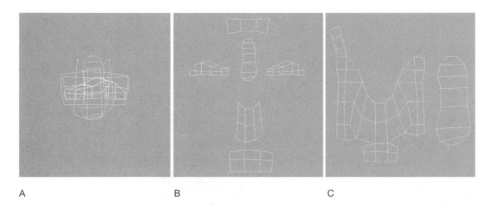

A                              B                              C

FIGURE 8.48 Adjust the layout of the foot
UVs in the UV Texture Editor.

D

As you can see in **Figure 8.48d**, with the UVs manipulated the foot looks a lot
cleaner.

### Head UVs

The head is relatively simple to map. As you can see in **Figure 8.49**, starting with a basic cylindrical map will give us a good starting base.

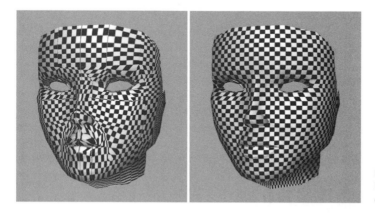

FIGURE 8.49 The head after a basic cylindrical map

Kila's eyelashes are going to be solid black, so we will map them separately. If we need to later, we can adjust these UVs so we can apply additional detail.

1   Select the faces that make up the eyelashes, as shown in **Figure 8.50** (top).

2   Because the eyelashes are a basic black, we don't need them to have separate UVs; they can occupy the same space on the texture page. And they won't have any detail, so we can afford for them to use just a small area of the page. So go ahead and apply a basic planar map to them, projecting from the X axis (**Figure 8.50**, bottom).

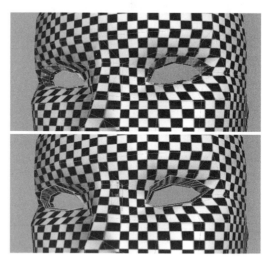

FIGURE 8.50 Select the eyelashes and map them separately.

**3**   While you still have the eyelashes selected, go to the UV Texture Editor window, change the selection to UVs and move them up so they will be above the head.

**Figure 8.51** shows the head UVs in their current state. As you can see, the eyelashes are now separate and above the head.

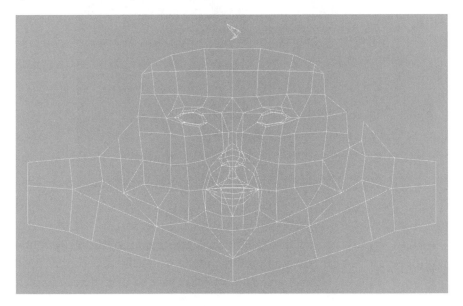

FIGURE 8.51 The current head UV layout

Let's stay in the UV Texture Editor and work directly on the UVs for the face. The actual geometry of the face has the eyes open, but in the UV layout they should be closed so that we can apply a texture to her eyelids.

**4**   As seen in **Figure 8.52**, manipulate the UVs so that the eyes appear to be closed.

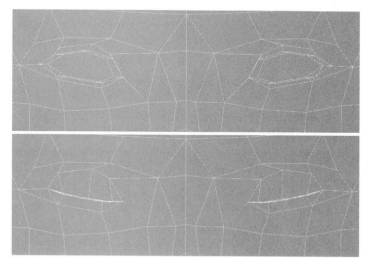

FIGURE 8.52 In the UV Texture Editor, close the eyes.

Next, you will separate her lips. This will give them nice clean edges, making the texture appear higher in resolution than it actually is. Secondly, it will let you give the lips a larger area on the texture page so that you can implement more detail in them.

**5**   In the UV Texture Editor, select the edges that mark the outline of the lips.

**6**   Go to Polygons > Cut UVs to separate the lips from the face.

**7**   Switch to face selection, and select the faces that make up the lips.

**8**   Go to Select > Convert Selection to UVs.

**9**   Move the lips away from the face, scaling them up slightly (**Figure 8.53**).

With the main areas complete, continue to work on the head, reducing any stretched areas in the texture. In particular, work on the nose area.

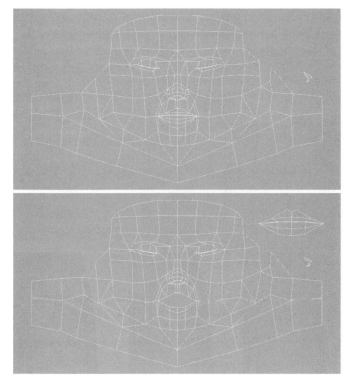

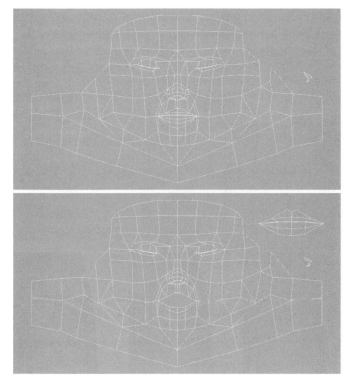

**FIGURE 8.53**
Separate the lips
in the UV Texture
Editor.

### Inner Mouth, Eye, and Ear

Let's stay with the head now and concentrate on the eyes, inner mouth, and ear.

1   Looking first at the eyes, apply a simple planar map here across the Z axis,
    scaling the UVs toward the back slightly. This will reduce the stretching
    along the sides. You can see the result in **Figure 8.54**.

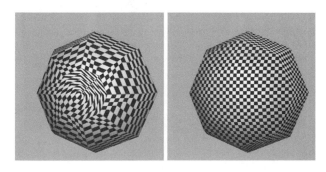

**FIGURE 8.54**
Planar-map the
eyeball.

**2** Next, consider the geometry that makes up the inner wall of the mouth. This, too, can have a simple planar map applied to it; this time, however, as shown in **Figure 8.55**, project it from the X axis.

You don't need to unwrap this area of the model, because at most it will have a basic gradient texture applied to it.

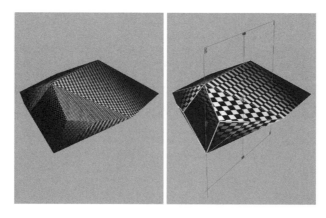

**FIGURE 8.55** For the inner mouth, project a planar map from the side.

**3** You can skip the teeth, which already have pretty good mapping on them. This leaves the tongue. This is another area that will not warrant much detail. This time, we will project the mapping along the Y axis (**Figure 8.56**). This means we can at least add some detail to her upper tongue.

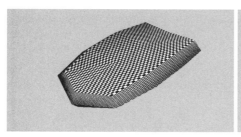 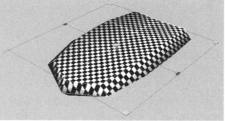

**FIGURE 8.56** Project the mapping down onto the tongue.

**4**    Now you've come to the ear. Again, a simple planar map will work well here (**Figure 8.57**), but unwrap the UVs that are behind the ear.

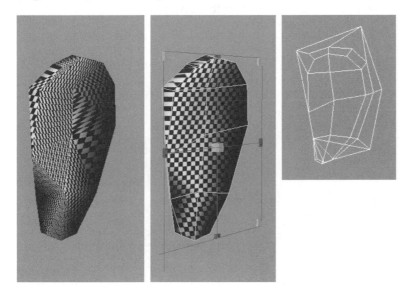

FIGURE 8.57 Planar-map the ear.

We are almost done; there are just a few more areas to work on. Coming up next is the hair.

## Hair UVs

The inner layers of the hair already have some basic mapping applied to them. This will allow us to use a single texture to map all of them.

### Outer Hair

The only area needing attention here is the outer layer of hair.

1   As shown in **Figure 8.58**, apply planar mapping to the outer layers on both sides of the hair, projecting along the X axis.

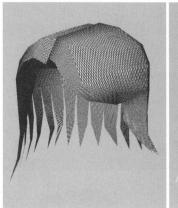

**FIGURE 8.58**
Apply planar mapping to the outer layer of her hair, on both left and right sides.

2   With the mapping applied, select Kila's left-side piece first and, as illustrated in **Figure 8.59**, adjust the UVs in the UV Texture Editor.

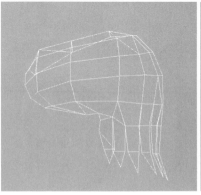
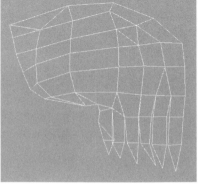

FIGURE 8.59 Adjust the UVs for the hair on Kila's left.

**3** Do the same with the hair on Kila's right, remembering to flip the UVs first (**Figure 8.60**).

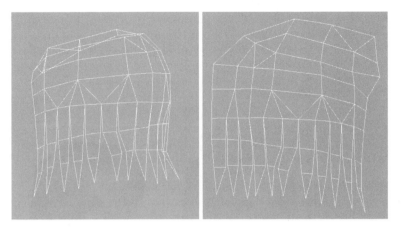

**FIGURE 8.60** Adjust the UVs for the hair on Kila's right.

Now comes the tricky part. We want both sides of the hair to be combined again—but if we do it now, the UVs will overlap. What we will do is separate the UVs before we combine them.

**1** First of all, separate the UVs, moving them apart.

**2** Combine both sides of the geometry making up the hair, welding the vertices down the center. With the left and right UVs now separated, we can work on them more easily.

We want to join the UVs across the top of her hair. Connecting them at the part will mean we can keep the flow of the hair while making sure the detail is not broken. So, we need to rotate them.

**3** Select the UVs for one side of the hair and go to Polygons > Rotate UVs, opening up the options. Here you can specify what degree of rotation you wish to apply.

**4**  Rotate both sides until the tops are facing each other (**Figure 8.61**, left).

**5**  Use the Sew UVs tool to connect the edges down the center (**Figure 8.61**, right).

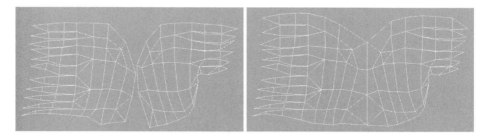

FIGURE 8.61 Rotate the UVs for the hair; then sew the facing edges together.

**6**  With both pieces of the hair connected now, edit the UVs a little more before moving on. Your goal is for the outer hair layer to look like that in **Figure 8.62**.

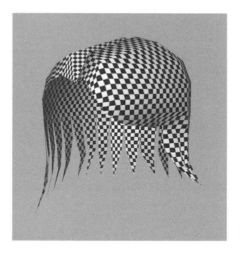

FIGURE 8.62 The outer hair, with mapping

With the main section of the outer hair mapped, our next task is to edit the UVs on the inner side of the hair at the brow.

### Inner Front Hair

To complete Kila's hair, we will now map the polygons that make up the inside layer of her hair at the forehead.

**1**   As you did in the preceding section, apply planar mapping to both sides of the front area of hair across the X axis (**Figure 8.63**).

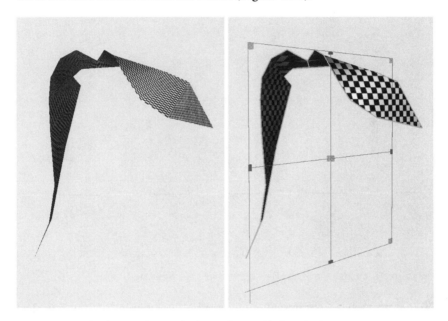

FIGURE 8.63 Apply mapping to the inner pieces of hair at the brow.

**2**   Tweak the UVs, removing any overlapping or stretching areas.

**3**   Separate both sets of UVs if they will overlap when the two pieces of geometry are combined.

**4**   Combine the meshes, welding the vertices down the center.

**5**   Next, you will join the two sections of UVs, using the center as the connecting point. Rather than having to manually move one set of UVs to the other, Maya will do it for you. In the UV Texture Editor, select the edges that connect, as seen in **Figure 8.64**, left.

**6** Go to Polygons > Move and Sew UVs. What you will see is that the smaller piece has not only been welded to the larger one but has moved, too (**Figure 8.64**, right).

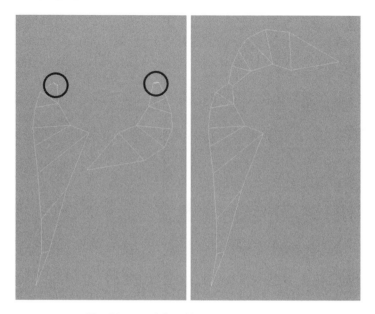

FIGURE 8.64 Use Move and Sew UVs to weld the separate UVs.

As shown in **Figure 8.65**, the inner pieces of the front hair are now complete.

FIGURE 8.65 Hair UV mapping applied and adjusted at the forehead

To finish the UV work on the Kila model, we still need to work on the hands and the belt. Let's look at the hands next.

## Hand UVs

The hand is another area to which applying mapping is relatively simple.

1    Begin by applying planar mapping downward on top of the hand, adjusting it to match the orientation (**Figure 8.66**).

> **TIP**  You can select both the top and bottom of the hand and apply the mapping to both areas at the same time.

2    As shown in **Figure 8.67**, first work on the top half's UVs in the UV Texture Editor. Move the UVs for the sides of each finger outward, so you can add a bit of detail to them when it's time to draw the texture.

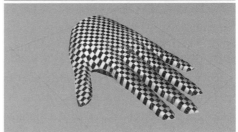

FIGURE 8.66 Planar-map the hand, projecting down onto it.

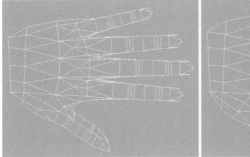
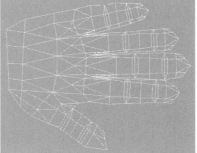

FIGURE 8.67 Adjust the UVs of the top half.

3    Do the same for the bottom of the hand, remembering to flip the UVs first.

The finished hand should look like that in **Figure 8.68**.

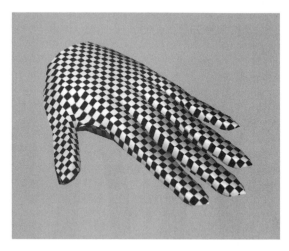

**FIGURE 8.68** The hand mapping is complete.

## Belt UVs

The final lower-body area to address is Kila's belt. Initially, the mapping here was fine (because this item of clothing was created from a basic cylinder, it had inherent mapping). We have since then adjusted it slightly, adding more geometry to the back of the body, so we need to address the resulting alterations in UVs.

1    Select the belt and look at its UV layout in the UV Texture Editor (**Figure 8.69**).

   You can see the main belt area in the center—the section that looks kind of like a UFO—but there are also lots of oddly shaped boxes around it. These are from the extra polygons you created on the inside of her belt. To start with, you will move these boxes away from the main belt's UVs, making it easier to work on them.

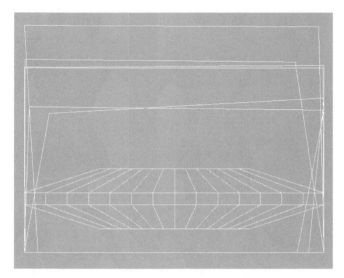

FIGURE 8.69
The belt's UV map

**2**    Go back to the 3D view, and select the faces you added to the inside of the belt (**Figure 8.70**). This will highlight them in the UV Texture Editor.

FIGURE 8.70 Select the belt's inner faces.

**3** Now that the faces are emphasized, go back into the UV Texture Editor and go to Select > Convert Selection to UVs. Follow the illustrations in **Figure 8.71**. Move the selected UVs up, away from the main belt's UV layout (**Figure 8.71b**).

**4** The shapes of the boxes need altering, to make them cleaner and more uniform. To help with this task, make sure the grid is visible by going to View > Grid.

**5** Select the UVs for each corner and, holding the X key, snap the UVs to points on the grid until they all match the same rectangular shape. You want it to look as if only one rectangle exists (**Figure 8.71c**).

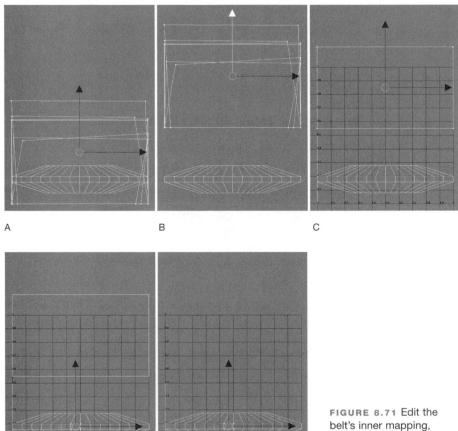

A    B    C

D    E

**FIGURE 8.71** Edit the belt's inner mapping, matching it with an appropriate section of the belt.

The texture for these inner sections of the belt can be the same as part of the outside, so what you can do next is move these UVs to the same place as a section of her belt—but which section?

6   Select a face on the outside of the belt (**Figure 8.72**). We'll use this section because it will have a basic texture applied to it, so no one will notice it's the same on the inside. If we were to use the front, where the buckle will be, then that texture would be repeated on the inside, which would look wrong.

FIGURE 8.72 Select a face on the outside of her belt.

7   With the face selected, go back to the UV Texture Editor, converting the selection to UVs (**Figure 8.71d**).

8   Now that you know where to move them to, hold down the V key and snap the UVs for the inner belt to the selected ones on the actual belt, as shown in **Figure 8.71e**.

9   All that's left to do now is edit the UVs for the top and bottom of the belt (**Figure 8.73**).

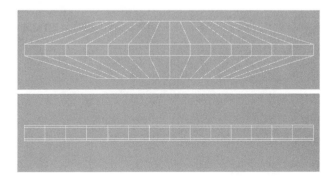

FIGURE 8.73 Adjust the top and bottom UVs for the belt.

**FIGURE 8.74** The belt's final UV mapping

We now have basic UV mapping applied to the entire mesh—but before we can sign it off as complete, some adjustments are needed.

### Extra Mapping Adjustments

There is one final thing to do before we can finalize Kila's UV work. On any normal model, we could use the same mapping for the left and right arms, essentially having to draw only one arm. Kila's arms are different, however; one has a tattoo. So we will need a separate set of mapping for each arm. The tattoo extends down onto her hand, so we will also need a separate set of mapping for them.

1  Duplicate and mirror the current arm and upper hand (**Figure 8.75**). Then go to Modify > Freeze Transformations; this will reset the −1 value on the Scale X attribute back to 1.

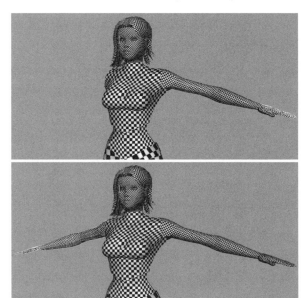

**FIGURE 8.75** Duplicate and mirror the left arm and upper hand.

**2**   Although you have duplicated these pieces of geometry, the UV coordinates they hold will still be the same. To fix this, first flip and then move the UVs so they no longer overlie the ones on the left side. Flip the arm UVs vertically, and do the hand UVs horizontally.

You can see the adjusted UVs in **Figures 8.76** and **8.77**.

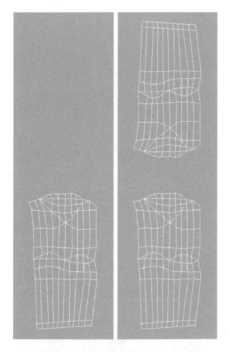

**FIGURE 8.76** Flip and separate the UVs for the new arm vertically.

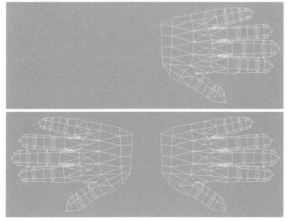

**FIGURE 8.77** For the new hand, flip the UVs horizontally before moving them.

The basic UVs are mapped now. As you can see in **Figure 8.78**, Kila's mapping is looking cleaner than the original. Currently, the squares of the grid are differing sizes, indicating that some areas occupy more texture space than others. This is not a problem, however; we can address this in the next section when we reposition the UVs so that they can be exported to an image file using UV Snapshot.

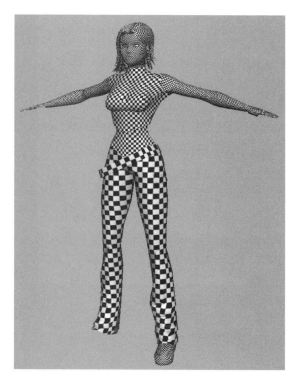

**FIGURE 8.78** Kila, fully mapped but not finished

# Exporting the UV Positions

With the help of Maya's UV Texture Editor, we can export the UV positions as a bitmap to use as a handy guide for creating the texture. First, we need to rearrange our UVs, attempting to fit them all into a square while making sure they don't overlap.

### UV Management

When the model is finished, she will be combined into a single piece of geometry. With that in mind, let's see how the UVs will look.

1   Select all of Kila's geometry and take a peek in the UV Texture Editor.

As you can see in **Figure 8.79**, things are a bit of a mess. You can make out a few of the body parts, but there is no chance you could draw onto this image and create a successful texture map.

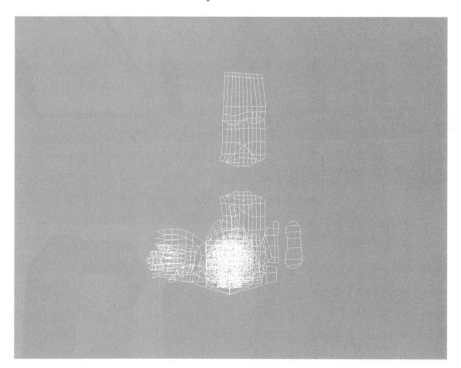

FIGURE 8.79 Kila's current UV mapping

**2** Spend some time selecting each separate piece of geometry and moving the UVs out, so you end up with everything laid out as seen in **Figure 8.80**. Each piece is now separate. This looks much better—you can tell what each part is.

FIGURE 8.80 The untangled UVs

The next problem to address is one of priority. At present the eyeball UV's are larger than her head, meaning the eye will have much more detail in the final texture. This is clearly wrong; you need to adjust the scale of each set of UVs, enlarging areas that need greater detail.

**3** To scale the UVs, simply select the piece of geometry in the 3D view. Then, in the UV Texture Editor, right-click and select UVs. Select all the UVs and press R to switch to the Scale manipulator.

While you are doing this scaling, you can begin to rearrange the UVs into their respective texture pages. Use the main grid to help you place them. Our budget is two 512x512 texture pages, so we can make use of this by dividing the UVs into three separate pages.

**NOTE** As a general rule, texture pages must conform to specific sizes, in powers of 2 (2, 4, 8, 16, 32, 64, 128, 256, 512, etc.). To be certain of what you are required to use, consult your manager.

**4** The first page to set up will contain the main head and hands, along with the feet and belt. This will be exported as a 256x256 texture page.

**5** In the next page, place all the main body parts. This will be a 512x512 page because we will need more detail in the body.

**6** Place the hair on a third texture page, also 256x256 in size. Parts of this page will be transparent, so we will keep it separate.

You can see the final UV layouts in **Figure 8.81**.

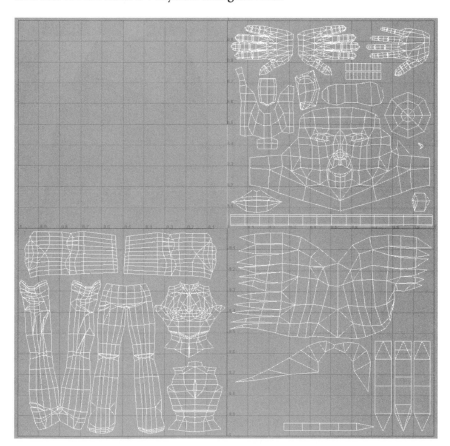

FIGURE 8.81 Kila's UV layout

There is one final adjustment we will make before we complete the mapping process: splitting the UVs in the T-shirt.

### Divide the Shirt

What we want to do now is split the UVs at the base of Kila's crop-top. This is necessary because, with the UVs attached, some of the color from her shirt may bleed through onto her stomach.

1   Select the edges across the base of the T-shirt, as shown in **Figure 8.82**. Go to Polygons > Cut UVs to cut them.

2   Select the faces that make up the bottom section of the torso. Convert the selection to UVs by going to Select > Convert Selection to UVs.

3   Move the selected UVs down slightly, creating a gap.

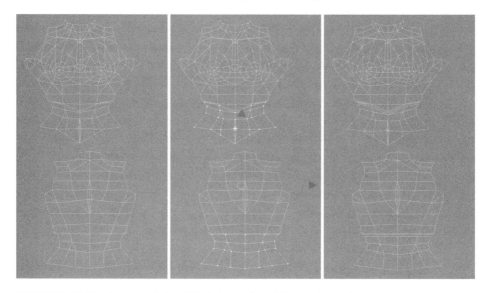

**FIGURE 8.82** Create a gap in the UVs between her shirt and stomach.

With this final adjustment made, we have completed the process of mapping UVs onto Kila. As you can see in **Figure 8.83**, the squares are now much more uniform in size. All we need to do now is export the UV layout, baking it out as an image we can use as a guide when we draw her texture.

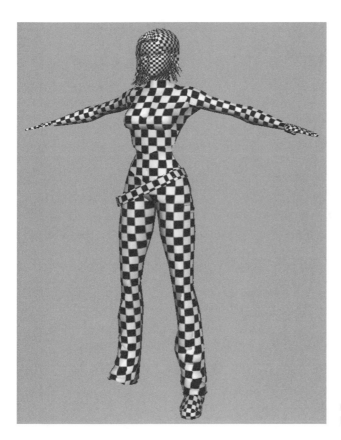

**FIGURE 8.83** Kila with her final UV mapping

### Taking a UV Snapshot

Using the UV Snapshot tool, we can export the UV layout as a bitmap, which we can then take into a digital imaging application to use as a guide for our texture.

**1**  Select the elements that make up the first texture page. These should be the head, eye, teeth, inner mouth, hands, tongue, shoe, eyelashes, and ear.

**2**  Look at **Figure 8.84**; these elements are already positioned correctly. To create a UV snapshot, the elements you want to capture must lie in the upper-right corner of the grid. This is the only area that Maya considers (positive 0 to 1 texture coordinate space) when saving out a UV snapshot image. Anything outside of +1u, +1v is ignored.

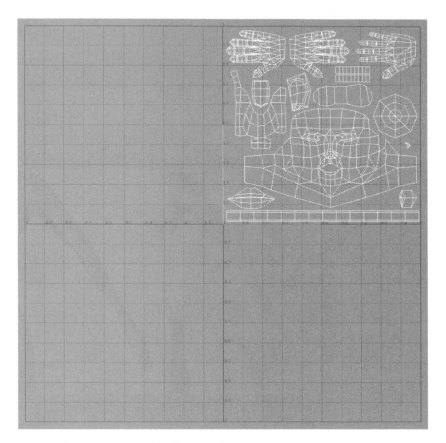

FIGURE 8.84 The head UVs in the correct position

So you are ready to create the base for the first texture page.

3    In the UV Texture Editor, go to Polygons > UV Snapshot. This opens the options dialog box seen in **Figure 8.85**.

FIGURE 8.85
The UV Snapshot
dialog box

**4**    This first texture is going to be sized at 256x256, so make sure the Size X and Size Y options are set to this.

**5**    Click Browse, and point to where you want the texture to be stored. Call it KilaHeadUV.tga.

**6**    Make sure Anti-alias Lines is not enabled; this will make the UV lines exported easier to manage and follow. Click OK, and the UV image will be created.

Before we look at the snapshot, let's create the base images for the other two texture pages.

**1**    Select the elements that made up the body page. This includes the legs, torso, and arms.

**2**    Move these UVs up to the upper-right corner of the grid (**Figure 8.86**); then open up the UV Snapshot options.

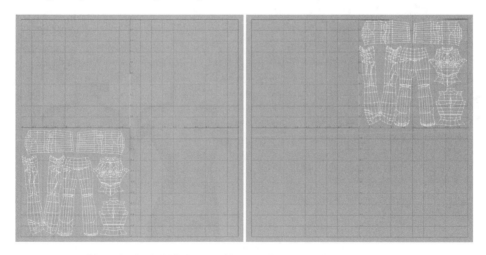

FIGURE 8.86 Move the body UVs into position to take a snapshot.

**3**    This time set the Size X and Size Y to 512.

**4**    Specify your place to save, naming it KilaBodyUV.tga, and click OK.

**5**    Finally, do the same with the hair UVs, saving these at a size of 256x256 with the name KilaHairUV.tga.

You should now have three images that you can use to guide you in creating your textures. These are shown in **Figure 8.87**.

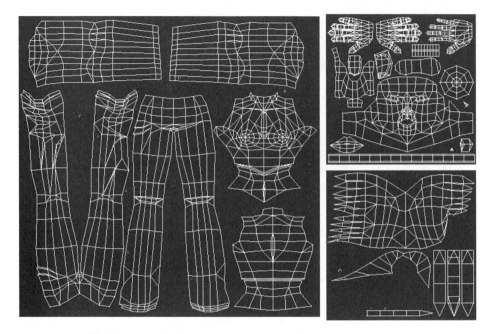

FIGURE 8.87 The three exported texture pages

The UVs have been successfully mapped and exported. What's needed now is to piece some of Kila back together and combine her.

## Recombine the Character

To begin, we need to create duplicates of the lower hand, the foot, and the eye.

1  We can mirror the hand and foot; go ahead and do this. But the eye must remain the same—simply copy this and move it across to where the right eye should be.

2  At this stage, we will only combine the main body. This will include the torso, legs, and arms. Make sure you weld the vertices afterward.

When mirroring and combining geometry, you must check the normals in particular. These are the directions in which each face is pointing. At present, she looks fine, but that is because Maya is displaying her as double-sided.

3    To check the normals, select the mesh and open up its attributes by pressing Ctrl+A.

4    Scroll down to the panel labeled Render Stats and open it up. Uncheck the checkbox labeled Double Sided.

5    Now look at your mesh; do any areas appear inside out? You can quickly fix them by going to Edit Polygons > Normals > Conform.

In most cases, all the polygons in the object will now be facing the same direction. If the problem remains, try selecting the faces and running Edit Polygons > Normals > Reverse, making sure the options are set to Reverse.

The Kila model is fully prepared now and ready to be textured. Delete the history and save the file as Kila_Mapped.mb.

## Mapping Grae

Using what you have learned in this chapter, load the divided Grae model (Grae_Divided.mb), and see if you can apply UV mapping to him.

> **TIP** ▶ If you are having trouble mapping an area, try dividing it further into more basic shapes, such as cylinders or planes. This will simplify the task of applying basic UV mapping. Concentrate then on getting each piece looking correct before combining them all again.

**Figures 8.88** and **8.89** show my finished Grae model and UV maps, which we can use in the next chapter. You can find this file on the CD as Project Files/08/ Grae_Mapped.mb.

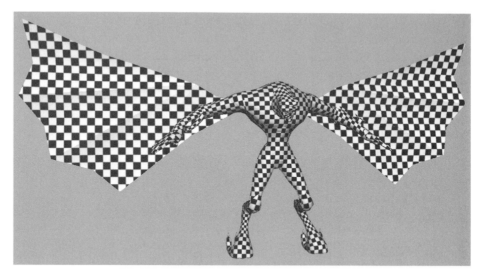

**FIGURE 8.88** Grae with full UV mapping

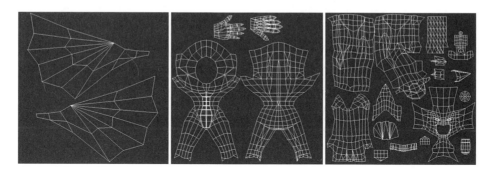

**FIGURE 8.89** Grae's exported texture pages

**NOTE** Exporting the UV maps does not mean that they are set in stone. You can edit them further if you like, as will be demonstrated in Chapter 9, "Texture Painting." Just remember that the images you export are the UVs at that stage, so if you drastically edit them before texture painting, you may need to re-export the maps.

## Summary

You now have the two models completely mapped and ready to be textured. This chapter on UV mapping has given you substantial knowledge and experience with Maya's UV editing tools, and you've created a basic material.

During the next chapter, we step outside Maya and, using the UV snapshots generated here, we'll draw the textures for our characters.

# CHAPTER 9
# Texture Painting

**THIS CHAPTER COVERS** various texturing techniques. It is not, however, a chapter on "how to draw." Rather, it explains how to use Maya in conjuction with Adobe Photoshop to prepare and paint your characters' textures. We also discuss how best to optimize your pages to get the file size as small as possible.

I chose Photoshop for our work in this chapter because it seems to be the industry standard; most companies I know of use it. Feel free to adapt this chapter to whatever digital imaging software you are using, or you can download a trial version of Photoshop from the Adobe Web site using the link on this book's CD.

The Photoshop toolbar shown in **Figure 9.1** holds most of the tools we will use to paint our textures. These tools are generally self-explanatory—for example, the Zoom tool allows you to zoom in and out of your image—and I'll briefly explain the others as we use them.

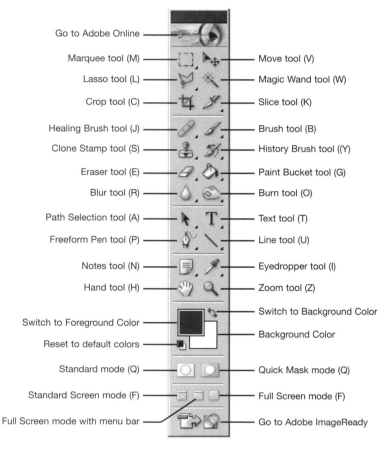

FIGURE 9.1 The Photoshop toolbar

For further information on Photoshop's tools, go to the application's Help > Photoshop Help, or press F1.

**TIP** For best results when creating any 2D artwork on a computer, I highly recommend purchasing a graphics tablet. A mouse is good for work that requires more precision, but for drawing it's not a very fluid tool. Graphics tablets are also pressure sensitive, meaning you can vary the thickness of the line you are drawing by applying more or less pressure. The two main suppliers of graphics tablets are Wacom (www.wacom.com) and Nisis (www.nisis.com).

## Image Preparation

To begin, we will load in our UV snapshot and prepare the image so we can use it efficiently. We need to invert the UV snapshot so we have black lines on a white background. We can then use this as an overlay, guiding us as we paint underneath it.

1    Open up Photoshop and load in the file called KilaHeadUV.tga.

2    Go to Image > Adjust > Invert (Ctrl+I/Cmd+I).

3    Now you need to duplicate this image and then create a separate layer with it, so first go to Select > All (Ctrl+A/Cmd+A) to select the entire image.

4    To remove the selected image from the background layer and place it in a layer of its own, go to Edit > Cut (Ctrl+X/ Cmd+X), followed by Edit > Paste (Ctrl+V/Cmd+V). This creates a new layer for you in the Layers window (**Figure 9.2**) called Layer 1.

5    Rename Layer 1 to UV Layout by double-clicking on the name itself in the window and then typing the new name.

6    Near the top of the Layers window is a white drop-down list with Normal currently selected. The options here alter the way the layer is displayed. Change this to Multiply.

**FIGURE 9.2** Photoshop's Layers window

Multiply will combine the current layer's colors with the ones underneath it. Multiplying any color with black produces black. Multiplying any color with white leaves the color unchanged. So in effect you have the black outlines in this layer while the rest of the layer appears transparent.

The initial preparation of the image is complete now. In the next section, we'll apply the base colors for our texture.

---

**Texture Page Size**

If you have the time, I recommend doubling the size of your texture pages before you begin painting. It can be difficult to include lots of detail in a smaller page. Painting it first on a larger page and then sampling it down will improve the overall image quality and retain most of the original's detail.

As a project progresses, you may be asked to provide some publicity renders for marketing; these might be used for magazine covers, POP displays, and Web site wallpapers. These renders will all need a better texture quality, and the characters will look much better if rendered with the larger texture pages.

---

## The Base Colors

The first stage in applying color is to lay down flat shades to act as a base.

Before we paint, we will create a new layer called Flats. To create it, go to Layer > New > Layer (Shift+Ctrl+N/Shift+Cmd+N), or click the New Layer button to the left of the small trashcan at the bottom of the Layer window.

> **NOTE**   When a new layer is created, it is always placed above the one you currently have selected. The new Flats layer should be in between the Background and UV Layout layers, so that the UV Layout layer always overlays your work. If things are not so arranged, you can simply select Flats in the layer window and drag it into the correct position.

We will now paint the base colors onto the Flats layer. These colors should be medium tones, because we will need to apply lighter ones for the highlights and contrasting darker ones for darker areas and shadows.

**1**   Use the Paint Bucket tool to fill the layer with whatever color dominates the page. In this case, there is more skin on this page than any other, so we will use that (**Figure 9.3**, middle). Click the Foreground Color box in the toolbar to open the Color Picker and select the color.

**2**   Continue around the page, blocking in the base color for each element. First select the area using the Lasso tool, and then fill it using the Paint Bucket tool and the appropriate color (**Figure 9.3**, right).

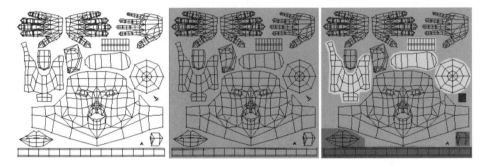

**FIGURE 9.3** Block in the base colors. (See page C1 for color version.)

Now save out two versions of this file, one to work on and a combined, flattened version to view in Maya. Note that if you are running Maya 6 or higher, you can use the .psd file directly. There is no need to save out a separate Targa file to use in Maya.

**3**   Go to File > Save As, saving the file as KilaHead.psd. This will be the main file that you work on. Saving it as a .psd (Photoshop) file means it keeps all the layer information.

**4**   With the .psd version saved, remove the UV Layout layer. You can make it invisible by clicking on the eye icon to the left of the layer, or delete it by dragging it to the trashcan at the bottom right of the Layers window.

**5**   Next go to Layer > Flatten Image. This will flatten all the layers, baking them onto the background layer. If you turned off the visibility for the UV Layer, you will be asked if you want to Discard Hidden Layer; select yes.

**6**    Now save this version as KilaHead.tga, saving it as a Targa file. After you click OK, you'll be given the option to change the file's bit/pixel setting. Since we don't have any alpha channels, 24 bits/pixel is fine (we will discuss bit depths later in the chapter).

Follow this procedure for all the other texture pages you have, saving them in both Photoshop and Targa file formats. You should have six pages for Kila, a .psd and a .tga each for KilaHead, KilaBody, and KilaHair. At this point, you can also work on the pages for Grae, calling them GraeBody, GraeMisc, and GraeWing and saving a .psd and .tga for each.

> **TIP** ▶ I recommend creating a separate layer for each item of Kila's clothing. This will make editing them much easier later on.

Before we add more detail to the textures, we will apply them to our models in Maya so that we can view them interactively as we work.

## Viewing the Texture in Maya

Let's now apply these basic textures to our geometry. Having them applied means we can switch between Maya and Photoshop as we work, keeping an eye on the way things are looking on the actual models.

**1**    In Maya, open up the file you created in Chapter 8, Kila_Mapped.mb. She currently has the checkered map applied to her, and we now want to swap this for the main texture pages.

**2**    First we need to create three new shaders, each one holding the Targa files we just saved. Open the Hypershade window or the Multilister, depending on which you prefer, and create three Lambert shaders. We use Lambert because these will give us flat, matte-looking textures.

**3**    Rename the new shaders to Kila_Head, Kila_Body, and Kila_Hair.

> **NOTE** ▶ Maya does not allow spaces to exist in the names of its objects and so will always replace spaces with underscores.

4 Open up each shader's Attribute Editor and click the checker button to the right of the Color slider (**Figure 9.4**). Choose File in the Create Render Node window that appears then point the Image Name to each corresponding Targa file.

5 While the Attribute Editor is still open, set the Diffuse values to 1. They are set to 0.8 by default; altering them to 1 will set the texture to be at full strength.

6 Now you can apply these materials to the model. Select the geometry that makes up Kila's hair. In the Hypershade, right-click the Kila Hair shader and select Assign Material to Selection.

7 Select the elements that exist on the body UV page. This should be a single mesh because we combined them earlier. Right-click the Kila Body shader, and select Assign Material to Selection.

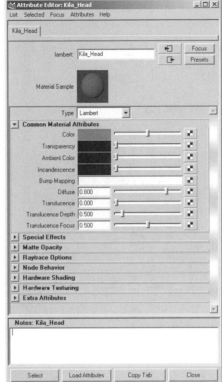

**FIGURE 9.4** Open each shader's Attribute Editor and assign the color texture.

8 Finally, select the rest of the geometry that still has the Check texture applied to it, right-click the Kila Head shader, and select Assign Material to Selection.

An easy way to do this is to right-click the Check shader and choose Select Objects with Material. This will select all the faces that house that material.

9 In the Hypershade window, select Edit > Delete Unused Nodes. This will delete the Check texture, as it is no longer used.

As seen in **Figure 9.5**, Kila now has color and is looking more like the original concept art. Save the file as Kila_Texture.mb.

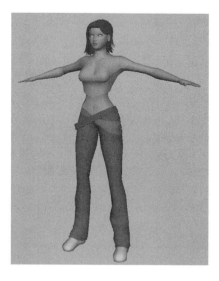

FIGURE 9.5 The Kila geometry with base colors applied (See page C6 for color version.)

Do all these same tasks on the Grae model, applying the base materials to him (**Figure 9.6**). Call this file Grae_Texture.mb.

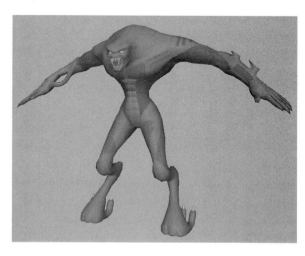

FIGURE 9.6 The Grae geometry with base colors applied (See page C1 for color version.)

With the base colors applied, we can now go on to check that each section lines up correctly. It's important to do this now, before we work the details into the texture pages.

### Texture Alignment

Because the UVs for Kila's top and sash have been split in two, we need to make sure they line up on the model before we begin adding details. Look at the armpit area shown in **Figure 9.7**, left. You can see that the front and back textures don't line up properly.

This alignment problem will often occur at seam locations, but correcting such areas will get easier as you become more experienced. To help reduce the misalignment, you can use the UV Layout to help guide the placement of your colors.

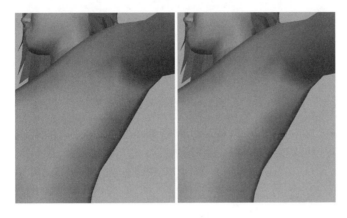

**FIGURE 9.7** Adjust the texture and UVs to line up the texture. (See page C1 for color version.)

1   Make sure you have both Maya and Photoshop open, with the model loaded into one and the texture loaded into the other.

2   Initially, look at the geometry in Maya, particularly at the seams, to identify areas that are not aligned properly. Then, in Photoshop, select the appropriate color and, using a small brush, work on the .psd file.

3   When you are happy with your work, flatten the file (Layer > Flatten Image) and overwrite the Targa file that is used by Maya. (Make sure to keep updating the .psd file with the unflattened version at regular intervals, too.)

> **NOTE**  Another way to do this realignment is to keep both the .psd and the .tga open in Photoshop. Tweak the .psd file, hide the UV Overlay layer, and then select all (Ctrl+A/Cmd+A). Use the Copy Merged tool (Ctrl+Shift+C/Cmd+Shift+C) to snapshot all the layers of the .psd file without having to flatten the file, and paste (Ctrl+V/Cmd+V) into the .tga file. Flatten the .tga and save.

> **TIP**  Setting up a shortcut key for "flatten image" is a great time-saver, too.

Move back into Maya and reload the texture so you can see it applied to the model.

1   In Maya, go to your Hypershade window and select the Textures tab above the main window. This presents the three main texture files used on Kila.

2   Open the texture for her body, which will open the Attribute Editor.

3   Click the Reload File Texture button to reload the texture. The view panel will now be updated.

Alternatively, you can use the first button, labeled Tex, in the GCDM shelf supplied on the CD. This will automatically reload all the textures in the scene.

**TIP** ▶ If you can't get the seam to line up perfectly by editing the texture, you can always fine-tune the UVs in the UV Texture Editor.

Now that you've realigned the armpit area, fix the strap of the T-shirt. Then work on the left and right sides of her sash (**Figure 9.8**).

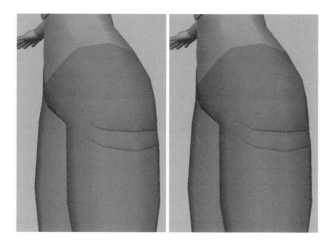

**FIGURE 9.8** Fix the texture on the sash. (See page C2 for color version.)

## Lighter Shades and Highlights

With the base textures complete and in position, we can begin to add some details. In this section we will paint in lighter shades and highlights.

First, let's follow the process illustrated in **Figure 9.9** to add lighter shades to the front of Kila's torso.

**1**　Start by creating a new layer named Lighter Tones. Set the foreground color to be a lighter shade of the skin tone. Don't just use white; it's not a realistic skin tone. Try a pale yellow or pink color.

**2**　Using the Paint Brush tool at a size of 3, roughly mark in the areas of the torso that would catch the light (**Figure 9.9b**).

**3**　Using the Blur tool, work your way around and blur the edges of the areas you just painted (**Figure 9.9c**).

**4**　You want the lighting to be more subtle here, so set the layer's Opacity to around 40%, toning down the lighter shades (**Figure 9.9d**).

**5**　Using the Lasso tool, select the areas that overlap onto the crop top, and go to Image > Adjustments > Desaturate. This will turn them from the lighter skin tone to white, which will work better for the T-shirt.

**6**　Use the Eraser tool to sharpen up some of the edges that are too blurred around her stomach muscles. Work on the area until you are happy with the results; take a look at **Figure 9.9e**.

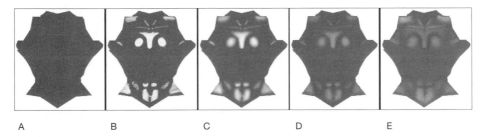

A            B            C            D            E

**FIGURE 9.9** Add lighter shades to the torso front. (See page C2 for color version.)

**7**　Save the image as a .psd. Then, hiding the UV Layout layer first, flatten it and overwrite the KilaBody.tga file.

**8** In Maya now, reload the Kila Body texture. What you should see is the texture applied as in **Figure 9.10**, left.

**9** To get a better idea of the texture's placement, go to the panel's Lighting menu and select Use No Lights. The image will now look like the one in **Figure 9.10** on the right.

> **TIP** You should work in Use No Lights mainly when you're applying textures. This is particularly useful when lining up the separate sections of the texture, as when matching the shoulder with the torso. Keep in mind that the better your characters looks in the "no lights" view, the better they will look in the game.

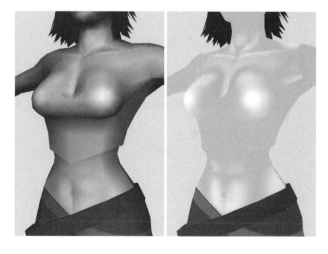

**FIGURE 9.10** Set Use No Lights to see the character unlit. (See page C2 for color version.)

Continue around the body and the head texture pages, filling out the lighter areas.

When you're done with those areas, create another layer called Highlights. Work on top of the lighter tones, implementing any highlighted areas (for example, her cheeks, nose, and breasts).

> **TIP** Feel free to create more layers when you are not completely confident about painting directly on top of your work. If another layer exists above the main one, you can always combine them after you've finished working, by going to Layer > Merge Down (Ctrl+E/Cmd+E). Also, instead of just merging with the layer below, you can merge all the visible layers by going to Layer > Merge Visible (Shift+Ctrl+E/Shift+Cmd+E). Another option is to merge all the linked layers by going to Layer > Merge Linked (Ctrl+E/Cmd+E).

You can still at this stage make minor alterations to the geometry—say, for example, you notice that the shape of the face needs a slight alteration. Major changes, though, will involve some editing in the UV Texture Editor and possible alterations to the texture. If you make considerable changes to the geometry and/ or UV Layout, you can always generate a new UV snapshot to replace the one in your .psd file.

At this point, Kila looks like the image in **Figure 9.11**, which uses the texture pages shown in **Figure 9.12**.

**FIGURE 9.11** Kila with lighter tones and highlights added (See page C3 for color version.)

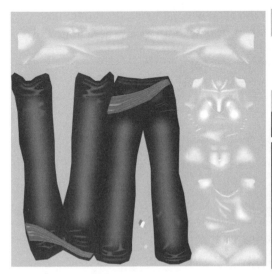 

**FIGURE 9.12** The texture pages, with lighter tones added (See page C3 for color version.)

We will edit the hair texture page later in the chapter, so let's work next in the darker contrasting areas of the main body and head.

## Darker Shades and Shadows

In order to bring the lighter tones out in the model, adding depth to the textures, we next need to add the darker areas.

As you did with the lighter tones, begin by creating a new layer named Darker Tones, and work your way around the texture pages, focusing on darker areas. These will include the creases in her jeans and recessed areas in her skin.

> **TIP** Remember, when texturing with darker tones, to use darker shades of the color you are painting onto, rather than black. Also, experiment with slightly different tones; for example, try making darker areas of skin slightly redder, and see what results you get.

When you're ready, create a fourth layer called Shadows. Now you can go in and add the darkest areas to the texture, while also implementing some of the minor shadows (**Figures 9.13** and **9.14**).

Notice in **Figures 9.13** and **9.14** that I have added the shadows that are cast by her hair, belt, and crop top, and in the crotch of the jeans. Although a few game engines do allow the character to receive shadows cast by itself, adding these shadows in the image will help give depth and detail to areas where none exists.

**FIGURE 9.13** Kila with darker tones and shadows added (See page C4 for color version.)

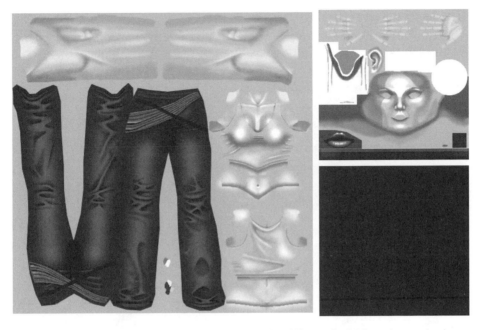

**FIGURE 9.14** The texture pages with darker tones added (See page C4 for color version.)

We are coming along well with the textures. We have added highlighting to them, to provide detail and form to the model. Next, we'll go in and add compelling details such as her hair, eyebrows, and tattoo.

## Final Texture Details

To complete the main textures, we need some particulars that don't yet exist. In addition to enhancements for her body and face, we will also add Kila's teeth and tongue. **Figure 9.15** shows the model with all these final details included.

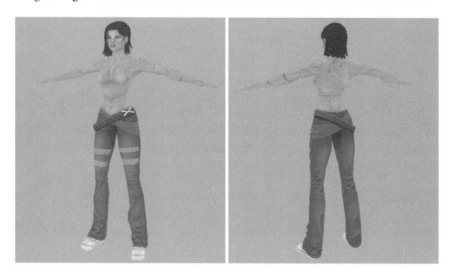

FIGURE 9.15 Kila with details added to the textures (See page C5 for color version.)

Start with a new layer for each detail you add—you can always collapse them later, merging them into a single layer.

### Face

Let's look at the face first; this is shown in **Figure 9.16**.

Remember—if you are at all unsure about how something should look, refer to a photographic reference. You can also search online for other artists' texture pages—just don't use the actual images in your artwork.

1    First, draw in the pupils and iris outlines of the eyes, but don't add any highlights to the texture; we will be putting these in later. Adding these eye elements will really make a difference—Kila will no longer look like a zombie!

The background text states that Kila's eyes will glow. You don't need to be concerned about that here because it can be better achieved by using an in-game effect.

Use a light gray rather than pure white for the "whites" of Kila's eyes. No one's eyes are pure white—more importantly, though, the light gray will make the highlights we will create later stand out nicely.

FIGURE 9.16 Add detail to her face, including the eyes, eyebrows, and hairline. (See page C13 for color version.)

**2**   Next, give her some eyebrows; these will help remarkably to complete the look of the face.

**3**   In the concept render, Kila has very dark eyes with pink eye-shadow, so implement these into the texture next.

**4**   Using the base hair color, carefully sketch in the hairline at the top of her forehead, applying the Blur tool to smooth it out a little. This will help break up the currently solid hairline.

Originally, the eyelashes were to be left black, but after consulting with the lead artist it is agreed that they would benefit from additional detail. We have the texture space available, so we will add this eyelash detail later on in the chapter.

> **NOTE**   You will find while working with your manager that the specifications of a character will often change, and the look may deviate somewhat from the main concept artwork. If lots of changes are planned, don't be afraid to voice your own opinion—schedules are very important, so if changes look like they're going to take an extra three weeks, let your manager know this. And do it before you begin editing; it may turn out that you won't have time to implement the changes. You don't want to end up having to cram three weeks of work into one.

Let's move on now and focus on the elements at Kila's waist.

### Waist Area

At the waistline, we have two main areas we can enhance. Kila has a chain that wraps around her stomach, acting as a belt. Below that, it looks like her navel is pierced, so we should implement this, too. Finally, there's the belt, which needs the buckle and some other details added to it.

You can see all of these details in **Figure 9.17**.

**FIGURE 9.17** Add detail to the belt and other items at the waist. (See page C13 for color version.)

### Jeans Detail

Continuing down the model, we next come to her jeans. At present, the jeans look fine, but there are a number of areas we can improve.

#### *Denim Grain*

Denim, like most cloth, has texture. In this case, it has a grainy look. Using Photoshop's Noise Filter, we will add this graininess to make our texture look more like real denim. (Later, this technique can also be adopted on Grae to give his skin more texture.)

1  On the Flats layer in Photoshop, use the Magic Wand tool to select the blue area of the jeans (**Figure 9.18a**).

2  Duplicate this area into a new layer; go to Edit > Copy (Ctrl+C/Cmd+C) and then Edit > Paste (Ctrl+V/Cmd+V).

**NOTE** Make sure the new layer exists above the Lighter Tones, Darker Tones, and Shadows layers. This will make the new layer appear to be overwriting the others, but don't worry—this layer will actually overlay the others (Figure 9.18b).

3   Go to Filter > Noise > Add Noise. This opens up the dialog box seen in **Figure 9.19**.

4   Set Amount to about 8.3, and set the Distribution to Gaussian. Make sure Monochromatic is enabled; this will keep the noise the same color as the jeans.

5   Click OK to apply the filter (**Figure 9.18c**).

6   You need to adjust this layer so that it loses its color information and also adjusts the saturation of the jeans. Do this by going to Image > Adjustments > Desaturate.

7   Adjust the overall brightness by going Image > Adjustments > Brightness/Contrast and setting Brightness to 35 (**Figure 9.18d**).

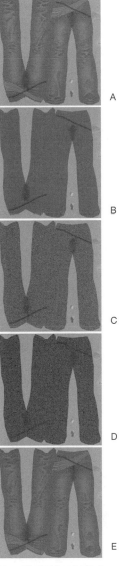

FIGURE 9.18 Use Photoshop's Noise Filter to add grain to the fabric of the jeans. (See page C6 for color version.)

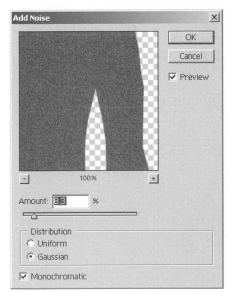

FIGURE 9.19 The Add Noise window

8   Finally, this layer must be transparent so that you can still see the detail below it. Set Opacity in the layer window to 15% (**Figure 9.18e**).

With the jeans grain complete, let's now add the seams, and finally the tears at the front of her thighs.

### Seams and Tears

To complete the jeans, we need to add the seams that run down the inner and outer legs, as well as the tears in the fabric at the front. Both these enhancements can be seen in **Figure 9.20**, and both features should initially be created on new layers.

As illustrated in **Figure 9.21**, the seams are created by using the Line tool with a lighter color to trace the inside edges of the UV Layout. The lines will be slightly too thick, so go in afterward and carefully trim off a few pixels. The idea is to give a slight hint of the detail needed.

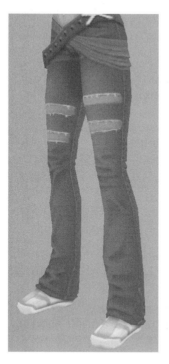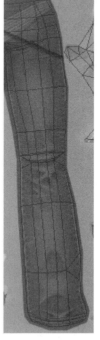

The rips in the jeans legs are initially created on a number of layers: the main skin color, then shading, and finally the white strands that hang over the tears. When you are happy with the results of your work on these layers, you can combine them into a single layer.

FIGURE 9.20 Kila's jeans with details added (See page C14 for color version.)

FIGURE 9.21 Run the seams down the inside and outside of the leg. (See page C14 for color version.)

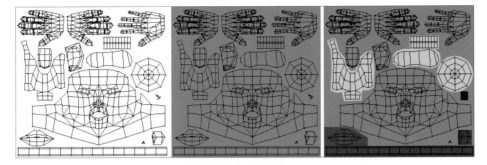

**FIGURE 9.3** Block in the base colors.

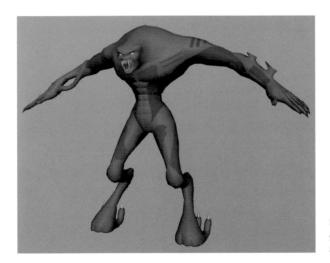

**FIGURE 9.6** The Grae geometry with base colors applied.

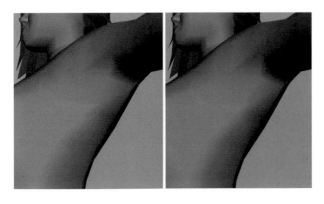

**FIGURE 9.7** Adjust the texture and UVs to line up the texture.

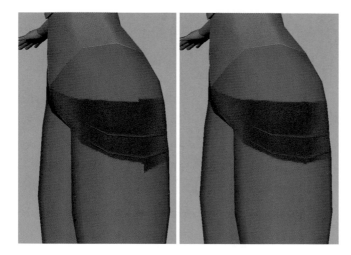

**FIGURE 9.8** Fix the texture on the sash.

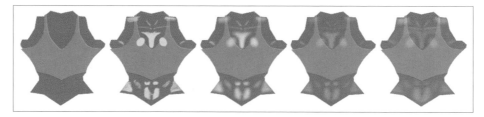

**FIGURE 9.9** Add lighter shades to the torso front.

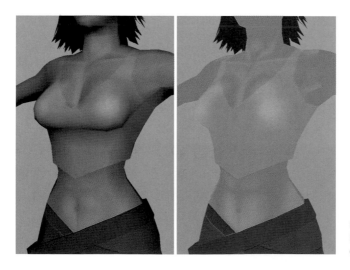

**FIGURE 9.10** Set Use No Lights to see the character unlit.

**FIGURE 9.11** Kila with lighter tones and highlights added.

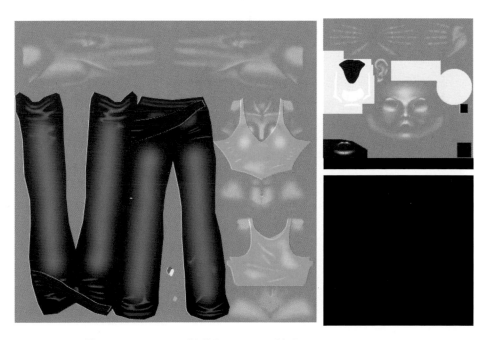

**FIGURE 9.12** The texture pages, with lighter tones added.

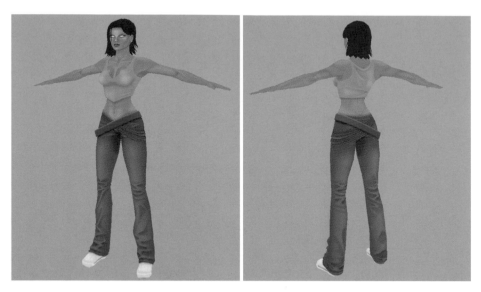

**FIGURE 9.13** Kila with darker tones and shadows added.

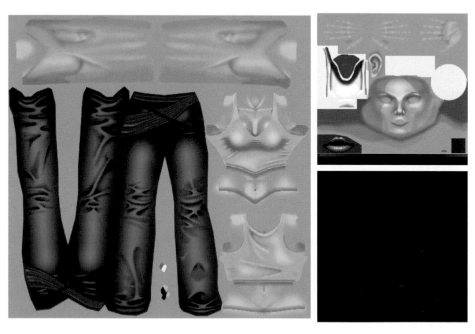

**FIGURE 9.14** The texture pages with darker tones added.

**FIGURE 9.15** Kila with details added to the textures.

**FIGURE 9.25** The current texture pages.

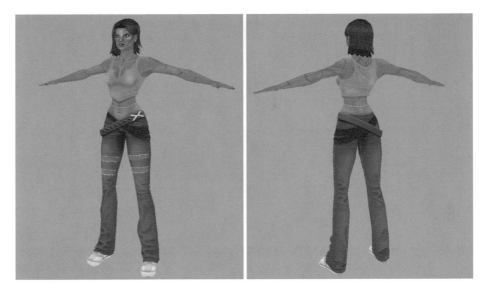

**FIGURE 9.27** The current Kila model with the hair now textured.

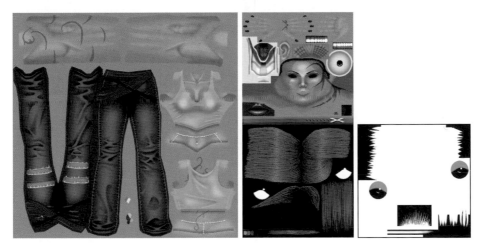

**FIGURE 9.42** Kila's texture pages.

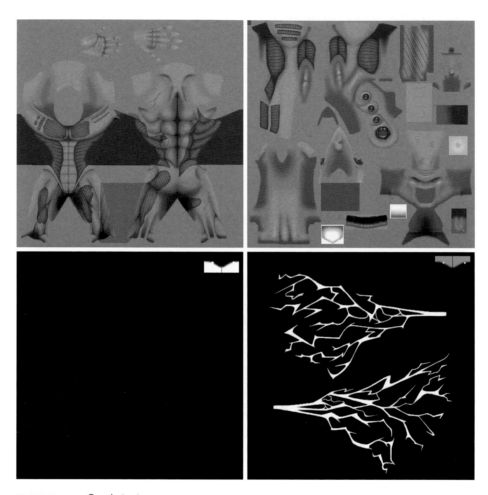

**FIGURE 9.43** Grae's texture pages.

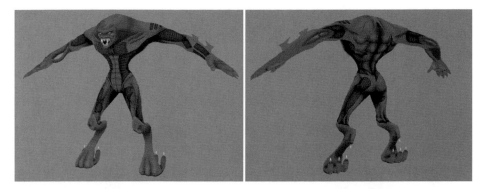

**FIGURE 9.28** Follow the same steps to texture Grae.

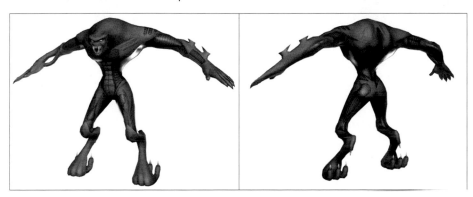

**FIGURE 9.46** Grae with specular map applied.

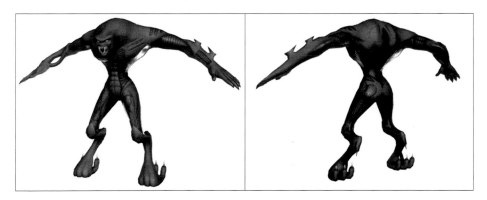

**FIGURE 9.48** Grae with both specular and bump maps applied.

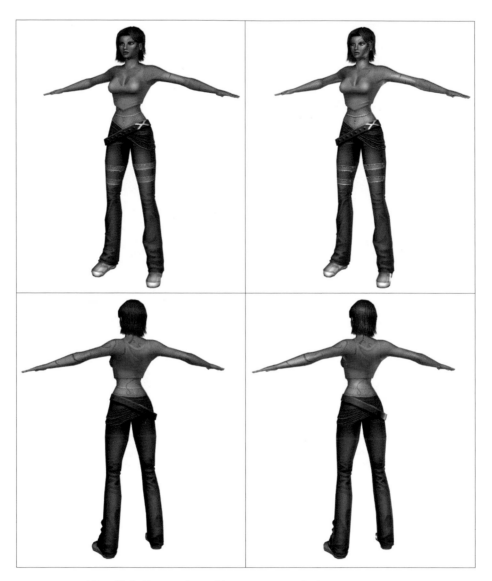

**FIGURE 9.49** Kila with both specular and bump maps applied.

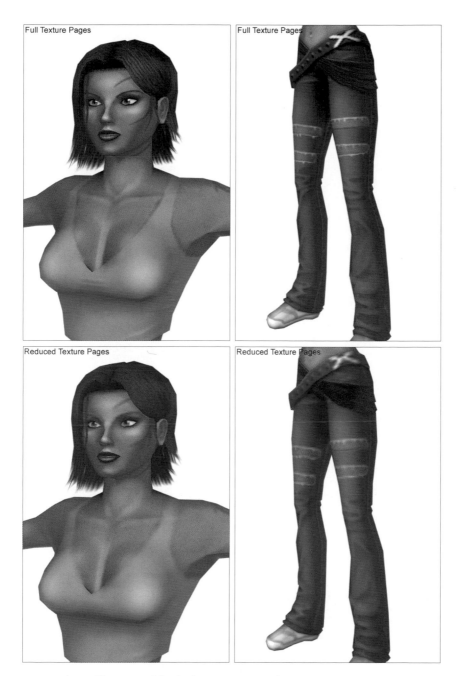

**FIGURE 9.54** Close-ups of the texture page comparison.

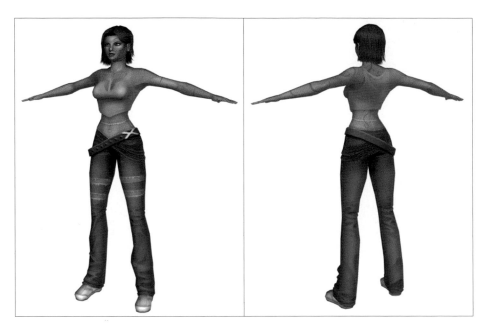

**FIGURE 9.58** Kila final model after texturing and tweaking.

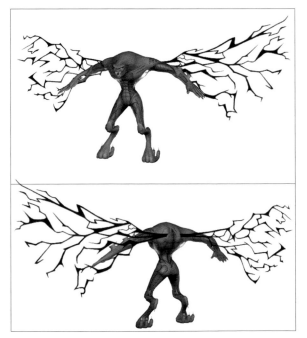

**FIGURE 9.59** Grae final model after texturing and tweaking.

**FIGURE 9.16** Add detail to her face, including the eyes, eyebrows, and hairline.

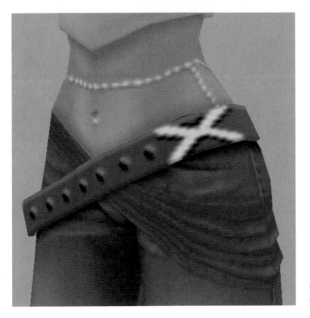

**FIGURE 9.17** Add detail to the belt and other items at the waist.

**FIGURE 9.20** Kila's jeans with details added.

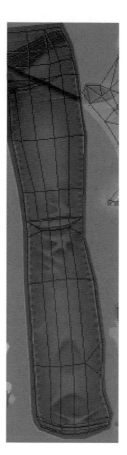

**FIGURE 9.21** Run the seams down the inside and outside of the leg.

**FIGURE 9.26** Build up the hair texture page.

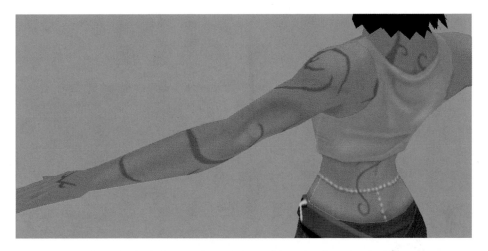

**FIGURE 9.22** Once the body is complete, we can add another layer for the tattoo.

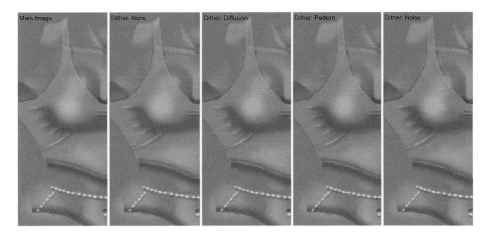

**FIGURE 9.56** Effects of the different Dither options.

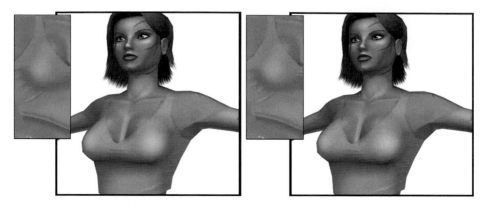

**FIGURE 9.57** The 24-bit and 8-bit comparison.

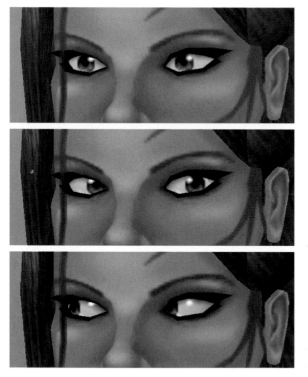

**FIGURE 9.36** The eyes with highlights and shadows applied.

### Tattoo

To finish off the main body of our character, we next will add her trademark tattoo that exists on her face, back, left arm, and hand.

The winding tattoo should first be created on a separate layer, since you will need to adjust the layer's opacity so that the tattoo appears to overlay the other details (**Figure 9.22**). Setting the Opacity to about 60% should work well.

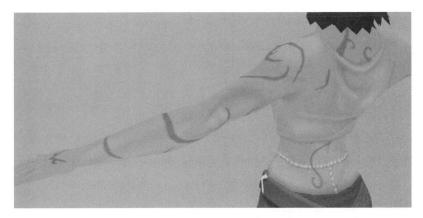

**FIGURE 9.22** Once the body is complete, we can add another layer for the tattoo. (See page C15 for color version.)

With all the main body textured now, let's look at the inside of the mouth.

### Inner Mouth

As seen in **Figure 9.23**, we next work on giving color to the inner mouth, tongue, and teeth—ready for any lip-synching she may need to do.

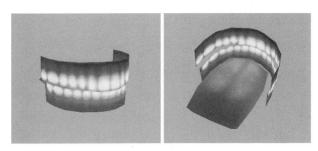

**FIGURE 9.23** The inner mouth with textures

At present, the UV Layout for the teeth is not very efficient. The entire rows of top and bottom teeth need to be squeezed into this small area. What we can do is assume that her teeth are perfect, so we create one half and mirror the geometry for the other half—meaning we only have to draw half of her teeth, allowing us to add more detail.

**1**    First delete the left side of the teeth geometry.

**2**    Adjust the UVs so they take up more space on the page (Figure 12.24).

**FIGURE 9.24** Adjust the teeth UVs to take up more space on the page.

**3**    Now duplicate and mirror the existing half of the teeth, creating the left side.

**4**    Finally snapshot the UV map again and load it into your .psd file for Kila's head in Photoshop. You can now draw the teeth onto the texture page. You can see the current texture pages in **Figure 9.25**.

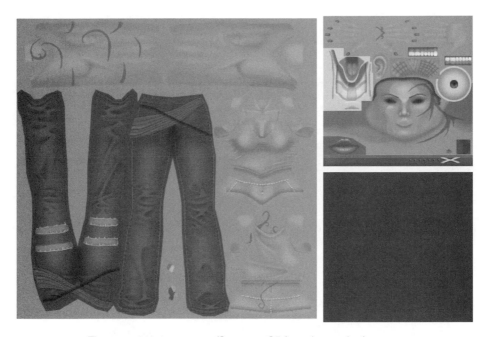

**FIGURE 9.25** The current texture pages (See page C5 for color version.)

## Hair

With Kila's main body and head nearing completion, let's work on her hair. As demonstrated in **Figure 9.26**, creating the hair is simply a matter of building up different layers of hair using gradually lighter tones.

> **TIP** Try to keep to individual strokes when building up this texture; don't be tempted to "scribble" the hair.

1   Working backward this time, first create a darker base layer (**Figure 9.26a**).

2   Add a lighter layer, drawing only where the light would strike the hair. In this case, the part and the area tucked behind her ear need to be darker (**Figure 9.26b**).

3   Again step up the lightness, adding a third layer to the hair. The three strips that exist under the outer layer of hair should remain slightly darker to help give the hair depth (**Figure 9.26c**).

**4** The basic hair is more or less complete now. The final steps are to add highlights, and to darken the area where the hair curves inward (**Figures 9.26d** and **9.26e**).

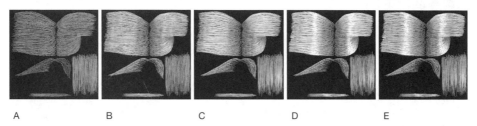

A       B       C       D       E

FIGURE 9.26 Build up the hair texture page (See page C14 for color version.)

Kila's texturing is finished (**Figure 9.27**). It's Grae's turn now; simply follow the same steps to create his textures (**Figure 9.28**).

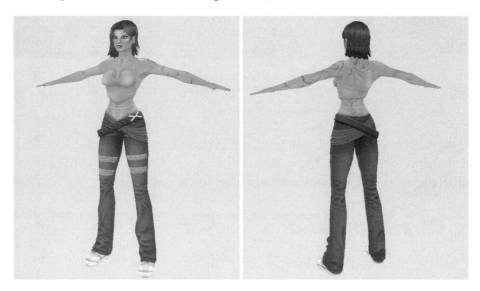

FIGURE 9.27 The current Kila model with the hair now textured. (See page C7 for color version.)

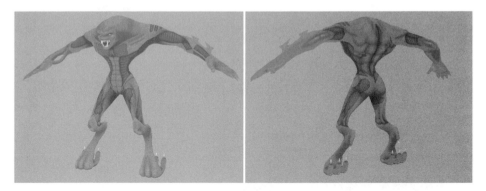

FIGURE 9.28 Follow the same steps to texture Grae. (See page C9 for color version.)

## Working with an Alpha Map

In this section we will add transparent areas to the geometry by using an *alpha map*. An alpha map is basically a grayscale image. This image tells Maya (or your game engine) which parts of the texture page are transparent and which are opaque. In Maya, areas that are pure white (values 255,255,255 in all red, green, and blue channels) will render opaque; black (0,0,0) will render transparent; and any values in between will be translucent to varying degrees. (Some game engines invert these values, so it's important to check with your manager to verify the final opacity values.)

There are five regions in our two characters on which we can use an alpha map. For Kila, we can implement alpha maps into her hair, eyes, and eyelashes. Grae only needs alpha maps on his eyes and wings.

### Creating the Hair Alpha Map

Let's look at Kila's hair first. At present, her hair is quite angular (**Figure 9.29**), and we can fix this by making the strands more transparent toward their ends, losing the sharp edges that the polygons form.

FIGURE 9.29 Using an alpha map, we can make Kila's hair less angular.

1   You first need to create the alpha map. Load in the current hair texture file, KilaHair.psd.

2   Create a new layer called Alpha.

3   The white areas of the image will be opaque, and black will be completely transparent. Most of the hair will be solid, so fill the layer in white.

4   In black, draw in all the areas that will be transparent. Thanks to the size of the page, you can afford to draw in a bit more detail in this step, allowing for additional hair strands that will "break up" and more clearly define the hair.

5   Use the Blur tool to smooth out some of the edges. The alpha map also works in different shades of gray, so the blurring will make the hair gradually fade out.

   Be careful not to blur the edges too much. Go in afterward and remove some of the blur with the Eraser tool. Areas that are gray will be semitransparent, so make sure areas that must be completely transparent are solid black.

   You can see the finished alpha map in **Figure 9.30**.

   **TIP** ▶ Before you save the alpha map, quickly invert it by going to Image > Adjustments > Invert. You will be able to see any subtle areas that you may have missed when painting on your image.

**TIP** You can use Photoshop's Eyedropper tool to sample the black and white colors to ensure that you have 0,0,0 and 255,255,255 values.

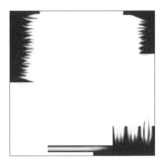

FIGURE 9.30 The hair alpha map

Most game engines require the alpha map to be a separate texture page, so at this point you could save the complete file as a .psd, then flatten it and save it as KilaHair_Alpha.tga.

### Viewing the Alpha Map in Maya

The main alpha map is complete. Next, we will bring it into Maya so we can see how it looks when applied to the character. To see the image in Maya, we will embed the alpha map into the main hair image.

1 Make sure KilaHair.tga is the active window in Photoshop. You need to work in the Channel window, so open it up by going to Window > Channels. This shows the different color channels that exist in the image: red, green, and blue.

2 Create a new channel. Just as in the Layers window, click the Create New Channel button at the bottom of the window, directly to the left of the trashcan. This adds a new channel, conveniently called Alpha 1 (**Figure 9.31**).

FIGURE 9.31 Create a new alpha channel.

3 Switch back to KilaHair_Alpha.tga or the .psd from which it was created. Select the entire alpha layer you drew earlier (Ctrl+A/Cmd+A), and make a copy of it (Ctrl+C/Cmd+C).

**4** Select the Alpha 1 channel of KilaHair.tga and paste the alpha map into it (Ctrl+V/Cmd+V).

**5** Flatten the rest of the image, leaving you with the hair texture. Save it as a Targa file, selecting 32 bits/pixel when prompted. The 32 bits/pixel option ensures that the alpha map is embedded in the image file.

**6** Move into Maya. Reload the textures and open up Hypershade.

**7** Double-click the material called Kila_Hair, opening up its attributes.

**8** Still in the Hypershade window, click the Textures tab to reveal all the texture files associated with the scene.

**9** With the middle mouse button, select and drag the hair texture over the Transparency attribute in the Attribute Editor. A box will appear around the Transparency attribute, showing you that it's all right to drop the texture here.

**10** Go back to the view panel, and you will see that the hair now has transparency (**Figure 9.32**, left).

> **NOTE** With the alpha map applied to the hair, you may experience some display problems. The lower layers of hair may pop through the outer one, as you can see on the right side of her hair in Figure 9.32. This is mainly due to the hair geometry's being separate from the rest of the image; combining them will reduce the problem. This issue is a display problem within Maya and not indicative of transparency errors in the alpha map.

**11** All that is left to do is adjust the vertices on the separate strands of hair, thickening them and widening them to fill in any large gaps in the hair (**Figure 9.32**, right).

**FIGURE 9.32**
After applying the alpha channel, fill in any gaps in the hair geometry.

The hair is now complete and ready. Next we will work on the alpha map for the eyes.

### Preparing the Eyes' Alpha Map

At present, the eyes don't look real; they have no depth, mainly due to the lack of highlights. Using the alpha map created for Kila's hair, we can add these highlights as well as a slight shadow to the whites of the eyes. First, you'll prepare the eyes to receive these details.

1   In Maya, hide everything except for the eye geometry (**Figure 9.33a**).

2   Duplicate the eyes, moving the copies slightly forward (**Figure 9.33b**).

3   You will apply the alpha map to the duplicates. This means the eyes as a whole can rotate, while the highlights and shadow stay static. You can therefore delete the back row of polygons from the duplicates (**Figure 9.33c** and **9.33d**).

4   Move the duplicate eyes back so they exist just in front of the original eyes (**Figure 9.33e**).

5   Finally, apply the hair material to the duplicate eyes. (We are using the hair page because it already uses an alpha map and has extra UV space in it.) They will be completely black for the time being, until you update the texture.

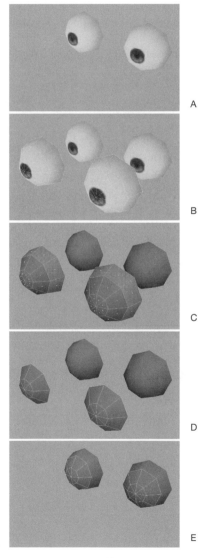

**FIGURE 9.33** Create duplicates of the eyes.

6   With the duplicate eyes still selected, open up the UV Texture Editor (**Figure 9.34**, left).

7   Separate the UVs for each eye so that they no longer lie on top of each other. Then reposition the UVs for both eyes so that they lie over the empty space on the texture page (**Figure 9.34**, right).

**FIGURE 9.34**
Apply the hair texture to the eyes.

8   Now we have extra information on our UV Layout. We need to export it as a UV Snapshot so we can use it in Photoshop. Export the eye UVs as a temporary file, making sure it is the same size as the hair texture page (256x256 pixels).

The geometry is prepared; now let's update the alpha map.

### Creating the Eyes' Alpha Map
Follow these steps to add the eye details to the alpha map.

1   Open the KilaHair.psd file.

2   Load in the UV snapshot you created for the extra eye UVs.

3   Copy and paste the new eye UVs into the KilaHair.psd file; this will create a new layer.

4   Using the new UVs as a guide, work on the alpha layer and create two black circles marking where the eye alphas are. This will initially make them completely transparent.

**5**   To create the shadow at the top of the white part of the eye, create a new layer and mark in the shadow; use white over the top of one of the black spheres. Make sure to blur the lower edge so the shadow is quite soft.

**6**   Duplicate this layer (Ctrl+C/Cmd+C and then Ctrl+V/Cmd+V) and mirror it, creating the shadow for the other eye. Adjust Opacity for both of the layers to about 60%.

**7**   With the shadow done, create another layer and mark in the highlights for one of the eyes.

**8**   Duplicate this layer and move it into position for the other eye. Your alpha map should now look like the one in **Figure 9.35**, right.

**9**   To complete the highlights, you will fill the same area in white on the color texture page (**Figure 9.35**, left). If you forget to do this last step, the highlight will be displayed in black because the area that is white (solid) on the alpha map is black on the color texture page.

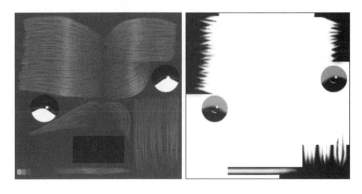

**FIGURE 9.35**
Update the alpha map and texture page to add eye details.

**10**   Update the Alpha 1 channel in the Channels window; then flatten and resave your image.

When you reload the texture in Maya, the shadow and highlights will be applied to the eyes (**Figure 9.36**, top). Furthermore, when the entire eye rotates, these highlights will stay static; this is demonstrated in **Figure 9.36** (middle and bottom).

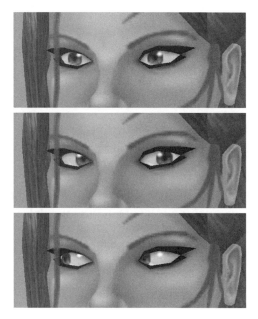

**FIGURE 9.36** The eyes with highlights and shadows applied (See page C16 for color version.)

**NOTE**  You may need to alter slightly the geometry that holds the highlights, to prevent the main eye geometry from popping through when the eyes move.

Kila's eyes now look much better and have more life. Next, we will address one last area that needs the alpha map: the eyelashes.

### Creating the Eyelash Alpha Map

At present, Kila's eyelashes are a little boring; at the same time, they're exaggeratedly thick. We will tone them down and make them more realistic by adding more detail.

1    Select the faces that make up the eyelashes and extract them, separating them from the main model.

2    Apply planar mapping to them along the Z axis. The UVs should now be laid out as seen in **Figure 9.37**, left.

**3**   Snap the UVs for the left eyelashes to the ones on the right, so that they all occupy the same space (**Figure 9.37**, middle).

**4**   Adjust both sets of UVs so that the top and bottom lashes overlap. This means the same texture will be applied not only to both the left and right sides but also to the upper and lower eyelashes.

**5**   Position the edited UVs over a blank area of the page (**Figure 9.37**, right).

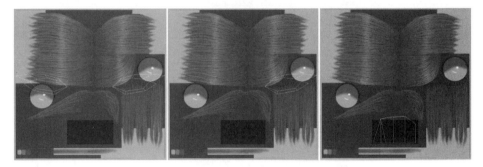

**FIGURE 9.37** Edit the UVs for the eyelashes so that they all occupy the same area on the texture page.

**6**   As you did with the eye highlights, create a new UV snapshot to work from, importing it into the .psd file in Photoshop.

**7**   As seen in **Figure 9.38**, draw the texture for the eyelashes on the alpha page, leaving the same section on the main color page black.

**FIGURE 9.38** Update the alpha map to include the eyelashes.

**8**   Edit the alpha channel, updating the image. Flatten and save.

What you should have now are better-looking eyelashes on your model, as shown in **Figure 9.39**.

FIGURE 9.39 The eyelashes before and after updating

We are finished with Kila's alpha map, so let's work on Grae's wings.

### Creating the Alpha Map for the Wings

Grae's wings are not just a single object; they consist of numerous tendrils that come out of his back. To keep the polygon count down, we created the wings from a number of larger polygons, intending to add the tendrils with the help of an alpha map. Because the tendrils are solid black, the main color page for the wings can be solid black, too. The alpha map will be the one that holds all the detail.

1    Load the file GraeWing.psd.

2    Create a new layer called Alpha, filling it in black (meaning it will initially be completely transparent).

3    Go in with solid white and draw the individual tendrils, as seen in **Figure 9.40**.

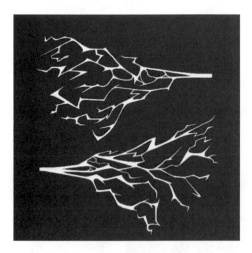

FIGURE 9.40 Draw the
tendrils into Grae's wing
alpha map.

Now copy the alpha layer into an alpha channel, hide the alpha layer so that the
color channels will be solid black, flatten the image, and save it. Then view it in
Maya (**Figure 9.41**).

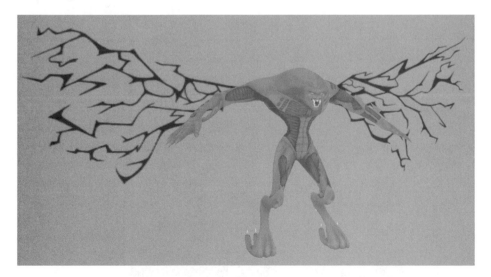

FIGURE 9.41 Grae with wings textured

Your next task is to go in and add highlights to Grae's eyes, as you did for Kila.
That will finish him up—all of your alpha maps are done.

The main textures for both Kila and Grae are now complete, and you can see them in **Figures 9.42** and **9.43**.

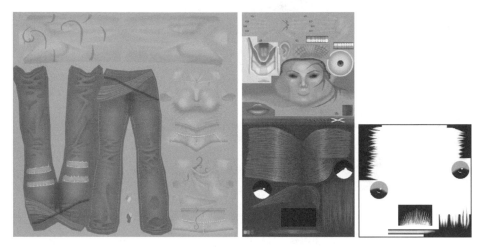

**FIGURE 9.42** Kila's texture pages (See page C7 for color version.)

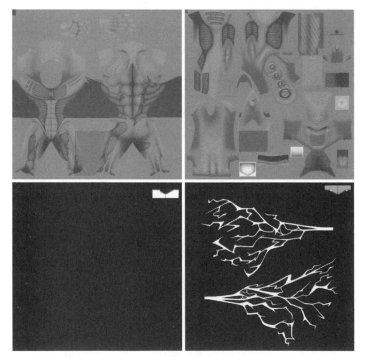

**FIGURE 9.43** Grae's texture pages (See page C8 for color version.)

# Bump and Specularity Maps

We can give the textures even more life by adding effects that will work on top of the base textures. Effects such as *specularity* and *bump maps* are included in most of today's games to add the appearance of shiny and rough surfaces.

> **NOTE** Of course, you will need to check whether the game engine can handle specularity and bump maps. Secondly, you must verify that you have the texture space available for these effects. Each added effect will add another version of the texture page to the overall texture page count.

Bump maps are used to give objects the illusion of having even more detail. The bump map uses a grayscale height map that works with the surface normals of the model. This map tells us which areas on the texture need to be bumpy, and the normals tell the map what direction to work in. This technique does not add any geometry to the model, and the silhouette stays the same.

The *specular map* simply specifies which areas of the texture are shiny and which ones have a matte finish. It does this by producing a central hotspot and the halo surrounding it; together, they provide an illusion of reflected light.

In much the same way as an alpha map, bump and specular maps work off a grayscale image. White areas indicate higher bumps or shiny areas; darker areas create recessed areas or matte areas. As described earlier for alpha maps, the values for black and white may be inverted in some game engines; be sure to check this out.

Now let's explore briefly how we can implement bump and specular maps into our characters, while also seeing how to apply them in Maya.

## Grae's Texture Effects

For a change, we will look at Grae first, because he will benefit more from these effects. His skin is quite bumpy, and in lots of areas the flesh is torn away to reveal muscle underneath. By applying a slight shine to this muscle, we can give the impression of moisture.

Use the main textures as a guide when creating your bump and specular maps. Working from these will help you to see which areas need to be shiny or how to judge the heights for the bump map.

For the bump map, begin with a 50% gray background. This will allow you to add darker colors to act as recessed areas on the character, as well as lighter areas to create bumps.

**Figure 9.44** shows the specular (top) and bump maps (bottom) we will be applying to Grae. You can find the completed maps on the CD in Project Files/09. Look for the files with _Bump or _Spec at the end of the filenames.

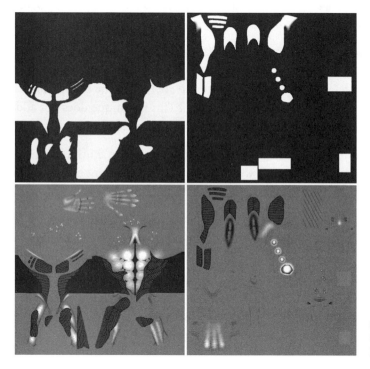

**FIGURE 9.44**
Grae's specular and bump maps

First we will apply the specular map. To apply a specular map, we first need to change the shader type. Lamberts are good for use with matte surfaces, but we cannot apply a specular map to this because it doesn't have the ability to be shiny. So we'll use a Blinn.

1    Open up the attributes for the Grae_Body material (**Figure 9.45**, left).

2    At the top of the shader's main attributes window, change Type from Lambert to Blinn. The layout should change to that seen in **Figure 9.45**, right. The name will also change, to blinn1; rename this back to Grae_Body.

By default, a Blinn material is shiny, so in effect you are telling Maya what levels of shininess each area of the texture should have.

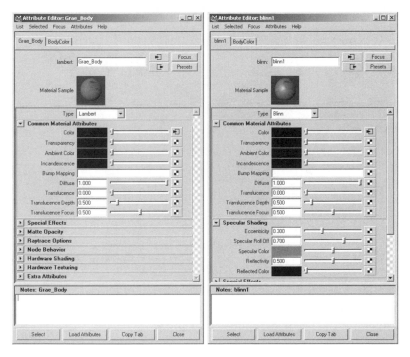

FIGURE 9.45 Change the Lambert shader to a Blinn.

3   To apply a specular map, you follow much the same procedure as for applying the basic color map, except in this case we will be editing the Specular Color attribute in the Specular Shading section. Simply click the button to the right of the attribute and point the file window to the file called GraeBody_Spec.tga.

4   To finish the application, adjust the Eccentricity and Specular Roll Off values to get the correct highlights.

*Eccentricity* controls the size of the highlights on the surface. The default value of 0.3 should work fine.

*Specular Roll Off* affects the intensity and sharpness of the highlight. Use 0.3 to get a good shine representing a wet surface.

Repeat the foregoing procedure, applying the GraeMisc_Spec.tga file to the Grae_Misc material. **Figure 9.46** shows Grae with the specular map applied. As you can see, only the areas you specified are shiny.

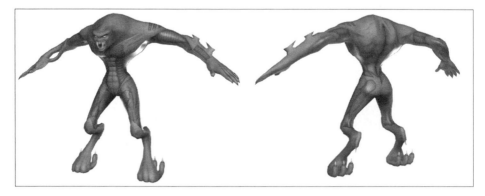

FIGURE 9.46 Grae with specular map applied (See page C9 for color version.)

Now let's add the bump map.

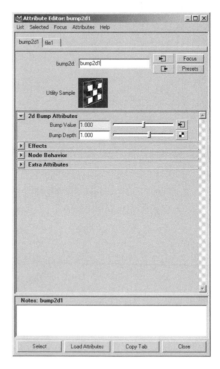

1   Look at the Grae_Body materials attributes in the Attribute Editor, and you'll see the Bump Mapping attribute under the Common Material Attributes heading. This is where we assign our bump map.

Click the small button to the right of the Bump Mapping text box; this opens up the Create Render Node window. As you did when you applied the color texture, select File.

Now something different happens. Instead of going directly to the file window, you go to the actual bump nodes attributes (**Figure 9.47**).

FIGURE 9.47 The Bump Node attributes

**2**   The only attribute we are interested in here is Bump Depth in the 2D Bump Attributes pane. Adjusting this will alter the emphasis your bump map has on the texture. A setting of 1 is usually far too severe, so set this to around 0.2.

**3**   To help keep things tidy, rename this node to BodyBumpValue.

**4**   Click the file1 tab at the top of the window; this brings you to the file's attributes. Select the bump map file called GraeBody_Bump.tga.

**5**   Finally, rename file1 to BodyBump.

There we have it—the bump map is applied. Do these same steps for the Grae_ Misc material.

With both the specular and bump maps applied, you can see in **Figure 9.48** that the Grae model has dramatically improved—and without having to add any extra polygons.

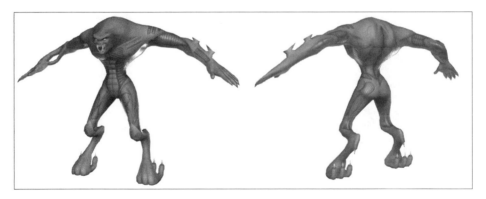

**FIGURE 9.48** Grae with both specular and bump maps applied (See page C9 for color version.)

### Kila's Texture Effects

The bump and specular maps for Kila will create effects that are quite restrained.

▶ Although Kila doesn't have any shiny areas, we can still make use of a specular map. The oils in our skin make it shine slightly when exposed to certain lighting conditions, so we can use the map to imitate this effect.

▶ We can also employ a bump map to bring out some of the smaller details in the model. The creases in her clothing, or detail in her hair could benefit from this.

**Figure 9.49** shows the character with the bump and specular maps applied. You can see a subtle difference, but you and your team may want to decide whether this subtlety is worth adding four more texture pages. Whatever you decide, once the maps are created you can always decide to apply them at a later stage.

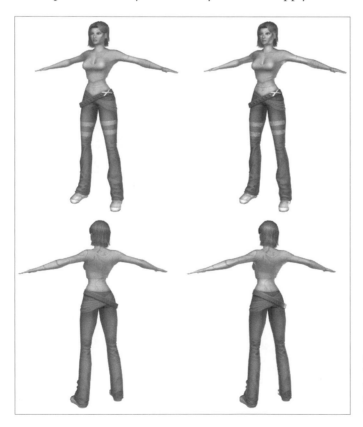

**FIGURE 9.49** Kila with both specular and bump maps applied (See page C10 for color version.)

## Topology Check

With the textures and their special enhancements completed, we can now take one last look over our models to see if we can fix any problem areas or remove any more polygons. Doing this now is a good idea because, with the textures applied, it is easier to spot potential problems. The two areas we are looking for, as we've done in earlier stages of the project, are polygon reduction and triangulation.

### Polygon Reduction

Now that we have finished the textures, we can reassess the geometry and remove anything that is no longer needed. The first area we can remove is where the polygons make up the upper spine; these are shown in **Figure 9.50**, left. Because her crop top falls quite high across her shoulder blades, we don't see her spine, so these polygons are no longer needed.

1   Snap the vertices to the inner ones and weld them. This should not involve altering any UVs.

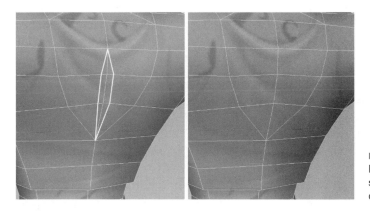

**FIGURE 9.50**
Remove the spine mesh detail.

2   The next area we can reduce is her navel. Originally, we built it in just in case we needed detail in this area, but the texture does a good enough job at providing definition. Select the vertices that make up the navel and weld them to each other, adjusting the remaining vertex so it is in the correct place.

**3**   The result should look like **Figure 9.51**, middle. The UVs need realigning slightly in the UV Texture Editor, giving you the result in **Figure 9.51**, right.

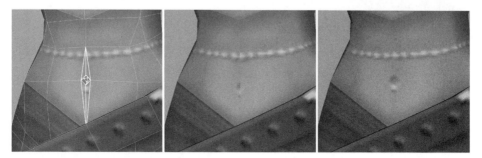

FIGURE 9.51 Remove the navel detail.

It's not likely there's much else we can reduce in Kila, but have a good look around anyway. Examine Grae, too, to be sure, before we continue on to check the triangulation.

## Triangulation

All engines (game engines and even Maya's own rendering engine) convert polygons to triangles at render time. You may see a "quad" in the viewport, but look closely and you'll see that the square is already divided into two triangles, whether there's a line being drawn there or not. For quads, Maya is making the division decision on-the-fly, depending on the planarity of the polygon's surface—and this might not be the decision that suits the surface of the model.

It's a good idea to do a pass on the model, slowly turning it around, looking to make sure that the quad decisions don't create concavities or bulges that are inappropriate to the anatomy. In those cases, you can manually create the desired edge with the Split Polygon tool. Or, if an edge already exists, turn it with the Flip Polygon Edge tool.

> **NOTE**   Because we are only splitting or flipping edges, the UVs will not be affected. If we were to delete polygons or dramatically alter the topology, the UVs would need to be tweaked or reapplied.

The main area containing some of these problems is Kila's face.

**1**  Hide the hair geometry so that you can concentrate on the face's topology.

**2**  Look in from the angle demonstrated in **Figure 9.52**, left. You will see a concave face causing the cheek to look angular.

**3**  Split these polygons as shown in **Figure 9.52**, middle, to smooth out the upper cheek (**Figure 9.52**, right).

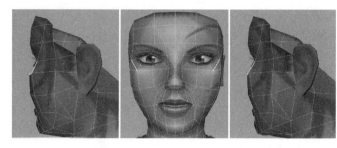

FIGURE 9.52 Split the concave faces to smooth her upper cheek.

**4**  Now look at the bridge of her nose (**Figure 9.53a**), where you can see a bad crease.

**5**  Our first step in reducing this crease is to split the polygons as shown in **Figure 9.53b**.

Next, split the polygons across her forehead as demonstrated in **Figure 9.53c**.

Finally, delete the edges highlighted in **Figure 9.53d**.

**Figure 9.53e** shows the reduced crease. Although it's not completely gone, it's better than it was.

Continue to look around both character models to see if you can see any more areas that need triangulating.

You've accomplished a great deal so far in this chapter. The textures are applied and enhanced, and the models have been fine-tuned. We're ready now to optimize the texture pages.

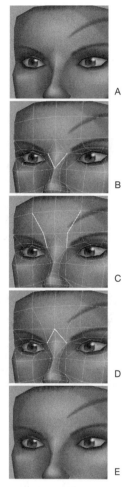

A

B

C

D

E

FIGURE 9.53 Reduce the crease on the bridge of her nose.

## Texture Bit Depth and Page Size

Texture memory is an important factor in game development. Keep your pages as small as possible—the image size as well as the file size is important. Although you may have been given a maximum texture limit, you'll get extra points if your character could look just as good in less.

There are two ways you can do this: reducing the actual page size, and reducing the bit depth. You can even combine reductions in both to get texture sizes down even more.

How far you can go with these reductions (or whether you can use them at all) depends on your managers and the game you are developing, so always check this out with your team. If you can, try and see both versions of the character—reduced and not reduced—running in the game engine, to get a realistic idea of how they will look. Remember that things look completely different on a television screen than they do on a computer monitor, so it may be that you can't see any difference in the reduced version. In that case, you have saved some memory that can be used to polish the game elsewhere.

### Page Size Reduction

Reducing the size of your texture pages is a dramatic way to reduce the overall file size, but on some characters this will leave you with unacceptable results. Let's begin by determining how big our textures currently are.

Without the alpha maps embedded, the main 512x512 pages are 769 KB each; the 256x256 pages are 193 KB each. Immediately we can see that if we reduce the highest ones to 256x256, we will be saving 576 KB on each; that's enough to add roughly another three texture pages for other characters. If we reduced the 256x256 pages to 128x128, we will save an additional 144 KB each.

This is all well and good—but how do the characters look after this sacrifice? On first glance, there doesn't seem to be much difference, but on closer inspection you can see that a lot of the detail has been lost. Also, some areas are slightly more blurred and pixelated than before the reduction.

Have a look now at the close-up shots in **Figure 9.54**. Getting in closer to the character makes it a bit more obvious that the pages are reduced.

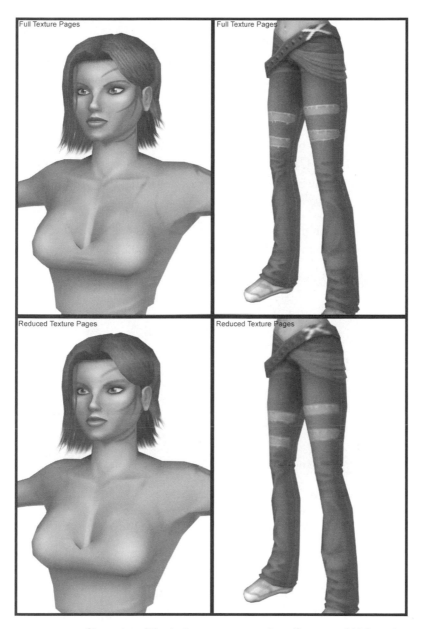

FIGURE 9.54 Close-ups of the texture page comparison (See page C11 for color version.)

Reducing page size is a quick and easy way to retrieve some memory, but it can affect the look of your characters.

## Bit Depth

What about altering the bit depth? Bit depth measures the amount of color information available in an image. Greater bit depth means more colors are available. An image with a bit depth of 8 has 256 possible colors; one with a bit depth of 24 has roughly 16 million possible colors.

Up to now we have been working with 24-bit images, but what would they look like if we reduced them to 8-bit (256 colors), and how much would the file size be reduced? A 512x512 image at 769 KB would be knocked down to 257 KB—not as much as reducing the image size, but we do get to keep the same amount of pixels.

1   To reduce the bit depth in Photoshop, go to Image > Mode > Indexed Color. This opens up the options window shown in **Figure 9.55**.

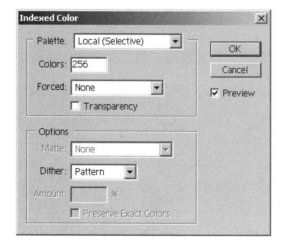

**FIGURE 9.55**
Indexed Color options

2   The Colors option should be automatically set to 256; if it's not, set it to this amount.

3   The other option to play around with is Dither. Because we are reducing the number of colors, we can specify whether we want Photoshop to try to blend the remaining ones using a method called *dithering*. The options are None, Diffusion, Pattern, and Noise. **Figure 9.56** shows the results of applying these options. I find Pattern to be the best choice here, but it does depend on the image you are reducing and your personal tastes.

**Figure 9.57** shows how reduced the bit-depth affects Kila. Although it does look pixelated in areas, there isn't much of a difference, and with a little work touching up the texture you won't see any noticeable degradation.

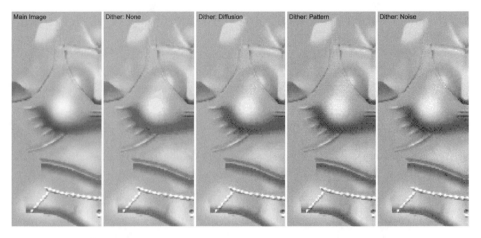

FIGURE 9.56 Effects of the different Dither options (See page C15 for color version.)

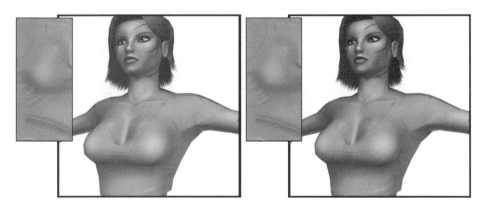

FIGURE 9.57 The 24-bit and 8-bit comparison. (See page C16 for color version.)

With the textures finished and optimization tasks done, we have completed our tasks for this chapter. **Figures 9.58** and **9.59** show the finished models.

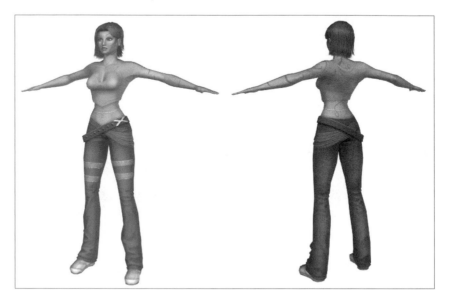

**FIGURE 9.58** Kila final model after texturing and tweaking (See page C12 for color version.)

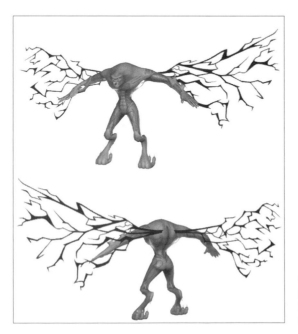

**FIGURE 9.59** Grae final model after texturing and tweaking (See page C12 for color version.)

The good thing about the textures is that you can continue to work on them throughout the project, so these versions do not need to be the final ones. Keep coming back to them throughout the rest of the book. (The best way to improve upon them is to forget about them for a few days and then have a fresh look.)

## Summary

Kila and Grae are now truly complete. They have been fully textured, giving them color to bring them to life in the game world. Throughout this chapter we have discussed how to create textures as well as how to reduce the file size of texture pages. With the models now finished, you're ready for Chapter 10, where you will explore levels of detail.

# CHAPTER 10
# Levels of Detail (LODs)

**NOW THAT OUR** characters are complete, including textures, and have been signed off by our managers, we can proceed to generate the *level of detail (LOD) models* needed to preserve processing power.

As we have already discussed (mainly in Chapter 5, "Model Optimization"), saving processor power and memory is very important when creating computer games. Here in Chapter 10 we will demonstrate how to gradually reduce a character to its lowest resolution, efficiently optimizing the model to get the various levels of detail needed in the game.

## Why Do We Need LODs?

When a character is far off in the distance, essentially taking up few pixels on the screen, there is no need for the character to have 4000 polygons when 100 or less will do.

This is where LODs come into play. What you do is take your main model and create four versions, or five, or however many are needed, each one stepping down in its polygon count. As the character moves away from the camera, a different version of the model is loaded in its place. The farther away from the camera, the lower the version, until the character can no longer be seen.

If we use Kila as an example, her main model of 4094 polygons would more than likely be used for close-up shots, or maybe just in cut scenes. The next LOD for Kila, then, would be the main one used in game, since we could remove around 1000 polygons and still retain all the detail needed. The LOD after that would comprise 1000 polygons; then we'd drop down to around 500; and the last one would be about 100 or 200. As you can see, we step down gradually at first, before dropping dramatically as distance from the character increases. We can do this because there will be decreasing need for detail as the character moves farther away.

> **TIP** The graphics programmer usually sets the number of LODs and the number of polygons in each LOD. The trick is to have as few LODs as possible. One rule of thumb in the industry is "The sum polycount of all LODs shouldn't exceed the main game model."

You can see Kila with her levels of detail in **Figure 10.1**. Although there are fewer polygons in the versions that are farther away, you cannot tell.

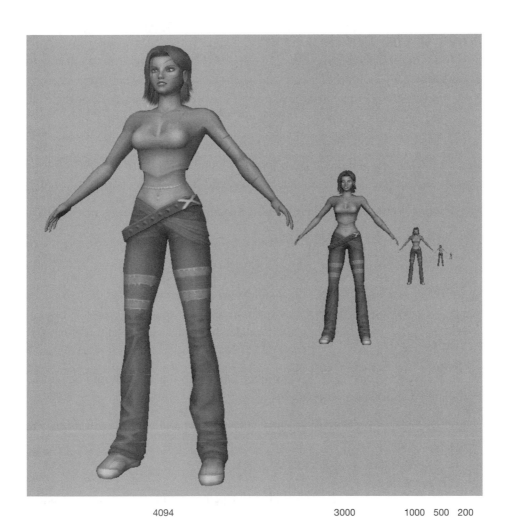

4094                                   3000            1000  500  200

FIGURE 10.1 Kila with levels of detail

Check out the games you play. Look carefully, and you will see characters or
objects "pop" as they move away from the camera. This is the game engine swapping the current model for a lower LOD.

## Setting the Binding Pose

Before we proceed to create LODs for both our characters, we need to alter their pose. We began with both Kila and Grae in the basic T pose, which made it easier to work with them, but we will need to alter the pose in preparation for the characters to be bound to a skeleton (which we'll do in the next chapter).

It's advisable to alter the pose now (you could even start off designing your models with the arms posed like this, to save time). Otherwise, once the level of detail models have been created, you would need to edit five models instead of just one.

The main areas that will need altering on Kila are the arm and finger positions.

### Arm Adjustment

The arm should be at the average position between the most-used extreme positions. If a character only ever walks with its arms down by its sides, it doesn't make any sense to raise the arms up to shoulder level when you bind it. This would just increase distortion to the shoulder area when the skeleton deforms the mesh.

Kila will be performing generally ordinary actions, so the arms should be set at about a 45 degree angle.

Before we adjust them, we need to make the arms separate objects so that they're easier to manipulate.

### Detach the Arms

Not only do we need for the arms to be detached from the torso, but also to be separated along their UV borders so that we keep the UV's intact.

Open up the file called Kila_Texture.mb.

1    Select the main body geometry and open the UV Texture Editor (**Figure 10.2**, left). Because we combined the body geometry, all the UVs are being displayed on top of each other. We need to separate the UVs in order to see the ones belonging to the arms.

2    You can tell Maya to show only the faces belonging to the background image, by going to View > View Faces Of Selected Images. As seen in **Figure 10.2** (middle), this will hide the other UVs not associated with this texture page.

**TIP** It may be that the incorrect image is displayed in the background, giving you the wrong UVs (Figure 10.2, left). To switch to the image you need, select it from the Image > Selected Images menu.

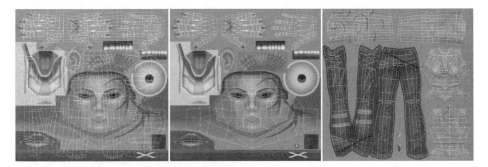

**FIGURE 10.2** Select the arms using the UV Texture Editor.

**3**  Select the faces belonging to the arms, and return to the main view panel.

**4**  Using the Extract tool, separate the arms from the body as seen in **Figure 10.3**.

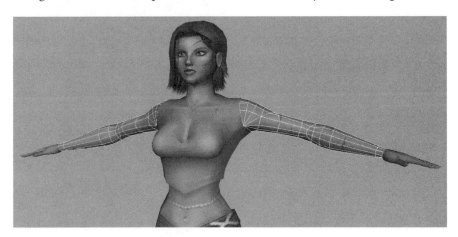

**FIGURE 10.3** Detach the arms.

The arms are now free for you to work on. (Notice your bonus: The hands are now separated, too, ready for LOD work later.) Next we will look into the best approach for rotating the arms.

### Rotate the Arms

We want to rotate both the arms the same amount and from the same pivot on either side. We could adjust the pivot as shown earlier in the book, snapping it to a vertex close to where our shoulder pivot would be. This wouldn't be very accurate, though, because the arm would rotate around the wrong axis. What we want is for the axis to follow the orientation of the arm.

For this purpose we will use a *locator*, which is a very simple dummy object that takes the shape of a cross. Locators have many uses: They can pinpoint positions in space; they can be used as a main controller; or, as in this case, they can be used to drive the rotation of a series of objects.

We will position a locator where the shoulder pivot is, and parent the arm and hand to it. When the locator is rotated, the arm will rotate correctly.

1   Create a locator by going to Create > Locator. Then move it up to the correct position over the shoulder's pivot point (**Figure 10.4a**).

2   To make the rotation more precise, switch to the top view (**Figure 10.4b**) and rotate the locator to match the orientation of the arm (**Figure 10.4c**). This rotation should only be around the Y axis.

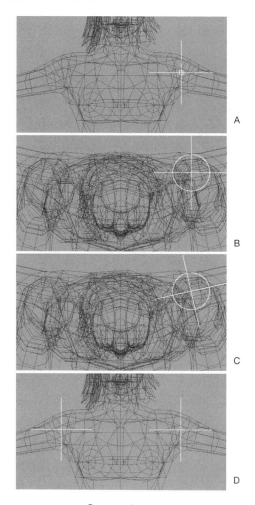

**FIGURE 10.4** Create a locator and position it at the shoulder pivot.

**3** Duplicate the locator, and make the Translate X and Rotate Y attributes negative values. This mirrors the locator for the other arm (**Figure 10.4d**).

**4** Now select the arm geometry for the first arm, then the hand, and then the locator last. To parent them, press P.

Do the same for the opposite arm, parenting the arm and hand to the other locator.

> **NOTE** By selecting the locator last, you are telling Maya that you want the objects you selected first to be parented to the locator.

**5** The rotations must be exactly the same on either side, so we will activate snapping on the Rotate tool. Double-click the Rotate tool icon, opening up the tool's options (**Figure 10.5**).

Enable Snap Rotate and set the Step Size to 5.0. This will make the tool rotate in units of 5 instead of flowing freely.

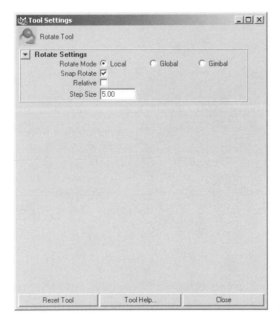

**FIGURE 10.5** Enable Snap Rotate in the Rotate tool's options.

**6** Rotate the locator around the Z axis (blue), using the manipulator and not the Channel Box. (If you used the Channel Box, the locator would not rotate around its local axis; instead, the Z axis might default back to the global axis.)

Rotate the locator by seven steps, and then do the same to the opposite arm (**Figure 10.6**).

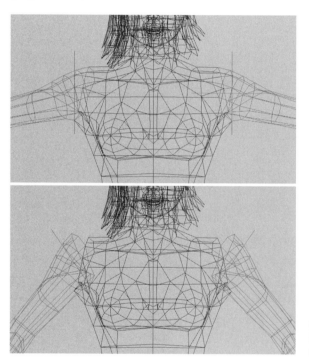

FIGURE 10.6 Rotate both locators seven steps.

The arms are now orientated correctly, meaning we can now reattach them to the torso. Make sure you deactivate Snap Rotate on the Rotate tool before you proceed.

### Reattach the Arms

Now the two arms are in position, and we can stitch them back onto the torso. First, we need to combine the three pieces of geometry into a single model.

**1** Select both arms and the torso and combine them (Polygons > Combine).

**2** Work your way around the shoulders, merging the vertices so that they lie in between the arm and torso geometry (**Figure 10.7**, right).

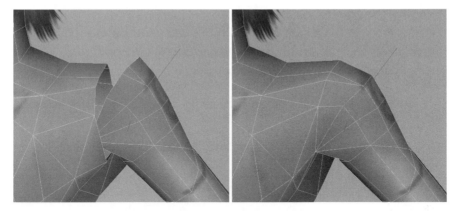

FIGURE 10.7 Weld the vertices around the shoulders.

3    As you can see in **Figure 10.8**, left, the shoulders are no longer shaped correctly, so work the vertices and smooth out both shoulders (**Figure 10.8**,
right).

> **TIP** Remember—to keep the shoulders symmetrical, select the opposing
> vertices and move them at the same time. If the vertices need to be moved
> away from or toward each other, simply use the Scale tool instead of transla-
> tion.

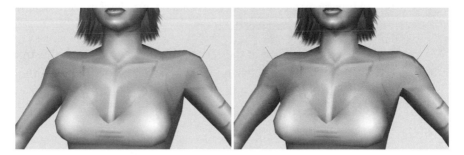

FIGURE 10.8 Smooth out the shoulders.

Now that the shoulders are repositioned and smoothed out, let's reposition
the fingers.

**Finger Adjustment**

Like the arms, the fingers should be between their most extreme positions. Currently they are flat, which is close to one extreme. We need to go in and bend them slightly so that they look more relaxed.

> **NOTE** Adjusting the hands is a good idea, but it's not strictly necessary, so feel free to skip this section if you like.

To save time, we can delete the right hand and work only on the left. We can do this because both hands have more or less the same UV mapping. Then we can duplicate the edited hand to replace the right hand.

**1**   Delete the right hand.

**2**   The left hand will still be parented to the locator, so unparent it by selecting it and going to Edit > Unparent.

The hand's orientation is currently correct, but to make editing the fingers easier, you'll need to rotate the hand in order to flatten it. Before you do, though, you need to store (freeze) its current position and rotation.

**3**   Freeze the transforms (Modify > Freeze Transforms). This will reset the translation, rotation, and scale values to zero, meaning that after you're done editing the fingers, you can just set the Rotate values back to zero again, resetting the hand to its correct position.

**4**   When you detached the arm at the very beginning of this pose-adjustment process, the pivot point for the hand defaulted back to the center of the world, and this will now make it difficult to manipulate. So center the pivot for the hand by going to Modify > Center Pivot.

**5**   With the translation, rotation, and scale values at zero and the pivot centered, you can now rotate the hand so it is flat, as shown in **Figure 10.9**, middle.

**6**   Adjust the fingers so they are like the ones in **Figure 10.9**, right, bending them into a more relaxed pose. Look at your own hand for reference.

FIGURE 10.9 Adjust the orientation of the hand before bending the fingers.

**7**  When you are happy with the shape of the fingers, reset the hand rotations back to zero in the Channel Box or by using the Modify > Reset Transforms tool, returning the hand back to its correct orientation.

**8**  Duplicate the left hand to create the right hand.

> **NOTE**  Make sure you snap the pivot point back to the world's center before you mirror it. Press Insert to activate the pivot point and then hold down X, which will snap the point to the grid as you move it.

**9**  With the right hand selected, open the UV Texture Editor and adjust the UV's so the back of the hand is over the section that does not have the tattoo on it. You can see this in **Figure 10.10**.

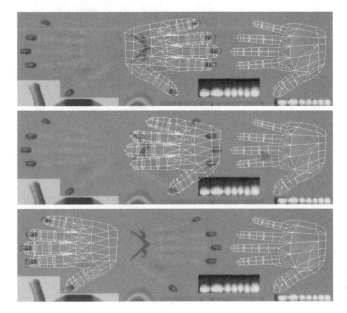

FIGURE 10.10
Adjust the new right hand's UVs.

**10** To finish your work on the pose, clean up all the geometry in the scene. Go to Edit > Delete All By Type > History. You have to delete the history first because (even though none of the geometry is still parented to the locators) the locators are still attached to the geometry via history. Once the history is cleared, you can safely delete the locators.

**11** Finally, save the scene as Kila_Pose.mb.

> **TIP** Now that you have a hand that is modeled, optimized, textured, and posed, I recommend saving it to your Morgue. It's a nice addition to your collection for use on future characters.

**Figure 10.11** shows Kila in her new pose.

Grae, too, needs to be posed, so load Grae_Texture.mb. Adjust his arms and fingers just as you have done Kila's. Save him as Grae_Pose.mb when he's finished.

When your models are posed and ready, you can begin generating the levels of detail.

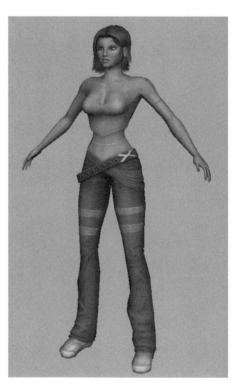

**FIGURE 10.11** Kila in her new pose

# Generating LODs

Creating the LODs is in some ways similar to optimizing the mesh. There are two principal stages:

▶ First, look for areas that can be sacrificed, or in this case, what can't be seen when the camera is at that particular distance. For example, if the individual fingers are not visible when you zoom out, you can combine the fingers to create a mitten-type hand.

▶ After you have removed any unnecessary detail, you can remove more polygons. Look for areas that create shallow angles and places that house unused polygons, just as you do in optimization. Continue to do this until you reach the polygon limit of the LOD you are creating.

Kila is currently made up from 4094 polygons. This will be the first LOD and the main model that will be used for close-ups. It's more than likely the next LOD will be the one mostly viewed in game. So let's create four more levels of detail for her at the following polygon counts: 3000, 1000, 500, and 150.

### LOD 2: 3000 Polygons

Make sure the Kila_Pose.mb file is open. Before creating the second LOD, we must duplicate the current character's geometry. We only need one copy at this stage, because the LOD after this one will be based on this LOD 2's complete geometry.

1   You should have all the pieces of the character in a group called Kila. Rename this to Kila4094.

2   Duplicate this group, calling the new copy Kila3000.

3   Create two new display layers (go to Layer > Create Layer in the Layer Editor), one for each separate version of the model. Call one Kila_4096 and the other Kila_3000, placing the appropriate group into each layer.

4   Hide the original file (Kila4094) by turning off the layer's visibility, so you are only working with the duplicate.

**5**   Position the model (by just moving the camera) as seen in **Figure 10.12**. She should more or less fill the screen; this will be the size of the full-resolution character.

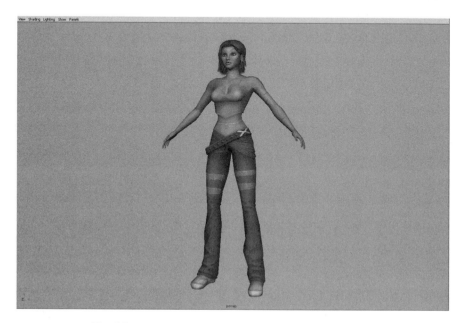

**FIGURE 10.12** The full-resolution model will be seen at this distance.

**6**   Now dolly out until she is roughly half-size (**Figure 10.13**). This is approximately the distance at which this model will be viewed when in a game. When the main model is this far away from the camera, the game will switch to this LOD.

**FIGURE 10.13** The distance of the next level of detail.

**7**   Now that you have a basic distance to gauge your model on, begin rotating around her and see what you can initially sacrifice. At this distance you can still see quite a bit of detail; even her individual fingers are still visible. What you can do, though, is

▶   Remove the highlights created for her eyes, and delete her eyelashes and her tongue. (If she does talk at this distance, you will not see it.)

▶   Remove the single strand of hair from the front of her head, as well as the first inside layer of her hair. After doing this, you will need to tweak the remaining inner layers of hair to fill the gap that now exists.

That's about as much as you can remove at this stage, but she is still using 3878 polygons. Next we will go in and remove some areas of small detail in order to get closer to our 3000 limit for this LOD.

### Hands

Although Kila's fingers are still visible at this level, they don't need to have much detail in them; it's sufficient if they merely "suggest" fingers. In designing the main hand, we included polygons around the joints so that the fingers would not pinch badly when bent. There is no need for these polygons at this distance, so we can remove them.

Reduce the fingers down to basic cubes like the ones seen in **Figure 10.14**, right. If you are merely merging vertices or collapsing edges, the UV information should stay intact.

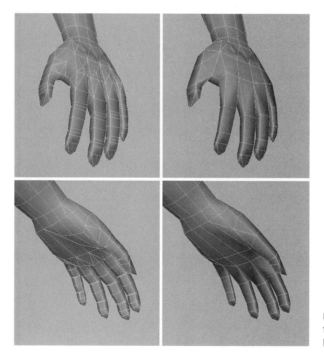

**FIGURE 10.14** Reduce the fingers down to basic cubes.

Reducing the fingers brings us down to 3236 polygons, not too far from our goal.

### Sash and Jeans Legs

Let's now reduce some areas of detail in the sash and the jeans legs, which won't be missed at this distance. When creating the main model, we built creases on her hip to give the sash additional detail, and creases and folds in the jeans. This detail can now be removed.

**1**   Begin by collapsing the main edges that create the overhang for the folds of the sash. These are highlighted in **Figure 10.15a**.

**2**   Remove the final set of edges that made up the folds (**Figure 10.15b**).

**3**   As you can see in **Figure 10.15c**, the UVs have been altered. So, open up the UV Texture Editor and fix the UVs using the main model (Kila_4096) as reference (**Figure 10.15d**).

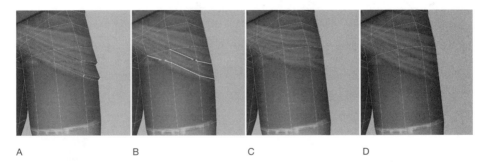

A            B            C            D

**FIGURE 10.15** Remove the folds from her sash.

**4**   Remove the similar folds in the jeans at the back of her knees. Do this by collapsing the edges highlighted in **Figure 10.16**.

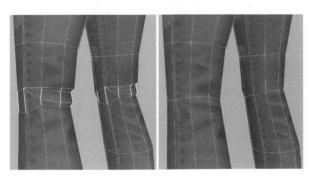

**FIGURE 10.16**
Collapse the folds at the back of her knees.

**5** Now focus on the folds at the base of her legs. Work your way around these, collapsing the majority of the edges until you have a more rudimentary-looking lower leg (**Figure 10.17**, right).

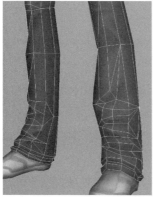

**FIGURE 10.17** Reduce the folds in the lower part of the jeans legs.

With these reductions to the sash and jeans, our polygon count now stands at 2948, just under the limit. This is great news—it means we can move on and begin work on the next LOD.

Before you do, rename the group and the display layer to represent the new polygon count. So Kila3000 would become Kila2948, and Kila_3000 would be Kila_2948. This helps to inform others of the polygon count and keeps you up to date.

**Figure 10.18** shows our second level of detail. You shouldn't see much of a difference in Kila's form at present, which is good because this model won't be too far away from the camera.

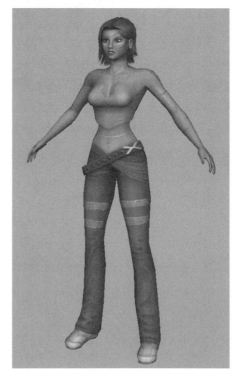

**FIGURE 10.18** The second level of detail, up close.

### LOD 3: 1000 Polygons

LOD 3 will be quite a dramatic step down because we will be able to remove a huge amount of polygons from areas where they are not seen at this distance.

**1** Create the base geometry to work on. Duplicate the previous LOD's group (Kila2948) and call the new copy Kila1000.

**2** Create a new display layer called Kila_1000, placing into it the Kila1000 group and its contents.

**3** Turn off the visibility for the layer called Kila_2948. This leaves you with just the new geometry to work on.

**4** As you did before, zoom out to about half the size of LOD 2 to get an idea of how the geometry will be viewed in a game. You can see this in **Figure 10.19**. From this distance, you can't see very much detail. Her facial features are lost, as are her fingers. It should be quite easy to reduce this version down to 1000 polygons.

FIGURE 10.19 Dolly out to about half the size of LOD 2.

**NOTE** We could even go lower than 1000 for LOD 3. Just because we have a limit doesn't mean we must hit it exactly; we just can't go over it. If areas are not seen, then there is no use for them, so we may as well delete them.

5 Let's first remove obvious things that can't be seen. This version of the model will not have any facial animation because you simply won't be able to see it, so you can remove the inner mouth, including the teeth, and weld her lips together.

6 Remove her eyes and her ear; they won't be seen, either.

7 Both inner layers of her hair can go, too. We can adjust the outer layer to compensate for this loss.

With these elements removed, we are down to 2692, so let's zoom in and begin reducing the main geometry.

### *Hair Reduction*

Begin by working on her hair.

1 Focus on her hair geometry by selecting it and pressing F.

2 Select the edges shown in **Figure 10.20** (left) and then collapse them (**Figure 10.20**, right).

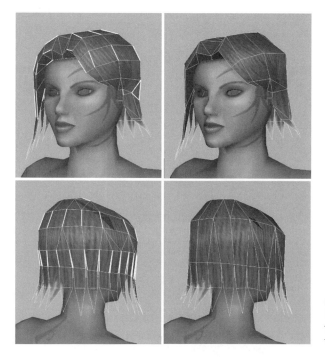

**FIGURE 10.20**
Begin reducing
the polygons in
the hair.

**3**  Delete the triangular faces at the very bottom of the hair and then weld the separate strips together, making the mesh solid.

**4**  Optimize the hair further, removing polygons not only from the outside, but from the fringe of hair at the forehead (**Figure 10.21**, left).

**5**  Extend the hair down to roughly match its original length on the higher-resolution model (**Figure 10.21**, right). It doesn't have to be exact; we can edit it more precisely in the next step.

**FIGURE 10.21** Make the outer hair solid before extending it down.

**6**  Because we have removed polygons, the overall shape of the hair will be less full. Make the LOD 2's display layer visible, turning the display type to Template. This will show the second LOD's geometry as a gray wireframe over the current model (**Figure 10.22**, left).

**7**  You can now work on the hair, shaping it as seen in **Figure 10.22**, right, "thickening" it to match its previous look.

**FIGURE 10.22** Use the wireframe of LOD 3 as a template to thicken the hair.

We will leave the hair as it is for now; this should be sufficiently reduced. Next we will trim down her face.

### Face Reduction

We only really need to keep basic features in the face. Take another look at **Figure 10.19**; you can't see any major details.

1  Focus in on the face. Feel free to hide the hair at this stage, to make working on the head easier. Then, as demonstrated in **Figure 10.23** (top-right), weld the eyes closed.

2  By now you should have a good grasp of polygonal modeling, so go ahead and work on the nose and then the lips (**Figure 10.23**, middle). Finally, work your way around the face, collapsing edges there until you have a basic face like the one in **Figure 10.23**, bottom-right.

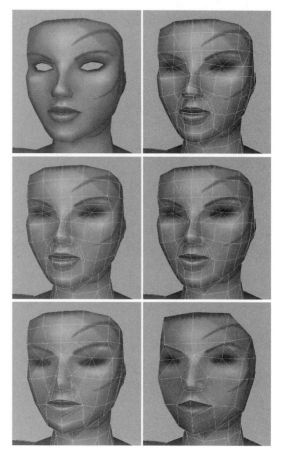

**FIGURE 10.23** Reduce the polygons in Kila's face.

> **NOTE**  Remember to keep updating the UVs as you work, as well as checking the shape against the next-higher LOD.

Don't worry too much about deciding where to remove faces. Once you start collapsing edges, you will notice other areas that can be collapsed. They will stand out because the detail in that area does not match where you are currently working.

> **NOTE** The model is starting to look quite odd now, but remember that this version will only ever be seen from a distance. Keep zooming out as you work, to get a realistic idea of how she will look in a game.

You will probably have the urge to continue reducing polygons on her neck and the rest of her body, mainly because the head and body don't match anymore. But wait; we will look at the rest of the body later on. Next up are the hands.

### Hand Reduction

The hands have far too much detail in them for this level. We no longer require separate fingers, for example, so we will convert them into flat, mitten-style hands as mentioned earlier.

1   Begin by welding the fingers together as seen in **Figure 10.24b**, making sure you delete the inner faces afterward.

2   Remove the finger ends, flattening out the end of the hand (**Figure 10.24c**).

3   Work on the whole hand, reducing the overall detail, and remember to fix the UVs afterward.

You should now have a low-polygon mitten-type hand like the one shown in **Figure 10.24d**.

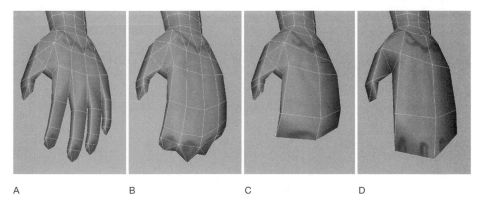

A                    B                    C                    D

FIGURE 10.24 Adjust the fingers to get a mitten-type hand.

The reduced hands can now be used to guide optimization of the arms.

### *Limbs Reduction*

Because we reduced the hands, triangles will have appeared at the wrist area (**Figure 10.25**). This is because the sections there no longer match up to the ones where the hands attach to the arms.

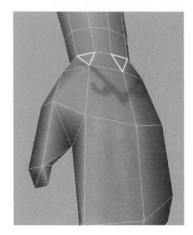

**FIGURE 10.25** Triangles have appeared because the hand and arm no longer match.

1 On each arm, follow the triangles, and select the edges all the way up Kila's arm. You should end up with each alternate strip selected (**Figure 10.26**, left).

2 As you can see in **Figure 10.26** (middle), collapsing these edges will reduce the arm from having ten divisions around the axis to five.

3 Optimize each arm further (**Figure 10.26**, right), removing most of the detail we added to allow it to deform correctly. At this camera distance, you won't be able to tell whether the elbow and wrist look wrong as they bend.

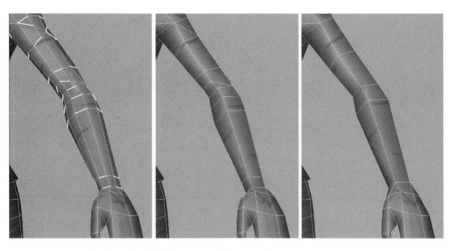

**FIGURE 10.26** Reduce the divisions around the arm's axis.

4 Now take a look at the legs. Remove most of the detail highlighted in **Figure 10.27**, left, following the polygons around to her buttocks. This will leave the legs in a more or less cylindrical shape.

**5**   We have a shallow angle on the thigh area. Select the edges shown in **Figure 10.27**, middle, and collapse them. The legs will look like those in **Figure 10.27**, right.

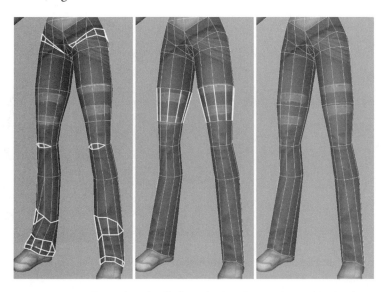

**FIGURE 10.27** Removing details from the legs leaves them with a basic cylindrical shape.

**6**   In the crotch and buttock area, remove the polygons shown in **Figure 10.28**.

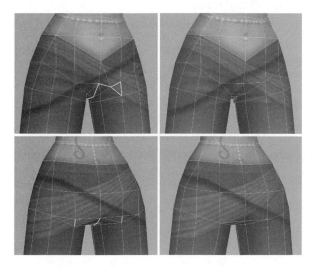

**FIGURE 10.28** Remove polygons at the crotch and buttocks.

**7**  Now repeat for the legs the steps used when you reduced the arms. Select the edges that make up every second vertical strip (**Figure 10.29**, left) and collapse them, reducing the divisions around the legs from ten to five.

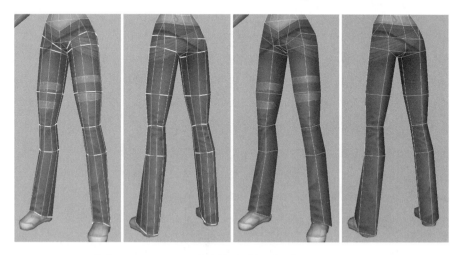

FIGURE 10.29 Collapse every second vertical strip of polygons.

The legs are now sufficiently reduced. Remember to use LOD 2 as a template to fill them out, since they will have thinned down when the edges were collapsed.

### Torso Reduction

Compared to the rest of the model, the torso now looks out of character; it has too much detail. We need to remove some of this detail to bring it in line with the rest of her reduced geometry.

**1**  Select the edges highlighted in **Figure 10.30a**, just at the base of her spine, and collapse them as shown in **Figure 10.30b**.

**2**  There are quite a few areas to reduce on the torso; let's do them all at once. Follow **Figure 10.30**, selecting and collapsing the edges that are marked in white on both front (**Figure 10.30c**) and back (**Figure 10.30e**). After you make these changes, the torso should now resemble **Figures 10.30d** and **10.30f**.

**3**  Next, collapse the edges that form the overhang of her top (**Figure 10.31**).

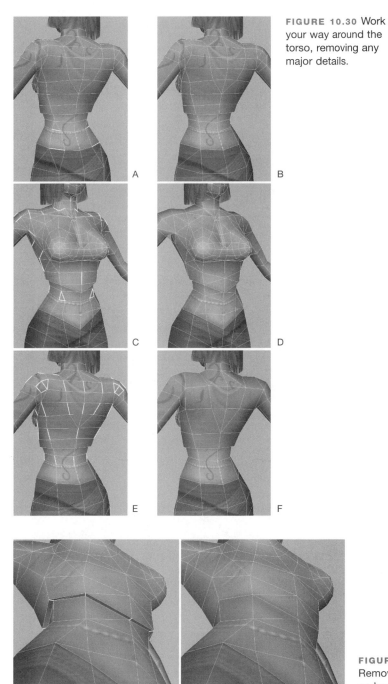

FIGURE 10.30 Work your way around the torso, removing any major details.

FIGURE 10.31 Remove the overhang on her top.

4   There are still quite a few polygons in her stomach that we don't need, so delete those (**Figure 10.32**).

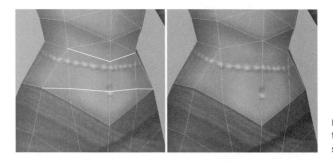

**FIGURE 10.32** Delete the extra edges in her stomach.

5   Work your way along as shown in **Figure 10.33** to collapse the edges on the breasts.

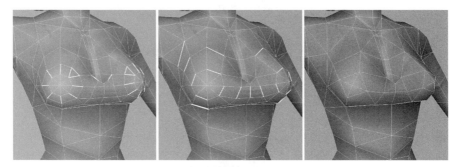

**FIGURE 10.33** Remove detail on the breasts.

6   Under the breasts, collapse the edges highlighted in **Figure 10.34**, left.

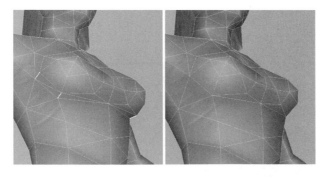

**FIGURE 10.34** Collapse these edges under the breasts.

**7** On the chest and at the cleavage, remove all of the geometry highlighted in **Figure 10.35**, left.

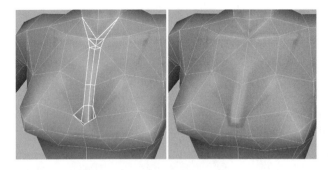

**FIGURE 10.35**
Optimize the cleavage
area.

**8** Finish off the chest area by working on its general shape (**Figure 10.36**). Remember to use LOD 2 as a guide.

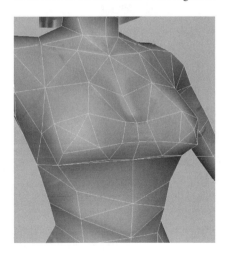

**FIGURE 10.36** The
optimized chest area

NOTE  Don't forget the UVs–correct any incorrect areas as you progress.

9   To complete your work in the torso area, quickly remove the division in her neck (**Figure 10.37**, left), making it a single flat area (**Figure 10.37**, right).

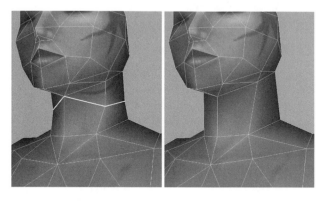

**FIGURE 10.37**
Remove the division in her neck.

Only the accessories are left to finish the reductions for LOD 3.

### Belt and Shoe Reduction

Although we could just delete the belt, it is still slightly visible at this distance, so we'll take the time to reduce the number of polygons used to construct it. Then we'll work on the shoes.

1   Remove the inside polygons on the belt, as well as the upper and lower edges (**Figure 10.38a**).

2   Collapse every other set of edges, removing every second polygon (**Figure 10.38b** and **c**).

3   Adjust the shape of the belt so it does not cut through the character model (**Figure 10.38d**).

4   To complete this LOD, reduce the shoes until they resemble **Figure 10.39**, right.

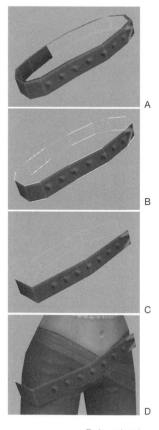

A

B

C

D

**FIGURE 10.38** Belt reduction

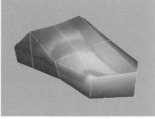

**FIGURE 10.39** The optimized shoe

LOD 3 is finished. Look at the polygon count to make sure you are below the limit of 1000. Good—the final count is 794, well under the limit. Rename both the geometry group and the display layer to reflect this number. **Figure 10.40** shows the third level of detail; as you can see, Kila is now starting to look quite different from her original form.

We are beginning to see some dramatic alterations to Kila's geometry. When we are finished with the next two LODs, she will be almost unrecognizable up close.

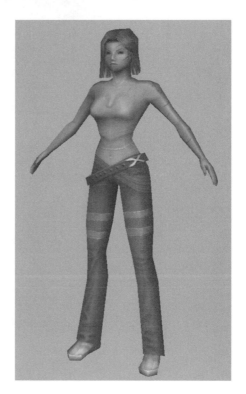

**FIGURE 10.40** LOD 3 up close

### LOD 4: 500 Polygons

**Figure 10.41** shows the next LOD's distance from the camera. As you can see, we are getting quite far from our character and can no longer see any details. All we can see is her basic shape.

**FIGURE 10.41** LOD 4's distance from the camera

1    Just as you did before, duplicate the previous LOD's group and rename it to Kila500, placing it into a new display layer called Kila_500.

2    Start by deleting her belt, which is no longer visible at this distance.

3    On the hands, remove the thumb before reducing both hands right down to their basic shapes (**Figure 10.42**).

4    The arms currently have five divisions around the axis, so we can reduce them down to four (**Figure 10.43**). Select the edges at the very front of the arm, and collapse them.

5    Now you can remove the polygons that add shape to the arms, shown in **Figure 10.43**, middle. Again, these won't be visible when the camera is at this distance, so it's safe to remove them.

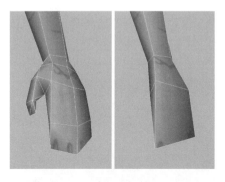

**FIGURE 10.42** Reduce the hands to basic shapes.

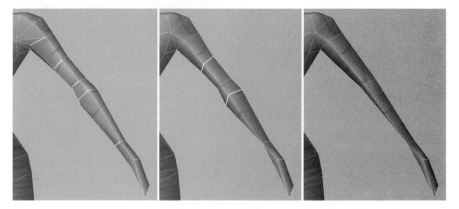

**FIGURE 10.43** Optimize the arms down to basic shapes.

6    Moving on to the hair now, this can be reduced to a basic box shape like the one in **Figure 10.44**, right. You can even remove all of the internal geometry, if any still exists.

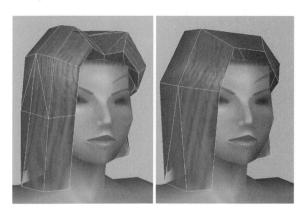

**FIGURE 10.44** Reduce the hair geometry down to a basic box shape.

**7** Reduce the face as demonstrated in **Figure 10.45**, removing the details for her eyes, nose, and lips and leaving her face more or less flat.

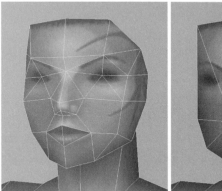

**FIGURE 10.45**
Remove details from the face.

**8** The legs can be reduced in the same way as you did the arms. Select the edges at the front and collapse them, reducing the divisions around the legs from five to four (**Figure 10.46**).

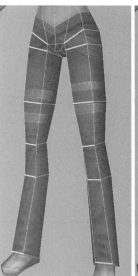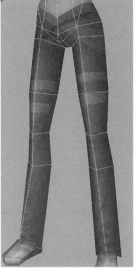

**FIGURE 10.46** Reduce the divisions around the legs.

9   When the legs are reduced, you will notice areas around the crotch and waist that can be optimized. At this level, polygons to aid deformation are not needed, so select and collapse the edges highlighted in **Figure 10.47** top-left and top-right.

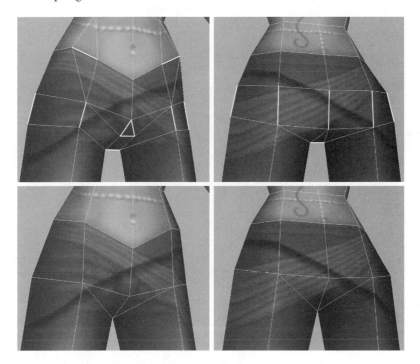

FIGURE 10.47 Optimize the waist and crotch.

10  Now you've come to the torso. You only need the basic shape to represent the character, so there are quite a few areas you can reduce here. Remove the edges shown in **Figure 10.48** top-left and bottom-left, giving you the torso seen in the top-right and bottom-right of **Figure 10.48**. After removing the polygons, you will need to fine-tune the shape slightly.

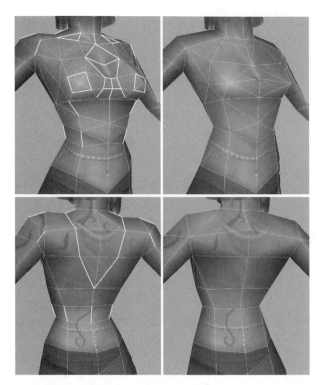

FIGURE 10.48 Remove most of the detail from her torso, leaving the basic shape intact.

**11** Finally, work on the shoe, reducing it down to the basic shape seen in **Figure 10.49**, right.

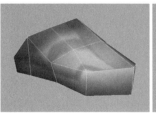 

FIGURE 10.49 You only need a very fundamental shape for the shoe.

LOD 4 is now complete and you can see it in **Figure 10.50**.

Checking the polygon count shows we are down to 309—another successful reduction. Rename the group and display layer to reflect the correct polygon count, and move on to create the final level of detail

### LOD 5: 150 Polygons

We are now at the final level of detail, the most basic version of our character. **Figure 10.51** shows the distance at which this version will be activated; not much at all can be seen. We can just about make out arms, legs, and a torso, so these are the areas we will concentrate on.

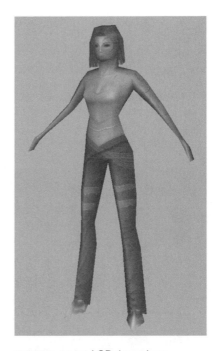

FIGURE 10.50 LOD 4 up close

FIGURE 10.51 LOD 5's distance from the camera

1 Create a copy of the LOD 4, renaming it to Kila150.

2 Place this copy into a new display layer called Kila_150, and hide the display layer of the previous version.

3 Delete the hair and shoes.

4 You only need a vague representation of arms, so completely remove the hands, merging the end of each arm into a single vertex (**Figure 10.52**).

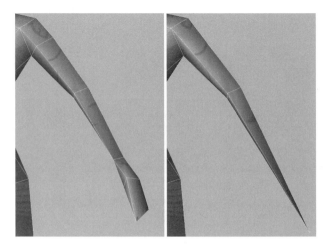

FIGURE 10.52 Remove the hands and merge the ends of the limbs.

5 You won't see the face at all at this distance, but you do need something to represent her head. Delete the faces under her chin, and then work on the head until it's a basic flat cube like the one in **Figure 10.53**. Not only will this use fewer polygons, but it will work well from a distance.

FIGURE 10.53 Reduce the head down to nothing but a basic cube shape.

**6**   Remove any extra polygons on the legs that add to their shape. All you need at this stage are very basic cube shapes (**Figure 10.54**).

FIGURE 10.54 Leave just two basic cubes for the legs.

**7**   Finally, there's no need for details on her torso, either. You just want a basic shape, so remove the areas highlighted in **Figure 10.55** top-left and bottom-left to make them like **Figure 10.55** top-right and bottom-right.

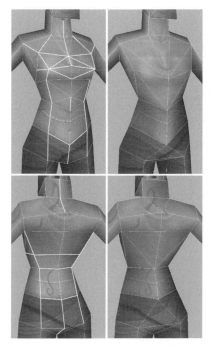

FIGURE 10.55 Optimize the torso area.

Our final level of detail weighs in at 120 polygons. She's not much to look at (**Figure 10.56**), but you have to remember she will never be seen this close in the game. Rename the final group and display layer to represent the polygon count (Kila_120) and save the file as Kila_LOD_Prep.mb.

Our LOD model for Kila is complete, but will it work? Once we have completed the reductions on Grae, we will test both characters' LODs to see how they will look in a game when the characters move away from the camera.

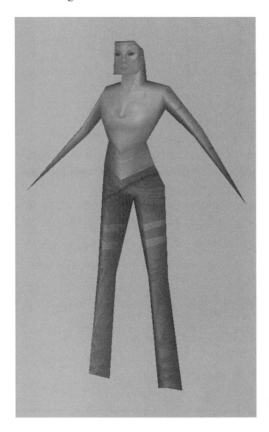

**FIGURE 10.56**
LOD 5 up close

## Grae's LODs

For Grae's LOD work, you'll be taking over.

Load in the file you created earlier, Grae_Pose.mb.

The main Grae model is 5174 polygons, so generate levels of detail at around the following polygon limits: 4000, 1500, 750, 350, and 150. He is a much larger character than Kila, so he will need an extra LOD.

Remember that each LOD will be roughly twice the distance away from the camera as the next-higher one, so keep zooming out to that level to check your progress.

Here are a few areas to consider:

▶  Grae's teeth and claws hold a lot of polygons and will ultimately not be seen from a distance. Try removing the back faces from his teeth first.

▶  If you are struggling to meet your LOD limits, consider removing the wings completely when he is far from the camera—but this is something you'd want to check out with your manager first.

▶  Remember to consider the hands for reduction as well as the limbs. Their need to deform correctly fades, the farther they get from the camera.

When finished, save your work as Grae_LOD_Prep.mb. You can see Grae's LODs in **Figure 10.57**.

**FIGURE 10.57**
Grae's levels
of detail

## Testing LODs: The Level of Detail Group

Knowing how the levels of detail will look in the game can be guesswork at times. It usually involves your actually seeing the character in the game—but Maya has a way around this requirement. Maya allows you to view the models interactively using a Level of Detail Group. The programmers on your team can then use the data in this group to help them set up the in-game LODs.

Much like a normal group, what the LOD Group does is group all the different resolutions together. Then you can designate at what distance each model should be viewed.

Let's apply this technique to our characters, Kila first.

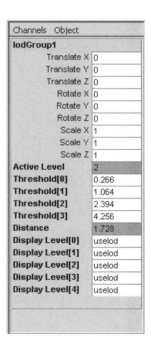

1   Load in the file called Kila_LOD_Prep.mb. Make all the LODs visible in the Layer Editor.

2   In the Outliner, select the highest LOD group first (Kila4096). Then, holding Ctrl, select the lower ones in order.

3   Go to Edit > Level Of Detail > Group. Each version of your character will now be placed into a new group called lodGroup1. This group will now control each LOD's visibility.

4   Try dollying the camera in and out of the screen; the character will change depending on its distance from the camera. The problem at the moment is that the distances are not set up correctly.

FIGURE 10.58 The Level of Detail Group options in the Channel Box

5   If it's not currently selected, select the lodGroup1 group and look in the Channel Box (**Figure 10.58**).

In the Channel Box, you'll see that we have some new attributes in addition to the usual translate, rotate, scale, and visibility attributes.

▶ **Active Level** tells you which LOD is currently being viewed.

▶ **Threshold[0]–[3]** are the distances at which the LODs change.

▶ **Distance** is the character's current distance from the camera.

▶ **Display Level[0]–[4]** hold various display options for each individual LOD.

6 We will use the Distance attribute to help us fill in the Threshold attributes correctly. Dolly out to the distance where the LOD will first change to level 2, using **Figure 10.13** as reference. When you're there, copy the value from the Distance attribute into the Threshold[0] attribute. It should be 5, or about that.

7 Do the same for the rest of the LODs, updating the associated Threshold attribute for each level. The values should be approximately 15 for Threshold[1], 43 for Threshold[2], and 123 for Threshold[3].

Now, as you move in and out from your character, the LODs will change according to the distances you have set.

8 Rename lodGroup1 to KilaLOD, and save the scene as Kila_LOD_Active.mb to show that the LODs are all set up accordingly.

Now you can follow these same steps on the Grae model; for him, set the LOD thresholds to 35, 90, 170, 330, and 700.

## Summary

With this chapter complete, Kila and Grae have been designed, modeled, optimized, and textured, and now we have generated their levels of detail in order to save processing power. That is all the modeling we will be doing for now.

In Chapter 11, we will get some experience with Maya's animation tools as we provide the skeletons that will enable our characters to move and interact with the gaming environment.

# CHAPTER 11
# Skeleton Setup

**IT'S NOT JUST** a character's look in the game that makes
that character appealing; a lot has to do with the way it moves. To bring
our characters to life, we give them a *skeleton*. This skeleton then drives
the geometry just as our human skeletons drive our muscles and, in turn,
our skin.

Over the next two chapters we will explore the process of creating an
"intuitive" skeletal structure that will make our characters move and
emote realistically and with ease. We will begin by inserting basic joints
into Kila and Grae, before adjusting the rotational axes to get the results
we require.

# The Base Skeletons

Creating the base skeletal structure is pretty straightforward—it's simply a matter of building up half the character and then mirroring it to create the opposite side.

As with many aspects of game artwork, we do have technical limits to adhere to. These limits vary dramatically depending on the format for which you are developing and the game engine you are using, but to be safe it's best to create the skeleton using as few joints as possible. A "safe" number for a main character is 64; this limit is a common one because it's the maximum for the PlayStation 2.

We have already touched on the basics of joint creation in Chapter 6, but before we proceed to building skeletons, let's have a closer look at the joint options.

### Options for Joint Creation

Open up the options for the Joint tool (**Figure 11.1**) found in the Skeleton menu. We are going to use the default settings in this chapter's work, but here's a list of all the options in the Joint Settings pane.

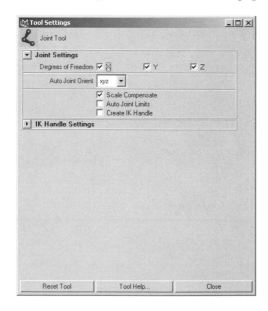

FIGURE 11.1 Joint tool options

**NOTE**   You can alter any of these settings after a joint has been created.

▶ *Degrees of Freedom* dictates which rotations are active. Disabling X, Y, or Z will remove the ability to rotate around that axis. Disabling some axes can be done, for example, on an elbow joint, where you would want to rotate around one axis and not the others.

▶ *Scale Compensate* (when enabled) automatically scales other joints in the same skeletal hierarchy when you scale joints above them. The default setting for this option is enabled.

▶ *Auto Joint Limits* lets Maya specify how far a joint can rotate around its axis.

▶ *Create IK Handle* automatically adds IK (Inverse Kinematics; see Chapter 12) to your character's joints as you create them. As tempting as this option might seem at first glance, it's rarely a good idea to use it.

▶ *Auto Joint Orient* determines how the axis on each joint will be set. In the default setting (xyz), X will always point down the bone. Y will attempt to point up, and Z will try to point out to the front (the Y and Z axes' positions are determined more by the orientation of their child bones than the effect of this setting).

You can see the effect of the xyz Auto Joint Orient setting demonstrated in **Figure 11.2**. In this example, there are two joints, and in the center of each you can see the joint's rotational axis: X pointing down the bone toward the next joint, Y pointing up, and Z pointing out to the front.

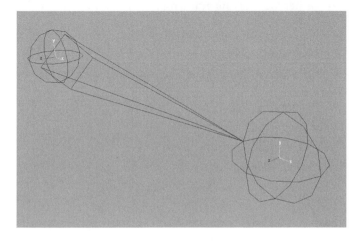

**FIGURE 11.2**
A basic two-joint setup with the rotational pivots visible

We will talk more about the rotational axis and joint orientation later in this chapter.

> **TIP** ▶ To show the selected object's rotational pivot, go to Display > Component Display > Local Rotational Axis.

Now that we know a little more about the options available for joint creation, let's continue on and build the skeletons that will animate our characters. We will work on Kila first.

### Kila's Skeletal Structure

For Kila we need an essentially standard skeleton to start us off. First we will create her limbs.

Load the file that contains all the LODs, Kila_LOD_Prep.mb.

Some joints may already exist in the scene; these were used back in Chapter 6 when we tested Kila's deformation. Delete these for now; we want to construct this skeleton from scratch.

We don't want to edit any of the geometry, so turn the display layer visibility off for the lower levels of detail, and set the highest LOD's display type to Template.

1  Switch to the front view and go to Skeleton > Joint Tool to begin building in the joints for Kila's arm, starting with the clavicle, or collarbone (**Figure 11.3**). Then build joints for her leg, starting at the hip.

   After placing each joint, you can manipulate its position by clicking on it with the middle mouse button. Press Enter to complete each chain. Make sure the joint chains for the arm and leg appear straight when you're looking at them from the front.

FIGURE 11.3 For the arm, begin the joints with the clavicle rather than the shoulder.

2   Next, using the top and side views, position all the joints of the arm and leg so that they lie down the center, or close to it, of the geometry (**Figure 11.4**).

TIP   If you need to move the joints after the chain is complete, press the Insert key. This allows you to move a joint without affecting others in the joint hierarchy.

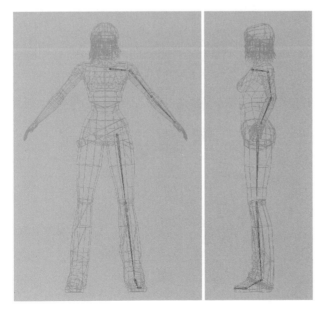

FIGURE 11.4 Position the joints down the center of the geometry.

**3** The main part of the spine is constructed from six joints, starting with the base joint located halfway between her navel and her crotch. The fifth joint in the chain should be at the base of her neck, leaving the sixth and final one to be positioned parallel to the neck but no higher than her mouth.

With the main spine done, create one additional joint out in front of her head, resting just outside her mouth.

You can see all seven of these joints in **Figure 11.5**.

**4** You currently have three separate skeletons; now you will combine them into a single one. Select the clavicle joint and then the spine joint that exists just below it. Press P to parent them (**Figure 11.6**).

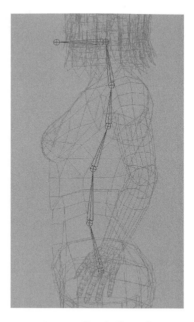

FIGURE 11.5 Create the spine, neck, and head joints.

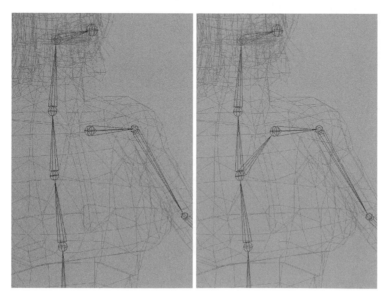

FIGURE 11.6 Parent the clavicle to the spine.

**5** Parent the thighbone to the first, base joint of the spine (**Figure 11.7**).

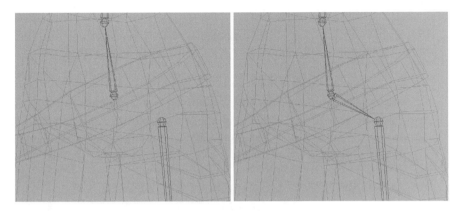

**FIGURE 11.7** Parent the thighbone to the base of the spine.

**6** The basic skeleton now exists for Kila's left side. You still need to add the joints for her fingers, which should be parented to the wrist (**Figure 11.8**). Create four joints for each of the five fingers, and then parent each root joint to the wrist.

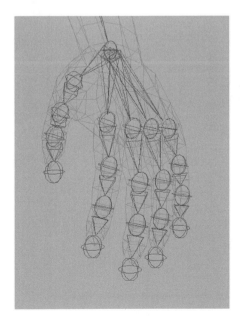

**FIGURE 11.8** Create the joints for her fingers.

With these basic joints in place, we can now copy and mirror them to create Kila's right side.

**1**   Open the Outliner, and Shift+click on the plus sign next to the joint hierarchy. This opens up the entire hierarchy as shown in **Figure 11.9**, left.

In the hierarchy's current state, you can't tell which joint is where, so let's go in and manually rename them all. Call the very first joint Root, and put the prefix L_ in front of the names of all the left-side joints. Add _Tip at the end of the names of the joints at the very end. See how the new hierarchy looks in **Figure 11.9**, right.

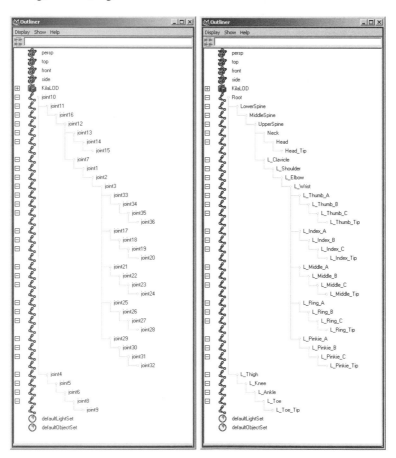

**FIGURE 11.9** Rename all the joints.

**2**   Now select the L_Thigh joint. Go to Skeleton > Mirror Joint and open the
options (**Figure 11.10**).

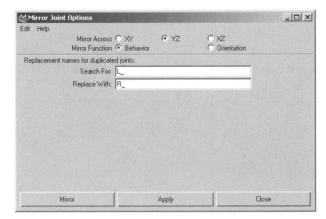

**FIGURE 11.10** Mirror
Joint Options dialog box

**3**   Set Mirror Across to YZ; this
will mirror the joints from +X
to –X. Leave Mirror Function
set to Behavior. In Search For,
type L_; and in Replace With,
type R_. This renames all the
mirrored joints beginning with
L_ so they begin with R_.

Click Apply when you're finished; you've now created the
right leg.

**4**   Select the clavicle and mirror it,
using the same options, to cre-
ate the right arm.

As you can see in **Figure 11.11**, Kila
now has a basic skeleton. Save the
file as Kila_Skeleton.mb.

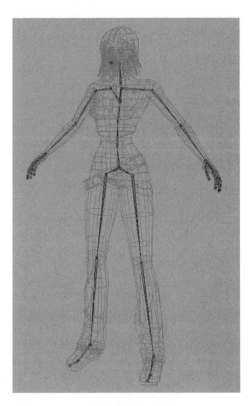

**FIGURE 11.11** Kila's basic skeleton

### Grae's Skeletal Structure

Now we will look at Grae's base skeleton.

Load the file Grae_LOD_Prep.mb, and prepare it by turning off all the display layers except the first one (Grae_5174). Set this level's display type to Template.

Remove any joints that currently exist in the scene, except for the ones you created for the wings (and keep these hidden for now).

1   Use the Joint tool to create the left arm and leg joints (**Figure 11.12**). Remember to begin the arm from the clavicle.

**FIGURE 11.12** Create Grae's left arm and leg joints.

> **TIP**  Because of the size difference between our two characters, Grae's joints may not be clearly visible, so adjust the display size of joints by going to Display > Joint Size.

2   Grae has individual toes, unlike Kila, so create the joints that will animate these (**Figure 11.13**).

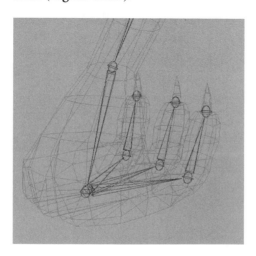

**FIGURE 11.13** Insert joints into the individual toes.

**3**    Next, implement the spine. Grae's will be quite different from Kila's, of course—try to follow the curve of his upper body as seen in **Figure 11.14**.

**FIGURE 11.14** Add the spine joints.

**4**    With Grae's spine in place, parent the clavicle to the joint nearest to it on the spine, and parent the thigh joint to the root of the spine.

**5**    To complete the left side, build the joints into the hand. Keep in mind that Grae has fewer joints in each finger than Kila does (**Figure 11.15**).

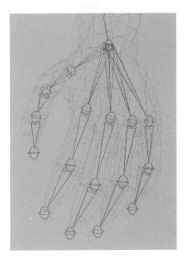

**FIGURE 11.15** Add the joints in his hand.

**6** To complete the base skeleton for Grae, rename all the joints (remembering to use the L_ prefix and place _Tip after the names of the end joints—these will be on the fingers, toes, wings, and head). Then use the Mirror Joint tool to create his right side.

The base skeleton is complete; you can see it in **Figure 11.16**.

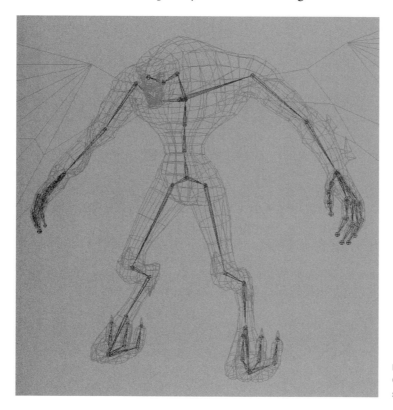

**FIGURE 11.16**
Grae's basic skeleton.

For both the basic skeletons that now exist inside each of our characters, we can improve on the way they animate by adding extra joints on top of the fundamental ones.

## Additional Joints

Working with the fundamental skeleton is ideal for animating a character's main body, but what about other areas such as the eyes, Grae's wings, Kila's hair, and even her chest? To make the character appear more realistic, these areas should animate, too.

### Eyes

Kila and Grae's eyes need the ability to move, so first we will create joints to animate them. Follow these steps for both characters, as their eyes will work the same.

**1**  Start by hiding all the geometry except for the eyes.

**2**  When we created the eye, we removed the back half because it wasn't needed. For the eye to rotate convincingly, we need the joint to be in the center of the original sphere.

So create a single joint and, looking from the front, position it over the center of the eye (**Figure 11.17**, left).

**3**  Switch to the side view, and move the joint to the very back of the eye geometry (**Figure 11.17**, right).

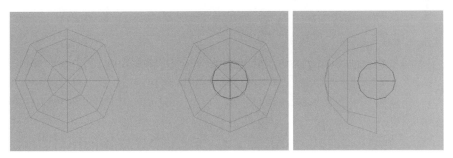

**FIGURE 11.17** Position a joint over the pivot for the eye.

4    With the eye in position, rename it to L_Eye and parent it to the head joint (**Figure 11.18**, left).

5    Use the Mirror Joint tool to copy the new eye across to create the right eye (**Figure 11.18**, right). This should automatically rename it R_Eye in the process.

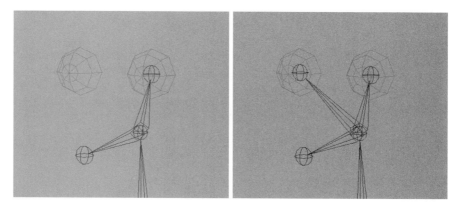

FIGURE 11.18 Parent the left eye joint to the head joint before mirroring it to create the right eye.

That's the eyes in position. We will look into adding more joints in the way of facial animation in Chapter 13.

### Kila's Chest

As Kila moves around, it would be nice to add a little bounce to her bosom, giving her a bit more life and making her seem more organic. We can approach this enhancement in two ways: using either joints rotations or translations to add animation.

If we use the translations method, we have freedom to move the joints anywhere in space. Also, the main pivot point will actually be inside each breast, meaning we are essentially picking each breast up and moving it around. Using rotations limits the movement to around the pivot point itself. This is ideal for rotational-based animation, on which the majority of the body is based. What you need to find out at this stage is how the joints are handled when they are exported and placed into the game. If the engine can only handle rotations, then the decision is made for you.

But which method is best? It depends on the area you are animating and what you need it to do; in this instance, both techniques will provide good results. Let's take a look.

Open up the file named KilaChestTest.mb.

Press Play in the Time Slider, and you'll notice that the movement of both breasts is almost identical, yet the one on the right is controlled via translations whereas the left side is controlled by the joints' rotations. The only initial difference can be seen when you look from the side. As the chest rises, the breast controlled via rotations tilts upward as it rotates.

Look at the joint configuration for the two techniques in **Figure 11.19**. As you can see, the joints on the left, which control the breast via rotations, have to be quite far back, just past the spine in fact. Having the joints too close to the breast will cause it to tilt upward unnaturally as it rises and falls.

With the joints placed actually inside the breast, as shown in the torso on the right of **Figure 11.19**, controlling them with their translations will initially give you a good idea of how they will move—as well as giving you more freedom over where they move.

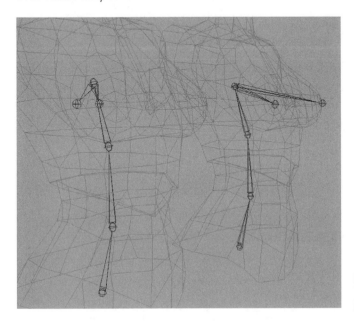

**FIGURE 11.19**
Two different chest
joint configurations

Using translations to manipulate your geometry will allow you to animate it through all three degrees of movement. With rotations, on the other hand, you are locked to the pivot point and so can only move the breast up and down and twist it. Using translations, however, lets you move it up, down, and in and out.

So for Kila, we opt for the translation method—but in other projects, make sure you check on which methods are possible for your game environment, and think first about what you want the area to do.

### Kila's Hair

Kila's hair is quite long, so if it doesn't have some movement it won't look natural. Ideally, the hair would be controlled by an in-game physics engine, but for the purposes of this book we will add some joints to give it basic movement.

We could create lots of joints, giving us the freedom to do anything we want with the hair, but its current topology and associated joint restrictions mean we have to rely on fewer joints.

1   First, hide the main skeleton. Then, as demonstrated in **Figure 11.20a**, create five individual joints along the bottom of her hairdo.

> **TIP** If the geometry layer is set to Reference instead of Template, joints can be point-snapped to vertices, which will aid in their placement.

2   Because we want the hair to swing, using rotations is the best way to animate it. Duplicate the five joints you just created, and move them up to the pivot points from which the hair "hangs." Halfway up the side of her head is an ideal position (**Figure 11.20b**).

3   Parent the lower joints to the upper ones (**Figure 11.20c**). Rename them all, adding _Tip  after the names of the lower joints so that you will know these are end joints.

4   Unhide the main skeleton, and parent the hair joints to the head. This gives you the setup shown in **Figure 11.20d**.

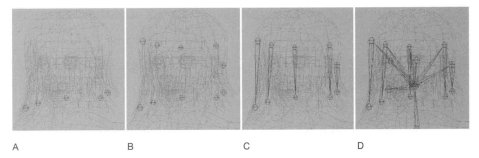

A            B            C            D

FIGURE 11.20 Hair joint assembly

We now have the ability to add some movement to her hair.

### Grae's Wings

Grae's wings, like Kila's hair, need the ability to move. You should already have a wing setup left over from Chapter 6. We can use that here, saving us the effort of creating a new one.

First we need to address the wings' ability to open and close. With the current joint hierarchy we can't do this (**Figure 11.21**, left). The single joint at the wrist rotates all the fingers of the wing; we need to be able to rotate these individually.

1    Select the middle joint of each wing finger, and go to Edit > Unparent (**Figure 11.21**, middle).

2    Now select the knuckle joint to which they were originally parented, and duplicate it four times. Call these duplicates L_Wing_Finger01_Base, L_Wing_Finger02_Base, L_Wing_Finger02_Base, and L_Wing_Finger04_Base.

3    Parent these new joints to the one from which they were duplicated, L_Wing_Wrist.

4    Now parent the ends of the wing fingers to the new joints. So L_Wing_Finger01 will be parented to L_Wing_Finger01_Base, and so forth. In effect, the wing will look no different than when we began.

As you can see in **Figure 11.21**, right, we can now open and close the wing by using the new joints we've created.

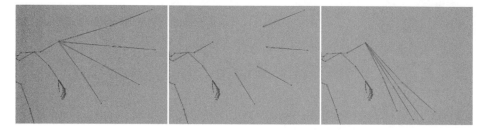

FIGURE 11.21 Adjust the wing hierarchy so that the wing can open and close.

Now that the wing is easier to pose, we can go about attaching it to the main skeleton and mirroring it for the wing on the right.

1    To start, simply parent the wing to the upper spine joint—the same one to which the clavicles were parented (**Figure 11.22**, middle).

2    To create the wing on the right, select the first joint belonging to the existing wing and use the Mirror Joint tool (**Figure 11.22**, bottom).

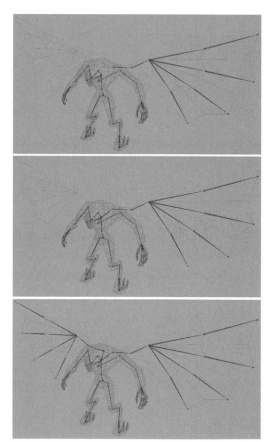

FIGURE 11.22 Parent the wing to the upper spine and then create a mirrored duplicate.

## Joint Cleanup

The principal skeletons for Kila and Grae are now complete, so let's find out how many joints make up each one. In this case, I have made this easy for you; the number of joints in the scene does not match the number that will be used in the game. All of the end joints are there merely as a visual aid; the actual geometry will not use them to move.

> **NOTE** You'll want to double-check this with the relevant programmer; it may be that your game engine does need these end joints.

Contained in the GCDM shelf is a button labeled jntCnt. Running this will give you an accurate joint count. It will not, however, include any of the end joints (such as the eyes), so you will have to add these to the count.

Using the jntCnt tool, we can see that Kila uses 57 joints, plus another 4 for her eyes and chest, bringing the count up to 61. Grae uses 66, plus 2 for his eyes, making the total 68.

In the next section, we will need to check how the skeleton will move—or, more accurately, rotate.

Depending on how you constructed the skeleton, there may be some values in the rotation attributes. Because the majority of the skeleton is controlled by its rotations, it's vital that these are zeroed out before checking the rotational axes. Having them all at zero will simplify animation and control.

Before we continue to the next task, quickly select all the joints and freeze the transforms, making sure to freeze only the rotations.

## Checking the Rotational Axis

One of the most important stages in character rigging, particularly in Maya, is to check the rotational axes. The way a joint rotates depends on how the axis is aligned. This is particularly important when you are using joint chains as we have done in Kila and Grae.

Look at **Figure 11.23**, left. Here we have our current hand for Kila, which looks fine. To get the fingers to bend and make a fist, we would select the root of each finger, then its hierarchy, and do a global rotation around the Z axis.

**Figure 11.23**, right, shows the result. Because all of the rotational axes are out of line at this point, the fingers are all bending in random directions.

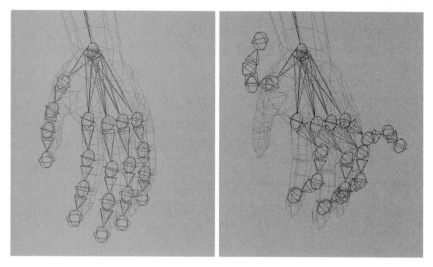

FIGURE 11.23 Rotating the fingers around the Z axis demonstrates that the rotational axes are not correctly aligned.

You'll find this misalignment in a number of areas around the skeleton as it is currently constructed, so let's fix them.

This gives us the opportunity to look at two more of the tools located on the GCDM shelf: rsJnt and orJnt.

▶ The rsJnt tool will reset a joint's axis to match the one above it in the hierarchy. If no joint exists above the joint being reset, rsJnt will match the world axis.

▶ The orJnt tool attempts to reorient each joint using the default xyz setting (in this case, X pointing down the bone, with Y and Z perpendicular to it).

> **NOTE**  Maya does have its own tool for reorienting joints (Skeleton > Orient Joint). I've found, however, that this tool doesn't operate as I'd expect when more than one joint is selected. Feel free to use the Maya command if you prefer.

1   Select the root of Kila's skeleton. Then select the rest of the joints below it by going to Edit > Select Hierarchy.

2   With the joints now selected, go to Display > Component Display > Local Rotation Axis. As you can see in **Figure 11.24**, right, each joint's axis is now visible.

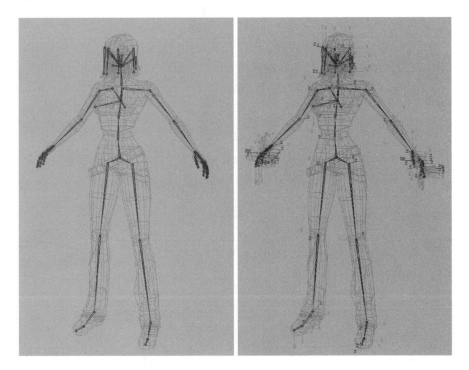

FIGURE 11.24 Make all the joints' rotational axes visible.

Now that we can see each axis, we can realign them.

3   To start, reset the spine joints. Select the main root joint and continue selecting your way up the spine, right up to the Head_Tip joint. Make sure you select the joints in order.

> TIP   It can be a little confusing having all the rotational axes displayed at once. I recommend hiding the ones you are not currently working on. Select a joint and go to Display > Component Display > Local Rotation Axis. You can go a step further by hiding the inactive joints, too, but be warned that hiding one will also hide all the ones beneath it in the hierarchy.

**4**    **Figure 11.25**, left, shows the current orientation of the axes. Click rsJnt, and these will be reset as seen in **Figure 11.25**, right—all nice and neat, with Z pointing forward.

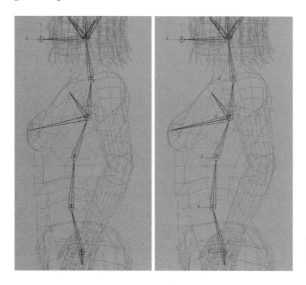

FIGURE 11.25
Reset the rotational axes on the spine.

**5**    Next, perform the same resetting process on the breast, eye, and hair joints (**Figure 11.26**).

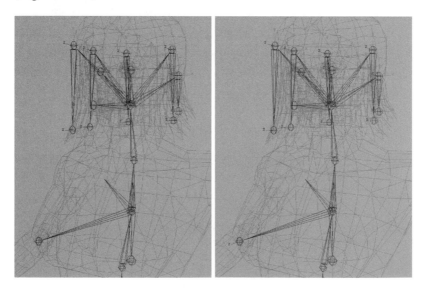

FIGURE 11.26 Reset the breast, eye, and hair joints.

**NOTE** ▸ Normally, a joint's rotation should match the orientation of the joint itself, with one axis pointing directly down the bone. We are ignoring this principle for the breast, eye, and hair joints, however, because we want the rotations to match Maya's world pivot. In Chapter 12, we will be assigning rigging controls to these joints, so having the axes at this default state will make them easier to control.

That's the center of the body complete, now, so let's proceed to the arms and hands.

To orient the arms correctly, we first need to temporarily reset the clavicles. We do this because the orientation of the arm joints will be based on their parent joints. If we simply fixed the clavicle without resetting, the shoulder's Y axis would not point directly up, and the arm's rotation would be off. Resetting the clavicle will allow the shoulders, and then the rest of the arm's axes, to orient correctly.

**1**   Select the clavicle joints and click on the rsJnt button.

**2**   Select the shoulder and elbow joints; this time click on the orJnt button.

**3**   Because the wrist joint has lots of children, we can't tell it to adjust the axis so that X points down one bone toward the next one. In this case, our hand is oriented the same as the upper arm, so we can use the rsJnt tool which will copy the previous joint's orientation.

You can see the arm orientations in **Figure 11.27**.

**NOTE** ▸ Think about how you want the hand to bend before you jump in and reset the orientation. If the alignment process described here is not going to work, then you will have to edit the rotational axis manually, which we will look into shortly.

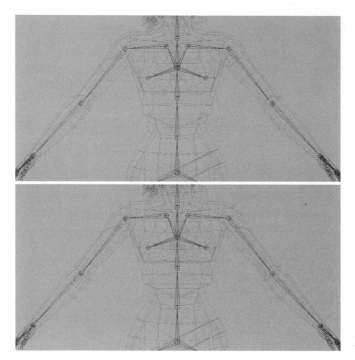

**FIGURE 11.27**
Reset the clavicle
and then reorient
the rest of the arm.

**4** For the fingers, simply select each joint and press orJnt (**Figure 11.28**, middle).

Now the thumb will have the same orientation as the fingers, but if you rotate your own thumb you'll notice it works on a different axis. To rectify this, the GCDM shelf has another button labeled rot45. This tool will rotate the joint's rotational pivot around the X axis at 45-unit intervals.

**5** On the left hand, select the thumb joints, and press the rot45 button seven times (**Figure 11.28**, right).

**6** For the right hand, you only need to press this once because the orientations are mirrored.

> **TIP** Make sure to double-check against your own hand to verify the proper effect is achieved, particularly for the thumb.

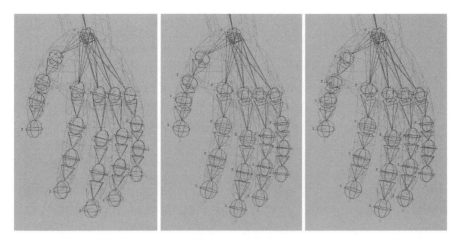

**FIGURE 11.28** Fix the orientation of the fingers and thumb.

The last joints to tackle are in the legs. Starting from the hip, select each joint and press orJnt. As you can see in **Figure 11.29**, this works well on the legs. The feet, however, are at an angle. We want the pivots to be flat (an axis flat and parallel relative to the grid) while also being aligned with the foot; otherwise, when we rotate the feet, they will skew off to one side.

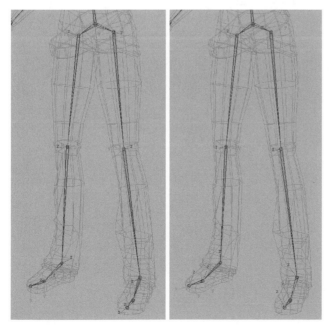

**FIGURE 11.29**
Reorient the rotational axes on the legs.

We could try resetting the ankle joints, but this won't work; they will only inherit the previous joint's pivot. So what we do is this:

**1**   Select the ankle joints and unparent them from the knees (Edit > Unparent); see **Figure 11.30b**.

**2**   Now reset the ankle joints. They will inherit the world pivot, making them nice and flat.

**3**   With the ankles set, you can select the rest of the foot joints and run orJnt on them (**Figure 11.30c**).

**4**   Parent the ankles back to the knees (**Figure 11.30d**).

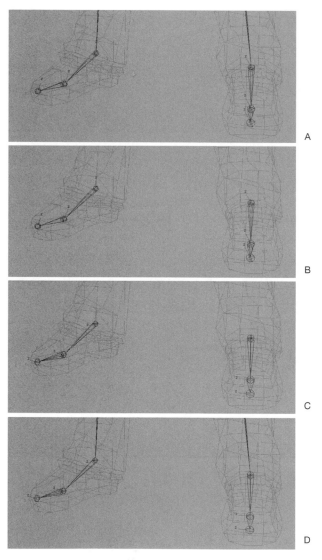

A

B

C

D

**FIGURE 11.30** Fix the orientation of the feet.

The feet aren't finished yet—we still need to fine-tune them. Look from the top view, as seen in **Figure 11.31**, top. Although the axes are flat, which is how we want them, they don't match the orientation of the foot. Each foot points slightly outward, whereas the axis is pointing dead ahead. We need the axis to match that shown in **Figure 11.31**, bottom.

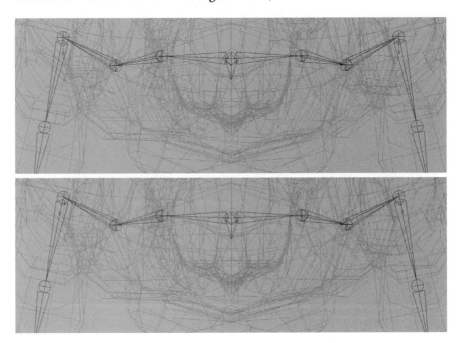

FIGURE 11.31 We now need to adjust the orientation from the top view.

**5** Go up to the status line and select the Select By Component Type button, the second button from the left in **Figure 11.32**.

You are now in Component mode, but you still need to tell Maya what components you want to edit.

**6** Right-click on the question mark toward the right end of the status line (**Figure 11.32**). On the menu that appears, select Local Rotation Axis.

FIGURE 11.32 Choose Select By Component Type then right-click the question mark in the status line.

**7** Now physically select the ankles' rotation axes and rotate them to match the joints, as demonstrated in **Figure 11.33**. Make sure to restrict your rotation to the Y axis, so that X remains flat relative to the ground/grid.

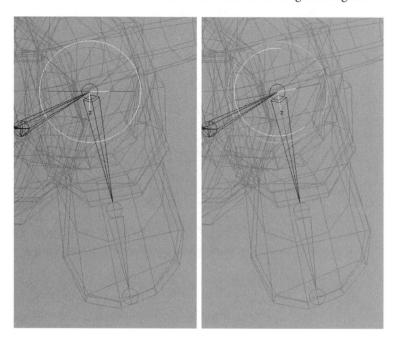

FIGURE 11.33 Fine-tune the rotational axes on the ankles.

**8** Press F8 when you are done to return to Object mode.

With the rotational axes cleaned up, the skeleton is complete (**Figure 11.34**). Save your work, updating the Kila_Skeleton.mb file.

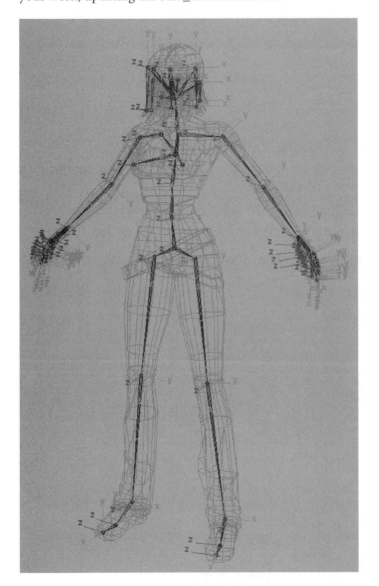

**FIGURE 11.34** Kila's completed skeleton with the cleaned-up rotational axes.

Grae's skeleton can be adjusted in exactly the same way as Kila's. Go ahead and work on this next, updating the file Grae_Skeleton.mb.

## Repositioning the Characters

Before we move on to Chapter 12, there is one final thing to check in our characters so far: their overall position in Maya.

Switch to the side view and make sure the grid is enabled (Show > Grid). You will see that the characters are not aligned with the world correctly (the left panels of **Figures 11.35** and **11.36**). The two thick black lines of the grid show the world's root; the horizontal one is our floor.

Select KilaLOD and Root in the Outliner, moving them up the Y axis and along the Z axis until their feet rest on the horizontal line, as seen in **Figure 11.35**, right. Do the same for Grae: Select GraeLOD and Root in the Outliner then move them up as seen in **Figure 11.36**, right.

When finished, freeze the transforms on their LOD groups, making sure you only have Translate selected.

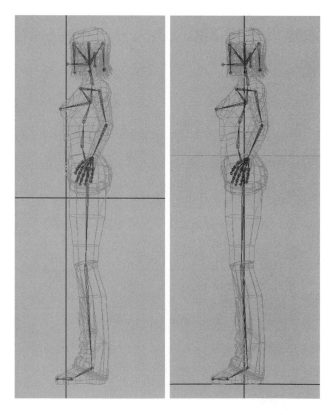

**FIGURE 11.35**
Reposition Kila
and her skeleton
in the world.

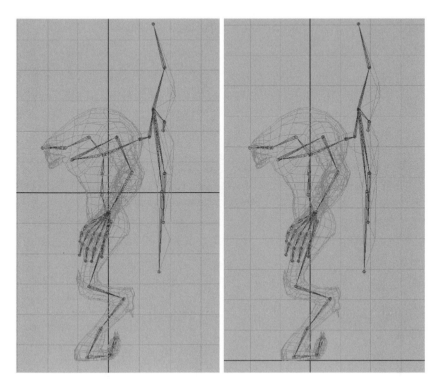

**FIGURE 11.36** Reposition Grae and his skeleton in the world.

## Summary

The first stage of character rigging for Kila and Grae is complete. We have created base skeletons and adjusted the rotational axes to correct orientations, allowing the skeletons to animate correctly. Next we will add controls to the skeletons, making it easier to pose and animate the characters.

# CHAPTER 12
# Character Rigging

**WITH THE BASE** skeletons in place, we could just bind the geometry to them and begin animating. At first this would work well, but sooner or later we would start to notice that our ability to make the character move is heavily restricted. At present, the character is like a car without seats, pedals, or even a steering wheel. We can get it to move and we can control it, but not without some difficulty.

This is where adding a rig will help. *Rigging* is the process of adding controls on top of the base skeleton. Initially these controls will act as a visual aid, helping us identify which area we are manipulating. On a deeper level, they will allow us to move and pose the character in ways we can't accomplish with just the base skeleton.

As you can imagine, rigging a full character can be a complicated task, and to the novice it can be quite daunting. You can't simply throw a rig together—you have to think about what you want each control to do, and whether it will make life easier in the end for the animator. The key is making a rig that anyone can just pick up and play, enabling them to get poses quickly and easily, while at the same time making sure no part of the setup can be damaged unintentionally in the process.

Rigs come in all shapes and sizes, and you will find that everyone has their own way of rigging. Rigging can be quite a personal thing, so don't be concerned if the rig you will create during this chapter is not the same as ones you may have seen in other books or on the Internet. Once you have an understanding of the fundamentals of rig building, you can then create your own to suit your needs.

With this in mind, we will take a different approach in this chapter than we have so far. We'll begin by spending some time learning the underlying theory and new terms involved before we proceed to the actual task of creating a rig.

## Why Use Controls?

With the character mesh visible, trying to select the correct joint can prove tricky and often frustrating. It would make things much less challenging if we could forget about the joints on the base skeleton, controlling it through other means. Adding intuitive controls to your rig will make the whole animation process easier and quicker.

Maya has a system on hand to help you with these controls. Every object has a built-in selection handle; this is displayed in the form of a small cross that you can position anywhere in the scene. You can activate these handles by going to Display > Component Display > Selection Handles.

The selection handle crosses work well to a point, but imagine that you have one cross for each joint. Looking at the example in **Figure 12.1**, left, can you tell which area of the skeleton is selected by which handle? Some of them are quite obvious from this angle, but imagine how difficult it would be if you were looking from the side.

This is where *icons* work well to represent controls. Custom-made using Maya's curve creation tools, an icon can be tailored to suit the area it will move—like the hand outline in **Figure 12.1**, right—so that you and other animators can easily navigate the scene.

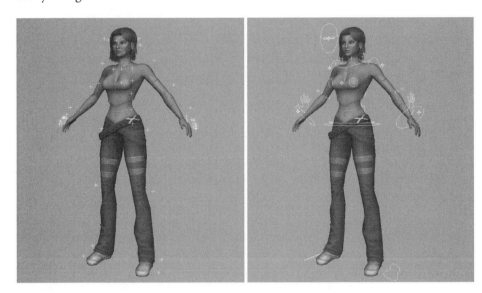

**FIGURE 12.1** Our Kila skeleton with two different control methods

Icons don't just help with navigation; they also help with positioning. All joints have translation values on them that cannot be frozen, and resetting them to zero will position each joint at the world root. Having icons drive the joints with an initial value of zero is useful if you need to reset the character or copy animation from one icon to another.

Another valuable asset is that you can add *dynamic attributes* to these control icons. A dynamic attribute added to the icon can then control a series of other attributes on a completely different object; this is done using the Set Driven Keys command under the Animate menu (which we will discuss later in the chapter). For example, you could have a single attribute on the hand icon that will pose the entire hand, making it into a fist; a value of 0 on this attribute would be the hand in its default pose, and 10 would be the fist. As you can imagine, animating the hand will go much more quickly using a dynamic attribute than it would if you had to rotate each finger joint individually and then set a key.

All that said, Maya's selection handles still have a great deal of use in our rig and, when used on a small scale, can prove invaluable.

### Icon Creation

You can use anything, from locators to default curves, as icons—as long as you make it easy to identify which area of the skeleton is represented. Having the same icon/locator for each control would be just as confusing as using the default selection handle, as shown earlier in **Figure 12.1**, left.

Maya has some default shapes that you can choose for icons:

▶ A plain circle shape can be created quickly by going to Create > NURBS Primitives > Circle.

▶ If you only want half of the circle, you can use Create > Arc Tools.

▶ You can always use a locator from Create > Locator.

The default icon shapes are good solutions for quick iconic representation, but you may need more specific shapes, too, such as feet or hands. To create these, you'll use the *curve tools* found in the Create menu.

▶ The *Control Vertices (CV) Curve tool* creates curves based on the placements of control vertices (CVs). Each CV contributes to the overall shape of the curve.

As demonstrated in **Figure 12.2**, the curve you build will not show up until you have placed the first four CVs. You will also notice that the CVs don't lie on the actual curve, so this method of creation is less helpful if you are making precise shapes.

▶ The *Edit Point (EP) Curve tool* is geared more toward accurate curve creation, because each point you place lies directly on the curve.

As you can see in **Figure 12.3**, unlike the CV Curve tool, the actual spline is visible once you have placed the second edit point.

▶ The *Pencil Curve tool* allows you to draw your curve freehand—ideal when you need to trace an image or create a more complex shape.

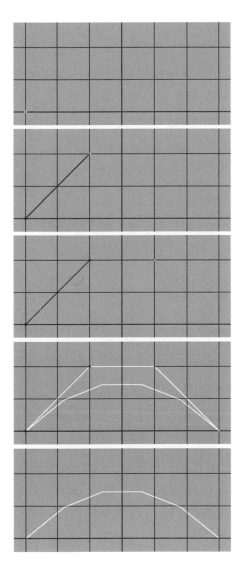

FIGURE 12.2 Creating a curve with the CV
Curve tool

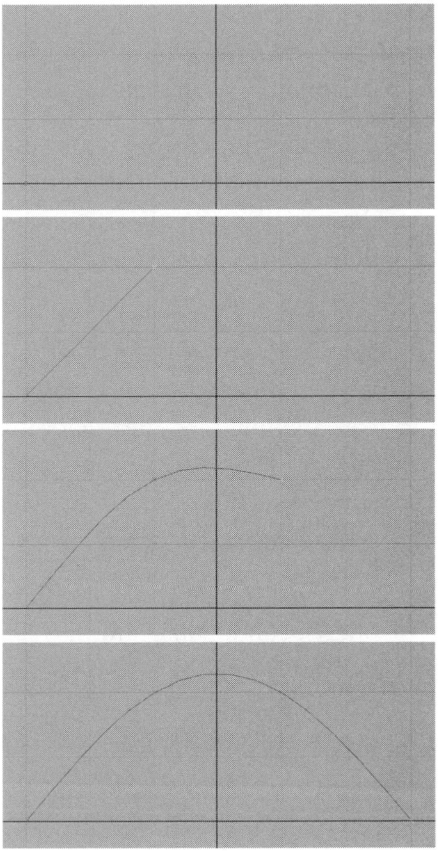

FIGURE 12.3 Creating a curve with the EP
Curve tool

### Curve Tool Options

Each curve tool has similar options for controlling the overall shape:

▶ *Curve Degree* is perhaps the most common option used; it controls the smoothness of the curve, as illustrated in **Figure 12.4**.

The setting 1 Linear will give you an angular shape, with the curve following a linear path between each control point. The effects of settings 2, 3 Cubic, 5, and 7 get gradually smoother, with 7 producing the smoothest version of a curve.

▶ *Knot Spacing* adjusts the position of each edit point. Uniform will give you a predictable distribution, whereas Chord Length will improve the overall curvature.

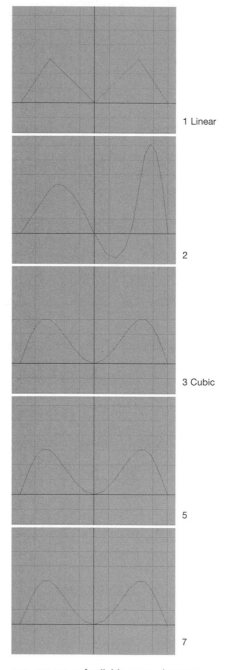

**FIGURE 12.4** Available curve degrees

Once the curve is created you can adjust the smoothness of a curve's display by selecting the curve and pressing 1 for a rough version of your curve, 2 for medium smoothness, and 3 for the smoothest display (**Figure 12.5**).

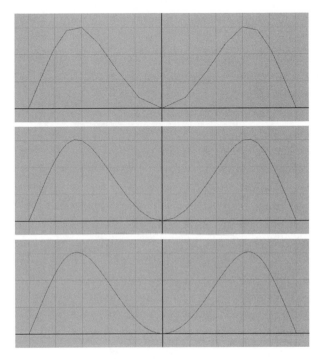

**FIGURE 12.5** You can adjust the curve's display smoothness by pressing 1, 2, or 3.

**NOTE** To help build our rigs during this chapter, we will use the ready-made icons found on the CD in Project Files/12/Icons. That folder also has a few extra icons for your convenience.

## Forward Kinematics and Inverse Kinematics

Before we work on creating controls for animating Kila and Grae, it's important to understand a major principle of character rigging: *forward kinematics (FK)* and *inverse kinematics (IK)*. FK and IK are two different methods of moving a character in a scene. Each has its advantages and disadvantages, depending on what you want the character to do, and so both should be implemented into the character rig to account for any eventuality.

*Forward kinematics* is the process of animating *down* the hierarchy. For example, to raise or lower a character's hand you would rotate the shoulder, then the elbow, and finally the wrist (**Figure 12.6**).

Animating with FK is highly recommended because in many cases it produces better, more natural looking movements—but it's not always practical. Say the character is leaning with a hand on a table; we would need the hand to stay locked while the character's upper body moves. Keeping the hand steady using FK would be practically impossible, but with inverse kinematics it's a piece of cake.

Inverse kinematics works opposite to FK. As suggested by its name, in IK the joint chain is evaluated *backward*. **Figure 12.7**, left, shows the hand on the table with an IK handle applied (the cross located at the wrist). The IK handle dictates the position of the wrist, locking it in place. The rest of the arm then follows. If we move the main joints of the body forward (**Figure 12.7**, right), you can see that the wrist stays where it is. The hand remains locked, resting on the table, because the IK handle is not parented to (controlled by) any joints in the skeleton. The shoulder and elbow joint rotations are calculated by the *IK solver* (explained shortly) to allow for the best possible position and orientation of the skeleton chain between the shoulder and the wrist.

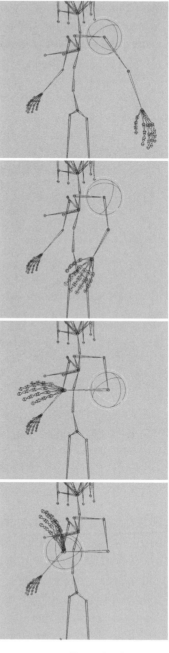

**FIGURE 12.6** Example of forward kinematics (FK)

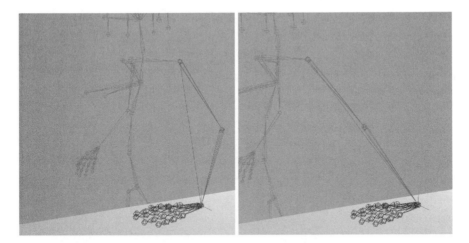

**FIGURE 12.7** Example of inverse kinematics (IK)

## IK Solvers

*IK solvers* are the brains behind IK handles. They work out how to rotate each joint in a joint chain controlled by an IK handle. There are three types of IK solvers in Maya: IK Single Chain solver, IK Rotate Plane solver, and IK Spline solver.

The *IK Single Chain* solver is the most fundamental way of manipulating a joint chain. Not only do you use the IK handle to manipulate the joints' position, you can also use its rotation to adjust the joint chain's orientation.

**Figure 12.8**, left, shows an arm with an IK Single Chain solver applied. Rotating the IK handle around the X axis will adjust the direction in which the elbow points (**Figure 12.8**, right).

On initial creation, the *IK Rotate Plane* solver looks the same as the Single Chain solver, except that you cannot alter the orientation of the joint chain by rotating the IK handle. Instead, the *pole vector* and *handle vector* (**Figure 12.9**) define the plane on which the middle joints lie. Imagine that the two vectors make up two edges of a flat triangle, with the arm joints lying on this triangle. Since the pivots for this triangle lie on the shoulder and wrist joints, moving the end of the pole vector will tip the triangle, forcing the joints to follow and affecting the orientation of the arm.

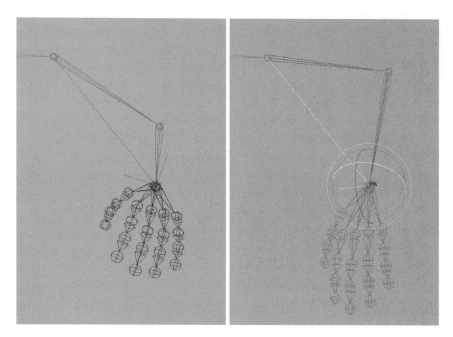

**FIGURE 12.8** An arm with an IK Single Chain solver applied

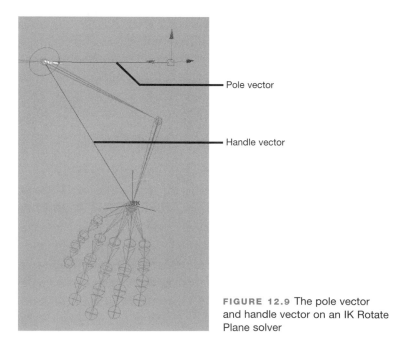

Pole vector

Handle vector

**FIGURE 12.9** The pole vector
and handle vector on an IK Rotate
Plane solver

You can move the pole vector by selecting the IK handle and pressing T to activate the manipulator tool. This will select the pole vector, allowing you to manipulate it. This can be very useful when animating arms or legs, because you can lock the pole vector to an object behind the arm using a *pole vector constraint*, meaning the elbow will point exactly where you need it to point. We will discuss the various constraints later in the chapter.

> **NOTE** Another way to manipulate the arm's orientation is to use the Twist attribute on the IK handle, although in this arrangement it can be difficult to keep the elbow steady when the arm has a lot of movement.

The IK Single Chain and Rotate Plane solvers are created in exactly the same way. Go to Skeleton > IK Handle Tool and open up the options. Following are some of the options associated with this tool (**Figure 12.10**).

▶ The *Current Solver* box specifies which of these two IK solvers you wish to create. You can change this after the handle has been created, allowing you to switch later if you need to.

▶ *Solver Enable* specifies whether the IK solver will be enabled upon creation.

▶ *Snap Enable* allows the IK handle to snap back to its origin (the second joint you selected in the handle's creation).

▶ *Sticky* allows the IK handle to stick to its current position while you continue to pose the skeleton.

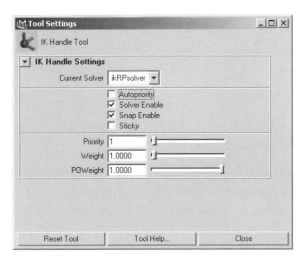

**FIGURE 12.10** IK Handle tool options

An *IK Spline* solver is a spline-based system best suited to long joint chains, like the kind you would see in a snake, a tail, tentacles, or even a spine. Once you create this solver, Maya gives you a spline with which you control the movement of the joints.

As you can see in **Figure 12.11**, manipulating the CVs on the spline will affect the rotations of the joints.

How can we apply these IK solvers to our characters Kila and Grae? The most obvious places are the characters' arms and legs, enabling the feet to lock to the ground as they walk, and the hands to be locked to specific objects. We could use the IK Spline handle on the spines, but Kila and Grae's spines are made from just a few joints, so it would not benefit the animator in the long run. Using the IK Spline would take longer

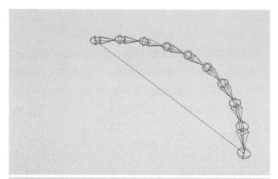
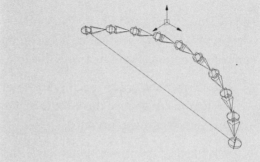
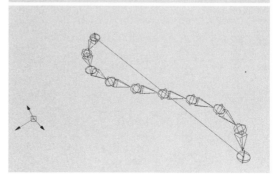

**FIGURE 12.11** Example of IK Spline solver

to animate; in addition, it could lead to restriction of the spine's movement since you would not be able to animate each joint separately.

On top of the IK, we will also need to add controls that will make it easier to use. All this can become fairly complex, so with this in mind let's start building the controls that will animate our base skeletons. We'll begin with the characters' arms and hands.

## Arm and Hand Controls

Kila and Grae's arms and hands, as is, are quite capable of giving us the animation we need. We can manipulate the shoulder and elbow joints to pose the
arms quite easily; we can even go in and animate the individual fingers. Adding
further controls to the arms and hands, however, will make posing them quicker
and easier to do.

### Arm Controls

Currently, Kila's arm inherits the rotations of the clavicle. As you can see in
**Figure 12.12**, when the clavicle rotates, so do the shoulder, elbow, and so on. So
we first need to lock the shoulder's rotation to another, independent control; this
will give us complete command over its movement.

Begin by loading the file Kila_Skeleton.mb.

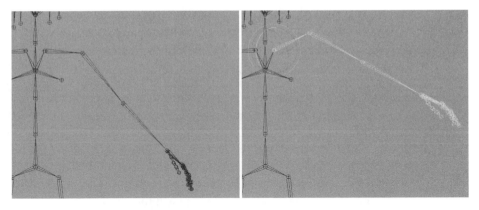

**FIGURE 12.12** Lock the shoulder's rotation so it's not dependent on the clavicle.

**1**   Select the left shoulder joint and create a duplicate of the arm, making sure
to set Group Under in the Duplicate options to World. This ensures that the
new arm is not parented to the spine or any other joint.

Move this duplicate back slightly so we can see it (**Figure 12.13**, middle).
This will be the control arm.

**NOTE**   Use a duplicate of the main joints in order to retain their orientations.

**2**  Delete the finger joints from the end of the control arm, leaving just the shoulder, elbow, and wrist joints (**Figure 12.13**, right).

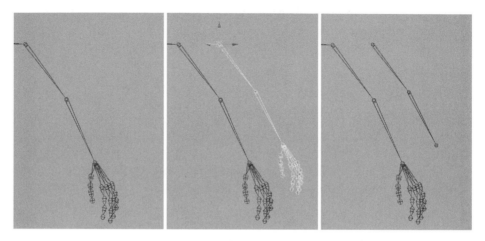

**FIGURE 12.13** Duplicate the arm and remove the fingers to create a control arm.

**3**  So that you can distinguish the control arm from the normal arm, rename the new joints to L_ConShoulder, L_ConElbow, and L_ConWrist

**4**  Lock the rotations of the normal arm to the control arm. Select the control shoulder first, then the normal shoulder, and go to Constrain > Orient and open up the options.

An *orient constraint* locks the orientation of one object to another, so in this case our normal arm's rotations will be locked to the control arm's rotations. When the control arm rotates, the normal one will follow.

**5**  Look at the options for the Orient Constraint in **Figure 12.14**. Turn off Maintain Offset, and set Constraint Axes to All. With the tool configured, click Apply. (If you now select the L_Shoulder joint, you will notice that the rotations in the Channel Box have turned blue; this indicates that they are being controlled by another object.)

> **TIP** The Maintain Offset option is useful when your initial rotation attributes are different on each object, yet you want to keep the current orientation. Without Maintain Offset enabled, the constrained object would inherit the control object's exact rotations, potentially flipping it.

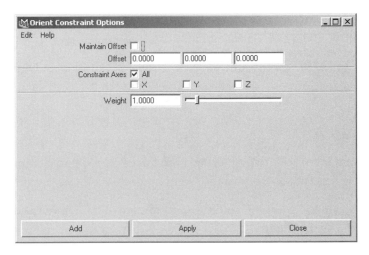

FIGURE 12.14 Orient Constraint options

**6**  Try rotating the control shoulder; the normal one will follow. Even better,
if you now rotate the clavicle, the shoulder will keep its original orientation
(**Figure 12.15**). This means the arm can hang free.

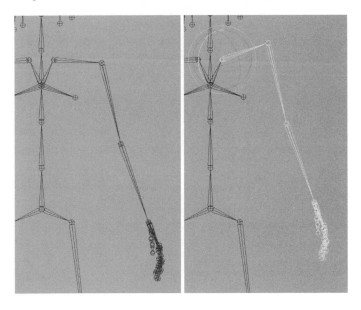

**FIGURE 12.15**
The shoulder's
orientation is no
longer affected
by the clavicle.

**7**  Continue this procedure, orient-constraining the main elbow to the control
elbow, and the main wrist to the control wrist joints.

The control arm is eventually going to lie over the main arm, so we need to make it easier to select. Here is where we will use Maya's selection handles.

**1** Select each joint in the control arm and go to Display > Component Display > Selection Handles. You will see the handles appear at the center of each joint.

> **TIP** If the handles are not visible, make sure their visibility is turned on in the current view by going to Show > Handles.

**2** Next, you want to move the handles away from the joints. Go into Component mode (F8), and select the cross next to the question mark in the status line.

**3** You can now edit the selection handles' positions, moving them out and away from the joints (**Figure 12.16**).

**4** Press F8 when you're finished, to leave Component mode.

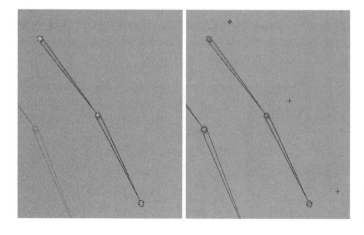

**FIGURE 12.16**
Edit the positions of the selection handles.

Finally, we need to lock the control arm's position to the main arm's shoulder, so the control arm will follow where the main skeleton goes.

**1** Select the main shoulder, and then the control arm's shoulder.

**2** Just as we locked the orientation, we can also lock the position. Go to Constrain > Point, and configure the options as you did for the orient constraint, turning off Maintain Offset and setting Constraint Axes to All.

The control arm will now be in exactly the same position as the main arm, and you can now control the left arm with the control arm. In addition, its orientation is free from the clavicle's, allowing the arm to hang free. Follow this same procedure to create a control arm for the right arm.

At this stage, I recommend creating two new display layers, one called Skeleton (with a display color of dark gray), and the second called Rig_Controls (with display color set to white or an equally light color). Place the main skeleton in the Skeleton layer, and the new control arms into the Rig_Controls layer. This will help us differentiate between the two objects.

### Arm IK

We already have FK control over the arms, because this is based on simple rotations of the joints, and we can quite easily work with the control arms to animate the main arm. Now let's add the option of IK so that we can lock the hand's position in space.

First, set the Skeleton layer to Template. We will be working only on the control arms, so we don't want to accidentally select the main skeleton.

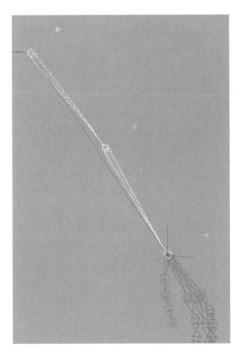

1   Go to Skeleton > IK Handle Tool and open the options.

2   Configure the options for a Rotate Plane solver, with the solver enabled and sticky, and then click Close. Your mouse pointer is now a cross.

3   Select the control shoulder joint, followed by the control wrist joint. The IK is then applied, giving you the main IK handle (**Figure 12.17**). Rename the IK handle to L_ArmIK.

**FIGURE 12.17** The arm with IK applied

The basic IK is now applied, but using the IK handle as an animation tool can cause problems because its translations cannot be frozen. We need all the main animation controllers to have default values of zero; otherwise, we might discover problems when we want to return to the default pose, or if we need to transfer animation between sides of the character or to other characters.

In addition there is currently no visual aid to tell us where the pole vector is, so we will add an icon to tell us this. That way, we always know where the elbow is pointing, and we have a means of easily positioning it.

With these aids in place, we can implement the final controls, allowing us to switch between IK and FK control.

1   To represent the IK in the left arm, a simple NURBS circle will do as our icon. Go to Create > NURBS Primitive > Circle. Snap the circle to the wrist joint (press V); then scale and rotate it so it loosely fits around the wrist (**Figure 12.18**).

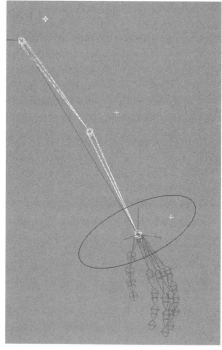

2   With the circle in position, freeze the transforms. Then delete the history on it so it is nice and clean, and rename it to L_Arm_IK.

To transfer between IK and FK control, we use the tools found in the Animate > IK/FK Keys menu. These allow us to turn the IK on and off, and to set keys on the joints affected. These keys, however, will only work on the IK handle. To make the rig more efficient, we want to transfer this control across to the circle icon.

3   Select the circle. Holding Shift, select the IK handle, and go to Animate > IK/FK Keys > Connect to IK/FK.

**FIGURE 12.18** Position the circle around the wrist.

With the icon selected, you can now turn the IK on and off via the Animate > IK/FK Keys > Enable IK Solver menu item.

4   You can now parent the IK handle to the icon so that it will move wherever the icon does. To do this, just select the IK handle, then the icon, and press P.

Next we will add control to the character's elbow by fixing the pole vector to a second icon.

1   Import the file Icon_Cube.mb (found in Project Files/12/Icons), and snap its position to the left elbow. Adjust its scale so you can see it clearly over the geometry, making sure you freeze the transforms afterward.

2   Select the cube, then the IK handle, and go to Constrain > Pole Vector. The elbow's position will now be locked to the cube.

3   Rename the cube to L_ElbowPos. Then hide the main IK handle, and assign both icons to the Rig_Controls display layer.

This completes one arm. Go ahead and work on the right arm (**Figure 12.19**) next. The control arms should lie over the main skeleton's arms.

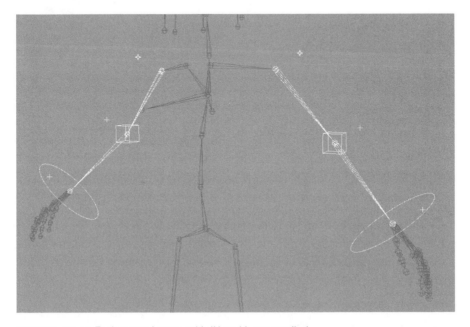

FIGURE 12.19 Both control arms, with IK and icons applied

Now follow the same procedure for adding IK to Grae's arms:

1   Duplicate the main arms to create the control arms, renaming the new joints accordingly.

2   Orient-constrain the main arm joints to the control arm so that they will inherit the control arm's movement.

3   Make the display handles visible on the control arm, and edit their positions.

4   Point-constrain the control shoulder to the main skeleton's shoulder so that the control arm always lies in the correct position.

5   Add the IK handle between the control shoulder and the control wrist.

6   Add two icons, one to control the IK and another to control the pole vector. Position the IK control over the wrist and the pole-vector control over the elbow.

7   Set up the FK/IK switch on the wrist icon; then parent the IK handle to the icon. Set up the pole vector constraint between the IK handle and the elbow icon.

8   Create two display layers for the skeleton and rig controls, assigning the appropriate elements to each.

With Grae at the same stage now as Kila, we can proceed with the rig on Kila.

### Wrist Controls

Like the shoulders, the wrist's rotations should be independent of the forearm's. This will give the animator greater freedom when animating, because the hand can be positioned and will stay in that pose regardless of how the rest of the character animates.

1   On the left arm, hide the selection handle you made visible for the control wrist joint (we are going to create a new wrist control, so we don't need this selection handle to be visible anymore). Select the control wrist and go to Display > Component Display > Selection Handle.

2   Duplicate the control wrist joint and move it back slightly (**Figure 12.20**). Rename it to L_ConHand.

Again here, we need to retain the correct orientation, so we are using a duplicate of the wrist joint as the main controller.

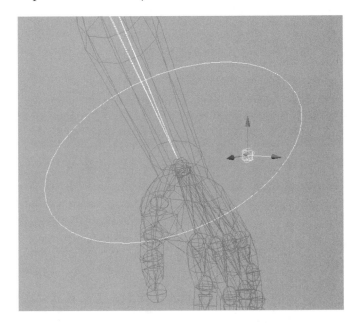

**FIGURE 12.20**
Duplicate the control wrist joint.

3   This will be the main controller, so make the display handle visible. It should retain the position of the joint from which it was duplicated, so you don't need to reposition it.

At present, the control wrist inherits its rotations from the elbow and shoulder joints, so we don't have complete control over it. Forcing it to follow the rotation on this new joint, which has no influences, will free up the control wrist's movement and allow us to pose it freely.

4   Select L_ConHand followed by L_ConWrist, and go to Constrain > Orient; your previous options should have been stored.

5   Select L_ConWrist followed by L_ConHand, and go to Constrain > Point to lock the new wrist control's translations to the old wrist controller.

The wrist is now free from the forearm, so go ahead and apply this to the right arm. Then add the same controls to Grae.

## Finger Controls

Animating the hands can be a time-consuming job, so we want a way around having to rotate each joint separately before setting a key. What we will do next is add controls to the fingers, allowing us to pose them quickly and easily. In this section you'll see how to use time-saving dynamic attributes, mentioned earlier in this chapter.

> **NOTE** The next two sections cover advanced character-rigging tasks. You may find that you don't need to animate the hands on your character, or the animators on your team may prefer to animate the joints directly. Feel free to skip this entire section on finger controls if you don't need it.

### Adding Quick Poses

Using the new hand-control joint we created in the preceding section, we can add extra *dynamic attributes* that, once configured, will automatically pose the hand.

Attributes are built into every object. Up to now you have used the primary Translate, Rotate, and Scale attributes, which control an object's movement, orientation, and scale. You know that changing the value of an attribute has an effect on the object. In addition to these default attributes, user-added dynamic attributes can control a number of characteristics on an object, or even on a completely different object.

Let's now add some dynamic attributes to Kila's control hand joints.

1    Select both the left and right hand controls (L_ConHand and R_ConHand), and go to Modify > Add Attribute. The Add Attribute dialog box illustrated in **Figure 12.21** appears. This is where you will add a new attribute to the selected objects.

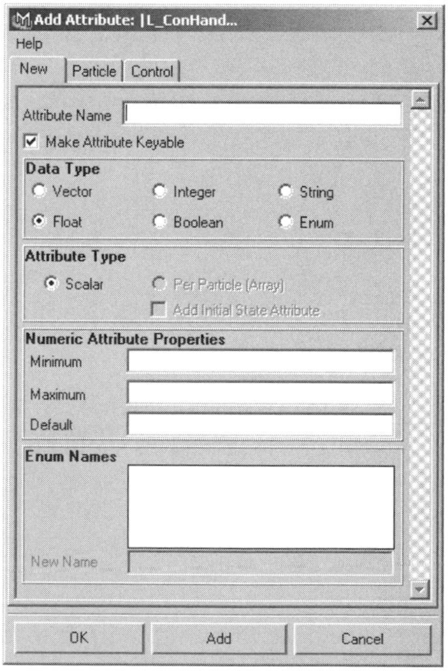

FIGURE 12.21 Add Attribute dialog box

## Dynamic Attribute Options

The following options under Modify > Add Attribute are available for creating dynamic attributes:

▶ *Attribute Name* allows you to give the new attribute you are creating a name. This should be a descriptive name that represents what the attribute is created to do.

▶ *Make Attribute Keyable,* when enabled, means the attribute can be animated.

▶ *The Data Type* is where you specify what sort of attribute you are creating:

Vector will give you three floating-point (integer or decimal point) values. So an attribute named Fist would end up with three attributes called Fist X, Fist Y, and Fist Z.

Float sets the attribute to be a single floating-point value.

Integer forces the attribute to accept only whole numerical values.

Boolean creates a simple on/off switch.

String creates an attribute that can hold a text string.

Enum gives the user a list of choices, which you specify in the Enum Names box at the bottom of the Add Attribute dialog box.

▶ In the *Numerical Attribute Properties* section, you can lock your attributes so they have a maximum and minimum value.

2  Let's now create our first attribute, called Fist. You only need a numerical value, so set the Data Type to Float (the default).

3  Clamp the attribute's values by setting Minimum to 0 and Maximum to 10 in the Numerical Attribute Properties section.

4  Click Add, and the new attribute will appear in the Channel Box (after Visibility, as seen in **Figure 12.22**).

**5** Repeat steps 2 through 4 to add attributes called Curl, Point, and Splay (**Figure 12.22**).

With these dynamic attributes added to the wrists, we next need to wire them up to the fingers. To do this, we will use the *Set Driven Keys options* (Animate > Set Driven Key > Set).

Set Driven Keys links one attribute to another (on the same object or a different one) using key frames. Unlike normal keys in Maya, driven keys are not set at specific times in the time slider; rather, they are set at specific values on another attribute. For example, the character's hand will be in its default pose when the Fist attribute is at 0. Change the Fist attribute to 10, and you will see the hand change into the fist pose. This is because driven keys have been placed on the hand for when the fist attribute is at 0 and 10.

Let's now apply this technique to our character's hand.

**1** Open the Set Driven Key dialog box (**Figure 12.23**, left) by going to Animate > Set Driven Key > Set and opening the options box. You will work on the Fist and Point attributes first, since these finger poses are similar.

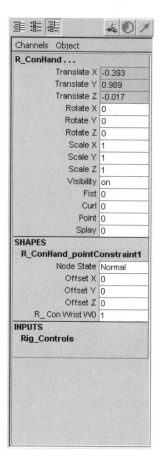

**FIGURE 12.22** Add Fist, Curl, Point, and Splay attributes to the wrist joints.

**2** Select the L_ConHand joint. In the Set Driven Key dialog box, click on the Load Driver button. On the left side of the Driver box, the name of the object will appear, with all its keyable attributes in the box to the right. From this list, select Fist.

**3** Next, select each finger joint except for the very end ones, and click Load Driven. In the Driven box, the names of all the finger joints will appear; select them all. Then, in the list on the right side of the Driven box, select the rotateX, rotateY, and rotateZ attributes (you only need to store the rotations).

Your Set Driven Key window should now look like that in **Figure 12.23**, right.

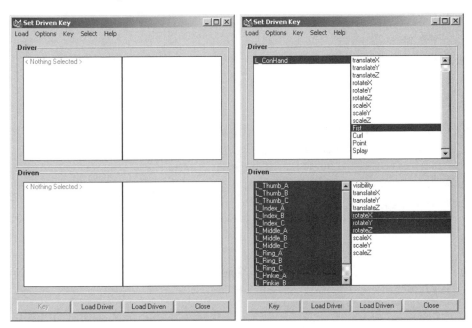

FIGURE 12.23 The Set Driven Key window before and after the attributes are selected

What we've just done is tell Maya that we want the Fist attribute to drive the finger joints' rotations. Now we will define the start and end poses associated with each attribute (Fist, Curl, Point, and Splay). First we will store the default pose into each of the four dynamic attributes.

> **NOTE**    Make sure all four of the dynamic attributes are set to 0. To do this, select L_ConHand in the Driver panel of the Set Driven Key dialog box. This will quickly select the object so that you can check the attribute settings.

**4**    In the Driver box, select Fist and then click Key. Continue, selecting Curl, Point, and then Splay, before clicking Key for each one.

The current hand's pose is now stored, so that when each attribute is at 0, the hand will be at this default pose.

**5**    With the Set Driven Key window still open, set the Fist and Point attributes to 10. (Don't set a key yet, though.)

**6** Adjust the finger joints to form a fist (**Figure 12.24b**).

> **TIP** Set the joint display size so the joints are the same thickness as the geometry for the fingers. This will give you a better idea of how the fingers will look as you pose them.

**7** Select Fist in the Driven box and click Key. Then select Point and click Key. Now if you adjust the Fist or Point attribute on L_ConHand, the fingers will animate to form a fist.

To get the point, set Fist back to 0 and Point to 10 so it makes the fist; then edit the index finger so it points (**Figure 12.24c**). To update the pose, select Point in the Driven box and click Key.

**8** Next we will work on the Curl. Make sure all the attributes are back to zero; then set Curl to 10.

**9** Adjust the fingers as seen in **Figure 12.24d**, rotating just the end joints of the fingers. Then select Curl in the Driver box and click Key.

**10** Finally, create the pose for Splay (**Figure 12.24e**). Remember to set all the attributes back to 0 and Splay to 10 before you begin to pose the fingers.

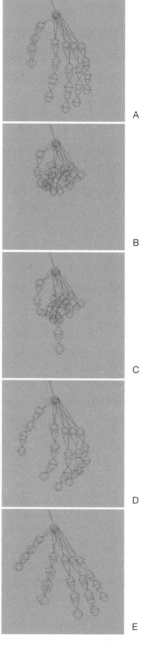

A

B

C

D

E

**FIGURE 12.24** Create the four hand poses for Fist, Point, Curl, and Splay.

Now we have the ability to get quick poses on Kila's hands. You may need more specific poses for your game; perhaps the character holds a gun or operates some kind of machinery. Now that you have learned the dynamic attributes technique, you will be able to add more poses if you need them.

> **TIP** To help create poses for the right hand, I have included a small tool on the GCDM shelf labeled mirPo. This tool mirrors the pose from one side of the skeleton to the other, in this instance saving you the effort of re-posing the right hand. Just get the left hand into its pose, select the wrist joint on the main skeleton (not the control wrist), and click the mirPo button. The right hand will now adopt the same pose.

The key poses are an excellent way to achieve quick animations. Now you need to add the ability to animate the fingers individually; we'll tackle that next.

### Full Animation of the Fingers

The quick hand poses are normally all you will need for in-game animation. The problem facing you now is that you can't edit the fingers individually because they are locked by the driven keys. We will now add full animation functionality back into the hands.

> **NOTE** Before you implement full animation into your rig, check with your manager; it may be that you don't need these controls and so don't need to spend time implementing them.

1   Import the icon file named Icon_Hand.mb. This contains a group called LeftHand, which contains individual finger icons.

2   Snap the main LeftHand group to the left wrist joint by holding V, and adjust the overall scale so it matches the size of the hand joints (**Figure 12.25**).

3   Freeze the transforms.

> **NOTE** The hand icon group's main pivot exists below the actual icons themselves. This is so the icons can stay out of the geometry while also being locked to the wrist's position.

> **TIP** You may want to turn off the Rig_Controls display layer so that you can concentrate on the hand itself.

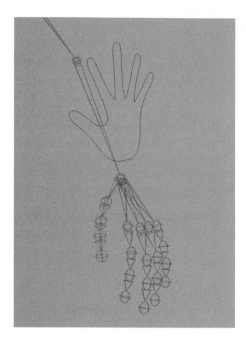

**FIGURE 12.25** Import and position the hand icon.

**4** We want the hand icon to stay locked to the wrist as it moves. Select the control wrist first, and then the main hand icon group (LeftHand). Then go to Constrain > Point, making sure Maintain Offset is disabled.

Now we will start to wire the fingers up using Set Driven Keys. Since the process for connecting each finger is the same, we will describe the process for connecting the little finger (pinkie); then you can apply the same technique to the rest of the fingers.

**1** Go to Animate > Set Driven Key > Set and open the options box.

**2** Select the icon for the pinkie finger. Then click Load Driver in the Set Driven Key window. You will notice that I have already added a series of dynamic attributes for you, so you should not need to add any.

**3** Select each joint of the pinkie finger, leaving the end one unselected, and click Load Driven. The three separate Pitch attributes (Proximal_Pitch, Middle_Pitch, and Distal_Pitch) correspond to each individual finger joint, so you only need to set keys for these attributes.

**NOTE** When you work on Grae, remember that he only has two joints in each finger. That means you can ignore his Distal_ Pitch attributes.

4   Store the finger in its base pose by first selecting the Proximal_Pitch attribute, and then just the L_Pinkie_A's rotateZ attribute (**Figure 12.26**). Then click the Key button. (We only need to work on the Z rotation because it's all that is needed to bend the finger.)

5   Select the Middle_Pitch and the L_Pinkie_B's rotateZ attributes, and set a key.

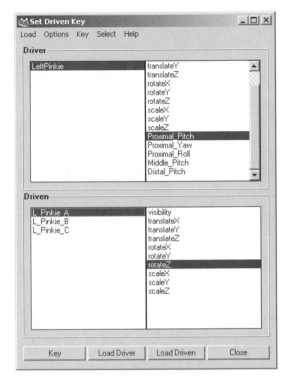

**FIGURE 12.26** Select just the Proximal_Pitch and the L_Pinkie_A's rotateZ attributes.

6   Finally, select Distal_Pitch and the L_Pinkie_C's rotateZ attributes, and set a key.

With the default pose stored, we can now begin to store the finger's maximum rotations.

1   Set each of the Pitch attributes (Proximal_Pitch, Middle_Pitch, and Distal_ Pitch) to –5.

2   Bend the finger back, using only the Z rotation (**Figure 12.27**, middle).

**NOTE** Setting Kila's joints to about 30 (and 50 for Grae) will bend the finger back farther than it naturally could go, but we need to give the animators some flexibility. And we will also want to apply the same rotations to the other fingers. So keeping this to a nice round number makes the value easier to remember.

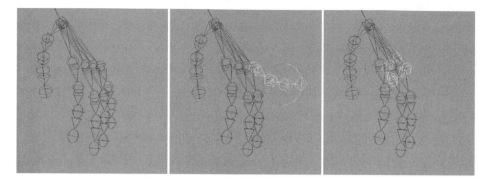

**FIGURE 12.27** Take the finger to both extremes and store each pose.

**3** With the finger in position, set a key on the three Pitch attributes, remembering to select only the corresponding joint in the Driven window.

**4** You will now take the finger to the next extreme, so first set the Pitch attributes to their maximum of 10.

**5** Rotate the finger around the Z rotation to –80 (**Figure 12.27**, right) and set a key on each Pitch attribute in the Set Driven Key dialog box.

Now as you move the three Pitch attributes in the Channel Box, the finger will quite happily bend. We still need to add lateral movement to the finger; this movement, however, will be restricted to the knuckle (Proximal) joint.

**1** Select the first joint of the pinkie, and reload it into the Driven section of the Set Driven Key dialog box.

**2** To get the finger to spread, we need it to rotate around the Y axis, so select rotateY in the right side of the Driven box. Make sure the joint's Y rotation and Proximal_Yaw are set to 0. Then set a key.

**3** Set Proximal_Yaw to –10, and the finger's Y rotation to 25. Set another key to define this pose (**Figure 12.28**, middle).

**4** Finally, set Proximal_Yaw to 10 and the pinkie's knuckle joint to –25, setting one final key to define this second extreme (**Figure 12.28**, right).

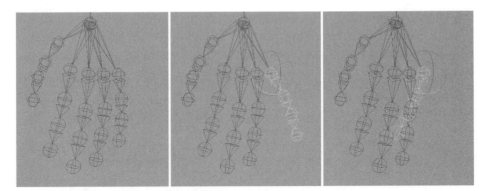

**FIGURE 12.28** Using the Y rotation, store the fingers' spread.

To complete the finger setup, we need to allow for the finger to roll, rotating around the X axis.

**1**   Set the base pose, with both the Proximal_Roll and L_Pinkie_A's rotateX attributes sct to 0.

**2**   Set Proximal_Roll to –10. Then set the finger to one extreme by rotating the X rotation to 30. Set a key.

**3**   Set the final key by defining the next extreme, setting Proximal_Roll to 10, and then the finger's X rotation to –30.

The pinkie is now fully posable; continue setting up the rest of the fingers for the left hand, using exactly the same values as we have established for the pinkie finger.

When all the fingers are set, import a second hand icon (or duplicate the first), remembering to rename the main group and the individual elements so they represent the right hand. Follow the same procedure to wire up the fingers on the right hand, but this time make the values negative (for instance, 30 should be –30). This allows the fingers to move in the same way as those on the opposite hand, making them easier to animate and transfer animation if needed.

We now have the ability to quickly pose the fingers as well as animate them individually; the arms and hands are fully rigged (**Figure 12.29**). Now would be a good time to save your work, naming it Kila_ArmRig.mb.

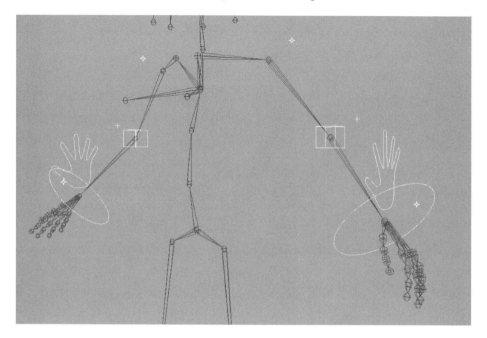

FIGURE 12.29 Kila's arms, fully rigged

When you're ready, start at the top and follow the instructions in this section to rig Grae's arms and hands. Save him as Grae_ArmRig.mb.

## Leg and Feet Controls

The rig for the legs is quite similar to the arms. We need to create control feet that will help us to drive the feet, add IK connecting the control feet to the main feet, and finish them off by adding further dynamic attribute–driven controls.

Because Kila's and Grae's feet are quite different, we will examine in detail the steps for creating the control feet for both characters.

### Basic Control Feet for Kila

Let's start by creating the basic feet that will control Kila's legs. After these are in place, we can add controls for animating the toes and knees.

For the basic feet, we will use a modified version of a technique that has been around for as long as I can remember: creating a duplicate of the foot joints and using them to drive the main joints. This differs from the techniques we've used so far in that the controlling hierarchy is drawn in reverse—toe to ball to ankle. So to move the foot, you rotate the toe, then the ball of the foot, and then the ankle joint, creating what's known as a *reverse foot*.

1   Before you get started, duplicate both the main skeletons' feet from the ankle down. Make sure that Group Under is set to World in the Duplicate options.

2   Place the duplicates in the Rig_Controls display layer. Then turn off visibilty for the Skeleton layer so that you can concentrate on the initial foot setup (**Figure 12.30**, top).

3   Reverse the order of the joints creating the reverse foot. This is easily done by selecting the end toe joints and going to Skeleton > Reroot Skeleton, which rearranges the order of the control foot. As you can see in **Figure 12.30**, bottom, the last joint becomes the first joint.

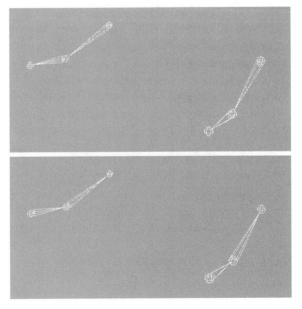

**FIGURE 12.30** Create the joints that make up the basic control feet.

**4** Now that you have the basic joints to create the control feet, go through them and rename each joint, starting with L_ConToe, L_ConBall, and finally L_ConAnkle. Do the same for the right foot (using a prefix of R_, of course).

**5** Now bring in the icons; import the file Icon_Foot.mb (**Figure 12.31a**). Following **Figure 12.31b**, position the icon so it's on the outside of the left foot.

**6** You want this icon to rotate the foot from the ankle, as your own foot does, so press Insert and point-snap (press V) the pivot point up to the ankle joint (**Figure 12.31c**).

**7** Create a mirrored duplicate of the foot icon, positioning it over the right ankle. Freeze the transforms, and rename the file to RightFoot (**Figure 12.31d**).

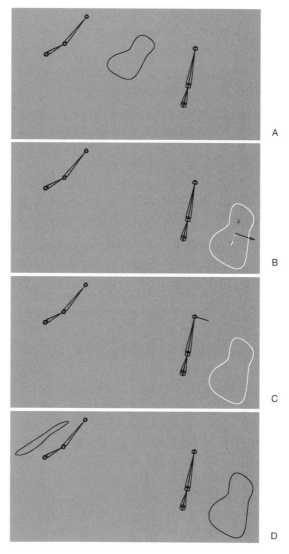

**FIGURE 12.31** Import and position the foot icons.

When we created the base joints for Kila's feet, in Chapter 11, we had to alter the rotational pivot of the ankles so that they lined up with the orientation of the foot. We will have to do something similar here—as you can see in **Figure 12.32**, left, the rotational axis for the foot icon does not follow the orientation of the foot joints.

1  Because you are working with an icon rather than a joint, you can't directly edit the rotational axis; nor can you rotate the joints of the feet, because they would no longer line up with the geometry. What you can do is alter the Y rotation of the icon so that the manipulator lines up with the foot (**Figure 12.32**, right).

2  When you have the Y rotation value for the left foot, copy it across for the right foot, turning it into a negative value.

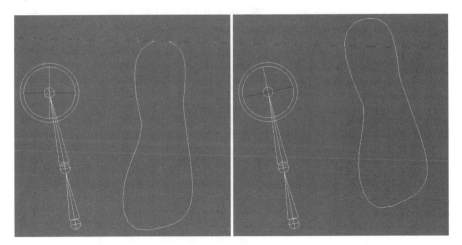

FIGURE 12.32 Adjust the rotation of the foot icons so they line up with the joints.

Note that this will add some rotational values to the icon, which we don't really want. Once the character is bound, we can zero these values out, which will make her feet point directly forward.

3  Parent the joints to the icons. Select the L_ConAnkle joint and then the left foot icon, and press P. Then select the R_ConAnkle joint and parent it to the right foot icon.

**4**   You have the controllers now, so you need to connect them to the actual base feet. Make the base skeleton visible once more, and turn off the Rig_ Controls layer, focusing in on the legs as seen in **Figure 12.33**, left.

**5**   For each leg, create an IK Rotate Plane handle from the hip joint to the ankle joint.

**6**   Again for each leg, create an IK Single Chain handle from the ankle joint to the ball joint, and another from the ball joint to the tip. You can see this in **Figure 12.33**, right.

Although it only controls a single joint, we add IK onto the ball and ball tip joints to help lock them down. They will then only move where the IK handles take them.

**7**   Rename these IK handles to L_AnkleIK, L_BallIK, L_ToeIK, R_AnkleIK, R_BallIK, and R_ToeIK.

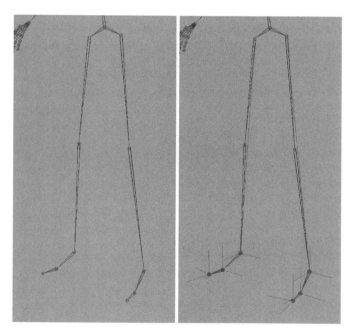

**FIGURE 12.33**
Add IK to the legs.

**NOTE**   We use a Rotate Plane IK Handle on the legs because we want to be able to control the direction the knees point. We will add this feature during the next section.

**8**  To make the control feet move the legs, you simply parent each IK handle to the joint over which it lies on the control feet. So parent L_AnkleIK to L_ConAnkle, L_BallIK to L_ConBall, and L_ToeIK to L_ConToe. Follow this pattern for the right leg's IK handles.

Now when you move or rotate the feet icons, the main feet and legs follow. What's more, you can adjust the position of the root and the feet will stay locked to their position.

> **NOTE**  In the traditional reverse foot setup, you would also have a heel joint to use as reference for the actual heel of the character. We don't need this joint here because, when the character gets animated, you will have the actual geometry to refer to.

### Additional Foot Controls for Kila

Being able to manipulate the feet is one thing, but we still have the knee position to consider. We can set up the knees in much the same way we did with the elbow, by using a pole vector constraint.

First we need some icons. To help indicate that these are for joint positions, we will use the same cubes that we used for the elbows earlier in this chapter.

**1**  Create two duplicates of the elbow cubes, and point-snap them to the knees as illustrated in **Figure 12.34**. Rename them to L_KneePos and R_KneePos.

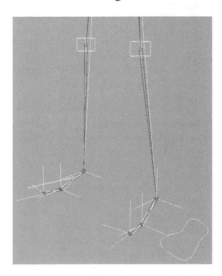

**FIGURE 12.34**
Duplicate the elbow cubes and point-snap them to the knees.

> **NOTE** Ideally, we need these knee controls to exist in front of the knees, but if we add a pole vector constraint it may adjust the knee positions slightly. We don't want this to occur until this character is bound to the mesh, so to keep the joints in position we will leave the icons over the knees.

**2**   Select the L_KneePos cube and, holding Shift, select the L_AnkleIK IK handle. Then go to Constrain > Pole Vector.

**3**   Do the same on the opposite leg, selecting R_KneePos and R_AnkleIK before applying the pole vector constraint.

The knees are now locked to the control cubes and will point toward them no matter where you position the cubes. Once the character is bound, we can put the cubes in a more suitable position.

Our next task is to add controls to the toes, making it easier to pose the feet. To begin, we need some dynamic attributes added to the foot icons; when connected, these will drive the toe and foot animation.

**1**   Select both the foot icons and go to Modify > Add Attribute. The default options are set just as we want them to be, so simply type in the names for each attribute and click Add. Call these Ball Rotate, Toe_Rotate, Tip_Toe, and Foot_Twist.

Now we will use Maya's Connection Editor to wire the attributes up. This tool directly connects one attribute to another; for example, our Ball_Rotate attribute will connect to the L_ConBall's rotate Z attribute. Then when we adjust the Ball_Rotate attribute's value, the actual joint will rotate for us even though we are not directly rotating it.

**2**   Open the Connection Editor window (**Figure 12.35**) by going to Window > General Editors > Connection Editor.

**3**   Open the Left Display and Right Display menus and make sure Show Non-Keyable is turned off for both. This will hide the attributes not relevant at this time, so the columns will be easier to read.

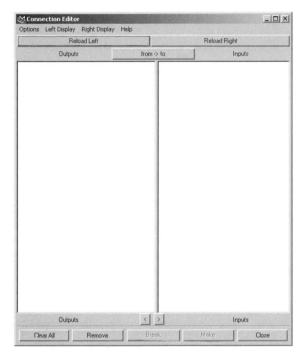

**4**  Select the LeftFoot icon and click the Reload Left button in the Editor. The keyable attributes belonging to the icon appear in the Outputs column (**Figure 12.36a**).

**5**  Select the L_ConBall joint and click Reload Right. All the related keyable attributes load into the Inputs column (**Figure 12.36b**).

**6**  Select the attribute Ball_Rotate in the Outputs column. The attributes to which it can connect in the Inputs column turn bold (**Figure 12.36c**).

**7**  In the Inputs column, open the Rotate menu by clicking on the + icon next to it, and select Rotate Z (**Figure 12.36d**). By simply selecting the two attributes, you have connected them, and their names turn italic to confirm the connection.

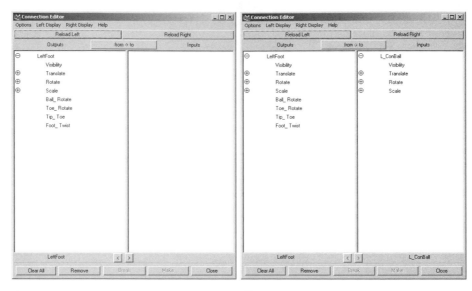

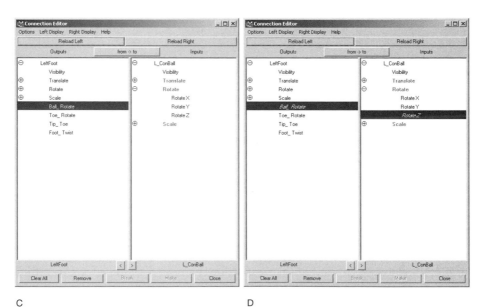

FIGURE 12.36 Connecting the LeftFoot's Ball_Rotate attribute to L_ConBall's Z rotation

Now, as you can see in **Figure 12.37**, the LeftFoot's Ball_Rotate attribute will drive the L_ConBall's Rotate Z attribute.

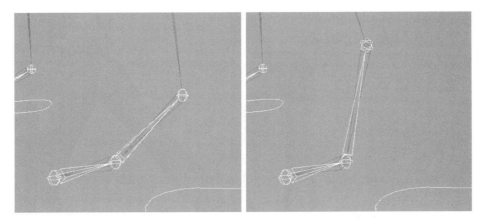

FIGURE 12.37 The LeftFoot's Ball_Rotate now rotates the L_ConBall joint.

Let's wire up the next attribute, Toe_Rotate. We want the toe joint to be able to rotate up and down, but right now it is tied to the position of the L_ToeIK IK handle. With that in mind, we could make the IK handle move, which in turn will move the toe joint.

First we need the toe joint's pivot to be in the same position as the L_ConBall joint so that it gives us the rotation we need: the ability to tap the toe. As it is, though, the IK handle stays locked to its pivot, causing the toe joint to point out to the side (**Figure 12.38**, right). To get around this, we will place the IK handle into a group; we can then adjust the group's pivot and connect its rotation to the Toe_Rotate attribute. This will then rotate the IK handle.

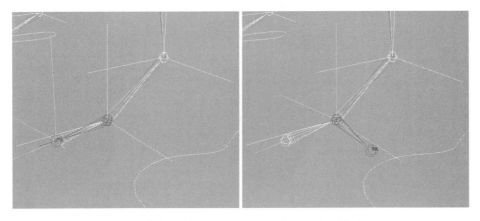

FIGURE 12.38 Moving the IK handle's pivot makes the toe stick out to the side.

**1**    Select the L_ToeIK handle and group it to itself (Ctrl+G/Cmd+G). Rename the new group L_ToeRotate.

**2**    Edit L_ToeRotate's pivot point, snapping it to L_ConBall.

**3**    Using the Connection Editor, connect the Toe_Rotate attribute on the LeftFoot icon to the Rotate Z of L_ToeRotate (**Figure 12.39**). Now when you adjust the Toe_Rotate attribute, the toe will "tap"—rotate up and down (**Figure 12.40**).

Notice that the joints on the control foot do not move. This is not a problem, though; all we will see when the character is completed is the actual geometry moving.

**FIGURE 12.39**
Connecting Toe_Rotate on the LeftFoot icon to the Rotate Z of L_ToeRotate

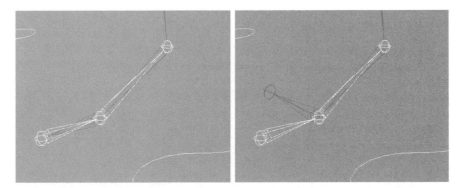

FIGURE 12.40 The Toe_Rotate in action

4   Next is the Tip_Toe attribute. This is quite easily set up; all you need to do is
    use the Connection Editor to connect it to the Z rotation on the L_ConToe
    joint (**Figure 12.41**). You can see this connection working in **Figure 12.42**.

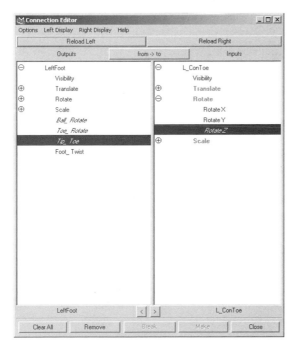

FIGURE 12.41 Connect
the Tip_Toe attribute
to the Rotate Z of
L_ConToe.

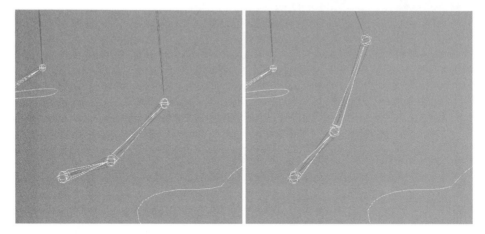

**FIGURE 12.42** Adjusting the Tip_Toe attribute will make the character stand on her toes.

The final attribute to connect is the Foot_Twist. This will cause the whole foot to rotate around the ball joint. We have the same issue here that we had with the Toe_Rotate attribute: If we connect to the Y rotation of the L_ConBall joint, only the back of the foot but not the front will rotate. This makes the foot take an unnatural bend (**Figure 12.43**, right). So, as we did with the Toe_Rotate attribute, we will use a group node to solve the problem.

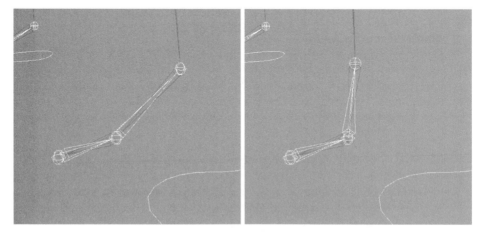

**FIGURE 12.43** Rotating the ball joint around the Y axis gives unwanted results.

**5**  Select the L_ConToe joint and group it to itself (Ctrl+G/Cmd+G). Rename the group L_FootTwist; then edit its pivot, snapping it to the L_ConBall joint.

**6**  Now you can connect the Foot_Twist attribute on the LeftFoot icon to the L_FootTwist group's Y rotation (**Figure 12.44**). You now have the ability to rotate the foot around the ball joint (**Figure 12.45**, right).

**FIGURE 12.44** Connect the Foot_Twist attribute to the Y rotation of the new L_FootTwist group.

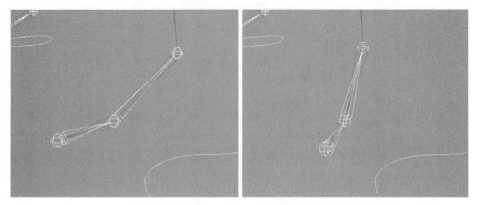

**FIGURE 12.45** The Foot_Twist attribute now rotates the foot around its ball joint.

The left foot is now set up, and we can do more with it than just the standard translation and rotation. Repeat the process, adding new attributes and connecting them up to the joints for the right foot. Remember to use the group nodes to help you achieve those tricky controls.

Next up is adding the ability to turn the IK off, so that you can animate using FK. To accomplish this, we'll follow the exact same procedure that we used earlier with the arms.

1   Select the LeftFoot icon. Holding Shift, add L_AnkleIK, L_BallIK, and L_ToeIK to the selection.

2   Go to Animate > IK/FK Keys > Connect to IK/FK.

3   Now, using Animate > IK/FK Keys > Enable IK Solver, you can toggle the state of the IK on the feet, turning it on and off.

4   Apply this same IK arrangement to the right foot.

5   We don't need the control feet and IK handles visible anymore because all the controls are tied into the feet icons, so select the L_FootTwist and R_FootTwist groups and hide them. This hides the objects within (**Figure 12.46**).

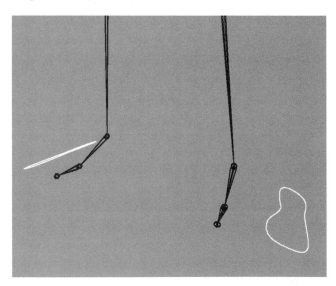

FIGURE 12.46 The rigged legs and feet

Kila's legs and feet are now completely rigged. Save the file as Kila_LegRig.mb, and let's move on to Grae.

### Basic Control Feet for Grae

Because Grae's legs will animate differently, the way we rig them is quite different from the process for Kila. We don't use a reverse foot in this instance because we don't need the ability to rotate Grae's ball or toe joints (that's not to say that using a reverse foot is the only way to achieve this). Instead, for Grae we will rely solely on the control icon.

1   Open the Grae_ArmRig.mb file, and import the Icon_Foot.mb file into the scene.

2   Using the geometry as a guide, position the icon next to the left foot, making sure it's scaled appropriately. Then freeze the transforms and rename it to LeftFoot.

3   Snap the pivot to the ankle joint on the skeleton (**Figure 12.47**).

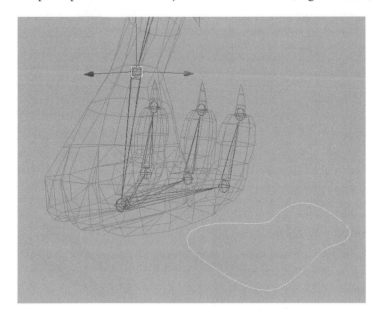

FIGURE 12.47 Point-snap the icon's pivot to the ankle joint.

**4** Create an IK Rotate Plane handle from the hip joint to the ankle joint, calling it L_AnkleIK.

**5** Create an IK Single Chain handle going from the ankle joint to the one immediately after it, the ball of the toes. Rename this one to L_BallIK.

**6** To help lock down the toes, create a second IK Single Chain handle going from the ball of the toes back to the first joint of the middle toe. Rename this to L_ToeIK.

You can see all of the IK handles applied in **Figure 12.48**.

> **NOTE** ▶ If Grae is lifted off the ground, leaving the foot behind will allow his toes to drag realistically and not be locked to the position of the ankle joint. This will help give the toes more weight.

**7** Finish up by parenting the three IK handles to the foot icon.

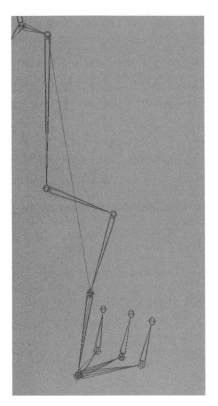

**FIGURE 12.48** Create three IK handles.

You can now fully manipulate the rotation and translation of Grae's foot via the icon. We can move ahead now to the additional attributes needed for his feet and toes, before you apply the same techniques to create the rig for his right foot.

### Additional Foot Controls for Grae

Simply moving the foot around in space isn't enough; we need to free up the toes and ankle. Enabling them to be animated individually will give the creature more life. As we've done before, we'll begin by adding attributes to the foot icon.

**1** Select the left foot icon, and go to Modify > Add Attribute to open the Add Attribute dialog box.

**2**  Create six Float attributes called Ball_Rotate, Ankle_Tilt, Foot_Twist, L_Toe_
Rotate, M_Toe_Rotate, and R_Toe_Rotate.

**3**  Connect the Toe_Rotate attributes to the actual toes, using the Connection
Editor (Window > General Editors > Connection Editor).

**4**  Select the foot icon and click Reload Left (**Figure 12.49**, left). Then select the
outer toe joint and click Reload Right.

**5**  Highlight L_Toe_Rotate in the Outputs list, and then Rotate X in the Inputs
section, connecting these attributes (**Figure 12.49**, right).

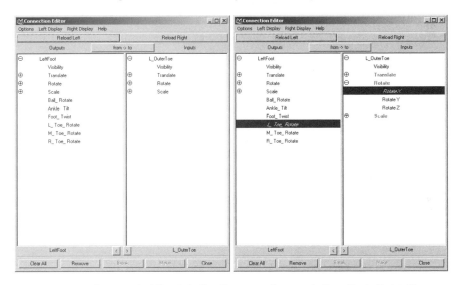

FIGURE 12.49 Connect LeftFoot's L_Toe_Rotate attribute to L_OuterToe's RotateX
attribute.

**6**  Repeat steps 3 through 5 of this procedure, this time connecting the M_Toe_
Rotate attribute to the middle toe's rotate X attribute, and finally R_Toe_
Rotate to the inner toe's attribute.

As you can see in **Figure 12.50**, you can now animate the toes individually and independently of the foot, simply by using the attributes on the foot icon.

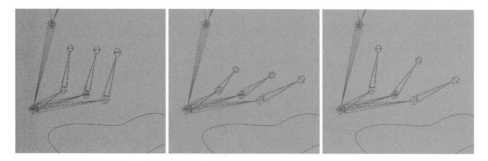

FIGURE 12.50 The toes now animate independently of the foot.

As we did with Kila's Foot_Twist and Toe_Rotate attributes, we now need to create extra group nodes on top of the L_AnkleIK and L_BallIK IK handles. The joints they are connected to are currently locked; by creating these extra groups, we can indirectly animate the joints.

1  Group L_AnkleIK to itself, and rename the group to L_AnkleTilt. Snap the group's pivot to the L_Toes joint (**Figure 12.51**).

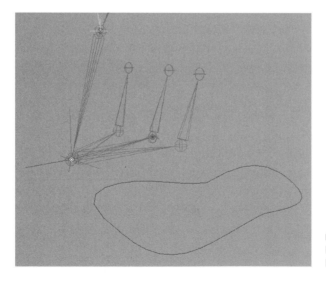

FIGURE 12.51 Snap L_AnkleTilt's pivot to the L_Toes joint.

**2**   Group L_ToeIK to itself, and rename the group to L_BallRotate. Snap this group's pivot to the same joint as the L_AnkleTilt group.

**3**   For the final group, select and group L_AnkleTilt, L_BallRotate, and the last IK handle that hasn't been grouped yet, L_BallIK. Name the group L_FootTwist. Again, snap the group's pivot to the same joint as the previous two groups.

**4**   Now that we have these control groups in place, we can connect them to the appropriate attributes on the foot icon. Using the Connection Editor:

Connect the LeftFoot's Ball_Rotate attribute to the L_BallRotate's Rotate X attribute (**Figure 12.52**, left).

Connect the Ankle_Tilt attribute to L_AnkleTilt's Rotate X (**Figure 12.52**, middle).

Connect the Foot_Twist attribute to L_FootTwist's Rotate Y attribute (**Figure 12.52**, right).

**FIGURE 12.52** Connect the remaining attributes to their corresponding groups.

We now have complete control over Grae's foot. One last thing to do is lock down the orientation of his leg using a pole vector constraint.

1   Duplicate the cube you used on Grae's left elbow, and snap it to the left-rear knee joint (**Figure 12.53**). Freeze the transforms and rename this to L_KneePos.

2   Select the cube (L_KneePos) and, holding Shift, select the L_AnkleIK IK handle.

3   Go to Constrain > Pole Vector to restrict the knee's movement. Now the rear knee joint will always point toward the cube.

As with Kila, we also want the ability to free Grae's feet from their IK constraints and animate them using FK.

1   Select the LeftFoot icon. Holding Shift, add L_AnkleIK, L_BallIK, and L_ToeIK to the selection.

2   Go to Animate > IK/FK Keys > Connect to IK/FK.

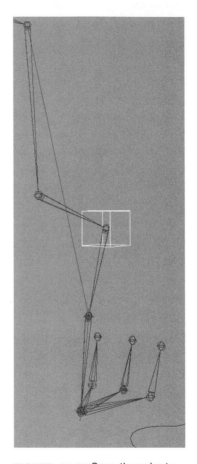

**FIGURE 12.53** Snap the cube to Grae's left-rear knee joint.

3   Using the Enable IK Solver tool in the same Animate > IK/FK Keys menu, you are now free to toggle the state of the IK on the foot.

To finalize the left foot, clean things up a bit. Place both icons into the Rig_Controls layer. Since we no longer need the IK handles, turn off the L_FootTwist's visibility, which will hide all the IK handles parented under it.

Now repeat the procedures for creating the basic control foot and adding its dynamic attributes to rig Grae's right foot. Then save the scene as Grae_LegRig.mb.

## Main Body Controls

With the rigging of the limbs for both characters completed, we can now move on to implement the main body controls. These will enable easier manipulation of Kila's hips, spine, and waist. Then we'll do similar work on Grae's body.

### Hips and Spine

Moving the main upper body of the characters will be done using the hips as the main control point. We simply need to create an icon to represent the hips' position and rotation.

**1**  Working in the Kila_LegRig.mb file again, create a third NURBS circle.

**2**  Snap the circle to the main Root joint of the hips. Then scale the circle as shown in **Figure 12.54**, so it lies outside the geometry of the character.

**3**  Freeze the transforms and delete the history before renaming the circle to Root_Control.

Before we connect this icon to the root joint, we need to create two groups; these will help us add further control to the waist later.

**4**  Select the main root joint and group it twice. Call the first group WaistControl, and the second one RootControl. Make sure the pivot for RootControl lies over the root joint, and the pivot for WaistControl lies over the first joint of the spine.

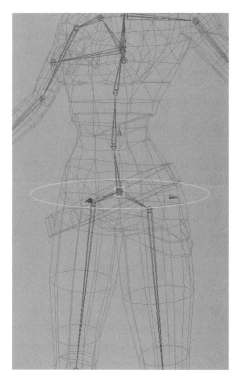

**FIGURE 12.54** Manipulate the circle so it lies outside Kila's hips.

**5**    Select the circle and, holding Shift, select the RootControl group (using Hypergraph or Outliner). Apply a point constraint followed by an orient constraint; for both, make sure that Maintain Offset is turned off.

Now the main root of the character can be translated and rotated via the Root_Control icon. The spine is made of very few joints, so we don't need any fancy controls to animate it. All we need is to create some iconic representation that we can use to pose it.

**1**    Import Icon_Arrow.mb, and point-snap it to the first joint on the spine (**Figure 12.55**, left). You may also need to adjust the arrow's scale so it is clearly visible.

**2**    Move the arrow back so that it exists outside the geometry, rotating it to point toward the joint it will be controlling (**Figure 12.55**, right). When you're done, freeze the transforms.

**3**    So the arrow will rotate around the correct pivot, snap its pivot back to the lower spine joint.

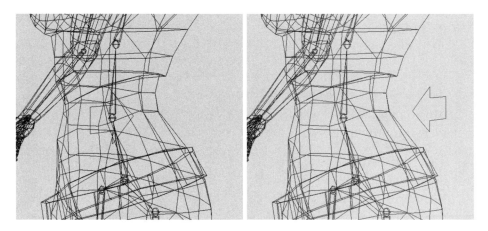

**FIGURE 12.55** Adjust the arrow so it points toward the joint it will control.

**4**  To connect the arrow and the spine joint, select the arrow first and then, holding Shift, the spine joint; perform an orient constraint on them.

**5**  Rename the arrow to Lower_Spine.

**6**  Repeat this procedure to create arrows for the other two spine joints, calling the arrows Middle_Spine and Upper_Spine and positioning them as seen in **Figure 12.56**.

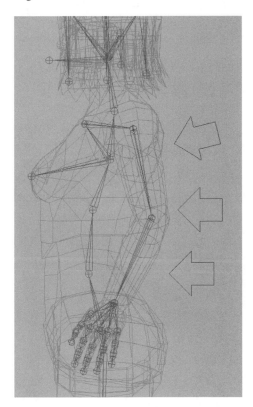

**FIGURE 12.56** Position all three control icons for the spine joints.

In the current arrangement, if we rotate one of the lower arrows, the pivots for the others become misaligned—when we animate them, they won't be moving around the correct pivots (**Figure 12.57**, left). We want them to stay locked to the joints they are controlling. We could use a point constraint to make this happen, but the spine will still animate unrealistically. Instead, we take a simpler approach.

**7** Parent the Upper_Spine arrow to the Middle_Spine arrow, and then the Middle_Spine arrow to the Lower_Spine arrow. Finally, parent the Lower_Spine arrow to the main Root_Control icon.

This ensures that the spine will animate correctly while keeping the controls in their correct positions (**Figure 12.57**, right).

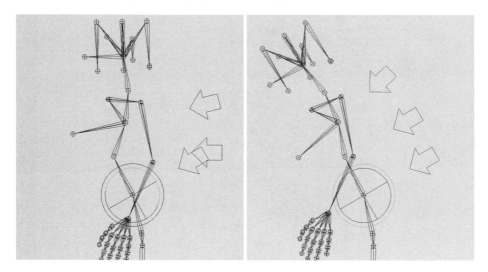

**FIGURE 12.57** Parent the arrows to maintain proper rotations.

**8** One last thing to do: Make sure all the new icons are placed in the Rig_Controls layer.

### Waist Control

Another icon to be added next will give us control of the pelvic area, independently of the upper body. We will use the WaistControl group created earlier.

**1**  For the icon to represent this control, create another NURBS circle and name it Waist_Control.

**2**  Position and scale the circle as shown in **Figure 12.58** (left), so it lies just above the Root_Control icon. Remember to freeze the transforms and delete the history afterward.

**3**  Point-snap the pivot for the circle to the lower spine joint (**Figure 12.58**, right).

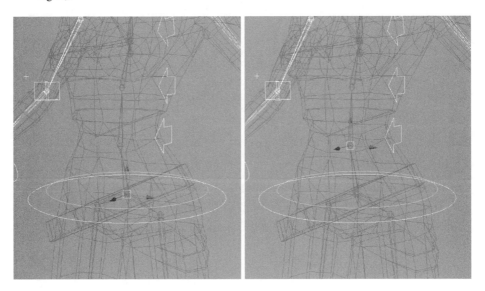

**FIGURE 12.58** Position the circle above the root control and snap its pivot to the lower spine joint.

**4**  So that you can control the waist with the circle, select the Waist_Control icon and then the WaistControl group and apply an orient constraint.

As demonstrated in **Figure 12.59**, the waist will rotate without affecting the spine—perfect for adding a feminine touch to Kila's walk and allowing her to dance if she is shown at work during the game (we know from the back story that she's a professional dancer).

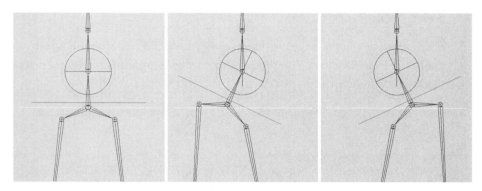

FIGURE 12.59 Kila's waist now rotates free from the spine.

**5** Parent the Waist_Control to the Root_Control so that the icon stays in its correct position.

Kila's spine and waist are now fully rigged; this is a good place to save the scene, as Kila_TorsoRig.mb.

Go ahead and implement the same spine and waist rig into Grae—it's a good idea to add the same waist controls to all your characters, as it adds further freedom to their movements. Save this scene as Grae_TorsoRig.mb.

## Upper Body Controls

We have arrived at the upper body controls. For both characters, these include the clavicle, head, and neck controls.

### Clavicle

For the clavicles, we could simply control them via an orient constraint, but this would not prove a very intuitive way of animating. Instead, we will use a constraint that we haven't used so far: the *aim constraint.*

1   Turn off the visibility on the Rig_Controls layer and make sure you can see the actual character geometry. Setting the geometry's layer to Template will allow you to see it but not edit it.

2   We need a new icon for the clavicle controls; this time, we will build it in Maya. Switch to the side view, and go to Create > Arc Tools > Three Point Circular Arc. We will use the default options.

3   With the Arc tool active, click once in front of the character's shoulder, then once just above it, and then a final time just behind it; this defines three points on the curve. You can see this process in **Figure 12.60**. Press Enter to complete the curve, and rename it to LeftClavicle.

**FIGURE 12.60** Create a three-point arc.

**4** Switch to the perspective view. Move the curve so it sits above the left shoulder (**Figure 12.61**, middle). When you are happy with the position, point-snap the pivot point to the actual shoulder joint (**Figure 12.61**, right).

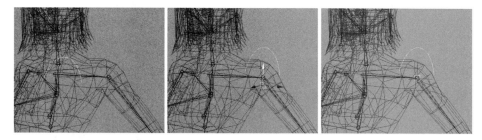

**FIGURE 12.61** Position the icon above the left shoulder.

**5** Freeze the transforms and delete the history.

**6** With the icon in place, connect it to the clavicle so that it will control the joint's rotation. Select the icon (LeftClavicle) first, and then add the corresponding joint (L_Clavicle) to the selection.

**7** Go to Constrain > Aim and open the options (**Figure 12.62**).

An aim constraint alters an object's orientation (the clavicle joint) to always aim at another object (the arc) along a set axis. See the sidebar "Aim Constraint Options."

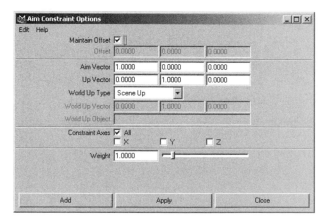

**FIGURE 12.62**
Aim Constraint options

## Aim Constraint Options

Here are some of the more important options for setting up an aim constraint:

▶ *Aim Vector* dictates which axis will point toward the target object's pivot point. The three boxes after it represent the X, Y, and Z axes. A value of 1 will fully influence the aim in that direction; however, a 1 in all three axes at the same time will give you a median position.

▶ *Up Vector* is the axis you want to point upward. By default, it will try to align itself with the World Up vector, which is Y.

▶ *World Up Type* alters the way the World Up vector is used and has the following options:

Scene Up will try to align itself with the current scene's Up axis.

Object Up causes the Up vector to try and aim at the origin of a specified object.

Object Rotation Up sets the World Up vector to use a specified object's rotations as a guide.

Vector makes the Up vector try to align with the World Up vector.

None uses none of the above and instead bases its orientation on whatever it was set to before you chose None.

**8**    Set the aim constraint's options as follows:

We know that X points down the bone. The first box next to Aim Vector represents the X axis; set this to 1 so we are aiming fully in that direction. Make sure the middle box (Y) and the last box (Z) are both set to 0 so these have no influence.

We also know that the Up Vector should be set to Y because the Y axis points up, so set the middle box to 1 and leave its neighboring boxes at 0.

Leave the World Up Type set to Scene Up.

Check Maintain Offset to enable it, since the joints may move slightly. With this setting turned on, they will stay in position.

9   Click the Apply button to apply your settings. Then set and Apply the same options for the right clavicle, except for the Up Vector's Y axis (the middle box); set this to −1 because the Y axis on this joint points down.

10  To finish up the clavicle controls, parent them to the Upper_Spine icon. This will keep them from drifting away from the body as it moves.

As you can see in **Figure 12.63**, we can now position the shoulders by translating the icons along the Y and Z axes.

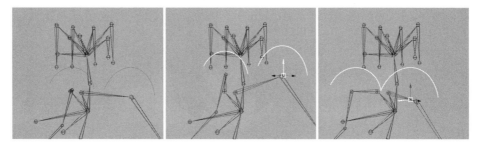

FIGURE 12.63 The clavicles are now controlled by the two icons.

Add these icons to the Rig_Controls layer and save the scene.

### Neck

We will use a simple icon to drive the neck's rotations, much as we did for the hips.

1   Create a NURBS circle, calling it NeckRotation.

2   Point-snap it to the neck joint. Then manipulate it as shown in **Figure 12.64**, left, so that the circle lies just above the shoulders.

> **NOTE**  When you set up the circle for Grae, you may need to alter its rotation, too, so that it follows the orientation of the neck.

3   Adjust the circle's pivot point so that it lies back over the neck joint.

4   Select the neck icon and, holding Shift, select the neck joint. Then orient-constrain them.

**5**    Parent the neck icon to the Upper_Spine icon.

The neck now has external control, meaning we don't need to edit the skeleton directly.

If you want, you can go in and adjust the CVs for the circle, curving the shape to fit the shoulders (**Figure 12.64**, right). This is purely for aesthetic reasons.

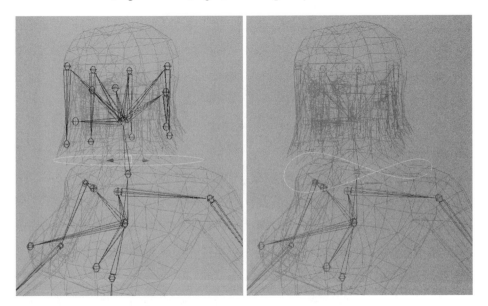

FIGURE 12.64 Add a NURBS circle to control the neck's rotations.

**Head**

The final area of our main rig, the head, tends to be the most unpredictable area of animation. In this section we will discuss an easy way to gain full control over where your characters are facing, allowing the head to move freely or to lock onto objects as the character walks by.

> TIP As an alternative to the following technique for head rigging, you could just add a control similar to the one we implemented for the neck. That will let you control the head's rotations directly.

1   Open the Kila file you have been working on so far, which should be Kila_
    TorsoRig.mb. So you can concentrate on the head, turn off the visibility on
    the Rig_Controls layer. Import the file named Icon_Head.mb. This will be
    our main head control icon.

2   Point-snap the icon to the head joint. Then scale and rotate the icon so it's
    facing the same direction as Kila's head.

3   Move the icon out in front of the head, as shown in **Figure 12.65**, and freeze
    the transforms.

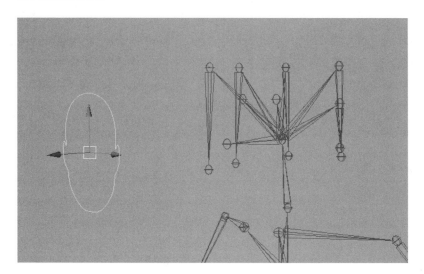

FIGURE 12.65 Import, scale, and position the head icon.

4   We are going to use an IK Single Chain solver that will enable us to posi-
    tion the head and lock it, so that the character can stay focused on one thing
    while her body does another. Go to Skeleton > IK Handle Tool. Making sure
    you have ikSCsolver selected in the options, and create a handle from the
    main Head joint to the Head_Tip joint (**Figure 12.66**, top). Call this handle
    Head_Direction.

5   We want the head icon to be able to control the IK handle, so parent the
    handle to the head icon.

**6**   Move the IK handle out so it lines up with the head icon (**Figure 12.66**, bottom). This makes the head's position more accurate.

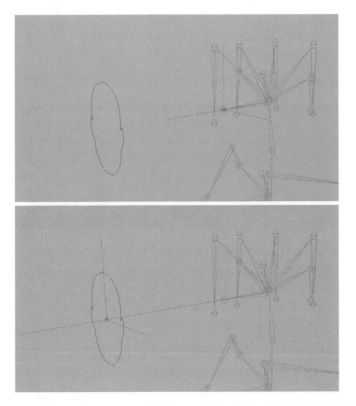

FIGURE 12.66 Create an ikSCSolver for the head and parent it to the head icon.

Now the head joints will track the head icon; you can see this in **Figure 12.67**, middle. You can even use the head icon's Z rotation to tilt the head. Before we finish with this stage of the rigging, we can add another effect.

**7**   Select the head joint and then the head icon, and go to Constrain > Aim. In the constraint options, set the Aim Vector to be –1 in the Z axis (with 0 in X and Y), and set the Up Vector to be 1 in the Y axis (with 0 in X and Z).

Now when the head icon moves, not only does the head joint track its movement, but the head icon stays oriented toward the head (**Figure 12.67**, right). This makes it easier to control.

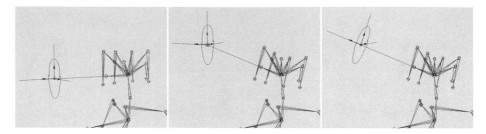

**FIGURE 12.67** Use an aim constraint to get the head icon to stay focused on the head.

The first stage of the head's setup is complete. Now we need to check the head's rotation order, altering it to prevent *gimbal lock*. See the sidebar "Rotation Order and Gimbal Lock."

## Rotation Order and Gimbal Lock

*Rotation order* indicates which rotations get evaluated first; the default order is xyz, meaning the Z axis is evaluated first, then the Y axis, and finally the X axis. This means that when you rotate around the Z axis, the Y and X move with it; rotating around the Y axis will move the X axis; and rotating the X axis will only move itself.

Having an incorrect rotation order will result in what's known as *gimbal lock*. This occurs when two axes end up existing along the same plane; you can't get the third degree of rotation because it clashes with another. This can cause your objects to flip, and ultimately not move as you require.

Unless you are animating using the gimbal setting in the Rotate tool options (the default setting is Local), this phenomenon is hidden to you. Maya will maintain the 90-degree offset of rotation planes by adding rotational values to the other axes as needed. By carefully considering your character's movements in advance, you can prevent some gimbal lock problems. Setting the correct rotation order (in the Attributes Editor) is a crucial step.

Look at **Figure 12.68**, left; these are our current gimbal rotational axes. To make these settings available, open the Rotate tool options and set Rotate Mode to Gimbal.

If we rotate round the Y axis, the X axis turns with it (**Figure 12.68**, middle), but the Z axis doesn't. This means the Z axis will eventually be in the same place as the X, resulting in gimbal lock. This happens because, by default, the Y axis is evaluated second, meaning the X axis will move with it but the z will not.

Changing the rotation order to zxy (or xzy, depending on how you wish the object to rotate) will mean the axes are evaluated correctly; as you can see in **Figure 12.68**, right, when the Y axis is rotated, all the other axes follow.

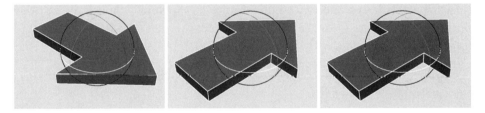

**FIGURE 12.68** Gimbal lock example

As our head icon moves around the head, it uses primarily the Y axis, with the X coming in a close second. We need these axes to remain intact so that we can then edit the Z axis, causing the head to tilt no matter where it is. Without correct rotation order, this would be difficult to achieve. Let's set this up now.

Select the HeadControls icon, open the Attribute Editor, and in the Transform Attributes, set Rotate Order to zxy. Make the same adjustment to the main head joint on the base skeleton. Now the head and the head icon will rotate correctly at any angle.

> **TIP** It's important to check other parts of your rig for areas where the rotation order may need altering, to reduce the possibility of gimbal lock.

With our head icon work done, and the rotational order adjusted, tidy the scene a little by placing the head icon in the Rig_Controls layer. Then hide the IK handle.

The base rig for Kila—limbs, body, and head—is now finished, so save your scene as Kila_BaseRig.mb. Work on Grae, following the same steps until you arrive at the same stage for him, saving his scene as Grae_BaseRig.mb.

## More Controls

Now that the main rig for both characters is complete, we can set up the other areas that need to have life. These are the eyes, Kila's chest and hair, and Grae's wings.

### Eyes

Both characters' eyes need the ability to move as they look around. The best way to achieve this is to create an icon that the eyes always look at, much the way the head follows the head icon. For the eyes, however, we can't use IK because we only have a single joint.

1   Import the file called Icon_Eyes.mb into your scene. You will now have two separate eye-shaped icons.

2   Point-snap each eye icon to its corresponding joint. Scale them and then rotate them so they are the correct orientation, as seen in **Figure 12.69**, top. Then move them out (using Z only) in front of the head until they line up with the head icon (**Figure 12.69**, bottom). Freeze the transforms.

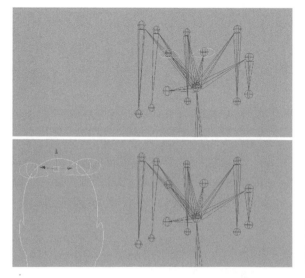

FIGURE 12.69 Snap the eye icons to the eye joints, and move them out to the head icon.

### Aligning the Eye Icons

As you can see in **Figure 12.70**, left, the eyes and the head do not line up correctly. This isn't a major problem and it's not important to fix. But if you want to, here's how:

Right-click the head icon and select Edit Points (**Figure 12.70**, middle). Select all the edit points, and move and scale them so they line up with the eyes (**Figure 12.70**, right). We edit the icon in Component mode, because we won't need to freeze the transforms or make further adjustments to the hierarchy.

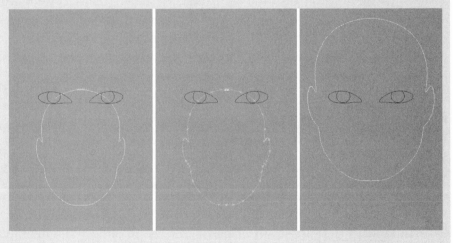

**FIGURE 12.70** You might want to adjust the head icon's edit points to match the scale of the eyes.

3   With the eyes in position, we can wire them up to control the joints. Select the left eye icon and then the left eye joint. Apply an aim constraint with Aim Vector set to 1 in the Z channel (0 in X and Y), and with Up Vector set to 1 in the Y channel (0 in X and Z).

4   Apply the same aim constraint to the right eye icon and the right eye joint, using the same settings as for the left eye.

5   The eyes are separate at present, but want to move them together. Select both eye icons and group them, calling the group EyeControl.

6    For all new groups, the pivot is placed at the world root, so go to Modify > Center Pivot and place the pivot between the eyes.

7    Make the group's selection handle visible so you can select it easily. Do this by going to Display > Component Display > Selection Handle.

8    To finish up, make the eye icons always face the eyes, as we did with the head icon. Select the main head joint and then the EyeControl group, and perform another aim constraint. This time set Aim Vector to −1 in the Z channel. Also, enable Maintain Offset if the eye group is higher than the head joint.

The eyes are now rigged, but as you move the icon around, you won't see much of a difference to the joints. To see the eyes moving, select the joints and go to Display > Component Display > Local Rotation Axis. Now you will see that the axes always follow the EyeControl icon because they were told to always aim at them.

### Kila's Chest

It's quite easy to rig Kila's bosom; we merely need to point-constrain each joint to an icon that will drive it.

1    Start by creating two more NURBS circles, calling them LeftBreast and RightBreast.

2    Position each circle as shown in **Figure 12.71**, left, so each circle is in front of a breast. Freeze the transforms.

3    Point-snap the pivot point for each icon to the joint it will control.

4    Select the left breast icon, then the corresponding joint, and do a point constraint. Do the same for the right breast icon, constraining the joint to the icon.

5    You now have icons that let you animate each breast individually. We also want to be able to animate them both at the same time. To set this up, select both icons and group them, calling the new group BreastControls. Center the pivot of the group by going to Modify > Center Pivot.

**6**  As seen in **Figure 12.71**, right, make the display handle visible (Display > Component Display > Selection Handles).

**7**  Parent the BreastControls group to the Upper_Spine icon so that the group will move with her upper body.

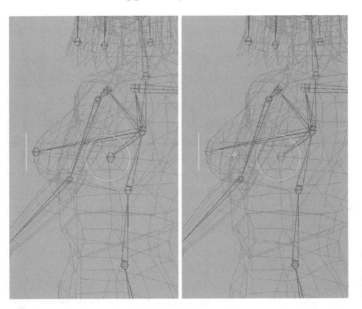

**FIGURE 12.71**
Add control icons to the breasts.

We now have the option to animate both breasts at the same time by using the BreastControls group, or move them individually via their icons.

## Hair and Wings

The final areas we need to rig are Kila's hair and Grae's wings. You should by now have a good grasp of the tools that are available to help you rig these areas, so take a stab at it yourself and see what you can come up with. If you have trouble or are struggling with something, you can always refer to the files called Kila_XtrasRig.mb and Grae_XtrasRig.mb on this book's CD.

Ideally, a dynamics engine will drive animation of Kila's hair. This would provide the best results and free up the animators to work on other things. Unfortunately, we don't have that luxury for Kila, so take the opportunity to try and add your own, simple rig.

Here are a couple of suggestions:

▶ You might give the hair a very basic rig, forcing the animator to supply every movement the hair needs. Simply implement some basic icons that will control the hair joints' rotations. This approach has its advantages, since there will be occasions where the animator needs complete freedom over the way the hair moves.

▶ You can use IK handles to control each joint. This technique allows you to pull the hair around from the base—it's a more user friendly way of animating.

Rigging Grae's wings can be approached in a much easier way: Import the file Icon_Wings.mb into the scene. You will find that I have already set up a series of attributes on the icons for you to use. Then use Set Driven Keys to generate poses for the wings, which correspond to each attribute.

Both Kila and Grae's bodies are now fully rigged, head to toe (**Figure 12.72**). The only other main controls we need to add are those to control facial animation, which we will discuss in the next chapter.

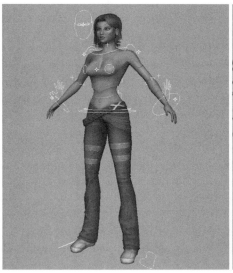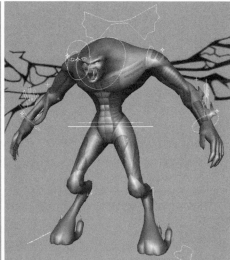

FIGURE 12.72 Kila and Grae, fully equipped with their rigs

# Visibility Controllers

With all these icons lying around, your Maya scene can become messy and difficult to navigate. The final tool we will use in this chapter is a *visibility control*, which lets us show or hide the various icons. For the animator, it's an easy way to identify what icons are needed and hide the ones not being used.

Before we implement the visibility control, we first need to take a broad look at our scene. Load the Kila_XtrasRig.mb file you have been working on so far, and open up the Outliner. As you can see in **Figure 12.73**, left, we have lots of new objects that are forming the rig. Let's compile them all into a nice neat group.

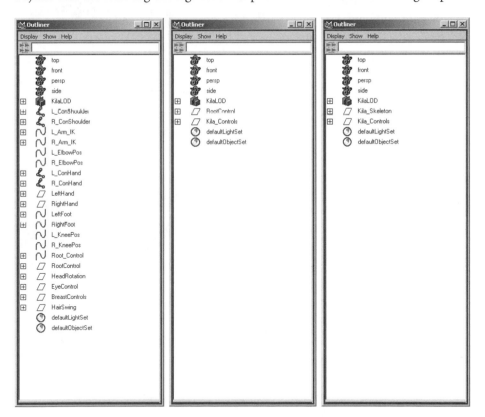

**FIGURE 12.73** Tidy up the Kila and Grae scenes' contents before you proceed.

Select everything except the main LOD group (KilaLOD), the main scene cameras, and the RootControl group. We omit this last element because it contains the main skeleton. For now, all we want are parts of the rig. So group everything you have selected into a new group, Kila_Controls (**Figure 12.73**, middle). Also, rename the RootControl group so that you have a better idea of what it is; call it Kila_Skeleton.

The scene is now much tidier, as seen in **Figure 12.73**, right. Anyone else coming in to use it will have a good idea of what's where.

Do the same tidying up in Grae_Xtras.mb.

Now let's implement our visibility controller.

1   Import the file Icon_Visibility.mb and rename the VisibilityControl icon to KilaVisibility. We do this because it will help us to differentiate her visibility controls if we were to import other characters into the scene.

2   Move the new icon up above Kila's head (see **Figure 12.74**). Freeze the transforms.

3   So that the icon stays with the actual rig as it moves, point-constrain it to the root joint. Select the root joint and then, holding Shift, add the visibility icon to the selection. Go to Constrain > Point, making sure Maintain Offset is enabled.

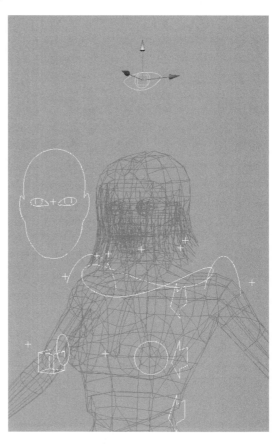

**FIGURE 12.74** Position the visibility icon above Kila's head.

Now that the icon is in place and fixed to the rig, we can start to add attributes to it that will control the other icons' visibility. Think carefully about what you want to be able to control. In this case, let's add the ability to turn all the icons on and off; we can add that control to the actual geometry, too.

**4**   Add two Boolean attributes to the KilaVisibility icon, called AllIcons and AllGeom. We can also add the ability to simply view the icons in certain regions. Add another three Boolean attributes called LeftIcons, MiddleIcons, and RightIcons.

Think of other visibility controls you'd like to have: Maybe you would like to control each icon separately? Feel free to add more if you want. Otherwise, let's go ahead and connect up the ones we've added so far.

**1**   Open the Connection Editor (Window > General Editors > Connection Editor).

**2**   Select the KilaVisibility icon, and click the Reload Left button to load the icon into the Outputs list. In the Inputs list, load the Kila_Controls group.

**3**   As shown in **Figure 12.75a**, connect the AllIcons attribute to the Visibility attribute.

**FIGURE 12.75a**
Connecting the new
Visibility attributes

**4** All the icons now disappear. This happens because the Boolean attributes you've created are set to Off by default. Go through each one now and set these to On.

**5** Load the KilaLOD group into the Inputs list, and connect the AllGeom attribute to the Visibility attribute (**Figure 12.75b**).

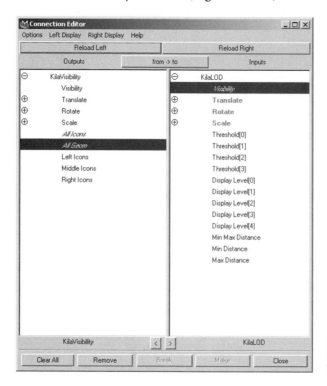

**FIGURE 12.75b**
Connecting the new Visibility attributes

**6**  For the next attribute, LeftIcons, we will need to control the visibility of a number of objects at once. Select all the left-side objects (L_ConShoulder, L_Arm_IK, L_ConHand, LeftHand, LeftFoot, and L_KneePos), and click Reload Right in the Connection Editor.

**7**  As shown in **Figure 12.75c**, select LeftIcons; then work your way down the Inputs list, selecting all the Visibility attributes.

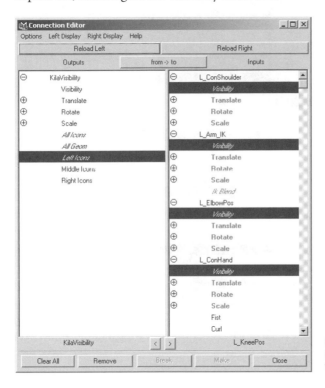

**FIGURE 12.75c**
Connecting the new
Visibility attributes

**8** For the MiddleIcons attribute, load Root_Control, HeadRotation, EyeControl, BreastControls, and HairSwing into the Inputs list. Then connect MiddleIcons to all their visibility icons (**Figure 12.75d**).

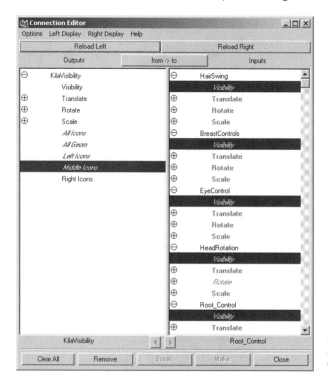

**FIGURE 12.75d**
Connecting the new Visibility attributes

**9** Select R_ConShoulder, R_Arm_IK, R_ConHand, RightHand, RightFoot, and R_KneePos, and click Reload Right.

**10** Connect the RightIcons attribute to all the Visibility attributes on the right (**Figure 12.75e**).

**FIGURE 12.75e**
Connecting the new
Visibility attributes

Save the scene as Kila_VizRig.mb—we now have complete control over how the icons are viewed. This should make the animation process much easier.

Follow this same procedure to apply visibility controls to Grae.

## Color Coding for Icons

There is one final visual aid we can add to help distinguish our control icons. We can alter each icon's wireframe color, essentially color-coding them.

At present, all of our controls are white. This is good because it makes them stand out. But what happens if we are looking from the side? Knowing whether you are selecting the left or right arm could be difficult. Adding colors to different areas of the rig will help to distinguish the side you are working on.

The color for each icon is currently locked to the Rig_Controls layer. Initially, this was a useful layer to have—we don't need it anymore, though, because we can now control the icons' visibility by means of our new visibility icon.

1   Delete the Rig_Controls layer by right-clicking it in the Layer Editor and selecting Delete. All the icons will return to the default color of dark blue.

2   Select the LeftFoot icon and open up its Attribute Editor by pressing Ctrl+A (**Figure 12.76**, left).

3   Open up the Attribute Editor's Object Display pane, and you'll see three more sections: Ghosting Information, Bounding Box Information, and Drawing Overrides. Open Drawing Overrides (**Figure 12.76**, right). Make sure Enable Overrides is enabled, and then you can edit the color swatch just below it to choose a color for your icon.

4   Now work your way around all of the icons, making the ones on the left blue, the ones in the middle green, and the ones on the right yellow. Choose any colors you prefer, as long as they are sufficiently different. You can even make every icon a different color if you like; just be sure the scene is easy to read.

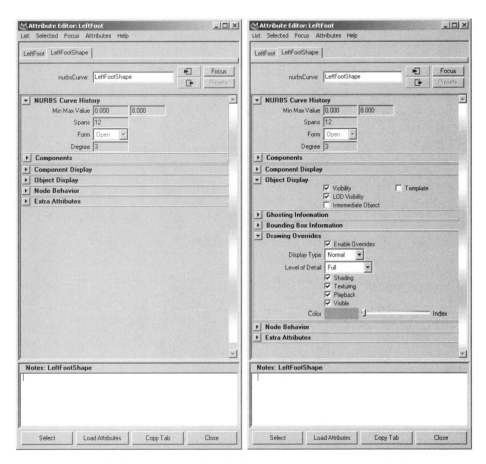

**FIGURE 12.76** Adjust the color swatch under Drawing Overrides to color-code icons.

You can see in **Figure 12.77** that the icons are distinctive now; you can easily tell which side is which. Save the scene with its new colored icons as Kila_MainRig.mb.

Apply color-coding to Grae's control icons, too.

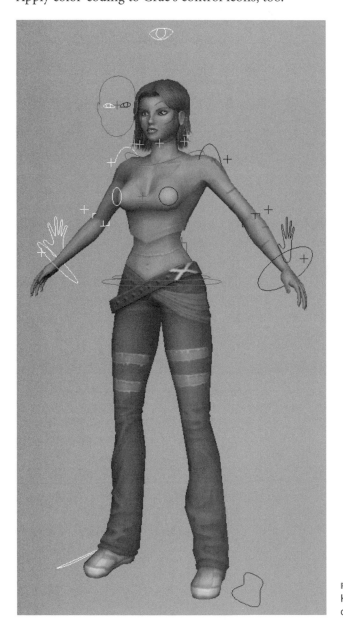

**FIGURE 12.77**
Kila with color-coded icons

## Summary

In this extensive chapter you have learned the benefits of using icons to animate your characters. You have also seen how best to implement these icons to drive your skeletons.

If you find rigging to be a long and tedious job, consider using the Creature Tools scripts provided on the CD. Creature Tools will automatically generate a rig to your own specifications and have you animating in minutes.

We have one final section to add to our rigs for Kila and Grae. Chapter 13 shows you how to rig for facial animation using both blend shapes and joint-based techniques.

# CHAPTER 13
# Facial Animation Setup

**WITH EACH GENERATION** of hardware comes more scope for graphical detail. Facial animation is fast becoming a major element of video games; characters can not only speak but also express emotions. It used to be that a simple joint acting as a jaw was enough. This allowed the character's mouth to open and close, but the illusion failed to bring the character to life; instead, it looked more like a puppet.

Two of the most popular methods today of real-time facial animation use either joints or *blend shapes*. Joint-based animation simply uses a series of joints placed around the face that, when moved, serve to animate the character's face. Blend shapes, or *morph targets,* use duplicates of the face as a reference. The main face then morphs into the vertex-modified reference shapes.

This chapter demonstrates how to set up your characters using joints and using blend shapes, so that you can make up your own mind about which one to use in a particular situation.

Your choice will depend heavily on the game engine, so consult with the lead programmer first before embarking on a particular method. In addition, discuss the matter with your manager before you start work. Find out exactly what the character will need to do. If all it will ever do is blink, then there is no need to spend time creating multiple face shapes.

## Joint-Based Facial Animation Setup (Kila)

The most obvious way to animate a character's face is to use joints, because we are already employing them to animate the body. We simply place joints at certain places around the character's face, which will then act like muscles, moving the vertices around and animating the face.

Where do we put facial joints to get the best facial expressions on Kila?

▶   We need one to operate the mouth, opening and closing the jaw.

▶   For the eyes, we'll add joints that operate the eyelids.

▶   Joints at several locations around the mouth will give movement to the lips, enabling the character to form words.

▶   The eyebrows contribute a lot to facial expression, so we can add joints to move these as well.

▶   If our budget allows, we can add the ability to animate the tongue.

▶   Two more joints will add movement to the cheeks.

This list includes quite a few extra joints, so for your own project, make sure you have room in your budget. In this chapter, we will implement them all.

## Joint Placement

As we did with Kila's breasts, we will rely mostly on the translations of joints to animate the face. We only need to add joints to the left side of her face, and then mirror these to create the right side.

**1**   Open up the file Kila_MainRig.mb and, using the visibility controller we added in Chapter 12, turn off all the icons.

**2**   Switch to the side view, and hide her hair and the main skeleton so you can concentrate on her face. Turn the geometry layer visibility to Template.

**3**   Using the Joint tool found in the Skeleton menu, place Kila's jawbone as shown in **Figure 13.1a**. Call the first joint Jaw, and the second Jaw_Tip.

**4**   Place three joints that will control her tongue, using the actual tongue geometry to guide you. Call these TongueBase, TongueMiddle, and Tongue_Tip, before parenting TongueBase to the Jaw joint (**Figure 13.1b**).

**5**   Following **Figure 13.1c**, place two single joints in exactly the same place as the eye joint. (You will need to make the base skeleton visible again for this step. Set it to Reference, so that you will be able to snap the new joints to the ones on the base skeleton.)

We need the eyelids to follow the same rotations as the eyes, so these joints need to be in the same position as the eye joint. Use the Point Snap tool to position them correctly, and call them L_UpperLid and L_LowerLid.

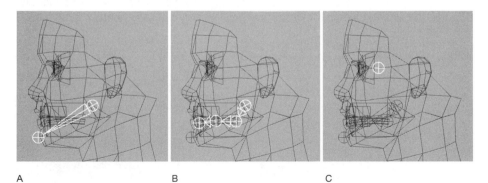

A                                    B                                    C

**FIGURE 13.1a–c** Place the joints that will animate the left side of Kila's face.

6    Add three separate joints around her lips, placing one at the top, one at the corner of her mouth, and a final one on the lower lip (**Figure 13.1d**). Call these L_UpperLip, L_OuterLip, and L_LowerLip.

7    Place two joints along the eyebrow, calling these L_InnerBrow and L_OuterBrow (**Figure 13.1e**).

8    Create a joint that will animate her cheek, calling it L_Cheek (**Figure 13.1f**).

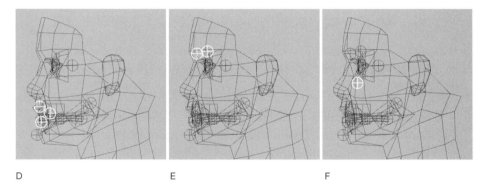

D                                E                                F

**FIGURE 13.1d–f** Place the joints that will animate the left side of Kila's face.

9    Switch to the perspective view now and move all except the jaw and tongue joints away from the center, placing them in the areas for which they were intended (**Figure 13.2**, middle).

> **NOTE**   As illustrated in Figure 13.2, right, make sure the joints lie half in and half out of the actual geometry. This way, they will give an accurate movement when animated.

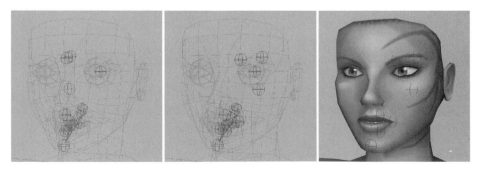

**FIGURE 13.2** Move the new eye, eyebrow, and cheek joints away from the center and into their correct places.

**10** The joints are now in position, so make the main skeleton visible again. Then parent all the joints except TongueBase, TongueMiddle, Tongue_Tip, Jaw_Tip, and LowerLip to the main head joint. Parent the LowerLip joint to the jaw joint because it will move with the bottom jaw.

> **TIP** You may find it easier to select the joints in the Outliner. A quick way to navigate through the hierarchy is to select any of the joints belonging to the face in the main view; then right-click in the Outliner and select Reveal Selected. You will be taken to the selected joint in the Outliner, which in turn will reveal the rest since they all lie in the same place.

Next, simply use the Mirror Joint tool to copy each joint across, creating the right side joints. Do all except for the jaw joints.

**1** Select one of the new face joints and go to Skeleton > Mirror Joint.

**2** In the tool options, set Mirror Across to YZ. Under the heading "Replacement names for duplicated joints," put L_ in Search For, and R_ in Replace With.

This will automatically rename the joints for you so that they represent the right side.

**3** Click on Apply to mirror the joint and keep the window open. Now repeat this for each of the remaining face joints.

> **NOTE** Remember to reset each joint's rotational axes, especially after you have mirrored them. Select all the new joints and use the rsJnt button on the GCDM shelf. Use the orJnt button on the jaw and tongue joints.

You can see in **Figure 13.3** that the face is looking pretty complicated right now, and to an animator this would be a nightmare to pose. But we can rig the face just as we did the body, making it easier to get basic poses and mouth shapes. In order to do this, the joints must first be bound to the mesh and their positions tested.

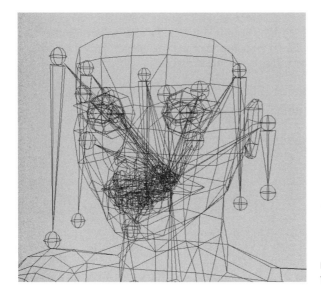

**FIGURE 13.3** The face with the full joint configuration

### Preparation and Binding

Although binding isn't covered until Chapter 14, "Final Character Deformation," we want to make a start now on this process so that we can fully rig the face.

To successfully bind Kila, we need her to be a single object. Your game engine may not handle multiple objects, so in this case it's safest to combine Kila's polygons.

1   Select each element that makes up the highest level of detail and go to Polygons > Combine. This will create a single object; rename it to Kila_LOD01.

2   Because she started out as separate objects, combining Kila won't have welded the vertices between each element. Look at **Figure 13.4**, middle. At the line where her head meets her hair, there are two vertices lying on top of each other. You can easily select one and move it down, which creates an undesirable hole.

To fix this, select all the vertices of her head and hair and go to Edit Polygons > Merge Vertices, setting the value to a small number such as 0.0001. This way, only vertices that lie on top of each other will be welded (**Figure 13.4**, right).

3   Double-check each area that this welding should have affected, including the hairline, eyelashes, and inner mouth. Make sure that the lips, though, have *not* been merged.

4   Combining Kila into a single object will have placed the geometry out of the LOD group, so quickly make sure she is again parented to the Kila4096 group. This will ensure the LODs still work.

5   Delete the history on the mesh.

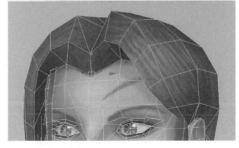

**FIGURE 13.4** Merge all the seams, welding the vertices together.

> **NOTE**  There may be a stray node still in the Kila4096 group; this may have been missed when we deleted her history. She is a single model now, though, so it's safe to delete this node. Use Hypergraph or Outliner to check for this issue.

The first LOD for Kila is now a single mesh, which will make her easier to work with. Now let's connect her to the base skeleton.

1   In the Outliner, navigate to the first joint of the base skeleton; this should be called Root. Select it and open up the hierarchy by Shift+clicking on the plus sign (+) next to Root.

2   Go to Edit > Select Hierarchy to select all the objects beneath Root.

**3**  Although the skeleton hierarchy is selected, you don't want to bind all the joints. Scroll down the Outliner and, holding Ctrl, deselect all the joints ending with _Tip. These are only here as visual aids and don't deform the character.

Also make sure you only have joints selected. Unselect any icons, constraint nodes, or effectors (which are part of the IK system and usually named "effector") that may also be selected.

**4**  With just the correct joints selected, hold Shift and add the Kila mesh to the selection.

**5**  Go to Skin > Bind Skin > Smooth Bind and open the options. For Bind To, choose Selected Joints, and for Bind Method, choose Closest Joint. Set Max Influences to 3, and Dropoff Rate to 4.

**6**  Click on Bind Skin, and the skin is now attached to the base skeleton. You can test this by moving some of the control icons (**Figure 13.5**, right).

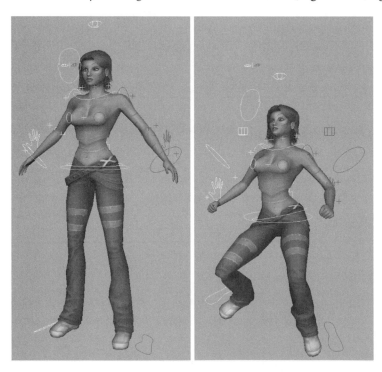

**FIGURE 13.5** Test the bind by moving some of the icons around.

**TIP** On the GCDM shelf, you'll find a button labeled Bind. This will automatically select the joints needed and bind the selected skin to them, while making sure no unwanted objects are included.

Save the scene as Kila_FaceBind.mb.

We will leave binding the rest of the body until Chapter 14. For now, let's concentrate on the job at hand and edit the weighting information on the face.

### Joint Weights

Since we covered the various weighting tools and options in Chapter 6, we can now get right to it and work on the facial joints.

**NOTE** Unless specified, we will mainly be using the paint operation Replace, from the Paint Weights pane in the Paint Skin Weights options.

We will be moving the joints around, so it would be prudent for us to first store their current translations. Since the joints' translations cannot be frozen, we will set a keyframe on them, thus storing their default pose.

**Figure 13.6** shows the Time Slider at the bottom of the Maya window (the main bar with numbers in it). This controls time in Maya; simply clicking in the slider will alter the frame you're on. We will discuss the Time Slider in more detail in Chapter 16, "Animating for Games."

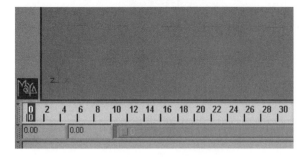

FIGURE 13.6
The Time Slider

On the Time Slider, make sure you have frame 0 selected; then select all the joints associated with the face. Right-click in the Channel Box and select Key All from the menu. The attributes will turn orange to indicate they are keyframed.

We have thus stored the joints' positions at frame 0; you will be able to see a thin red line indicating that the selected object has a key set on it. We can still move the joints around, but to return them to their default pose we need only click on frame 0 in the Time Slider. The only way to store a new pose would be to set another key.

With the joints, positions safely stored, let's look at adjusting the weights on her jaw and lips.

### Jaw and Mouth Weights

The jaw joints are first; they'll allow us to open and close her mouth.

1   Make all the icons invisible. Focus in on the face and make sure you can see the base skeleton (**Figure 13.7**, left).

2   Following **Figure 13.7**, right, rotate the main jawbone down to where the mouth would be open. As you can see, the weights are not distributed properly, so you need to go in and tweak them.

**FIGURE 13.7**
Rotate the jaw joint so that you can see how the weighting looks.

3   Select the main character model, and go to Skin > Edit Smooth Skin > Paint Skin Weights Tool and open the tool's options.

4   Set both Brush Opacity and the Paint Weights Value to 1, and select the Jaw joint so that you can edit its weights (**Figure 13.8**).

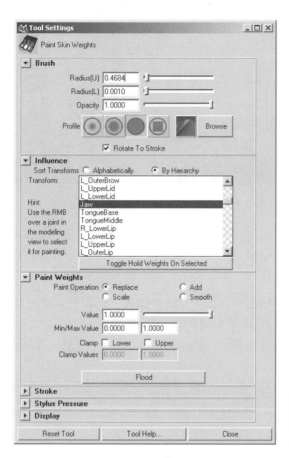

**FIGURE 13.8** Set the Paint Skin Weights tool settings and select the Jaw joint.

5   Using the solid brush, fully weight the bottom of the jaw (including her bottom teeth and tongue) to the Jaw joint.

6   Reset the Paint Weights Value to 0.5, and paint over the middle of the mouth at the corners and cheeks (this is the area halfway between the upper and lower lips), as seen in **Figure 13.9**, left.

7   Select the head joint, and set Paint Weights Value back to 1. Fully weight the top of her head (including her upper teeth and lip) to this joint (**Figure 13.9**, middle).

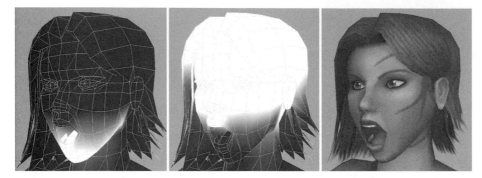

FIGURE 13.9 Adjust the weights for the jaw and head joints, fixing the mouth.

As you can see in **Figure 13.9**, right, the mouth now looks better when it is open. But the problem now is that it's too round when open, so we need to bring the sides of the mouth in.

We will now adjust the weighting for the lip joints we created. This will help to adjust the shape of her mouth when it is open.

**1**   Reset the joints back to their default positions by moving the Time Slider to a different frame, and then back to frame 0.

**2**   Move outward all six joints that will operate the lips (**Figure 13.10**, right). When they're weighted, these joints will open the lips but keep the teeth together.

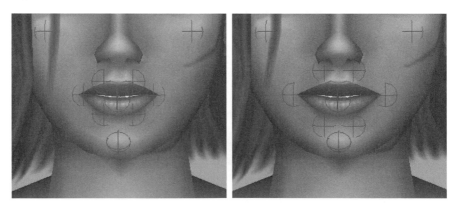

FIGURE 13.10 Move the joints for the lips slightly outward from the mouth.

Because we fully weighted them to the jaw and head joints, the vertices around the mouth are being told to ignore the lip joints. Let's attend to this next.

3    With a softer brush and a smaller Opacity value (say, 0.10), start to add weighting information for just the left three lip joints. Make the vertices on the inside of her lips almost fully affected by the joints, with the influence gradually fading as you get farther from the mouth. This will cause the lips to flatten slightly as they part, just as they would do naturally.

As you are adding the weights, you will see the lips begin to open up, with the vertices moving gradually toward the joint you are working on (**Figure 13.11b**).

4    When you are happy with the weights, you can mirror them across to the joints on the right side of her mouth. First, though, you have to reset the joints back to their default position; if they are not reset, the weights will not mirror properly. In this case, it's as simple as returning to frame 0.

5    Select the geometry and go to Skin > Edit Smooth Skin > Mirror Skin Weights, setting Mirror Across to YZ and enabling Positive to Negative as the Direction. The weights will now be copied across, as shown in **Figure 13.11c**.

Work more on the shape of the lips; they should look like those in **Figure 13.11d**. To add additional realism to the face make the upper lips influence her nose slightly. Keep opening the mouth up (**Figure 13.11e**) to get a better idea of how the mouth looks with the new weights. Remember, though, that you will now have to position the outer lip joints, too, since these will control the corners of the mouth.

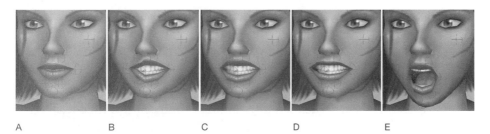

A          B          C          D          E

FIGURE 13.11 Add weighting to the lip joints

When you've finished this phase of weighting and adjusting, Kila's jaw and lips will be fully controlled by the joints.

## Deleting History

While manipulating the lip joints, you may notice that the inner mouth pops through the teeth or gums. You can at this stage flip or delete any edges that do this, but at the cost of creating history on the model.

If you are using Maya 6, you can delete the construction history without losing the weighting information. Simply select the mesh and go to Skin > Edit Smooth Skin > Delete Non-Skin History.

If you are using an earlier version of Maya, however, there is unfortunately no easy fix. What you can do, once the face and rest of the body are fully rigged and you've made the necessary mesh modifications, is duplicate the mesh—this will delete the history on the duplicate.

Make sure the duplicate is placed inside the correct LOD group; then bind it to the skeleton, making sure you bind it using exactly the same joint selection. If you originally used the Bind button on the GCDM shelf, use it again here; this will guarantee the joint selection is the same.

Select the main mesh. Then Shift+select the duplicate and go to Skin > Edit Smooth Skin > Copy Skin Weights. All the weighting information will now be copied across to the duplicate character model; you can delete the original mesh, leaving a clean character.

Now we will complete the mouth by adding control to her tongue. Again, it's quite difficult to get to the tongue in order to weight it properly, so first open Kila's mouth some to expose the tongue more. We will now isolate it so that we can work on it more easily.

1  Right-click on the Kila model and select Face, switching to face editing mode.

2  Go to Edit Polygons > Selection > Selection Constraints, which opens the dialog box seen in **Figure 13.12**. This tool allows you to alter the way you select things.

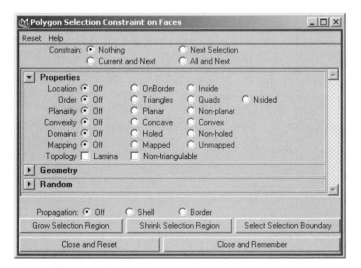

FIGURE 13.12 Polygon Selection Constraints dialog box

**3**    Near the bottom of the dialog box are the Propagation radio button selections. Selecting Shell will automatically expand our next selection to contain all the connected faces.

**4**    Navigate inside Kila's head to the tongue and select any face on it; with the new selection setting, this now selects the entire tongue.

**5**    Click on the Close and Reset button in the Polygon Selection Constraints dialog box.

**6**    With the tongue selected, go to Show > Isolate Select > View Selected in order to work on just the tongue (**Figure 13.13a**).

**7**    You want the joints to be visible, too, so use the Outliner to select the TongueBase and TongueMiddle joints. Then go to Show > Isolate Select > Add Selected Objects to make these visible (**Figure 13.13b**).

**8**    As seen in **Figures 13.13c** and **13.13d**, rotate the tongue joints down along the X axis. Then select the tongue geometry and open the Paint Skin Weights options.

**9**    Fully weight the whole tongue to the TongueBase joint (**Figure 13.13e**).

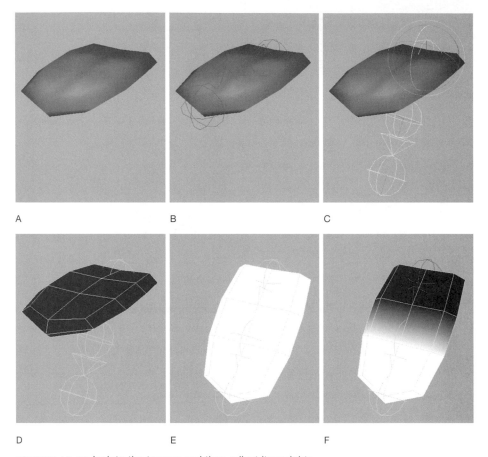

A          B          C

D          E          F

**FIGURE 13.13** Isolate the tongue and then adjust its weights.

> **TIP** Although you can't see the rest of the geometry, the paintbrush will still be able to select it, so make sure you are actually on the tongue before you apply any weights. Once you know you're on the right spot, try to keep the mouse button held down because the brush will then move over the adjoining faces.

10  Finally, weight the lower half of the tongue to the TongueMiddle joint (**Figure 13.13f**).

11  When you're finished, reset all tongue joint rotations back to 0.

The mouth area is now complete; so let's continue on to the eyes.

### Eye and Eyelid Weights

We need to add control to the eyes and eyelids so the character can look at things as well as blink.

Getting to the geometry for the eyes might be tricky, so we'll isolate just the general area we need to work on. To do this, simply select the faces around the area of the eyes and, on the current view, go to Show > Isolate Select > View Selected. As you can see in **Figure 13.14**, only the faces you selected are visible, allowing you to work more easily and quickly.

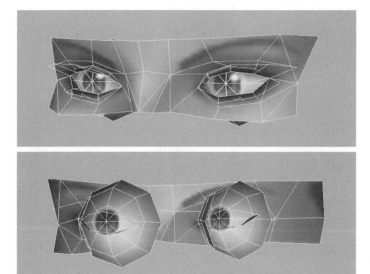

**FIGURE 13.14**
Isolate the faces around the eyes.

Go to Skin > Edit Smooth Skin > Paint Skin Weights, open the options, and set both Brush Opacity and Paint Weights Value to 1. Fully weight the left eye's geometry to the L_Eye joint (**Figure 13.15**, top) and then the right eye's geometry to the R_Eye joint (**Figure 13.15**, bottom).

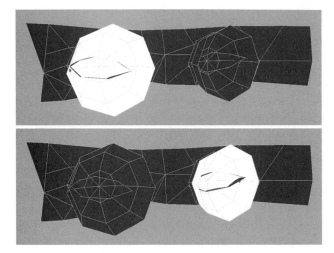

**FIGURE 13.15**
Add weighting to
the eye joints.

Now, as you can see in **Figure 13.16**, when you move the EyeControl controller around, the eyeballs will follow.

**FIGURE 13.16** After weighting the eyes, test to see how they rotate.

Next let's look at the eyelids. For this task we will work on the left side and then mirror the weights.

**1**   Select the joint named L_UpperLid and rotate it around the X axis about 15 units. Rotating the joint allows you to see what effect the weights will have on the mesh. **Figure 13.17**, top, shows you the current influence this joint has, which is none.

**2**   Open up the Paint Skin Weights options. In the Influence pane, select L_UpperLid. Set Brush Opacity and Paint Weight Value to 1.

**3**  Paint on the lower vertices of the left upper eyelid and eyelash, leaving the very corners of the eye alone (**Figure 13.17**, middle).

**4**  The eyelid now has quite a harsh, angular look to it; let's fix that. Turn Value to 0 and Opacity to around 0.1; then reduce the amount the eyelid affects the outer vertices, rounding the eyelid as it closes (**Figure 13.17**, bottom).

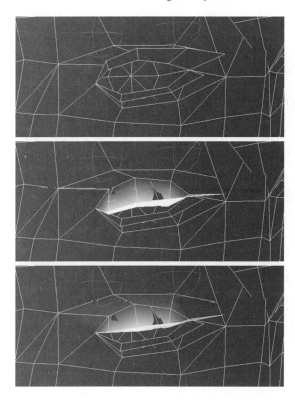

**FIGURE 13.17** Adjust the weights on the upper eyelid.

The upper eyelid is complete; now to repeat the procedure for the lower lid.

**1**   Set the L_LowerLid joint's X rotation to -7.

**2**   With Value and Opacity set to 1, fully weight the upper vertices of the lower eyelid to the joint (**Figure 13.18**, middle).

**3**   With Value reset to 0 and Opacity reset to 0.1, go in and smooth out the lower lid, giving it a better curve (**Figure 13.18**, bottom).

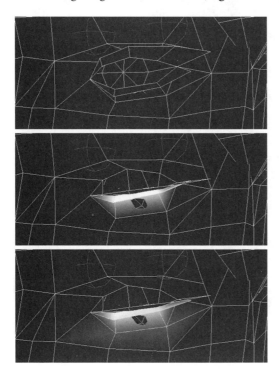

**FIGURE 13.18** Adjust the weights on the lower eyelid.

**TIP**   Don't worry about the eye geometry popping through the eyelids at this stage. Later, when we rig them, we can make the eyelids move forward slightly, which will hide this problem.

Mirroring the weights of the eyes isn't as straightforward as it was for the lips. Currently we have three joints residing in the same place on either side. This will confuse Maya when we ask it to mirror the weights because it won't know which joint to copy the weights to. To prevent this, simply move both UpperLid joints up slightly and the LowerLid joints down. Giving them their own individual locations will help Maya choose which joint to mirror across to. As long as the rest of the body is in the default position, the weighting should mirror successfully.

Select the mesh and go to Skin > Edit Smooth Skin > Mirror Skin Weights. There is no need to set the options; Maya will have retained the previous settings. When you're done, snap the eyelid joints back to the eye joints.

We will be mirroring the weights in the eye area quite often, so I suggest moving the eyelid joints and setting a key while on frame 1. This way, you will merely need to switch to frame 1 when mirroring weights, rather than having to move the eyelids each time.

**1** To set this key, first move along to frame 1 in the Time Slider.

**2** Move each of the joints into position.

**3** Select all four joints and set a key in the Channel Box, by right-clicking it and selecting Key All from the menu.

As shown in **Figure 13.19**, the eyelids now follow their joints and can be made to open and close.

FIGURE 13.19 The eyelids now open and close.

We are almost done with adjusting the weights on the face; all we need to do now is work on the eyebrows and cheeks.

### *Eyebrow and Cheek Weights*

First, the eyebrows.

1   Start by moving each of the left eyebrow joints up slightly so they are away from their default positions.

2   Select the mesh and open the Paint Skin Weights tool. Set Paint Weights Value to 1, Brush Opacity to 0.5, and select the joint named L_InnerBrow.

3   Using a softer brush, paint in the area of the eyebrow. Make the vertices closest to the eyebrow almost fully affected by the joint; allow the influence to fade out as it moves away (**Figure 13.20**, middle).

4   Select the joint named L_OuterBrow. Apply weighting similar to the inner section of the eyebrow (**Figure 13.20** bottom).

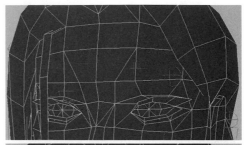

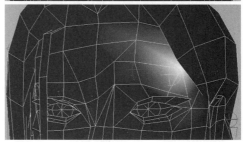

**FIGURE 13.20** Add weighting to the left eyebrow.

5   Mirror the weights by first going to frame 1 and then selecting Skin > Edit Smooth Skin > Mirror Skin Weights. Although the eyebrow joints exist in their own space, the mirror weights tool works globally; so even though we are mirroring the new eyebrow weights, the eyelids will be mirrored, too.

Try the eyebrows in different poses before you decide they are complete (**Figure 13.21**). It may be that they look fine in one pose but do not work in another and so will need some minor tweaking.

FIGURE 13.21 Try the eyebrows in a number of poses.

> **TIP** When mirroring weights, always check the vertices down the center of the model. These tend to end up with incorrect weighting information, so make sure to check them after mirroring.

The last area to edit is the left cheek. You want to add more subtle movement to the face as she talks, giving her a more organic feel. The cheeks need a soft influence on the geometry, so use a soft brush and apply a higher influence close to the joint, then gradually fade this out (**Figure 13.22**).

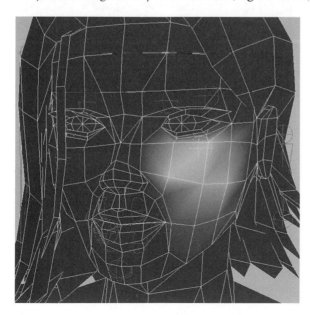

FIGURE 13.22 Add weighting to her cheek.

We have one final tweak to perform before our weighting tasks are complete. Select the head joint in the Influences pane of the Paint Skin Weights settings, and make sure the main sections of hair are weighted fully to it (**Figure 13.23**, left). Switch the Paint Operation to Smooth, and set both Value and Opacity to 1; then give the edges of the cheeks and eyebrows a general smoothing (**Figure 13.23**, right). This will be a subtle change, but it will smooth out the overall movement of her skin.

**FIGURE 13.23** Smooth out the edges of the cheeks and eyebrows.

The facial joints are now bound and weighted to the character's skin and ready to be rigged. Save the file as Kila_FaceWeight.mb.

# Facial Rig (Kila)

Now that each joint manipulates the mesh, we can animate them to create various facial expressions. In the model's present state, this would be a long and tedious job, so we will add a rig to the joints much like the one we created for the hands.

We will first add the ability to create quick poses for common facial expressions, and then we will create a small library of mouth shapes to help speed up any lip-synching. Finally, we will create individual controls for the eyes and eyebrows.

## Rig Preparation

Before we implement the rig controls, we will need something to manipulate them, so let's first create a series of dynamic attributes that will drive the joints.

1    The most obvious place to put attributes is the HeadControls icon, so select this first.

>    **NOTE**  The HeadControls icon already has quite a few attributes on it, but we'll hide some of these later in Chapter 15, "Finalize and Clean Up."

2    Go to Modify > Add Attribute to open the Add Attribute window.

3    Start with a basic Boolean called _ (a single underscore). This may seem to be a strange name, but this is going to be a dummy attribute, acting as a divider to help us quickly navigate the Channel Box and get to the attributes we need.

4    Right-click on the new attribute's name in the Channel Box, and select Lock Selected from the menu. This turns the attribute gray, which will also help us visually.

5    Now we will create the first section of actual attributes. Create four Float attributes called Happy, Shock, Angry, and Injured, giving them a minimum value of 0 and a maximum of 10. These will form the main facial poses.

6    Create a second divider attribute, this time called __ (two underscores); you can't repeat attribute names on the same object. Remember to lock this, too, using the same method as in step 4.

Now we will add the attributes that will drive the mouth and form the various mouth shapes we need for lip-synching.

7  Create 10 attributes this time, all with a Data Type of Float and having a minimum value of 0 and a maximum of 10. Call these O, CDENSZ, AKI, L, MPB, FV, Ooo, Ahh, Smile, and Frown. These names represent the sounds the mouth will form.

8  Create and lock a third and final divider named ___ (three underscores). You will now add attributes to control the eyelids and eyebrows.

9  Create six new float-type attributes named LeftInnerBrow, LeftOuterBrow, RightInnerBrow, RightOuterBrow, LeftEyeLids, and RightEyeLids. Give these a minimum value of –10 and a maximum value of 10.

Your Channel Box should now resemble that shown in **Figure 13.24**.

We have all the attributes we need for now, but feel free to add more if you want them. In the next section, we'll wire them up.

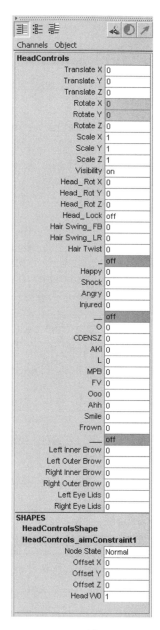

**FIGURE 13.24** The HeadControls icon with extra facial animation attributes added

### Rig Creation, Main Poses

With the main controls for the facial rig created, we will now use Set Driven Key to connect the controls to the joints. First we will define the main facial poses.

1   Open the Set Driven Key dialog box (Animate > Set Driven Key > Set), and load HeadControls in the Driver section. (Select HeadControls and click on Load Driver.)

2   Next select all the joints associated with the face, and click on Load Driven.

3   Select the Happy attribute next to HeadControls, and select all the translation and rotation attributes next to the joints. Your Set Driven Key dialog box should look like that in **Figure 13.25**.

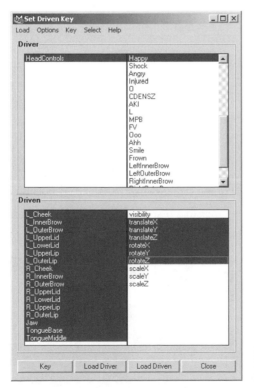

**FIGURE 13.25** Set Driven Key with all needed objects loaded

4   Click on Key to store the base pose for the Happy attribute.

5   Repeat steps 3 and 4 for the Shock, Angry, and Injured attributes, storing their base poses.

Now we can start building individual poses for Kila.

1  Select the HeadControls icon, and set Happy to 10 in the Channel Box.

2  Position each face joint, using rotations and translations so that Kila looks happy (**Figure 13.26a**). Make sure you use a facial expression reference at this stage, or even grab a mirror and copy your own smile.

3  Click on Key in the Set Driven Key dialog box, and then test the Happy attribute.

4  Set Happy back to 0. Set Shock up to 10 in the Channel Box, and select Shock in Set Driven Key. Remember that moving the timeline back to 0 will pop the joints back to their default position.

5  Adjust the face joints so that Kila appears shocked (**Figure 13.26b**), and set a key to store this pose.

6  In Set Driven Key, select Angry next. Then set the Shock attribute back to 0, and Angry to 10.

7  Give Kila an angry-looking face like the one in **Figure 13.26c**. Press Key in Set Driven Key to store it in the Angry attribute.

8  Finally, set Angry back to 0 and Injured to 10, and then select Injured in Set Driven Key.

9  Give Kila a face expressing that she has just been hurt and is about to cry (**Figure 13.26d**). Set a key to store it.

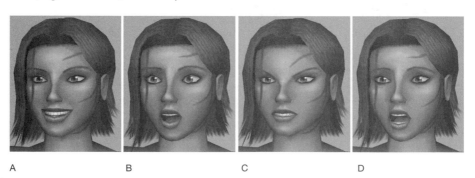

A          B          C          D

**FIGURE 13.26** The four main face poses: Happy, Shocked, Angry, and Injured

Setting these poses means we can quickly give her face movement and the ability to express emotion.

### Rig Creation, Mouth Shapes

Using Set Driven Key again, let's connect up a set of attributes that will make Kila talk.

You should still have the Set Driven Key dialog box open; if it's not, reopen it. Reload HeadControls into the Driver section.

**1**  You will only be controlling the mouth area, so reload just the jaw, lips, and tongue joints into the Driven section. Select the rotation as well as the translation attributes in the list on the right.

Work your way down this section of attributes, starting with O and ending with Frown, setting a key on each one to store the default pose.

**2**  Select O again in Set Driven Key, and set the same attribute to 10.

Now adjust the joints of the mouth to make her look like she is saying the letter O (**Figure 13.27a**).

> **TIP** Try to exaggerate the mouth shapes slightly when you create them. This will give the animators a bit more flexibility when they are doing lip-synching.

**3**  Set O back to 0, and set the attribute named CDENSZ up to its maximum of 10.

Our mouth shape is similar when we say any of the letters *C, D, E, N, S* or *Z*, so we can combine them into a single attribute for Kila. Adjust the mouth as seen in **Figure 13.27b**. Make sure CDENSZ is selected in Set Driven Key, and then set a key.

**4**  Next up is AKI. Set this to 10, remembering to reset the CDENSZ attribute to 0.

As you did for CDENSZ, pose the mouth so she is saying the letter *A, K,* or *I* (**Figure 13.27c**). This is quite similar to the CDENSZ mouth shape, but the mouth is open slightly more. Then select the AKI attribute and set a key.

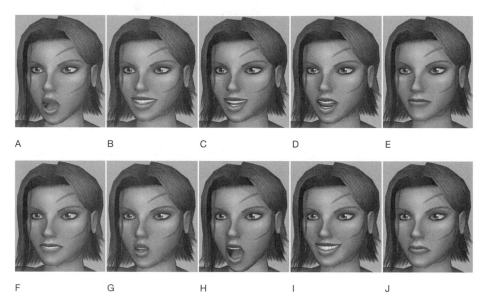

A    B    C    D    E

F    G    H    I    J

**FIGURE 13.27** Kila's mouth shapes

**5**  The L pose is next (**Figure 13.27d**). Set the L attribute to 10 and the AKI attribute to 0. Pose the mouth, this time remembering to pose the tongue under the upper teeth. Then store the pose by setting a key on the L attribute in Set Driven Key.

**6**  Set MPB to 10 and reset L back to 0.

You could just use the default pose to get the look of *M, P,* or *B,* but as you can see in **Figure 13.27e**, creating a pose where the lips are closed tighter will emphasize the shape. When you're done, set a key on the MPB attribute in Set Driven Key.

**7**  Next is FV. For this shape we want to tuck the lower lip under the upper teeth (**Figure 13.27f**). First set up the attributes by setting FV to 10 and MPB back to 0. Pose the mouth and, with FV selected in Set Driven Key, set a key.

**8**  Next set Ooo to 10 and FV to 0. Pushing the lips forward and together slightly will give us the Ooo shape seen in **Figure 13.27g**. Set the key for Ooo in Set Driven Key.

**9** For Ahh, you want just a general open-mouth shape. Manipulate the jaw joint and then position the outer lip joints so you end up with a mouth like the one in **Figure 13.27h**. When you're done, set the key.

**10** Kila won't be miserable all the time, so you need to make her smile. Set the Smile attribute to 10 and reset the Ahh attribute to 0. Give her a lovely big smile as in **Figure 13.27i**, and set a key on the attribute.

**11** Finally, implement the Frown. Set Frown to 10 and Smile back to 0. Then adjust the joints to make her look sad (**Figure 13.27j**), and set a key on the Frown attribute.

The principal shapes for the mouth are now set up and ready to be animated. Because we're using joints, we're not restricted in the number of poses we create for this element, so feel free to make more if your character needs them. You might want to assign more options to the tongue, allowing her to stick it out or something similar, but only add what will actually be used. It's a good idea to consult with your manager to make sure vital expressions are covered, but a conversation with the animator is also important at this point. There may be some mouth shapes needed for quick lip-synching.

**Rig Creation, Eyebrows and Eyelids**
The final facial areas we will rig are Kila's eyelids and eyebrows. These are key areas in expressing emotions, so it's crucial that we add the ability to animate them quickly and easily.

You should be getting the hang of setting driven keys by now, so in the procedures from this point on we can safely leave out some of the details.

**1** With the Set Driven Key dialog box open, make sure HeadControls is loaded into the Driver section, and that the four main eyebrow joints are loaded into the Driven section.

We first need to store each joint's default position, but each eyebrow attribute should only affect one joint, so we will need to work on the joints individually.

**2** As demonstrated in **Figure 13.28**, select LeftInnerBrow next to HeadControls, and then all the translations and rotations next to L_InnerBrow. Set a key.

Do the same for the other three Brow attributes, making sure you have only the corresponding joint selected in the Driven section.

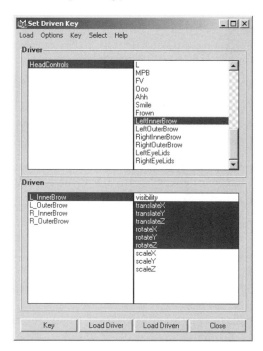

**FIGURE 13.28** Select a single attribute and a single joint and set a key.

With the base pose keyed, we can now define the extremes these joints can move to.

**3** First set the four eyebrow attributes to 10; then adjust each eyebrow joint so they are raised as far as they can go (**Figure 13.29**, middle).

**4** When you are satisfied with the pose, store it in the Set Driven Key dialog box. Do this by going through each individual attribute on the HeadControls icon and setting a key on the joint it will control. *Don't* select all four joints at the same time.

**5** Now set the attributes to -10 so that we can define the lowest point to which the eyebrows will go. Move the joints so that the eyebrows are like those in

**Figure 13.29**, right, and set a key on each—one attribute to one joint—in Set Driven Key.

FIGURE 13.29 Key both extremes for the eyebrows.

Now rig the eyes.

1    With Set Driven Key open and Head Controls loaded in the Driver section, load all four eyelid joints into the Driven section.

2    Select the LeftEyeLids attribute in the Driver section, and then all the rotations and translations for L_UpperLid and L_LowerLid in the Driven section (**Figure 13.30**). Set a key to store the default pose.

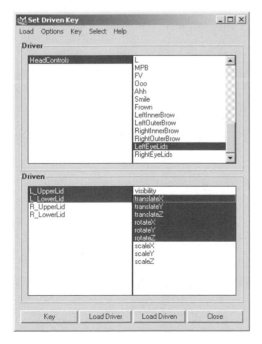

FIGURE 13.30 Select the joints and attributes associated with the left eyelids.

**3** Store the default pose for the right eyelids, selecting RightEyeLids and then the R_UpperLid and R_LowerLid joints.

**4** Now work on closing her eyes, as shown in **Figure 13.31**, left. Start by setting the LeftEyeLids and RightEyeLids attribute to –10.

**5** Close the eyes by rotating both the upper lid joints around the X axis so that they cover most of the eyeball. Then rotate the lower lids up to meet them.

**6** Before you set a key to store the pose, translate all four joints out along the Z axis so that the eyeballs don't pop through the lids.

**7** Follow the same procedure for storing the default pose (steps 2 and 3) to store this one.

**8** Now we will widen her eyes. This time set the LeftEyeLids and RightEyeLids attribute to 10, which will reset the eyelids for us. Then, rotating around the X axis, open her eyes wider (**Figure 13.31**, middle). Store the pose in Set Driven Key.

Kila's facial rig is complete now. Not only can she open and close her eyes, but she can also open each eye independently (**Figure 13.31**, right). Save the scene as Kila_FaceRig_Jnt.mb.

FIGURE 13.31 Rig the eyelids so she can open and close both eyes or either eye.

This completes the tasks of this section. With the facial rig you've constructed, Kila can communicate with the player. If you'd like to, you can add further controls to the joints to allow extra manipulation of her lips and jaw (as I have in the Kila_FaceRig_Jnt.mb file on the CD).

Let's now explore the other method for creating facial movement: blend shapes.

## Blend Shapes Facial Animation Setup (Kila)

Blend shapes work by referencing the vertices from a duplicate of the main mesh. The duplicated vertices are edited to create a facial expression into which the main head will morph on command. Suppose the duplicate face is edited to represent an open mouth. Using the Blend Shape window, you can then tell the main face to gradually morph into the duplicate, making the character's mouth open and close.

Depending on the system for which you are developing, the number of available blend shapes might be restricted, so always check with your manager first. Work with as few blend shapes as possible. In this section, we will work with just a few basic shapes, and you can add more if you have the budget to do so.

Our first step is to prepare the geometry.

### Preparation for Blend Shapes

Open up the file called Kila_MainRig.mb and turn off visibility for all the icons. We can't use the geometry in its current state for our work with blend shapes, so (as we did with the joint rig) we need to combine all the separate elements of Kila into one object.

With the first LOD combined into a single element, we could duplicate the whole figure and use that as our morph target, but that would be a huge waste of memory and processing power because we only need to alter her face. So we will separate her face from the rest of the body, and then combine the rest. In effect, there will be two separate mesh objects.

1   Switch to the side view and hide her hair, as seen in **Figure 13.32**, left.

2   Following **Figure 13.32**, middle, select the faces that make up her principal face area, as well as the ones under her jaw (these will move as she opens her mouth).

3   With these faces selected, go to Edit Polygons > Extract. This separates the face from the body (**Figure 13.32**, right).

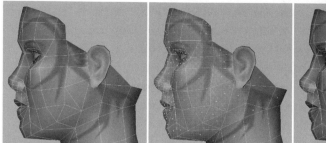
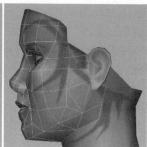

**FIGURE 13.32** Extract Kila's face.

4   Because the eyelashes, inner mouth, teeth, and tongue will move as the face moves, you need to combine them with the face's geometry. (This can be done much more easily in perspective view.) Select all these elements, and go to Polygons > Combine to combine them.

> **NOTE** When blend shapes morph from one shape to another, the vertices follow a linear path. This won't work for elements that rotate, so we'll leave the eyeballs with the main body, controlling them with joints instead.

5   Now you need to weld all the duplicate vertices that lie in the same place; this stops the mesh from tearing as it moves. Select all the vertices of the combined face, and go to Edit Polygons > Merge Vertices and set the value to a small number (say, 0.0001).

Double-check that coincident vertices are indeed merged and that areas with deliberately small gaps (like the mouth) were not inadvertently merged.

6   Center the pivot for the face (Modify > Center Pivot). This will make it easier to manipulate later.

7   The face is now its own object and perfect for creating Kila's blend shapes. Delete the history on both the separated face and body geometry.

8   Unhide the hair; then combine all the other pieces that make up her body, including the eyes and belt. You could at this stage hide the face to make this step easier.

9   Weld the vertices around the ear and hairline with a small value like 0.0001.

10   Finally, delete the history on the body.

The mesh is now ready for generating face shapes. Move the geometry for both the face and the body back inside the Kila4095 folder in the Outliner. Then rename the body to KilaBody and the face to KilaFace. Save the file as Kila_ Combined.mb.

With the face detached and the rest of the body combined, we can start to build up our library of face shapes.

### Generating Face Shapes

Creating blend shapes is a simple task involving nothing more than editing vertices. The faces we create will essentially be the same as the poses we generated for the joint-based facial rig.

To start, we will generate the Ahh shape so that we can test the mouth before continuing on to create shapes that will animate the eyelids and eyebrows. We will then create the O, L, MPB, FV, Ooo, Smile, and Frown shapes. You will notice that, unlike the joint-based facial setup, we don't create face shapes for CDENSZ and AKI. Since we are limited in the overall number of blend shapes we can use, we will use the Ahh and Smile shapes together to create CDENSZ and AKI. Efficiency is also called for in the creation of some base facial poses, including Shock, Angry, or Happy. These can all be done via the other basic shapes.

> **NOTE** It's important that the geometry is fully tested and complete before you create the blend shapes. If the topology is altered in any way afterward, they will have to be redone. Each vertex is assigned a number in Maya, and blend shapes work with these numbers. Altering the topology means altering the vertex numbers, so the face shapes will no longer work. You can still flip and edit edges, as that doesn't affect vertex numbers.

> **TIP** Do not freeze the transforms on any of the face shapes. The vertices work on a relative basis, so all transforms should remain intact. If not, when you blend the main face to one of the others, the whole face will move to its target.

Let's create the Ahh shape.

**1** Duplicate the face and move it over to the left of the main model. Name this copy Ahh.

**2** Hide the main model. Then, following **Figure 13.33**, left, select all the vertices that make up the bottom jaw, teeth, and tongue, but *not* the vertices that lie on the edges of the model.

**3** Press E to switch to the Rotate manipulator; then press Insert and move the pivot point to the spot from which the jaw will rotate. You can see this in **Figure 13.33**, middle.

**4** Rotate the jaw around the X axis so that the mouth is open (**Figure 13.33**, right).

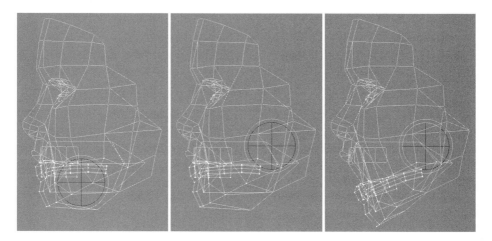

**FIGURE 13.33** Rotate the vertices of the jaw.

**5** As you can see in **Figure 13.34**, left, the mouth doesn't look right yet. Spend some time editing the vertices on the head to sculpt the shape of the mouth (**Figure 13.34**, right).

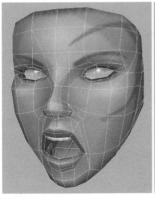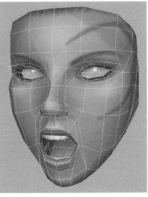

**FIGURE 13.34** Sculpt the vertices to fix the mouth area.

The first mouth shape is complete and we haven't noticed any problems. One good feature of blend shapes is that, even after they have been applied to the main model, you can still tweak the vertices to get the shape just right.

We'll do the eyebrows next, and learn a technique of creating two face shapes from one.

1   Duplicate the main face again, and this time call it LeftBrowUp. Position it to the left of the Ahh face shape.

2   Edit the vertices, this time to raise both eyebrows as shown in **Figure 13.35**.

> **TIP** To save time, select the same vertices on each side of the face. This way, when you move them, both sides will be exactly the same.

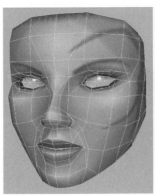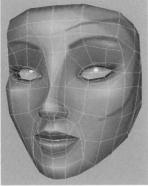

**FIGURE 13.35** Adjust the vertices to raise both eyebrows.

This shape is acceptable for moving both eyebrows at the same time, but we want Kila to be able to move them individually, as well.

3  Duplicate this face, calling it RightBrowUp, and move the copy over to the left (**Figure 13.36a**).

4  On LeftBrowUp, select all the vertices you edited on Kila's right side (**Figure 13.36b**).

5  Look in the Channel Box, and you'll see a new heading labeled "CVs (click to show)," as seen in **Figure 13.37**, left. Click on this heading to reveal all the selected vertices, plus their current positions relative to the face's default pose (**Figure 13.37**, right).

6  Select all the coordinates and set them to 0. This resets the selected vertices back to their default positions (**Figure 13.36c**).

7  Select the central vertices (**Figure 13.36d**), and in the Channel Box set them to be half of their current values.

Why are we setting the central vertices to half? Each blend shape works relatively; that is, the vertex positions are added to any that are already applied. So if the left eyebrow and right eyebrow shapes fully affected the central vertices on the head, when both shapes were applied these vertices would move double the distance.

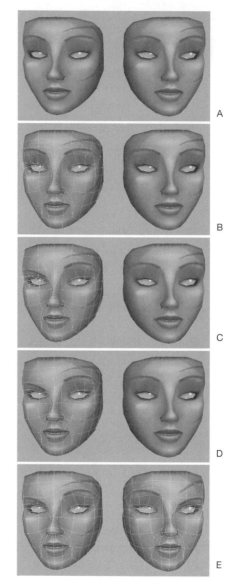

A

B

C

D

E

**FIGURE 13.36** Use the Channel Box to reset the eyebrows.

So when we set vertices that may need to share their values to move half the amount for each eyebrow, it means that when both are applied at the same time, the central vertices won't move too far up. They'll wind up where you actually want them to be.

**8**  On the RightBrowUp model, reset the vertices on its left and center (**Figure 13.36e**), just as you did for LeftBrowUp.

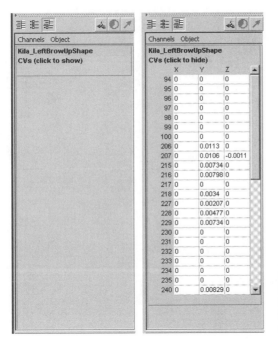

**FIGURE 13.37**
Reset the values in the Channel Box to return the vertices to their default positions.

The technique you've just used is a quick and easy way to get two shapes out of one; plus, you will know that each side will be the same. It may be that you don't want the face to be symmetrical, which is fine, but this way you get a good starting point from which you can tweak later.

Go ahead and create the rest of the face shapes needed, by simply duplicating the main head and editing the vertices. You should have the following:

▶  Both the left and right eyebrows, lowered.

▶  Both individual eyelids opening wider and closing.

▶  The remaining facial shapes L, MPB, FV, Ooo, Smile, and Frown.

**TIP** For the eyelids, you will need to use the shape of the eyes as a guide, so keep the duplicated head in its default position until you are happy with the eyelid shape.

You can see all of these shapes in **Figure 13.38**. These represent a good initial group of face shapes for a character. If your budget allows, you can add more to get more refined manipulation of the face.

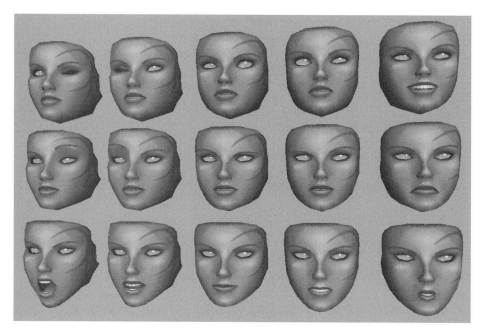

FIGURE 13.38 Blend shapes for Kila's face

With the entire library of face shapes complete, we can now apply them to our main model.

## Blend Shape Application

The geometry shapes are ready, so now we can connect them to the main face model, allowing us to morph the face into any of the new shapes.

**1**   Select all the face shapes, adding Kila's main face to the selection last.

**2**   Go to Deform > Create Blend Shape, and set the options seen in **Figure 13.39**.

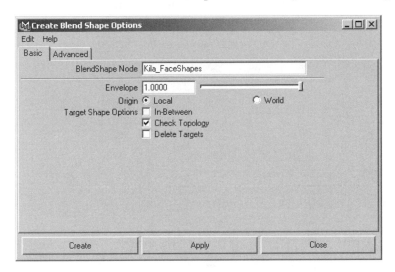

FIGURE 13.39 Create Blend Shape options

**3**   We will use the default options, so just set BlendShape Node to Kila_ FaceShapes; this defines the name for the actual blend shape controller.

**4**   Click on Create to create the blend shape controller.

To animate the blend shapes, go to Window > Animation Editors > Blend Shape, which opens up the window shown in **Figure 13.40**, left. Moving the sliders will animate the main face, morphing it into its target shape. Pressing Select will select the node, enabling you to animate it via the Channel Box (**Figure 13.40**, right).

**NOTE** You can change the orientation of the sliders by going to Options > Orientation and selecting either Horizontal or Vertical. Vertical is the default view.

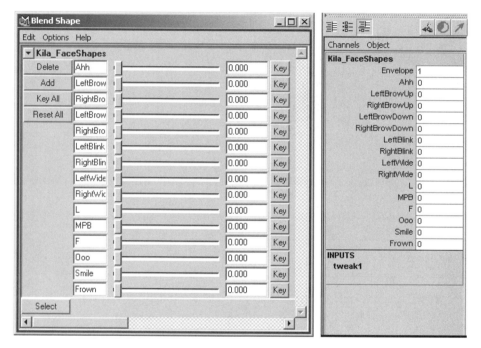

FIGURE 13.40 The Blend Shape window

Now that the blend shapes are set up, take some time to edit each face, tweaking the vertices until you are satisfied with the final shapes.

Place all the face shapes in a new group called Bshapes; then move this node so it is under the Kila4095 group.

Create a new display layer called BlendShapes, add the BShapes group to it, and save your scene as Kila_FaceRig_BS.mb.

> **TIP** ▶ Once the face shapes have been applied to the main face, you can delete them. However, I recommend keeping them in the scene for as long as you can. This allows you to easily edit them if you need to.

The animator will quite happily use the Blend Shape window to animate the character. If you like, though, you could use Set Driven Key to tie the blend shapes into the main head controller, as you did with the joint setup.

### Facial Animation and LODs

You have now worked through two approaches to facial animation on Kila, but what about the LODs? Giving a character the ability to be seen talking might be unnecessary at a distance, but you may need it for the next level of detail.

For the joint-based face, all the hard work has already been done. Because all the animation is applied via the joints, we can simply bind the lower LODs and then copy the weighting information across. We will be covering this process in Chapter 14.

The blend shapes, however, will need further work in terms of LODs. These shapes reference a copy of the face's geometry, so we will need to create the required blend shapes for all the LODs. This might seem a daunting task, but getting organized ahead of time will help. Before you start, consider what will actually be seen at that distance and what the geometry will allow. Dolly out until Kila is just about to switch to her next LOD; then use the Blend Shape window to see what face shapes are visible and actually distinguishable.

Certainly at this distance you can see that her mouth is open or closed, her eyebrows are raised or lowered, and her eyes are open or closed. The smile is clearly visible, but the rest of the mouth shapes can hardly be seen, so it wouldn't be advisable to re-create these for the lower LOD.

With the blend shapes created and applied, you can use the Connection Editor to connect the lower-LOD blend shape nodes' attributes to the higher ones. When you animate the highest LOD, the lower ones will follow; that means you and the animator don't need to animate each individual LOD.

## Grae's Facial Animation

Now that we have some experience working with the two main styles of facial animation, it's time to take a brief look at Grae.

Whichever animation method you choose, rigging Grae's face will be simpler than doing Kila's, mainly because he does not speak. Nevertheless, his jaw will need some slight movement, as will his upper lips. So we'll do some rigging for these, in addition to his eyes and eyebrows.

When it comes to rigging the joint-based face, you can skip most of the attributes we included for Kila. Just use JawOpen to control how the mouth opens, and add JawSlide to enable the jaw to move left and right as he grinds his teeth. Add some poses for his tongue, too; you should be able to see it moving because his mouth can open quite wide.

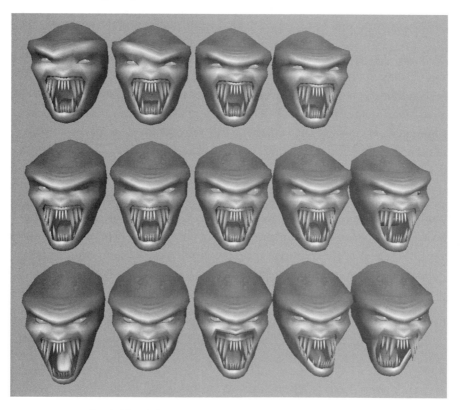

**FIGURE 13.41** Grae's blend shapes

For the lips, create a LeftUpperLip and RightUpperLip attribute, and connect them to the upper lip joints. These will enable the animator to make him snarl.

In addition, you can copy Kila's final six attributes: LeftInnerBrow, LeftOuterBrow, RightInnerBrow, RightOuterBrow, LeftEyeLids, and RightEyeLids.

For Grae's blend-shape animation version, stick to more or less the same face shapes as Kila's, which can be seen in **Figure 13.41**.

## Which Is Best?

Now that we have explored both ways of generating facial animation in game characters, let's have a look at the issues, pros, and cons for both methods.

▶ The big question concerns which version the game engine, or indeed the target platform, can handle. Chances are any one of them could use joints, since they will already be doing so to move the character around. You may even find that blend shapes are not eligible and need not be considered.

▶ The way each type of animation works and looks can be drastically affected by your budget. Having too few joints, or too few blend shapes, will make the face look stiff. The freedom to include all the joints needed would allow you room to create an almost limitless number of facial poses and movements. With blend shapes, each new face would add to the overall size of the character in memory, so eventually you could reach your limit. Even so, this can be overcome through clever use of your shapes; you can mix existing ones to create new ones.

▶ The initial setup of the joint-based face rig can be quite cumbersome and tricky, since you're having to use Set Driven Key to store each pose and area of movement. However, once they are complete, redoing them shouldn't be necessary, even if the character's topology is changed.

The blend shapes setup is simpler but does rely heavily on the main face's geometry being locked. Any alteration in the facial topology could result in your having to redo all the existing blend shapes.

▶ With the joint setup, you can't get the facial expressions vertex-perfect, because each vertex's position is merely influenced by the joints. With blend shapes, on the other hand, you are physically sculpting each face, allowing you to get each pose perfect.

If you are lucky enough to be able to choose either method, it will come down to your own preference or style of working.

## Summary

This chapter's discussion of the use of joints and morph targets to achieve facial animation will help you decide which one you prefer and which is appropriate for your project. Next, we will move to the chapter on the final binding—attaching our characters' geometry to their skeletons and then adjusting the weighting information to enable correct deformation.

**CD Files**

Kila_FaceRig_BS.mb
Kila_FaceRig_Jnt.mb
Kila_Bound_BS.mb
Kila_Skinned.mb
Grae_FaceRig_BS.mb
Grae_FaceRig_Jnt.mb
Grae_Bound_BS.mb
Grae_Skinned.mb
KilaBody.tga
KilaHair.tga
KilaHead.tga
GraeBody.tga
GraeMisc.tga
GraeWing.tga
GraeBody_Bump.tga
GraeMisc_Bump.tga
GraeBody_Spec.tga
GraeMisc_Spec.tga

# CHAPTER 14
# Final Character Deformation

**WE HAVE A MODEL** and a rig for both Kila and Grae, and now we need to connect the rigs to the models so that one will drive the other. We'll do that here in this chapter, using techniques already discussed: mesh binding and painting weights. You've worked with these techniques in Chapter 6 and extensively in Chapter 13, so you should be well acquainted with using them.

## Preparation and Binding

Before we can test our completed characters' deformations, we need to prepare the geometry and bind it to the skeleton. If you followed the joint-based facial setup in Chapter 13, your geometry is already bound to the skeleton, so feel free to skip along to the next section. If, on the other hand, you are using the blend shape method, follow the instructions here for attaching the mesh to the base skeleton. This will drive the characters' movement, deforming the mesh so that the character can achieve poses and, ultimately, animate.

Load the file called Kila_FaceRig_BS.mb, (or Grae_FaceRig_BS.mb if you are working on him). The geometry for the first LOD is already prepared—in Chapter 13 we combined it into a single mesh and cleaned it up, so it is ready for final weighting. The face and body must remain separate because blend shapes manipulate iterations of all the vertices of Kila's face, allowing her to talk.

**1**   In the Outliner, navigate to the first joint of the base skeleton, called Root. Select it and open up the hierarchy.

**2**   Go to Edit > Select Hierarchy to select all the objects beneath Root.

**3**   Although we have the skeleton hierarchy selected, there are some joints we don't want to bind. Scroll down the Outliner and, holding Ctrl/Cmd, deselect all the joints that end with _Tip. These are only here as visual aids; they do not deform the character.

Also, make sure no icons or other nodes are selected, we want only the joints to deform the mesh when moved.

**4**   With the correct joints selected, hold Shift and add the KilaBody mesh to the selection.

**5**   Go to Skin > Bind Skin > Smooth Bind and open the options. For Bind To, choose Selected Joints; for Bind Method, choose Closest Joint; and set Max Influences to 3 and Dropoff Rate to 4.

**6**   Click on Bind Skin; the body geometry is now attached to the base skeleton.

> **NOTE**   Alternatively, you can select just the body geometry and press the Bind button on the GCDM shelf. Provided that the base joint is called Root, this button will automatically select the proper joints and bind the mesh to them.

We now have to attach her face in a slightly different way. Because in this case the vertices of her face are controlled via blend shapes, certain game engines will have trouble if the vertices are also controlled by a number of joints. As far as I am aware, this conflict is due to the game engine's having to handle two types of deformation at the same time: It can be quite processor intensive, so using just one method is preferred. However, we still need the head to move with the skeleton, so it will have to be affected by one joint (the head joint). Sometimes simply parenting the face geometry to the head joint will suffice, but you can also bind it, and making sure it is only influenced by the head joint will certainly please the programmers.

For either method, binding or linking, all of the face vertices will essentially be controlled 100 percent by the head joint alone. With that in mind, it's crucial to also make sure that all vertices bordering the face mesh are also 100 percent bound to this same joint. If not, the mesh will break apart at those seams during posing and animation.

> **NOTE** It's a good idea to talk through this issue with your team's lead programmer, who may have specific ideas on how it should be handled.

**1** Select the main head joint, called Head.

**2** Holding Shift, select the face geometry.

**3** Go to Skin > Bind Skin > Smooth Bind, and set Bind To to Selected Joints, and Bind Method to Closest Joint. Set both Max Influences and Dropoff Rate to 1, which will fully weight the face to the Head joint. We don't need to do any more work on it.

**4** Save the file as Kila_Bound_BS.mb.

Both the blend-shapes and joint-based versions of our characters are now at exactly the same stage. This means we only need to edit the weighting information on their bodies, because the joint-based faces were completed in Chapter 13. So we will just look at the joint-based version. The same weight-painting techniques can easily be applied to the blend-shapes version if need be.

## Painting Kila's Weights

In Chapter 6, we used weight painting briefly to get an idea of how the geometry would deform. Now we will be applying the final weights, so we have to make sure all areas of her body move correctly.

We will concentrate on her left side, and then copy the weights across to the right when we are done.

Load the file Kila_FaceRig_Jnt.mb and we will start work on her arms.

### Arm Weights

The arms are probably the most important area to weight correctly. They are always in motion and can move dramatically in all directions, which unfortunately will show off any badly weighted areas.

#### *Shoulders*

The shoulder is capable of moving around in all three axes. Not only does it raise and lower, it can move forward and backward, and also twist. Obviously, depending on what your own character's primary actions will be, some of these poses will be more important than others.

Let's first look at the shoulder as it is raised and lowered.

1   Using the visibility icon, turn off the middle and right icons so that we can concentrate on her left side.

2   Focus in on her left arm; rotate the shoulder down and look at how the mesh deforms when it's in this rest position.

    As you can see in **Figure 14.1**, the area under her arm moves into her torso, which we don't want it to do.

3   Select the geometry itself. Then go to Skin > Edit Smooth Skin > Paint Skin Weights Tool and open up the options. Set Value to 0 and Opacity to 1, and in the Influence pane make sure you have L_Shoulder selected.

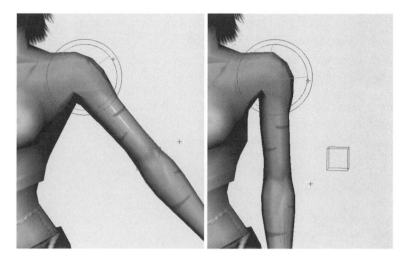

FIGURE 14.1 Lower the arm by rotating the shoulder.

> **TIP** > If you need to see the actual texture of the model while you edit the weights, open the Display pane found in the Paint Skin Weights window and uncheck Color Feedback. In some instances, the actual texture will play a part in disguising some of the pinching as the character deforms, so it's good to keep checking the textured version of your model, too.

4    As demonstrated in **Figure 14.2**, right, paint just under her arm, doing the front of the torso as well as the back. Also paint above the shoulder, removing the influence the shoulder has over this area.

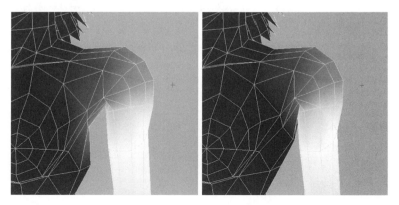

FIGURE 14.2 Remove the shoulder's influence from the torso.

5    Select Smooth as the Paint Operation. With a softer brush, edit the shoulder itself, smoothing it out and rounding it off. Using Smooth will average out the distances between each vertex, adding a subtle change to the weighting values but smoothing the overall shoulder as it deforms.

6    Rotate the arm as shown in **Figure 14.3**, so it is almost horizontal. (If you raise your own arm, you will notice that it will not rotate above this level; it is your clavicle that takes over and raises the arm further.)

Check to see how the shoulder and armpit areas look. You may need to smooth the armpit slightly but other than that it should look fine.

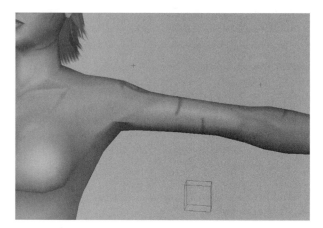

**FIGURE 14.3** Raise the arm so it is horizontal.

Now let's examine the shoulder as it rotates forward and backward. With the arm still in its horizontal position, rotate it forward around the Y axis (**Figure 14.4**). As you can see, we have some severe pinching that needs attention.

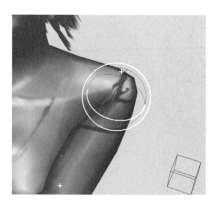

**FIGURE 14.4** Rotate the arm forward around the Y axis.

1   Reduce Brush Opacity down to around 0.15, and keep Paint Weights Value
    at 1. Using either Replace or Add, try and tweak the weights around the
    shoulder to minimize the pinch (**Figure 14.5**). You won't be able to remove
    it completely; just try to make it less obvious.

FIGURE 14.5 Tweak the weights to reduce the pinch.

2   Reset the arm back to its default position; you can do this quickly by setting
    the shoulder rotations to 0, 0, 0 or right-clicking on the selection handle and
    selecting Assume Preferred Angle. Now rotate the arm forward, making the
    geometry deform in a different way.

    Edit the pinching as needed.

3   Now test how the shoulder looks when the arm is bent backward. Again
    here, the arm has limited movement when rotated backward from a raised
    position.

## Manual Assignments Using the Component Editor

If you are having trouble editing the weights on a particular area, you can go in and manually assign certain joints to affect certain vertices and by a certain amount, on a per-vertex level. To do this:

**1** Select the character model and go to Window > General Editors > Component Editor (**Figure 14.6**, top).

**2** Select a vertex from the character model, and then select the Smooth Skins tab in the Component editor (**Figure 14.6**, bottom).

At the left of the window, you will see all the vertices you have selected (listed vertically). In this case, we have vtx[1816], which is vertex number 1816. All the joints that have influence over it are listed across horizontally. You can scroll over and assign each joint's influence over that vertex; 0 is no influence, and 1 is the maximum influence.

Although this method does allow you to be more accurate with the weight assignments, keep in mind that going through every vertex on your character can become quite tedious.

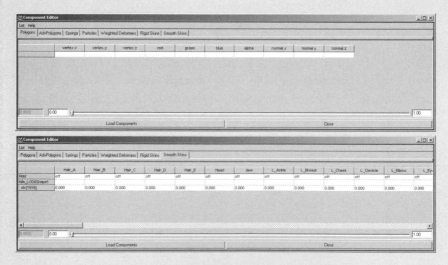

FIGURE 14.6 Making manual assignments in the Component Editor

With the first two rotations fixed, we can now test the twist, which is the rotation of the arm around the X axis.

The problem we get to now is one of priority. If we remove some of the shoulder's influence from the shoulder joint to make this pose look good, another pose will look wrong because the weights are then different. We wind up continually altering weights to fix one pose and then having to redo weights on another.

What you have to do is decide which poses the arm will be in for the majority of the time and concentrate on these. For the others, you can get away with the odd pinch or crease because these poses are not seen very often.

> **TIP** The character's texture can play a role in disguising areas that don't deform well. Using darker areas will hide any pinching in the geometry; areas that are lighter or include lots of detail serve to highlight creases and areas that stretch.

The twist pose will be the lowest priority for Kila, so let's see how it looks.

**1** Put the arm back into its default pose and, following **Figure 14.7**, rotate it forward around the X axis. Try to match your own arm's boundaries when it's rotated like this.

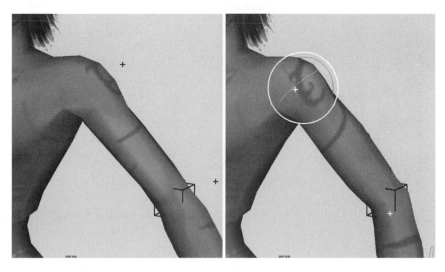

**FIGURE 14.7** Rotate the arm forward around the X axis.

**2** Judging by how things look in **Figure 14.8**, the front and back are acceptable. This is a low-priority pose, so we can leave it as is.

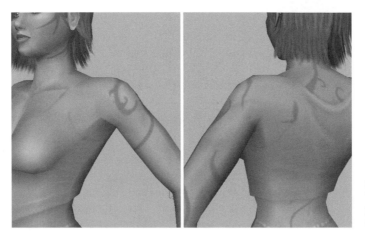

FIGURE 14.8
The shoulder
looks fine with
this rotation.

**3** Next, rotate the shoulder the other way around the X axis. As you can see in **Figure 14.9**, this time the back looks fine but we have a nasty crease at the front.

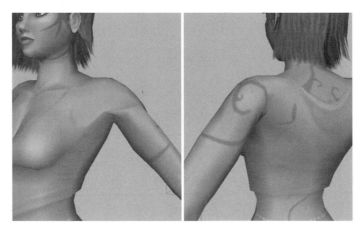

FIGURE 14.9
Rotated the
other way,
the shoul-
der shows a
crease at the
front.

**4** To reduce this crease, first smooth the weights around it. Don't get carried away, though; this smoothing will affect the shoulder when it adopts other poses.

**5**    Notice that the edge highlighted in **Figure 14.10**, middle, is the major cause of the crease: It is flipped the wrong way. Select this and delete it; then delete the same edge on the opposite shoulder.

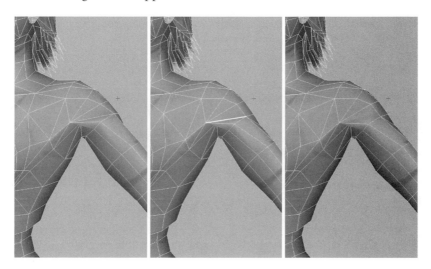

FIGURE 14.10 Smooth out the weights and delete the offending edge.

Now the shoulder should look pretty good in the major poses. Before you move on to the elbow, rotate the shoulder around and double-check all the weighting.

### Elbows

The elbow is slightly easier than the shoulder to weight because it only rotates around one axis.

**1**    Raise the arm to make the elbow easier to edit. Then rotate the elbow joint around the Y axis (**Figure 14.11**).

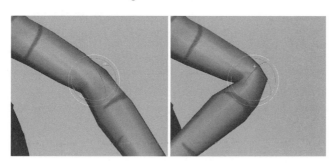

FIGURE 14.11
Raise the arm, and rotate the elbow around the Y axis.

**2**   Set the vertices below the elbow (**Figure 14.12a**) to be fully influenced by the elbow. Next, set the Paint Weights Value to 0 and paint on the vertices above the elbow (**Figure 14.12b**), removing its influence.

**3**   Now set Value to 1 and Brush Opacity to 0.10. With a soft brush, work on the elbow area, filling out the pinch that currently exists.

You can see the final elbow in **Figures 14.12c** and **14.12d**.

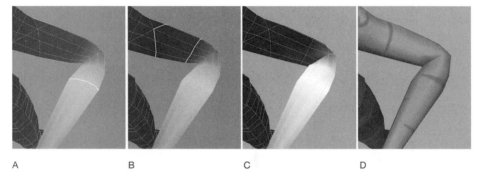

A            B            C            D

FIGURE 14.12 Adjust the weighting on her elbow.

> **NOTE**  It's important to realize that you will not get every joint to deform realistically. We are limited to the geometry and the skeleton that we use to deform it, so all we can do is work toward the best possible result. With joint and polygon restrictions, you won't get the character to deform perfectly in all situations.

### Wrist

We've arrived at the wrist. Like the shoulder, it needs all degrees of freedom weighted correctly, but here the weight painting is pretty straightforward.

Again we have to think about priority when working on the wrist. We can achieve a good bend when the wrist rotates around the Y axis or Z axis, but this is at the sacrifice of the X rotation, which makes the wrist twist. Think about what actions your character is most likely to do more—if they are holding weapons, the Y and Z rotations will more likely take priority; but if the character's actions cause the wrist to twist a lot, then the X rotation will have to offer better deformation.

First, rotate the wrist around the Y and X axes to see how it deforms. You will no doubt notice that the geometry moves with the action in a way that makes the wrist appear to bend unnaturally. This is because the weights are evenly distributed between the forearm and wrist joints. We now need to lock some of these weights down.

**1**    Select the mesh and open the Paint Skin Weights window. Set Opacity to 1 and Value to 0, and select L_Wrist in the Influence pane.

**2**    Paint the vertices just above the wrist, removing the wrist joint's influence (**Figure 14.13**, middle). Then make sure the vertices immediately below the wrist are fully weighted to it (**Figure 14.13**, right).

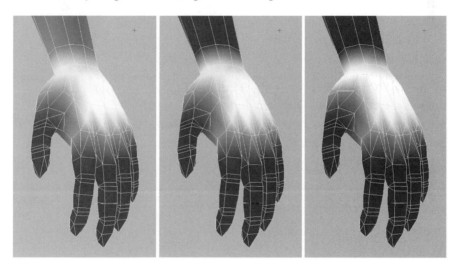

FIGURE 14.13 Change the priorities of the weighting around her wrist.

Now the hand will move quite nicely up and down, left and right—but look at what happens when you twist it (**Figure 14.14**). You get quite a bad deformation around the wrist area.

In a real arm, the wrist doesn't actually twist around the wrist joint. Instead, it's the ulna and radius bones in our forearm that twist around each other, making the hand seem to rotate. To implement this properly into our character would involve adding an extra joint halfway up the forearm; we didn't include this in our rig because we required a simpler setup.

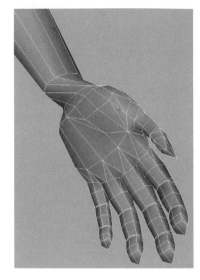

**FIGURE 14.14** The wrist deforms badly when twisted.

Many studio's add gloves or long sleeves to their character designs, which can disguise the twist of the wrist. This usually works well, because the hand is essentially detached from the arm and the wrist is hidden beneath the sleeve or glove.

The only solution we have is to continue to pose the hand and edit the weights until we reach a satisfactory result. So let's leave the wrist as is and look at what we can do with the hand and fingers.

## Hand Weights

We will skip the main palm area until the fingers are done, since these are more important to get right. After the main finger weights in place, we can then go in and make any minor alterations to the palm.

If the geometry making up the fingers doesn't deform correctly, the hands will not work visually. The best approach is to work on the fingers one at a time.

1   Select the icon for the index finger. Set the Proximal_Pitch, Middle_Pitch, and Distil_Pitch to 5.

   With a single finger bent, you can now see how the weights have been distributed. As you can see in **Figures 14.15a** and **14.15b**, the index finger's joints are affecting the middle finger's geometry.

**2** Paint the main area of this section of finger so it is fully influenced by the joint (**Figure 14.15c**), and remove any influence it has over any neighboring fingers. Do this by reducing Paint Weights Value to 0 for this task.

Then change Value to 0.5 and paint over the vertices that lie down the middle of the knuckle, making it half influence both sections of the finger.

**3** Move to the next joint, L_Index_B, and repeat step 2. Fully weight the section to the joint, while removing any outside influence. Then make the center knuckle vertices influenced by both the L_Index_A and L_Index_B joints.

**4** Now work on the tip of the finger. Weight it fully to the L_Index_C joint, removing any influence it has over the middle finger.

**5** To finish, set Opacity to a smaller value, select a soft brush, and work on the base of the digit, underneath where it meets the palm. Try to get the finger to pinch less as it bends.

As shown in **Figure 14.15d**, the main finger is now weighted correctly.

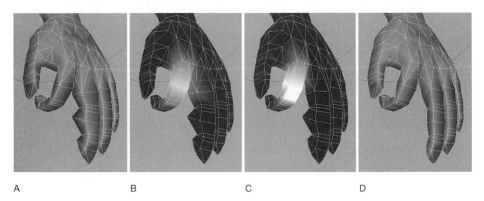

A          B          C          D

**FIGURE 14.15** Paint the individual sections of the finger.

Repeat these steps for the other three fingers and the thumb. First bend the finger, then work on each section until the weighting is correct and doesn't influence any of the other digits.

> **NOTE** This procedure will obviously be different if you are using the lower-resolution hands that may have fewer fingers. Just make sure that each section is fully weighted to the joint that rotates it.

Now when you bend all the fingers, they should deform correctly without moving any of their neighboring fingers (**Figure 14.16**).

The final stage for the hands is to weight the palm area so it is almost completely controlled by the wrist joint (**Figure 14.17**). This will also help you to fill out the base area of the fingers if they are pinching.

FIGURE 14.16 The fingers now deform correctly.

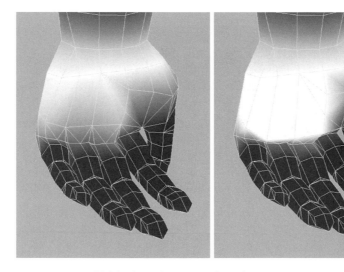

FIGURE 14.17 Weight the palm area to the wrist.

## Leg and Waist Weights

For the legs, it is best to begin at the top in the waist area, because the hip can rotate in a number of directions. When that is done, we can address the knee, ankle, and finally the foot.

1   To start, move the foot icon as demonstrated in **Figure 14.18**, first out in front of the leg, then up, and finally out to the side. You will also need to move the knee position icon, or the leg will flip and the knee will point backward.

2   Now focus in on her left hip. Begin by editing the weights for the Root joint. As you can see in **Figure 14.19**, left, the weights are distributed quite softly in this area, making it quite flexible and squashy. You need to lock down some of the weights, making the hips look more solid when she moves.

**FIGURE 14.18** Position the leg and knee to see how they deform.

3   Set both Opacity and Value to 1, and paint around the main hip area with the solid brush. Also paint around the back of the hip, under her crotch, and the belt. Paint only on her left side (**Figures 14.19b** and **14.19c**).

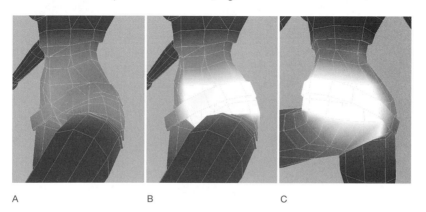

A                         B                         C

**FIGURE 14.19** Fully weight her left hip area to the Root joint.

Now that we have the main hip area locked, we can go in and work on the rest of the vertices, smoothing out the general area while also removing any pinches or creases. To help with this, we will first edit the weights on her thigh. At present, this is partially weighted to the Root joint, causing it to flatten as she raises her leg. Fixing this now will help show us exactly what we need to do to complete the hip.

1   Fully weight the main bulk of her thigh to the left thigh joint, painting over the vertices highlighted in **Figure 14.20**, left. The thigh should literally pop out, back into its original form (**Figure 14.20**, right). This means we can go back and tackle the rest of her hip.

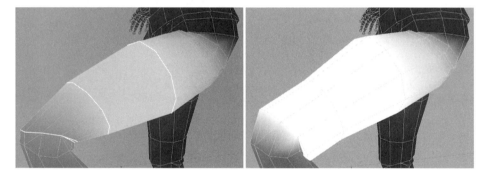

FIGURE 14.20 Correct the weights on her thigh.

2   Still focusing on the L_Thigh joint, select a softer brush. Then paint around her buttock, softening the curve and averaging out the distance between the vertices (**Figure 14.21**, left).

3   Next, work on the front of her thigh. In this area, try to reduce the amount of pinching that occurs. Removing it completely will be nearly impossible, so just make it less obvious by closing any large gaps in the geometry (**Figure 14.21**, right).

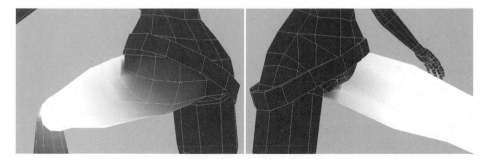

FIGURE 14.21 Tweak the weights around her hip.

Finally, be sure to remove any influence the left thigh has over the right.

We have now corrected the hip in one position, but it also rotates backward and out to the side. Move the foot icon back, so the leg resembles that in **Figure 14.22**.

FIGURE 14.22 Move the foot back to see how the hip deforms from a different position.

Check to see how the front and back of the thigh look. In **Figure 14.23**, left, the front looks fine. Maybe a little bit of tweaking is needed to straighten out her sash, but there are no major problems. The rear will need a bit more work. In **Figure 14.23b** we can see that there is a sharp polygon sticking up; that will need to be fixed.

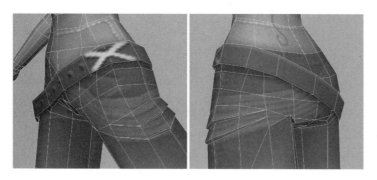

FIGURE 14.23
The front weights look fine, but the rear needs work.

1   Open the Paint Skin Weights tool; you should still have all your previous settings stored, so edit the front and rear of her hip until the weights resemble those in **Figure 14.24**.

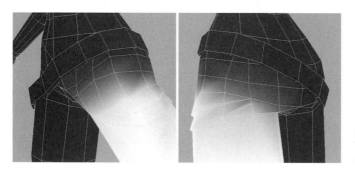

FIGURE 14.24
The edited front and rear weights

2   Now recheck how the hip looks with the leg bent forward. Make any minor tweaks needed, before moving it out to the side (**Figure 14.25**) so we can test the final position. The weights on the hip should really look fine in this pose. If you do need to make any adjustments, it will only be to the side.

**FIGURE 14.25** Move the leg out to the side to test the final pose.

Now move the leg around and double-check each position, making sure the hip looks as good as it can before we work on the knee.

As we did earlier with the thigh, we need the lower leg to maintain its volume as it moves. Right now the thigh joint affects it, so we need to remove this influence first.

**1**   With the L_Thigh joint still active, set Value to 0 and Opacity to 1 before painting the lower section of her leg (**Figure 14.26**, middle).

**2**   Tweak the weights around the knee (**Figure 14.26**, right) trying to smooth out any harsh lines.

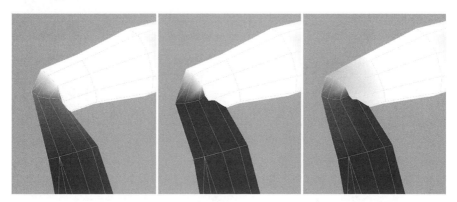

**FIGURE 14.26** Adjust the weights on the lower leg and knee.

That's the knee area more or less complete now; we have adjusted all the weights we need to by just using the L_Thigh joint.

> **NOTE** ▶ Don't be discouraged about areas that intersect when they deform, like the knee and thigh, upper arm and lower arm, and so forth. This happens all the time in video games—unfortunately, it's the only way to allow the limbs to keep their shape and achieve the most realistic and lifelike deformations. Once the character is in game and running around, you probably won't even notice these little flaws.

Now let's look at the base of her leg and the foot.

1   First reset the position of the leg. Then rotate the foot so it is pointing downward, before using the Toe_Rotate attribute to point the toe upward (**Figure 14.27**).

Although things in this area may initially look all right, the main foot area's weights are distributed between three joints—the ankle, toe, and tip—making it flatten as the foot rotates. Let's fix this, weighting the main bulk of the foot to one joint, the ankle joint.

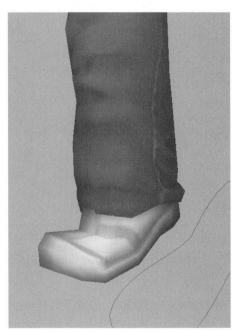

**FIGURE 14.27** Pose the foot to see how the weights are distributed.

2   Highlighting L_Ankle as the joint to edit, fully weight the heel of the shoe and the lower part of the jeans to this L_Ankle joint (**Figure 14.28**, right).

3   In the Paint Weights pane, select the Smooth paint operation to smooth out the lower section of jeans, but don't paint over the very bottom since this needs to stay locked to her shoe.

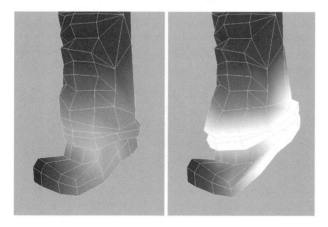

FIGURE 14.28 Set the ankle to fully influence her heel and lower jeans.

As a final test, rotate the foot into a few different poses to see how the jeans deform. As you can see in **Figure 14.29**, the folds in the jeans compress nicely and work quite well, so there is no need to do any further work on this area.

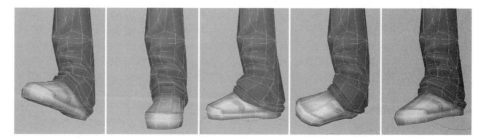

FIGURE 14.29 Test the lower leg's deformation in other poses.

The waist, leg, and foot have now had their weighting reworked and should now deform correctly when Kila is animated. Try putting the leg into some different poses to see how different areas deform, making any changes you need before you proceed.

## Head and Neck Weights

Before we move into this section's steps for the head and neck weights, let's make sure we have the face all set. Regardless of which version of the character you are working on, the face area will have already been weighted, either earlier in this chapter (for blend shapes) or in Chapter 13 (for joint-based).

The blend-shapes face is already a separate object, meaning we can't accidentally edit its weighting. Be careful on the joint-based face, though, since the weights can easily be damaged.

If you are working on the blend-shapes model, make sure the vertices around the face are fully weighted to the head joint. The face geometry's weighting is fine, but because it's a separate object we need to guard against tearing around the edges where it joins to the body mesh. To do this, work on the body geometry, fully weighting the vertices around the face to the head joint.

In the joint-based version, make sure all but the face is fully weighted to the head joint. You can do the hair for now, if you want; just make sure not to touch the face's weights.

You can see both versions of the head in **Figure 14.30**. The joint-based Kila is on the left, and the blend-shapes version is on the right.

**FIGURE 14.30**
Fully weight the head and hair to the head joint, but leave the face as is.

This preparation leaves the neck, shoulders, and the outer areas of her head to work on. We will need the head icons visible, so turn the left icons off and the middle icons on. Now we can proceed to look at the neck and shoulders.

First of all, the hair joints will be affecting the neck and the top of the shoulders. Since the hair geometry is at present controlled by the head, we can safely remove its influence from the model and reapply it to just the hair later.

1   In the Paint Skin Weights window, set Value to 0 and Opacity to 1, and select Hair_A as the joint to work on.

2   Instead of painting on the model to remove the influence, click on the Flood button at the bottom of the Paint Weights pane. This applies the current settings to the entire model, so in this case Hair_A will have a value of 0 on every vertex. In other words, this joint won't be affecting any vertices in the model.

3   Next, select Hair_B and click on Flood, and then do the same for the other three hair joints, to make sure none of them influences the neck or shoulders.

With that done we can now work on the necks weights.

1   Following **Figure 14.31**, move the head icon up, exposing the neck and showing you how it currently deforms.

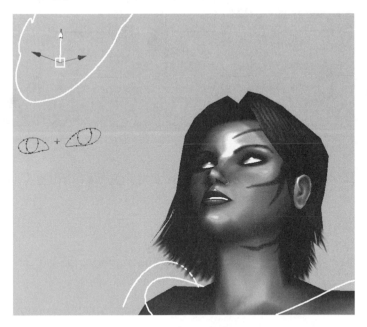

**FIGURE 14.31**
Raise the head icon, tilting the head upward.

2   Edit the weights around the center of her neck so that they are fully weighted to the neck joint.

3   Use a smaller Opacity setting and work around the upper and lower sections
    of her neck so that they are evenly influenced.

4   Check to see that the neck joint affects no other areas on her back or outer
    shoulders. If it does, you can remove the influence by setting Value to 0 and
    Opacity to 1 before painting over the vertices.

The final neck weights should resemble those seen in **Figure 14.32**, right.

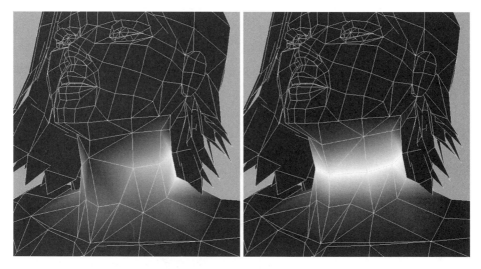

FIGURE 14.32  Edit the neck's weighting.

Check the neck's actual rotation, using the control icon to make sure it deforms
correctly, and make any needed alterations to the weights.

## Main Body Weights

All that is left in painting Kila's weights is adjusting the weighting on her torso
area. After that, we can mirror the weights across to the right side.

The torso is quite easily fixed; you just have to keep the deformation smooth so
that the body maintains its overall shape as it moves.

> **NOTE**   Be sure to take care when editing the waist area, because we have
> already applied some weighting to it earlier in this chapter.

**1**    Make all the icons visible again and, as demonstrated in **Figure 14.33**, bend Kila backward a little. Then go in and fully weight the vertices to the joints closest to them.

**Figure 14.34** shows the weights for the Upperspine (top), Middlespine (middle), and Lowerspine (bottom). As you can see, the weights are like strips around the body. The upper spine joint also includes her chest and the upper parts of her back, right up to the base of her neck.

With these weights blocked in, we can now test the torso in other poses.

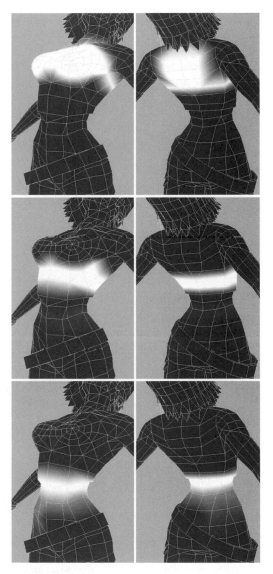

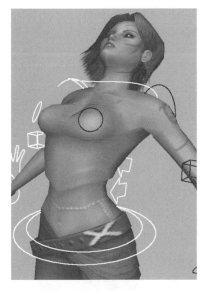

**FIGURE 14.33** Bend Kila backward so you can weight the torso.

**FIGURE 14.34** Weight the torso vertices to their closest joints.

**2** First, using the spine icons, rotate her so she is bent forward (**Figure 14.35**). As you can see, we have some pinching and bad deformation on the front. Tackle this by using a smaller Opacity value and a softer brush to adjust the weights. When you're done, go in with the Smooth paint operation and smooth out any harsh edges, averaging out the vertices.

> **TIP** To help keep the shape of Kila's stomach, try adjusting the weights so that the Root joint has more influence on the vertices that form the inside of her crop top.

**3** Reset the spine back to its default position. Then rotate it around the Y axis this time, as shown in

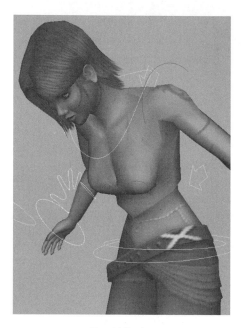

**FIGURE 14.35** Bend Kila forward to test her torso deformation.

**Figure 14.36**. The twist should initially be fine; if there are any areas that don't appear to twist nicely, go in with the Smooth tool and a small Opacity value and paint over the area.

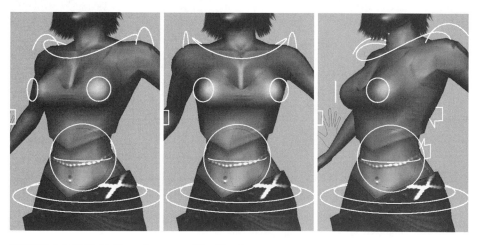

**FIGURE 14.36** Twist the spine around the Y axis.

**4**  Finally, test how she looks when bent over to the side, around the Z axis (**Figure 14.37**). This position, too, should be fine, although you may need to weight the actual hip area to the Root joint more, to prevent it from moving inward.

You've got the main torso area complete now. Before we move on to do her chest, it's a good idea to test the shoulders' deformation when the clavicle controls are moved.

Move the left clavicle control up slightly and see how the shoulder looks. As shown in **Figure 14.38**, left, the main shoulder moves up fine, but the area just at the neck stays where it is, causing an unnatural indentation. With Value set to 1 and Opacity set to

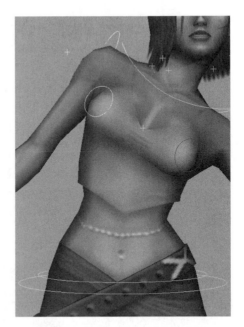

**FIGURE 14.37** Twist the spine around the Z axis.

a small value, gently paint over the area between the neck and shoulder, bringing it up in line with the shoulder's position (**Figure 14.38**, middle).

Now that the main torso is complete, we will reinstate the controls for her breasts.

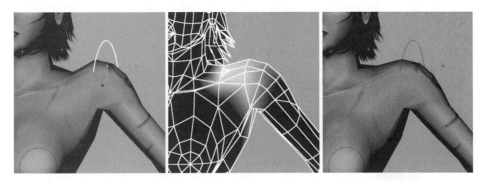

**FIGURE 14.38** Adjust the shoulder so that it deforms correctly when the clavicle control is moved.

1   As demonstrated in **Figure 14.39**, left, move the LeftBreast controller up. This won't affect the actual geometry because the vertices making up her chest are fully influenced by the upper spine joint.

2   Go back into the Paint Skin Weights tool and select the L_Breast joint. Set Opacity to around 0.3. You can see that there is currently no influence because the mesh remains black (**Figure 14.39**, middle).

3   Now work your way around her left breast, starting from the center and working your way outward. What we want is for the middle to be more or less fully controlled by the joint, with the influence fading as it moves away from the joint itself (**Figure 14.39**, right).

4   Make sure to add a slight influence to her crop top as well.

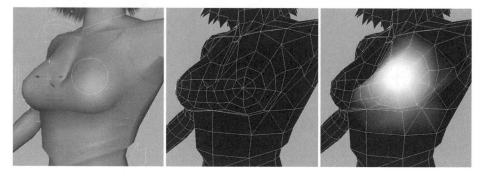

FIGURE 14.39 To finish the torso, add weighting back to her breast.

The main body area is complete—that is, her entire left side is finished. It's time to mirror the weights.

> **NOTE**   You may have noticed that the hair area is not yet properly weighted. We want to mirror the weights first, before finishing the hair, because her hair is not symmetrical; that means the weights will not mirror properly in that area. We can, however, adjust these weights afterward.

## Mirroring Weights

With one side of Kila completely weighted, we can now save ourselves a lot of work by copying the weights across to the right side of the body.

Before you begin, make sure she is back in her default pose so that Maya can tell which joints it is copying from and to. Also, if you are using the joint-based facial rig, move the Time Slider to frame 1, separating the eyelid joints.

1   Select the character mesh. Go to Skin > Edit Smooth Skin > Mirror Skin Weights and open the options (**Figure 14.40**).

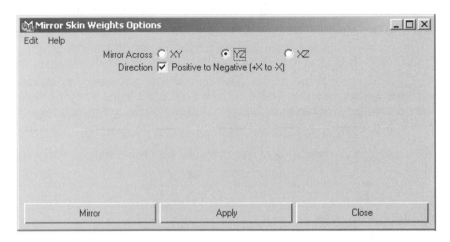

FIGURE 14.40 Mirror Skin Weights options

2   The way Kila is placed in the virtual world means her arms span the X axis. Therefore, you need to mirror the weights across the Y and Z axes, so set Mirror Across to YZ.

3   Her left side lies in the positive section of the axis, but her right side is in the negative. Because you are mirroring from the left, enable Direction Positive to Negative so that Maya knows which side to mirror from and to.

4   Click on Apply, and the weighting information will be copied across.

Maya's Mirror Weights tool doesn't always do a perfect job; the weighting tends to get confused down the center of the model, and often weights are assigned incorrectly. You may find, for example, that the vertices down the center of her T-shirt move with the right breast but not with the left. These kinds of problems will need fixing before you move on; make sure that each side equally affects the vertices in between.

Other areas to check include the crotch, which needs to stay fixed to the Root joint. The upper spine and even the base of her neck may need to be corrected, too.

Look also at areas such as her belt, which isn't symmetrical. This lies across an area that dramatically deforms, so it will be impossible for the belt not to intersect with the mesh at some point; just try for the best result you can get.

> **TIP** The best overall way to check your weighting is to put your character into some extreme poses. These will reveal any faults in the way the weights are distributed. You can then go in with a lower Opacity setting and tweak the weighting values until they are correct.

With the main body-weighting mirrored we can now move on and work on her hair.

## Hair Weights

Because the hair joints are not symmetrical, we can't rely on weighting the left side and mirroring the weights across for the right.

> **NOTE** Before continuing with the work in this section, It's important that you are entirely finished with all Mirror Weights operations on this character. If you proceed with any nonsymmetrical work and then notice problems that require remirroring, you'll have to redo all your nonsymmetical work. In addition, it's a good idea to keep saving your work as you go, so you can easily refer back to some previous weights if you make a mistake.

At this point it would be useful to turn on the base skeleton so you can see the positions of the hair joints.

**1**  As shown in **Figure 14.41a**, move the individual controllers for the hair outside the head.

> **TIP** You can quickly turn off all the icons by going to the view's Show menu and disabling NURBs Curves.

**2**  Select the character mesh and open the Paint Skin Weights tool, highlighting the first hair joint, Hair_A (**Figure 14.41b**).

**3**  With both Value and Opacity set to 1, begin to paint over the polygonal strands of hair that are closest to the joint. Start on the outside and work your way in, making sure you don't paint too far up the head (**Figure 14.41c**).

**4**  Repeat these steps for the remaining strands of hair, weighting them fully to their closest joints (**Figure 14.41d**).

A

B

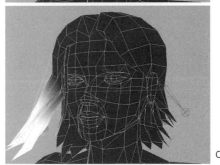

C

D

**FIGURE 14.41** Fully weight each strand of hair to its closest joint.

**5**   At present, if the hair moves, it will look quite rigid because we have fixed the vertices rigidly to each joint (**Figure 14.42**, left). To help free the hair, allowing it to flow more naturally, paint over the strands again, but this time use the Smooth paint operation (**Figure 14.42**, right).

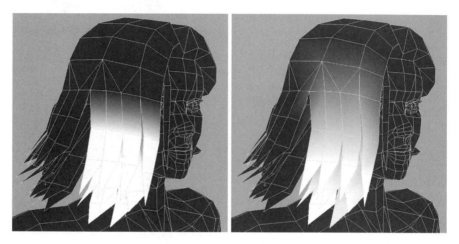

FIGURE 14.42 Smooth out each strand of hair, allowing the hair more movement.

Our aim was to give Kila's hair some life, "unlocking" it from her head, and we have achieved that. You can now animate the controls, and the hair will follow smoothly.

You have one more step to complete the weighting process on Kila, and that is to remove any small weights that have been applied as you worked. While painting the weights, you may have applied smaller weighting values to other joints without really noticing. These are often relics of using the Paint Skin Weights tool's Smooth or Replace paint operations. Upon export into the game engine, these might be removed, but if they are not they could have an impact on the processing power of the system.

So let's get rid of them. Select the character mesh and go to Skin > Edit Smooth Skin > Prune Small Weights. The default value of 0.01 will work well in most cases, but to be safe, save your scene before applying this to your model. Any values below 0.01 will be reset to 0, and the remaining weights will be normalized to add up to 1.

## Final Rig Adjustments

When we created Kila's rig, we had to keep the elbow and knee position markers locked to the elbow and knee joints. This was to prevent the base skeleton moving before it was bound. As you have probably noticed, this can cause problems—especially in the case of the knee icons being actually on the knee. When you move the foot, the knee tries to stay pointing at the icon, causing the leg to flip.

Now that the mesh is bound to the skeleton, we can move these knee icons into more suitable positions.

**1**   Move the knee position icons out in front of the knees (**Figure 14.43**, left).

**2**   Make a note of the Rotate Y attributes currently set for both feet (you will need to reapply these values later). Reset the Rotate Y attribute on both feet back to 0 so that the feet point exactly forward (**Figure 14.43**, middle).

**3**   Parent each knee icon to its corresponding foot icon.

**4**   Freeze the transforms on both knee icons and reset the Y rotation on both feet icons back to their original values.

> **NOTE**   It's important to again reset the feet back to 0 before you pass the completed rig to the animators. This will give them a clean rig to work with. Setting it to 0 now, however, will mean the character is no longer in her bind pose, which could cause problems later when we bind the LODs.

Now the knees will naturally follow the feet as they move (**Figure 14.43**, right). Plus, you have the ability to tweak the knees' positions should you need to.

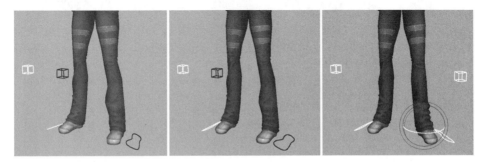

**FIGURE 14.43** Move the knee icons and parent them to the feet.

We can also do this same adjustment for the elbow positions. Like the knees, the arms will flip when the IK is enabled, to stay pointing at the icons. Moving the elbows back slightly will prevent this from happening (**Figure 14.44**). In this instance, we don't need to parent them to anything; just freeze the transforms when you have finished moving them, to store their new default positions.

> **NOTE** Consult with the animators about how they would like the pole vector icons set up. It may be that they should all be parented to a certain node, or not parented at all.

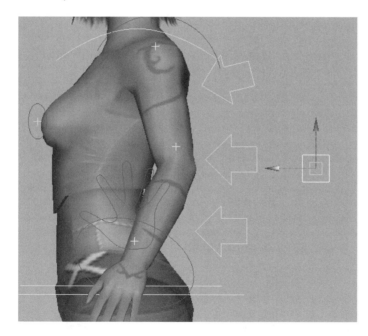

**FIGURE 14.44**
Move the elbow
position icons back.

The main Kila model is now bound and ready to go to the next and final stage, but what about the other LODs?

# Level of Detail Weights

We have worked hard to tweak the weights on the first LOD until Kila deforms accurately as she moves. Now we need to apply the same weighting values to the other four levels of detail. This does seem like a huge task, but luckily Maya has a handy tool—Copy Skin Weights—that lets us copy the weights from the first LOD across to the others.

We first need to prepare the geometry as we did for the main model. Select the LOD group in the Outliner, and make sure all the layers are visible and that each LOD is set to "show" in the Channel Box (**Figure 14.45**).

1   At present, your Outliner should look like the one in **Figure 14.46**, left. Go through each individual LOD and combine the geometry into a single mesh (Polygon > Combine), remembering to merge the vertices around her hair with a small value of 0.001.

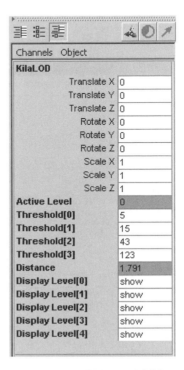

**FIGURE 14.45** Make each LOD visible by setting them to "show."

**NOTE**   If you are using the blend-shapes version, remember to keep the faces separate wherever blend shapes have been applied.

**2** Place the models back inside their LOD group. Delete the history and rename them to Kila_LOD02, Kila_LOD03, Kila_LOD04, and Kila_LOD05 (**Figure 14.46**, right).

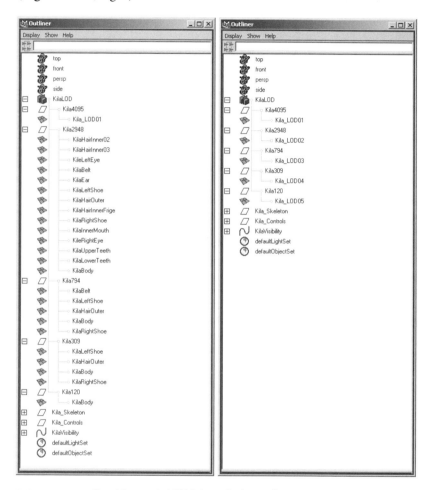

FIGURE 14.46 Combine each LOD into a single mesh.

**3**   When copying weights, the number of joints to which the source and destination mesh are attached has to be the same. Therefore, you have to be sure each LOD model is bound to the base skeleton in exactly the same way as the original. A quick way to do this is to select each new LOD model in turn and click on the Bind button on the GCDM shelf. This will ensure each level is bound to the base skeleton just the same way as the original.

With all the geometry attached to the skeleton now, we can copy the weights across. We simply tell Maya which mesh we are copying from, and which we will be copying to.

**4**   Select the first LOD that you have already weighted, Kila_LOD01. Now, holding Ctrl, select the next LOD (Kila_LOD02).

**5**   Go to Skin > Edit Smooth Skin > Copy Skin Weights.

**6**   Repeat steps 4 and 5 for the other LODs, selecting first the main LOD (Kila_LOD01) and then the one you wish to copy the weights to.

All the LODs now have the same weighting applied to them, so they will deform nearly the same as the first LOD does. This also means that the facial animation setup for the joint facial rig is carried across to the second LOD, saving us from having to set it up again.

Now go through each LOD and check that the weighting is correct on each model. Due to the change in topology, there will be areas where the weighting has accidentally affected some vertices incorrectly. This shouldn't take much work; the majority of the weighting will have passed across just fine.

> **TIP** ▶ Remember that these are LODs—try to view them from the same distance at which they will ultimately be viewed in game. There is no point in spending time adjusting weights on areas that will never be seen.

When you are completely happy with the weighting on each level, set the Display Level on each LOD group back to "uselod," and make all the display layers visible.

As demonstrated in **Figure 14.47**, all versions of Kila are now weighted and checked, allowing us complete freedom to put her into any pose. Save this version of Kila as Kila_Skinned.mb.

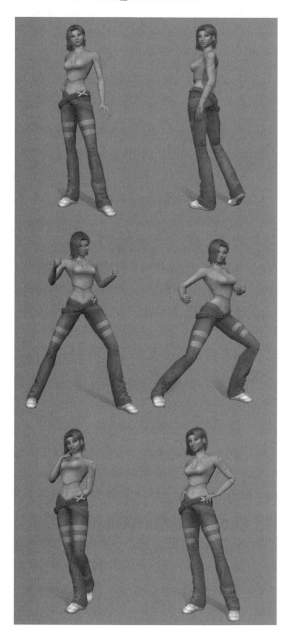

**FIGURE 14.47**
Kila, fully weighted

# Painting Grae's Weights

You should now have a good grasp of what to look for when adjusting the weighting on your characters, so I will leave the Grae model more or less up to you. If you are working with the blend-shapes version of Grae, you will first need to prepare and bind the geometry to the base skeleton. Start with Grae_FaceBind_BS.mb, bind the body mesh to the skeleton and the face to just the head joint, and save the file as Grae_Bound_BS.mb.

Before you begin to work on Grae's weights, you need to alter the designation of which joints actually affect the mesh. In an earlier chapter, we added four extra joints to the wings so we could control Grae's fingers, enabling us to open and close them. We don't need these joints bound to the mesh, however.

Specifically, these are the wing finger "base" joints. They all lie on top of one another at present, and the Wing_Wrist joint is there, too. Deciding which joint to weight to could be a nightmare, so to make things easier we will remove the influence of the four main finger joints. The fingers will still work as they should because the middle joints will control the wing's main movement.

Load the file Grae_FaceRig_Jnt.mb.

**1**    To remove a joint's influence, first select the mesh and then the joint.

**2**    Next go to Skin > Edit Smooth Skin > Remove Influence.

Follow these steps for all of the following joints: L_Wing_Finger01_Base, L_Wing_Finger02_Base, L_Wing_Finger03_Base, L_Wing_Finger04_Base and R_Wing_Finger01_Base, R_Wing_Finger02_Base, R_Wing_Finger03_Base, and R_Wing_Finger04_Base.

The weights these joints had will be distributed to the surrounding joints.

After removing the influences, go ahead and work on Grae's weights. Here are a few tips to help you out:

▶    Start by fully weighting each wing to the wing's root joints. This will simplify the task of working on the body.

▶    When you work on the wings, fully weight the vertices to the joints they are closest to. Then make sure the vertices that lie in between are half weighted to the joints on either side.

▶ When working on the main body, make sure you pose the area you are working on, verifying that the weights look as good as possible at each extreme.

When you're done, save his file as Grae_Skinned.mb. You can see the results of Grae's weighting in **Figure 14.48**.

FIGURE 14.48 Grae, fully weighted

## Summary

Here in this chapter we have covered the process of adjusting weighting values to make the mesh deform correctly when posed. Both of our characters are now more or less ready to be animated. We can now move on to the final step of our characters' setup. Chapter 15 discusses cleaning up the scene and locking off any unused controls on the rig. This readies the file to be handed over to another member of your team, without fear of the character's being accidentally broken by additional editing.

**CD Files**

Kila_Skinned.mb
Kila_Final.mb
Grae_Skinned.mb
Grae_Final.mb
KilaBody.tga
KilaHair.tga
KilaHead.tga
GraeBody.tga
GraeMisc.tga
GraeWing.tga
GraeBody_Bump.tga
GraeMisc_Bump.tga
GraeBody_Spec.tga
GraeMisc_Spec.tga

# CHAPTER 15
# Finalize and
# Clean Up

**YOU HAVE YOUR MODEL;** it's rigged and ready to go, right?
Wrong. If you pass Kila and Grae to your animator in their present state,
it's a sure thing that within a week he or she will have broken them by
accidentally moving some part of the rig they shouldn't have.

Here in this chapter we will talk about how to clean up the scene and
lock off any controls to which the animator should not have access.
Additionally, we will introduce the use of character sets and the
significant role they play in animation.

## Scene Optimization

While working in Maya, your scene file will slowly grow in size. This isn't just due to elements left over as you work; residual nodes from imported scenes can remain, too, slowing down your workflow and increasing file sizes.

What we want to do now is a final major clean up of the scene, removing anything that is no longer of use. Both rigs are almost identical, so we'll concentrate mainly on Kila. Along the way, I'll point out places where the workflow may differ when you work through these steps on Grae.

Load in the file called Kila_Skinned.mb (for Grae, load Grae_Skinned.mb).

> **NOTE** Be sure to save your scene before running the Optimize Scene Size tool in step 1. This tool is not undoable, so it's wise to have a backup just in case the command deletes something you need.

1 Go to File > Optimize Scene Size and open the options (**Figure 15.1**). This tool will scan the scene and delete any unused objects and nodes.

2 Enable all the options. Click on Optimize, and the scene will quickly be optimized.

3 You no longer need the image planes, so remove them next, by going to Edit > Delete All by Type > Image Planes.

4 Look at the Layer Editor. There are no longer any image planes in the scene, so delete the ImagePlanes layer by right-clicking it and selecting Delete.

5 Because the visibility of the layers is now controlled with the LOD group, there isn't much point in having separate layers for each of Kila's LODs. Delete all but the first layer and rename this to Kila. (For Grae, remember that he has one more LOD than Kila.)

6 Use the Outliner to select the KilaLOD group. Place it in the Kila layer, setting it to Reference when you're done so that nobody can select the character mesh.

7 If two characters were in the same scene, their skeleton layers might be easily confused. To avoid this, rename the Kila layer to Kila_BaseSkel. (Create a similar layer name for Grae.) Turn off its visibility and set its display type to Reference.

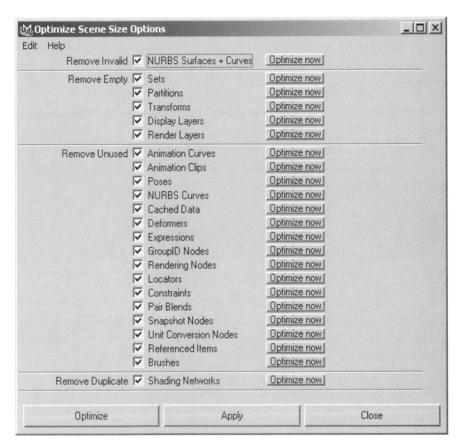

FIGURE 15.1 The Optimize Scene Size options

The scenes are now clean and tidy, with nothing remaining that is not relevant to the character or their rigs.

> **TIP** If you want the scene to be completely clean, leaving just the objects needed, you can use File > Save Selected. Simply select the objects you wish to keep and save them out into a separate file. This will strip out anything not required by the scene.

## Make Your Rig Idiot-Proof

The base skeleton and character meshes are now locked by the Layer Editor, meaning no one can edit them by mistake. The rig, however, still needs some protection.

In its present state, the rig can easily be broken. Almost all of the controls can be moved away from the rig, but they need to stay locked to it. Another concern is that you want only the rotations to be available to the animator; as it is, however, the translations and even the scale attributes are freely available to edit. All of this can have disastrous results.

In this section we will look into locking off all the attributes we don't want anyone to use, with the help of the Channel Control window. This tool allows us to make attributes *nonkeyable,* meaning the animator cannot place keyframes on them. The animator can still move an object using the manipulators, but we can lock the specific attributes that we don't want to be editable.

The beauty of the Channel Control tool is that with "Change all selected objects of the same type" enabled you can work on a number of objects at the same time (as long as they are of the same type), which speeds up the whole process.

1   Open the Channel Control window by going to Window > General Editors > Channel Control. As you can see in **Figure 15.2a**, the window is empty because we don't have anything selected.

2   Select all the finger icons for both hands, including the thumbs and the palm area. These will be automatically loaded into the Channel Control window (**Figure 15.2b**).

3   You are now in the Keyable tab of Channel Control. This tells you that the attributes on the left can have keyframes applied to them; the ones on the right cannot.

>   **NOTE** Whichever object you selected last will be the main one visible in the Channel Control window, so don't worry if the window looks different from Figure 15.2b.

As demonstrated in **Figure 15.2c**, select all the rotate, scale, translate, and visibility attributes in the Keyable list on the left.

**4**   Notice that the Move >> button is now enabled; click on this now to move the selected attributes across to the Non-Keyable list on the right, leaving only the ones we want available to animate (**Figure 15.2d**).

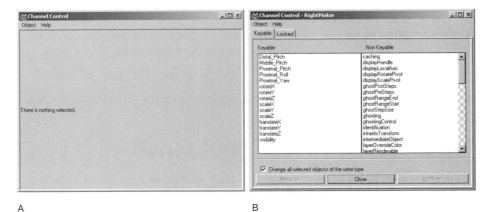

A

B

C

D

FIGURE 15.2 Move all the basic transformation attributes to the Non-Keyable list.

Although you've now ensured that keys can no longer be set on the finger icons' main attributes, they can be selected and moved, rotated, or even scaled, which we don't want to occur. We need to lock these attributes so that their values cannot be altered.

**1**  Click on the Locked tab; the window will change to show what is currently locked in the left panel, and unlocked in the right panel (**Figure 15.3**, top). At present, nothing is locked.

**2**  Scroll down the Non-Locked list on the right and select the translate, rotate, scale, and visibility attributes.

> **TIP**  Holding Ctrl/Cmd lets you to select multiple attributes.

**3**  Now the << Move button is enabled. Click on it to move those selected attributes across to the Locked list (**Figure 15.3**, bottom).

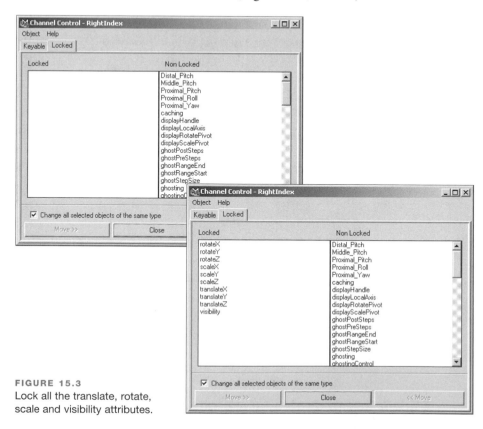

**FIGURE 15.3**
Lock all the translate, rotate, scale and visibility attributes.

> **TIP** You can also lock attributes directly in the Channel Box if they are keyable. Simply right-click on the attributes you wish to lock, and select Lock Selected.

So the hand icons are locked, and only the attributes that control the fingers are available to be animated. Let's now clean up the rest of the hand.

1  Select both the palm icons again and press the Up Arrow key, which will select the groups above these icons in the hierarchy. Although these are not visible, the animator could quite easily select them and probably animate them. We need to lock all the attributes as well as make them all nonkeyable.

2  In the Keyable tab of the Channel Control window, make sure all the attributes are moved across to the Non-Keyable side.

3  Switch to the Locked tab, and move the translate, rotate, and scale attributes across so that they are locked.

You will notice that we omitted the visibility attribute in the preceding steps. This is because, unlike with the other finger icons, the visibility icon controls this attribute. Locking the visibility attribute here would lock it in its current state, so the visibility icon would have no effect.

> **TIP** You can quickly see if a visibility attribute is connected to the visibility icon by looking in the Channel Box. If the attribute is colored yellow, it has an incoming connection.

Now that we know how the Channel Control window operates, we can start to work on a larger scale. Let's start with all the icons whose movement is based only on rotations.

1  Select the control handles that allow you to animate shoulders, elbows, and wrists on both the left and right sides.

2  Make the translate, scale, and visibility attributes all nonkeyable, and lock them in the Locked tab. (In this case, we can lock the visibility attribute because it isn't directly controlled by the visibility icon.)

**3**   Select the waist control icon, the neck rotation icon, and all three spine icons and make them nonkeyable. Lock the translate, scale, and visibility attributes.

Note that we have to do these separately from the arms because they are different object types.

Next, we will look at the icons that translate only.

**1**   Select both arm IK controllers and all four elbow and knee position icons.

**2**   Add to this selection both breast icons and the main chest group—just select the handle in between each breast icon. (Needless to say, you can skip this step for Grae.)

**3**   We aren't finished yet. Also include in this selection the main head icon, both eye icons, and the main eye group.

**4**   Finally, add all five of Kila's hair control handles and the two clavicle controllers.

**5**   Now make all the rotation, scale, and visibility icons nonkeyable and lock them.

For the last group, we just need to lock and make nonkeyable the scale attributes, since we need to animate the translations and rotations.

**1**   Select both feet and the main root control.

**2**   Make them nonkeyable, and lock the scale attributes.

**3**   The visibility icon controls the visibility attributes on these icons, so you can't lock them; but do set them to be nonkeyable.

That's it; the main rig is cleaned up nicely. Now we need to go in and lock the controls that are not immediately visible.

1  Using the Outliner, select the HeadRotation and HairSwing groups that exist just above the hair and head controllers in the hierarchy. If you are working on Grae at this point, select the WingControls group, too.

2  Add to this selection the KilaVisibility (**Figure 15.4**) icon.

3  In the Channel Control window, make all the translate, rotate, scale, and visibility attributes nonkeyable, and lock all the same attributes except visibility.

> **TIP** If you know the exact name of an object or series of objects, you can use the selection field on the status line to select them, rather than having to trawl through the Outliner. And when you need to select a number of objects whose names are almost the same, you can use wildcards: Simply enter *Bone* in the selection field, and anything with Bone in its name will be selected.

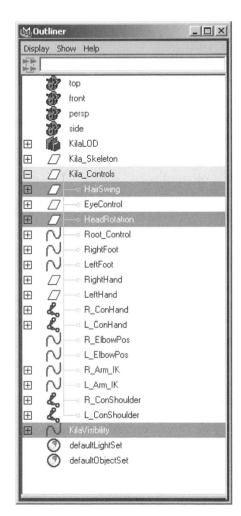

**FIGURE 15.4** Select the HairSwing, HeadRotation, and KilaVisibility objects in the Outliner.

For the next step, let's try selecting using the selection field rather than the Outliner.

**1**  In the selection field on the status line, type in HairHelper (**Figure 15.5**). This selects the locator we created to help us control the hair's movement.

FIGURE 15.5 Make quicker selections using the selection field on the status line.

**2**  Now lock and make nonkeyable all the main translate, rotate, scale, and visibility attributes.

**3**  We don't directly manipulate the IK handles in the scene, so we can safely lock these. First select them all by going to Edit > Select All By Type > IK Handles. Make everything nonkeyable, but only lock the main translate, rotate, scale, and visibility attributes.

**4**  Finally, there are two joints that have evaded us so far. These exist at the end of the control arms and are called L_ConWrist and R_ConWrist. Like the IK handles, these joints are not animated directly; instead, we use the L_ConHand and R_ConHand joints to animate them. Therefore you can safely make all attributes of these joints nonkeyable, and lock the main translate, rotate, scale, and visibility attributes.

> **NOTE**  If you haven't done so already, now is a good time to zero off those rotation values lingering on the Rotate Y attribute on the character's feet. This additional clean-up will make the rig even better for an animator to work with.

Your rig should now be tamper proof; having available only the attributes that should be animated will avoid future problems with the rig.

Check to make sure you have not missed any controllers, visible or otherwise, before you continue. It's best to do this first in the Outliner because each object will be clearly listed. In addition, go through each icon in the view panel, since this is how the animator will interact with the character.

## Character Sets

Our rigs are is clean and tidy now and can be animated easily (and safely)—but they're still quite complex in construction and don't allow for any quick and convenient way to access the character as a whole. What we can do now is define a series of *character sets* for the characters. A character set stores all the attributes associated with the character's animation in one central place. The animator can then access these attributes quickly and easily in order to edit the character as a whole.

Another benefit of character sets is that you can use them in conjunction with the Trax Editor (Window > Animation Editors > Trax Editor) to store the animation data in *clips*. These can then be exported and stored for future use, even on other characters. You'll find more discussion of the Trax Editor in Chapter 16, "Animating for Games."

In addition to the main character set, you can have subcharacter sets that lie beneath the main one. These are useful when you need to divide up your character. For our Kila and Grae characters, we'll set up a subcharacter set for the upper body animation and another for the lower body animation. We can then export and import animation onto these subcharacter sets separately, enabling the mixing and matching of various animations to create new ones. We can even have another separate subcharacter set for Grae's wings.

So let's first create the main character set for Kila.

1   Go to Character > Create Character Set and open the options seen in **Figure 15.6**. This is where you will give the character set a name and ask Maya to include some attributes in its initial creation.

2   Name the character set Kila_CS to indicate that it belongs to Kila and that it's a character set, just in case more than one character is imported into the scene. In the Character Set Attributes, enable the From Channel Box item.

3   We want this main character set to hold all the facial animation, so before we create it, select the main head icon. In the Channel Box, select all the attributes associated with facial animation.

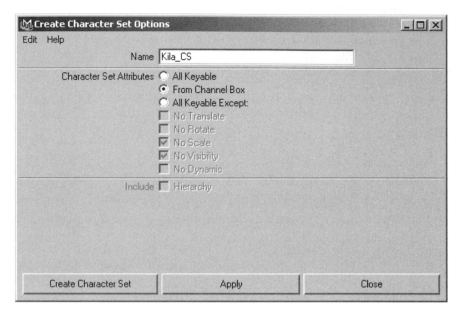

FIGURE 15.6 Create Character Set window

**NOTE** If you are using the blend shape version of the character, highlight all the attributes on the blend shape node.

**4** When everything is selected, click on Create Character Set. In the bottom-right corner of the window, below the Time Slider controls, you will see that the character set has also been activated (**Figure 15.7**).

You will also notice that for the selected objects, the name Kila_CS will appear under the Inputs section in the Channel Box. This is to indicate that the character set is connected to the object's attributes.

FIGURE 15.7 The Kila_CS character set is active.

Now we need to add the eyes to this character set as part of the facial animation.

**1**  Select each eye icon and then the main eye controller group.

**2**  Select all the translate attributes in the Channel Box.

**3**  Go to Character > Add to Character Set, and the selected attributes will be added.

We now have our main character and it holds all the relevant attributes that can have animation applied. Let's now create the two subcharacter sets, which will hold all the attributes for the upper and lower body.

**1**  Go to Character > Create Subcharacter Set and open the options. As you can see in **Figure 15.8**, they are identical to the ones for the main character set.

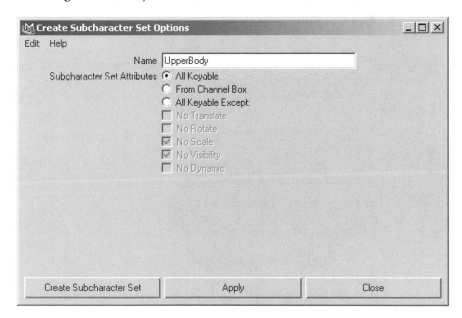

FIGURE 15.8 Create a subcharacter set for the upper body.

**2**  First type in the name UpperBody and set Subcharacter Set Attributes to All Keyable. Making sure you have nothing selected in the scene, click on Apply. (You want to leave this character set empty for now because you're going to create the lower body set directly after this.)

**3**   Type the name LowerBody into the Name field and, using the same settings as for UpperBody, click on Apply. Close the window when you're done.

**4**   Because these are subcharacters, they will not be activated, so now we need to activate the UpperBody set. You can do this in either of two ways:

▶   Click on the red down arrow to the right of the Time Slider, where Kila_CS is currently displayed as the active character set. Then select the appropriate subcharacter set from the menu.

▶   Go to Character > Set Current Character Set Kila_CS > UpperBody.

Now all you need to do is add all the upper body icons' attributes to the subcharacter. You will work your way through each of the upper body icons, the spine joints, clavicles, arms, hands, hair, neck, and head.

**1**   First select an icon and then highlight all its attributes in the Channel Box.

> **NOTE**  When working on the head, ignore the facial animation attributes you already assigned. Also ignore all the ikBlend attributes because these control the ability to switch between IK and FK. If you add these to the character set, they won't work.

**2**   Go to Character > Add to Character Set, and the attributes are added.

**3**   Finally, switch to the LowerBody subcharacter set and add to it the Waist_Control, Root_Control, both knee controllers, and foot icon attributes. Remember to ignore the ikBlend attributes.

The main character sets are now set up and can be used to safely store and transfer animation between characters.

At this point you might want to store the default pose so you can quickly get back to it. In doing this, you will get your first taste of animation by setting a keyframe. With most game engines, the first frame (or in some cases frame -1) has to be the character in this default pose. Now that we have the character sets, we can do this quickly.

**1**   Either select the Kila_CS character set in the Outliner, or go to Character > Select Character Set Node > Kila_CS.

**2**   Then, making sure the Time Slider is set to 0, right-click in the Channel Box and select Key All.

**3**   Do the same for the UpperBody and LowerBody subcharacter sets, and you're done.

Save this final scene as Kila_Final.mb.

If you haven't already, clean up Grae's scene and rig. Then create character sets for him similar to those you've done for Kila. Save his scene as Grae_Final.mb.

> **NOTE**   Now that both characters are truly complete—geometry, LODs, rigging, animation setup, binding—and have been finalized and cleaned up, I recommend making one last check, if you have the time available. It's not impossible that your characters might benefit from further work on the textures or the weighting.

## Summary

Congratulations! Both characters are now ready to be passed on to the animators or to be animated by you. You have successfully designed, modeled, optimized, textured, LODed, and rigged Kila and Grae. This final chapter in the characters' creation showed you how to clean up the scene and prepare the rig to be animated safely, as well as how to add the capability to quickly export and import animation onto the character.

There's one final chapter for you to work through. Now that the characters are completely modeled, rigged, and optimized, you're ready to study the techniques for animation in games.

# CHAPTER 16
# Animating
# for Games

**ANIMATION IS TRULY MAGICAL:** Being able to make an inanimate object move and show emotion is a powerful skill. There are many aspects of animation, enough to fill a book in itself; in this chapter we will focus on real-time animation and the various aspects of its creation, with the goal of bringing our Kila and Grae characters to life. Once we have established a few ground rules, I will demonstrate how to generate a basic walk cycle.

> **NOTE** If you would like to learn more about the basic principles of animation, many helpful books are recommended in Appendix B, "Reference and Further Reading."

To prepare for animation, you must know everything your character will do and how they should do it. Your lead animator will work closely with the designer on the project to compile an animation list that will then be passed to you.

In Chapter 1, we introduced some of the design elements associated with our characters. You read a brief background story that helped to portray the characters' personalities, and basic information in the form of bios offered more insight into who they are and why. All this character information will now help us decide how Kila and Grae will walk. We know Kila is a dancer, so we can enhance her feminine walk, adding a bit more sway to her hips and giving her a sexier look. Grae, on the other hand, is a colossal beast; we want to feel the power behind each purposeful step as he lumbers around.

With these ideas of how the characters will move and interact with the game world, you can then go on to gather some reference material. More than likely this will be in the form of movies (DVDs, videos downloaded from the Internet, or something you have filmed yourself). Once you have a solid idea of the movements required, you and your team can discuss how they will be implemented into the game engine and what techniques will be used to save memory.

## Animation Optimization

As you are now well aware, in every aspect of real-time artwork you have to keep within specified boundaries, and the same applies to animation. If your character can perform a hundred moves, all these will have to be stored in memory. Add to this the animations for all of the nonplayer characters, plus scenic animation, and your allotted chunk of the memory is soon gone.

Restricting the number of animations used isn't the best approach for today's games; in-game animation is a huge draw these days, and variety is the key to making your characters interesting and believable. Instead, you can explore the following options for saving processing power.

## Mirroring Animations

Normally, if you wanted your character to be able to step left as well as right, you would have to create two separate animations, both of which would be stored in memory. Such doubling-up on so much of the animation data can soon reach the limits of your resources. One way to remove the need for mirrored versions is to see if the programmers on your team can do the mirroring in the game engine. (By this I mean mirroring only the joints' rotation and translation values; mirroring the whole skeleton would also flip the character mesh.)

Having this aspect of animation handled in the game engine can cut almost in half the amount of data being stored, leaving you room for more animations.

## Dividing Animations

Another way to reduce the memory consumed by animations, without losing any of the animation, is to divide them up. Say your character is running, which is one animation. Then she needs to hold a variety of weapons, say five. In all, you have six separate running animations.

What you can do is divide them into upper- and lower-body movements. The hips and legs from the primary run animation could also be used with the upper body animation from each of the six variations.

Storing upper and lower body data will itself save a lot of memory. If you can, you could even divide the animations further, into individual limbs—but this can lead to a reduction in the quality of the animation.

As always, talk these options over with your manager; implementing this technique into the game engine can be a big job.

## Skeleton and Animation Sharing

For games in which you have many characters that potentially will do the same things, you can create one set of generic animations that can be applied to all. In this case, it's wise to use the same skeleton structure in order to maintain the correct motion, but slight variations in size and proportions can also work.

This sharing technique is particularly useful on more generic, nonplayer character animations—civilians, for example—where the repeated use of the same animation is not obvious.

## Animation Categories

Real-time animation is handled differently from big-screen animation. To make the game truly interactive, each animation has to be handled separately, so that the correct one can run when the player requests it.

In all, real-time animation can be separated into the five principal categories discussed in this section. Each animation you create will fit into one of these categories.

### Idle and Fidget Animations

When the player stops controlling the character, it will begin to cycle randomly through various animations. If, for example, the character is standing still, a default breathing animation will play, in which the shoulders and chest rise and fall and the arms swing slightly—this is the *idle animation*. Once this has played for a while, another animation will randomly kick in; this could involve the character's looking around aimlessly, tapping a toe, or picking their nose; the intent is to give them variety and some feeling of life. These variants are know as *fidget animations*. Both idle and fidget animations need to be looped or cycled and so could also come under the next category, *cycle animations*.

### Cycle Animations

Almost all the animations involving the character's physical movement (except idle or fidget animations, where the character is standing still) will be based on a single sequence, looping. A walk cycle is a good example of a cycle animation; this begins at the crossover point of the animation (the stage when the legs cross over from the side view) and ends in the same place. The animation can be looped seamlessly, giving the impression that the character can walk continuously.

### Four-Stage Animations

The four-stage animation can also be described as a Move In, Hold, Cycle, and Move Out sequence. This sequence can be used when the character needs to change states temporarily; say climbing a ladder, for instance.

For the Move In, you need a starting animation where the character grabs hold of the ladder and moves into a pose where they can ascend or descend it easily. The Hold is this pose held while the player decides what they want to do; this

Hold can be classed as an idle animation and so could possibly have other idle or fidget animations branching from it.

Next you have the Cycle. In the ladder-climbing example, the Cycle would be a short sequence involving the character climbing up or down the ladder. This would then be looped for the duration of the movement.

Finally, we have the Move Out, which is simply the character leaving the ladder and returning to the default idle animation or rest pose.

### Blending Animations

Blending animations are used to transition the character smoothly from one animation state to another—for example, from walking to running. Switching from one animation directly to another can cause the character to stutter or to jump obviously—blending animations are intermediate animations that take the character smoothly and seamlessly from the walk to the run. These animations can even be taken a step further so that you have different animations based on which foot the character is currently on when triggered to change to a different animation.

With the exception of major change-of-venue actions such as the ladder climbing example, blending animations are rarely used in games. Blending is usually handled by the game engine, which tweens the position of the character in a frame of his current animation to the newly called animation. Obviously, tweening isn't the most visually appealing or accurate solution, but it is fast; and if the programmer is willing to tweak the parameters a bit, it can have a quite passable result.

### Custom Animations

These are simple animations that are specific to a character or to the game itself. Custom animations can include things such as operating a computer or transforming into a beast, but they are not the normal set of animations used by the majority of in-game characters.

### Cinematic Animations

More and more games are relying on cinematic animations—real-time cut scenes—to help the story progress. These are scenes played using the actual game engine rather than showing a prerendered movie. This method is beneficial because it can help keep the flow of the game intact. These "scripted" events usually involve an animated scene being played when triggered in the game.

## The Animation List

Most of the animations you create will rely heavily on animations you've created previously. Therefore, it's important to follow the structure of the *animation list,* which your lead animator and project designer will have compiled in advance.

You would think a list containing the animations a character performs in a game would be pretty straightforward. They walk, run, jump, maybe have some fight moves or shoot a gun. In actual fact, however, a lot more animations than these explicit ones are involved in getting your characters to move, most of which you may not even realize are separate animations.

The animation list will tell you what movements are required, but not how the character will perform them. A walk cycle, for example, can be one of the most difficult animations to create because it can be interpreted in any number of ways—each person has their own way of walking. So creating a unique animation that also has to loop is tricky. Since most animations are based upon it, the very first pose that needs to be defined is the *rest pose.*

### Defining the Rest Pose

With any third-person-perspective game, the main character has to be interesting even when the player is not controlling him. Look at any game you play, and when you're not controlling the character, he will first adopt the idle animation before looping through any fidget animations he has. Before these animations can be created, a *rest pose* needs to be defined.

It's important to lock the rest pose early on, since changing it later will involve altering many of the animations based on it. For example, consider a crouching position. The animation would start with the character in the rest pose and end in the crouch position, which can be classed as another rest pose. Then when the character stands again, the rest pose is where the animation would end. So altering the rest pose would also mean editing all these other animations.

Initially, the rest pose need only be a single frame, just one pose. At this stage you don't need any animation, because this is the pose used as the starting point for many others.

You may find that you will need a number of rest poses, each depending on the character's state of health or current mood. For Kila, we might have the following (the first three are illustrated in **Figure 16.1**):

▶   The default posture used in game: relaxed yet dynamic, and—most important of all—in keeping with her personality. Also, don't have the feet too far apart, or it will be difficult to get other animations back into this pose.

▶   A posture to indicate when she is low on health.

▶   A fight stance; Kila will use hand-to-hand combat to defend herself.

▶   Various weapons, ranging from a metal post to a machine gun, will be available to Kila. To avoid having a different rest pose for every weapon, you could create the same rest pose for weapons that are held with one hand, like a pistol or Uzi. Even the default pose could be used for these stances.

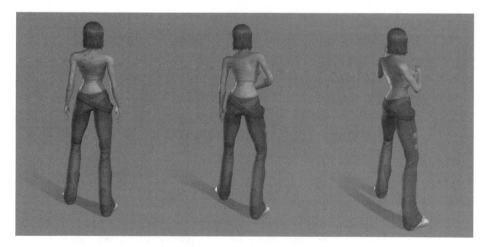

**FIGURE 16.1** Examples of rest poses

TIP ▶   Try viewing your character from an in-game view. This will help you to see if certain poses or animations, including the rest pose, read well at that distance. It may be that you have been too subtle, in which case you will need to exaggerate the pose more.

With the rest pose(s) defined and signed off by your manager, you can then proceed to generate all the animations that begin or end in this pose. The idle animations, for example, all need to start and end in the same place so that they can flow into each other smoothly.

Take a good look at your complete animations list and make sure you know which ones need to be done first. Before we look at creating an animation in Maya, let's examine some of the program's animation tools.

## Animation Tools

There are many ways to produce and control animation in Maya (in fact, whole books are written about them), so we'll just look at the main animation controls.

### Animation Controls

At the bottom of the Maya user interface are various animation controls; these can be seen in **Figure 16.2**.

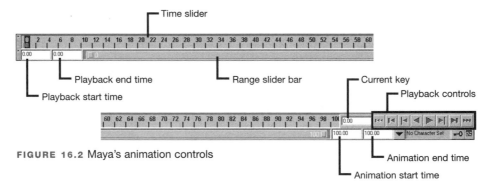

FIGURE 16.2 Maya's animation controls

Let's first look at the Time Slider. This bar shows the range of frames you are currently working on. Clicking anywhere in here with the left mouse button will highlight the selected frame with a black box and update the view to show that frame of the animation.

**TIP** Clicking with the middle mouse button in the Time Slider will select that frame but not update the time in the views. This is handy if you want to quickly copy the pose from one frame to another. You simply select the object whose keys you want to copy, select the frame you wish to copy to with the middle mouse button, and then set a key on the object at this new frame.

Right-clicking on the Time Slider will open up a new contextual menu (**Figure 16.3**). These options allow you to cut, copy, and paste selected keys, snap them to specific times, and adjust the playback and range of the animation. We'll look at other contextual menu items (such as Tangents and Playblast, which play a valuable role in animation) later in the chapter.

The Range Slider sets the current visible range in the Time Slider. This is useful if you need to work on a specific section of the animation, while also maintaining the full animation timeline.

Setting values for the Animation Start Time and Animation End Time will set the overall animation's timeline.

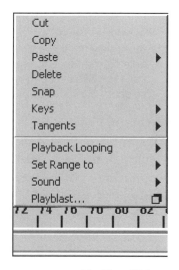

**FIGURE 16.3** The Time Slider contextual menu

You can use the Playback Start Time and Playback End Time to manually set the Range Slider. To interactively edit the Range Slider, use the Range Slider bar. At either end of this bar are two small squares; click and drag these to specify the Time Slider range in which you want to work.

The Playback Controls are very much like a remote control, allowing you to play the animation, step along a frame at a time, or even move along to the next keyframe.

Now that we know how to control time in Maya, let's now look at how to set keyframes.

### Setting Keyframes

When you set a *keyframe,* you are actively storing that object's attribute values at that specific time. Storing particular values at specific spots in the Time Slider instructs Maya to create the in-between positions of those values that ultimately provides the illusion of movement.

> **NOTE** Although they are related, setting a key is not the same as setting a driven key. As you may remember from Chapter 12, driven keys link one attribute to another, but are set at specific attribute values, not specific frames in the Time Slider. Ordinary keys are set at a specific frame, storing the currently selected attributes at that time.

When keys are set on an object, they show up in the Time Slider as red lines (**Figure 16.4**, top). You can then interactively edit these keys, moving and scaling them in the Time Slider itself. To do this, hold down Shift and drag over a selection in the Time Slider. Your selection will be marked with a red box, with arrows at either end and in the center (**Figure 16.4**, bottom). Selecting the center arrow lets you drag the selection, in effect moving the entire set of selected keys as a group. Selecting and moving one of the end arrows lets you scale the selected keys in that direction.

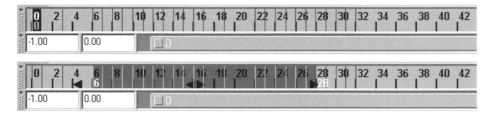

FIGURE 16.4 Working with keys in the Time Slider

So how do we create a keyframe? There are a number of ways to do this in Maya; here are the most common ones:

▶   In the Animation menu set, go to Animate > Set Key (you can also access this tool by pressing S). By default this will set a key on all the selected object's keyable attributes, but it can be configured to work however you like, using the options seen in **Figure 16.5**. The best thing to do is play around with this tool until you find a setup that works best for you.

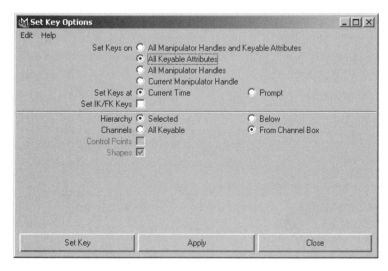

▶ In the Channel Box, simply right-click on a single attribute and choose Key Selected to set a single key. Key All will set a key on all the keyable attributes of the object.

▶ Moving away from the main Maya UI, you can also set keys in several other windows. For example, in the Attribute Editor you can right-click on an attribute and select Set Key.

▶ You can also add keys to objects in the Graph Editor and Dope Sheet, both of which are discussed next.

### The Graph Editor

Setting keys to move an object is only half the job; the other half is working with *animation curves.*

To get from one keyframe to another, a curve is drawn between them, sort of like a path to be followed by the object's attributes. This is called *interpolation,* and it's Maya's way of predicting how the object should move from one keyframe to another. The Graph Editor allows you to edit not only the keys themselves, but also these curves. The *tangents* of a curve dictate the way the curve enters and exits a keyframe. Editing these tangents can have dramatic results on how the animation flows from one keyframe to the next.

Open up the file Cube_Example.mb. All of these cubes are identical and have exactly the same keys set on them at the same times; but when you play the animation, each one moves differently. This is because each cube's tangents are different.

Open the Graph Editor by going to Window > Animation Editors > Graph Editor. You'll see the window in **Figure 16.6**. (Your Graph Editor window may differ slightly, depending on the version of Maya you are using. All the basic tools will still be present, however.)

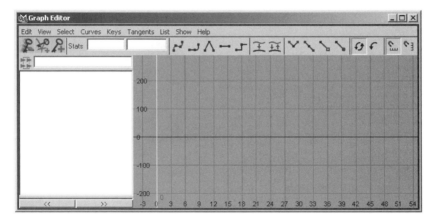

FIGURE 16.6 The Graph Editor

Let's have a quick look at some of the tools on the Graph Editor's toolbar.

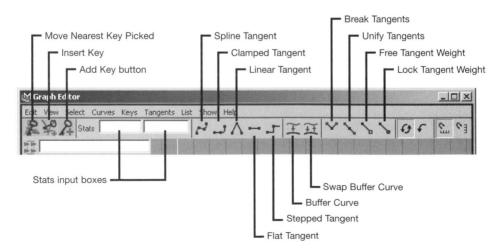

The first few buttons at the left end of the toolbar are the key manipulation tools:

▶ **Move Nearest Picked Key.** When this tool is active, only the key nearest to the cursor will move regardless of how many keys you select in the Graph Editor.

▶ **Insert Keys.** With this tool active, simply select the curve with the left mouse button, then click and drag with the middle mouse button until you reach the place where you want to insert a key.

▶ **Add Keys.** This tool works similarly to Insert Keys, except that clicking with the middle mouse button will dictate where the new key is placed. Holding the middle button allows you to move the key around; it will not be committed to the curve until you release the button.

> **NOTE** There is an important difference between the Insert Keys and Add Keys tools: Insert Keys will add keys at the position in time that you designate, but only on the existing value curve. Add Keys will add a key wherever you designate, but will not preserve the value curve.

Next on the toolbar are the two **Stats** input boxes. The first box shows you the frame number of the selected key, and the other box shows the key's attribute value. With a key selected, you can type absolute values into these input boxes to place the key in an exact place or time.

The five **Tangent buttons** are (left to right) Spline, Clamped, Linear, Flat, and Stepped. Clicking on these will apply a particular tangent to the whole curve or to the selected keys. Tangents are discussed in a later section.

After the tangent buttons are two **Buffer Curve** buttons. The first one allows you to store the current curve in a buffer. You can then make changes, enable View > Show Buffer Curves to display the buffered curve in gray, and compare the new curve with the buffered curve. If you want to revert back to the stored curve, click on the second button, **Swap Buffer Curve.**

Next on the toolbar are two tangent-editing tools. The first, **Break Tangents**, lets you edit the in and out tangents for each key individually. The **Unify Tangents** button will fix this break, so if you manipulate the in tangent of a curve, the out tangent will also be affected. All tangents are unified by default.

Next to the two tangent-editing buttons are the **Free Tangent Weight** and **Lock Tangent Weight** buttons. By default, all curves are created nonweighted; this means you can only edit the tangents vertically—the handles will only move up and down, pivoted around the key. When the tangents are weighted, you have complete freedom over where the handles can be placed; that means you can move them horizontally as well as vertically, adding more weight to each key. To convert a nonweighted curve to a weighted one, select the attribute in the list on the left in the Graph Editor and go to Curves > Weighted Tangents.

> **NOTE** If you prefer, you can change your general animation preferences to make weighted tangents the default rather than nonweighted.

Now that we have an understanding of some of the Graph Editor's tools, let's get some exposure to working with animation curves and tangents. You should still have Cube_Example.mb open, along with the Graph Editor.

1   In Maya's main view, select the first cube, named Cube_Spline.

   **Figure 16.7a** shows the Graph Editor with the selected cube listed on the left. Below this is a list of all the cube's attributes that have animation applied to them. Currently only the Translate Z attribute has animation applied.

2   Press F in the Graph Editor's main window to frame the animation curve. As you can see, this first cube has a Spline Tangent applied to it. This makes the curve flow smoothly between all the keys.

3   Select the next cube, Cube_Clamped. This tangent is a hybrid of two others, the Linear and Spline tangents. Unless two keys are similar in value, all the tangents will be set to splines. As you can see in **Figure 16.7b**, the first two keys have the same value, so their tangents are set to Linear; the third key has a higher value, so the tangents leading out of the previous key and into this are set to Spline.

4   Next, look at the cube called Cube_Linear. This type of tangent creates a simple linear path between keys (**Figure 16.7c**).

**5**  Now select Cube_Flat. As you can see in **Figure 16.7d**, instead of the cube following a straight linear path from key to key, it now moves along to the second key and then eases out of it before easing into the final key. This creates a gradual smooth motion when the object starts to move or comes to a stop.

**6**  Finally, look at the Stepped tangent shown in **Figure 16.7e**; this is applied to Cube_Stepped. Unlike the others, this one does not flow along a path as such; rather, it will snap from key to key without being interpolated.

Each of these tangents discussed here can be applied to any curve, by either clicking on the tangent's button found on the Graph Editor toolbar, or from the Tangents menu in either the Graph Editor or the Time Slider contextual menu.

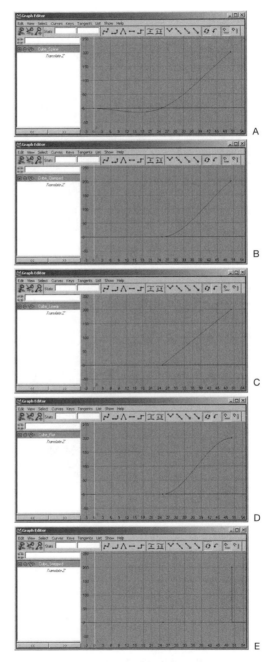

**FIGURE 16.7** Spline, Clamp, Linear, Flat, and Stepped tangents

As well as altering the tangents on a whole curve, you can also select each key and apply them individually. With a key selected in the Graph Editor, you can also edit the curves manually using the two handles that appear. These can be moved around until you achieve the motion you require (**Figure 16.8**).

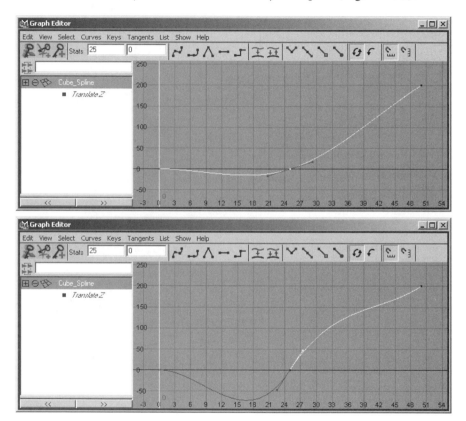

FIGURE 16.8 Editing tangents manually in the Graph Editor

## Dope Sheet

The Dope Sheet is used primarily to edit the timing of your animation because it gives you access to the keys for the whole scene. This can be very useful when you need to quickly speed up or slow down areas of your work.

To open the Dope Sheet, go to Window > Animation Editors > Dope Sheet. In **Figure 16.9**, top, we have the window displaying the basic scene summary, which shows us all the keys that exist in the scene.

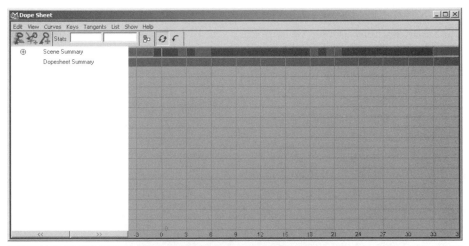

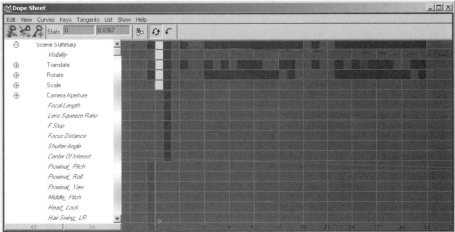

FIGURE 16.9 The Dope Sheet

**NOTE** This display option is not available by default. To make the scene summary visible, go to the Dope Sheet's View menu and enable Scene Summary.

As you can see, the toolbar is a cut-down version of the Graph Editor's, allowing you to add/insert new keys and input absolute values for existing keys. Next to the Stats boxes is a new button for turning hierarchy on and off. When this is enabled, the keys are displayed on objects that exist below the active object, meaning you can work on an entire hierarchy at once.

You can also display each separate attribute in the scene by clicking on the plus icon next to Scene Summary, which will open up its contents (**Figure 16.9**, bottom). You can then select the keys, represented by black blocks; the blocks turn yellow when selected. You are then free to move or even scale them using the middle mouse button to achieve the animation you require.

### Playblast

Depending on the specifications of the computer you are working on and the complexity of your scene, it can be difficult to get a realistic idea of how your animation is going to flow when put into the game. Producing a *playblast* allows you to quickly output your animation as a movie, play it back, and see how the animation will look when run at an exact frame rate.

To produce a playblast, right-click on the Time Slider and select Playblast from the contextual menu. Maya will then run through the animation, taking screen grabs of the selected view, and storing them either as a movie file or separate images.

If you open the Playblast options (**Figure 16.10**), you can configure what Maya will capture and how it is stored. Most of the options are fairly self-explanatory, so let's just have a brief look at the less obvious ones.

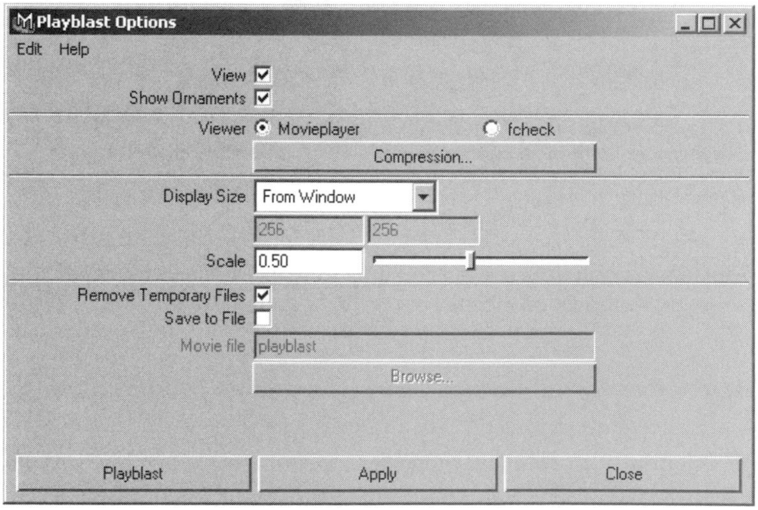

**FIGURE 16.10** Playblast options

▶ **View** automatically opens the movie for you after Maya has finished capturing it.

▶ Having **Show Ornaments** enabled keeps the camera name, axis, and other onscreen displays visible in the playblast.

▶ The **Viewer** options let you specify how you would like the playblast to be output. The Movieplayer viewer will use your operating system's default movie-viewing software, and will more than likely output the playblast as a single movie file. Fcheck is Maya's own viewer and can only handle images. Thus, the playblast is output as individual frames—but this can produce a better, cleaner playback of your animation.

As you begin to animate later in the chapter, don't be afraid to generate any number of playblasts; they are an invaluable means of making sure your animation is headed in the right direction.

## Creating a Walk Cycle

In this section we will produce a walk cycle for Kila. First we will block in the basic motion; once this is in place, the animation can be easily tweaked and refined.

Since this is an in-game animation, it's best to exaggerate the movements slightly at the beginning. If they look "over the top" from the game camera, you can easily reduce the exaggeration using the Graph Editor.

### Scene Preparation

We will start by preparing the scene, getting it ready for animation.

1 Open the Kila_Final.mb file. (You don't need to use the Rest Pose file here because the walk cycle will not begin or end in it.)

Make sure you have a key set on frame –1, storing the file's base pose. Do this by selecting each character set (Character > Select Character Set Node), then right-clicking in the Channel Box and selecting Key All.

**NOTE** Depending on how your game engine handles animation data, you may or may not need to store this base pose. When the character animation is exported, you may need the skeleton to be keyed in this bind pose at the beginning of each animation. It's best to discuss this with your team's technical artist or lead programmer to be sure.

2    Go to Window > Settings/Preferences > Preferences and, as shown in **Figure 16.11**, select Keys in the Categories list.

3    Set both Default In Tangent and Default Out Tangent to Linear. Every new key you create will now have Linear tangents, which will initially be easier to work with. You can alter these tangents again later.

While you work on these steps, you will animate Kila physically moving forward; this will help you visualize how the walk is shaping up. You also need to see how the animation loops, as if she were walking in place. This is because, once the walk is complete, you will have to remove any forward motion, as the game engine will implement that for you.

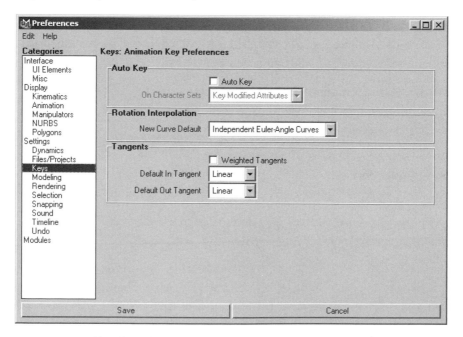

FIGURE 16.11 Alter the default tangents in the Preferences window.

**TIP** Some animators prefer to go straight in and create the animation on the spot, without the forward motion. I find it useful to have both versions at hand just in case I need to generate an animated sequence in which the character must physically walk a distance. With the forward motion included, I don't have to try and put it back in, which can make the feet appear to slide if not done correctly.

To help us see both versions, we can parent a camera to a point at the character's feet. This means the camera will move with the character, giving the illusion of Kila walking in place. We can look through a different camera to see her actually moving along.

1   Make sure you are still on frame −1, and create a new Locator (Create > Locator).

2   Set the Kila_BaseSkel display layer so you can see the joints. Select them, and then select the main Root joint.

3   Holding Shift+Ctrl/Cmd, select the locator and apply a point constraint just on the Y axis, making sure Maintain Offset is enabled. (If for some reason you can't see the locator, check the visibility in the panel's View menu. Or simply make the selections in the Outliner or Hypergraph.)

Now as Kila moves, the locator will follow but will stay locked to the floor.

4   In the side view, position Kila so you can see her legs and waist in the center of the window.

5   go to View > Select Camera. Holding Shift+Ctrl/Cmd, select the locator and parent the camera to it by pressing P.

6   Now you need to set up the Time Slider to cover the time it will take Kila to perform a single cycle of her walk. Set the start frame back to 0, and the end frame at 32.

**NOTE** When creating the walk, the first and last frames must be the same so that the animation loops. This will cause the animation to pause slightly when played, so remember this when you play it back, or create a playblast that only runs up to frame 31.

We use a power-of-two range (0 to 32) because it's then easier to divide the animation into stages. For example, the first and last poses of the walk are on frames 0 and 32; these key poses are known as "extremes." Halfway, we would place a new pose (when the legs cross over the opposite way) on frame 16; this is known as a "breakdown" or "passing position." We can then place additional poses called "in-betweens" on frames 8 and 24, before breaking down the animation further if we need to. With all the main keys evenly spaced, the animation will play at a steady pace throughout.

Now that we have a locator acting as a basepoint for the character, you can parent other cameras to it in order to see the character cycling from other angles. With the scene ready now, we can begin to animate.

### Legs and Waist: Blocking Out Poses

The first step in creating any animation is to block out the main poses. These are the extremes, breakdowns, and any in-between poses needed. This not only gives you a good idea of how the timing feels as the character moves, but also how each pose looks.

Before you do anything else in Maya at this point, get out of your seat and walk around the room. Observe where your waist and feet are at certain stages in your walk. See how they rotate, what speed they move. When do your hips dip? If you are a male animating Kila, try to imitate a feminine walk. It's one thing to watch someone else walking—but to physically do it yourself will give you insight for applying it to your character. Try to do this for all your animation work; don't be afraid of looking silly—in the long run, your animation will be better for it.

1   Let's create our first extreme. With your own walk fresh in your mind, move along to frame 0, switch to the side view, and position Kila's feet to match the crossover point in the walk (**Figure 16.12b**).

Move the right foot up slightly and rotate it so it is tilted forward. Move the hips down and forward, too.

Set a key on the translate and rotate attributes for the icons of both feet and Root_Control.

Normally we would now place the second extreme on frame 32, then the breakdown at frame 16, and so on. However, since our character is moving forward, it makes sense to place each pose as we come to it in the timeline.

This will allow us to see where the hips and feet should be placed on the subsequent poses.

2  Move along to frame 8 and create the second pose. Move the right foot forward until it is just about to plant itself, pose the left foot so it's just about to leave the floor, and move the hips forward, keeping them in between both feet at all times (**Figure 16.12c**).

Set a key to store this pose.

A  Frame −1                B  Frame 0                C  Frame 8

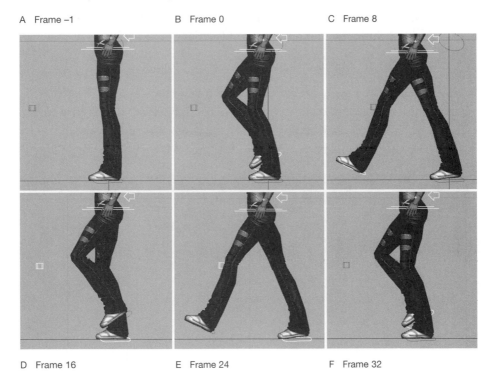

D  Frame 16               E  Frame 24               F  Frame 32

**FIGURE 16.12** From the side view, block in the basic leg poses.

3  Now we come to what would be the breakdown and the next crossover. Move along to frame 16 and try your best to replicate the pose on frame 0 (**Figure 16.12d**), but on the opposite feet. Set a key to store it.

4  Now add the second in-between. The left foot needs to plant, so move to frame 24 and do your best to replicate the pose on frame 8, again on the opposite feet (**Figure 16.12e**).

**TIP** An easy way to do this is to use the middle mouse button to go to frame 24. Line up one of the feet on top of the opposite one in the view, and set a key just on the one you moved. Left-click to move back to the reference frame, then repeat on the other foot and the root. The poses will be nearly identically mirrored in just a few seconds, with no guesswork.

5  The pose in frame 32 (our second extreme) needs to be the same as frame 0 so that it can successfully cycle (**Figure 16.12f**). To quickly accomplish this, simply copy the keys from frame 0 to frame 32 and then adjust the Z translation.

Now we will clean up the Root_Controls keys a little—it's important to keep your animation clean, removing any unused keyframes.

1  Select the Root_Control and open the Graph Editor.

2  Delete all the keys, except the first and last ones on the Translate Z curve. You want its Z translation to be a continuous straight line, as it is in **Figure 16.13**. This will allow the character to move forward smoothly; any extra keys might cause her to pause as she steps.

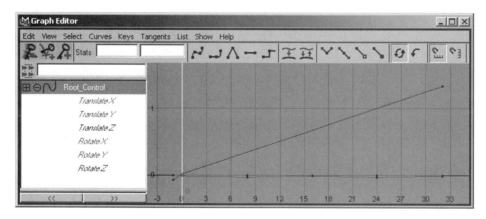

FIGURE 16.13 Ensure that the Root_Control's Translate Z curve only has keys at either end.

3  Removing these keys may mean you have to go back and tweak some of your poses, so go back and do that now before we continue.

From the side, the walk is shaping up nicely; but what about the front? As shown in **Figure 16.14a**, by switching to the front view we can see that her legs are too far apart. In a more feminine walk, the feet tend to cross in front of each other, almost as if she is walking on a tightrope.

**1**   Select the LeftFoot icon and, in the Graph Editor, highlight just its Translate X attribute (**Figure 16.15**, top).

**2**   Now select all the keys except the one that lies on frame –1, and move them down (**Figure 16.15**, bottom). This should also bring the foot in toward the center in the view panel, as seen in **Figure 16.14b**.

   Move the keys down to about –0.138 and make a note of the value.

**3**   Now apply this same technique to the RightFoot icon. Edit its Translate X attribute by moving the keys to a value of 0.138 (**Figure 16.16**, bottom). This brings the foot in the opposite way (refer back to **Figure 16.14c**).

The problem we have now is that the feet will go through the legs as they pass by. We can fix this easily in the Graph Editor. We know that frames 0 and 32 are the same; these are the crossover frames for the right foot, so we need to edit both.

**4**   Select frames 0 and 32 in the Graph Editor and move them both down, to a value of around 0.075. This should move the foot back out in the main view panel (**Figure 16.14d**).

**5**   Select the LeftFoot icon and move its key to where the crossover exists (frame 16) out to around –0.075.

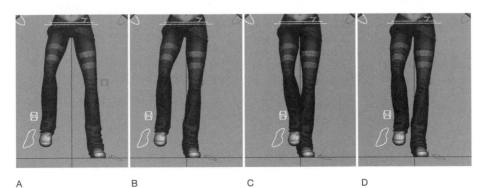

A          B          C          D

**FIGURE 16.14** Adjust the feet so her legs are not too far apart.

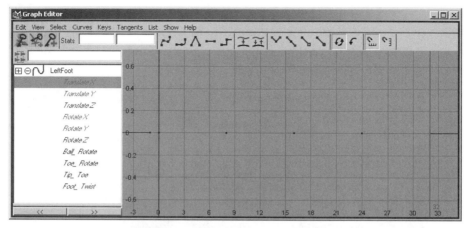

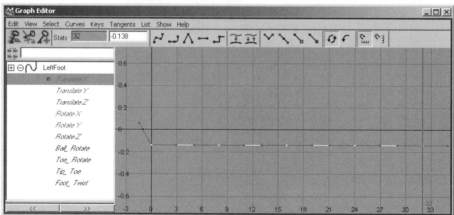

**FIGURE 16.15** Edit the Translate X keys to bring the feet in.

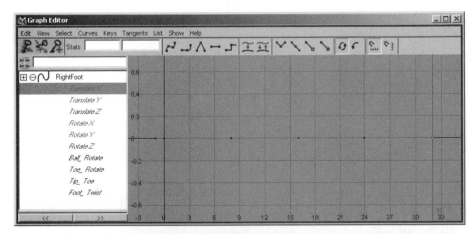

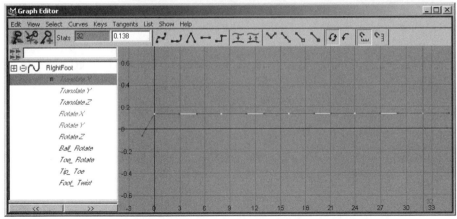

**FIGURE 16.16** Edit the Translate X keys to bring the feet in.

We have now blocked in the animation for the waist and legs. You may need to play the animation through, or create a playblast, to check how she looks from the side again before we proceed:

▶ Altering the feet positions probably means the hips are now too low; if this is the case, select the Root_Control's Translate Y keys and move them up slightly.

▶ Make other final adjustments to the basic poses and timing as needed, but keep the keys at the times already specified: frames 0, 8, 16, 24, and 32.

### Legs and Waist: Refinement

With the poses established, we can now refine the basic animation, giving Kila a smooth and realistic walk cycle by adding extra keys and poses.

Moving along the timeline, the first thing we can work on is the way the feet plant after each step. At the moment, they don't spend enough time on the ground, giving the impression that she is floating along and has no weight.

1   Working on the left foot first, move the keys set at frame 8 to frame 10. This will keep the foot grounded for longer.

You can use any method you like to move the keys: in the Graph Editor, in the Dope Sheet, or by simply highlighting them and moving them in the Time Slider.

2   Move along to frame 32. Then select frame 28 with your middle mouse button and set a key at this frame. You've just copied the pose from frame 32, essentially moving the keys back. We need to keep the keys at frame 32 because it is the very end of the animation.

3   To achieve the same results for the right foot, move the keys set at 16 back to 12 and move the keys at 24 up to 26.

Now that the feet have changed, you will also need to alter the hips. You want them to drop just as each foot plants on the floor and takes the weight.

1   Select the Root_Control icon, and select just the Translate Y attribute in the Graph Editor. You will see the curve for the Y translation, as demonstrated in **Figure 16.17a**.

2   We now want to offset the hips' dip so it happens when the foot plants. Select all the keys except for the one at frame –1, and move them along the timeline until the two lower keys, which currently lie on frames 8 and 24, lie on frames 15 and 31 (**Figure 16.17b**).

3   You will now need to set new start and end keys, or the animation will not loop. Move along to frame 32 and set a key on just the Y translation. This will store its current value and maintain the curve's current shape.

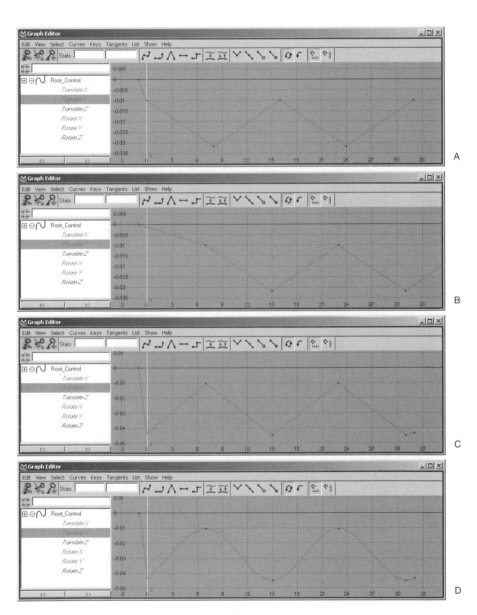

**FIGURE 16.17** Adjusting the hips' Y translation

**4**  To create the seamless loop, you will copy this exact key to frame 0. Select frame 0 using the middle mouse button, and set another key on the Y translation.

**5**  Clean up the curve by deleting any keys after frame 32 (**Figure 16.17c**).

**6**  Flatten the tangents on the middle three keys only, by selecting them and clicking on the Flat Tangent button.

Your new curve should resemble that in **Figure 16.17d**.

We have now smoothed out the waist's animation, so let's do the same on the feet.

**1**  Select the right foot. In the Graph Editor, flatten all the tangents by clicking on the Flat Tangent button (**Figure 16.18**, bottom). This will initially soften all the animation on the foot.

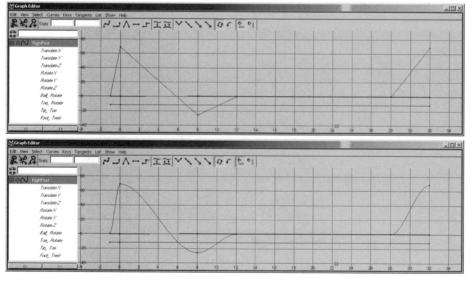

**FIGURE 16.18** Flatten all the tangents on the right foot.

**2**    Now select only Translate Y. As you can see in **Figure 16.19**, top, on frame 8 there is a key that breaks up the nice arc between frames 0 and 12. If you play the animation, you'll probably notice that this causes the foot to pause just before it is planted on the floor. We want to remove this so the foot can flow freely.

Select the key at frame 8 and delete it, which will give you the cleaned-up curve in **Figure 16.19**, bottom.

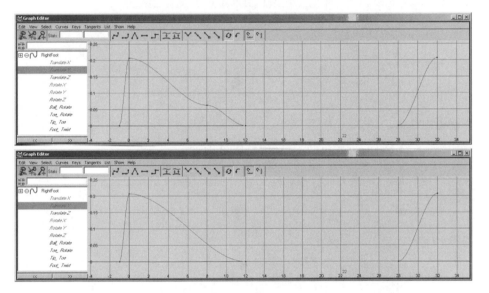

**FIGURE 16.19** Remove the extra key in the Y translation.

**3**    The same correction can be done on the Z translation, except that the key you want to remove lies on the very first and last frames. Instead of deleting this one, we simply select the keys and click on the Linear Tangent button, straightening out the curves so that they run in a more linear fashion (**Figure 16.20**).

**4**    Now select the left foot and follow the same procedure. You want to remove the extra key from the Y translation. For the Z translation, this time the key we require is in the middle of the curve, meaning we can simply select it and delete it (**Figure 16.21**).

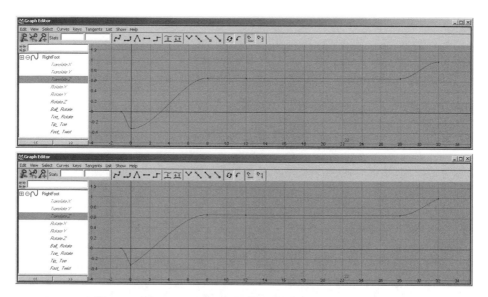

**FIGURE 16.20** Make the first and last keys' tangents linear.

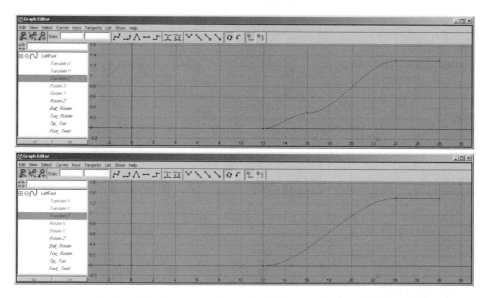

**FIGURE 16.21** On the left foot, you can simply delete the extra key on the Z translation.

We still have work to do on the feet, but that should wait until after we work on the hips. We'll do these now because their positions could affect the feet's animation later on.

We are now going to add a bit of weight to Kila as she moves. To do this, we will shift her hips over the foot that is currently on the floor and taking all her weight.

**1**   Switch to the front view first. While on frame 0, move the Root_Control over her left foot using just the X translation. Use a small value of around 0.015, this will also give her hips a subtle sway as she moves (**Figure 16.22**).

When you're done, set a key on just the Translate X attribute.

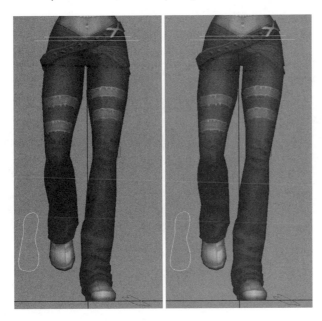

**FIGURE 16.22** Move the Root_Control over her left foot.

**2**   Now move to frame 16 and set the same value, but this time make it negative: −0.015. Then set another key.

**3**   Set a key on frame 32; set this one to be the same as the original value, which was 0.015.

**4**   Now look in the Graph Editor and make sure you have keys only on frames 0, 16, and 32 of the X translation. Remove any keys that lie in between.

**5**    Finally, flatten all the tangents on the curve, to smooth out the sway of the hips.

Now we will give her a little wiggle as she walks, by animating the waist controller. The first thing we will alter is the amount of tilt on her hips. When one of her feet is placed on the floor, it's taking all the weight of her body, so her hips will tilt away from that leg.

**1**    Starting on frame 0, rotate the Waist_Control around the Z axis until you reach a value of around 7. The hips should tilt like those in **Figure 16.23**, middle.

**2**    Set a key on just the Rotate Z attribute on both frames 0 and 32.

**3**    Move along to frame 16 and set the Z rotation to –7, tilting her hips in the opposite direction (**Figure 16.23**, right). Set another key.

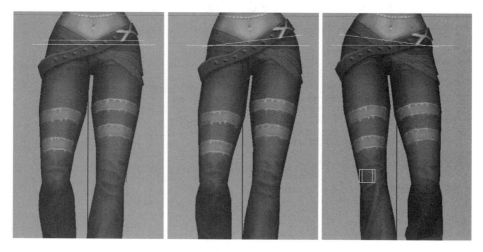

**FIGURE 16.23** Tilt the hips around the Z axis.

**4**    Go to the Graph Editor and make all of the Rotate Z curve's tangents Flat to soften their movement.

When women walk, their hips' movement is in relation to the placement of their feet. The hip doesn't begin to tilt in the opposite direction until the foot has been placed, because it's the shift in weight that straightens the leg out; this then forces the hip to tilt away from it. We need to insert a few more keys to implement this detail.

**5**   Move along to frame 11 in the Time Slider and set a key on the Rotate Z attribute. Follow that with another key placed at frame 27. You are adding keys here because these are the frames just before each foot plants.

**6**   Now, using the Graph Editor, edit the keys so that the hips don't tilt immediately. Set the key at frame 11 to 1.7, and the key at frame 27 to −1.7.

As demonstrated in **Figure 16.24**, the hips will begin to gradually tilt until they reach frame 12, the point where the foot connects with the floor. Then they'll tilt more quickly before moving gradually again over toward the other foot.

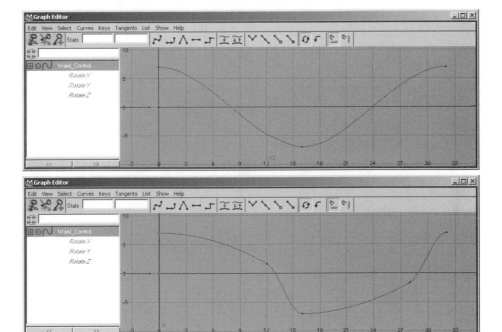

**FIGURE 16.24** Edit the Waist_Control's Z rotation to make the hips tilt correctly.

Now that we have the hips' tilt, we can implement a slight rotation to make the hips move forward with each leg.

**1**   Move along to the first frame where the right leg is about to plant; this should be around frame 10. Set the Waist_Control's Rotate Y attribute to 10, and set a key on it.

**2**  Move along until the left leg is in the same position; this should be at frame 26. Set the Y rotation to –10 and set another key.

**3**  Move along to frame 32, and set the Y rotation to 0 so that it's the same as on frame 0. Set another key.

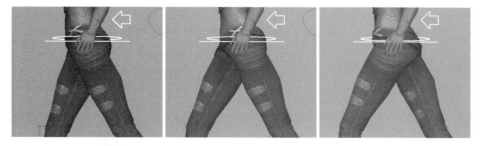

FIGURE 16.25 Add rotation to the hips around the Y axis.

**4**  Now open the Graph Editor so we can see the curve (**Figure 16.26**, top). You want the two middle keys to run smoothly, but because this animation loops you want to keep the first and last keys as they are. If their tangents were set to Smooth, it would cause the animation on the hips to pause as it reaches the end of the cycle.

So select the middle two keys and make their tangents Flat, producing a smoother curve like that in **Figure 16.26**, middle.

Finally, you need to make sure this curve loops correctly. Looking at its current path, the tangents are shallower at the beginning than they are at the end—the start and end keys need to be updated so the animation will run smoothly. Our animation's midpoint is at frame 16, but we offset the animation by two frames; so the new midpoint is 18.

**5**  Move along to frame 18. With your middle mouse button, select frames 0 and 32 and set a key on the Rotate Y attribute. The curve is now correctly balanced, making for a better loop (**Figure 16.26**, bottom).

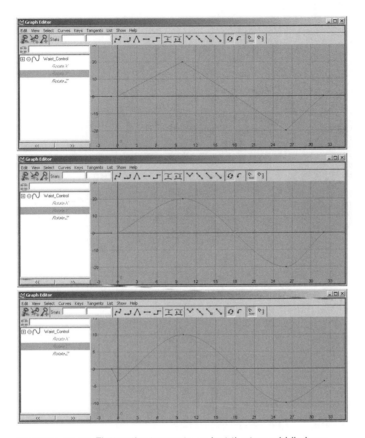

**FIGURE 16.26** Flatten the tangents on just the two middle keys.

The majority of the hip work is complete. So we can now return to the feet and finish them. We'll use the Ball_Rotate control we added to the rig, so as each foot moves back, Kila will eventually end up on just the ball of her foot.

1   Use the gridline as a floor marker, and move along the timeline until the left foot starts to prematurely leave the floor. This should be around frame 4.

2   This marks where the ball of the foot should start to rotate, so move back to frame 3. Set a key on the Ball_Rotate attribute, storing the value of 0 on this frame.

3   Now move along to where the foot *does* leave the floor; this should be at frame 10 (**Figure 16.27**, left). Set the Ball_Rotate attribute to –45, which will plant the ball of the foot back on the ground (**Figure 16.27**, right). Set a key.

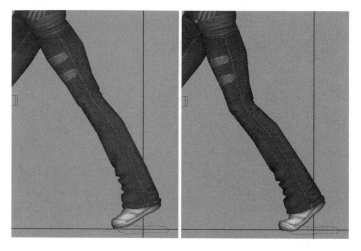

**FIGURE 16.27**
Add animation to the Ball_Rotate attribute.

4   Set the Ball_Rotate attribute back to 0 where the foot has fully left the floor, which should be around frame 16. Set a key here, too, effectively removing the rotation around the ball of the foot.

5   Now repeat the procedure on the right foot. Set the Ball_Rotate attribute to 0 on frames 19 and 32, and then plant the ball of the foot on frame 26 with a value of -45.

6   All that remains is to flatten the tangents on both Ball_Rotate attributes, to smooth out the animation.

Now you have all the basic keys in place for Kila's lower body. Go through the animation again, adjusting it in the Graph Editor until you are happy with the walking movement of her legs. Here are a few things to look out for:

▶   It may be that the feet raise too high off the ground, making her look like she is walking in water. If need be, simply move the highest Y translation keys for the feet down slightly.

▶   You may want to add a slight twist to the feet as they come forward. Do this by placing keys on the Z rotation of the feet.

▶   You can also adjust the knee positions, pointing her knees inward as she walks.

Play through the lower body animation a few times, and maybe even generate a playblast to see how it runs in real time. Once you are completely happy with it, we will continue on to the torso.

### Torso Animation

The animation in Kila's legs and hips will guide the movement of the rest of her body. To add movement to her torso, we only need to animate the main spine controls.

To make sure we have complete control over the animation, we will animate one attribute at a time, but to speed things up we can animate all three spine joints together, giving her back a smooth, gradual arc as it moves.

We will begin with the Rotate Y attribute, making her torso twist slightly with each step. As you walk, your upper body tends to mirror the lower body's actions. That is, when your right leg is out in front, it's the left arm that is in front. As the arm moves to the front, the torso twists, bringing the related shoulder out with the arm. This is the movement we will now add into Kila.

1   Select all three spine controls. At frame 0, neither leg is out in front, so we will keep the torso's rotations at 0. This is the crossover point in the animation.

   Set a key on the Y rotation on frames 0 and 32 on all spine controls. These frames need to hold the same pose.

2   Move along the Time Slider until the right leg is as far forward as it can go; this should happen on frame 8.

   Using just the Y rotation, twist the torso so that the left shoulder moves forward. Inputting a value of -2 directly into the Channel Box will affect all three spine controls and should be sufficient; we don't want the torso movement to be too dramatic. Set a key when you're finished with the rotation.

3   Move along until the left leg is all the way forward; this should be on frame 24. Set a value of 2 in the Rotate Y attribute, and set another key.

   **NOTE**  We use the same values on both sides so that Kila's walk is even. If one side moved more than the other, she might have a limp or some other unnatural movement. In some parts of the game this will be what you want; for instance, when she is injured.

**4** With all the main keys applied, go into the Graph Editor. Flatten the tangents on the new keys, but leave the first and last ones Linear. As you can see in **Figure 16.28**, you can work on all three attributes at once.

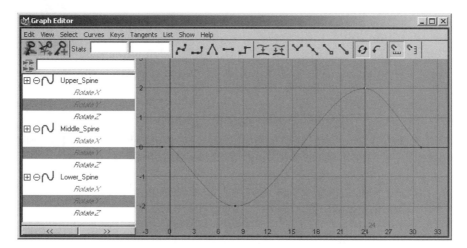

**FIGURE 16.28** Animate the spine's Rotate Y attributes, then flatten the two central tangents.

Kila's torso will now twist slightly as she walks.

To help show the weight behind each step, we can use both the Z and X rotations to dip and tilt the upper body. As each foot plants on the ground, the hip tilts away from it; this also causes the body to tilt. Gravity and momentum then make the weight of her upper body dip slightly before catching up with the rest of the body.

> **NOTE** When you're creating a walk cycle, as a general rule the shoulders should tilt opposite to the hips. So when the left hip is raised, the left shoulder is dipped.

Let's implement the Z rotation first.

**1** You should still have all three spine controls selected; if not, select them all again and switch to the front view.

Unlike the Y rotation, the shoulders need to be tilted when the legs are at their crossover point, which is at frames 0, 16, and 32. On frame 0, set the Rotate Z attributes to -1.5, tilting the shoulders to her left, as seen in **Figure 16.29b**. Set a key to store this at frames 0 and 32.

**2**   You now want the shoulders to tilt to her right (**Figure 16.29d**), so move
along to frame 16 and set a value of 1.5. Set a key.

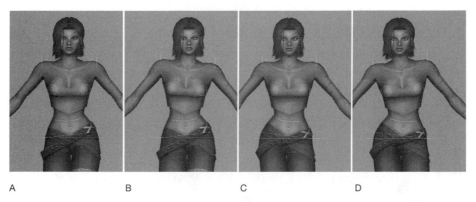

A                              B                              C                              D

**FIGURE 16.29** Use the Z rotation to tilt the shoulders at frames 0, 16, and 32.

**3**   Finally, smooth the keys out in the Graph Editor by making all the tangents
Flat (**Figure 16.30**).

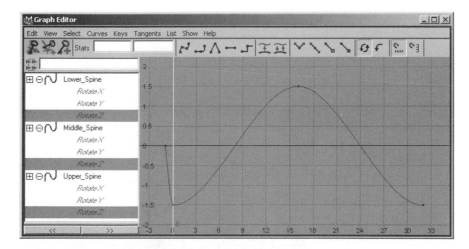

**FIGURE 16.30** Flatten the tangents on the Z rotations to smooth out the animations.

The final torso attribute to animate is the X rotation. Although this will give a
forward dip to her walk, placement of these keys is different from the Z rotation.
This is because the dip needs to start just after the foot has planted and then rise
at the crossover point, before dipping again when the next foot goes down.

**1** Switch to the side view and, with all the spine controls selected once again, move to frame 0. As seen in **Figure 16.31b**, set the X rotation to 2, which should give a subtle dip. Set a key on frames 0, 16, and 32.

**2** Move along to frame 8 and set the Rotate X attribute to -0.7 (**Figure 16.31d**). In this instance we don't mirror the first value because that would cause her to bend too far backward. Set a key on frames 8 and 24.

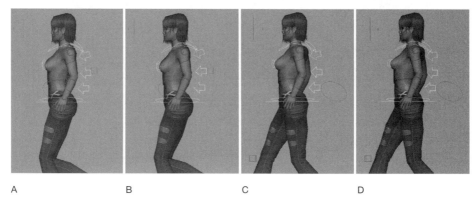

A           B           C           D

**FIGURE 16.31** Implement the forward dip by animating the X rotation.

**3** Flatten the tangents in the Graph Editor. Your curves should now resemble those in **Figure 16.32**.

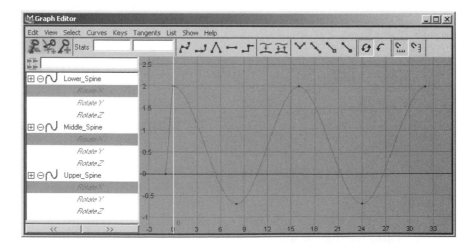

**FIGURE 16.32** Set all the X rotations' tangents to flat in the Graph Editor.

The torso area is complete. Looking at Kila's walk from the front, she sways quite a lot. This could work well for a character with real "attitude," but for Kila we want to calm this down a bit. We want her head to be almost stationary as her hips sway from side to side. We can fix this easily by animating the Rotate Z attribute on the main Root_Control. (If you like the attitude and want to keep the exaggerated sway, you can skip this step; or you could reduce the amount that we're going to edit the animation, to give her even less of a sway.)

1   Switch to the front view and make sure you have the grid visible. As you can see in **Figure 16.33a**, on frame 0 Kila's head is over to the left of the main gridline. We want her head to stay more central to that line.

2   Select the Root_Control, and rotate around the Z axis until her head lines up with the gridline (**Figure 16.33b**). Use the part in her hair as a guide.

3   Now set keys on the Rotate Z attribute on frame 0 and frame 32.

4   Move along to frame 16 (**Figure 16.33c**), and again rotate the Root_Control, this time backward so her head stays fixed to the line (**Figure 16.33d**). Set a key.

5   Flatten all the tangents in the Graph Editor.

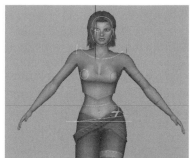
A

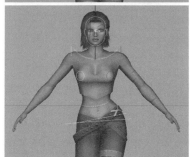
B

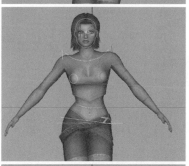
C

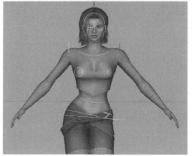
D

**FIGURE 16.33** Use the Root_Control to compensate for the movement in her upper body.

> **NOTE** You could, if you want a more precise movement, apply the same value to Root_Control's Rotate Z attribute in frames 0 and 16; just remember to make the one in frame 16 a negative number.

The torso movement is now complete. After the rest of the animation is applied, you can look at the character's walk as a whole, seeing how everything works together. At that stage you can play around with the keys for the torso until you get the animation just right.

### Arm and Clavicle Animation

Animating the torso helped show us where the shoulders will be at specific times in the walk cycle. With those keys in place, we can begin work on her arms.

At present, Kila looks like she is shrugging her shoulders a little, so let's begin by animating the clavicle controls and reducing this shrug. Select both clavicle controls and move them down slightly, as shown in **Figure 16.34** on the right. Then set a key on just the Y axis, on frames 0 and 32.

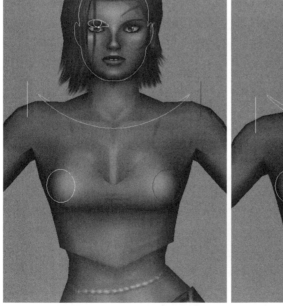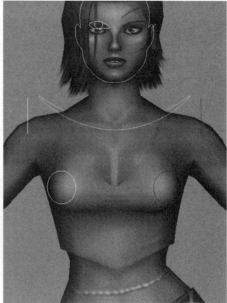

**FIGURE 16.34** Lower the clavicle controls.

That could be all that's needed for the clavicles, but feel free to add some slight animation to the Z and Y translations to give the shoulders some movement—a slight bounce with each step.

Now let's turn our attention to the arms. First prepare the scene by using the visibility controller to hide all the icons except for those on the left side. You will be working in both the side and perspective views, so in each one's View menu make only polygons and handles active. This will hide all the other icons we don't need at present.

In a basic walk cycle, the arms tend to mirror the legs' movement, so when the left leg is forward, the right arm is also. We're going to concentrate on creating a full swing of her left arm, using the FK controls. Employing forward kinematics will give a better simulation of a swinging arm because it's a rotational-based movement. If we used IK, the wrist would follow a linear path between each key set, which would be difficult to animate and would look unnatural in the end.

Because the animation starts at a crossover point, we will start this swing at frame 8, where Kila's right foot is forward, and end it at frame 24 where her right foot is behind her.

1   Move along to frame 8. As demonstrated in **Figures 16.35b** and **16.35e**, rotate just the left shoulder, moving it forward slightly. Then set a key on all the rotation attributes.

2   Move on to frame 24. Here, rotate the shoulder again, moving it backward this time (**Figures 16.35c** and **16.35f**). Set a key on the rotations.

The main swing is in place, so we can use the arm's pose in between these two keys, which is a crossover point, to define the first and last keys for the animation.

A B C

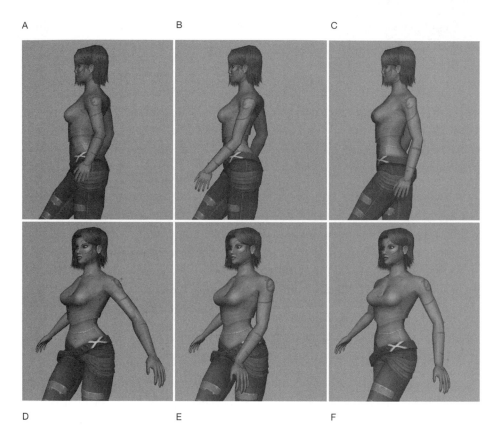

D E F

**FIGURE 16.35** Start by rotating the shoulder at frames 8 and 24.

**3** Move to frame 16, which is the point of the second crossover. Click on frame 0 with your middle mouse button, and set a key on all the rotation attributes of the shoulder.

**4** Click on frame 32 with the middle mouse button and set another key here.

**5** Finally, go to the Graph Editor and flatten all the tangents on just the middle keys.

With the basic movement for the arm in place, next up are the elbow and wrist joints. If we key the elbow's rotation at frames 8 and 24, the elbow will appear rigid because it will move at exactly the same times as the shoulder. We want to offset the elbow animation, making the arm appear to move freely.

**1**  Move along to frame 11, which is just after the shoulder has reached its first key. Rotate the elbow, just around the Y axis. This is demonstrated in **Figure 16.36**, left. Set a key on the Rotate Y attribute.

**2**  Move to frame 27, and rotate the elbow back so that the arm is almost straight, as in **Figure 16.36**, right. Set another key on the Y rotation.

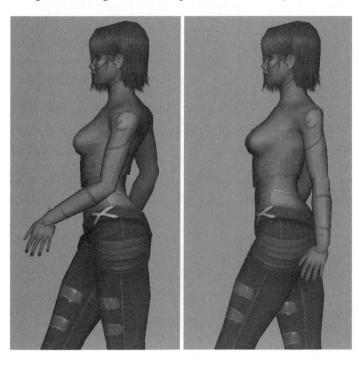

**FIGURE 16.36**
Pose the elbow at frames 11 and 27.

The basic swing is in, but we can no longer use frame 16 as our middle point of reference to help us on frames 0 and 32. Instead, we need to work out where the new middle pose will be.

**3**  Count the number of frames between the last key created (at frame 27) and the final frame (frame 32). There are five.

**4**  Now select frame 27 and move back five frames to frame 22. This is the frame where the elbow should be as it's rotating back.

**5**  Use the middle mouse button to select frame 32, and set a key on the Y axis. Do the same on frame 0.

**6** Flatten the tangents on the two middle keys to smooth out the animation.

For the wrist, follow the same procedure as for the elbow, to give it a bit of swing.

**1** Start by moving along to frame 11; then pose and set a key on the hand (**Figure 16.37**, left).

**2** Move on to frame 27, and pose and key the hand (**Figure 16.37**, right).

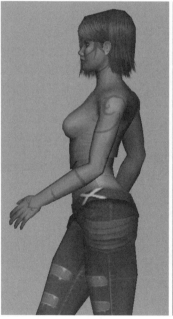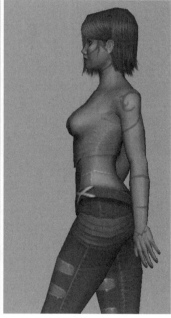

**FIGURE 16.37**
Key the hand's pose at frames 11 and 27.

**3** Using the method we employed for the elbow, work out the frame for the middle pose that the hand should be in for frames 0 and 32. You should land on frame 22.

**4** With the middle mouse button, select frame 32, and set a key on all the hand's rotations. Do the same at frame 0.

**5** Flatten the tangents on both the middle keys.

The entire arm now swings nicely, but it moves a bit too freely. When our arms swing forward and backward, they pause slightly just before they change direction. We will now implement this into the shoulder; you can then apply the same procedure on the rest of the arm.

**1**   Select the shoulder and open up the Graph Editor. As you can see in **Figure 16.38a**, the curves are nice and smooth.

**2**   Move along to the first set of keys, which in this instance lie on frame 8. Hold down the middle mouse button, and move along the timeline to frame 12. Set a key on the shoulder; this will give us a pause of 4 frames (**Figure 16.38b**).

**3**   Move along to the next set of keys at frame 24. Again holding the middle mouse button, move ahead another four frames and set a key (**Figure 16.38c**).

**4**   The new keys' tangents are quite angular, so select them keys and flatten the tangents (**Figure 16.38d**).

The final things to alter are the start and end frames, which need to be updated to take into account the change in the curve. Our new last key was placed at frame 28, so that means there are four frames between that and the end frame 32.

**5**   Move four frames back from frame 24; this is now where the arm ends its cycle. With the middle mouse button, click on frames 0 and 32 and set a key on both. This gives you the final curves seen in **Figure 16.38e**.

The shoulder will now pause slightly before it changes direction. Apply this arrangement to the elbow and hand animations.

The left arm now has motion, so follow the steps in this section again for the right arm.

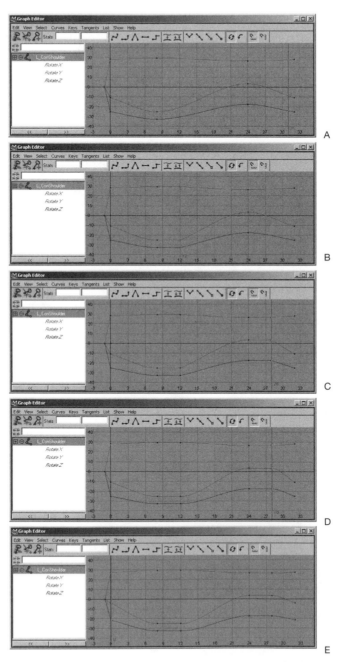

**FIGURE 16.38** Add extra keys to make the arm pause slightly
before it changes direction in its swing.

When both arms are at this same stage, it will give you a better idea of how the animation feels as a whole, so create a playblast and spend some time tweaking things until you are happy with the results.

▶ Try playing around with the timing of both arms so that they are not exactly symmetrical; this can add interest to the animation.

▶ Try moving the keys back a frame or two, so the arms' animation happens slightly sooner.

That's it for the primary animation included in Kila. If you want, go ahead and add movement to her head, breasts, and even her hair. Stick to just simple animation for these parts; all they really need to have are slight bounces. Tweak the overall walk cycle, refining her movements until the walk is perfect.

Save the finished file as Kila_Walk.mb.

Creating a walk cycle for Grae is a little more difficult, because of his unusual leg conformation. The basic principles remain the same, but you may want to give him more vertical movement as his knees unbend. Also, his wings would move in the same pattern as his arms, but you may wish to give them even more sway to indicate their less-solid construction. Save the file as Grae_Walk.mb when you're happy with it.

## Running in Place

When the animation for Kila is played in-game, it's the game code that will actually cause her to move. So we now need to alter our animation, removing her forward movement. (If you animated the character without this forward movement, you can skip this section.)

Normally, removing the forward movement would involve editing the Root_Control and both foot controls' Translate Z attributes, working out where they should be at specific times—as you can imagine, this can be a very difficult and time-consuming task. To make this much easier, I have supplied a script on the GCDM shelf called **Spot**. As long as you have followed the same naming conventions I have used during the creation of the rig, this script will pull the animation back for you.

> **NOTE** If you are using a different rig or if your names are different, you can simply rename the main controls to Root_Control, LeftFoot, and RightFoot, and the script will work. When you're done with this task, you can change the names back to the ones you prefer.

All the Spot script does is work out the distance of each foot from the hips on each keyframe. The keys are then pulled back while maintaining this offset. You can do this just as easily using the Graph Editor, but it will take a while longer to complete.

Once you've run the script, all you need to do is make sure the first and last keys (0 and 32) are exactly the same, to ensure that the loop is seamless.

You can see both Kila and Grae's walk cycles by loading the files Kila_Walk.mb and Grae_Walk.mb from the CD. You will also find a selection of QuickTime movies in this chapter's Movies directory, showing both characters walking from different views.

## Animation Archive

Keeping all your previous animation works in an archive will add efficiency to all your animation projects. These archives can then be called upon when needed, potentially saving you days of work.

Because we have built character sets into our characters (see Chapter 15), we can use these to export the animation data and import other animations onto the Kila and Grae characters. We do this using the Trax Editor.

The Trax Editor is a fantastic tool for manipulating existing animations. Each animation is stored as a clip, which can then be imported onto a character to create whole sequences of animation. You can even manipulate the timing, blend animations, and work on top of each clip to add improvements to the existing animation.

As you can see in **Figure 16.39**, the Trax Editor has been dramatically improved in the transition from Maya 5 to Maya 6. In this section we will focus more on the Maya 6 version because it is the most current, but most of the basic principles remain the same for both versions.

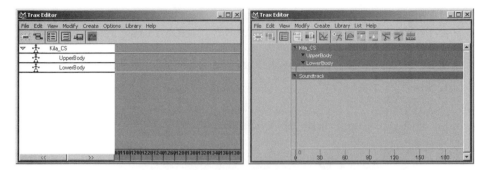

FIGURE 16.39 The Maya 5 Trax Editor (left) and the improved Maya 6 version (right)

Now that we have the walk cycle completed, we can create a clip. This takes all the animation data associated with the selected character set(s) and places it into a single node. This node can then be worked on or even exported as a separate file to be used on a separate character. Note, however, that you must be using the full version of Maya to export a clip; the Personal Learning Edition does not support this feature.

Let's first look at creating and exporting a clip.

1   Open the Trax Editor by going to Window > Animation Editors > Trax Editor.

2   First select the character set by going to Character > Select Character Set Node > Kila_CS. (If you are using Maya 5, the character sets in the scene will already be loaded into the Trax Editor.)

3   Load the character set into the Trax Editor by clicking on the Load Selected Character button (this is the seventh button from the left on the Trax Editor toolbar).

    The Trax Editor will now have the current character active; it should look like **Figure 16.39**. Notice that the subsets are also brought into the Editor.

4   There are two ways to create a clip. The first and quickest way is to click on the Create Clip button, which is the first one on the toolbar. This will create a clip for each character set (the main set and both subsets) using the current settings.

If you want to configure the settings before you create the clip, however, go to the Create > Clip and open the options (**Figure 16.40**).

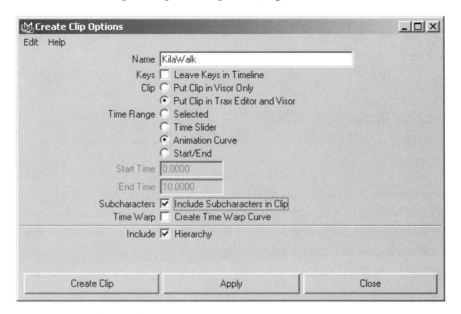

5 In the options, call the clip KilaWalk, specify that the Time Range will be dictated by the Animation Curve, and make sure to enable Include Subcharacters in Clip. Click on Apply, and three new clips will be created (**Figure 16.41**).

6 It's a good idea to rename each of these clips to match the animation it stores—simply double-click the clip's name in the Trax Editor. For example, rename KilaWalk1 to KilaWalk_LB for the lower body animation. If this clip is exported later, people will be able to tell what it is.

7 To now export all the clips together, select the main KilaWalk clip by clicking directly on it in the Trax Editor; then select File > Export Clip in the Trax Editor. Because you selected the main character set to export from, all three clips will be exported and stored.

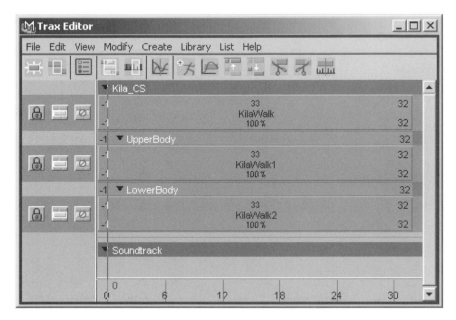

**FIGURE 16.41** Three clips are created, one for each character set.

With the animation safely stored, you can now import it back onto your character. To do this, simply select the character onto which you want to import the clips, and go to File > Import Clip to Characters.

We have barely scratched the surface of what is a very powerful tool in Maya, but by delving deeper into the Trax Editor we might find ourselves in a whole different book. If you intend to do a lot of animation work, I recommend you spend some time with the Trax Editor to see what it has to offer.

## Summary

For the final chapter in this book we have discussed some of the fundamentals of real-time animation. We have also explored Maya's animation environment and its tools; we learned how to create a simple walk cycle.

You now have the basic knowledge needed to tackle almost any animation sent your way, as well as the breadth of knowledge to take on nearly any task in game character creation.

# Normal Mapping in Maya

**A TECHNIQUE USED** in many of today's games is *normal mapping*. This is a method of making a low-polygon object or character appear to have more surface detail than it actually has, by collecting intricate lighting detail from a high-polygon version and applying it to the normals of the low one. *Normals* are the vectors (direction) a surface is facing.

Actually an application of bump mapping, normal mapping also works from a bitmap image. Normal maps are different from bump maps, however, in terms of the information they store. Bump maps work off a grayscale image that only registers changes in height; a normal map uses an RGB image, which contains enough information to store not only height but direction as well.

Red is the direction across the object, from left to right. Green goes from top to bottom, and the amount of blue dictates the height. The stronger the color, the more that normal faces in that specific direction.

Normal maps are becoming a key part of game development, so it's important to have some experience with creating them in Maya.

## System Requirements

To generate a normal map, you have to be running Maya 6 or later. This version has all the appropriate tools that allow you to generate and apply normal maps.

There's a plug-in available for previous versions of Maya, called RayDisplace, that will generate normal map data within Maya, but it's a bit unstable. There are also stand-alone utilities from the major card manufacturers that process the high-polygon model data to produce the normal map data. But Maya 6 is the first in-software implementation of normal mapping.

In addition, your video card must be able to support normal maps. Maya will generate the data regardless of your graphics card's abilities, but without the proper video card, you won't be able to use Maya's High Quality Interactive Render option to view the maps.

## Generating a Normal Map

First you need to get Maya set up for generating normal maps.

Go to Window > Settings/Preferences > Plug-in Manager. You will see the Plug-in Manager shown in **Figure A.1**. This is where you control the plug-ins that are loaded into memory. Work your way down the list until you reach the plug-in called TransferSurfaceInfo.mll. Check the boxes for "loaded" and "auto load"; the plug-in will be automatically loaded the next time you boot up Maya.

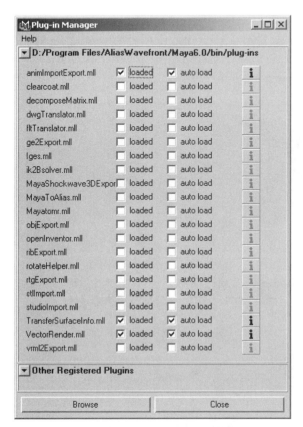

**FIGURE A.1**
The Plug-in Manager

With this plug-in enabled, you can use the Transfer Surface Information tool found in the Lighting/Shading menu. We will cover this shortly.

To generate a normal map, you need to create two objects:

▶   A higher-resolution mesh, from which you will extract the normal map information

▶   A lower-resolution model, to which you will apply the normal map

**1**   Create the first of two polygon planes. Go to Create Polygon Primitives > Plane. Set both Subdivisions Along Width and Subdivisions Along Height to 20. This will give you the high-resolution mesh to work with (**Figure A.2**, top).

2   Call this new plane HighRes. Then move it across in the X axis and edit it, raising the vertices as shown in **Figure A.2**, bottom, to give it some detail. You just need something simple for this example; we are only using the geometry to demonstrate how normal maps work.

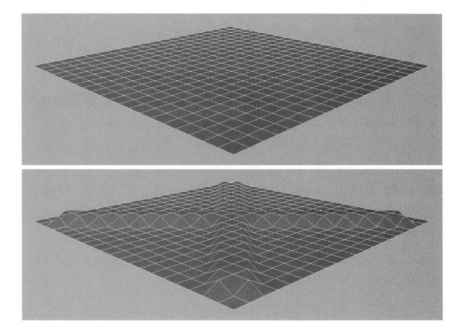

FIGURE A.2 Create the first, high-resolution polygon plane and give it some detail.

3   Create a second polygon plane, setting Subdivisions Along Width and Subdivisions Along Height to 1. This will be the low-resolution plane, to which the normal map will be applied. Call this plane LowRes.

4   Delete the history on both planes.

You now have your basic models (**Figure A.3**). Our aim is to get the same detail into the lower-resolution model that we have in the higher-resolution one.

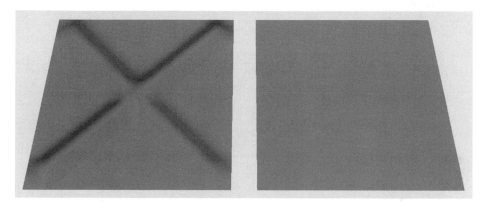

**FIGURE A.3** The high-resolution and low-resolution models

Before we can generate the normal map, both sets of geometry must exist in the same place. This is so that Maya knows which object the normals will be generated from as well as what UVs to fit into on the lower-resolution mesh.

**1**   Select the HighRes model, and set the Translate X attribute back to 0.

**2**   Using the Outliner, select the HighRes model. Then, holding Shift, select the LowRes model.

**3**   Switch to the Rendering menu set, and go to Lighting/Shading > Transfer Surface Information. Open the options (**Figure A.4**).

   The Transfer Surface Information tool will transfer surface information from a model to an image file. We can use it to generate our normal map.

**4**   Under Target Options, set Transfer to export the Tangent Space Normals. These normals are evaluated locally and can be rotated to point in the direction of the polygon.

   Object Space normals always point the same direction, so they are no good for defining our map. (Make sure to consult your lead programmer on which coordinate system to use; there are some appropriate uses for object space normals.)

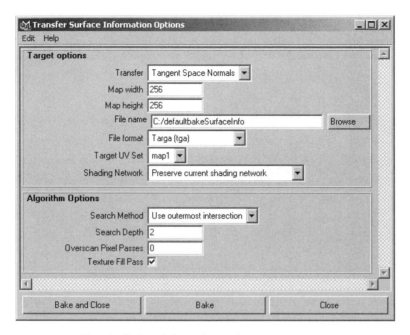

FIGURE A.4 Transfer Surface Information options

**5** The Map Width and Map Height values define the size of the bitmap image; 256×256 is fine for this example.

**6** Specify a filename and location, and the format for the image to be exported.

**7** Set Shading Network to "Preserve current shading network." You will need to edit the shader when you apply the normal map, so there is no point in creating new ones.

**8** Now set the Algorithm Options:

Set Search Method to "Use outermost intersection." This controls how each object's intersections are handled.

Set Search Depth to 2. This specifies the farthest distance to which the algorithm will go to look for these intersections.

**9** Click on Bake and Close, and the normal map will be generated.

Your resulting normal map will look like the one in **Figure A.5**, although it will be predominantly in blue and not grayscale.

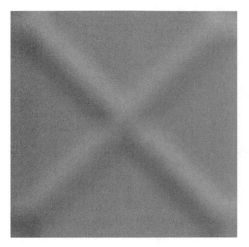

**FIGURE A.5** The normal map

The normal map is now exported. We can apply it to the lower-resolution model and view it interactively in Maya.

## Viewing Normal Maps

We can now create a new shader that we will apply to the low-resolution polygon plane.

**1**    Start by moving the HighRes plane across again in the X axis, so that you can see each model separately.

**2**    In Hypershade, create a new Lambert material and call this NormShader. Apply it to the LowRes plane.

When you created the normal map, Maya also created a new texture file node pointing to it. You can see this in the Hypershade Textures tab and in **Figure A.6**. We now want to connect this to our new Lambert shader.

**3**    Open the Connection Editor (Window > General Editors > Connection Editor), and load the texture node, which should be called file1, into the Outputs section. Load the NormShader into the Inputs section.

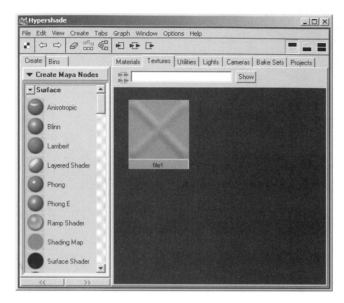

**FIGURE A.6** Maya also creates a file node pointing to the normal map.

4    As demonstrated in **Figure A.7**, connect the Out Color attribute of the file1 node to the Normal Camera attribute of the NormShader node.

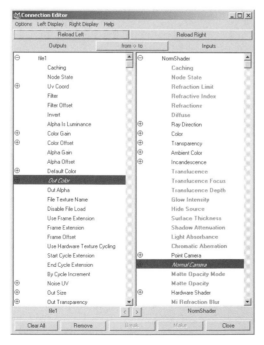

**FIGURE A.7** Connect the Out Color attribute to the Normal Camera attribute.

**5**  Now the material is set up; all we need to do is configure the view so that we can see the normal map. Go to the view's Shading menu and turn on High Quality Rendering, Smooth Shade All, and Hardware Texturing.

| | |
|---|---|
| ✔ High Quality Rendering | ▢ |
| Wireframe | 4 |
| ✔ Smooth Shade All | |
| Smooth Shade Selected Items | |
| Flat Shade All | |
| Flat Shade Selected Items | |
| Bounding Box | |
| Points | |
| Shade Options | ▶ |
| Interactive Shading | ▢ |
| Backface Culling | |
| Smooth Wireframe | |
| ✔ Hardware Texturing | ▢ |
| Hardware Fog | ▢ |
| Apply Current to All | |

**FIGURE A.8** Configure the view panel so we can view our normal map.

Now you will see the normal map applied to the geometry. As you can see in **Figure A.9**, bottom, this works quite well and gives the flat plane the illusion of detail. Next let's see how it reacts to light.

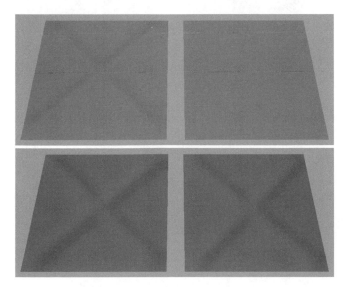

**FIGURE A.9**
The normal map is now visible in the view.

**1** In the view's Lighting menu, activate Use Selected Lights. The geometry will go black because there are currently no lights in the scene.

**2** Create a new Point Light by going to Create > Lights > Point Light.

**3** Move this new light around, and you'll notice that both objects' surfaces react to it as if they had the same topology; yet there is a difference of 798 faces (**Figure A.10**).

The only drawback to normal maps (as with bump maps) is that they don't physically alter the geometry, so when the plane is viewed from the side, as in **Figure A.11**, the illusion is shattered.

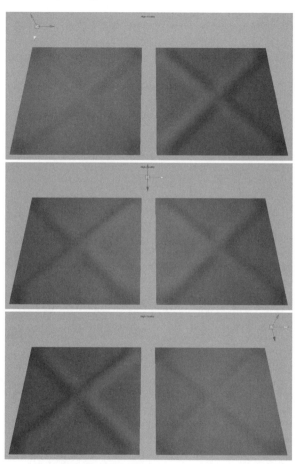

FIGURE A.10 Both objects react the same to the light as it moves around the scene.

FIGURE A.11 When not viewed directly, the normal map does not work as well

# Reference and Further Reading

Contained in this section are a number of books and Web sites that are valuable sources of reference. I have included a description for many of them; they are all worth your time to explore.

## Anatomy Books

▶ *Anatomy for the Artist,* Sarah Simblet and John Davis (DK Publishing, 2001)

This is a magnificent book, featuring more than 250 photographs and 100 drawings depicting the human body in various poses, while focusing in on various parts in detail.

▶ *How to Draw Manga: Bodies & Anatomy,* Society for the Study of Manga Techniques (Graphic-sha Publishing, 2002)

This book teaches you how to draw characters in the manga style, but it does so using some of the best and most useful illustrations I have found. Not only are these images clean and well drawn, they also examine parts of the body from different angles and poses.

▶ *Dynamic Anatomy,* Burne Hogarth (Watson-Guptill Publications, 2003)

Hogarth has a unique style of drawing, one that demonstrates particularly well the surface features of musculature for figures in motion.

▶ *Human Anatomy for Artists: The Elements of Form,* Eliot Goldfinger (Oxford University Press USA, 1991)

If you're looking for an anatomical reference with a medical emphasis, this is it. Goldfinger's book examines every muscle in the body individually, covering structure, function, and relation to the body as a whole.

▶ *Strength Training Anatomy,* Frederic Delavier (Human Kinetics Publishers, 2001)

*Strength Training Anatomy* was created as a guide for weight lifters to show exactly how certain exercises were affecting muscle shapes and structures. For artists, the book is an excellent visual cue for how muscles work in relation to each other and how their shapes change in different circumstances.

▶ *Bridgman's Complete Guide to Drawing from Life,* George Bridgman (Sterling Publishing, 2003)

Bridgman's approach to drawing focuses on structure, body mechanics, and rhythm lines.

▶ *Cyclopedia Anatomicae,* Gyorgy Feher and Andras Szunyoghy (Black Dog and Leventhal Publishers, 1999)

Containing pencil drawings of human and animal bones and muscles, this is one of the reference books of choice for creature TDs.

## Animation Books

▶ *The Animator's Survival Kit,* Richard Williams (Faber and Faber, 2002)

Veteran animator Richard Williams has written a veritable bible for the aspiring animator. It covers every aspect of animation and is useful for both traditional and computer animators.

▶ *Teach Yourself Body Language,* Gordon R. Wainwright (Hodder & Stoughton Educational Division, 1999)

Not exactly an animation book, but having knowledge on why we do what we do is essential to any animator.

▶ *The Artists Complete Guide to Facial Expressions,* Gary Faigin (Watson-Guptill Publications, 1990)

This is an exhaustive reference guide to facial expressions and the psychology behind them.

▶ *Cartoon Animation,* Preston Blair (Walter Foster Publishing, 1995)

Good supplemental animation book from one of the traditional masters, this book is chock full of animation breakdowns, both human and animal.

▶ *How to Draw Animation,* Christopher Hart (Watson-Guptill Publications, 1997)

▶ *The Human Figure in Motion,* Eadweard Muybridge (Dover Publications, 1989)

## Web Sites

For those on a budget, the Internet is a rich source of reference material, home to hundreds of Web sites dedicated to various techniques and applications.

### Anatomy Reference

There are hundreds of anatomy-related Web sites. Following is a selection of some of the best and most useful. (Be warned, though, most of these do contain nudes.)

▶ **Human Anatomy** www.3d.sk

(Subscription required) A fantastic site developed specifically for 3D artists and game developers. This houses lots of very useful images of people in various poses and states of dress. Even better: the photographs are specifically taken with the 3D artist in mind.

▶ **Human Anatomy Pictures for Artists** www.fineart.sk

The sister site of 3d.sk offers free images as well as a selection of online Andrew Loomis books to help the budding artist on a budget.

▶ **Met Art** www.met-art.com

Met Art offers the largest, freshest, classiest collection of nude art and fine photography in the world.

▶ **Simple Nudes** www.simplenudes.com

▶ **Online Medical Anatomy Atlas** www.rad.washington.edu/atlas

▶ **Henry Gray's Anatomy of the Human Body** www.bartleby.com/107

The Bartleby.com edition of *Gray's Anatomy of the Human Body* features 1,247 vibrant engravings—many in color—from the classic 1918 publication. There's also a subject index with 13,000 entries ranging from the Antrum of Highmore to the Zonule of Zinn.

## Miscellaneous References

Here are various sites that have other uses, including references for poses and general information on traditional artists and beauty analysis.

▶ **Posing Guide** www.photographytips.com/page.cfm/375

(Subscription required) Although this site is aimed at photographers, it offers good advice on creating poses, as well as images ideal for posing your 3D character.

▶ **Skulls Unlimited** www.skullsunlimited.com

▶ **Marquardt Beauty Analysis** www.beautyanalysis.com

▶ **Art Renewal Center** www.artrenewal.com

High-resolution images of classic figurative painting through the ages.

▶ **Web Gallery of Art** http://gallery.euroweb.hu

The Web Gallery of Art contains over 11,600 digital reproductions of European paintings and sculptures created from 1150 to 1800. A considerable number of the pictures are commented, and there are biographies of the significant artists.

▶ **Google**  www.google.com

The best reference of all: Click on the Images tab, and the entire world's collection of reference imagery is at your fingertips.

### Computer Graphics

If you are interested in creating artwork for games, it's likely that you have at least a small interest in the world of computer graphics. Here are a few Web sites I visit quite often.

▶ **CG Networks**  www.cgnetworks.com

▶ **CG Channel**  www.cgchannel.com

▶ **Polycount**  www.polycount.com

The original and currently best site for all things real-time. Forums, utilities, tutorials, industry news, and mod assets are just a small part of what this site has to offer.

▶ **The 10 Second Club**  www.10secondclub.net

Monthly animation contest, forums, and advice for aspiring animators.

▶ **Real Time CG**  www.realtimecg.com

Home to a very popular monthly competition sponsored by Peachpit Press and New Riders. Entrants are given a game-art-related brief each month that they must complete and submit to a panel of industry professionals. The site hopes to one day be a complete resource for the professional and aspiring game artist; this is one to watch.

▶ **Forums.** The following sites are home to some of the most popular CG-related forums on the Net. Discussions span everything related to computer art and animation, so sign yourself up and post your work to get constructive feedback and help.

www.conceptart.org

www.cgchat.com

www.cgtalk.com

http://cgchar.toonstruck.com/forum/index.php is a character animation forum that evolved from the original CGCHAR mailing list.

### Maya Sites

There is an enormous Maya community available online, where you'll find excellent tutorials, scripts, and plug-ins available for free. Here are just a few sites I find useful.

► www.highend3d.com

► www.learning-maya.com

► www.simplymaya.com

► www.zoorender.com

► www.digital-tutors.com

► www.3dcafe.com

► www.3dluvr.com

## Graphics Tablets

As mentioned in Chapter 9, graphics tablets are the only way to create professional 2D artwork on your home PC (along with a decent 2D graphics application, of course).

► Wacom (www.wacom.com) does a nice range of graphics tablets that offer high-quality results, although they can be expensive.

► Nisis (www.nisis.com) has a more affordable range of products for those on a strict budget.